Kosova 2: The Ottoman Empire

Series Editors

Jason L. Frazer
Besa T. Pinchotti
Diane Tafilaj
Ramadan Musliu

Series translated by:

Avni Spahiu
Getoar M. Mjeku
Faton Bislimi

Originally issued 2012 in Albanian
by Jalifat Publishing in Houston and Faik Konica in Prishtina as
Kosova 2: Perandoria Osmane

Published by Jalifat Publishing
Houston, Texas

JUSUF BUXHOVI

KOSOVA

Volume 2

The Ottoman Empire

JALIFAT PUBLISHING
Houston USA
2013

To my wife, Luljeta,
and children: Arsim, Njomëza, and Arta

CONTENTS

9

NOTE ON SPELLING, NAMES, AND PRONUNCIATION

This volume contains a multitude of reference to foreign places, people, titles, honorifics, and socio-political and philosophical concepts, for which there is no universally accepted variant or spelling in the Latin alphabet. To avoid political biases and reader discomfort, this translation primarily adapts to prevailing English use with certain exception.

Generally, whenever available and appropriate for modern use, an established Anglicized version of historical names and terms is preferred. Variations in the other relevant languages and historical contexts are given in parentheses when a foreign name or noun is introduced. For example, the volume uses *sanjak*, instead of the Modern Turkish *sancak*, to denote the Ottoman administrative division; likewise, the translation gives *Skanderbeg* and *Murad* over the modern native variants, *Skënderbeu* and *Murat*.

However, we have given preference to modern native spellings for names such as *Pjetër Bogdani* and *Arsenije III Crnojević*, whose Anglicized versions are inexistent, inconsistent, or unduly archaic. Certain terms, such as *Rilindja*, *bölükbaşı*, or *Načertanije*, or even placenames such as *Štip*, do not have an established English spelling either; those and other modern names are usually given in their native orthography.

Unconventional or non-English names and spelling are also retained to preserve the work's originality and the author's choice and to avoid the translator's own prejudice. Most notably, the official Albanian (and Turkish) variant, *Kosova*, as used in the country itself, takes precedence over *Kosovo* (in reference to both, the Ottoman vilayet and the modern state). Other cases may include default names for Balkan places of a historical significance to the Albanians (*e.g.*, *Shkup* instead of *Skopje* or *Üsküb*; *Janina* over *Ioannina*) and the author's deliberate resort to archaic or poetic terms (*e.g.*, the ancient name *Dardania* to refer to Kosova; *Vuçitërn* for the town of Vushtrri).

Abbreviations

These abbreviations are followed by a colon when a foreign name or term is introduced in parentheses, as for example: Skanderbeg (Alb.: Skënderbeu); they are italicized and followed by a comma when preceding an explanation or the English meaning of a foreign word—*e.g.*, besa (*Alb.*, oath, word of honor, trust, or covenant).

Alb. – Albanian

Arb. – Arabic

Grk. – Modern Greek

Ita. – Italian

Mac. – Slavic Macedonian

Mont. – Montenegrin (occasionally, Serbian may be given when historically relevant)

sing. – singular (for terms introduced in their plural form)

Srb. – Serbian

Trk. – Turkish, including Ottoman Turkish

Pronunciation

The majority of foreign names and words are written in the Albanian, Turkish, or Serbo-Croatian (Slavic) alphabet. Pronunciation is akin to English with the following exceptions:

Albanian *ë* – a schwa sound as the *a* in *America*; it is usually omitted in speech when it appears at the end of a word or unstressed syllables;

Turkish *ı* (dotless i) – similar to the Albanian *ë*, but with the tongue positioned higher to the roof and further back in the mouth;

Turkish *ö* – similar to *i* in the South African pronunciation of *bird*;

Albanian *y* and Turkish *ü* – equivalent to the French *u* or German *ü*;

Albanian *q*, Turkish *k* (before e, i, ö, and ü) – a softer, palatal version of the English *ch* (certain Albanian dialects pronounce *q* like *ç* or the Slavic *ć*, see below);

Slavic *ć* – a softer version of the English *ch*;

Albanian and Turkish *ç* and Slavic *č* – English *ch* (as in *check*);

Albanian *gj*, Turkish *g* (before e, i, ö, and ü) – a softer, palatal version of the English *j* (certain Albanian dialects pronounce *gj* like *xh* or the Slavic *đ*, see below);

Slavic *đ* (also written as *dj*) – a softer version of the English *j*;

Albanian *xh*, Turkish *c*, Slavic *dž* –equivalent to the English *j* (as in *John* or *George*);

Slavic *h* – similar to *h*; same as the Scottish *ch* in *loch* or the Spanish *j*;
Turkish *ş* and Slavic *š* – pronounced like the English or Albanian *sh*;
Slavic *ž* and Turkish *j* – equivalent to *zh* in English or Albanian;
Albanian *dh* – voiced English *th*, as in *the* or *other*; and
Albanian *th* – always unvoiced, as in Eng. *theme*.

TRANSLATOR

INTRODUCTION

If we ought to accept the premise that the Ottoman Empire is, in many regards, the successor to the Byzantines—albeit with Islamism as a different component that in its Ottoman form implied tolerance to other faiths—one might say that the succession is not a continuation of the Byzantine achievements, but of failures. The Byzantine Empire abandoned the ideals of world universalism and of the Western civilization, giving in to pressure from invading "barbarians," such as the Slavs, Bulgarians, and Avars, who continued to challenge the empire with their incursions from the north. While previous emperors of Illyrian-Dardani origin—Diocletian, Constantine the Great, and Justinian—imposed imperial law over the invading tribes, Heraclius and later rulers allowed the newcomers to govern through their "barbarian" structures. In many instances, the new tribes were at odds or even against the imperial order; Bulgarians and later Slavs shrunk the empire from within and brought about its end.

In the process of the Byzantine decline, the idea of cosmopolitism was gradually replaced by the Eastern mentality, whose foremost carriers were the Slavs and other "barbarian" peoples. As a result, Illyricum was renamed Balkans, while the vision of universality came to an end with the fatal Western-Eastern schism. The divide, marking a clash of civilizations, brought disastrous consequences for the West. Upon the appearance of the Ottomans in the region, the Orthodox Slavs became, not incidentally, the first and the most trustworthy allies of the new invaders. Meanwhile, Albanians, Hungarians, and other Western peoples, defied the Ottomans as their worst enemies.

Such a synthesis of the past, well beyond the conventional understanding, is seemingly stringent and—especially due to the stereotypes that the 20th century historiography, inundated with nationalistic and ideological tones, has created—appears incomprehensible. Nevertheless, the approach is well founded on the role of the main historical actors as well as on the social, political, and cultural concepts they espoused. Here, the Seljuk Turks and the Slavs, along with the Avars, Mongolians, and the like, were the "barbarian" peoples of Asia, sharing a mentality that sought to conquer, not to build. On the other hand, the Western peoples, rooted in antiquity, were preoccupied with the creation of a world empire, as a civilizing mission that their status of "divine people" assigned them. In the Balkan Peninsula, the undertakings of Alexander the Great and later Pyrrhus of Epirus represent the commitment of the Western people to that mission. Moreover, several emperors, such as Diocletian, Constantine the Great, and Justinian, ascribed Illyricum and Dardania, as ancient foundations of the realm, the task of preserving and spreading the Western civilization.

It is likely the same responsibility fell also on the Albanian national hero, Gjergj Kastrioti Skanderbeg (also George Castriota Scanderbeg, Alb.: Skënderbeu). Taken to the Ottoman court at an early age, he gained the trust of the sultan and became a prominent figure in the military, responsible for the rising empire's westward expansion. Yet, Skanderbeg refused to assist the Ottomans; he defied the sultan and sided with the West. Doing so, the Albanian leader offered the West a great historic service that once was much extolled but has now almost slipped into oblivion. Deserting the Ottoman army on the eve of the Battle of Nish, where he was to clash swords with the West, Skanderbeg returned to the castle of Kruja and reestablished the old Albanian kingdom. At the same time, he became a defender of Christianity and herewith a supporter of the Western civilization.

Skanderbeg's quarter-century war against the Ottomans reveals the pro-Western role of the Albanians, while the Orthodox Slavs, as allies rather than vassals of the new empire, appear as a historical embodiment of the Eastern conscience. Both sides, Albanians and Slavs, were faced with the critical dilemma: to fight or to join the Ottomans. Here, Despot Stefan Lazarević and other Serbian rulers served as the right-hand men of Sultan Bayezid I; later leaders also maintained cordial relations with Mehmed I and Murad II. The Albanians did not join the Ottomans, even after the forceful subjugation that ensued Skanderbeg's resistance. The Serbs, on the other hand, cooperated with the Ottomans and—as in decisive expeditions such as the final Siege of Constantinople—allied with them in battle.

After the loss of a Balkan Christian coalition in the 1389 Battle of Dardania Field, Serb rulers accepted Ottoman vassalage; they served, however, as allies rather than as inferiors who paid tributes to their master. Serbian units repeatedly took part, alongside Bayezid's army, in Ottoman expeditions against the Hungarians and Romanians. Later, Serbian troops aided the campaigns of Mehmed I and Murad II. The despots of Rascia were present and played a crucial role even in the internal struggles for power, which broke out between Bayezid's sons, following his death. The Serbs sided with both Musa and Mehmed I, only to switch sides and align with the apparent victor in the finals stages of the struggle for power. In a similar fashion, they came to the aid of Murad II, who furthermore took Branković's daughter, Mara, for a bride. The marriage turned out an important factor in strengthening the Ottoman-Slavic ties, adding a spiritual component, especially during Skanderbeg's wars against the Turks. The Orthodox Church was granted autocephaly (ecclesiastic independence) along with other great privileges under the Ottoman Empire. Mara, as the sultan's consort, was instrumental in obtaining permits for new Orthodox places of worship; imperial decrees, moreover, protected the Serbian monasteries, allowed for the expansion of their property, while the Slavic Orthodox clergy grew manifold.

The course of Serbian cooperation with the Ottomans impeded the creation of a Western alliance against the new empire's expansion to the center of Europe. The injury suffered by the West is most evident in two major events: first, in 1448, in the Second Battle of Dardania Field, which was to take place in the same venue as the 1389 encounter, the Serbs worked against the broad European coalition; and second, they aided the conquest of Constantinople, finalized in 1453. These turning points determined the direction of Ottoman conquests and the rise of the Turks as a new world power, the status the empire would enjoy for about four to five hundred years.

In both, the Second Battle of Dardania Field and the Siege of Constantinople, the Serbs played a pivotal role. In Dardania, they contributed to the loss of the first European Christian alliance; during the battle for the city, Serbs fought against the last Byzantine fortress, whose fall buried the hopes of Christians that the West could defend itself at its very roots. Even after the Slavic Orthodox ceased to be important allies to the Ottomans, as they once were during the reigns of Bayezid I, Mehmed I, and Murad II, they remained docile and cooperative with the regime. Seeing no need for their services, the Ottoman Empire put an end to all vassal despotates—Serb, Bulgarian, and Greek—in the Balkans and placed the newly occupied territories under direct imperial administration. Adhering to the famous speculative doctrine that "where there is no Serbian state, the Church is in change," the Orthodox Church came to the aid of the Ottoman governance. Collecting taxes from the *râya* (Christian subjects), on behalf of the empire, the clergy secured substantial revenues for the Church.

The Serbian Church adhered to this policy of cooperation until the 19th century. Then, after the Russo-Ottoman wars over Crimea, Bessarabia, and the Caucasus, the Slavic Orthodox in the Balkans came under the spiritual and political auspices of Saint Petersburg. Russia, meanwhile, began to pursue its hegemonic policy on Europe, using the Balkans as a gateway. Beginning with the Great Eastern Crisis—the political upheaval that sprung with the decline of the Ottoman Empire—Serbia became a driving force of pan-Slavism in the Balkans (it even used the new ideology to blackmail the West into lending its support in addition to the Russian backing). With the publication of the *Načertanije* (*Srb.*, A Draft) of Ilija Garašanin (followed by a similar Greek program, *Megali Idea*, and a Bulgarian one), the Serbian state called for a solution to the national issues based on the "historical right." To this goal, Serbia promoted war for the annexation of the Albanian lands, in order to separate them from the territories that had to be divided among the Balkan states after the retreat of the Ottoman Empire.

The expansion, however, was sought under the anathema that the Albanians were "supporters of the Ottomans"! As a main argument, Serbs postulated the mass conversion of Albanians to Islam of during the 17th and 18th centuries. This contention, however, ignored the secular nature of the Albanian national movement. As part of *Rilindja Kombëtare*—the National Renaissance, which began around the same time as the publication of the *Načertanije*—the ethnic group not only disregarded religious affiliations and the East, but returned to antiquity, claiming descent from the Pelasgians, the old inhabitants of the Balkans. Seeing themselves as founders of the Western civilization, the Albanians used Western ideals as a foundation for their national movement.

Rilindja was but an expression of the political and spiritual will of the people to return to the West, where Gjergj Kastrioti Skanderbeg had adhered to five centuries prior, when alone he repelled the Ottoman invasion and fought against Slavs and others who allied with or became vassals of the Ottomans in a war against the West. *Rilindja*'s pro-Western demands were primarily presented by the 1878 League of Prizren, the political organization that sought the establishment of an Albanian state. The League, endeavoring to protect the Albanian lands from annexation into the regional states, later became a provisional government—the Albanian state was thus revived, although its authority was limited to the then Vilayet of Kosova.

Through this historical movement for independence, the Albanians gained the respect of Western powers, principally Austria-Hungary and

Germany. To a certain extent, Great Britain and Italy were sympathetic to Albania's independence, although they were tied to political conjunctures and conflicting spheres of interest arising due to the Great Eastern Crisis. The Albanian struggle for statehood underwent grim trials such as in the aftermath of the First Balkan War when each—Serbs, Montenegrins, Greeks, and Bulgarians—occupied parts of Albania. Under such circumstances, it was only the recognition of an independent state that saved Albania from vanishing altogether.

The entire process of the Albanian return to the Western family, from where their ancestors had been forcibly expelled—as at the time of Skanderbeg, they were the first and only people that attempted to separate from the Ottomans—ended with the fall of the Ottoman state. But unlike neighboring Slavic Orthodox nations that had declared war on the Ottomans and fought for the immediate destruction of the empire, the Albanians propagated a gradual political process, seeking equality through the unification of the four Albanian-inhabited vilayets of the Ottoman Empire into a single autonomous state. This entity would represent the so-called *Ottoman Albania*, which would eventually yield way to a *European Albania*, noting in the process but a historical compromise between the ethno-cultural and the socio-political reality created during five centuries of Ottoman rule.

The idea of an Ottoman Albania, as a transitional solution leading to the establishment of a Western state, was unacceptable for the Ottoman Empire, which insisted in preserving its administration in the European territories before they were claimed by the Russian-backed Balkan nations. However, the autonomous Albanian state was the preferred choice for many of the Great Powers of Europe. The support was most apparent in the British proposal at the Ambassadors' Conference of the Congress of Berlin; in April 1880, the representative of the United Kingdom suggested that the Albanian vilayets be merged into a single autonomous province.[1] And the British idea was not incidental. In fact, it came two years after the decisions of the Congress of Berlin, which set a framework for future reform in the Ottoman Empire. Article 23 of the Berlin agreement allowed for the autonomy of Christian peoples as a solution to internal problems of the empire.

Earlier, the Albanian League of Prizren had also demanded autonomy. In a memorandum signed by two prominent leaders, Abdyl Frashëri and Mehmet Ali Vrioni, the League requested that the participating nations at

---

[1] Buxhovi, *Kongresi i Berlinit 1878*, 651.

the Congress of Berlin deliberate an autonomous Albania. The letter, being a delayed reaction, did not specifically address the unification of the four Albanian-inhabited vilayets. Yet, even if the memorandum had arrived in a timely manner, the Congress of Berlin would hardly consider the Albanian demands since the Sublime Porte (Ottoman government), did not recognize the Albanians as a nationality. The Porte placed Muslim Albanians under the *millet-i osman* (Ottoman nationality), along with all those who had accepted Islam. The categorization caused further complications with non-Muslim Albanians, forming one-third of the population, of which two-thirds belonged to the Orthodox Church and one-third were Roman Catholic. *Rilindja* activists, mainly Albanian intellectuals in the Ottoman Empire, mobilized in demands for their nationality rights. To further their goal, the Albanians formed in Constantinople the Central Committee for Defending the Rights of the Albanian Nationality (*Komiteti Qendror për Mbrojtjen e të Drejtave të Kombësisë Shqiptare*). Abdyl Frashëri was elected head of the group, while his brother Sami led another newly-founded group—the Society for the Printing of Albanian Letters (*Shoqëria e të Shtypurit Shkronja Shqip*), which is widely known as the İstanbul Society. Intellectuals played a vital role in presenting to the international community a clear and precise understanding of the political aspirations of the Albanians. Autonomy for Albania was set forth as a solution within the 1856 Peace Treaty of Paris where the Great Powers agreed to preserve the *status quo* in the Ottoman Empire and prevent changes imposed from the outside and without internal agreements.

The British proposal for Albanian autonomy under the Ottoman Empire failed to gain the support of the six Great Powers of Europe; Russian opposition was categorical, while France was supportive in principal, but demanded a broader assessment of the situation. However, the Ottoman representative did not object. The proposal meandered for about two months around the diplomatic circles in İstanbul, but was likely ignored by Sultan Abdul Hamid II. The Ottoman ruler seems to have been more concerned about retaining his control of his Balkan dominions and may have disregarded the Europeans' intention to use Albania as a barrier against the Slavic Orthodox occupation of the lands the Ottomans would one day have to surrender. Abdul Hamid's infatuation with Albania, whom he called the "caliph's castle" and like terms, were purported for internal consumption. This did not mean that the sultan was ready to treat the Albanians outside the *millet-i osman*, since through such a move he would lose his Albanian card as he had lost the Serbs, Greeks, or Bulgarians as their autonomy under European supervision culminated in independence. To avoid such a development, the Muslim monarch turned to the Islamic-Ottoman emancipation of the Albanians as a last chance to keep them on his side.

In other words, the Ottoman Empire sought a social and political emancipation of the Albanians, but in compatibility with Islam. The rapid opening of state schools in the Albanian vilayets, beginning in the second half of the 1800s, was intended to serve that goal.

Education was indispensable and although it entailed attending Ottoman or foreign schools (in Greek or the Slavic languages), it allowed the Albanians to undergo an internal emancipation that strengthen their national identity. This warned that internal reforms—earlier reorganization known as *Tanzimât* or later ones taken after the Great Eastern Crisis—would not suffice to secure the empire's continuity or, at least, formal presence in Europe; the Albanians and the Porte's behavior towards them could keep the empire in the old continent. But the ethnic group conditioned its role to the recognition of their nationality, independent of the *millet-i osman* (as hoped for by Sultan Abdul Hamid II and other conservatives). The Albanians demanded they be recognized as a separate nationality, contending that the Islamic identity of the majority could help maintain ties with others, but could not be taken for granted.

That the Ottoman Empire hoped to retain Albanian within its borders is later seen at the London Conference in 1912-13. After the Ottomans lost to the Balkan alliance (Serbia, Montenegro, Greece, and Bulgaria) in December 1912, they waged a full-scale diplomatic battle with the Great Powers to keep Albania as an autonomous state under the sultan's sovereignty. Then, Albania had already declared its independence, and in April 1913 the Conference agreed to return it under Turkish suzerainty; but the decision was retracted three months later, when Albania was recognized as an independent country to be supervised by the international community. The Great Powers chose a foreign prince to rule the new country and demanded that the Ottoman Empire leave Albania, whose fate now was bound to Europe.

The Ottoman position on Albania reflects not only the epilogue of the Turkish presence in the region; it also represents the challenges that the Albanians, along with other Balkan peoples, faced repeatedly. On the one side, the Albanians lived through the Ottoman invasion that stripped them of their spiritual identity to make them part of the imperial blend. On the other hand, they experienced destruction at the hands of neighboring states: Serbia, Montenegro, Greece, and Bulgaria associated their liberation from

21

the Ottoman Empire with the Albanian question and attempted to physical exterminate the Albanians.

For that reason, with the onset of the Great Eastern Crisis, the Albanians had fewer problems with the Ottomans and increasingly more trouble with their traditional adversaries. Here, the Albanians—having maintained their identity despite Turkish efforts at assimilation—were in a political struggle against the Ottomans, which they could not lose but through an untimely agreement; with the neighboring states, however, they were waging a war of life or death.

CHAPTER 1
THE OTTOMAN EMPIRE AND MEDIEVAL ALBANIA

The Ottoman Arrival in the Balkans

The first Ottoman incursions into Europe and the beginnings of vassal states in the Balkans: The Byzantine emperor allies with the Ottomans. After a victory at Savra in 1385, the Ottomans extend their sovereignty over Albania; the 1389 Battle of Dardania Field marks the beginning of Ottoman rule over the Balkans. Sultan Bayezid I forges his strongest alliance with the Serbian despots—Stefan, the son of Lazar, and the succeeding Branković dynasty—who will serve as the empire's right-hand men.

The years 1354, 1371, and 1389 are of great importance for the Ottoman conquests in Europe and the developments they brought about. In the history of Medieval Albania, the year 1385 is yet another turning point, marking the beginning of Ottoman vassalage in the face of disunity and internal strife among local rulers. The quarrels were a handicap to the Albanians, who remained in a weaker position throughout the Ottoman period. Other groups in the region, however, used the Ottoman invasion as a cause for unity and political alignments that would prove more beneficial under the new circumstances.

In 1354, the Ottomans, having conquered Bursa, crossed the Dardanelles and set foot in the Balkans. There, in 1364, they seized Adrianople, which they renamed Edirne and turned into their new capital. During the Bursa campaign in 1326, Sultan Osman I had advised his son and crown prince, Orhan, to infiltrate the leadership of the Byzantine Empire. Therefore, Orhan I, who took power shortly after, forced the Byzantines to enter into an alliance, forged by the sultan's marriage with the daughter of Emperor John VI Kantakouzenos. Through such a calculated move, the Byzantines apparently hoped to send a strong message to their adversaries. The Byzantine-Ottoman alliance warned internal opponents, the Serbs and Bulgarians, that they ought to cease abating the empire from within. Moreover, John VI cautioned Western enemies—the papacy in particular, but Venice and Genoa, too—that he "was not alone." He had a strong ally who would help the oriental empire assert influence over any opponent, including the West. Nevertheless, as the Byzantines would later witness, the alliance did not prevent the loss of their few remaining territories. The new friendship, the first of its kind between the two realms, induced Byzantine adversaries to enlist as Ottoman vassals. The alliance hence only set a new approach, also embraced by the Eastern Church and the Slavic peoples, in that the Byzantines would rely, as they did on many occasions, on the Ottomans and Muslims for assistance in the war against the Western Church and the West in general.

The year 1371 marks another important stage in the Ottoman incursions and continued expansion into Europe. After conquering Adrianople, the rising power annexed additional land in Thrace, causing the independent Balkan leaders—mainly Serb and Bulgarian nobles—to feel the threat of the Ottoman advance. The Byzantines, as well as Venice and Genoa, encouraged the region's lords to act before it became too late. Consequently, Balkan leaders formed their first military alliance under the command of the Mrnjavčević brothers, Vukašin and Uglješa, who were joined from the Albanians by Alexander of Vlora (Alb.: Aleksandri i Vlorës). The alliance met the Ottomans on the banks of the Maritsa River in Bulgaria, but suffered a heavy defeat, as a result of which the Turks began a process of forcing Balkan lords, primarily princes of Rascia and Bulgaria, into vassalage.

In 1389, a coalition of regional leaders, assisted by Hungarian, Polish, and other Christian volunteers, lost the decisive Battle of Dardania Field, which paved the way for the quincentennial Ottoman rule. However, the Ottomans had already established their sovereignty over Albania as of 1385, at a time of disunity among the local rulers. That year, in the Battle of Savra, the Myzeqe region of Albania, the Ottoman commander, Timurtaş Pasha, decapitated Prince Gjergj I Balsha of Shkodër (also George I), who fought without the aid of prominent noblemen such as Lord Thopia of Durrës. In fact, the latter had his own stakes in the Ottoman victory. After the Balshas and their allies, including the Muzakas (Ita.: Musachi), lost to the Ottomans, Lord Thopia regained his own (but "scorched" city) of Durrës (Ita.: Durazzo).[2] Therefore, while the battle was a part of the Ottoman campaign in Albania, it was not entirely distinct from the frequent quarrels between the local dynasties. After the death of Tsar Dušan, who for a brief period ruled most of Albania earlier in the century, the local noblemen plunged in disputes over the previously occupied territory. They rushed to regain their lands individually and outside a political union, although the circumstances called for unity, given the imminent threat of an Ottoman invasion.[3]

Unlike the Slavic, Bulgarian, and other Balkan leaders who joined arms in battle despite their longstanding hostilities, the Balshas and the Thopias, the most prominent ruling families of Albania, were not united. The loss of one and the gain of the other indicate the special circumstances under which Albania existed since the 13th century when the Latin Empire of Constantinople was founded. The Albanians were sandwiched in between the West's war against the Byzantines. In other words, the war was waged between the Western Church and the Eastern Church, whose westernmost territories began in Albania, inevitably tying military allegiance to ecclesiastic affiliation. Under such circumstances, the feudal lords of the Albanian countries found it difficult to unite, since their political positions were determined by others—usually victors, even if temporary ones—while the church would lead them the "Lord's Way," which was but affiliation with one or the other side. Moreover, the Albanians faced numerous invasions from the Slavic state of Rascia and the Bulgarian kingdom, which ruled over parts of Albania twice for periods spanning over a century.

The Albanians were under the same social and political framework when the Ottomans first arrived in the Balkans. At the time, the regional powers, such as the princes of Rascia who controlled major parts of Albania, held sway over Albanian princes. As the Ottomans defeated the Balkanians in one battle after another (at Maritsa, Bulgaria; at Beliche, Bosnia; and at Dardania Field) and placed them under their imperial command, the Albanians became "vassals of the vassals" and had their political alignments directed from above. Therefore, the Ottomans, who first appeared on the eastern borders of the Byzantine Empire and later penetrated to the western parts of the realm, attained influence over all contemporary social and political developments in the region.

---

[2] For more, see H.P.Sh. 1 (2002), 287-292.

[3] For more, see Konstandin Jireçek, *Historia e Serbëve* II (Tiranë: 2010), 137; Georg Ostrogorski, *Historia e Perandorisë Bizantine* (Tiranë: 2002), 382.

The Ottomans were descendants of the Oghuz Turks, who began to pierce into the eastern parts of the Byzantine Empire after they split off their primordial homeland in Central Asia. Initially, the empire did not pay due attention to their incursions, given the ongoing internal conflicts with the Slavs and the Bulgarians. Additionally, the Byzantines struggled to contain the Arabs, with whom they had continuous and extremely challenging confrontations since the 7th century. The first Byzantine encounter with the Seljuk Turks occurred in 1071, when the imperial forces suffered a hefty defeat, resulting in the loss of a substantial part of the eastern dominions.

The Oghuz Turks entered modern history when the Seljuk sultan granted their leader, Ertuğrul, a small dominion on the banks of the Sangarius (Sakarya) River; in 1243, however, a Mongolian invasion defeated the Seljuks and their state soon broke into numerous smaller entities.[4] As a result, Ertuğrul's son, Osman I (1290-1323), expanded his father's dominion and turned it into an independent state known as the Ottoman Emirate. The monarch attained the title of Sultan and his subjects, who would later form the Ottoman Empire, became known as the Ottoman Turks.[5]

In 1354, the Ottomans landed on the Balkans, setting the stage for further invasions. When they arrived in Albania, they found the local princes in a struggle for the lands that had been previously occupied by Rascia. After the death of Tsar Dušan in 1355, the *župans* (sing.: *župan*) and other noblemen who had been subjected by Rascia, launched their efforts for independence. As a result, the Balshas founded their principality in the north, the Thopias controlled central Albania, and the Muzakas had their possessions in the south; other families also created their own states (a more detailed overview of the pre-Ottoman Albanian principalities is given in volume 1 of the series).

As part of such developments, which may be termed internal (since the Albanians acted within their lands and, whenever inevitable, with only superficial loyalty to the Byzantine state or as vassals of Western powers such as Venice), the Albanians felt the Ottoman threat, but had no direct encounter with it. They avoided such contact even in 1364, when the Ottomans defeated the Byzantine army at Adrianople and, renaming the city to Edirne, made it their capital.

Furthermore, in a vortex of territorial expansionism, even to their own detriment, as was the case with the Balshas and the Thopias, the Albanians

---

[4] H.P.Sh. 1 (2002), 373.
[5] *Ibid.*

remained vassals of the lords of Rascia, Vukašin and Uglješa Mrnjavčević. The Rascian brothers, aided by Bulgarians and Greeks, led a Balkan coalition against the Ottomans. As a consequence of the Balkan defeat at Maritsa in 1371, the princes of Rascia and Epirus agreed to become vassals to the Ottomans.

Soon afterwards, the Ottomans reached the Albanian territories. Having taken Plovdiv, the capital of the Bulgarian kingdom, and coerced the Bulgarians into vassalage, the Ottomans appeared in Thrace and Epirus. There, the Turkish forces conquered the cities of Štip, Prilep, Manastir (also Monastir; Mac.: Bitola; Trk.: Manastır), Kostur (Grk.: Kosturia), and Ohër (Mac.: Ohrid; Trk.: Ohri). In addition to the ruling Palaiologos family, some Albanian noblemen in the Despotate of Epirus were also forced into vassalage, enabling the Ottomans to approach the coastal towns. The penetration, however, could provoke a confrontation with the Venetians and other Western powers. To test the Western stance on the region, the Ottomans launched a campaign in the Albanian countries, which were already at war with each other.

The Battle of Savra was a beneficial undertaking for the Ottomans whose participation in the conflict decided the outcome. Subsequently, they withdrew so the victory could be handed to the Thopias. Yet, the Thopias became vassals of the empire and the Muzakas and other noblemen from southern Albania followed suit, signifying but the beginning of an endless Ottoman presence in the region.

Ultimately, the temporary "retreat" of the Ottoman forces, lasting for about two years, was a test to see how Venice and other Western factors would react in the face of Turkish expansion. Then, the rising power would seek to submit all local rulers into vassalage, a relationship that curried great favors from them. The Ottomans benefited from the tributes they levied on their vassals who would also have to "accommodate" to a new imperial regime and a different civilization. Additionally, the new vassalages allowed the Ottomans to prepare for further campaigns in the West, since the new order "pacified" the areas that served as a bridge between the East and the Occident.

Certainly, "peace" between the Balkan vassals, who now included the majority of the Albanians with nobility titles and possessions that carried little importance, could have continued for a while, had the West remained inert. But aware that the *status quo* would favor the Ottomans in their planned invasion of Central Europe, the Western powers began to encourage the Balkan nobles to fight against the new empire. The West was aware that such endeavors would result in defeat, but sought to buy time, regardless of the price the Balkans, already accustomed to sacrifice, would pay.

The new situation, marked by hesitation and yet hopes of defense, created the impression that the Balkan lords would abandon their known quarrels and unite against the common enemy. However, political calculations soon became apparent. With the support and advice of missionaries from Catholic nations, Balkan leaders initiated their efforts for a broad regional coalition in 1387. Although the movement is credited to Rascian Knjaz Lazar Hrebljanović, whose office sent invitations for mutual action, the true initiative was taken by the Holy See, Venice, and above all Hungary. The latter in particular had multiple reasons for its involvement, since the Ottomans had targeted and would inevitably pass through the Magyar lands in the next European campaign.

The West directly instigated the Balkan alliance under the banner of Christendom, the sole "unifying" emblem for the divided region. However, the movement also induced the Ottomans. To secure their back and to rule out any possibility of a Bulgarian involvement, the new empire concentrated its forces in Plovdiv and prepared them for a march to Nish (Srb.: Niš), a city they had conquered two years prior. In the meantime, territories ranging from Rascia to the Dardani towns of Prishtina and Shkup (also Shkupi, Scupi, Scopia; Mac.: Skopje; Trk.: Üsküb, Üsküp) remained outside Ottoman control. Those appear partially as possessions of Prince Vuk Branković, who was likely of Triballi descent (and of the same family as Vojsava, the mother of the Albanian national hero, Skanderbeg),[6] and partially under the lordship of Balsha. The Lezha-Prizren highway was under the custody of Dhimitër Jonima. Upon passing Nish, Ottoman forces headed towards Dardania Field, where they faced the troops of the Balkan coalition. Alongside the armies of Albanian rulers—Gjergj II Balsha of Shkodër, Teodor Muzaka (Ita.: Theodore Musachi) from Myzeqe, Dhimitër Jonima, lord of the lands along the Lezha-Prizren highway, and Andrea Gropa of Ohër—the Turkish troops encountered the forces of Rascian Prince Lazar and his son-in-law, Vuk Branković. The Romanians under Voivode Mircea the Elder, Croatian troops

---

[6] See Boban Petrovski, "Vojsava Tribalda," *Symposium on Gjergj Kastrioti Skanderbeg* ([Shkup]: 2006): 67-77. Among others, Marin Barleti and Gjon Muzaka (John Musachi) also contend that the Brankovićis were Triballi, thus a remnant of a Slavicized Dardani tribe; in reference to Gjon Kastrioti's wife, Vojsava, the early Albanian writers note that her father was a Tribald.

led by Ban Ivan Horvat, and the army of Bosnian King Tvrtko were also part of the coalition.

Many historical sources note that the Battle of Dardania Field began on June 15th of 1389 and ended the same day, sometime in the evening, with the defeat of the Balkan Christian alliance. Sultan Murat I of the Ottomans found his death at the battle at the hands of Milesh Kopili, by many accounts an offspring of a local Albanian tribe (in Slavic literature, his name initially appeared as Miloš Kobilić, and later as Obilić). Kopili was a son-in-law of Knjaz Lazar who was also killed at the battle, as a sign of revenge, after he was caught prisoner. Meanwhile, the Ottomans also executed Kopili, who is revered as a double hero—by Albanians and by Slavs. Among Albanian nobles, Teodor Muzaka fell in the battle. The same day, Bayezid I, nick-named *Yıldırım* or "the Thunderbolt," succeeded his late father as the new Ottoman sultan.

The tragic epilogue at Dardania Field opened the way to further Otto-man conquests in the West, while sealing the fate of the Balkan peoples who, after their participation in combat, would suffer five-hundred years of oppression under the new empire.

Yet, while Bayezid I defeated the Balkan coalition, he did not chastise his enemy, as was expected. To the contrary, he made Vuk Branković a vassal. By several accounts, the new tributary had sabotaged the battle due to disagreements with his father-in law. Other sources indicate that Branković had welcomed the Ottomans so he could free himself of Rascian pressure, because, like Kopili (Lazar's other son-in-law), he was not a *Serb*. The Serbian historical epic, albeit fabricated in the 19th century to further the hegemonic ideology of the state, questions Branković's and Kopili's loyalty to Lazar, but such doubts would never be raised about a "true" Serb.[7] Using folklore and without sufficient historical references, Albanian scholars also support the assertion that Milesh Kopili and others were of Albanian ethnici-ty.[8] Meanwhile, independent academics, openly question the Slavic-

---

[7] See: Dena Debeljković, "O Kosovskom Boju," *Antologija Srpske Narodne Epike Kosova i Metohije* (1964); Dragutin Kostić, "Miloš Kopilić-Kobilić-Obilić," *Revue Internationale des Etudes Balqaniques* I (1934); Dragutin Subotić, *Yugoslav Popular Ballads* (Cambridge University Press, 1932); Tihomir Đorđević, *Boj na Kosovu* (Beograd: 1934).

[8] Fatos Arapi, *Këngë të moçme shqiptare* (Tiranë: 1986); Jahja Drançolli, *Në kërkim të origjinës së Millosh Kopiliqit* (Prishtinë: 2006); Muhamet Pirraku, "Pjesëmarrja e Shqiptarëve në betejën e Kosovës 1389," *Gjurmime Albanologjike*, seria e shkencave historike (1990); Selami Pulaha, *On the Presence of Albanians in Kosova During the 14th-17th Centuries*

Orthodox identity of Branković,[9] Kopili, and other despots of Dardania, back the thesis that the noblemen were *Slavicized, Christian Dardani*, mainly of the Triballi branch. The group, described by many historical accounts, was a mix of the ancient ethnic stratum and tribes invading from the east in the 7th century and onward. Later, after the newcomers accepted Christianity, around the 10th century, the mixed population turned into an important local factor.[10] While academic work on the topic is inconclusive, this position may be a starting point for further research, which may relieve scholars of fanatic entrapments, which have served the political conjunctures of the past.

The historical epics of both Serbs and Albanians used Kopili and Branković in myths purported to revive the national conscience in the 19th century and after. Nevertheless, the crucial Battle of Dardania Field was decisive in the rise of the Ottomans to the status of a world empire. The Turks would retain their eminence for five consecutive centuries until the 19th century, when Dardania became again a crucial factor—this time for the demise of the empire.

The rise of the Ottomans was to the detriment of the Balkan Christians, but was nevertheless made possible by them. After they first opposed the Ottomans at Maritsa and Dardania Field, the Balkanians submitted to vassalage, which enabled the empire's consolidation and westward expansion. Among the sultan's assistants, the first and the most useful were the so-called Slavic Hasians. Since Bayezid I, the Ottomans maintained sustainable alliances with the Hasians whose siding with the Turks was unfavorable to Balkan Christians. Here, the Albanians appear to be among the greatest victims, facing multiple punishments. The Ottomans held a grudge against the Albanians because of their loyalty to the Byzantine Empire at a time when even the rulers had turned their coats (the Palaiologos dynasty had accepted vassalage). Additionally, the Turks distrusted the Albanians as potential allies to Venice and main supporters of the West—the Catholic Church in particular. The small ethnic group also experienced harassments from the Rascians who, as vassals and principal supporters of the Ottomans

---

(Tiranë: 1993); Skënder Rizaj, *Falsifikimet e Historiografisë Serbe/The Falsifications of Serbian Historiography* (Prishtinë: 2006); Thoma Murzaku, "Lufta e banorëve të tokave lindore," *Konferenca e Dytë e Studimeve Albanologjike* [2nd Albanian Studies Conference] (Tiranë: 1969).

[9] Petrovski, "Vojsava Tribalda," *supra*, 67-77.

[10] Buxhovi, "Raportet shoqërore dhe politike midis Dardanëve dhe pushtuesve sllavë në shekujt XIII-XV," *Kosova* 1.

in the Balkans, took advantage of their new position to settle disputes with their neighbors in all respects.

In fact, the Rascian-Ottoman alliance had begun prior to the Dardania encounter. Later accounts refer to such a foreplay in which the sides prearranged the Ottoman victory in the battle. As a result, Rascian-led Orthodox princes would then benefit from a peace treaty with the Ottomans and retain religious and political privileges within the new empire. However, the Orthodox gave no thought to the fate of the Balkan Catholics.[11] Furthermore, the army of a Rascian nobleman, named Dejanović, joined forces with the Ottomans well before the battle. Likewise, many Rascian Vlachs fought alongside the Turks, who recorded their allies' participation in combat.[12] Indeed, Ottoman sources support the conclusion that the Rascians deliberately aided the Ottomans, seeing them as the only "savior" who could defend the Orthodox from the "Catholic threat" that relentlessly pursued them.[13]

Notwithstanding the consequences of the Balkan defeat at Dardania Field, Bayezid's approach to the Orthodox Slavs indubitably indicates he intended to use their military power, now under his behest, as a buffer against Hungary. The sultan felt the indispensable need for allies in the most vital parts of the Balkans to support his military expeditions. Bayezid also sought to subdue the smaller Seljuk principalities in Asia Minor,[14] in addition to the westward expansion; hence the overall stability the empire was essential. To reach his objective, the Ottoman ruler allowed Prince Lazar's sons to reign over the Slavic principalities according to their laws and customs. Nevertheless, the princes were to submit to the sultan's suzerainty and pay him the *jizya* tax and conscript a certain number of soldiers into a

---

[11] See the works of Jozef von Hamer, M. Šufflay, F. Babinger, S. Skëndo et al. in support of the theory. They refer to Lazar's son, Despot Stefan, who was among the first to accept Ottoman vassalage and participate with his army in the future battles, alongside the sultan, against the Hungarians and the Polish. Similarly, to back the theory, the scholars mention Đurađ Branković's sabotage of the Second Battle of Dardania Field and Mark Kraljević's alliance with the Ottomans.

[12] Bogumilj Hrabak, *Katoličko stanovništvo u Srbiji 1470-1700* (Beograd: 1978).

[13] See Ralf Bierman, *Lehrjahre im Kosovo* (Bonn, 2006), describing the Serbian comportment vis-à-vis the sultan prior to the Battle of Dardania Field: "Serbs have greater fear of an occupation from Catholic Hungary, than the Muslim Turks." [translated] The issue is addressed in a relation by the Bishop of Tivar, Guiliame Adea, *Directorium ad passagium faciendum* (1332), to Philip VI Valois, King of France.

[14] Muhamed Ali Salabri, *Perandoria Osmane: faktorët e ngritjes së saj* (Prishtinë: 2009).

separate unit that would participate in Ottoman campaigns. The sultan also married Lazar's daughter, Olivera, also known as Despina by other accounts.[15] The patriarch and the Orthodox clergy approved the matrimony and the bride was sent to the great harem in Bursa, where she met numerous royal consorts of noble Greek, Frankish, and Seljuk origin.[16] Stefan and Vuk Lazarević were to report twice to Bayezid's court and to assist him militarily upon request (other rulers—such as Marko Kraljević; Constantine, Despot Esau of Janina; Angelos of Thessaly; and, the Byzantine co-emperor, Manuel Palaiologos—were in an analogous relationship with the sultan). Multiple contemporary accounts note that King Sigismund of Hungary built a defense line against the sporadic excursions by Ottomans and Slavs, who operated jointly in the frontier areas. In 1390, the ban of Severin and a magistrate by the name of Ladislav captured in Braničevo Ottoman and Slavic flags.[17]

The Ottomans also gained the support of Vuk Branković, whose Dardania dominions extended from the town of Zvečan (Srb.: Zvečan) to Prishtina and then south to Shkup; they had been mainly under Rascian control since Stefan Nemanja's incursions beginning in 1191 (there were sporadic interruptions after the death of Dušan, when the Balshas and then the houses of Dukagjini and Kastrioti ruled over those areas). As a fallback—in case the Hungarians, Turks, or another power expelled him from his realm—Branković petitioned the coastal city-state of Ragusa for asylum for himself, his wife Mara, and sons (Đurađ, Grgur, and Lazar). Once the Ragusans granted his request in May 1390, Branković handed the city of Shkup to the Ottomans; later, he also surrendered Zvečan, Prizren, and a significant part of his Dardania domains.[18] Consequently, the old Dardani town of Shkup, where only two generations prior the Slavs had launched their attacks on the Albanian lords, became the offset of the Ottoman invasion.

Moving south from Shkup, the Ottomans captured the city of Ohër from the Gropaj family in 1394. To further weaken the Albanian nobility and seize more of their territories, they torched all of the Albanian castles in the area. Struga, Pogradec, and Starova were all destroyed, and the same strategy was also pursued during the invasion of Janina, Korça, and Përmet. For reasons noted before, the Ottomans were suspicious of Albanians and took a toll on them; they trusted, however, the princes of Rascia and the Greeks, who since

---

[15] *Ibid.* 87.

[16] Jireček, *Historia e Serbëve* II, 153.

[17] *Ibid.* 153.

[18] *Ibid.* 155.

inception showed a tendency for political intrigues, furthering the destruction of the Albanian nobility.

The northern campaign—from Zveçan to Shkodër (also Shkodra or Scutari) and Ulqin (Mont.: Ulcinj), then to Deja (Lat.: Dagnum) and Kruja—followed a similar pattern, although the Ottomans took care to preserve the mines, which they would later use for the needs of the empire. Therefore, they did not burn the castle at Zveçan, but placed it under an Ottoman *kefalos* (*Grk.*, headman). Meanwhile, they appointed an administrator (*kadı*) to manage the iron mine on the outskirts of Ras.

Nevertheless, the Ottoman conquest of northern Albania did not occur without military confrontations, which were absent in the former domains of Branković (as mentioned before, he became an Ottoman vassal in order to preserve his dominions in Dardania, but also because he would gain much greater influence than what he enjoyed under the Rascians).[19] The Ottomans fought the Balshas over Ulqin, the seat of the family, and over Shkodër. In 1391, Gjergj II Balsha called on Pope Boniface IX for aid, but little help arrived. Bayezid's army held the prince as a prisoner of war and only released him a year later when he agreed to surrender Shkodër, Drisht, and the port of Shëngjin.[20] Another nobleman, Dhimitër Jonima, did not follow Balsha's example: he accepted vassalage and held on to his strategic domains between Shkodër and Durrës.[21]

After Gjergj II Balsha, who was forced into vassalage, and Jonima, whose voluntary submissions spared him his lands, the Dukagjini brothers, Progon and Tanush, stood on the Ottomans' way. In the summer of 1393, the Dukagjinis handed Lezha to a Venetian admiral and, when the Ottomans reached the Adriatic Sea through the Buna River, the admiral occupied the nearby mouth of the Drin.

The Ottoman expansion continued until 1402, when it came to a halt for about a decade. The reason for the stagnation was the Ottoman defeat that year in the Battle of Ankara (Angora). In this confrontation with the Mongolian army of Tamerlane (Timur Lang), Bayezid fought with Stefan and Vuk Lazarević and their nephews, the Branković brothers, on his side.

Bayezid died a year after, while a prisoner of Tamerlane in Akşehir, where once stood the old kingdom of Phrygia; then, the Ottomans engaged

---

[19] See Buxhovi, *Kosova* 1 [Mesjeta], "Raportet etnike midis Arbërve dhe pushtuesve sllavë në shekujt XIII-XV."

[20] For more, see, Josef von Hamer, *Geschichte des Osmanischen Reiches* II, 175-183.

[21] *Ibid.* 183.

in a decade-long internal war of succession, with the late sultan's sons vying for the throne. Ottoman vassals also participated in the struggle: the Lazarevićis supported Musa, while the Brankovićis sided with Mehmed I (Trk.: *Mehmet*), nicknamed "the Wrestler" (Trk.: *Küreşci*). Leading his army from Asia into Europe, Mehmed encountered Musa's units at Philippoli and, after killing his own brother, acceded to the throne in July 1413. The beginning of Mehmed's eight-year rule also saw the resumption of Bayezid's conquests. In the Balkan campaigns, the new sultan had the assistance and advice of regional allies, the Brankovićis and other Orthodox noblemen. He had to begin by pacifying the Albanians in their entirety. Owing to its strategic position, Albania was conducive to an anti-Ottoman cohesion; an Albanian alliance with the West could cost the Ottomans hopes of reaching their ultimate target, Central Europe. In fact, they had already seen the Albanians turn the tide against the empire; during the interregnum period following the Battle of Ankara, local noblemen created several new entities. For instance, Niketa Thopia took over the former lands of the Venetian vassal, Konstandin Balsha, who ruled the city of Kruja. Gjon Kastrioti, son of Pal Kastrioti, established his dominion in the adjacent Mat region, and within a short period he was able to expand to the coast. In fact, he gained control of lands ranging from the Cape of Rodon near Durrës to Lezha and Shkodër and, as citizen of Venice and Ragusa, was put in charge of the highways leading to Prizren and Shkup. Like most feudal lords in northern Albania, Kastrioti swung between the two churches: there were Catholic clergy and abbacies in his dominions, but records also note that his endowments supported the Orthodox Hilandar Monastery on Mount Athos (present-day Greece).[22] At the beginning, he was a vassal of Venice, but by 1410 he was forced to submit to the Ottomans.[23] With Mehmed's return to the Balkans (where he preserved the alliance with the Slavic Orthodox princes, who not were his obedient vassals but his comrades-in-arms in all campaigns, including the ones against Hungary, Bosnia), the Ottomans focused on Albania and its Adriatic coast, seeking to eliminate all Albanian ties with Venice or other Western powers. To succeed in the Albanian campaign, Mehmed I continued to strengthen his main allies and vassals—the Rascians, but not excluding the Palaiologoi and the Greeks, who at the time were almost entirely under the Slavic Orthodox. The sultan granted Despot Stefan several lands,

---

[22] Jireček, *Historia e Serbëve* II, 173.
[23] See Thálloczy, Jireček, "Zwei Urkunden aus Nordalbanien," *Arch. Slav. Phil.* 21 (1899).

including the Koprijan castle in the vicinity of Nish, the Znepolje region in Trn, and the mountain range between Nish and Sofia. Likewise, the vassal emperor of the Byzantines, Manuel, regained the cities he had lost to Musa. Rascians and Greeks also established closer ties: the nephew of Despot Đurađ married Irene Kantakouzene, and Byzantines, including Irene's brother, Thomas, joined Rascian service.[24]

However, the Rascian lords, who were then Mehmed's right-hand men, hoped that the Ottoman campaign would not only subdue the recently-consolidated Albanian nobility, but put an end to the latter's alliances with Venice. If that were impossible, then the Serbs expected to oversee those alliances, a role for which they had the Ottoman support.

The Ottomans favored the Serbs; for instance, in 1412, imperial forces attacked and besieged Novobërda, and then handed the town to an offspring of Knjaz Lazar. After the death of Niketa Thopia in early 1415, the Ottomans conquered Kruja; in 1417, they seized Berat from Teodor Muzaka and Kanina along with Vlora from Rugina Balsha, whereas a year later they took Gjirokastër, the seat of the Zenebishi family.[25]

These conquests were made at a time when the Venetians defeated Mehmed I at sea near Gallipoli (1416) and forced him to make peace. The treaty implied that the Ottomans had agreed with the Republic of Venice over their interests in Albania, where the Turks would rule the interior and the Venetians would be in charge of the coastal town.

The last head of the Balsha family, who had then lost much of his realm, declared war on Venice with the support of his uncle, Despot Stefan Lazarević and his step-father Sandalj. These noblemen had defeated Sigismund of Hungary over coastal dominions. A Republic of the Adriatic was established in Split, Trogir, and the Brač, Korčula, and Lesina islands; the Kotor gulf was also included in the new state.

Seven years later, Balsha attached Venetian domains and sieged the castle of Drisht. The Venetians backfired by seizing Budva. This move led to peace negotiations, but as envisaged by Serbian Despot Stefan, Balsha did not take part and his principality was represented by the Serbs. Balsha, who had no son of his own and had appointed Stefan as his heir, was ill and died shortly thereafter, on April 28, 1421, and his successor buried him with honors.[26]

---

[24] For more, see "Glasnik," *Serb. Annalen*, 53-80; Mijatović, *Despoti Đurađ . . .*, 77.

[25] H.P.Sh. 1 (2002), 377.

[26] See Stanojević, *Arch. Slav. Phil.* 18 (1896): 459, cited in Jireček, *Historia e Serbëve* II, 186.

The last remaining Rascian leaders influenced the fate of a great part of Dardania. The Ottomans gave the region to Vuk Branković to rule as part of his vassal state. However, due to the economic importance of the Novobërda and Zveçan mines of Dardania, between 1394 and 1444, the Ottomans put their civil servants and soldiers in charge of the mineral production. Therefore, products could no longer be delivered to Ragusa or Venice, as had previously been the case, but would directly pour into the Ottoman treasury. Before the final conquest of Dardania in 1455, Branković's local government and the Ottoman authorities "coexisted," although the latter had the final word.[27]

Most of Dardania, north of Shkup and Tetova (Trk.: Kalkandelen; Mac.: Tetovo), fell to the Ottomans during the reign of Sultan Mehmed II, the Conqueror (1451-1481). Of course, the Ottoman target were the renowned mineral excavations at Novobërda, Zveçan, and Gllahovica (this one was rich in iron). Several sources indicate that "the sultan had gathered the Islamic army and had taken off for holy war from Shkup, from where he would pass along the Kara Tonlu Mountains [*i.e.*, Karadak of Shkup] to Novobërda." This town, which the Saxon German miners called *Neuberge* and the Italians *Novomonte*, had a strong fortress and several miner settlements around. There was the main Ragusan colony, but some Italians, especially Venetians, lived there, too. Many local noblemen resided in Novobërda, from where they oversaw the extraction, processing, and shipping of minerals. Because of their importance, the sultan had decided to place the mines under his absolute authority. To achieve his goal, he had to resort to his military, since the domestic noblemen insisted on the 1441 agreements with the Ottomans for joint use of the mines. The sultan first dispatched the unit of an officer by the name of Isa Bey, who called on the garrison chief to surrender. When the local commander refused to obey, the sultan himself marched into Novobërda with the rest of the army. A forty-day siege began immediately. Following several bombardments, as the defense walls of the castle began to fall, the city surrendered on June 1, 1455. The Ottomans eliminated much of the city leadership and took 320 young men to be trained as janissaries.[28] It was rumored that the sultan's soldiers discovered a great silver treasure that Vuk Branković's son had kept in the castle and took it to Constantinople.[29]

---

[27] For more, see K. Jireček, J. Radonić, *Istorija Srba* I (Beograd: 1952), 369, 422.

[28] Babinger, *Mehmet Pushtuesi dhe koha e tij*, 145.

[29] Rizaj, *Kosova gjatë shekujve XV, VI dhe VIII*, 20.

The fall of Novobërda, hailed as a bastion of Christendom, was ill-received news in Italy and Hungary. Despot Đurađ Branković learned of the defeat on June 21, while at a convention of noblemen in Rab, Hungary. There, the region's lords were preparing for a Christian campaign against the Ottomans.[30]

Unmoved by the Christian plan, Sultan Mehmed II led his army to Trepça and easily seized the town's castle. There, too, he found a great treasure and in the meantime gained control of the rest of the silver mines. On his way back, he rested in *şehitlik* (*Trk.*, martyrdom), the site where Sultan Murad I had been killed in 1389. Mehmed then headed to Salonika (Thessaloniki), and from there returned to Edirne.[31]

The Beginning of Ottoman Rule in Medieval Albania

The defeat at Maritsa paves the way for vassal states in the Balkans; the Battle of Savra marks the beginning of Ottoman rule in Medieval Albania. The Balkan peoples suffer a historical defeat in the Battle of Dardania Field. The Ottomans gradually install their administration in the occupied territories; the first sanjaks—including Arnavud-İl, Vuçitërn, Dukagjin, Prizren, Shkup, and Shkodër—are formed in the Elayet of Rumelia or the European territories. The timar system undermines the Albanian nobility; the Albanian lords oppose the expropriation and organize their first uprisings. The Thopias and Arianitis rebel; the noninvolvement of Kastrioti, Dukagjini, and other families furthers the occupation of the country. Venice divides Albania and signs a peace treaty with the Ottomans to the detriment of the Albanians. Albanians join the ranks of spahis and subaşıs for the first time.

The Ottomans established their rule over Albania in several stages. First, the Turks turned the local realms into vassal states (after the 1371, 1385, and 1389 battles). Then, direct conquest took place—in central and southern Albania between 1412 and 1420 and in Dardania from 1445 to 1456, culminating in 1479 with the fall of Shkodër. For most of its part, the Ottoman expansion ruined the Albanian principalities and the like social structures;

---

[30] Babinger, *Mehmet Pushtuesi dhe koha e tij*, 146.
[31] *Ibid.* 20.

the Kastrioti, Dukagjini, Jonima, Arianiti dynasties suffered defeat. In Dardania, on the other hand, the Ottomans put an end to the bicentennial rule of the Nemanides (Srb.: Nemanjići) and succeeding dynasties of Rascia. In the last two hundred years, the Rascians had not only prevented but fought against any state of Albania, including entities such as the Kingdom of Albania (the House of Anjou, instrumental in the foundation of this state, added the royal crown as a symbol of Albania's political union with their other domains).

In parts of Albania, the Ottomans appeared as invaders; in others, such as in Dardania, they were the "liberators" from the Slavic Orthodox occupation. But the new circumstances allowed the Albanians, albeit under foreign rule, to unite. As a consequence, they appeared as a single social and ethnic unit, which during the five centuries of the Ottoman period would be known as *Arnavudluk* (or *Arnavutluk*, *Trk.*, Albania), regardless of whether the people would be treated as *Arnavud* (*Trk.*, Albanian) or within the *millet-i osman* (Ottoman nationality).

The unification of the Albanians, however, should not be so one-sidedly assessed as to allow fictive conclusions on the "benefits" of occupations (though we may not disregard the facts either). After the conquest, the Ottomans installed their administration, which involved a type of military feudalism known as the *timar* system. A *timar* was a fief, after the Byzantine model, which allowed the Ottoman authorities to oversee defense, production, and taxation.

The administrative system of the Ottoman Empire evolved hand-in-hand with the territorial growth of the state. The map of the empire underwent significant changes since the time the Ottomans set foot in the Balkans and began their westward expansion. The state was divided into several administrative units: the *sanjak* (Trk.: *sancak*, banner) was originally the largest and a subdivision of a sanjak was known as a *kaza*, further divided into *nahiyes* (*subaşılık* was also a subdivision of the sanjak of which more will be said later). During the reign of Murad I, the *elayet* or *beylerbeylik* (*Trk.*, a dominion under a "lord-in-chief") as a top-level administrative division of the empire. Initially, there were only two elayets: Rumelia (from *Rûm*, from *Arb.*, Rome; Turkish for Christian), formed in 1362, and Anadol (Anatolia) since 1393. The administrative seat of Rumelia was first at Edirne, then Galipoli, and later Plovdiv. In the 15th century, the elayet capital was moved to Sofia and then to Manastir.[32]

---

[32] Rizaj, *Kosova gjatë shekujve . . .*, 41.

Although the Ottomans espoused the idea of a centralized administration, the conquered areas were governed in different ways, depending on the local peculiarities. Besides the elayets, the empire created another administrative unit known as *hükümet* (plural *hükümetler*), which were self-governing tribal territories ruled by tribe leaders, the *ahiret*.[33] According to this form of governance, the Albanian highlands enjoyed internal autonomy. The Ottoman *kanunnames* (codified laws) note that "the Kurdish, Albanian, and Arab *bajraktars* (tribe leaders) were secure and independent, but they were very poor and powerful [sic], while the voivodes of Wallachia and Moldavia were not as secure and independent."[34] In the Balkans, Montenegro was also organized as an autonomous tribal territory, known as the Kara Dağ Vilayet; it was supervised by the sanjak of Shkodër and Dukagjin and made up of 9 *nahiyes* (sing. *nahiye*).[35]

According to known sources, the Ottomans created several sanjaks in Albania during the 15th century, including the Pashasanjak of Shkup (Trk.: Üsküb) consisting of 344 timars, and the sanjaks of Vuçitërn (also Vushtrri; Trk.: Vıçıtırın), Prizren, Shkodër (also Shkodra, Trk.: İşkodra), Dukagjin (Trk.: Dukacin), Elbasan, Ohër (Trk.: Ohri; Mac.: Ohrid), and Vlora (also Vlona; Trk.: Avlonya). (See Table 1 in Appendix.)

The sanjaks of Preveza and Janina and *Sancak-i Arvanid* (*Trk.*, the Sanjak of Albania or the Albanian sanjak; Alb.: Sanxhaku i Arbrit, Albania), among others, were also established in Albania.[36]

Sanjak of Shkup appeared as the most important; its 22 nahiyes extended over a large area from Salonika in the southeast to Gostivar and Kërçova (Mac.: Kičevo) in the northwest. *Sancak-i Arvanid*, with Gjirokastër as its administrative center, was another large division, covering the territories from Çamëria in the south to the Mat River in the north. *Sancak-i Arvanid* was divided into smaller units, including several *nahiyes*.[37]

A sanjak was governed by a *sanjakbey* (Trk.: *sanjak beyi*, sanjak lord), who commanded the sanjak army, made up of hundreds of *spahis* (Trk.: *sipahi*). A *vilayet* was led by the *subaşı*, the commander of the spahis who had

---

[33] *Ibid.* 42.

[34] Albert Howe Lybyer, *The Government of the Ottoman Empire in the time of Suleiman the Magnificent* (Cambridge: Harvard UP; London: Oxford UP, 1913), 297, cited in Rizaj, *Kosova gjatë shekujve XV, XVI dhe XVII*, 42.

[35] B. Đurđev, *Turska vlast u Crnoj Gori u XVI i XVII veku* (Sarajevo: 1959), 95.

[36] H.P.Sh. 1 (2002), 379.

[37] *Ibid.* 379.

their timars in the region. In every vilayet, the *subaşı* was assisted by the *kadı* (from Arb.: *qadi*, judge), heads of the Sharia (Islamic law) courts, who performed administrative, civil, judicial, and religious tasks. Besides the *kadı*, the Ottoman administration included other civil servants, including the *naivs*, the *kadı* deputies, and the *imams*, as religious leaders. City castles also had a *dizdar*, a garrison commander; each was granted his own *timar*. The non-Muslim population, *i.e.*, the Christians, was known as *râya* (*Trk.*, subjected).[38]

The status of the *râya* developed from the idea of *holy war* (Trk.: *cihad*, from Arb.: *jihad*) as a fundamental principle in the establishment and the growth of the Ottoman state. The first Ottoman principality, formed in 1302 after a victory over the Byzantine army at Nicaea (a former Byzantine capital), completely adhered to the principles of *dar-ul-islam* (Arb., the Islamic world). The conquests to the West were achieved under the motto of turning the whole world into an Islamic empire. Yet, the *holy war*, which was successfully waged by the Ottomans, did not aim at destroying but at subjecting "the infidel world," the *dar-ul-harb*. Therefore, the Ottomans founded their empire by uniting under their rule Muslim Anatolia with Christian Balkans. Although permanent *holy war* was a fundamental principle of the state, the Ottomans appeared at the same time as protectors of the Orthodox Church of millions of its followers.[39]

Islam guaranteed the life and property of Orthodox Christians and the Jews, on the condition that they remain obedient and pay per capita taxes. They were allowed to practice their religion and live in accordance with their religious law. During the early years of the empire, the Ottomans followed a policy of seeking the peaceful and voluntary submission of Christians before resorting to war.[40]

After the Ottomans landed in the Balkans in 1326, there were no more "voluntary" submissions. Lastly, Mikhail Gazi, a Greek nobleman near the Turkish border, embraced Islam and cooperated with the Ottomans.[41] However, submission through war was soon to follow; the vassal states were only a transitional period that set the stage for later conquests. Vassalage developed as a general phenomenon in the Balkans after the 1371 Battle of Maritsa, and one Balkan state after the other became vassals of the Ottoman

---

[38] *Ibid.* 380.

[39] Inalxhik, *Perandoria Osmane*, 19.

[40] *Ibid.* 19.

[41] *Ibid.* 19.

Empire. This practice of submission was also aided by the Byzantine emperor, Palaiologos, who pled Ottoman assistance in retaining his throne.

Since the Ottomans respected the principles of feudalism, the vassal states were initially requested only a small annual *haraç* tax. This tribute was paid as a sign of submission to the Islamic state and did not impose a material burden on them. However, as the Ottoman Empire needed increasingly higher tax revenue to cove the military expenses, the vassal princes began to feel the growing encumbrance. This led to open conflicts with the Ottomans, especially between 1441 and 1460, when Sultan Mehmed II put an end to the vassal principalities, turning them into integral parts of the empire. As a consequence, the old system was replaced with the new Ottoman system and the previous vassal feuds were placed under state custody, converted into *timars*, or distributed as *yaya* (compensation for military services for Ottoman farmers who had joined the army). Therefore, the Ottoman regime placed a centralized administration instead of a decentralized feudal system, which had gained momentum in the later stages of the Byzantine period. The Turks imposed universal regulations instead of taxation right and other privileges that the previous feudal lords had enjoyed under the Byzantines.[42]

In the Ottoman system, the *timar* was the state-owned land, representing the basic factor providing for the revenue as well as the defense of the empire. A *spahi*, as *timariot* (*i.e.*, holder of the land grant), was responsible not only for defense, but also for the agricultural production of his feud. Therefore, the empire made sure that, once it established its rule over newly-conquered territories, a local administration was set up and a land and population census was carefully carried out. Then, the state delegated additional authorities to the *spahi*, entrusting him with maintaining order in the countryside.

The *timar* system intended to secure troops for the sultan's army, which kept a large cavalry under central command. When the sultan ordered a war campaign, the *spahis*, under the leadership of the *subaşı*, came together under the banner of the *sanjakbey*. The *sanjakbeys* united around the standard of the *beylerbey*, while each *beylerbey* would in turn the sultan's army at the order place and time.[43]

The *timar* system, as an administrative organization, from the *beylerbey* to the *spahi*, represented the sultan's executive power in the provinces. The

---

[42] *Ibid.* 31.
[43] *Ibid.* 217.

imperial officers constituted a type of police force responsible for protecting the *râya*, but they also collected taxes and implemented property laws. The head of the police administration in the province was the *beylerbey*.[44] Below his rank, there was a *defterdar* and *defter ket hüdası*, who administered the *timars*, and a *hazin-e defterdar*, financial secretary overseeing revenue for the imperial treasury.

As noted, the sanjak was the original top-level administrative division; then, several sanjaks formed a *beylerbeylik* or an *elayet*. One of the sanjaks within the elayet was under the direct administration of the *beylerbey* and was known as *pashasanjak* (Trk.: *paşasancak*, sanjak of the pasha). A smaller division, known as *subaşılık*, was a component of a sanjak; the *subaşı*, the head of a *subaşılık*, resided in the city and controlled the *spahis* who dwelled in the surrounding villages.[45]

The *beylerbey* also had other property called *has*, dispersed throughout the sanjaks of the elayet. Similarly, a *sanjakbey* also had *has* estates throughout the sanjak's *subaşılıks*.

Another administrative division of the provinces was the *kadılık*, the territory under the jurisdiction of a *kadı*. The *kadıs* lived in towns and made up the backbone of the Ottoman administration; in the 15th century, a *kadı* could also be promoted as *sanjakbey* or *beylerbey*.[46]

The third pillar of the provincial administration was the *hazin-e deftedar* as the financial officer who, like the finance minister of the empire, protected the sultan's treasury. Therefore, the centralized governance helped prevent the provincial pashas from obtaining excessive power. To this goal, the sultan was also served by the *janissary* (Trk.: *yeniçeri*, Alb.: *jeniçer*) garrisons,[47]

---

[44] *Ibid.* 223.

[45] *Ibid.* 224.

[46] *Ibid.* 225.

[47] The Janissary corps represents the elite contingent of imperial troops, established in the 15th century, during the Ottoman incursions into the Balkans and the West. Janissaries were usually children of Christians subjected to the *devşirme* or blood tax given to the sultan. The children taken under the system were sent to Constantinople, where they were diligently trained as future soldiers. In addition to the military training, they underwent a spiritual education under the supervision of the Bektashi religious order. The janissaries did not have the right to have a family. The order became synonymous with the military successes of the Ottoman Empire. In the 18th century, Sultan Selim III decided to dissolve the janissaries in favor of a professional army. The janissary order was forcefully abolished in 1836 when Mahmud II massacred thousands of fanatic dervishes and janissaries, who rebelled against

which were stationed in towns as an additional force to keep the local authorities from exercising arbitrary power.[48] The janissary units were made of three to five hundred soldiers who acted only under the direct orders of the sultan.

The Ottomans installed this system of administration in Albania as well, although it was done, as said, in two stages: between 1441 and 1455 when Mehmed II conquered Dardania, and between 1479-1485 when the whole country fell under the Ottomans.

It is noteworthy that the conquests of both phases ended with Albania's inclusion in the Elayet of Rumelia, which in Turkish meant *land of the Christians*. Since the Albanians, like the other peoples of the region, were Christians, it was a natural decision of the Turks to include the Albanians in a Christian administrative unit, where they remained for the entire Ottoman period.

Besides the elayet, the Ottomans established the *vilayet* (province), as a special unit within *sanjaks*. The *vilayet*, however, only covered newly-conquered Christian land, and were usually governed by locals.[49]

The vilayet was therefore the model administration in the country, since Islam had not yet considerably spread in the European dominion of the empire. The size of a vilayet varied; only by the second half of the 1800s did the vilayet become the highest-level administrative division in the Ottoman Empire.[50]

The establishment of Ottoman rule in Albania, like in other parts of the empire, was followed by the *defters* (sing. *defter*, register). The earliest known document of this kind is a cadaster of the year 835 hegira (1431 or 1432), titled *Defter-i Sancak-i Arvanid* (Cadaster of the Sanjak of Albania). It covers a part of the western territories, spanning from Çamëria to Mat. Along with the distribution of timars at the time of the survey, the register contains notes on earlier periods, the reign of Sultan Bayezid I (Trk.: Beyazıt, 1389-1402) and Sultan Mehmed I (Trk.: Mehmet, 1413-1421).[51]

---

the sultan. Since then, the Ottomans banned the Bektashi order and destroyed all its tekkes in the Constantinople area. A part of the Bektashis, however, took shelter in Albania and Bosnia, where they continued their activity. During the Albanian Renaissance (Alb.: *Rilindja*), the Bektashi community supported the national movement and many Bektashis became militants of Albanianism (Alb.: *shqiptarizma*).

[48] Inalxhik, *Perandoria osmane,* 226.

[49] Rizaj, *Kosova gjatë shekujve . . .,* 50.

[50] *Ibid.* 50.

[51] H.P.Sh. 1 (2002), 378.

Another early *defter*, dealing with Dardania, is that of *Vilayet-i Vlk* (Vilayet of Vuk), compiled in 1455 (that year, Mehmed II personally led a campaign for the conquest of Dardania, bringing an end to the Rascian occupation that began with Župan Stefan Nemanja in 1191, continued through the reign of Stefan Dušan in 1343-1355 to the despotate of the Triballi Brankovićis).

According to *Defter-i Mufassal Vilayet-i Vlk*, the province was divided into seven *nahiyes*: Trgovishta (Rožaje), Kllopatnik (Drenica), Dollc, Morava (Gjilan), Vuçitërn, Toplica, Prishtina, and Llab. The vilayet spread south all the way to Shkup, eastward to Lebanje, and northeast to Bllaca (Srb.: Blaca) and Prokupa (also Procopia; Srb.: Prokuplje), to the north to Priboj, to the northwest to Rožaje.[52] Later, from the vilayet's territory, the Ottomans formed the Sanjak of Vuçitërn, which is covered in 1477-1478 *defters*, encompassing timars in the *subaşılıks* of Vuçitërn, Llab, Upper Obrovc, Prishtina, Morava, and Toplica. Later, other areas were added to the sanjak. In the 1521-1522 *defters*, the sanjak included lands up to Kopaonik and Gollak, and extended south to the Karadak Mountains of Shkup; cities like Prishtina, Vuçitërn, Trepça, and Novobërda were part of the sanjak.

The disbandment of the Vilayet of Vuk and the appearance of the Sanjak of Vuçitërn is not only a simple administrative reform that accompanied the installation of Ottoman rule after the end of the vassal states, such as the despotate of Vuk Branković (the sultan's last allies in the area). In fact, the change from the vilayet to the sanjak reflected the ethnic makeup of the local population. Later assessments reveal the majority were indigenous Christian Albanians of the Orthodox rite; the Slavic Orthodox Church had long endeavored to strip them of their native identity in favor of the Slavic one. In the 1530-1533 defters, the Sanjak of Vuçitërn was divided into four *kazas* and nine *kasabas*. The sanjak had 26,573 inhabitants, only 283 of whom were Muslims (see Appendix, Table 2).[53]

The Sanjak of Vuçitërn was of great importance throughout its existence and, it would in away become a barometer of the social, economic, and spiritual developments—since these areas would witness the most dramatic conversions from Christianity to Islam. The changes also reflected the ethnic character of the population. The indigenous Albanians would up to the 19th century be recorded in a compact area that also included the Sanjak of Nish.

---

[52] Hadžibegović et al., *Oblast Brankovića* (Sarajevo: 1972).

[53] Rizaj, *Kosova gjatë shekujve . . .,* 53.

From this standpoint, the Sanjak of Prizren was also important, as were those of Shkodër and Dukagjin. The registers of these sanjaks between the 16th and 18th century clarified the Albanian border with Montenegro and Serbia, which appeared as autonomous provinces in the 1800s and were recognized as independent states at the 1878 Congress of Berlin. As instigators of the conflicts that culminated during the First Balkan War, these Balkan countries returned, after five centuries, parts of Albania under Slavic Orthodox rule.

Before that development, which would return to the pre-Ottoman state of the 15th century, the sanjaks of Prizren, Shkodër, and Dukagjin represent the changes through which those areas passed through from 1420 to 1479—from the beginning of the Ottoman vassal states to the complete conquest. The Ottoman occupation reclaimed the importance that these areas had for the construction of what later appeared as an ethnic entity with its own particularities, such as self-governance and the special statutes that the lands enjoyed even under Turkish rule.

Therefore, it may be noted that since 1455 when Dardania and northern Albania fell under Ottoman control, they were administered by the sanjaks of Vuçitërn and Shkup as well as the sanjaks of Prizren, Shkodër, and Dukagjin, which belonged to the Elayet of Rumelia. The Sanjak of Vuçitërn was the first sanjak of Dardania. Formed after 1455, it included a large part of Dardania—the areas from Kopaonik in the north to the Shkup Karadak in the south; from Toplica, Llap, and Gollak in the east to the Sirenica parish, Sharr, and Drenica in the west—which naturally interconnected the Albanian-inhabited lands. This sanjak remained intact until 1689 when it was brought under the sanjak of Shkup.[54]

The Sanjak of Prizren, formed after 1459, included a broad area, from Sharr in the south to Yeni Pazar, Bihor, and Brvenik in the north; from Drenica in the east to Peja and Gjakova in the west. This sanjak, too, reclaimed the importance of the roads connecting Dardania with other regions.

On the other hand, the Sanjak of Dukagjin, whose history dates since 1462, with its seat at Peja and in Lezha, included the *nahiyes* of Montenegro (as vilayet), the *nahiye-kaza* of Peja (İpek) and Altın-İli (the highlands from Gjakova to Tropoja) in the north, and extended to Dibër and Mat in the south; from Luma and Opoja in the east to Lezha and the Adriatic Sea in the west.[55]

---

[54] *Ibid.* 65.
[55] *Ibid.* 65.

The Sanjak of Shkodër was formed after the Ottoman conquest of the city in 1479. Several regions of the Dukagjin Sanjak will be added to Shkodër. According to the 1485 defter, the Sanjak of Shkodër contained four *kazas*: Shkodër, Podgorica, Peja, and Bihor. The kaza of Peja was made up of the *nahiyes* of Peja and Altın-İli (the areas between Gjakova, Junik, and Tropoja).[56] But, the Peja *nahiye*, by the end of 1578, is registered under the Sanjak of Dukagjin. Meanwhile, Montenegro was returned to the Sanjak of Shkodër earlier, in 1576.[57]

The arrangements of the sanjaks, despite the numerous changes, such as the swapping of territories, can only be understood through the lens of the new property organization that provided the basis for the social, economic, and political development of the empire. The *timar* system was a type of state feudalism; as such, it enabled a more advanced social order than its contemporary European counterpart, which at the time was in a process of disintegration. However, as of the second half of the 16th century, the new Ottoman system began to loosen up and the early *çiftlik* estates appeared, marking the beginning of a new feudal system.[58]

Nevertheless, until the final establishment of the *çiftlik* system, a process that took over 150 years, the conquered land in Rumelia had the status of *miriye* (Trk.: *eraz-i miriye* or *eraz-i memleket*, state-owned land). This means that the ownership of the land was not conveyed to Ottomans servicemen; instead, the real property was only given for use as a compensation for service. Such a land grant was known as a *dirlik* (also *derlik*) and could belong, according to its size and income generated, to one of three categories: *has, ziamet* (also *zeamet*), or *timar* (hence the name of the system). The *dirlik* was land given for subsistence, for the maintenance of an army, and the generation of an income; this type of land could not be inherited or sold. The *has* was the largest type of *derlik* with annual revenue of 100 aspers (Trk.: *akçe*). The *defters* of 1256-28 note that the sultan had a *has* estate in Prishtina, Trepça, and Novobërda; mines, including Novobërda, Trepça, and Janjeva, were also declared a *has* of the sultan.[59] Furthermore, the sultan had a *has* in Gjakova and its vicinity, which provided revenue of 3,000 aspers. The *zeamet* or *ziamet* was the second-category *dirlik* with its annual revenue between 20,000-99,000 aspers. This estate was given to *alaybeys*, fleet com-

---

[56] Selami Pulaha, *Defteri i regjistrit të Sanxhakut të Shkodrës i vitit 1485*, I, II (Tiranë: 1974).

[57] Rizaj, *Kosova gjatë shekujve . . .* , 63.

[58] *Ibid.* 78.

[59] Rizaj, *Rudarstvo Kosova i susednih krajeva od XV do XVII veka* (Prishtinë: 1968), 3-22.

manders, or *defterdars* (bookkeepers) or the *timars*; their use of the *zeamat* was known as *zaim*. The *timar*, in turn, was the third category of *dirliks* with revenue between 3,000 to 19,999 aspers. In the sanjaks coverings Dardania, there were 939 timars, of which 344 were in the Sanjak of Shkup, 53 in the Sanjak of Dukagjin, 225 in the Sanjak of Prizren, and 317 in the Sanjak of Vuçitërn.[60]

In addition to the *derlik*, there were other types of land grants: *vakıf*, *ocalık*, and *mukata*. These were property that the state distributed to public institutions such as *mosques, madrasas, hospitals, and dormitories*. Among those types of estates, the *ocalık* was instrumental in the erection of social and government structures in the conquered lands in accordance with the political principles of the empire. Thus, besides the janissary commanders, known as *dizdars*, *ocalıks* (ojaluk; *Trk.*, hearth) were given to local landowners who embraced Islam and gained the right to join the higher ranks of the Ottoman administration. Among the beneficiaries were the Rrotullaj, Mahmutbegolli, Bushati families, which governed the sanjaks of Prizren, Dukagjin, and Shkodër.[61]

Although the state-owned land was not alienable, the Ottomans allowed for another type of estate, called *bashtina* (Srb.: *baština*, inheritance), which could be inherited. This kind of property included vineyards, gardens, and houses of Christians. The *bashtina* was land passed down from the father.

Nevertheless, the timar system, especially in Albania, was a step backward that in effect returned to the earlier Byzantine land grants known as *pronoia*. The structure affected different social classes in various ways. The peasant, for instance, was given land, in which he toiled and brought revenue to the state and the superior structures—the spahis and the rest of the hierarchy. At the same time, the local nobility also declined, having generally lost its land. Only a part of the noblemen integrated among the spahis and the leaders of the Ottoman state.

However, the new system did not completely eliminate the previous local nobility from the social and political life. The timar system radically changed the concept of property and its use, making the land state property under tight supervision. But it did not prevent the local noblemen from being included in the system. In fact, there are indications that the Ottomans had quite a principled approach to the Albanian nobility in order that it

---

[60] Rizaj, *Kosova gjatë shekujve . . .*, 78.
[61] *Ibid.* 79.

would become part of the new system they installed. Therefore, in the early stage of the timar system, many Albanian aristocrats became spahis without any religious requirements. However, even before the timar system, during the period of vassal states, which could be seen as a stepping stone into the subsequent full conquest, the Ottomans coerced or stimulated the Albanian lords to send their young sons as hostages to the sultan's court. These boys were called *iç oğlans* and educated as part of the elite; after they converted to Islam, they were educated in a spirit of loyalty to the sultan. After a decade, when it was thought that these young men had become true Ottomans, they were given timars and great offices, according to their aptitude. Through the *iç oğlan* system the Ottomans had educated Gjon Kastrioti's son, Skanderbeg, Teodor Muzaka's son, Jakup Bej, Gjon Zenebishi's son, Hamza Bej, and many others who became important figures in the higher ranks of the Ottoman service.[62]

Another measure that stimulated the integration of the Albanian nobility in the Ottoman administration and military was the education of the *gulams* (adult sons). Sons of Albanian noblemen would stay with the *beylerbeys* and *sanjakbeys*; through services, the *gulams* would prepare for their career as feudal lords. After this stage, those who embraced Islam could be given not only timars but also the lands of their family and relatives. Yet, the *iç oğlans* and *gulams* of Albanian descent gained timars and positions not only in their land, but in other parts of the Ottoman Empire, too.[63]

Despite the integration, the timar system did not implement as expected in Albania. While the expropriation of the nobility gave land to the peasantry (a positive development on its own), the process was difficult and marred by severe disputes that even lead to various uprising.

The opposition to the timar system was expected, since the whole development was accompanies by violent measures, including the land and population census (Trk.: *mufasal*). This was marked by numerous irregularities, with the spahis making arbitrary decisions in order to gain more land, regardless of the local reports and peculiarities. In addition, the local landowners opposed their expropriation without any due compensation. The opportunity to join service as spahis was unacceptable to many because of the conditions such as conversion to Islam. The new religion was not openly

---

[62] H.P.Sh. 1 (2002), 328.
[63] *Ibid.* 382.

required—and there were instances where Christians became spahis made it to the higher ranks of the empire—but it was in most cases implied.

To implement the timar system, the *sanjakbeys* often used military power. They attacked disobedient villages, turning them into ruins, and crushed armed uprising. The targets of such revolts were the violent spahis, usually from the non-native military class. A register, compiled in 1431 or 1432, notes that in the vilayets of Pavël Kurti, Çartalloz, Tomorica, Këlcyra, among others, no timar belonged to the spahis of foreign origin who were present during the previous census.[64]

The uprisings of the Albanian nobility against the Ottoman rule in their land (the Arianiti revolt in 1420-1430 and later Skanderbeg's resistance) are noted by two factors. First, there was the expansion of the Pashasanjak of Shkup under the Evrenoz family. This dynasty had consolidated economically, and its growth ran counter the Albanian landowners, who suffered their demise. The other factor had to do with the Ottoman-Venetian war over Thessaloniki (1428-1430): the Albanians hoped to gain from the conflict as it was expected to weaken the Ottomans. However, as was later attested, the Albanians suffered setbacks for halting the Evrenozes was impossible. For instance, the Evrenozes and Đurađ Branković attacked Gjon Kastrioti's domain and only after his sons, Skanderbeg and Stanisha, then in Ottoman services, intervened at the higher imperial authorities, was the Kastrioti principality spared; the dispute was resolved by an agreement with Isak Bey Evrenoz. In the meantime, the Ottomans did not include their Albanian vassals in the relations with the West; the peace treaty with Venice that concluded the Thessaloniki war was of no benefit to the Albanians. The exclusion was most unfavorable to the Kastrioti principality that, even after becoming an Ottoman vassal in 1410, continued to maintain parallel ties with Venice. Gjon Kastrioti signed several agreements with the Venetians, granting them access to the Lezha-Prizren highway and addressing other matters of interest to Albania.

Gjon Kastrioti's agreement with the Evrenoz allowed the Albanian state to recuperate. However, the peace treaty with Venice encouraged Sultan Murad II to concentrate his military in Albania; having secured the port city of Thessaloniki, Murad II planned to further the western expansion with a campaign against Hungary. For this reason, the sultan spent the 1432-1433 winter in Serres (in modern-day province of Macedonia, Greece), waiting to

---

[64] *Ibid.* 385.

attack the Albanian troops of Gjergj Arianiti. This nobleman had escaped imprisonment in the sultan's court and returned to Albania; as leader of a growing rebellion, Arianiti was then threatening the recently-installed timar system in his homeland.[65]

However, before settling accounts with the Arianitis, the sultan had to suppress yet another Albanian rebellion. An Ottoman vassal, Prince Andrea Thopia resisted his suzerain, when the 1432/1433 census (Trk.: *mufasal*) expropriated Thopia's dominions in Durrës, Petrela, and Kruja. Although the direction of the campaign against Thopia is uncertain, records note that he lost a good portion of his possessions, including the castles of Kruja, Petrela, and Deja (Dagnum); Thopia continued his resistance in other areas, reaching Lezha's vicinity.[66]

Nevertheless, Thopia's uprising did not spread to Lezha due to Venetian influence. Venice held Lezha, Durrës, and Shkodër, but having lost Thessaloniki to the Ottomans, did not allow the Albanian lords to affect Venetian relations with the sultan. Likewise, the republic did not permit Nikollë Dukagjini, lord of a Venetian protectorate, to reclaim the city of Deja. In fact, the Venetians not only did not permit Dukagjini's plan, but they sent their own troops to ensure Deja's delivery to the Ottomans. In a letter to the sultan, the Venetian senate called him "brother"; for that reason, it had ordered the Count of Shkodër not to give support—shelter, property, or money—to any rebellious lords, including Nikollë Dukagjini.[67]

Since Venice, Albania's greatest ally, had made peace with the Ottomans, while Kastrioti kept restraint with agreements with his parallel agreements (with both, the Venice and the Ottoman Empire), the Thopias and Dukagjinis could only hope that uprisings would occur further from the Venetian territories. This came from Gjergj Arianiti (also Arianit Komneni or Komnenos); after his escape from imprisonment in Edirne, he returned to Albania and declared the rebellion by killing the spahis who had settled on his lands.[68]

Following the initial success, the uprising spread to the southwest of the country where Arianiti hoped to capture Gjirokastër, the capital of *Sancak-i*

[65] K. Bozhari, "Lufta shqiptaro-turke e shekullit XV," *Burime bizantine* (Tiranë: 1967), 44-46.

[66] Buda, et al., "Dokumente rreth kryengritjeve shqiptare kundër pushtuesit osman në vitet 30 të shek. XV," *Studime historike* 1 (1967): 147-162 [document no. 9: Venice, Feb. 19, 1432].

[67] *Ibid.*

[68] Bozhari, *Burime bizantine*, 44-46.

Arvanid. The sultan, observing the events from Serres, ordered the commander of Shkup, Ali Bey Evrenoz, to crush the Albanian uprising. But Arianiti defeated Evrenoz in the Shkumbin valley; owing to their high mobility, the Albanians were able to avoid frontal confrontation and maintain an upper hand over the Ottomans. Far from capturing Arianiti's son as the sultan had desired, Ali Bey barely escaped from the battlefield and reunited his disbanded troops in Epirus.[69]

The uprisings of Albanian princes—Arianiti, Thopia, and Arnith Spata who ruled over parts of Epirus—were an uneasy challenge for the sultan, too. In 1434, Murad II personally led a large army into Albania. Both sides suffered heavy casualties, but Andrea Thopia and Arnith Spata, commander of the Albanian troops, forced the sultan to retreat without any gains. By the end of the year, the same Albanian commanders caused as heavy of a defeat to Isak Bey Evrenoz who, encouraged by the freezing weather, had pierced into the area to annihilate the Albanian population.[70]

The achievements of the Arianitis incited the hopes that the sultan would give up the military campaigns and resort to vassalage agreements (the vassal states retained their autonomy and paid a poll tax called *haraç*, as a tribute to sultan) or at least abandon them for an indeterminate period. The Ottomans did not cease their expeditions, but for a decade (just as they were contemplating an invasion of Hungary), their military intensity diminished. Two factors made it possible for the Ottomans to pursue their Albanian campaigns: on the one hand, Gjon Kastrioti, Nikollë Dukagjini, Andrea Thopia, and lesser noblemen agreed with the new situation as long as they retained some of their privileges, albeit not guaranteed; on the other, Venice was cautious of Albanian actions that could endanger its dominions in Albania, which it had secured with the 1430 peace treaty.

At the time, Sultan Murad II even tried to garner support from the noblemen who maintained ties with the local Ottoman administration. Between 1432 and 1438, the sultan relied on the Evrenozes, who remained at the head of the Pashasanjak of Shkup. In 1441, he also appointed Teodor Muzaka's son, Jakup Bej, as *sanjakbey* of *Sancak-ı Arvanud-İl*. Jakup Bej, one of the most prominent officers in the Ottoman military, was killed in 1442 in war against the Hungarians. His brother, Kasim Pasha, is referred to as *bey* of *Sancak-ı Arnavud-İl*, while another brother, Sulejman, was serving as *subaşı*

---

[69] *Ibid.*

[70] See Rizaj, *Kosova gjatë shekujve . . .* , 25; K. Frashëri, *Skënderbeu . . .*, 109.

of Berat in 1449. In 1434, the Ottomans appointed Ballaban Bej of Albanian descent as *dizdar* of Kruja. Hamza Bej of the family of Gjin Zenebishi served as subash in Kalkandelen (present-day Tetovo), while Ishak, a commander in the border troops of Murad II, was also Albanian.[71]

The Albanians, as cofounders and main supporters of the Byzantine Empire and the eponymous people of several independent states that existed in their lands, were at the brink of disintegration. In the 1430 Ottoman-Venetian treaty, the Albanians were only a bargaining chip; in their uprisings against the timar system, the Albanians fought without many of their princes. Only with the appearance of Gjergj Kastrioti Skanderbeg did the Albanians reclaim their place in history; this was an unexpected yet glorious resurrection.

Skanderbeg and the Early War against the Ottomans

Skanderbeg returns to Kruja, beginning the first anti-Ottoman war in Europe. The Albanians unite at the Congress of Lezha. Branković sides with the Ottomans; Europe is defeated in the Second Battle of Dardania Field of 1448. Skanderbeg wages heroic battles in defense of Christianity; the disunited West fails to join the anti-Ottoman war. Venice plays a divisive role in the formation of anti-Ottoman alliance, working behind the scenes against Skanderbeg.

The life and deeds of Gjergj Kastrioti Skanderbeg, the son an Albanian nobleman, Gjon Kastrioti, lord of Kruja, covers one of the most important periods in the history of the Albanian people. Although his father had switched churches three times (between Catholic and Orthodox Christianity), Skanderbeg's war proved highlighted the western Christian identity of the Albanians in what was spiritually a clash of civilizations and politically a confluence of eastern and western spheres of interest.

In fact, Skanderbeg attained significance after he abandoned his prestigious position in the Ottoman army and returned to serve his home country. Otherwise, his name would have likely lurked among the many ordinary Ottoman servicemen, regardless of the rank he could have obtained. In November 1443, Skanderbeg was in charge of the Ottoman army that was to meet the Hungarian troops led by John (Janos) Hunyadi in Nish. On the eve

---

[71] *Ibid.* 391.

of the battle, Skanderbeg abandoned the imperial troops and returned to Albania where, assuming the leadership of the country, he launched a war on the Ottomans—at the time the world's largest empire, in whose army Skanderbeg had gained both fame and experience. This event represents the great turn that would elevate Skanderbeg to the status of the national hero and the greatest figure in the Albanian history. At a time when the West had been overwhelmed by panic and fear of the Ottomans (and the western powers only hoped to avoid the Ottoman threat by trickery and had not conceived the idea of a united defensive front), Skanderbeg led the Albanians in war for the preservation of the Western Christian civilization—a struggle that was rightly considered among the most important and the most dynamic of the era. In those moments of anxiety for Europe, the bells of the Notre Dame Cathedral in Paris tolled only for the Ottoman defeats; suddenly, the bells became the triumphant crier of the good news arriving from a remote castle, then almost unknown to Europe—Kruja, where the Ottoman flag had been lowered and replaced by the double-headed eagle of the House of Kastrioti. Soon afterwards, the flag became the symbol of the united Albanian state, but also served as hope for Western Christianity in the war against Ottoman incursions and Islam in the old continent.

Skanderbeg also presents a dilemma. His return to Albania was viewed as an act of a wise military officer of imperial dimension in service of his fatherland. Due to his war against the green flag, Skanderbeg the appellation *savior angel of Christianity* among many others; contemporary chroniclers compared him with prophets and like figures.[72] Other historians, however, hold that Skanderbeg's resistance was rooted in his patriarchal beliefs that inspired him to seek revenge against the sultan who had insulted his family and homeland; fame or power in the world's strongest military or the sultan's fondness did not cure the vindictive nature of the Albanian hero.[73]

---

[72] Contemporary European authors and chroniclers wrote tens of works about the life and deeds of the Albanian national hero, Gjergj Kastrioti Skanderbeg. Their works were written in different languages and pertained to various genres; some works reach the level of apotheosis. Later, there were multiple studies and chronicles that, recognizing Skanderbeg's merits as a defender of Christianity and the like, specify his Albanian nationality. In the 19th century, the hegemonic Serbian propaganda—seeking to deny the Western identity of the Albanians and their contribution to the West—tried to appropriate Skanderbeg, presenting him as a Montenegrin, Bosnian, or even Macedonian. However, such speculations had no repercussions for either history or politics.

[73] Recently, a Swiss historian, Oliver Jens Schmitt, has laid out the "thesis" that, when Skanderbeg deserted the Ottoman army at Nish as to return to Albania, he had no other

Both Albanian and foreign scholars have thus far rectified a monumental theory that Skanderbeg alone defied the Ottoman Empire because his return to Albania was unexpected and his role was unique. It is therefore the uniqueness of Skanderbeg that allows for a reassessment of the inner motives and external factors that convinced the Albanian national hero to take the challenges he met.

Here, it is worth considering the possibility that Skanderbeg sought glory and power; his time with the sultan may have led the Albanian lord to develop such a desire that only few people can satisfy. Therefore, to achieve his own grandeur, he had to work for an equally sublime goal—the Albanian war against the Ottomans. In fact, many contemporary scholars and important figures of the time indicated that Skanderbeg had such aspirations. They suggest that Skanderbeg, in addition to leading war and state-building efforts in Albania, was inclined to the role of the protector of the Western civilization and Christianity in the war against the Ottomans and Islam. That is a plausible and natural contention.

Nevertheless, Albanian scholars have been cautious of such a representation of Skanderbeg. Therefore, they tend to view him within the social and political dimensions of 15th century Albania, not in a broader historical context that emphasizes his role as a defender of Christianity and the Western civilization. Focusing on Skanderbeg's intention to reclaim a fief or

---

motives but revenge, which is *tied to the Albanian tribal mentality of vendettas and parallels the acts of an outlaw.* Schmitt's book was translated by Ardian Klosi and published as *Skënderbeu* in Tirana, Albania, in 2010. It comprises of a work, presented as a monograph, but has yet to see the light of publication in German. Schmitt also holds that Skanderbeg was a vassal of the Kingdom of Naples and a subject of Venice, among other contentions he presents as original arguments or as constructions of various documents and secondary sources. Albanian historians have criticized Schmitt's work; namely, Kristo Frashëri published a rebuttal titled *Skënderbeu i shpërfytyruar nga një historian zviceran dhe disa analistë shqiptarë* (A Travesty of Skanderbeg by Swiss Historian and Some Albanian Analysts).

Historians have long ago attempted to downgrade Skanderbeg's image with untruths and even insinuations. For instance, authors like the 18th-century English historian, Eduard Gibson, remains influential. In his *History of the Decline and Fall of the Roman Empire*, published in London, 1900, Gibson attacks Skanderbeg for, among others, his "betrayal" of the sultan as the starting point of Kastrioti's political career. Fan S. Noli addressed those criticisms in detail in his work *Gjergj Kastrioti Skënderbeu*, published in Boston, 1947 (an Albanian translation appeared in Albania in 1967).

principality, which was his homeland, the Albanians adopted their national hero's deeds to the educational goals and the patriotic folklore during the communist period in the 20th century. Since the communist ideology favored isolation and hostility to the outside world, Skanderbeg was viewed as an embodiment of the ideal of seclusion and war against others. But the view has outlived the regime and continues to preclude Skanderbeg's image as a rare personality who could alter the turn of epochs.

Another aspect of Skanderbeg's biography that deserves our attention is the time he spent with the Ottomans. While that does not cover a particularly long period, its historical accounts are overfilled with muddiness. As Gjon Kastrioti, Lord Kruja and the surrounding areas, became an Ottoman vassal with the hope for survival, he was required to send his own sons as hostages to the Ottoman court. However, it was his younger son, Gjergj Kastrioti, whom the Ottomans called Skanderbeg, who refused to accept vassalage as a permanent condition; he would rise up to the higher ranks of the Ottoman military, but later used this achievement for a higher goal.[74]

Despite the many accounts on the Kastrioti dynasty and their growth, historians have been unable to locate accurate records on the detainment of Gjon Kastrioti's sons in the Ottoman court. The main dispute surrounds Skanderbeg's age at the time he was taken and the fate of his elder brothers, two of whom many have been poisoned with the order of the sultan. The uncertainty has prevailed despite records indicating that the eldest of Gjon's sons, Stanisha, and the third, Reposh, were released from the Ottomans. Furthermore, based on Skanderbeg's early biographer, Marin Barleti (Lat.: *Marinus Barletius*), Stanisha accompanied his brother on his return to Kruja and during the takeover of the castle.

The first issue, that of Skanderbeg's age, which by accounts varies from eight, as put forth by Barleti,[75] to eighteen,[76] according to Fan S. Noli, is of central importance in assessing his motives. Because, as Noli says, "[W]hen

---

[74] Historians disagree as to Skanderbeg's age at the time he was taken to the Ottoman court. Marin Barleti writes that Gjergj was nine years old. Kristo Frashëri, in his monograph on Skanderbeg (2002), disputes Barleti's statement. Some other European sources also raise the issue.

[75] See *Historia e jetës dhe e veprave të Skënderbeut,* translated from the Latin by Stefan I. Prifti (1989).

[76] See *Histori e Skënderbeut* (1947).

Skanderbeg was taken hostage, he was not a little boy, but [a youngman] wellaware of his homeland's tragedy."[77]

Various historical sources support Noli's contention that Gjergj Kastrioti was taken by Sultan Murad II at age eighteen. Skanderbeg was recruited through the *devshirme* (Trk.: *devşirme*, collection [of children]) process as an *ichoghlan* (also *ichoglan*; Trk.: *iç oğlan*, boy servant), at the imperial court or the Palace (Trk.: *Saray*), where the Ottomans educated the sons of aristocrats. The theory that Skanderbeg was eighteen at the time is braced by Murad II's campaign in Albania, which took place between 1423 and 1425. The chroniclers—Ottoman Ashikpashazade (Trk.: Aşıkpaşazade) of the Ottomans, Latin-writing J. Pontono, and the Byzantine Laonikos Chalkokondyles—do not speak of great Ottoman success against the Albanian princes (*i.e.*, Gjon Kastrioti and Arianiti). The writers note, however, that the Ottomans reached an agreement with Kastrioti over a renewed vassal relationship. As part of the deal, Kastrioti assented to the further implementation of the timar system, while giving his youngest son, Ioan (Gjergj), as a guarantee. Ashikpashazade notes the Ottomans also brought Arianit Komina (Gjergj Arianiti) and one of his sons to the sultan's court.[78]

The second issue, of Skanderbeg's brothers, could also be helpful is assessing his motives, which have often been linked to revenge and the like. Here, there is a parallel issue involving the third of the Kastrioti brothers, Reposh, who is known to have served as an Orthodox priest at the Hilandar Monastery in modern-day Greece, where he died at a young age. However, his burial in the narthex of Despot Milutin with the epitaph *Duke of Illyria*[79] raises the question whether he was a priest or a military officer—for as a priest, he could have not had the title of duke. Furthermore, there is a dilemma about Kastriotis' ties with the princes of Rascia.[80] Likewise, the

---

[77] Cited in Tajar Zavalani, *Histori e Shqipnis*, 118.

[78] For more, see Pulaha, *Lufta shqiptaro-turke në shekullin XV: burimet osmane* (Tiranë: 1968), pp. 28-29, 31, 34-42.

[79] Shyqri Nimani, *Onufri dhe piktorë të tjerë mesjetarë Shqiptarë* (Prishtinë: 1987), citing the epitaph on Reposh Kastrioti's grave under the narthex of King Milutin: "Reposh, Duke of Illyria, 1430/31."

[80] Marriages were common among the nobles as a means of consolidating, maintaining, or expanding power. Gjon Kastrioti was married to Vojsava, who was a Triballi, most likely from the Brankovićis family, which had expansive dominions in parts of Dardania. Such nuptial politics continued with Gjon Kastrioti, who gave his eldest daughter, Mara, in

family's affiliation with the Orthodox Church is another point of discussion. The Kastriotis demonstrated a strong Orthodox faith as indicated in the family chronicles; the noble house handed several villages as gifts to the Church and entrusted the Hilandar Monastery with many family documents as well as the notes and the treasury.[81] There is, however, a layer of opacity about the Church the family belonged to from Gjon to Gjergj: Gjon switched several times between Catholicism and the Orthodoxy and was buried at Hilandar; Skanderbeg, on the other hand, was interred at a Catholic Church in Lezha. This in turn brings up the next and key issue about Skanderbeg's return to the "faith of [his] ancestors": did he convert while briefly serving as a subashi of Kruja in 1438 after his father's death, or after his permanent return to the city in 1443?

If there are no disagreements that upon return to his father's castle in Epirus (*i.e.*, Albania)[82] Skanderbeg tore his Ottoman uniform and started the rebellion against Murad II, it is unclear whether he also reverted to Christianity at the same time. Barleti contends that Skanderbeg was re-baptized right after he took over Kruja, but there are suggestions that the "misled" and the "coerced" did not immediately return to the old religion. For instance, many Muslims, including Skanderbeg's nephew, Hamza, became Christians during the first Christmas celebration on December 25, 1443.[83]

Barleti hold that the morning after his return to Kruja, Skanderbeg declared his return to the "faith of the ancestors," and called on all Muslim colonists and officers to publicly embrace Christianity. Doing so, not only would their life would be spared, but they would gain "many other benefits"; otherwise, they would be considered enemies and Skanderbeg would allow

---

marriage to the ruler of Zeta, Stefan Gjurashi (Crnojević); his second daughter, Jella, married Stres Balsha of Kurbin; the third, Angjelina, wedded Vladan Arianiti.

[81] Several sources refer to the documents and a part of the treasury of the Kastrioti family that was entrusted to the Serbian Orthdox monastery at Hilandar. None of the sources, however, identify the content of the documents. The Serbian Orthodox Church has given rise mystery by placing a permanent seal on the items, which may not be revealed to the public. That the documents may be of great historical importance is suggested by a publication of the Serbian Academy of Sciences on the treasury stored at Hilandar; the Academy has omitted a description of what the Kastrioti family documents contain.

[82] See Barleti, *Historia e jetës dhe e veprave të Skënderbeut*, 126.

[83] *Ibid.* 127.

"any punishment" against them.[84] Some sources note that Skanderbeg was indeed harsh against those who refused to be baptized.[85]

Such actions are in line Skanderbeg's repudiation of his Ottoman past. In fact, Ottoman records also indicate the persecution of Muslims. In the *Chronicle of the Father of Conquests* (*i.e.*, expeditions of Mehmed II), Tursun-bey writes: "Thus [Skanderbeg] put on the garment of apostasy, which is the dirtiest of all clothing, to become commander of a pack of infidel sinners."[86] Moreover, Kemal Pashazade says that Skanderbeg "ran away to the French and became a renegade."[87]

Such interpretations are highly reliable. Yet, for a leader such as Gjergj Kastrioti, religion had to do more with politics than faith. This would become apparent later during his reign.

What remains obscure is the fate of Skanderbeg's brothers and his age at the time when he was taken to Edirne. Once he is brought to the sultan's court, accounts are generally clear about his education and rise in the military. Within a short time, his exceptional aptitude helped Skanderbeg reach the higher ranks and gain even the personal trust of the sultan.

His achievements as well as his premeditated return to Albania were likely motivated by his belief in a great historical turn. Owing to his *will for victory*, Skanderbeg developed a vision rather than illusion of turning his back on the Ottoman Empire and claiming the leadership of his own country. His return was not conditional upon support with the West, including those with whom he would later cooperate and enter into somewhat unfavorable alliances (because of his ties with Venice and Genoa among others, several historians have suggested that Skanderbeg became a vassal of the West). But the creation of the Albanian state fell within the developments of the time, including the clashes between the West and the East, or Christianity and Islam.

The war for the state of Albania became the hope for Christian Europe— at least for a while, until it would be able to revive itself. On the other hand, the Ottomans saw Skanderbeg as a traitor and worse as a barrier to their expansion. Fearing that others may follow his example, the Ottomans sought

---

[84] Aurel Plasari, *Skënderbeu: një histori politike* (Tiranë: 2010), 319.

[85] See statement Dhimitër Franku, a soldier and later treasurer of Skanderbeg: "Thus, he ordered that all Turks who refused to be baptized be killed" (Franco, *Gli Illustri et Glorios Gesti*), cited in Plasari, *Skënderbeu . . .*, 320.

[86] Tursun Beg, *Tarih-i ebül'feth*, 136.

[87] Kemal, *Tevarih-i Al-i Osman VII Defter*, in *Lufta shqiptaro-turke*, 197.

the most severe punishment for Skanderbeg, even though they could at least temporarily bypass Albania and proceed to the West through conquests across the Danube River, towards the German countries.

Albania as a factor put an end to the Western fear that the Ottomans were invincible without unity among Christian nations. Although war against the Turks threatened their very existence, the Albanians were able to hold off their enemy owing to a new military strategy. Avoid the frontal combat that—besides the lack internal cohesion, mutual trust, and a strategy of joint command—had contributed to the Christian defeat at Maritsa and Dardania Field, Skanderbeg resorted to smaller and mobile units that would carry out surprise attacks on the enemy in multiple locations. His doctrine, which changed the nature of future wars, placed Skanderbeg among the greatest military strategists.

Skanderbeg's victories earned him the attribute of a world statesman, arguably the greatest and the most important of his time.[88] The Albanians meanwhile also gained momentum; for the first time, they were able to direct their relations with the West, straying from the previous pattern in which Albania had been a means to Western ends.

This affected the direction of West-East clashes, for both sides became dependent on the Albanian power or lack thereof. Prior to Skanderbeg, the fate of Albania had hinged on the outside powers; moreover, both the Byzantines and their adversaries had used the Albanians for their own goals.

Since early 10th century, the West had maintained an interest in Albania. Initially, the country was but a port at the disposal of Western powers in their struggle against the Byzantine Empire. In the 13th century (after the Principality of Albania, founded in 1190, broke into smaller feudal entities), the Western powers supported the creation of a unified state. In 1272, the Anjou Kingdom of Sicily established the Kingdom of Albania (Lat.: *Regnum Albaniae*; Alb.: *Mbretëria e Arbërisë*) with Charles I as king. This event represents the attempts to make Albania a factor that would defend Western interests in the East, albeit a satellite state at the pleasure of Western powers.

---

[88] See comments by popes, Voltaire, Marx, and other leading historical personalities on Skanderbeg and his contribution to Chistendon as well as his role in defending Europe from the OTtoman invasions in Aleks Buda, "Gjergj Kastrioti – Skënderbeu dhe epoka e tij," *Konferenca e Dytë e Studimeve Albanologjike* (1968) [Tirana]: 19-44; Nando Bulka, "Figura e Skënderbeut në letërsinë franceze," *Konferenca e Dytë e Studimeve Albanologjike*: 439-443.

Under Skanderbeg, Albania was consolidated from the inside and became an ineluctable state actor.[89] As such, it no longer appeared as a catapult for Westerners hurling into the East, as for instance, during the Crusades and then the period of the Byzantine decline. Yet, with Skanderbeg, Albania not only became a factor on its own right; situated in the border between civilizations, it befitted *the* shield of the West. The Albanian leader may have not foreseen either role, at least not to the extent they reached, but time made them inevitable. As will later be seen, the fate of Skanderbeg's Albania was tied to its political independence and successful war against the Ottomans.

The State of Skanderbeg, Military, and Church

> *The Albanian League of Lezha serves an institution of the State of Skanderbeg. To consolidate the state, Gjergj Kastrioti seeks the dissolution of independent dominions. As a consequence, the League of Lezha weakens and disintegrates after the Dukagjini, Muzaka, and Arianiti families leave or side with Venice or the Ottomans. Skanderbeg, supported by the lesser landowners and peasantry, creates a regular army and reserve volunteer units. Foreigners and paid knights serve in his praetorian guard. Skanderbeg's fair and equal treatment of the Churches, Catholic and Orthodox, helps consolidate the anti-Ottoman resistance and hails the Albanian leader as a unifier of Christendom.*

---

[89] The Lezha Convention was held in 1444 and presents the first and most important step that Skanderbeg took to unite the independent Albanian princes and noblemen into common state under his leadership. The meeting began on March 2 at the Cathedral of Saint Nicholas in Lezha. Among the noblemen attending were leaders of previous uprisings: Gjergj Arianti, Andre Thopia, Nikollë Dukagjini, and Theodor Korona Muzaka. Other important personalities included Pal Dukagjini, Lekë Zaharia, Lekë Dushmani, Gjergj Stres Balsha, Pjetër Spani, and the ruler of Montenegro, Stefan Crnojević. Representatives of highlander tribes also took part in the Convention. Participants agreed on forming a union known as the Albanian League or the League of Lezha. Skanderbeg was elected leader of the League. Another important decision was the formation of an army consisting of regiments recruited by Skanderbeg as well as the other noblemen. Skanderbeg was appointed commander-in-chief with the title *Capitanes generalis* (*Lat.*, general captain). See H.P.Sh. 1 (1969), 256.

Deserting the Ottoman army before the Battle of Nish in 1443, Skanderbeg enabled the Hungarian victory over the Ottomans. Returning to Albania, in the meantime, he declared a general uprising, defeating the enemy in most encounters. Thus, he resumed the creation of a unified Albanian state, a process the Ottomans had interrupted half a century prior.[90] The successful 1443 rebellion was a pre-condition to the formation of the state; beginning on March 2, 1444, the Albanian League of Lezha served as an institution.[91]

The Albanian League of Lezha, the basis of the state's creation, was not a "league of princes,"[92] but a union of lords, nobles, and headmen. The noblemen pledged to assist the liberation war with fighting men and finances, but they retained their feudal rights in their own dominions; they held their armies and castles. The highlanders also reserved their rights; they pledged to contribute only with soldiers, while they would continue to govern themselves according to their customary law.[93] Implicitly, the highlanders were at liberty to withdraw anytime without any consequences.[94] Therefore, the League elected Skanderbeg as its leader *only* for the mutual war against the Ottoman Turks. He remained otherwise a feudal lord confined to his domains and could command the League's army solely during the war. Among the League members, Skanderbeg was *primus inter pares* (first among equals).[95]

However, the League was unable to meet the growing demands of the escalating war. The particularistic power of noblemen, their immunity, rivalries, and greed for territorial expansion presented an obstacle to the anti-Ottoman war. The conflict required the mobilization of all human and material sources of the country, requiring coordination under a centralized government.[96] In 1447, at a time of conflict with Venice, Pjetër Spani and Gjergj Dushmani withdrew from the League of Lezha; later Gjergj Arianiti and Pal Dukagjini would also leave. Independent actions and walkouts from League members became a permanent threat to Skanderbeg. The menace was even greater when the Turks would stimulate the vacillation and Venice

---

[90] K. Frashëri, *Skënderbeu . . .*, 176.

[91] *Ibid.*

[92] Fan Noli: *Vepra* 4 (1947), 66.

[93] K. Frashëri, *Skënderbeu . . .*, 176.

[94] A. Luarasi, *Shteti dhe e drejta shqiptare në shtetin e Skënderbeut* (Tiranë: 1998), 128-130.

[95] K. Frashëri, *Skënderbeu . . .*, 177.

[96] *Ibid.* 177.

would use it for its benefits as it did when Arianiti and Dukagjini withdrew from the League.[97]

Despite the political challenges, Gjergj Kastrioti reached several military victories, most notably in the First Siege of Kruja. After routing Murad II from the walls of the city, Skanderbeg recovered from an earlier loss in Sfetigrad two years prior, gaining an increasing popularity among the masses. Meanwhile, the population began to despise as traitors the noblemen who had joined the sultan during the Kruja campaign. Most importantly, the prestige of Dukagjini, Arianiti, and Muzaka was also waning, as they remained indolent in face of sanguinary battles in the vicinity of their dominions.[98]

The fragmentations in the League compelled Skanderbeg to "violate" a part of the Lezha agreement regarding the sovereignty of the feudal lords. His first step was the reorganization of the armed forces ahead of ever more challenging Ottoman invasions.

Many authors, including his early biographer, Marin Barleti, note that by 1447, Skanderbeg raised an army of 15,000 soldiers; 3,000 of them were part of his professional personal guard, trained for the most difficult combat actions. Due to the federal nature of the League of Lezha, Skanderbeg had little elbowroom as commander-in-chief of the League Army. For that reason, he outwitted the League and built his own forces under his direct command, which would be able to keep up with the powerful, well-equipped, and increasingly sophisticated Ottoman military. An experienced commander, Skanderbeg trained his army in guerrilla warfare of surprise attacks and withdrawals. He divided his forces into two groups: the permanent army and the auxiliary or reserve units. The *permanent army* included Skanderbeg's Praetorian Guard, dominated by a lightly-armed but highly mobile cavalry, prepared for unforeseen encounters with the enemy. The rest of the military, or the *auxiliary army*, was composed of bands of peasants, who would mobilize at Skanderbeg's orders. Their task was to attack the rear line of the Ottoman army, to block the roads and ambush the enemy, and attack the caravans supplying the Turks with food and armaments.[99] Usually, the peasants in the auxiliary army were freemen volunteering on the *one man per house* principle. When the war ended, the peasant warriors would return

---

[97] *Ibid.* 177.

[98] *Ibid.* 177.

[99] *Ibid.* 193.

home and worked on the fields, but they kept their weapons with them and were ready for Skanderbeg's war cry.[100]

Officers had no ranks. Each was called a *kapedan* (captain, from Latin *capitanes*) and fell into either category: commanders of the greater formations, known as *Skanderbeg captains*; and *ordinary kapedans*, serving at the command of *Skanderbeg kapedans*.[101]

Later historians, using archives of contemporary source—especially those of Ragusa, the Vatican, and Venice—estimate that Skanderbeg's army did not exceed 6,000 troops ready for combat. The rest of his soldiers were volunteers, gathered, as needed, from different fiefs of the country.[102] Skanderbeg's military reorganization affected the command system, too; he replaced the *kapedans* from among the irresolute aristocrats with loyal and highly disciplined officers. Moreover, the Albanian lord hired foreign military advisors. Taking those steps, Skanderbeg not only violated feudal immunity of other noblemen: not only did he demote the suspicious and infective commanders; he also annexed the lands of the less powerful, including Topia, Stres, Muzaka, and Gropaj.[103] Consequently, the borders of the previous realms transformed into administrative lines, and independent

---

[100] Marin Barleti, *Skënderbeu: jeta dhe vepra* (Prishtinë: 1968).

[101] Demetri Franco, *Commentario dell Cose dei Turchi e del Signor Giorgio Scanderbeg* (Venetia: 1539), noting: Moisi of Dibër, a captain under Skanderbeg (*capitano di Scanderbeg*, p. 20), Muzak Thopia, captain and brother-in-law of Skanderbeg (*cognato et capitano suo*, p. 19), or Moisi and Gjurica, as captains (*sui capitani*, p. 9). At the Lezha Convention, Skanderbeg was appointed *capitano generale di tutti li altri* (general captain of all others)— thus captain-in-chief (p. 9).

[102] For more, see Fallmerayer, *Das Albanesische Element in Griechenland*, 9; P. Jovius, "Sub effigie Georgii Castrioti Scanderbeschi," *Elogia virorum*; D. Franco, *Commentario dell cose de Turchi et del s: Geogio Scanderbeg, principe di Epyrro*; Gegaj, *L'Albanie et L'Invasions Turque au XV siècle*.

[103] For more, see Gjon Muzaka, "Historia e Genealogija e Shpis së Muzakajve e shkrue prej zotni Gjon Muzakës, Princ i Epirit," in *Leka* review (Shkodër: 1932). It notes, among others: "Once Skanderbeg became commander of the lord of Albania . . .he decided to bring the whole country under his control; he imprisoned lords such as Gjon and Gjin Balsha (his nephews, sons of his sister, Jella), and took over their state, which lay between Kruja and Lezha . . . he annexed the state of Moisi Komneni, situated in Dibër . . . and after my father's death, he took Tomorica—the Lesser Myzeqe—from us, and he also annexed, from other lords, the countries of Komni and Ranci, but such lords had no means to resort to as [Skanderbeg] controlled the army and they could also face the Turks at any time . . ."

domains gradually melted into a single entity. This process led to the unification of the Albanian state.[104]

The expropriation, often by violent means, and the replacement of the command, frustrated many of the noblemen. Some left the Albanian League of Lezha and approached Venice, Naples, or even the Ottomans. With the withdrawal of the peers and as Skanderbeg assumed uncontested authority over state matters, the League became virtually defunct. It was supplanted by the State of Albania, a growing entity with an increasingly centralized government.[105]

The State of Skanderbeg, *i.e.*, the State of Albania, raises two questions worth answering: over its territory, and its recognition. These two add a third issue, that of the state's identification with Skanderbeg or his identification with the state.

Formed in 1451, the state initially covered only a part of Central Albania, bordering the Dukagjini domains to the north and Arianiti to the south. The Dukagjinis never joined the State of Skanderbeg, despite conciliatory gestures made by their Prince Leka; to the contrary, they made peace with the sultan and on many occasions worked against Kastrioti.[106] On the other hand, Skanderbeg developed fragile ties his southern neighbors when in April of 1451 he married Donika (Andronika), the daughter of Gjergj Arianiti.[107] But shortly after, Arianiti broke off with his son-in-law and allied with Venice. After his death in 1461, Arianiti's domains were merged to the State of Skanderbeg.

According to contemporary sources, the western border of the State of Skanderbeg was the Adriatic Sea. At the state's heyday, Skanderbeg's rule spanned from Velipoja to the Seman Island, with the exception of Lezha and Durrës. In the east, the Kastrioti realm extended beyond the Black Drin, up to the Korab, Kërçin, and Stagova mountains and the Radika gorge; to the north, the state border the Albanian principality of Dukagjini, roughly in

---

[104] K. Frashëri, *Skënderbeu . . .*, 179.

[105] Luarasi, *Shteti . . .*, 130.

[106] K. Frashëri, *Skënderbeu . . .*, 180.

[107] Barleti calls her *Donika* (Donica), while Gjon Muzaka, in his *Memorandum*, calls her *Andronica*, adding that she was the eldest daughter of Gjergj Arianiti. A 1469 document from the archives of the Aragonese chancellery in Naples refers to Skanderbeg's wife as Donika, while on her grandson's epitaph she is mentioned by the name Andronika (*Andronica Cominata*). Dhimitër Frëngu, who knew her personally, calls her Donika (*quella bellissima et virtuisissima figliola di Arianit Comina che si chiamava Donica*).

along the northern boundaries of the Mat region; in the south, Skanderbeg's Albania included the previous lands of Arianiti and Muzaka. Along the coast, Gjergj Kastrioti had two fortified harbors, including the renowned Rodoni Castle (previously Shufadaja) at the mouth of the Ishëm River.

The State of Skanderbeg at the time did not encompass a vast territory, but the name of its leader became world-famous and became the recognizable reference to Albania. Skanderbeg gained such stature in history, although his state was a type of feudal monarchy; it was moreover ruled despotically and had no monarch, but a "lord."

Historical accounts have led to confusion about Skanderbeg's official title as a head of state.[108] Marin Barleti styled Gjergj Kastrioti as "Prince of the Epirotes" (Lat.: *Epirotarum Princeps*).[109] Dhimitër Frangu (Lat.: Demetrius Francus) referred to the Albanian leader as "Prince of Epirus" (Ita.: *principe di Epyrro*) in a 1539 publication, while in 1636 Frang Bardhi (Francus Blancus) used the title "Prince of the Epirotes," in the same fashion as Barleti. Many foreign historians seem to have followed Barleti's use of *prince*.[110]

In the official European correspondence with Skanderbeg as well the letter bearing his signature, the Albanian hero makes no use of the styles *king* or *prince*; he simply used the tile *lord* (Latin *dominus*, Italian *signor*, Spanish *senyor*; Slavic *gospodin*). In a letter dated December 14, 1447, King Alfonso I of Naples (Alfonso the Magnanimous, or Alfonso V of Aragon, etc.), addressed Skanderbeg as "Lord of Kruja and the provinces of Albania" (Lat.: *Domine Croi provinciarumque Arbanie*).

Unlike Naples, the Republic of Venice did not *de jure* recognize Skanderbeg by any official title in the Veneto-Albanian peace treaty of October 4,

---

[108] K. Frashëri, *Skënderbeu . . .*, 188.

[109] Barleti, *Historia e Skënderbeut* (1986), 46.

[110] For more, see P. Jovi (1551) to F. Cunberti (1898). Some writers refer to Skanderbeg as *king*: for instance, J. De Lavardin (*Roy d'Albanie*, 1576), or Cl. C Moore (*King of Albania*, 1850). Such styles may have influenced the Albanian Renaissance writers, especially Naim Frashëri, who thought that Skanderbeg was the king of Albania and referred to him as such in a poem dedicated to him (1899). In addition, Fan Noli, in his early work on Skanderbeg, in 1921, used the title "King of Albania" (*Mbret i Shqipërisë*); in 1950, he simply referred to Skanderbeg as *Kryezot i Arbërisë* (Supreme Lord of Albania). Kristo Frashëri disputes the "Supreme" qualification of the title, since there were no vassal lords in the state of Skanderbeg, before or after 1450. That is further supported by a letter, dated October 31, 1460, that Skanderbeg wrote to Prince Feranti G. A. Orsjini. Although Skanderbeg mentions "my vassals" (Lat: *mihi vasali*), the reference is to his subordinates and not feudal lords under Skanderbeg's souzeranity.

1448. De facto, Venice treated Gjergj Kastrioti as the representative of the lords of Albania. The reasons that Venice avoided such recognition are known: the republic had specific agreements with the Ottoman Empire over their domains in the Albanian coast; depending on the Albanian-Ottoman war, the Venetians hoped to expand their possessions.

In fact, even Skanderbeg's style depended on his war against the Ottomans. After defeating Murad II at the walls of Kruja, in the fall of 1450, Skanderbeg acquired the title *Lord of Kruja* (Lat.: *dominus Croie*), or *Albanian Lord* (Lat.: *dominus albanensis*), or *Lord in Albania* (Ita.: *signor in Albania*)—although he was not styled *Lord of Albania* (Lat.: *dominus Arbaniae*). In the summer of 1451, Skanderbeg adopted the official title *Lord of Albania* (Lat.: *dominus Albaniae*). A month later, the Duke of Milan addresses Skanderbeg by the new title, which the Albanian leader used for the rest of his life. In fact, after 1451, all foreign chancelleries use *Lord of Albania*. The heraldry also honored the tile by engraving DA for *dominus Albaniae* on Skanderbeg's coat of arms and seal; the initials appeared on both sides of the double-headed eagle.[111] This eagle has ever since appeared on the Albanian national flag, too. (Yet, besides his arms and great seal that portrayed the double-headed bird, Skanderbeg also used a signet-ring or *sigillum annulare*; its negative had been deposited in the Bank of Ragusa, serving as a secret code or *sigillum secretum* between Skanderbeg and the financial institution.)

Besides the internal governance, military leadership and finances, another feature that led to the consolidation of state power was the fair treatment of all the people; Skanderbeg did not discriminate against either of the two Christian rites, Roman and Byzantine, which were practiced in Albania. For that reason, Fan S. Noli concluded that "religion gave the Albanians the unity that, [scattered in many political entities], they lacked in their state, and since [religion] also served as a bond connecting them with the West."[112]

In fact, Skanderbeg would not succeed in his war against the Ottomans without a platform of unification of the Churches, proclaimed at the Council of Florence on July 5, 1439. The council gathered important religious and political figures, including Pope Eugene IV, Byzantine Emperor Johan VII Palaiologos and his brother, Demetrius, Patriarch Joseph of Constantinople, and Bishop Visarion of Nicaea. They agreed in principle to reverse the 1054 ecclesiastic schism, whose boundaries directly fell on the Albanian lands,

[111] K. Frashëri, *Skënderbeu . . .*, 191.

[112] Noli, *Gjergj Kastrioti Skënderbeu* (1967), 43.

creating a war line. The unification of the church was contemplated extensively. In an elaborate ceremony at the Florence cathedral, the council
participants signed a bilingual agreement in Latin and Greek; the deal,
however, focused on plans on restoring the Roman Empire under the slogan
of expelling the "infidels" from Europe all the way to the lands that had once
belonged to the empire.[113]

The unification of the Church did not succeed, since the East had seemingly succumbed to the defeatist Byzantine slogan that "the Turk is better
than the French [*i.e.* the Roman Catholic]."[114] This was the view of some of
the Orthodox clergy who had seen the inevitable Ottoman growth as an
opportunity to revenge, as they did, against the Catholics. However, in face
of the Turkish threat, the Hungarian hoped that the "unifying" spirit of the
Council of Florence could lead to a collective war against the Ottomans.
Optimists, such as Giovano Torzelo, a high Byzantine official of Italian
background, even regarded Albanian power as highly significant in such war
efforts, since the Albanians had two lords who could recruit up to 20,000
knights and, once a Christian army came to their aid, they would fight
against the Turks.[115] The "unification" council could have influenced Skanderbeg's resignation in 1440 from his position as *subaşı* of Kruja, which he
held after the death of his father, Gjon Kastrioti.[116] If that was indeed the
case, Skanderbeg did use the spirit of "unification" to his advantage in
domestic politics—to avoid any possibility of schism, which could create
barriers for the future. In fact, Skanderbeg used the council to further an
existing trend among Orthodox churches, which began their affiliation with
the Roman Church, albeit maintaining their ties with Constantinople. Such
relations with Rome had begun in the last quarter of the 13th century among
the Orthodox churches—from Rubik in the north to Himara in the south—
in the Kingdom of Albania; the Catholic king, Charles I Anjou, a French
aristocrat residing in Naples, had those churches linked with the West, but
they retained their Byzantine ecclesiastic tradition. Then, affiliation with
Rome would not occur without the political pressure from the Anjous, who
aspired to reestablish the Eastern Latin Empire, dissolved in 1260. However,
the Albanians, worried about the expansionist policies of the Orthodox
rulers of Rascia, were also supportive of the ties with Rome. The Albanians

---

[113] For more on this "union" see Erhard, *Geschichte des Wiederaufblühens* (München: 1980).

[114] Noli, *Gjergj Kastrioti Skënderbeu* (1967), 55.

[115] Plasari, *Skënderbeu . . .*, 296.

[116] Inalxhik, "Iskender Beg," *Encyclopédie de L'Islam*, nouv. ed., vol. II (Paris: Leyden, 1961).

regarded the Catholic Anjous rather than the Orthodox Byzantines as their defenders from the Rascian threat since the Byzantines had not only weakened by then, they were also allies with the Slavs.[117]

One the early Orthodox dioceses to turn to Rome was the bishopric of Kruja. This district was until under the Orthodox archdiocese of Durrës, ultimately under the Patriarch of Constantinople; the Krujan see retained the status at least between 879, when it was first attested in the Council of Constantinople, and 1282, when it was last mentioned in the list of Eastern churches, in the *Escorial Taktikon* of Michael VIII Palaiologos. Similarly, other dioceses in the Orthodox metropolitan see of Durrës came under the pope. The bishoprics of Cernik, Kurnavia, Drisht, Pult, Shkodër, and Tivar converted to the Catholic rite; others, such as the dioceses of Stefaniaka in the Lower Dibër (Lat.: *episcopus Stephaniensis*), Lis in the Mat region, Pulheriopol, and Vlora (which had replaced the bishopric of Apolonia), established ties with the Holy See, but retained their Byzantine rite.[118]

The jurisdiction of the Roman Church extended in most of the Albanian countries. This happened party because of the threat of a Slavic invasion, especially after the conquests of Stefan Dushan in the first half of the 14th century, and partly with the demise of the Byzantine Empire, whose rule over Albania ended in the middle of the same century, leaving the Albanians to seek salvation from the West.[119] As a result, when Skanderbeg raised the flag of the liberation war, the ecclesiastic map of Albania appeared in three colors: the Catholic Church, tied to Rome in the canonical, ritual, organizational, and political aspects, dominated in the north and northeast; in the south and southeast, the Orthodox Church prevailed and, although weakened by the Ottoman occupation, it maintained its ties with the Patriarch of Constantinople; meanwhile, between the two zones, there would later appear the *Uniate* churches, which respected the traditional Byzantine rite and liturgy, but followed the Roman Holy See in the organizational and political facet. Yet, despite his preference of the Roman Church, Skanderbeg stood and acted above the ecclesiastic denominations.[120] For instance, in his ranks he employed commanders of all three confessions—captains such as Tanush Topia of the Catholic church of Durrës, Zakaria Gropa of the Orthodox church of Ohër, and Pal Kuka

---

[117] K. Frashëri, *Skënderbeu . . .*, 185.

[118] For more, see doc. no. 57 in *Acta et Diplomata res Albaniae Mediale Aetis Illustratia* I (Vienna: 1913); D. Farlati, *Illyricum Sacrum*. VII (Venetis: 1817), 414.

[119] K. Frashëri, *Skënderbeu . . .*, 186.

[120] *Ibid.* 187.

of the Uniate church of Stefaniaka. Furthermore, the Albanian diplomats at the time included Catholic prelates, such as Pal Engjëlli, and representatives of the Eastern rite, such as Stefan, the bishop of Kruja.

Skanderbeg's impartiality in ecclesiastic matters is also represented in a hagiographic work on the life and deeds of Niphonos—an Albanian from Morea (Peloponnesus, modern-day Greece), who became patriarch of Constantinople in the last decades of the 15th century. Before he was crowned head of the Eastern Church, he traveled with Zakaria to Kruja, where they met Skanderbeg and witnessed the great respect the Albanian lord nurtured for the Orthodox Church.[121]

Skanderbeg and the West

Skanderbeg's vision for a powerful Christian state within the ethnic borders of Albania: If proven in the war against the Ottomans, the State of Albania could become the basis for the revived Roman Empire, at least in its European part. The Christian states of the Adriatic hesitate to accept Skanderbeg as leader of the Western crusade against the Ottomans. The Albanian lord, however, suffers the greatest misfortune from his neighbors, the Greeks and Orthodox Slavs. At the Second Battle of Dardania Field in 1448, the Orthodox Slavs disrupt a regional anti-Ottoman coalition Skanderbeg has hoped for. Venice maintains disingenuous relations with Skanderbeg, while working with the Ottomans behind the scenes.

Having united the feudal lords of Albania, Skanderbeg concentrated on his state-building efforts. The West—his potential allies across the Adriatic and the Vatican, as the spiritual leader of Christendom—came to his aid. The successful war against the Ottomans had made Skanderbeg a defender of the West and Christianity; hence he needed the Western unification in a common front. Christians, in fact, had agreed as of the "Unification" Council of Florence on a joint campaign, in which Skanderbeg and Albania were likely to play an important role.

Despite the country's strategic position, Skanderbeg did not dither in his conviction that he had to wage a war even on his own and by all means. The

---

[121] For more, see Beduli, "Disa të dhëna lidhur me periudhën e Skënderbeut nga një vepër hagjiografike e shekullit XVI," *Konferenca e Dytë e Studimeve Albanologjike* I (Tiranë: 1969): 629.

West supported the State of Albania, but the greatest support for Skanderbeg would be if the Christian countries—jointly or even individually—went to war against the Ottomans. Some states could fight on the first line of defense against the enemy that had reached the gates of their castles; however, all Christian nations could join in a common war against the Turks, regardless of the geographical distance from the empire.

As a battlefield of constant Ottoman defeats, Skanderbeg's Albania sought to unify the West in the war. Christian nations could succeed in a united front if they deferred to the collective interests. Until then, the Europeans had fought in isolated fronts (at Maritsa in 1371 and twice in Dardania, in 1389 and 1448) and participants of such battles were typically from the Balkan and Central European peoples. In the meantime, some Europeans fought against the Turks, while others rested stood by or even entered into agreements with the Ottoman Empire; benefiting the Turks and damaging the warring Europeans.

Skanderbeg became aware of the inconsistencies between what the Christian West hailed as its common interest and the actual comportment of the Western countries, which rather favored their individual interests. For that reasons, some countries welcomed the Albanian war against the Ottoman Empire, but made their best efforts to confine the conflict to Albania. The Westerners expressed their support for Skanderbeg, praised his deeds, and here and there and with much pomposity sent him material assistance. Yet at the same time, the Western countries, including Venice, conducted secret talks with the Turks, often reaching agreements that sidelined the strategic interest of the West. This may have even brought about the failure of what Pope Pious II had envisioned as a crusade that Skanderbeg would lead against the Ottomans. Pious II died during the final stage of preparations and after Skanderbeg had already cancelled a peace treaty with the sultan. The untimely passing of the Holy Father could have only postponed, not call off the planned crusade. But the campaign never took for, as time would prove, the West was not ready and did not even desire to become involved!

Skanderbeg envisioned Albania as a powerful Christian state within the Albanian ethnic borders. If proven in the war against the Ottomans, the State of Albania could form the basis for the revival of the Roman Empire, at least in its European part. However, Skanderbeg's vision encountered barriers from among the Europeans themselves. In addition to the hesitations of the Christian countries along the Adriatic to accept Skanderbeg as leader of a Western crusade against the Ottomans, his neighbors—primarily the Slavs and the Greeks—gave the Albanian leader the greatest setback. The Orthodox Slavs not only did not fight alongside the Albanians against the Ottomans, but gave their best efforts to prevent the Albanian war from reaching regional dimensions, as Skanderbeg had hopes with the Second Battle of Dardania Field in 1448.[122] This encounter, which was expected to unite the Hungarians, Croatians, Poles with the Rascians, Albanians, and Greeks, presented a unique opportunity to make up for the 1389 defeat.

Nevertheless, multiple accounts indicate that the Europeans had lost the battle before it even began. Prince Đurađ Branković, known as a vassal and ally of the sultans Bayezid I, Murad II, and Mehmed II, agreed to fight alongside Janos Huniyadi and Skanderbeg. But not only did the Rascian despot not join his fellow Europeans; through ruse and trickery he prevented Hunyadi's arrival in Dardania, where the Brankovićis had their domains. Later, in pursuit of a secret deal with the Ottomans,[123] Branković ordered some of his units into war against the Hungarians, even prior to the battle, which had been scheduled for October 19, 1448 in Dardania.

Branković's treacherous stabbing of Hunyadi—before the Hungarians, as the main European units, arrived in Dardania—correlates with another factor: Venice. The maritime republic was, in one way or another, a part of the political games against Skanderbeg and the Christian alliance. Once Skanderbeg and Hunyadi, in cooperation with Branković, set the date for the battle, the Venetians began their military operations in the northwest of Albania, hoping to reclaim previous domains that Gjergj Kastrioti had taken from them in war. Out of fear that it may lose its other possessions in the Albanian coast, ceded certain areas to Skanderbeg, on the condition that he proceed no further with his military. Moreover, according to an accord with Kastrioti, Venice had agreed to pay him an annual tribute of 1,400 ducats.[124]

The unexpected skirmish with Venice held Skanderbeg off for several days. The main Albanian units, therefore, under Skanderbeg's personal command, departed on October 4, three weeks late. The delay would be fatal in war against the Ottomans; approaching Dardania Field in two routes, via Prizren and Shkup, Skanderbeg's army encountered Hungarian soldiers in flight. There, Skanderbeg learned the bitter news and quickly returned to Kruja, since the loss of the battle represented much more than a military defeat; it represented the loss of hope for an anti-Ottoman coalition of the frontline states. This alliance

---

[122] See Malcolm, *Kosova: një histori e shkurtër* (Prishtinë: 2001).

[123] *Ibid.*

[124] *Ibid.*

would bring together the Albanians, Serbs, and Hungarians with assistance from the Bulgarians, Greeks, and Vlachs; the Croats and Bosnians would also join. The ultimate assistance would in turn come from the Germans, Poles, French, and the Italian and Spanish principalities and kingdoms that would join in a crusade against the Ottomans, as Pope Pious II had planned.

Some sources, however, emphasize that Skanderbeg punished Đurađ Branković near Kruševac, but this remains an unconfirmed account. Later, retreating via Shkup, Skanderbeg took necessary measures to fold up the frontline in the Albanian countries. The defeat at Dardania Field and the correlation of the Slavic-Orthodox and Venetian backroom deals were a lesson to Skanderbeg. His family had maintained ties with the princes of Rascia (many of them of Triballi origin or a Slavicized Illyrian tribe; thus, of the same Illyrian-Dardani roots) and with the Slavic Orthodox Church. Skanderbeg had hoped that those relations would serve the common interest in face of the Ottoman threat. However, the ties turned out to have been illusory, as were the Venetian promises for a Western alliance against the Ottomans. But not only did Saint Mark's republic not join those endeavors; it undermined them by all means.

Later, after Mehmed II, the Conqueror, acceded to the Ottoman throne, Branković supplied 1,500 soldiers for the conquest of Constantinople in 1453. The Rascian role was two-pronged: on the one hand, it challenged the State of Albania; on the other, it lent a hand to the Ottomans to the detriment of Catholicism and the West. Later, the Serbian stance on the Albanians turned into open hostility, especially during the Great Eastern Crisis and onward, to continue with the Balkan wars, the interwar period up to the final decade of the previous century. In 1999, it took the Western military intervention against Serbia to halt the oppression of the Albanians—that which had first taken place during Stefan Nemanja's and Stefan Dushan's war with Albania (initially, the Albanian Principality under Progon, then the Anjou Kingdom of Albania, and the independent Albanian domains).

Nevertheless, the political games—Skanderbeg may have as well anticipated some of them, for he was aware of the circumstances—the lord of Albania did not wage his epic war alone. Important factors, such as the Papacy, the Kingdom of Naples, and the City of Ragusa, backed Skanderbeg. The Republic of Venice was also supportive, despite the disputes with Skanderbeg.[125] The Venetians controlled the main cities with an outlet to the

---

[125] Noli, *Gjergj Kastrioti Skënderbeu*, 37.

Adriatic—Durrës, Lezha, Drisht, Ulqin, Tivar, and Shkodra—as well as other territories in the north, known collectively as the *Venetian Albania*.[126] Venetian rule in the Albanian lands sought to disempower Skanderbeg, rather than carry out specific political goals, such the increased Western presence in Albania. This strategy, which aimed at consolidating Albania's adherence in the West, served as a basis for Skanderbeg's war as well as the aid the Christian world pledged for Albania.

Since Albania was the last remaining Roman Catholic bastion in the Balkans, which the Vatican endeavored to preserve and expand, the West was obviously expected to assist Skanderbeg with money and soldiers. Ultimately, the West had made support for any anti-Ottoman resistance a priority as of the Council of Florence in 1443. Authors such as Foigt and Falmeraier hold that the papal provision for Skanderbeg consisted only of apostolic benedictions and panegyric lectures.[127] However, documents prove that popes Nicholas V (reigned 1447-1453), Callixtus III (1453-58), and Pious II (1458-1473), gave Skanderbeg sound money in thousands of gold ducats from the papal treasury.[128] Thus, in 1467, Skanderbeg received 1,500 ducats from Ferdinand of Naples, 3,400 from Venice, and 9,250 from Pope Pious II.[129] The reasons behind the support, according to Noli, were clear: Skanderbeg was their most faithful ally, as for almost twenty-five years he fought against the common enemy with only two interruptions of about six months each.[130] In fact, Pope Callixtus III wrote that Skanderbeg had done more for the Christian faith than all other Catholic princes; therefore, the leader of the Church advised his legate to give the king of Bosnia a portion of the funds raised in Dalmatia for the new crusade so that the Bosnian monarch, motivated by the financial assistance, became "another Skanderbeg."[131]

---

[126] For more, see Schmitt, *Skënderbeu* (Tiranë: 2009).

[127] Johann Philipp Fallmerayer, *Das Albanesische Element in Grichenland* IX (Münich: 1866), 88.

[128] For more, see Farlati, vol. VII, p. 421; Ludwig Pastor, *Geschichte des papstums* IV (1891), 86; Athanas Gegaj, *L'Albanie et l'invasion turque au XVème siècle* (1937): 144.

[129] See Trichera, *Codice Aragonese*, p. 90, app. no. 40; Sime Ljubić, *Isitine o odnosu izmedju južnog slovenstva i Mletačke Republike* (Zagreb: 1875-1891): vol. X, no. CCCCI, p. 387; Pastor, vol. IV, p. 86; Gegaj, *L'Albanie et L'Invasion turque au XV-eme Siècle*, 144-45.

[130] Noli, *Gjergj Kastrioti Skënderbeu*, 49.

[131] See Augustinus Theiner, *Monumenta Slavorum* I (Rome: 1863), no. DCII, pp. 427-8, app. no. 15; Wikentije Wasilević Makuszew, *Istorićeskia Razyskania o Slawjanah v Albanii v Srednieg Weka* (Warsaw: 1871), 93.

After the Holy See, the Kingdom of Naples was Skanderbeg's greatest partner. The support was reasonable since the city of Brindisi, on the eastern coast of the Neapolitan realm, was no further than fifty miles away from the Albanian of Vlora. Therefore, to defend itself, Naples helped Skanderbeg maintain his resistance in Albania, which was a bridge onto the Apennine Peninsula.[132] Besides, the Neapolitan monarchs dreamed of a Catalan Mediterranean Empire, spanning from Barcelona to Constantinople.[133] In addition to Naples and Sicily, Alfonso the Magnanimous, King of Aragon, inherited his predecessors' (Frederick II, Robert Guiscard, and Charles of Anjou) ambitions over Albania. Between the years 1272-1332, the House of Anjou ruled over the Kingdom of Albania, the entity that for the first time united the Albanian nobles around a project for their own state (an earlier endeavor was the Principality of Albania, founded in 1190). Therefore, Naples supported Skanderbeg, but the Albanian leader also came lent a hand to his allies, disembarking with his army in Naples when Alfonso's royal crown was at risk. Here, Fan Noli rejects such the contention that the Albanian ties with the West had rendered Skanderbeg a simple *condottiere* (*i.e.*, a mercenary) of Naples and Venice, as other authors, including Nicolae Jorga and Langer, suggest.[134] Their theory has, in fact, survived to this day, reappering in modern discussions on *Venetian Albania*.[135] The Albanians maintained trade relations with Venice, but also developed coercive alliances with the republic before and during the Ottoman occupation while Skanderbeg was pushed as to recognize the Venetian possessions in some parts of Albania in order to keep them out of Ottoman rule. However, the ties with the republic could not represent the Venetian social, cultural, and political "domination" of the Albanian world, as modern writers maintain. It was the unyielding reality of the time that, even though the Albanians could have accepted and ever desired such an influence by the Venetians, the circumstances did not allow for the ties to extend beyond mere trade.

While Jorga and others overestimate the Venetian role in Skanderbeg's Albania, there are scholars who present an extremely different view. Among them, a Polish author, Wikentije Makuszew, regards the Venetian rule in Albania as lacking any civilizing attribute and Western character. The Venetian policy, as an alternative to Byzantism and Slavic expansionism, is

---

[132] Noli, *Gjergj Kastrioti Skënderbeu*, 50.

[133] See Nicolae Jorga, *Brève Histoire de l'Albanie et du Peuple Albanais* (Bucaresti: 1919), 47.

[134] Noli, *Gjergj Kastrioti Skënderbeu*, 51.

[135] See Oliver Jens Schmitt, *Shqipëria veneciane* (Tiranë: 2007).

described as "a war of extermination against the Albanian social classes."[136] Furthermore, Makuszew offers this image of the Venetians:

> In the Albanian cities of Durrës, Lezha, Shkodër, Drisht, Ulqin, and Tivar, annexed to Venice, the aristocracy was humiliated, the borgeoise was overrun, free peasants were made serfs. In general, the annexation of the Albanian land was the final stage of the process. The heads of the Albanian tribes were subsided and pushed into war against Turkey until they were overwhelmed [by the enemy] and agreed to unconditionally surrender to Venice, as a lesser evil than Turkey. After their subordination, [the tribes] were treated as slaves from a colony. When the tribe leaders were too powerful for Turks to defeat them, Venice did not hesitate to stab them on the back, inciting internal war and even declaring war on them. [Venice] had overrun the Balshas, and hoped to use the same tactic against Skanderbeg. At least three times, Skanderbeg offered to hand over Kruja to the Venetians, hoping to save it from the Turks (in 1449, 1450 and 1466), but the Venetians did not accept, because they believed Skanderbeg and his highlanders were too powerful to become their obedient servants. They would rather see Kruja under Turkish rule than under their own reign if the residents had not been crushed. Hence they assumed the responsibility to defend the town after Skanderbeg died in 1468 and annexed it in 1474, when the people were worn out and could certainly be enslaved. This way, the Venetians allowed all the cities in southern Albania to fall to Turkey, although they had occasionally been given the opportunity to place the [towns] under their protection, but had not agreed. Clearly, the Venetians thought that Albania could be taken from the Turks much more easily than from the Albanians themselves. It is quite dazzling that, except for some minor interruptions, they continued to subsidy Skanderbeg, although they wholeheartedly hated him! They followed such a policy, at times, because they wanted to wage a war against the Turks, but covertly, so they would be able to spare their colonies in Albania.[137]

In a similar fashion to the Polish historian, the Romanian Jorga believes that the Venetians were compelled to make peace with Skanderbeg.[138] For instance, in 1448 and 1451, Kastrioti was reaching victory after another and could endanger the Venetian colonies. Later, the republic made peace because it feared for its existence, such as when Mehmed II conquered

---

[136] See Makuszew, *Istorićarski Rasyskania o Slovjanah v Albanii v Srednie Vek.* (Warsaw: 1871), pp. 132, 146-47, cited in Noli, *Gjergj Kastrioti Skënderbeu*, 51.

[137] *Ibid.* 52.

[138] See Jorga, *Brève histoire . . . .*

Constantinople in 1453. Again, between 1463 and 1468, Venice was in dire need of Skanderbeg as an ally against the Turks.[139]

This position is also supported by a Croatian author, Sime Lubić, contending that "even during this final period, the Venetians were allowed their *proveditors* (governors) in Albania in order to obstruct Skanderbeg in every step he took and to stab him on his back. At last, Skanderbeg did not wish to accept Venetian auxiliary troops, unless they were placed under his direct command."[140]

During the Albanian-Ottoman war, Skanderbeg's ties with the Holy See, Naples, and Venice were at times imposed by circumstances. However, the relations with Ragusa were exceptionally friendly and mutually beneficial.

The affluent city-state of Ragusa did not abandon its Roman roots and continued to use Latin and Italian as official languages, although it was thoroughly slavicized. Money and trade were the only weapons that the Ragusan patricians used to support the war against the Ottoman Empire, the most perilous conqueror of the time.[141] Since Skanderbeg had assumed the flagship in the struggle, he was Ragusa's natural ally as well as a trade client. He was also a patron of the city's bank.[142] However, the ties were made friendlier by the significant Albanian presence in the city-state, where many Albanians had risen to the upper class. Among the patricians, there were members of several families from Drisht—Suma, Polombo, Lapore, and Span. In addition, like all towns in southern Dalmatia, Ragusa had many Albanian clergymen and monks, in charge of almost all ecclesiastic services.[143] This explains the cordial relations between Ragusa and Skanderbeg as well as the excellent reception he was given during his visit to the coastal city. Therefore, it was not by chance that, after Skanderbeg died, Ragusa declared a permanent day of mourning.

---

[139] *Ibid.* 46.

[140] Lubić, *Istine o odnosu između južnog slovenstva i Mletačke Republike* X (Zagreb, 1875), 334.

[141] Noli, *Gjergj Kastrioti Skënderbeu*, 52.

[142] Franz Miklosich, *Monumenta Serbica Spectantia Hisoriam Serbia, Bosna, Ragusi* (Vienna: 1858), 442.

[143] See Šufflay, *Acta et Diplomata* and *Illyrisch-Albanische Forschungen* 1: 265.

Endeavors to Restore the State of Albania

Skanderbeg's death and the dissolution of the State of Albania: The Otto-mans land on Otranto, Southern Italy; the West support an Albanian up-rising to prevent Ottoman incursions into Italy. Skanderbeg's son, Gjon II Kastrioti, returns to Albania to lead an anti-Ottoman war. Venice con-tinues its diplomatic games with the Ottomans, using the Albanians for its own interest. Gjergj II Kastrioti, Skanderbeg's grandson, leads another ex-pedition into Albania, but dies in mysterious circumstances. The Otto-mans take a hefty revenge on the Albanians, forcing many to migrate across the Adriatic. As the nobility and many clergymen left the country, the migrations were disastrous for Albania.

Skanderbeg's death in 1468 from malaria fever represents the beginning of an end of one of the major historical efforts of the Albanians in the fight against the Ottomans, a war which, owing to the victories achieved during more than a quarter century, once again turned into the struggle to protect the Western civilization from an eastern invasion, and then, depending on the perspectives, received various praises ranging from the highest papal honor, that was the proposal to crown him *King of Albania*,[144] to the epithets such as "angel savior of Christendom" and the like, which vested even mythical overtones in Skanderbeg's public figure.

However, it remains undeniable that the Albanians entered this war as first rebels to defy the Ottoman occupation, and emerged from it with the first victory the Europeans achieved against the Ottomans. While the victo-ries did not materialize as Skanderbeg had hoped, they did give hope to Western Christianity, even if temporarily or when used in different ways as moral and spiritual capital to further the fight against the spread of Islam.

Although Albania was left without its leader, the nation continued to re-sist the Ottoman attacks for several years, but it was unable to avoid the fatal scenario—the Ottoman reconquest. A harsh punishment and five centuries

---

[144] See Unpublished Codex of Pal Engjëlli in Latin, hosted at the Laurentianis Library at Florence, Italy, where Pope Pious II is believed to have proposed that Skanderbeg be crowned *King of Albania*: "The general decree of our lord, Pious II, sanctified with the divine grace as Pope, upon request of the Most Honorable Cardinal of the Holy Roman Church, Archbishop of Durrës, Monsignor Pal Engjëlli, has declared the indomitable fighter against the Muslim sect, Lord Skanderbeg, *King of Albania*." Cited in Kristo Frashëri, *Skënderbeu i shpërfytyruar* (Tiranë: 2009), 112.

of occupation followed. The Albanian defeat, along with military defeat and destruction of the entire state edifice built with great efforts during the quarter-century war against the greatest military power of the world, was a profound loss with multiple repercussions. The tragic consequences of the fall have led many critics, former and present, to ask whether the struggle was worth it for, according to them, the country was severely punished, while the loss continued to produce serious consequences for the Albanians—as far as to forget, as some have suggested, the medieval name of the country, *Arbër* (also *Arbën*, *Arbënia*, or *Arbëria*; thus, Albania), and adopt instead the modern name *Shqipëria* (often Anglicized as *Skyperia*)?[145]

Those who think so have in mind what happened to Albania after the reconquest by the Ottomans, when the whole country was subjected to an unprecedented terror. On one side, it was a revenge for the losses that the two powerful sultans of the time, Murad II and Mehmed II, had suffered before the walls of Kruja, and, on the other hand, a harsh punishment that would serve as a deterrent to others, as they could face the same fate if they were to resort to rebellion.

Initially, those actions led to the displacement of a large part of the Albanian population across the sea towards the south of Italy and in other parts of Europe. Later, the Ottomans continued numerous repressive measures against those who remained. Contemporary sources note that the migration began before Scanderbeg's death, but it reached a worrisome scale after his death, when Skanderbeg's own wife, Donika, along with their 13-year-old son, Gjon, joined their brethren in the exodus.[146] In a way, exile in Italy was provided for by an agreement that Skanderbeg did with Alfonso of Naples. Accordingly, relatives of Skanderbeg and a part of the nobility would be sheltered there, not indefinitely, but to protect themselves and prepare their return home at the fortunate moment. As a result, in addition Skanderbeg's family, most of the upper class—landowners, merchants, and some of the lords—left the country. Later, they were joined by Skanderbeg's soldiers and guerrillas, who entered the military of the maritime republics Venice, Genoa

---

[145] See Eduard Gibson, *History of the Decline and Fall Roman Empire* (London: 1900); Oliver Jens Schmitt, *Skënderbeu* (Tiranë: 2009); Husamedin Feraj, *Skicë e mendimit politik shqiptar* (1998); Driton Egro, *Një qasje kritike studimeve osmane në historiografinë moderne shqiptare* (Tiranë: 2007).

[146] Donika and Gjon II Kastioti moved to their lands in Italy (Monte santa Angelo near San Giovani Rotodo).

and Naples, while many others went as far as Spain and other countries, serving as paid men-at-arms.

Before the great exodus, the Albanians, and especially the nobility and the important lords who had supported Scanderbeg until the end, continued the fight he had begun. However, the new circumstances, in the absence of a personality that would match the national hero, the political life, along with the popular resistance, began to revert to the pre-Skanderbeg era of independent fiefdoms acting in accordance with their own interests. Thus, some noble families resumed their independence and turned to Venice for help, while some even began, hoping to protect themselves, to look to the Ottoman Empire and the renewal of the previous vassal relationships.

Venice soon appeared in support of a continued resistance, under its own supervision, in accordance with its own interests. Likewise, the maritime republic hoped to preserve its colonies and dominions in Albania, without any hesitation to enter into an agreement with the Ottomans, as it eventually did, to reach such an aim. The Venetians' first step in taking matters in their own hands was to send Pal Engjëlli, Skanderbeg's perennial envoy to the republic, back to Albania to convince the Kastrioti family to hand Kruja and other dominions to Venice.[147]

The proposal was another instance of Venetian presence as well as interference in the post-Skanderbeg era, which was addressed in the previous chapter. Then, the maritime republic undertook to supervise the military resistance against the Ottomans, as it did until 1479, when Shkodër fell to the Ottomans. However, it also divided the Albanian nobility, a part of which, including Lekë Dukagjini, turned to the Ottomans. Later, such nobles became Ottoman vassals. The new climate, in which Venice became the "master of the house" in a good portion of the territories that Skanderbeg had turned into the state of Albania, initially benefited from the Ottoman military hiatus for a period of two to three years. At the time, the Empire was carrying out campaigns elsewhere, including the Hungarian front, through which they hoped to penetrate into central Europe. The Ottomans returned to Albania in May 1474, but, this time, they did not march against Kruja, where the Venetians were now in charge. Instead, they headed to Shkodër, a city of a particular importance at the time. The battle for Shkodër lasted three months and, by mid-October, the Ottoman armies, led by the *beylerbey* of Rumelia, Sinan Pasha, lifted the siege. Their scorched earth withdrawal left

---

[147] H.P.Sh. 1, 466.

the country in devastation; in particular, the Ottomans took a toll on the castle of Deja, which Lekë and Nikollë Dukagjini protected for so long until it was destroyed by the *beylerbey*'s forces. Two years later, the Ottomans deployed a much larger army. This time, they encircled Kruja, where a joint Albanian-Venetian formation, aided by 300 *stratioti* from the Morea, was in charge of the defense. The siege continued for two years, until June 16, 1478, when Ottoman forces, led by Mehmed II, forced the city defenders to surrender and promised their a safe passage.[148] The Ottomans, however, did not live up to their work. With the exception of the Venetian governor and his guard, who left the castle intact, the locals were massacred without exception. Sultan Mehmed II then marched northward and, on his way to Shkodër, razed the town of Drisht and entered castle of Lezha, after the Venetian commander of the garrison abandoned the city. Here, likewise, the locals who had taken part in the anti-Ottoman war were left at the mercy of the enemy. Thus, the refuges in the island of Lezha were caught and massacred at the gates of the Rozafat Castle at Shkodër.

Mehmed II did not stay to supervise the takeover of Shkodër. Since conquering Albania was no longer a matter of military prestige, but of longstanding diplomatic games with Venice, the sultan left for Constantinople in September, the same year. Although Ottoman troops were ordered to continue the siege of Shkodër and force the Albanians to surrender or face starvation, it is likely that Mehmed II sought a deal with Venice in order to keep it away from Hungary and the other countries he wished to invade. With a peace agreement signed on January 25, 1479, Venice retained its possessions in the Mediterranean, but ceded Shkodër as the coastal towns of Himara, Sopot, and Kastrovila to the Ottomans. The parties agreed that the castle of Shkodër be handed to the Turks, and that its residents would be free to leave their city. On April 25, 1479, the Ottomans entered Shkodër. Almost all inhabitants of the town and its vicinity, including noblemen Lekë and Nikollë Dukagjini and Gjurash Crnojeviqi (Mont.: Đuraš Crnojević), left for Venetian-held territories.[149]

The fall of Shkodër and other important coastal towns and the Ottoman conquest of the Otranto castle led Western countries—including Venice, which had signed an agreement with the Ottomans and had sacrificed a part of the Albanian resistance for its own interests—to form an anti-Ottoman

---

[148] *Ibid.* 470.
[149] *Ibid.* 471.

alliance. The front would concentrate on Albania, since that would erect an efficient barrier to the Ottoman troops deployed in Italy. Furthermore, the death of Sultan Mehmed II and the crisis it sparked in the empire allowed for the Albanians to resurge, at least temporarily, in support of the West. To achieve this, Naples and other Western allies urged Skanderbeg's son, Gjon II, to return to his homeland and lead the anti-Ottoman resistance, which had begun with uprisings in various parts of the country. Meanwhile, Lekë and Nikollë Dukagjini, Konstandin Muzaka, and Gjurash Cërnojeviqi also returned to Albania. Cërnojeviqi entered into an agreement with the Ottomans and became their vassal, but other returning noblemen were not too far from following his path.

With a strong backing from the West, Gjon II Kastrioti landed south of Durrës. Meanwhile, Kosntandin Muzaka disembarked in Himara, and the Dukagjini brothers aided in the north, as they arrived in the vicinity of Lezha and Shkodër. The anti-Ottoman insurgency was initially successful, especially in the central and southern part of the country, where the junior Kastrioti relied on his well-trained troops, including Western volunteers and stratioti. Moreover, in August 1481, Muzaka routed the forces of Suleiman Pasha and seized Himara. Suleiman Pasha, then *beylerbey* of Rumelia, was captured and handed over to Gjon II Kastrioti, who then sent the Ottoman officer, as a trophy of war, to the king of Naples.[150]

Gjon II Kastrioti's victories in Albania made the Ottoman forces deployed in Italy particularly vulnerable. In 1481, the Kingdom of Naples freed the Otranto castle, expelling the Ottomans from the Apenine Peninsula. Therefore, the Western nightmare, which had begun with the Ottoman arrival in Italy, came to end, owing to the rearguard war that the Albanians waged in their homeland. Seeking to reestablish the state of Skanderbeg, Gjon II led his troops towards Kruja, but backed off at the city gates amidst waning Western support. As the West had already achieved its goals through the Albanian campaign—that is, the Ottoman withdrawal from Italy—it no longer supported Kastrioti's troops. As a result, the Albanians lifted the siege of Kruja, the Ottomans reclaimed the Himara castle, and Gjon II Kastrioti returned to Italy, where he died in 1502. He was survived by his sons, Gjergj II, also known as Skanderbeg the Junior (Alb.: Skënderbeu i Ri); Konstandin (Constantino, c.1530-1550) who served as bishop of Isernia;

---

[150] *Ibid.* 474.

Ferrante (d. 1561); and Federiko (c.1488-1503), honored by a royal funeral at Valencia, Spain; and a daughter, Maria, who was an patron of the arts.[151]

The West continued to rely on the Albanians for their political needs. The last effort was undertaken through Skanderbeg's grandson, Gjergj II Kastrioti, who was sent to his ancestral land to reclaim the *Great Age* (Alb.: *Moti i Madh*). However, the expedition was an adventure destined to fail; it served, in reality, the interests of the Republic of Venice in redefining its relations with the Ottomans rather than the hopes to recreate the Albanian state. Two years after the campaign began, the Ottomans conquered Durrës (until then, a Venetian possession), forcing the maritime republic to abandon plans for an Albanian front. Pursuant to the peace treaty Venice had signed with the Ottomans, Gjergj II Kastrioti, Progon Dukagjini, and other Albanian nobles, went to Shkodër to request that they be allowed to govern their former dominions under the sultan's sovereignty. The *sanjakbey* of Shkodër, Feriz Bey, reached a deal with many of the Albanian leaders, but refused an agreement with Kastrioti, who was forced to return to Italy. Thereafter, Skanderbeg's grandson moved to Cyprus, where he passed away under suspicious circumstances.

Nevertheless, awaiting the call of the *Great Age*—that one day they might return to serve their homeland—the Albanian elite units, known as *stratioti*, continued to fight under foreign banners and, for a lengthy period, remained the most successful soldiers of their time.

On the other hand, Albania itself suffered numerous misfortunes. Having lost its social and military elite, which left the country after Skanderbeg's death, Albania experiences a massive exodus. Many city dwellers sought shelter in the highlanders, where they underwent an acculturation process, while others sailed to Italy during a process that lasted for almost half a century. Likewise, the people of Morea (present-day Peloponnesus), who had begun their migration to Calabria and Sicily even before the anti-Ottoman war, were joined by innumerous Arvanites (*i.e.*, Albanians from Greece), who, defeated in the war, also lost their homeland

It is estimated that one third of the Albanians left their country permanently. Those who remained, lacking a sufficient number of priests and a minimal spiritual guidance, were faced with no choice but to accept Ottoman rule in accordance with the law of survival, which prescribed Islam as an inevitable factor.

---

[151] *Ibid.* 457.

Formally, acceptance of Islam was not a condition, since the Ottoman Empire preserved the religious tolerance as best attested in the relations with the Orthodox Church, which almost "voluntarily" surrendered its autocephaly to the sultan in exchange the freedom the Christian population needed to preserve its spiritual identity. However, the Albanians were the only of the Christian peoples in the Balkans who were unable to use their Christian identity to preserve their existence, as did other nations, such as the Slavs, Greeks, and Bulgarians. The reasons were simple: the ecclesiastic schism, in the 4th century AD, during the reign of Emperor Theodosius I, and the final division, in the 11th century, into the Constantinople-based Eastern Orthodox Church and the Roman Catholic Church. The Albanians were split and continuously shifted back and forth between the two groups depending on their political allies. If it can be asserted that, before and during Skanderbeg's epoch, the ecclesiastic geography—composed of three markers: the Catholic, Orthodox, and Uniate churches—was apparently favorable to the Roman Church (while the Orthodox dioceses of the Albanian Kingdom, under Charles I Anjou, were linked to Rome, albeit they retained their Eastern rite), the Ottoman reconquest turned the tide in favor of the Orthodox Church. Contemporary sources note that, in addition to the "unstable" dioceses (*i.e.*, the Orthodox parishes tied to Rome) that returned to Constantinople; Catholic regions were also forcibly converted to the Orthodox rite, since that allowed them to avoid the merciless persecution at the hands of the Ottomans. The latter had declared war on Catholics and considered the Catholic Church as belonging to Skanderbeg "the traitor," whose legacy they sought to eliminate.[152]

The Albanian began their life under Ottoman rule with a double handicap. Having no autocephalous church of their own, Orthodox Albanians belonged to the spiritual authority of the Slavic and Greek churches. In the meantime, the Catholics were left without spiritual guidance for a substantial period as they remained cut off from the Vatican. Moreover, even after a Holy See agreement with the Ottoman Empire, the organization of the Catholic Church in Albania was subject to the "territorial filters" of the Slavic Orthodox Church that, with the new administrative reform, supervised the Albanian areas.

As a result, the majority of Albanians of the Orthodox tradition, regardless of their will, were forced to accept Slavicization or Hellenization (since

---

[152] Julius Ernest Pisko, *Skanderbeg, Historiche Studie* (Wien: 1894), 162.

the Slavic and Greek churches preached in the respective tongues). Meanwhile, Catholics received their Mass in Latin from a non-Albanian clergy. Only with the appearance of the Dominican and Franciscan orders later on did changes occur in the ethnic and linguistic structure of the Catholic clergy, but such changes were unable to improve the difficult state of Catholics in Albania, especially in dioceses under Orthodox jurisdiction.

The preservation of a Christian identity, therefore, did not provide the Albanians with their spiritual freedom. To the contrary, the Orthodox Church added to the burden of its Albanian followers. The Constantinople Patriarchate had accepted the status of a vassal to the sultan and, in certain segments, such as the tax system, had become a state mechanism in the Ottoman Empire. Meanwhile, as the Holy See sought to maintain a centralist supervision of its congregation—celebrating Mass in the Latin language and without a physical presence among the believers—Albanian Catholics became doubtful about their sacrifice in the name of religion. It is under such a scenario that the Albanians were faced with doubts of an existential nature. For the first time, they lived in a socio-political landscape that turned them to the East. But the inevitable interaction with the East also gave rise to doubts as to how the Albanians would comport in circumstances that indicated a clash of civilization (even though the Ottoman Empire, having adopted religious tolerance, at least formally, rejected the idea of such a clash). Therefore, if up to then, shifting between the Eastern and Western rites had been accompanied by a change in the political leadership within the same (*i.e.*, Christian) civilization, the new reality brought more profound changes. It faced the Albanians with the pros and cons of maintaining or abandoning Christianity, especially that of the Orthodox branch, which risked the Slavicization or Hellenization of the Albanians. On the other end, the Albanians began to massively convert to Islam that—while preventing their Slavicization and Hellenization—opened the way for a new civilization and an existential dilemma.

Undoubtedly, the dilemma would remain a superficial issue were it to be addressed independently of the developments of the time. The social circumstances in which the Albanians lived during their forcible inclusion into the Ottoman Empire (when the Ottomans began to install the timar system in their European dominions, after the Battle of Dardania Field and the "transitional period of vassalages") were marked by a series of dichotomies. On the one hand, the rural population benefited from the distribution of land and the *haraç* poll tax levied for land use and products. In the meantime, howev-

84

er, the highlanders—defined by a patriarchal structure and situated in the north and northeast, but also in some parts of the south—opposed the timar system, since it threatened the continuity of the domestic law and patriarchal lifestyle. The opposition led to an armed resistance and continuous uprisings, which convinced the Ottoman Porte to give up the establishment of the timar system in certain parts of Albania. In those areas, the Empire permitted home rule for tribes and, later *bayraks* (Trk.: banner, an administrative unit). For that purpose, the Ottoman government created the office of *bölükbaşı* (Trk.: captain), who served as a mediator to resolve conflicts between the native customary law and the Sharia law (with the latter holding supremacy) in the self-governing areas.

The application of home rule in parts of Albania created two distinct realities in the country. In certain areas where the Kanun was followed, self-governance permitted the preservation of Christianity, mostly of the Roman Catholic rite; in other parts of the country, home rule provided the Albanians with an incentive to embrace Islam, as a facilitation and opportunity for advancement in the imperial system. Owing to their military affinities, Albanians were to advance even after they were subdued and, those serving in the armed forces, in certain cases, were to subdue others on behalf of the Ottomans; for, as Muslims, Albanians were able to reach the highest levels of government.

The manifold archives, however, note that, during the 1400s and 1500s, only a limited number of Albanians converted to Islam. The new faith spread rapidly over the next two centuries, which brought changes to urban life. In the meantime, as crafts and commerce gradually replaced the ancient feudal structure, the new professionals became increasingly dependent on the state and public infrastructure. In return, craftsmen and merchants gained certain privileges that elevated them to the ranks of the ruling class.[153]

Yet, despite the benefits of the religious conversion, the Islamic conscience of a considerable part of the Albanians (of whom details will be provided further in this chapter) remained superficial. As such, it remained throughout Ottoman rule, since conversion was conditioned by economic factors, including tax incentives. Meanwhile, Christianity continued to serve as a spiritual, as well as civilizing, designation.[154] The Porte sought the true Islamization of the Albanians as a means to consolidate its strategic positions in the European dominions of the Empire, but its efforts succumbed to

---

[153] See Pulaha, *Pronësia feudale në tokat shqiptare (shek XV-XVI)* (Tiranë: 1984).
[154] H.P.Sh. 1 (1969), 342.

manipulations. However, even when resorting to heavier measures—which included an increased *jizya* (a fiscal tax on property) for the Albanian *kazas* with a Christian majority—the Ottoman Empire failed to fully accomplish its proselytizing mission. For instance, only the head of a family converted to Islam for purposes of avoiding the jizya; the rest of the family retained their Christian faith. In other situations, all family members would declare Muslim names on the Ottoman census, but would retain their Christian names in private use.[155] Similarly, converts celebrated the old religious holidays in addition to the new ones, nurturing a spirit of tolerance in their families and beyond. The incomplete conversion led to a syncretic practice among converts. Known as *laramanë* (sing.: *laraman*, literally "piebald") in Albanian, such converts developed a doubled identity, retaining Christianity as a spiritual element, while embracing Islam as a political designation. Such a confluence of religions is reflected in the widespread occurrence of a Muslim given name followed by a Christian surname.[156]

Syncretism among Albanians differs from other forms of crypto-Catholicism, not so in its concept, as in the inclusion of the national identity in their perseverance to maintain their Christian faith. In fact, this strengthens the argument that Christianity, as retained by Albanians in the circumstances of the time, remained—despite the manipulations—a decisive factor for the future social and political orientation of the nation. That became evident particularly in the 19th and 20th centuries, when the national revival movement drew its support from the Western identity and civilization, dating back to the ancient times.

Before reaching the historic decision of the national revival era, the Albanians underwent significant developments, between the 1400s and 1700s, which nevertheless preserved the nation's political orientation. The Albanian demonym *Arbër* was gradually replaced by *Shqiptar* (Anglicized as *Skypetar*), while *Shqipëria* was substituted for *Arbëria*. Meanwhile, the Catholic clergy, in its efforts to halt the spread of Islam, became a vanguard of the Western identity through an increasing use of the Albanian language in publications and liturgy.

---

[155] See Iniac Zamputi, *Dokumente për Historinë e Shqipërisë*, vol. I; *Dokumente të shekujve XV-XVII për Historinë e Shqipërisë, vol. IV (1675-1699)*, I. Zamputi, S. Pulaha, eds. (Tiranë: 1990); Zamputi, "Dukagjini dhe Pulti në gjysmën e parë të shekullit XVII," *Buletini i Universitetit Shtetëror të Tiranës*; D. N. Ukgjini, "Malësia e madhe dhe kontributi i saj në mbrojtjen e katolicizmit gjatë pushtimit osman (shek. XV-XX)" [separate source].

[156] For details on Albanian *laramans* and the extent of their lifestyle, see Gjini, *Skopsko Prizrenska Biskupija kroz stoljeća*.

The Reestablishment of Ottoman Rule and Islamization

The imposition of the timar system and the new property structure brings about social change. Christian lords join Ottoman service as Spahis, while those who embrace Islam retain their social and economic positions. The new administrative division has Arnavutluk—or Albania—broken into sanjaks, kazas, nahiyes, and other units within the elayet of Rumelia. The first legal code, Kanuname, is adopted in 1529; a body of law is also codified for the sanjak of Shkodër. The Islamic Sharia gains usage in parts of the country. Areas such as the highlands maintain home rule according to the Law of Lekë Dukagjini, while a bölükbaşı is appointed to ensure the local law's compatibility with the Sharia. Conversions to Islam begin, influenced in part by the devşirme—or the blood tribute. Massive Islamization takes place in Dardania, parts of which were liberated from the violence of the Slavic-Orthodox Church and relieved of the Slavicization process begun under the previous Rascian occupation after the 1200s. The early civil registers, from the 1431 census in the Sanjak of Albania and the Vlk Vilayet in Dardania, indicate the Albanian identity of a majority of the population, which the Slavic-Orthodox Church had endeavored to assimilate.

The end of the Albanian resistance, under the leadership of Gjergj Kastrioti Skanderbeg, marked not only the end of the Albanian state, but also the reestablishment of Ottoman rule in the country. After the subjugation of Skanderbeg's state, twelve years after his death, the Ottomans returned to Albania and were to remain for the next five centuries.

The reestablishment of imperial authority in Albania was in contrast to the "usual" model followed elsewhere in the region. In the neighboring countries, the Ottomans initially sought a vassal relationship with the local rulers, who paid a tribute to their masters. The vassalage then served as a preparatory phase for a transition into full occupation. Thus, only at a later stage would the Ottomans install their administration, laws, and, most notably, the timar property system. In imposing the new structure, the empire easily incorporated even the impoverished castes of the population, which benefited from the land grants it was given to improve their living.

Nevertheless, since Albania had seceded from Ottoman rule under Skanderbeg and had rebelled against the two of the most powerful sultans—Murad II and Mehmet the Conqueror--the empire's reprisals were clearly foreseeable. As a result of the Ottoman revenge, Albania lost nearly all of its nobility. Most members of the elite either migrated to Venice and other Western countries or suffered annihilation at the hands of their enemy; the very few who remained hastily accepted Islam.

As a result, Albania and its people came under Ottoman rule through sub-jugation, expropriation, and punishment, which would have severe social, economic, and spiritual consequences for the nation. As a result, two phenome-na took place: a mass exodus and mass conversion to Islam. As to the first, the displacement did not only occur as the people migrated across the sea to Italy, as was usually the case with the nobility; "internal" displacement was also noted. Many fled to "Orthodox centers" under Greek and Slavic jurisdiction, for the two churches, having pronounced their loyalty to the sultan, enjoyed the protection of the state. However, Albanians who, unable or unwilling to flee, remained in their homes largely saw Islam as the only opportunity for survival. Migration and Islamization, as the choices that the people faced, was detri-mental to the Albanian identity. On the one hand, it prompted assimilation into the Slavic or Greek Orthodox communities. Meanwhile, Muslim converts were automatically inducted into the Ottoman nation (*millet-i osman*), or the imperi-al amalgamation that served as a shield against Slavicization and Hellenization, but nevertheless marked the beginning of a new occupation. Since Muslims were better able to avoid oppression than the *râyas* (Christian subjects), mass conver-sion to Islam was a natural development. Besides, the new religion also permitted peasants to receive land grants. Meanwhile, the newly-converted lords, serving as *spahis*, were able to keep their land and even rise to the ranks of the Ottoman system, which offered opportunities to those who took their chances.

While the Ottoman Empire retained its supreme authority, the social and economic life witnessed significant improvements from the oppression that accompanied the later stages of Byzantine rule. Initially, the Ottomans organized their administration into *elayets*, *sanjaks*, *vilayets*, *kazas*, and the like. In creating such division, the empire retained the country's name (albeit in its Turkish form, *Arvanudluk*) and considered the ethnic makeup. Subsequent-ly, the new regime installed the timar system, which took the land from the former states and nobility. The feudal principalities, autocratic in their govern-ment and so often oppressive of the toiling serfs, disappeared. A military-feudal order, rising on the ruins of the old system, in fact, was equally threatening as it aimed to restrict even the most established of rights that had survived the war. Namely, the new administration eyed on ending self-governance that certain communities such as the highlands had enjoyed even under the Byzantines. A shift in Ottoman policy, nonetheless, not only restrained the plans to vanquish the unruly highlanders, but led the state to supporting the autonomous communities and incorporating them into the imperial system.

After the Ottomans were in full control of the country, under the reign of Suleiman the Lawgiver (Suleiman I, Trk.: Kanuni Sultan Süleyman), the padishah's legal scholars codified the laws of the empire. For each of the sanjaks, there was an individual code, known as a *kanuname* (literally, book of laws). The oldest such code, known and surviving, from Albania is that of the sanjak of Shkodër, compiled in 1529. The sanjaks of Prizren, Ohër, Vuçitërn, Vlora, and Elbasan also had their own *kanunames*.[157] These compilations of laws always derived from the Sharia, or the holy law, with ultimate references to the Quran, which served as an eternal constitution for the Ottoman Empire. As noted, however, the codification process took into account the social and economic peculiarities of each sanjak, including the customary law passed down from earlier generations. The *kanunames* of the Albanian sanjaks included provisions on land ownership, status of spahis and rayas, and the native population's duties to the state.[158]

To regulate all matters affecting its administration, the Ottoman Empire conducted a census in 1506 in all parts of *Arnavudluk*. The regions of the country were classified into two zones or categories. One such group, referred to as the *üşür* or tithe areas, included the arable lands under the timar system. The other category comprised of the *self-governing* highlands, where timar was not in place. As they paid a fixed tax, known as *haraç*, the highlands were known as *haraç* areas.

The *haraç* areas, or the highlands, were in fact autonomous provinces, officially recognized by the central government. The areas had previously resisted the implementation of the timar system, which was not suited to the conditions of the country. Ottoman sources refer to autonomous territories in northern Albania and Dardania. They included a significant portion of the Dukagjin region in addition to Hot, Pult, Shala, Shosh, Nikaj-Mertur, Kelmend, parts of Iballa, Fan i Madh, Fan i Vogël, Mirdita, Puka, and Dibër. Meanwhile, self-governing areas were also recorded in southern Albania, such as the provinces of Kurvelesh and Bregdet, which consisted of thirty-three villages, and the Sul region, to the southwest of Janina.[159]

---

[157] H.P.Sh. 1 (2002), 517.

[158] *Ibid.* 517.

[159] *Ibid.* 530.

The autonomous provinces had their own authorities, which governed according to the customary law, an evolving legal corpus adaptable to the social developments of each region. For example, the *Kanun of Lekë Dukagjini* was the legal tradition of the Dukagjin highlands; the Kruja, Mat, and Dibër highlands were governed under the *Skanderbeg Kanun*, which adopted new doctrines from the Lekë Dukagjini school; whereas Malësia e Madhe had its own Highlands Kanun or *Kanun i Maleve* (literally, Kanun of the Mountains). The regions of Kurvelesh, Himara, Sul, and the like, also relied on *kanuns* of their own to govern the social and economic aspects of their communities. Ultimately, the highlander rule was depended on the empire's judiciary (Trk.: *kadılık*), as the *bölükbaşı* was the final interpreter of the law. In need of new conscripts to carry out further conquests, the Ottoman Empire used the office of the *bölükbaşı* to establish ties with the native strongmen. The relationship gave rise to a new institution, that of the *bajraktar*, literary the standard-bearer, holding authority over a namesake entity, the *bajrak* (Alb.: *bajrak* or *flamur*; from Trk.: *bayrak*), meaning standard or banner. These new leaders, entrusted in their positions by the aristocracy, became immensely powerful, such that they literally raised their own *bajraks* in lieu of the old flags. The *bajraks* as such became a military-administered territorial unit at the command of the native chieftains. As a result, in certain areas the *bajrak* was coterminous with a self-governing province, but in others it span across two or more such areas; meanwhile, multiple *bajraks* operated within the larger provinces. For instance, Malësia e Madhe alone had twenty-two *bajraks*; eight resided in Dukagjin, seven in Puka, five in Mirdita, four in the Lezha Highlands, and three in the Kthella Highlands (also known as the Ohër *bajraks*, as they bordered on the sanjak of Ohër). As heads of the several units, the *bajraktars* served as representatives of the Ottoman state, while their position became hereditary along male lines.[160]

It is noteworthy that the *bajrak* became a core element in the governing structure that encompassed over half of the ethnic Albanian domains. A union of *bajraks* constituted a single, larger administrative unit. The head of such a division was the *kapedan* (meaning *captain* in Albanian), who governed with the assistance of a *kuvend* (*Alb.*, cognate of the English "convention"), the assembly of representatives from the several *bajraks*. Accordingly, the five *bajraks* of Mirdita formed a distinct administrative unit. The Shko-

---

[160] *Ibid.* 537.

dër-based House of Bushati, for instance, obtained the title of *bajraktar*-in-chief (Alb.: *kryebajraktar*), rising to prominence as a feudal dynasty. The free highlands would also recognize the authority of such powerful families, albeit retaining their self-governance and customary law. In the free highlands of the south, however, the *bajraktars* were titled *kapedans*. They continued a tradition of paid military service, that of the renowned *stratioti*, who had served in the military forces of Venice, Naples, and other Mediterranean powers. Southern Albanians preserved their titles and social rank even through the new system, while those who accepted Islam, such as the Suliotes in the 18th century, gained additional feudal titles and other offices of importance.[161]

Islam, nevertheless, was not a matter of privileges alone. Indeed, rising to the ranks of the Ottoman service implied had become increasingly dependent on one's acceptance of the new faith, unlike in the earlier days when spahis and feudal lords, including *beylerbeys* of certain sanjaks, counted Christians in their midst. More than a device used to gain promotion, the youngest of the Abrahamic religion was a defining feature of the Ottoman state. The Ottomans saw their conquests as inseparable from the task of spreading Islam and, although tolerant to Christians and other believers, the proselytizing efforts engaged every mechanism of the empire.

Although Albanian Muslims remained a minority through at least the 1600s, Islam had its beginnings in Albania well before the Ottomans reoccupied the country in 1479. The *devşirme*, or the education of Christian children at state institutions, brought the Islamic creed to a new perspective. Appearing as a means of Islamization as early as 1402, the *devşirme* was a duty imposed on Christian families that had accepted Ottoman rule, even as vassals. Accordingly, such families surrendered their sons to the Ottoman state. The boys, each known as an *acemi oğlan* (*Trk.*, cadets), were to be trained as janissaries, while the *iç oğlans*, educated at the Palace (Trk.: *Saray*), served other needs of the imperial administration.

Devşirme, however, was more than a *blood tax*, as it was often called. In line with its rules, it initially involved only Christian children, aged 12 to 15. A special commission, in close cooperation with the local chieftains (Trk.: *kocabaşı*), selected the boys, who were taken at a one-fifth ratio from each family. The draftees were not discriminated against in that they were not converted into casual prisoners or slaves, as had been the case with prisoners of war during the Byzantine period. In fact, the boys were exposed to a

---

[161] *Ibid.* 537.

privileged educational regime, which afforded them the opportunity to become part of the military or even civilian elite of the empire. Dressed in solemn robes, the draftees were sent to the capital of the empire, where the local families sheltered the youngsters in groups of two. Afterwards, the *ağa* (commander) of the janissaries led the boys in a presentment before the sultan, who then kept his preferred ones at his court. The rest was sent to Ottoman families in Rumelia and Anatolia, where they learned Turkish and performed agricultural labor and, in two to three years, as needed, the boys would leave the host families to serve in various state institutions.[162] After converting to Islam, some of the janissaries were transferred to serve at the palaces of sanjakbeys or *beylerbeys*. Known individually as a *gulam*, such janissaries appear frequently in Ottoman records from the 1500s as timariots and as successful military men.[163]

The practice of *devşirme*, which lasted to the end of the 1600s, played a key role in the creation of the Albanian military elite as a constituent part of the Ottoman military class. As such, *devşirme* affected the social and political life of the country as Albanians collected through the *devşirme* process later formed the Ottoman administration in Albania (*Arnavudluk*). As recipients of land grants (*timars*, *ziamets*, and *hases*), former *devşirme* boys became crucial factor in diffusing Islam to other parts of the population. The latter considered converting as an opportunity for economic as even social and political gains. Prominent families, such as the Arianitis, Dukagjinis, Muzakas, and others, were also influential in the pragmatic approach of the population. With the collapse of the military resistance after Skanderbeg's death, some of the noble families accepted Islam as a means to preserve their lands. In doing so, they set an example for other layers of the populace to embrace the Muslim creed, at least formally. Ottoman records on the the Sanjak of Arnavud-İli indicate a sharp decrease of Christian landowners between the 1431-1432 census and the 1485 registration. While the early records note thirty-six out of 335 timariots were Christians, their number decreased to only sixteen some fifty years later. Although the transition was less rapid in other areas (particularly in Kruja and Dibra), the absence of Christian fieftains in the next century emphasizes the influence of the Timar system in bring about the mass conversion to Islam. Ultimately, regardless of whether such conversions were sincere and how it affected the religious

---

[162] *Ibid.* 588.

[163] Rizaj, *Kosova gjatë shekujve . . .*, 25.

identity of the masses, Islam did not—as attested in the 19th century—impede the emergence of a modern national identity.

Aside from *devşirme*, other factors contributed to the Islamization of Albania. Urban life was a noteworthy influence for cities served as seats of the empire's local authorities, including sanjakbeys, *alaybeys*, and *kadıs*. Additionally, the nature of urban settlements changed. Cities had previously served as outposts of feudal entities, which lived in seclusion and often in enmity with each other. United in a single imperial market, however, the cities established lasting ties that proved of great economic benefit. Concomitantly, the local ruling elite in the cities would spearhead the growth of Islam, owing to the economic opportunities the religion provided for the general population. In the meantime, even towns of smaller size played their part as they became administrative centers of *kazas* or *nahiyes* and engaged in commerce and craftsmanship. The two industries commenced their development at the request of the Ottoman administration, which then included locals who had converted to Islam. Ottoman registers for the Albanian sanjaks—reflecting the 1431 census in the sanjaks of Shkodra and Arnavud-Ili, the 1455 census of the Vilayet of Vlk (in Dardania); and later registrations conducted through the early 1600s—clearly indicate the vigor of the Islamization process, which mainly takes place among Christians in the larger vibrant cities. Then, Islam gradually diffused to the smaller towns such that, by mid-17th century, Muslims made up the majority in such urban settlements. For example, the 1478 register notes thirty-three Muslim households of the 107 recorded in Vuçitërn. The same year, the Islamic community in Prishtina counted fifty-one houses of the city total of 299. Meanwhile, by 1468, forty-one households had converted to Islam in Tetova (Trk.: Kalkandelen, Mac.: Tetovo), a town of 264 homes. Similarly, in 1485, only twenty-six homes belonged to the Islamic faith in cities such as Shkodër and Peja. A century later, in the 1598 and 1610 censuses, the number of Muslim households had sharply increased, having attained an overwhelming majority or remaining on the rise in many towns. In the first decade of the 17th century, the state religion prevailed in the greater towns such as Shkodër (almost entirely), Peja (90 percent), Vuçitërn and the vicinity (80 percent), Elbasan (79 percent), Kruja (63 percent), Prishtina (60 percent), Prizren (55 percent), and Dibër (51 percent). Fewer converts lived in Novobërda (37 percent), Trepça (21 percent), and Janjeva (14 percent), where the Roman Catholic Church retained the upper-hand.

Economic growth in the city remained a pillar in support of islamization as large number of residents from the rural areas poured into the booming towns in search of opportunities. There, newcomers accepted Islam without complaint. While peasants had little to gain in the countryside, ridden by the timar system, moving to the city and embracing the now prevailing religion opened doors to integration and prosperity.

Nevertheless, Ottoman records note a pervasive spread of Islam even in the rural areas of Dardania. (The historical region, comprising of the sanjaks of Vuçitërn, Shkup, Prizren, and Dukagjin as well as parts of the Sanjak of Shkodër, was reorganized into an administrative unit, known as the Vilayet of Kosova or *Kosovo*, in the second half of the 19th century. While the new name was unknown to the majority population, the Ottoman Porte adopted it at the behest of, and under pressure by, Serbia and Russia during the Eastern Crisis.) The causes of the mass conversion were primarily social and political since it is in these aspects that Dardania stood apart from other regions on the eve of the Ottoman conquest. Nevertheless, there are other factors, too, focusing on Dardania as an important geographical node from the ancient times up to—and throughout—the Ottoman period.

Back in 870, Dardania fell under the ecclesiastic jurisdiction of Constantinople. Meanwhile, the Bulgarians twice occupied the region, under kings Boris (852-879) and Simeon (894-927). Beginning in the mid-13th century, and up to the mid-14th century, Dardania was occupied by the Rascian Nemanide dynasty, which lasted until the reign of Stefan Dušan (1335-1355). Thus, Albanians had lived through a Slavic-Orthodox occupation at a time when the Orthodox Church did its utmost to uproot Roman Catholicism from the area. The enmity began during the rule of Urosh II and reached its peak at the time of Dušan, who waged a merciless war against the non-Orthodox. It is likely that, under such circumstances, the Albanian nobility and those appearing as *župans* were part of the Orthodox Church and subject to forced Slavicization. As a result, historians, including Serbian ones, have raised doubts about the Slavic origin of the Nemanides. Therefore, the dynasty is described as originally Triballi, a Slavicized tribe of the Dardani or Illyrian stock. While conclusions are tentative at the present, future discussions may bring the issue to greater light, should they be derailed from the non-academic approach of the past.[164] Ultimately, hints that the Nemanides

---

[164] For more on the topic, see vol. I of the series on the ethnic rapports between Albanians and Slavic invaders during the Middle Ages.

may be of non-Slavic origin are contained even within the pro-Serb writings of the 19th century. An offspring of the nationalist *Načertanije* project, the non-academic propaganda of the time attempted to forge a wide variety of documents, including ecclesiastic archives, which could serve the creation of a medieval Serbian myth. In such works, Serbian authors speculate on Prince Lazar's "betrayal" by his sons-in-law, for which they blame their "distinct" origin. If not Slavic, the allegedly disloyal men could not have been other than Albanian nobles, serving as vassals of their father-in-law.

Regardless of the origin of Lazar's subordinates, the mass acceptance of Islam among the people of Dardania is a crucial indicator of the ethnic makeup of the region. Through conversion, the people of Dardania sought an opportunity to free themselves of over a century of Slavic occupation. And, more importantly, they sought a way out of the oppressive Slavic Orthodox Church., the source of Slavicization. Owing to its cooperation with the Ottoman Empire (even against the Catholics), the Slavic Church retained its power after the conquest, maintaining authority over the Orthodox Albanians as well as those who had been forcibly Slavicized during the Rascian occupation.

Here, it is worthy to distinguish the Orthodox of Dardania with Orthodox Albanians of the coastal areas and northern Albania. The latter would preserve Christianity for the most part, for they had been part of the Orthodox Church owing to natural historical developments, outside of Slavic rule. Between the 13th and 14th centuries, however, the Dardanian Orthodox had been subject to Slavicization, which process came to an end after the arrival of the Ottomans. The distinction explains, moreover, the survival of Albanian Catholics in Dardania, while Orthodox Albanians were no longer present in the region. The Slavic Orthodox Church had nevertheless held on to its institutions in Dardania, such as the Patriarchate of Peja and the monasteries of Graçanica (Srb.: Gračanica), Deçan (Srb.: Dečani), Prizren, Shkup, etc. Thereby, the Slavic Church maintained a presence sufficient enough to limit Islam in the vicinity of churches and monasteries and to completely prevent it among the Slavs and the fully-Slavicized; elsewhere in Dardania, Albanians turned to Islam or followed Roman Catholicism.

The permanence of Catholics in Dardania is evident, but its extent does not compare to the region such as Shkodër and Mirdita. There, Christians of the Roman rite remained in greater numbers all the while Dardania enjoyed more favorable economic conditions than the other areas. Economic opportunities, nevertheless, had spurred a wave of mass conversions in Dardania to a much higher degree, leading in meantime to the practice of a clandestine Christianity, known as *crypto-Christianity*. The practice, noted only among Catholics, represents a transitional, syncretic phase of what Albanian speakers call *dybesim* (literally, *bi-faith*) or among Christians who accepted Islam only formally, in order to avoid the *haraç* or *jizya* tax and enjoy social equality with their Muslim compatriots. The so-called *laraman* practice was very common in Dardania and developed its distinct features. For example, many *laramanë* retained two given names—a Muslim name for public use and a Christian name in the family. In certain cases, only the head of a household would convert to Islam and declare the new religion, while the rest of the family would remain Christians. Instances were numerous (such as in the Gjakova area and other parts of Dukagjin) a Muslim convert continued to live with his Catholic brother within the same household unaffected by the religious diversity. Many families in those areas have preserved the practice of two religions to this very day.

The prevalence of Islam among Orthodox Albanians as opposed to the Catholics is also attested in the Ottoman registers or *defters*, containing data from the land and population census. While the registers mainly served for taxation and other administrative purposes, they also reflect the ethnic makeup of the population. For instance, the 1455 cadaster, or the so-called *Tapıdefteri*, records by name of household heads in 600 villages of the Dardania Field, or the eastern half of Dardania. As noted in charts provided in the Appendix to this book, a significant number of Albanians appears in the cadaster. Only individuals with a typical Albanian given name or patronymic are listed, since given names of Greek Orthodox, Latin Catholic, and Slavic Orthodox origin may be misleading. In the meantime, the Albanian presence in the Dukagjin Plateau, western Dardania, was even more substantial.

CHAPTER 2
BETWEEN EAST AND WEST

Efforts for Renewed Ties with the West

> *Although in a state of trouble, The Catholic Church tries to improve spiritual protection for Albanians: The Council of Trent of mid-1500s leads to the establishment of the College of Saint Athanasius in 1572, the Illyric College of Loreto is founded in 1580, and Basilian monks begin their mission in Albania. The new Propaganda Fide plays a role in Albania, opening of the first religious schools to conduct lessons in Albanian—in Kurbin, Kruja, in 1632, and Janjeva, Kosova, in 1671. The beginnings of the Classical Albanian literature are marked with the works of Budi, Bogdani, and Frang Bardhi as well as the seminal discovery of Buzuku's* Meshari *in 1740 by Gjon Nikollë Kazazi.*

A correct observation has been made that, while the Ottoman Turks gave a fatal blow to the cultural life of the country, they were unable to immediately impose their Islamic culture. In the 15th and 16th centuries, the Turks were, in terms of cultural developments, behind the Balkan countries. While they represented themselves as successors of the Islamic culture, as developed in the Arab and Persian languages, few Turks even understood the two languages. The ruling class of the landowning spahis and the Muslim clergy, which was to carry the Islamic culture in Albania, was generally of Albanian ethnicity and had little proficiency of Turkish, Arabic, or Persian. Furthermore, the timar system, of a heavy military nature, was not particularly supportive of cultural development, for the main objective of the feudal class was to obtain rent payments from the peasantry. All of these circumstances caused for Albania to plummet into a significant cultural backwardness in the 16th century.[165]

As records indicate, it took Ottoman authorities more than a century to set up few Turkish-language schools. Supported by Islamic endowments (Trk.: *vakıf*, from Arb.: *waqf*) of wealthy Muslims, the so-called *mektepler* (sing.: *mektep*) were religious institutions of the elementary level, which taught students to read the Quran, preparing them to serve in local mosques. Therefore, the Ottomans did not seek to emancipate the masses or to culturally enlighten the believers; the intention was to keep the people in a state of complete ignorance, dependence, and obedience to the empire. This aspect would become most evident in the final years of Ottoman rule, when ninety-seven percent of the population was illiterate.

The Christian clergy, even though affected by the German Reformation, served its congregation, with a focus on preparing native Albanians for priesthood. At the Council of Trent, beginning in the mid-1540, the Catholic Church decided to reorganize its clergy in the Balkans. The Council paid special attention to Albania, where the pre-Ottoman clergy, consisting of twenty monasteries and 120 monks, shrunk to only four monasteries and eleven monks by 1570. In a later session of the council, the Church approved the establishment of several special colleges for the local clergy in several parts of the world, including Albanian and other Balkan ecclesiasts. One of the early schools was the College of Saint Athanasius, established in Rome, in 1572, under the leadership of Basilian monks. The school served primarily Albanian and Greek students from Italy of the Uniate churches. A special school for the Catholics of Dalmatia was founded in 1580 in Loreto bearing the name Illyric College (*i.e.*, Illyrian college). The institution also became the alma mater of Albanian clergymen who, as will be noted later, were instrumental in the early development of a continuous Albanian education and literature.[166]

The two schools, however, implied a new agreement with the Porte on the presence of the Catholic Church in the occupied territories. As a first imperative, the Church sought to preserve its geographical boundaries vis-à-vis the Orthodox Church, which maintained an advantage owing to its status as an institution under the sovereignty of the Porte; secondly, the Catholic Church was to sponsor the publication of liturgy in Albanian, a particularly

---

[165] H.P.Sh. 1 (1969), 347.
[166] *Ibid.* 348.

difficult task for the time. To achieve the first goal, a Catholic campaign focused on creating new Uniate churches, by attracting Orthodox Albanians to separate from the Eastern Church and unite with Rome.[167]

For that reason, the Uniate movement sent Basilian monks as its missionaries in Albania. As early as the 16th century, numerous Basilians sailed from Italy to central and southern Albania. In Himara, they achieved great success, since they promised the Himariotes that, by uniting with the Catholic Church, Rome would offer weapons and aid in the war against the Turks. The Uniatization campaign continued through the next century, but the Patriarchate of Constantinople, owing to its close relations with the Porte and the sultan, was able to regain its foothold. The Orthodox efforts were fruitful especially in light of Rome's undelivered promise of aid for liberation. In fact, from the 16th century onward, the Orthodox Church opened several Greek-language elementary schools in southern Albania.[168] Serbian schools also began to operate later on in Kosova and Macedonia, laying favorable foundations for the Hellenization and Slavicization of a significant part of the Orthodox congregation in those areas.

The lost Uniate battle in southern Albania, Dardania, and Macedonia shifted the focus of the Catholic Church to Albanians of the Western rite, mainly in northern Albania and Kosova, but also in central Albania. Faced with Ottoman rule and throughout continued anti-Ottoman uprisings, efforts to salvage the Christian faith had not only a religious meaning; they were noted by patriotic undertones, even among conscientious clergymen. Defending Christianity against Islam, the Catholic clergy worked to hinder the assimilation of Albanians into Ottoman Turks.[169]

One such conscientious priest, who pursued the patriotic mission of the clergy, was Don Gjon Buzuku. In 1555, Buzuku published *Meshari* (*Alb.*, the Missal), an anthology of his Albanian translations of excerpts from the gospels, rituals, and liturgy. However, the work later slipped into oblivion until 1740, when it was discovered by another Albanian prelate and classical writer, Gjon Nikollë Kazazi from the town of Gjakova. Then student at the College of Propaganda Fide, Kazazi elatedly copied a fragment from "the ancient Albanian missal, worn with age" and sent it as a token to Father Gusetta, the founder of the Palermo Seminary, with the dedication. Later

---

[167] *Ibid.* 348.

[168] *Ibid.* 348.

[169] *Ibid.* 350.

rectors of the seminary, Pal Parino and Sepë Krispi held the fragment and cited it in their writings.

Meshari, nevertheless, was forgotten of, once again. Towards the end of the 18th century, the Library of the Propaganda Fide transferred it to the Cardinal Stefan Borgia collection of oriental books. Finally, the entire collection, including *Meshari*, ended up at the Vatican Library, where it is located under the call number *R(accolta) G(enerale) Liturgia. III. 194*, as the only copy known to date.[170]

The first study of *Meshari* began among the Italo-Albanians, or the Arbëreshë of Italy. In 1909, their bishop and scholar, Pal Skiroi, began his perennial work using a photographic copy of the book. Skiroi produced a full transliteration of *Meshari*, but his scholarly work was not published in its entirety. Later, in 1929, Justin Rrota secured three photocopies of the book from the Vatican library. Through his publication of excerpts along with his commentary, Rrota contributed to the monumental book's rising popularity.[171]

After *Meshari*'s publication, there was an increasing activity of Albanian writers and translators, focusing on Christian liturgy. In 1952, Lekë Matranga (also Matrënga, Ita.: Luca Matranga) published his *E msuame e krishterë* (*Alb.*, The Christian Doctrine). Matranga (1560-1619), an Albanian from Hora e Arbëreshëve (Ita.: Piana Degli Albanesi) of Sicily, was one the early students at the College of Saint Athanasius in Rome. In addition to its religious significance, *E msuame e krishterë* is of literary value since, along with the main catechism text, the author provides a poem of eight verses, inviting believers to always attend Mass.

At the same time, Albania began receiving a number of Catholic missionaries, primarily graduates of the Illyric College of Loretto, who opened elementary schools at their congregations and parishes.[172] While serving in the mission, the Albanian prelate, Pjetër Budi (Ita.: Pietro Budi; 1566-1622), was noted for his activities. Budi, a native of Guribardhë, Mat, translated *Doktrina e Kërshtenë* (*Alb.*, Christian Doctrine; Lat.: *Doctrina Christiana*),

---

[170] For more on *Meshari* by Gjon Buzuku, see the multivolume edition of *Meshari*, published by Rilindja, 1978. In addition to a facsimile and a transliteration of the text, the edition includes a preface by Eqrem Çabej. Professor Çabej offers a detailed commentary not only on the linguistic value of the work, but also its importance for the Albanian culture in general. Likewise, he analyzes the context in which the work was written, providing a great secondary source for future researchers.

[171] *Meshari i Gjon Buzukut 1555* (Prishtinë: Rilindja, 1978) 7.

[172] H.P.Sh. 1 (1969), 350.

published in 1618, and *Pasqyra e të rrëfyemit* (*Alb.*, The Mirror of Confession; Lat.: *Speculum Confessionis*) and *Rituali roman* (*Alb.*, The Roman Ritual; Lat.: *Rituale Romanum*), which were printed as a single volume in 1621. Alongside the translations, Budi added a large number of religious poems of an artistic deliberation.[173]

Despite the Church activities and the spread of religious books in Albanian, the Catholic Church remained in a difficult state. Owing to the fast expansion of Islam in Albania, the Catholic area shrank from day to day. To improve the situation, the Vatican founded a new powerful, Rome-based body, the Propaganda Fide (*Lat.*, for the propagation of the faith), which directed the faith-spreading efforts in the East from 1662 onward. The institution established, from time to time, additional schools for the needs of the Albanian clergy. In 1633, Propaganda Fide founded the Illyric College of Fermo, which was led by the Jesuit Order. Meanwhile, the Franciscans were in charge of the newly-formed the Montoriso School in Rome and the Basilian monks supervised two other schools servicing students of the Uniate congregations. The most successful graduates of such schools and colleges went on to study at the Urban College of the Propaganda. Upon completion of their higher education, the young clergymen were sent to Albania as "soldiers" of the Propaganda. Yet, suffering from the unfavorable political climate and their own ignorance of the Albanian language, missionaries often failed to cater to their flock, yearning for practical support rather than philosophical guidance. Albanian prelates, such as Pjetër Budi, wrote to Propaganda Fide, advising that vicars ought to speak Albanian before they are assigned to the country. The communication, however, strained Budi's relations with the Vatican to the point that Church leaders are considered to have plotted the priest's tragic drowning in the Drin River in 1622.[174]

Regardless of the concerns surrounding Catholic missionaries in Albania, their work is significant in that they opened the first schools with Albanian as the language of instruction. A religious primary school was founded in Kurbin, Kruja region, in 1632, where ten students enrolled to receive a clerical education. Four years later, Franciscan missionaries opened a school in Pdhana, along the Mat River. The year after, at the request of Blinisht (Zadrime) inhabitants, Franciscans founded a congregation, with a secondary school (gymnasium). The first Albanian school in Dardania was that of

---

[173] *Ibid.* 350.
[174] *Ibid.* 351.

Janjeva, established in 1671.[175] Similar schools operated also in Velje, Mirdita, and Shkodër. To fulfill the educational needs of the schools, the Albanian priests served also as teachers. They prepared relevant textbooks in the Albanian language. They were primarily religious in content, as was, for instance, the work of Pjetër Budi; but original opus was also noted, such as in Pjetër Bogdani's *Çeta e profetënve* (*Alb.*, Band of Prophets). [176] Some of the works were entirely didactic in character. They include a 1635 Latin-Albanian dictionary by Frang Bardhi (1606-1643) and Andrea Bogdani's Latin-Albanian grammar, a manuscript that was lost, along with other handwritten religious texts and dictionaries, during the Turkish expeditions of 1683.[177]

Owing to the activity of early writers, the publication of Albanian books, which had begun as an undertaking for the needs of the clergy, came to reflect the artistic and scholarly oeuvre of the classical Albanian literature. For that reason, the religious books called the attention of the Ottoman authorities. Meanwhile, as Albanian schools proliferated throughout the country, the regime became even more distressed, ordering measures to obstruct or even close the schools. Due to the repression that ensued, several schools switched to different buildings or locations, but they did not cease their work. Albanian priests were able to organize many of the schools at their congregations, although Serbian Orthodox clergymen would often denounce their Albanian colleagues before the Ottoman officers.

To preserve the spirit of engagement, despite the difficult circumstances, Pope Clement XI, himself of Albanian descent, came to the aid of the Catholic clergy in Albania. In 1703, he encouraged and supported a gathering of bishops of Albania, known as the Council of Arbën (Alb.: *Koncili i Arbënit*). Besides the more ecclesiastic issues, the Council approved of the religious publications in the Albanian language. In 1711, with Pope Clement's blessing, an Albanian-language chair was created at the Montoriso School in Rome.[178] The Albanian cathedra, preceded in time by the affluent activity of the several schools and colleges, created a basis to safeguard and consolidate

---

[175] See Gaspër Gjini, *Skopsko Prizrenska Biskupija kroz stoljeća* (Zagreb: 1986).

[176] Pjetër Bogdani's *Çeta e Profetënve* is considered to be the classical Albanian masterpiece since, in addition to discussing religious doctrine, the work explores philosophy, focusing on contemporary social and historical issues. The work includes many literary texts—author's original compositions in a pure language and fluent in style. The poems "Sibilat" (*Alb.*, Sybiles) appear as the first lyrical verse in Albanian literature.

[177] H.P.Sh. 1 (1969), 352,

[178] *Ibid.* 353.

the Western heritage among Albanians, even at a time of Islam's significant growth in the country.

As they carried out their religious mission, numerous clerics labored for social reform, resorting even to calls for an open confrontation with the Ottomans. Conscientious bishops, such as the homonymous Pjetër Budi and Pjetër Bogdani, became directly involved in such activities. Budi propagated an armed uprising of northern Albanian highlanders, calling for a Western knight to serve as their leader. Later, Bogdani led an army in the Austro-Turkish War in the 1680s as an ally of the Viennese general Piccolomini, who captured Prishtina and penetrated as far as Shkup, reviving the Christian population's hope to see an end to Ottoman rule. Yet, neither bishop reached ultimate success. Budi's project for an uprising remained a request, which is believed to have cost him his life. Meanwhile, Bogdani's participation in combat was futile and entailed severe repercussions for the Albanian population. The bishops' endeavors, however, remain an indication that historic change is possible and appears only when intellectuals, as a conscientious layer of a society, assume the leadership.

Efforts to Break Away From the East

The Albanian prelate, Pjetër Budi, presents his project to the Pope in 1616, proposing the great Albanian uprising against the Ottomans; the West ignores Budi project. Albanians participate in the Austro-Hungarian wars between 1683 and 1735. Pjetër Bogdani plays a role in those wars; the Albanians suffer the consequences of defeat. Following the Austrian defeat, many Albanians migrate to the north; Serbian history later manipulates with the exodus, presenting it as the "Great Serbian Migrations."

The Great Age of Skanderbeg nurtured a sense of pride among Albanians. Yet, Skanderbeg's era also reminded them of the misery that followed, inciting fears that, should the Albanians not rise to fight, they would live forever under oppression. Historical sources note that the Albanian resistance continued well after Skanderbeg's death, despite the terror and oppression that ensued after the Ottoman conquest, on the one hand, and the Western diplomatic games, on the other. During at least the first half-century under Ottoman Empire, Albanians forcefully rejected the new rulers and organized a series of uprising. The movement posed serious military challenges to the Porte such as, to quell the uprisings, the sultan would often have to personally lead his armies. Among such combats is the 1492 expedition that Sultan Bayezid II took against Himara. In what the Ottomans called a "successful" campaign, the Ottomans reached a deal with the Himariotes, granting them a type of extensive autonomy known as *venoma*.[179]

Western allies generally had an interest in retaining their ties to the Albanians, who would halt the Ottoman advance to the West. In fact, just as they conquered Albania, the Ottomans reached the southern coast of Italy and set sail for the Spanish shores. Faced with the situation, the Westerners resorted to their Albanian allies, inciting them to rise against the Ottomans in several parts of the country. But Western support was of a shaky character. For instance, while Skanderbeg's son, Gjon II Kastrioti, led a successful uprising in southern Albania, he failed to consolidate power as his main supporter, Venice, withdrew its support. Having encouraged the Albanians to fight against the Ottomans, the maritime republic delivered revoked its alliance with Kastrioti when it reached a peace treaty with the Porte, gaining Corfu and retaining Ulqin and Tivar (Mont.: Bar).

Therefore, with the beginning of the 16th century, the Albanians no longer sought to drive the Ottomans out of their country, but instead to prevent the complete installation of the Ottoman regime. The focus of the uprisings shifted to opposing the timar system and demands of local autonomy, which would permit their patriarchal, tribal society to survive. Retaining their ancient customary law, certain regions of the country remained self-governing for virtually the entire duration of Ottoman rule.

In light of the shifting affairs in Albania, Western powers maintained diverging strategies. The Vatican believed that Catholicism had its best chances of survival under the constructive conditions of autonomous regions, which ordinarily appeared in the highlands. Meanwhile, Venice had its eyes on Albanian "oases" outside Ottoman jurisdiction. Through such entities, the Venetians hoped to hold the Porte accountable to its agreements with the maritime republic with respect to the strategic coastal cities of Albania.

The two approaches relied on the same means, but pursued different ends. The Holy See regarded local autonomy as a factor that helped preserve a Western spiritual identity among the Albanians; in other words, Catholicism would retain a stronghold in an important eastern frontier. On the

---

[179] *Ibid.* 297.

other hand, Venice was concerned with its economic and political interests with respect to the Ottoman Empire. To serve such preoccupations, the maritime power was unhesitant to use Albania as a political tool. This strategy, which had been the Venetian attitude even during Skanderbeg's time, was noted again in 1594 when Venice and other European powers instigated a Balkan-wide uprising. The Western plan was to have the Albanians rise against the Ottomans in a campaign that would include the Serbs, Bulgarians, Greeks, and Bosnians. Gathered at a convention in Mat, Albanian leaders agreed on an uprising with the blessing of the pope and assistance of other Christian nations. Albanians appointed Tomë Plezha and Mark Gjini, two knights in service of the Republic of Venice, and Bishop Nikollë Mekajshi to enter into talks with the Papacy. Venice, nevertheless, took care to ensure the Albanian failure. Two years later, a second convention at Mat sent the same envoys to Holy See only to have them return barehanded for Venice convinced the Pope to await the end of the Hungarian-Ottoman war. This, Venetians held, was of greater importance to the West than the limited prospects of an Albanian victory.[180]

Venice objected to Albanian uprising in many later requests that local Albanian assemblies made to the Western powers. In 1601, the greater Dukagjin region held a convention in Mat, electing Nikollë Bardhi and Pal Dukagjini as emissaries to Venice, but the republic rejected Dukagjin's prayer for aid as "the time ha[d] not come for a general war against the Turks." Conscientious clergymen, therefore, demanded that Venice cease to regards the Albanians as a tool against the Ottomans. The prelates also supported the consolidation of self-governing areas for it was such entities (primarily those encompassing Malësia e Madhe, Dukagjin, Mat, Mirdita, and parts of the Gjakova Highlands) that could prompt a new war on the Ottomans. The initial success of a highlanders uprising, thought the clergymen, would inevitably bring Christian Europe to the aid of Albanians.

In addition to the Albanian conventions in Mat, regional efforts were also under way at the beginning of the 17th century. Balkan leaders assembled in a series of meetings at Kuç, Prokupa, and Belgrade to discuss anti-Ottoman movements. While the regional initiatives yielded no fruit, participants of former assemblies continued to push for an anti-Ottoman war. The Albanian prelate, Pjetër Budi, presented a project to the Vatican and other European countries, noting military preparations that Albanians, including

---

[180] *Ibid.* 335.

those who had accepted Islam, were to carry out. The description is sufficiently detailed and convincing, suggesting that military strategists were
heavily involved in the preparatory process. In 1616, Budi travelled to Rome
to personally deliver his detailed plan. At the Vatican, he requested weapons
and military experts from the West to assist the Albanians. Five years later,
Budi would again appear in Rome in pursuit of the same mission, handing
his war plan to a cardinal named Gozzadino. Specifically, in 1621, Budi
proposed that the war leadership be entrusted to a Bosnian knight, Bertucci,
who had expressed his willingness for the office and reportedly enjoyed the
backing of Germany and Austria.[181]

Budi's plans garnered no support. Venice intermeddled and the Papacy
gave no green light for a general uprising in the Balkans. Devastated by the
rejection and suspicious of Catholic clerics whom he regarded as very close
to Venice, Budi returned to Albania in early 1622. There, he summoned in a
special assembly the Catholic clergy of the area—the dioceses of Zadrima,
Shkodër, and Lezha—and convinced them not to accept any foreign bishops
in their districts and, should the Church have appointed a foreigner, to have
him ousted on the pretext that he knows neither the language nor the customs of the country. Pjetër Budi's rebellious stance exceeded the contours of
the ordinary. Ten months later, his enemies had him drowned as he was
crossing the Drin River on route to Malësia e Madhe.[182]

Along with the Albanian prelate, the Drin River swallowed several important documents that Budi was carrying on him. The nature of his death
reasonably suggests that the papers—because Budi was known for his
research in the Vatican archives and practice of archeology in Albania—were
of a historic significance. The tragic death also illustrates Holy See's fears
about the "excessive" involvement of Albanian clerics in social and political
affairs that could impact the Pope's relations with the Sublime Porte. After
the Reformation, the Vatican expressed an interest in the state of its Balkan
clergy, but was also cautious to restrain a Protestant spirit that would give the
Church in the Ottoman-held territories any ethnic attributes, even if that
would be required for the Church to survive. A livening example of the
situation is found in a letter that Domenic Andreas wrote to Cardinal
Barberini in February 1623. Assisting Barberini in his investigation of Budi's
death, Andreas writes that the Albanian prelate "had sin[ned] for he had

---

[181] Zamputi, *Dokumente . . .*, vol. III, p. 376-377.
[182] H.P.Sh. 1 (1969), 341.

requested that priests sent to Albania know the Albanian language." To Andreas, Budi's request was unacceptable, and the Church should continue to deploy foreign bishops from abroad.[183]

Meanwhile, the content of Pjetër Budi's letter to Cardinal Gozzadino in 1621 reveals the political influence of the Albanian priest.[184] For that reason, he was viewed as a threat not only by the Ottomans; the centralist movement of the Catholic clergy vehemently opposed ethnic attributes in the Church, while Venice, seeking to maintain the Albanians under its control, rejected their emergence as an independent political factor.[185]

Pjetër Budi's assassination in the Drin River slowed the anti-Ottoman momentum, especially among Albanian Catholics. The resentment remained, however, and whenever needed, it led to the battlefield. Half a century later, during the Austro-Turkish War, thousands of Albanians joined the Austrian armies once they reached the country.

Catholic Albanians responded en mass, when the Austrian emperor, Leopold I, called on them for a war against the Ottomans as early as 1687. Two important factors favored the Austrian monarchy: since 1615-1616, Austria had been the official protector of Catholics in the Ottoman state; meanwhile,

---

[183] See Domenic Andreas's letter to Cardinal Barberino, the investigator of Budi's case, as cited by Iniac Zamputi in *Dokumente . . .*, vol. III:

> After such an exasperating journey through weather of great wickedness, on land as well as at sea, I reached the diocese . . . And I learn that it is true that which some people worthy of trust have told me that the bishop of Zadrima, when he reached his bishopric, called a meeting with a clergy, at which [meeting] he said that from no on [they are] not to accept bishops or abbots in those areas if [such priests] are not native and he has made all the prists sign the reuqest and has thus acted against ecclesiastic freedom . . .
>
> Nevertheless, with immense sorrow and sadness I learned that as he travelled, recently, while crossing a river (which is called Drin), accompanied by five people, he was drowned in a certainly miserable way . . . It has not even been possible to locate his body. May God have mercy for that soul. He has also committed other sins . . .
>
> Therefore, illustrious lords, please, along with the Reverend Cardinal, do not allow crude bishops to be elected, because such and even more severe mistakes are made . . . It is necessary that foreigners continue to be appointed bishops here, as has mainly been the custom . . .

[184] Due to its historical importance, Budi's letter to the cardinal is reproduced in the Appendix.

[185] Zamputi, *Dokumente . . . .* III, 377.

Leopold I promised the Balkan peoples, including the Albanians, their right to self-governance, freedom of religion, along with the right to develop a national identity—including the national language and flag.[186]

The first factor, Austria's role as a protector of Catholicism, would have both positive and negative effects. Catholic Albanians would benefit from such protection, especially when impacted by the hegemonic and assimilationist approach of the Slavic and Greek Orthodox churches. Yet, Vienna's engagement led to a rivalry with the Holy See over the Albanians. Initially, the two powers disagreed over ecclesiastic matters, but later drifted into the social and cultural spheres. The animosity affected the Albanian people for centuries, especially during its later war for statehood. Beginning with the second half of the 17th century, the rivalry excluded the Vatican as a factor of influence on Catholic Albanians. Meanwhile, in its attempts to retain the Albanian coastal towns, Venice became an apparent opponent of Vienna; meanwhile, through its continued alliances with the Ottoman Empire and other powers, the maritime republic remained a detriment to the Albanians. Under such circumstances, the Albanian clergy would naturally support the Austrian call for war. Therefore, it would be expected that—once the Austrians reached Nish and, on September 24, 1689, a Count Ludwig lead his army to victory—the Albanians would support the Austrians. After Nish, the Austrian army would split into two directions, with one unit marching to Vidin, Bulgaria, under the orders of Count Baden, while General Piccolomini led the rest of the army to Kosova. It was at that time that the Albanian Catholic clergy began preparations to welcome the Viennese general and enter service at his command.

According to contemporary sources,[187] Albanians in Prishtina welcomed Piccolomini in an elaborate ceremony. The Albanian bishops, Pjetër Bogdani and Toma Raspasani, who received the general, had gathered numerous

---

[186] Skënder Rizaj, *Kosova dhe Shqiptarët: dje, sot dhe nesër* (Prishtinë: 1992), cited in Petrika Thëngjilli, *Shqiptarët midis lindjes dhe perëndimit* (Tiranë: 2003), 298.

[187] Multiple secondary sources discuss the Albanian involvement in Austro-Ottoman war of 1683-1735 using on the relations of Albanian prelates with the Vatican and military and diplomatic documents of Vienna. While Albanian historians, I. Zamputi, S. Rizaj, and S. Pulaha, have zealously studied the matter, their work lacks a critical and comprehensive approach and at times appears fragmentary and incompatible. It is particularly important to study the true character of the war, since it is known that Christian Albanians entered Austrian service, either as an insurgent group or as part of the liberation war.

volunteers who waited to join the Austrian army and continue southward to Shkup.[188]

No documents bring doubts about Pjetër Bogdani's involvement on the side of the Austrians. Multiple sources note that he was not only an ecclesiastic official, but a local leader, who viewed the arrival of the Austrian army in the Albanian lands, as liberation from the Ottoman violence. However, it is unclear whether Bogdani was directly involved in leading war efforts. Certain sources imply that the Albanian prelate was involved with the creation of a police service. In a meeting that was also attended by the Serbian Orthodox patriarch, Arsenie III Crnojević, Bogdani reached an agreement with the Austrian regarding an Albanian police that would join the Austrian army. However, official ecclesiastic records do not admit such an event and the Church position is understandable since clerics are prohibited to serve in the military.[189]

Ottomans, nevertheless, treated Bogdani with extreme scorn and brutality. In Prizren, the authorities beat the prelate in public, humiliating him before the eyes of the world; or, after his death, Ottomans disinterred his body and fed it to dogs. This indicates that Bogdani had become an im-

---

[188] Rizaj, *Kosova dhe Shqiptarët . . .*, 57, cited in Thëngjilli, *op. cit.*, 301.

[189] *See* Gjini, *op. cit.*, 174-175, describing the relation of Pjetër Bogdani to the Congregation, sometime towards the end of 1685. In the relation, Bogdani discusses the Austro-Turkish war and refuses a proposal that he lead about 300 of his Catholic followers to take the castle of Novobërda, on grounds that he is a prelate, not a military officer. That Bogdani did not participate in war activities during the Austro-Turkish war is noted also in Odette Marquet's book, *Pjetër Bogdani – letra dhe dokumente* (*Alb.*, Pjetër Bogdani: Letters and Documents), published in Tiranë 1997. The publication includes letters Bogdani sent to Propaganda Fide and several letters from the secret Vatican archives. Bogdani speaks of consequences of war, especially for the violence that Turkish units would exercise for revenge; he also notes that he suffered a punishment carried out in public by a pasha in Prizren, on a market day, but does not make references to his direct military involvement. His nephew, Gjergj Bogdani, wrote e relation to the cardinals the day Pjetër died, on December 6, 1689. Gjergj admits that his uncle had travelled to Shkup, then held by General Piccolomini, to encourage soldiers to fight, but he had fallen ill with the plague and, upon returning to Prishtina, had passed away (p. 509). Nevertheless, even without a direct participation in the war, Pjetër Bogdani was an influential leader. Gjergj Bogdani, then a missionary in Janjeva and Administrator of Prishtina and Vuçitërn, wrote a letter dated December 20, 1698 to Propaganda Fide, informing the institution that Turks had disinterred Pjetër Bogdani's remains and fed them to dogs while the corpse still had the miter on the head (p. 516).

portant authority, whom the Ottomans wished to eliminate by any means. It is through the prelate's influence that one also observes the support the Albanians maintained for their Christian identity and the Western civilization in general, despite the fact that a part had accepted Islam; for the conversions, as was evidenced, were a means to avoid discrimination or to enjoy social privileges rather than because of spiritual convictions.

The Austrians penetrated deep into the Albanians lands, while Albanians of the Catholic faith, but converts to Islam, too, joined their ranks. Yet, as the Austrian campaign failed, Albanians remained in service of the Ottoman Empire. A powerful vizier of Albanian descent, Mustafa Pasha the Cypriot (Trk.: Kıbrıslı Mustafa Paşa; Alb.: Mustafa Pashë Qypriliu), assumed the task of resuming the Ottoman occupation of the Albanian lands. There, the Ottoman Empire would remain for another two centuries, while many Albanian faithfully served in its ranks, composing a tragic chapter of the Albanians' direct involvement with both sides in the war between the East and the West. As contemporary sources attest, the war brought much suffering to the Albanians. At first, as the Austrian army advanced, retreating Ottomans razed entire Albanian villages to the ground. The Austrian would also leave carry out a scorched earth, while the scorching would intensify further as the Turks returned, punishing Austrian collaborators.[190] As a result, a good portion of Christian Albanians from the affected areas left the country together with the Austrian army.

Numerous sources note that after Skanderbeg's death, the Austro-Turkish wars, which intermittently lasted for about half a century, would cut off a significant part of ethnic Albanians living in the north and northeast of the ethnic territory. As war refugees, Albanians migrated to the north, settling permanently in parts of the Austrian Empire, from Banat and Srem to Ukraine.[191]

To make matters worse, Albanian of the Orthodox religion, for the most part, followed Patriarch Arsenie II Crnojević, such that they were recorded as

---

[190] Gjini, *op. cit.* In a relation that the Albanian prelate from Gjakova, Gjon Nikollë Kazazi, sent to Propaganda Fide in 1743, he notes the repressive measures the Turks had taken against the population after the Austrian retreat. Kazazi speaks of entire villages destroyed and the murder of Catholic vicars (p. 80).

[191] According to the Austrian sources, the number of Albanians who migrated from areas explicitly marked as Albania reaches 20,000. Vatican and Venetian sources confirm this. *See* H. Gera, *Die Kaiserlichen in Albanien 1689* (Wien: 1888); C. Contanrini, *Storia della gurra di Leopoldi primo imperadore e de principi collogati contra il Turco dall 1683-fino alla pare* ([Venice]: 1710).

Serbs.[192] Scholar Skënder Riza holds that the Serbian propaganda has greatly benefited from a misinterpretation of the word Serb, which—according to Ottoman, Serbian, Greek, and Russian sources—also included Orthodox Albanians, while the term Albanian was applied solely to Catholics and Islamized Albanians were known as Turks.[193]

Notably, Albanian historians made no contribution on the issue until as late as 1982, when a zealous and authoritative scholar, Selami Pulaha, published a work titled *Autoktonia e Shqiptarëve në Kosovë dhe e ashtuquajtura shpërngulje e Serbëve nga Kosova* (Alb., The Albanian Autochthony in Kosova and the So-Called Serbian Migrations from Kosova).[194] In his study, Pulaha rejected the theory supported by the Serbian propaganda that a mass emigration of Serbs and an Albanian "invasion" followed the Austrian defeat in Kosova. Pulaha's rebuttal consists of four parts. First, the scholar presents evidence of Albanians as an indigenous population from antiquity up to the Austro-Ottoman wars. Then, he shifts to Austrian archives, bringing to light new documents on the active participation of Kosova Albanians in the war. In the third part, Pulaha consults the Ottoman cadastral registers. Noting details for the northern Albanian highlands, the work discards the theory of Albanian highlanders repopulating Kosova after the Serb migrations. Finally, in a fourth part, Pulaha rejects a related speculation that Slavs were albanianized as they accepted Islam.

---

[192] Serbian historiography has made continuous efforts to manipulate the accounts of the Austro-Hungarian war and the exodus of refugees. In doing so, Serb academics downplay the Albanian participation in the war as an unimportant occurrence, while they exaggerate the role of Serbs. Specifically, they focus on the migrations, presenting them as a fatal loss of Kosova. The Serbian view holds that the majority of the population fled in fears of Turkish revenge, while Albanians descended from the highlands of Albania to populate Kosova's lowlands. Serbian authors who support the thesis include J. Cvijić, *Osnove za geografiju i geologiju Makedonije i Stare Srbije* (1906); Vladan Đorđević, *Die Albanensen und die Grossmächte* (Leipzig: 1913); B. Nušić, *Kosovo: opis zemle i naroda* (Novi Sad: 1962); D. Popović, *Velika soba srba* (Beograd: 1954); *Istoria naroda Jugoslavije* 2 (Beograd: 1960).

[193] *See* Rizaj, *Kosova dhe Shqiptarët* . . . .

[194] Several studies on Albanians as indigenous to Kosova are available as a rebuttal of Serbian theories. Notably, S. Pulaha studied the complexity of the Albanian autochthony in their ethnic homeland since the ancient times; among others, Professor Skënder Rizaj has conducted substantial research using Ottoman sources, while Dr. Muhamet Tërnava has focused on medieval Serbian documents.

Voskopoja and the Albanian Orthodox Identity

Orthodox Albanians endeavor to resist Hellenization and Slavicization through the Church. Emancipation in a Western spirit takes place in Voskopoja, as the town becomes the seat of the New Academy in 1744. Theodor Kavalioti completes the first translation of the New Testament into Albanian in 1770. Greek chauvinists murder Dhaskal Todhëri in 1805 as he is journeying back to his country with custom-made typefaces for Albanian printing.

Ever since it was drawn on their lands, during the reign of Emperor Theodosius in the 4th century, the borderline between the East and the West held the Albanians in a constant struggle between the two civilizations. While Albanians of the Roman rite retained an attachment to the West, those of the Eastern tradition were also favorable to the Occident. As the Church split in 1054, a perpetual struggle began within the Albanian Orthodox community to maintain ties with the West, despite the confrontation that Constantinople, as the capital of the Orthodox world, pursued against Rome. While persistent, the Albanians pursued a difficult plan; the Byzantine dogma and the inexistence of an autocephalous church of Albania hindered the Orthodox identity to serve the national interests of the Albanians.

Albanian nobles and princes worked to avoid siding exclusively with one party of the ecclesiastic schism. Such efforts began at the time of the Despotate of Epirus and the Anjou Kingdom of Albania, when the first structures of Albanian statehood appeared during with the dissolution of the Byzantine Empire. Nevertheless, with the later return of the Byzantine Empire and the reign of Dušan of Rascia, the war on Catholicism would intensify the religious divisions. Likewise, the arrival of the Ottoman Empire enforced the East-West schism even further. Instead of forming an anti-Ottoman alliance with the West, the Orthodox Patriarchate of Constantinople accepted the power of the sultan and came under the supervision of the Sublime Porte. In exchange for their submission, Orthodox Christians retained their freedom of religion, while the Catholic Church faced two joint rivals: Islam and the perfidy of the Orthodox Church, which desired to preserve its political position through means that would necessarily cause a detriment to Catholicism. The Orthodox approach had the support of Slavic and Greek princes, who vassals of the sultan. As a result, Orthodox princes came out openly against the Catholic countries and peoples, while the latter were waging their defensive war against Ottoman incursions. Slavs, in particular, were noted for their participation against Hunyadi of Hungary and in other Ottoman campaigns against the West. Moreover, Rascian troops, which served in the first line of attack during the final siege of Constantinople, diligently assisted their Ottoman allies to take the city.

As the period of vassalages and the acceptance of Ottoman rule unfolded, Orthodox Albanians were faced with Serbization and Hellenization, as both phenomena benefited from the autocephalous churches that used the liturgy in the respective national languages. Meanwhile, the Albanians of the Orthodox rite not only lacked the right to use their own language, but suffered strict persecution whenever they attempted to do so, even if such an act would have contributed to consolidate the Orthodoxy. This would be one of the reasons why so many Albanians would accept Islam without hesitation. The same fate would follow other defenseless groups such as the Bogumils in Bosnia, who were also threatened by the ecclesiastic hegemony of the Orthodox Church.

At the beginning of the 17th century, the Orthodox Church was reorganized and the Russians gained their ecclesiastic independence. Nevertheless, the Patriarchate of Constantinople, owing to the trust of the Porte, continued to regards itself as the spiritual leader of all Orthodox believers. Taking advantage of its leadership role, Constantinople resorted to a policy of complete Hellenization, but caused heavy resentment among the Serbian, Romanian, and Bulgarian churches. As a result, the Romanians and Bulgarians sought to establish special ties with Rome in order to overcome the threat of Hellenization, while the Serbian Church inclined towards its Russian counterpart. The Patriarchate of Ohrid (Ohër), which supervised the dioceses of Albania of Bulgaria, had the greatest urge to oppose the Greek ethnocentrism. That is not only because Constantinople denied the existence of Bulgarian and Albanian identities; to preserve its authority, the Greek Church sought to curb the Western spirit of the Renaissance humanism, which had begun to blossom on the eastern shores of the Adriatic.

As illuminist ideas began to spread in the Western Balkans, particularly in Albania and Greece, the Albanian town of Voskopoja (Arom. Moscopole) emerged as a cultural center. Albanians, mainly of the Orthodox faith, made up the bulk of the population, which also consisted of a Vlach minority. As early as 1710, a college was founded in the town and, even though it used Greek as a language of instruction, remained outside Hellenist influence. Ten years later, Voskopoja was furnished with a printing press, which provided city intellectuals a material basis for a rapid cultural development. In 1744, a group of intellectuals founded the New Academy (Alb.: Akademia e Re), an educational institution with a program comparable to secondary schools of Europe.[195]

The first rector of the Academy was a graduate of the University of Padua, Sevast Leontiadhi from Kostur (Gr. Kosturia). He was succeeded in office by Theodor Kavalioti, a native of Voskopoja and prominent thinker of the 18th century. Kavalioti was an ardent follower of Leibnitz's philosophy and to this day is known as the first translator to complete a rendering of the New Testament into Albanian. In 1770, he published a trilingual Greek-Aromanian-Albanian dictionary, which—two centuries after Gjon Buzuku's *Meshari*—set the national foundations of the Albanian Orthodox Church. It would take another two centuries for the latter to declare its independence, marking a victory over the Hellenist notion that "every Greek is an Orthodox and every Orthodox is a Greek."

The rise of Voskopoja as a cultural center in a Western spirit afforded Orthodox Albanians an opportunity to translate ecclesiastic works into their own language, as a first step in removing the shackles of Hellenism. Yet, alarmed by the developments, the Greek Patriarchate of Constantinople initiated a campaign, in concert with the Porte, to put an end to the Western-oriented town. As part of a complot, Constantinople dissolved the Patriarchate of Ohrid in a first move against Voskopoja. Later, in 1779, during the Russo-Ottoman war, the Orthodox clergy and the leadership of the town supported the Himara highlanders, who rose against their Ottoman rulers. It is likely that Voskopoja's interference in the local uprising was regarded as supportive of the Russians in the war, giving the Ottomans a pretext to revenge against the flourishing city. The opportunity came when Voskopoja residents failed to make timely payments to derebeys, who served as contracted city defenders. The Sublime Porte hence pitied the derebeys, allegedly discontent with the delays in pay, to attack, plunder, and burn the town.[196]

Voskopoja suffered a similar destruction again, in 1772 and 1789. Besides, the Patriarchate of Constantinople took sever measures against Voskopoja in the cultural sphere. The authorities expelled previous educators, replacing them with pedagogues close to the Patriarchate to ensure that the New Academy would serve Hellenist interests. The new teachers brought a spirit of chauvinism to the institution, while schoolmaster Daniel produced

---

[195] H.P.Sh. 1 (1969), 387.
[196] *Ibid.* 390.

texts that called on Albanian, Vlach, and Bulgarian students to give up "their barbarian languages" and learn only Greek. Under such circumstances, the Academy ceased to exist.[197]

Vokopoja's destruction has been depicted in many sources as "a pre-meditated revenge of Albanian Muslims against the influence of Orthodox Athens" and as a preventative measure against Hellenism. The situation on the ground, however, gives of a different account—that is, the Patriarchate of Constantinople and the Sublime Porte feared the spread of Western illumi-nist ideas among Orthodox Albanians, who threatened to break away from the Greek influence. Therefore, the measures were taken particularly against Ohër as an Orthodox center, which supported the liberation movements of the Balkan peoples, primarily that of the Bulgarians and Albanians. Ohër was likewise supportive of the Bulgarian and Albanian national identities, which were to be reflected in the use of the national languages at Mass and in liturgy. This is evidenced in the continued efforts that Kavalioti's students made to translate ecclesiastic books, even after Voskopoja was destroyed and the New Academy closed. Thus, in a war against the Greek reaction of Constantinople that prohibited the ecclesiastic use of national languages, Albanian clerics not only translated church books into Albanian, but for that purpose they invented unique Albanian scripts that did not resemble the Greek alphabet.

One of the early translators was the bishop of Durrës, Grigor Durrsaku, who translated parts of the New Testament in 1761. Following Durrsaku's footsteps, Dhaskal Todhëri, also known as Theodor Haxhi Filipi, also trans-lating parts of the New Testament and liturgy. In addition, Todhëri tried to set up an Albanian printing press in Elbasan. However, in 1805, as he was travelling back from Venice with the necessary supplies, he was killed by unknown assailants and was hence unable to fulfill his mission.[198]

Dhaskal Todhëri's death, similar to the tragic drowning of Pjetër Budi in the Drin River, after the prelate had demanded that Catholic priests know the Albanian language, did not halt the efforts of Albanian clergymen for a national awakening. Just like the Catholic prelates, Orthodox Albanians continued to work for the emancipation of their people in a Western spirit. In later centuries, the activists of the Albanian national rebirth, Rilindja, would wholly embrace the Western civilization and look to it for guidance in the movement for national liberation and independence.

---

[197] *Ibid.* 390.
[198] *Ibid.* 391.

CHAPTER 3
ALBANIANISM, ISLAMISM, AND OTTOMANISM

The Tanzimât Reforms and the Albanians

Mustafa Pashë Bushati of Shkodër and Ali Pashë Tepelena of Janina rebel; the Albanians emerge as a distinct factor in relations with the Ottoman Empire and the European powers. The Greeks benefit from the Albanian uprisings, while Serbia and Greece pursue hegemonic programs to the detriment of the Albanians.

The beginning of the 19th century brought perplexing days to the Ottoman state, as the once mighty empire struggled for its very existence. After repeated territorial losses to Russia in the eastern front, the Ottomans turned to their domestic affairs, hoping to save the state through reforms. The dated mechanisms of the state were to open way to practices from the West and feudal despotism and religious obscurantism to be replaced with a constitutional monarchy. This had now become the mutual position of both the sultan and the European powers, which had an interest to see the Ottoman Empire regain its previous authority as a reformed, modern state.

Formally, the Ottoman Empire implemented major reforms with the announcement of the seminal decrees, *Hatt-ı Şerif*[199] and *Hatt-ı Hümayan*.[200]

---

[199] *Hatt-ı Şerif* was drafted by Grand Vizier Mustafa Rashid Pasha, who was one of the leading reformers of the time. On November 3, 1839, Sultan Abdul Mejid I solemnly declared the document at *Gülhane*, meaning the Hall of Roses; owing to the ceremony, the decree is also known as *Hatt-ı Şerif of Gülhane*—that is, the Holy Decree of Gülhane. The document ended the spahi order, replacing it with the *çiftlik*, a type of private property, which could be owned by any subject of the empire, regardless of religion or race. The decree hence bestowed Christians with the right to own property. The sultan announced,

But, before modernization could begin, even just in formal terms, there were difficult ordeals to overcome. First, the state had to curb the influence of the janissaries, who had become a threat to the central power. Second, the Porte had to put down unruly pashas who had gained power as regional despots and sought to split off from İstanbul. Such rulers—the Bushati (or Bushatliu) dynasty of Shkodër, Osman Pazvantoglu of Vidin, and later Ali Pashë Tepelena of Janina—presented an even greater threat for they inspired further separatist efforts in the Balkans. To make matters worse, this happened at a time when Russia sought to use such movements to boast its own influence in the region. Meanwhile, even other European powers, which formally welcomed the Ottoman Empire in their midst and guaranteed its territorial integrity at the 1856 Congress of Paris, looked for opportunities to exert greater impact in the peninsula.

The two great challenges of the empire enormously affected the state of affairs in the Balkans. The region saw a surge of nationalism among Christian peoples, such as the Serbs, Greeks, Montenegrins, Romanians, and Bulgarians. Meanwhile, the empire embarked on an on-and-off relationship with the Albanians; the latter cooperated and shared certain interests with the Ottoman state, but disagreements over other matters also caused distrust and quarrels between the two sides. As a result of the modernization efforts, the Albanians lost the individual opportunities and community privileges they had enjoyed under the previous system. The Ottoman government disbanded the janissary corps, depriving Albanians of an important military institution they had dominated for some 300 years. Moreover, the reforms affected the local power that Albanian landlords had come to amass over the centuries. By the 1800s, the Albanians had built an economy and administration that functioned almost independently of the Porte, as Albanian pashas had assumed leadership of territories known as *pashaliks* (Trk.: *paşalik*; Alb.: *pashallëk*). This authority, however, was to come to a rapid end in the 19th

---

inter alia: "From this day onward, all of my Muslim and *râya* subjects shall have perfect security for their honor and property... From now on, the highest and the lowest [by rank] in the state, the vizier and the shepherd alike, each shall have their property as they please and none shall have the right to deprive them of [their property]."

[200] *Hatt-ı Hümayan* was announced in İstanbul in 1856, marking the most important step in the Ottoman transition to constitutional monarchy. The document guaranteed religious equality, formally stripping Islam of its supremacy, but also depriving Christians and Jews of their previous right to self-administration. As self-governed communities, certain groups enjoyed cultural development in accordance with their religious and linguistic affiliation.

century, as the empire extinguished the two great pashaliks of Albania, named after their capitals, Shkodër and Janina. Primarily, the changes affected Muslim Albanians for the Christian minority in the Albanian territories also greatly consolidated after Russia became the spiritual and cultural protector of the Slavic Orthodox peoples and Austria was permitted to guide the Catholics in the Ottoman Empire.

This development inevitably influenced the rise of a new ideology. Albanianism thereby appeared either as a need to express a national identity, which would enable the much-needed social and political progress; or, as a countermeasure to expansionist projects, such as the Greek *Megali Idea*[201] and the Serbian *Načertanije*,[202] which threatened the very existence of the Albanians as a distinct ethnic group. A defensive posture and the counter-efforts taken, nonetheless, would often place the Albanians in seemingly absurd situations. This was because, to protect their vital interests, they had to oppose modernization, by resisting the centralization of power that occurred at the expense of the traditional provincial and local establishments.

The central government had a reason to assume power in its own hands. Undoubtedly, the powerful and unruly janissaries and the semi-independent pashas were gravely troubling to the empire. The two groups, whose concerted anti-modernization actions would later appear as a rebellion against the central authorities, were founded on principles of feudal despotism and, owing to their strength, kept the empire immune from the positive changes in the social and political life of other European countries. Thereby, no true progress could take place unless a dedicated and active strongman was to deal with the janissaries and the pashaliks. The occasion arrived with the accession to the throne of a reform-oriented sultan, Selim III, in 1789. Before coming to power, Selim spent his youth in detention at the golden cage of the

---

[201] *Megali idea* (*Grk.*, Great Idea) appeared in November 1844. Greek Prime Minister N. Koletis sought to recreate the Byzantine Empire, under the leadership of Greece. The proposed entity would include all of Greece and central Balkans, in accordance with the territorial extent of the Orthodoxy. In fact, this hegemonic project aimed at occupying a large part of Albania (up to the Shkumbin River), Macedonia, and Bulgaria.

[202] *Načertanije* (*Srb.*, A Draft) was announced by Serbian Foreign Minister Ilija Garašanin. The project was based on the so-called historical right of Serbia over the Balkan territory that was once included in the medieval state of Dushan. According to Garašanin, Serbia would assume the role of the Slavic Piedmont in the Balkans and unite the Slavs in a greater state, spanning from sea to sea (*i.e.*, the Aegean and the Adriatic seas).

imperial palace. While he was not allowed to leave or travel, he was permitted several meetings with high-ranking officials, Ottoman and foreign, who convinced him of the need for reform and innovations.[203] Finally, when he left the cage, Selim III had no experience in the real world, but had at that point become an ardent proponent of change. He was determined to reassert state authority throughout the country and to reclaim the empire's place among the Great Powers. Because, in the initial years of his rule, the Ottoman Empire was at war with the Habsburgs, Selim III was unable to tend to the planned reforms until 1794, when he announced his vision for the New Military Order or, as originally called, the *Nizam-ı Cedid*.

The essence of the plan, which marked the beginning of the *Tanzimât* (*i.e.*, reform) period, was to create a modern military. The government hired French officers to train the Ottomans in accordance with the recent advancements of the military science and to prepare them for the challenges of the time. The reform, however, came to the dismay of the janissaries and the higher officers, who dominated the old-school military. A privileged class that wanted to halt the advancement of time, they launched a campaign to undermine the New Order.[204]

In reality, the anti-reformists were waging a battle for the survival of dated despotic and obscurantist feudal structures. For over three centuries, their establishment held sway over the empire, leading it to great victories. But, it was also responsible for the recent stagnation and failures and could seriously endanger the country if it were to remain in power. The establishment was not ready to accept any change, even as the Ottoman Empire lagged so far behind as to raise concern well beyond imperial borders. To bolster their cause, thereby, the hardliners recruited the janissaries, the last remaining institution on which the old establishment could rely. While the janissaries were no longer a formidable group, their retained pride and glory became a disadvantage at a time when the central authorities, which had established the order, worked to institute military discipline and political supervision from the capital. Meanwhile, the janissaries insisted in preserving the old system intact, as they announced shortly after the proclamation of the New Order. In 1801, members of the old group assassinated the popular governor of Belgrade, Haji Mustafa, who was serving as a viceroy to the reformist sultan. With the killing, old-school janissaries declared open

---

[203] Misha Glenny, *Historia e Ballkanit 1804-1999* (Tiranë: 2007), 3.
[204] *Ibid.* 4.

war to maintain the *status quo*, in which the conservative elite, including the hard-line Islamic clergy, was indifferent to any change that reflected the contemporary advancements taking place elsewhere in the content. As the assassination opened way to major developments in the Serb-dominated pashalik of Belgrade, the janissaries set off—likely inadvertently—a historic, dynamic process that included the advent of nationalist and separatist currents in the Balkans. During this period, the Porte's efforts to implement the military reforms, in favor of centralization and to the detriment of provincial despotism, would provide ground for Balkan nations to split off from the empire. Meanwhile, taking advantage of the independence movements, the Great Powers of Europe would interfere in the Porte's domestic affairs. Hoping to keep a balance among their own, the European states sought to preserve the Ottoman Empire in an effort that eventually led to the very dissolution it tried to desist.

The reform-minded Porte and the conservative establishment were unable to find common grounds for modernization. As a result, the very announcement of the reforms created ongoing internal conflict between the two sides. The inevitable reforms, which would eventually replace religious obscurantism with a constitutional monarchy, required a fresh social and political approach that embraced parliamentarism and (along with it) the concept of equality. Even after it became astoundingly clear that the era of Ottoman despotism had ended—and the only possibility of salvaging the empire was a new social contract respectful and accepting of cultural, ethnic, and national diversity—another impediment emerged with the spread of a new nationalist movement. The Young Turks (Trk.: *jön türkler*, Alb.: *xhonturqit*; from French: *jeune turcs*)—propagating radical reforms after the model of developed European nations—reverted to Ottoman ultranationalism, undoing much of the progress that the Tanzimât era reached in certain fields.

Nevertheless, it was not the announced reforms that would pave the way to the troubling developments that persisted until the dissolution of the empire; it was the contradictions within the reform process and the opposition to it (initially, that included a rebellious trend against the central government in different parts of the empire; then, there were the janissary mutinies against the New Military Order, with the support of the feudal class and the religious leadership, to end with the Young Turk Revolution in the final years). The opposition would be used for popular uprisings that would take on a nationalist character, as was the case with the Serbian Uprisings beginning in 1804 and other similar movements that later began in Romania,

Greece, and Bulgaria, leading to the Porte's recognition of those countries as autonomous principalities or independent states.[205]

The struggle with the janissaries dragged on much longer than Sultan Selim III had envisioned. Understandably, the reasons were also tactical and practical, since the empire aimed at replacing the janissary structures with the new military. This was being formed under the guidance of foreign experts who were primarily from France, but included Germans and others, too. To avoid the expected revolt of the janissaries, the reform-minded sultan lured many of them to the New Order, with promises of high ranks in the new hierarchy. Meanwhile, the janissary corps was stripped of its spiritual asset—that is, its patronage of the Bektashi religious order. Members of the military group were also permitted to raise a family and own property. The janissaries, thus, lost their zeal of professional soldiery, which had turned them into an elite imperial guard, meritorious of recognition for the great military successes between the 15th and the 17th centuries. Economic and political privileges incentivized many to abandon the traditional group and the idea of a military career was replaced with the pursuit of wealth and social status. Consequently, the janissary cult and its prestige declined significantly. The privileges handed out at the heart of the empire were fatal to janissaries on the periphery. It was precisely there where the ancient infantry units maintained their greater power and that came primarily to the advantage of provincial authorities. Most of the peripheral strongmen relied on members of the corps to oppose what both groups regarded as a common threat to their existence—the central government. At the time, provincial leaders had begun to increasingly disobey the sultan and, as they consolidated their own pashaliks, they would even cut off ties with the Porte; such was the case with pashas of Shkodër, Vidin, and Janina.

The cooperation between the janissaries and the break-away pashas remained a major cause of alert throughout the reign of two successive sovereigns. Sultan Selim III, and his successor, Mahmud II, regarded the janissary struggle as closely linked to the rebellious pashaliks. The two sultans hence undertook to quell the revolts, beginning with the Pashalik of Shkodër, then moving on to Vidin, before the finally reasserting control over Janina. To the Ottoman Empire, the Albanian pashaliks presented a strategic concern, because of their key geographic position. The Albanian lands offered the Porte an opportunity to defend itself against foreing enemies, but European

---

[205] *Ibid.* 2.

powers also had their eyes on the area as a means to destabilize the Ottoman Empire for their own interests. On multiple occasions, between the end of the 1700s and the beginning of the 1800s, Austria, Russia, France, and even England approached the Albanians for that purpose.

The rise and fall of the three great pashaliks present the lengthy overture of the internal Ottoman struggle against the feudal-despotic establishment. The empire had relied on the old structures for an extended period, but the day had now come to settle accounts with them, for their consolidation and independence threatened the central authority of the state. However, since Ottoman politics relied on a strong-arm mentality, which often helped resolve disputes among provincial contenders, the Ottoman Empire was at times interested—for strategic reasons—in robust Albanian pashaliks. For that reason, the empire refused to protect some of the sanjakbeys it hasd appointed in Ohër, Durrës, and Berat, when the Bushati pashas of Shkodër, Mehmet, and later Kara Mahmut, mounted attacks on the sanjaks. The Porte maintained the same stance towards local fieftains elsewhere in Rumelia when Pazvantoglu compelled into his tutelage. In certain cases, the Porte itself encouraged Ali Pashë Tepelena to subdue neighboring sanjaks and annex them into his Pashalik of Janina. Confrontations with the Porte began only after the pashas took a slash on their tax payments to the central government or unilaterally ceased all contributions. One such example is Pazvantoglu, who even went as far as to declare his independence from the empire. Later, Kara Mahmut Pashë Bushatlliu comported similarly as he entered into unsuccessful relationships with foreign powers, claiming that the move was needed to maintain the pashalik's army.

Sultan Selim III, and later his successors, Mustafa IV and Mahmud II— the latter was instrumental with his abolishment of the janissary corps and the persecution of the Bektashi religious order that serves as the spiritual protector of the military group[206]—used the joint pashas-janissaries revolt as

---

[206] The Bektashis first appeared as an order of Dervishes in Anatolia—*i.e.*, the Asian part of the Ottoman Empire. The founder and protector of the mystic order was Haji Bektash, who was born in Iran in 1224 and moved to Anatolia in 1284. A particular influence on Haji Bektash came from his contacts with Asian religions, such as Buddhism and Hinduism, during his travels to India, Tibet, and China. Bektashis later arrived in the Balkans. Their beliefs were well received in Albania, where Bektashism spread throughout the country. It is estimated that the Bektashi teachings attracted a sizable number of Albanians to accept Islam outside the dogma. In fact, as a period of national revival began in Albania, Bektashis became militants of Albanian nationalism. For more on Bektashism in Albania see: Stephen

grounds to extinguish the pashaliks. The first of the rebellious pashas, Pazvantoglu, returned to Vidin after he served in the imperial army during the Austro-Ottoman War of 1789-1792. He was determined to regain dominions that had belonged to his family, while hoping to create an influential pashalik, on the route that linked the Ottoman Empire with the West. On the pretense for a limited provincial force outside imperial control, Pazvantoglu was able to raise within a year an entire army of pirates and janissaries and other deserters who had grown discontent of the increasingly disorganized Ottoman military. When the loyalist governor of Vidin sent his troops to end Pazvantoglu's disorderly behavior, the unruly pasha achieved an uncontested victory.[207] He then braced his military further with janissaries and other Ottoman defectors and notably hired many of the infamous *kerjali* marauders, notorious for their devastating attacks.[208] So empowered was the pasha of Vidin such that in 1795 he declared independence from the sultan. This became the first, but not the last, instance that a pashalik in the European dominions of the empire would break off from the Sublime Porte; a year later, Kara-Mahmut Pashë Bushati, the pasha of Shkodër, came out against İstanbul; Ali Pashë Tepelena of Janina also followed the example in 1822. As the pashaliks split off from the empire, Sultan Selim III did not take much offense at the situation. He thought of the unrest as a great opportunity for a decisive and final blow to the unruly pashas and, even more so, to the janissaries, whom he viewed as the main obstacle to reform. The sultan, however, was forced to take a detour on his plan. As his forces prepared to take off for a march onto Vidin, Napoleon Bonaparte landed with his French troops in the then-Ottoman province of Egypt.[209] Thereby, the rebellious pashas set off a more complex state of affairs, as it involved not only the empire's internal dissolution, but also opened way to foreign hands to manipulate the break-away movements. The European powers became involved in the provincial strife, despite their formal commitment for the Ottoman territorial integrity and the maintenance of the *status quo*.[210]

Schwartz, *Islami tjetër: Sufizmi dhe rrëfimi për respektin* (Prishtinë: 2009); Schwartz, *Bektashizmi si model universal* (Tiranë: 2003); Schwartz, *"Two Books on Bektashi Islam in Albania," Albanian Catholic Bulletin* (Tiranë: 1991); Jashar Rexhepagiqi, *Dervishët dhe teqetë në Kosovë, në Sanxhak dhe rajonet e tjera përreth* (Pejë: 2003).

[207] *Ibid*. 5.

[208] *Ibid*. 5.

[209] Glenny, *Historia e Ballkanit 1804-1999*, 5.

[210] See the decisions of the 1856 Peace Conference of Paris.

Foreign interference was most evident in Vidin, whose pasha would not have initiated his rebellion without an instruction by Austrian and Russian representatives. The two powers had just recently concluded a war with the Ottoman Empire and, despite the peace agreement, endlessly sought means to weaken their enemy. Thereby, Pazvantoglu of Vidin tried to forge an alliance with Russia and other Orthodox nations in order to strengthen his position. He sent a similar offer to Vienna, too. However, his diplomatic efforts did not last; right after quelling a Serbian uprising in 1813, the Porte turned to Vidin, terminating Pazvantoglu's rule.

At nearly the same time, and using the same methods, the central government acted against the Bushati dynasty of Shkodër, whose attempted alliances with foreign powers ended in vain. The pashalik rose to prominence under the leadership of Mehmet Pasha, and later, his son, Kara-Mahmut. They ruled over a province that—unlike the Pashalik of Vidin, whose geographic proximity to İstanbul was less attractive to foreign powers—lay in a highly strategic node. The Albanian pashalik came to the attention of European monarchies and republics at a time when Austria longed to annex Bosnia, France had an eye on the Adriatic coast, while Russia was interested in Serbia and Montenegro. Initially, it was the 1789-1792 war against Russia and Austria and later Napoleon's invasion and the Montenegrin issue that elevated the Pashalik of Shkodër vis-à-vis the Ottoman state and other rival pashaliks (in conflict with the Bushatis or in pursuit of gains through political maneuvers against the dynasty). Under the circumstances, Kara Mahmut Pasha thought of direct dealings with the Porte's opponents as beneficial. He thus pursued consequent friendships with Russia, Austria, and then France; nevertheless, he paid a hefty price for the ties as he lost his own head in pursuit of joint plans with the French. The diplomatic efforts began in 1788, when Kara-Mahmut received at the Rozafat Castle a representative of the Russian ambassador to Venice. At the meeting, the Bushati leader agreed to sustain the uprising against the "common enemy" and vowed to facilitate Russian invasion of İstanbul; the Russian plan also included the occupation of Albanian lands in the Manastir area and a part of Macedonia, all the way to Thessaloniki.[211]

For his participation in the war, Mahmut Pasha demanded money so that he could bring other Albanian pashas to his side; he also requested that the Russians send a squadron of warships to the Albanian coast to threaten

---

[211] H.P.Sh. 1 (2002) 627.

or, if needed, bombard those cities that would side with the Porte.[212] Realizing, in the meantime, that the Romanov monarchy had its own plans and could keep him hanging by a treacherous thread, the Bushati leader deigned to enter into a similar agreement with the Habsburgs, too, hoping to receive an even more profitable bargain this time. For that purpose, the Archbishop of Tivar, Gjergj Radovani, reportedly relayed the pasha's request that Austria send a representative to Shkodër to negotiate a potential regional alliance against the Porte.[213]

Austria and Russia did not need the Albanian pasha's assistance. In 1792, to avoid the threat from the French of Bonaparte, Vienna and Saint Petersburg signed a peace treaty with the Ottoman Empire. For the time being, Mahmut also received signs of rapprochement from Sultan Selim III, who viewed the Pashalik of Shkodër as a key stronghold of the European frontier, from where he could control the unstable territories of Montenegro and Bosnia. Therefore, the sovereign made Mahmut Pasha a vizier and promoted Mahmut's brother, Ibrahim, to the rank of pasha, while also giving the Bushatis authority to govern the sanjaks of Ohër and Elbasan. Mahmut Pasha, however, did not perceive the imperial awards properly. After Selim III decreed the *Nizam-ı Cedid*, the ulama (*i.e.*, religious leadership) and the landowning class convinced him to oppose the reforms by force. Therefore, relying on the power of the janissaries, the group that was most threatened by the reforms, Kara Mahmut Pashë Bushati began his second insurgency against the central government of the empire.

In addition to the domestic anti-reformers who insisted in the rotted old system of the empire, the Albanian pasha looked to external support. In lieu of Austria and Russia, he now pursued a partnership with France, who was looking to expand its influence on the Adriatic just as they did elsewhere in the Mediterranean Sea. Napoleon's ambassador to Venice, who—having subdued northern Italy in 1796 and amidst plans to occupy Dalmatia, a coastal region of the Western Balkans—encouraged the Bushati pasha to declare war on Montenegro, while submitting his pashalik to French tutelage. Moreover, Mahmut Pasha received financial and military aid for that purpose. The French sent, among others, seven specialists, who were to assist with the modernization of the pashalik's army, ahead of the Montenegrin

---

[212] *Ibid.*
[213] *Ibid.*

expedition.[214] The Albanian pasha failed to realize the potential troubles with Russia, the defender of Slavic Orthodox nations such as Montenegro; neither did he consider the reaction of Austria, which would never permit a French ally on the borders of Bosnia. Thus, the French were decisive in eliciting Mahmut Pasha into war against Montenegro. First, before he could engage the Montenegrins, he had to reassert control at home. In July 1796, he hiked with his troops to the pashalik's mountainous communities, but was repelled by a surprisingly fierce resistance of the highlanders. Bypassing of the Albanians in September proved nevertheless more disastrous, for Montenegrin fighters ambushed and killed the Albanian strongman before he was able to live his dream of an independent pashalik. Remarkably, the movement for independence did not develop as an internal process hand-in-hand with the reforms, but it ran on the opposite direction—relying on the dated feudal establishment. Mahmut Pasha's attempts to obtain the assistance of foreign powers seeking to weaken the Ottoman Empire internally were equally unsuccessful. In particular, this happened was because none of the Great Powers was ready, under the circumstances, to permit the Albanian factor to gain momentum, especially when it appears as a distinct ethnic entity.

More or less, the same fate followed the Pashalik of Janina and its leader, Ali Pashë Tepelena. He began to rise right after the last sunset over of the Pashalik of Shkodër. In fact, the Janina pasha had also contributed to Bushati's demise. Yet, not only would the *Lion of Janina* fail to learn a lesson from the *Wolf of Shkodër*; Ali Pasha was to follow Bushati's exact path, applying the same methods to strengthen his power. Just like the previous break-away pashas, Tepelena relied on janissaries and other disintegrating military forces, undermined the domestic landlords and local chieftains, and pursued relations with foreign powers, only to end up lone against a whole empire. Having used all his cards and unable to resist the Porte's vigorous response, Ali Pasha had but an epic death as a consolation for his capitulation—a tragic event for him, but beneficial to his Greek subjects. The pasha of Janina began to consolidate power as he appropriated small and mid-size fiefs, whose activities were a heavy burden on the trade of goods in the area. Even though he often relied on violent means, the leader of Janina encountered no objections from the Porte. After the Shkodër crisis, the Ottoman Empire believed that the rise of Janina could increase the sultan's influence in a region marked by separatist movements. The Ottomans feared losing Bosnia and

---

[214] *Ibid.* 629.

Montenegro at a time when Serbs successfully gained their autonomy after two lengthy uprisings and Greeks were preparing for a war of independence in the southern Balkans. Just as he had death with the Bushati to entice them to his side, the sultan awarded the pasha of Janina the rank of vizier in 1799, using Tepelena's war merits as a pretext for the promotion. Earlier, Ali Pasha defeated the French on the Ionian coast, where he seized control of Butrint, Preveza, and Vonica.[215]

The Janina leader, however, was dissatisfied with the promotion and even viewed it as a cover-up for how the sultan had previously treated Ali. After the French war, the pasha was forced to surrender to the Porte the cities he captured from the enemy. Furthermore, the Ottoman government had entered into unfavorable deals with the foreign powers, including the Russo-Ottoman agreement of 1800 that created the so-called the pro-Russian Septinsular Republic, right off the coast of the pashalik. Therefore, as French expansion in the early 19th century inspired many anti-Napoleonic alliances, Ali Pasha thereby contemplated the benefits of his involvement with the foreign powers. Like the Bushatis in the earlier decades, Tepelena established ties with European empires, but to an even greater extent, coherence, and duration than his Shkodër counterparts. While Ali Pasha's diplomacy failed to support the pashalik's independence, his external relations transiently empowered him for the interests of foreign powers. In this regard, his cooperation with England—while Ali broke off ties with France and supported the wars against Bonaparte and later Russia— helped reclaim Albania's image internationally. Owing to Ali's friendship with prominent Europeans, Britain as well as continental mainland heard of the Albanians and their country as an "exotic" jewel of ancient European roots. Contemporary authorities on Albania included the renowned British poet, George Byron, who spent much time in Janina during Ali Pasha's rule. From there, in pursuit of Albanian and Greek uprisings against the Ottoman Empire, the British enthusiast moved to Misolongi, where he died of tuberculosis in 1824. Lord Byron became one of the early poets to represent the Albanian world in romantic tones, including vivid depictions of the powerful pasha of Janina.[216]

In this regard, Ali Pasha earned skills of politicking, which he mainly to amass power internally, ruling in a despotic fashion that quite frequently reached the level of tyranny, but not the fulfillment of a historic mission. The pasha of Janina used his diplomacy and military power against domestic rivals,

---

[215] *Ibid.* 643.

[216] See Xhoxh Bajron, *Udhëtimet e Çarl Haroldit . . .*

including the pashas of Berat, Delvina, Elbasan, and Shkodër. His dealing with the highlands of Suli and Himara was notably critical. The two regions, which had enjoyed local autonomy for over three centuries, so greatly suffered under Ali's rule such that they no longer retained their Albanian ethnic makeup. The oppressive measures, however, proved costly to the pasha. When the Porte began its final expedition against Ali in 1822, he had virtually no company, for even his own sons had abandoned him and joined Ottoman service.

Nonetheless, the rise and fall of the Pashalik of Janina, as a precondition to the Tanzimât reforms, had its peculiarities, for it shed light the importance of the Albanian factor in the Ottoman Empire. The pashalik's history also noted the ethnic borders of the Albanians, who had maintained their territorial extent and had grown in number during four centuries of Ottoman rule. In the new political landscape, however, the Albanians were to take further steps to become a recognizable entity. For that reason, the Albanian community needed a clear political program, especially after nations in the region came up with their own national projects. Notable, the Greeks had their *Megali Idea*, which paved the way for the Hellenic expansions in the Balkans. Meanwhile, a Serbian government minister, Ilija Garašanin, drafted the *Načertanije*, providing for a vision of a Greater Serbia, a hegemonic state with territorial claims against the Albanian ethnic area. Thus, the Albanian national awakening—and the need for unified actions and political programs that would ensue—were closely tied to the events that preceded the Tanzimât reforms. The process was inevitably influenced by the two Serbian uprisings and subsequent autonomy in 1817 and Greece's independence in 1830. These two nations greatly set off the Albanian movement for their expansionist plans threatened their ethnic territory from all sides. Although both the *Megali Idea* and the *Načertanije* appeared at roughly the same time and were based on hegemonic expansionism, they differed not to their unfavorable intentions towards Albanians, but as to the methods used. Serbs assigned themselves the role of the Pan-Slavic Piedmont in Southeastern Europe, for which they also the Russian blessing and, to some extent, the support of France that generally appeared as more cautious in regards to the interests that other peoples and the Great Powers had in the region. Meanwhile, the Greeks focused on the Orthodox faith and the paradigm that "whoever is Orthodox is Greek and whoever is Greek is Orthodox," which would serve that to build a Hellenist plan for the expansion of the Greek state since its creation.

Many Orthodox Albanians failed to grasp the perfidiousness of the Hellenist plan and stalwartly took part in the wars of 1822-1829 that led to an independent Greek state. Moreover, it would be some of the key activists of the Albanian national awakening, such as Thimi Mitko and others, who initially viewed Hellenism as a co-agent or supporter of Albanianism. The activists hence began to identify with the Greek current and build plans for a common state for the two people, an idea that certain political and intellectual circles sustained in various forms up to the independence of Albania. Therefore, during the next phase of their national movement, the Albanians had to carve out a distinct line between Albanianism and Hellenism, equating the latter with the then-rejected ideology of Islamism. The move enabled the Albanian movement to eliminate the confusion that the Greek *Megali Idea* and the Orthodox trap caused among the people; for in the cultural, social, and political aspects, the religion-based Hellenism was similar to Islamism.

In the meantime, one ought to consider the Serbian and other Slavic movements for independence as well as the difficulties that the Hellenist *Megali Idea* would impose, particularly on Bulgarians and Albanians. Realizing the extent of the Greek influence, the Ottoman Porte permitted an independent Bulgarian *exarchate*,[217] which would practically stir a Bulgarian movement for statehood, while also creating a preprogrammed Macedonian crisis. The exarchate produced an ecclesiastic split that gave rise to a highly dangerous rivalry in the European dominions, most notably in the Macedonia region—*i.e.*, the vilayets of Selanik (Thessaloniki) and Manastir. The mixed population of the two provinces was mainly Albanian and Bulgarian, but it also included Greeks and Serbs; the minority groups opposed division along ethnic lines, maintaining hence a position that greatly disadvantaged the Albanians. Therefore, the two provinces became the locus of an inter-ethnic conflict to such a scale that attracted the intervention of the Great Powers. In October 1903, Austria-Hungary and Russia signed the Mürzsteg Agreement.[218] This was purported for peace in the Macedonia region;

---

[217] In this case, the *exarchate* was an ecclesiastic institution of provincial leadership. The Sublime Port permitted the Bulgarian Exarchate to function independently of the patriarch. The Bulgarians were hence relieved of the supervision of the ecumenical Patriarchate of Constantinople, which was controlled by the Greeks. This decision of the Porte in 1870, albeit of a religious nature, brought significant changes, since the Bulgarians gained their autocephalous church and the right to express their religious identity outside of Greek influence. Until then, the Greeks had successfully maintained a synonymy of religion with the national identity, precisely as desired under the *Megali Idea*. As their church became independent, the Bulgarians were able to advance their movement for national independence.

[218] The Ilinden Uprising broke out in May 1903 in Macedonia with the formation of the so-called Republic of Krushevo, which was brutally put down by the Sublime Porte. As the

instead, the deal galvanized the processes leading to the First Balkan War of 1912, which had the Ottoman Empire expelled from its European dominions and led to the Albanian declaration of independence the same year.

Faced with the developments, the Albanians had no choice but to defend their own existential interests. Albanians began to rethink their rapport with the Ottoman government, neighboring nations, and the Great Powers in order to find the indispensable balance that would permit the small European nation to form an independent state. This approach reflected on the cautious behavior of the Albanians after the initiation of the reforms. Instead of seeking independence, the ethnic group waged a war for territorial, administrative, and political autonomy within the Ottoman Empire. But the idea of an Ottoman Albania was in fact a transitional project; when the Ottoman state was no longer able to sustain itself, the Albanians eventually opted for national independence, which had then become inevitable and the Great Powers would inevitably support it.

Albanianism and the Challenges of National Identity, Islamism, and Ottomanism

Albanians make their early efforts to promote an internal unity on the basis of Albanianism as a reflection of their national identity, while avoiding conflicts with Islamism and Ottomanism. That "the Faith of the Albanians is Albanianism" serves as an important metaphor for the political unification of the Albanians as a nation with a common language, tradition, and ethnicity. Saffet Pasha drafts a memorandum on the Albanians as defenders of the Ottoman Empire in the Balkans. Meanwhile, the nation's leadership demands a unified Albanian vilayet.

violence incited fears among the Great Powers, Austria-Hungary and Russia, as respectively protectors of the Catholic and the Slavic Orthodox in the Ottoman Empire, reached an agreement on reforms in the vilayets of Manastir and Selanik and parts of the Vilayet of Kosova. The deal intended to improve the position of Christians in the local administration, such as the court and the police. Russia undertook to supervise the reforms in the Vilayet of Selanik, while Austria-Hungary assumed responsibility over Manastir and Kosova. Since the Austro-Hungarian plan was met with opposition of the Albanian majority in the vilayets, the dual-crown monarchy gave up its reform efforts in the Albanian areas. But the attempted reforms ultimately failed throughout the region as Serbia, Greece, and Bulgaria endeavored to occupy as much territory from the contested vilayets.

131

In addition to the Serbian and Greek statehood and the fall of the great pashaliks, the 19th century brought additional challenges for the Ottoman Empire as the Great Powers pushed for internal reforms. As part of a plan for transition to constitutional monarchy, the Ottoman state was to provide for the equality of its subjects based on their ethnic and religious affiliation. The reform, however, was not flawless when it came to the Albanians, who adopted a double strategy to protect their national interests. While supporting the institution of equal rights on the one hand, the Albanians also worked against impediments that threatened to exclude them from the reform process. For instance, the Ottoman government failed to recognize a distinct Albanian community, including Muslim Albanians into the *millet-i osman* (*i.e.*, the Ottoman nationality) and grouping others in accordance with Church affiliation. Furthermore, the Albanians became increasingly cautious about anti-Ottoman rebellions, for previous attempts at independence under the the Bushati dynasty and Ali Pashë Tepelena had benefited other Balkan peoples rather than the Albanians. The simple answer for the Albanian failure in such uprisings was that the small nation had no natural friends in the way the Slavic Orthodox peoples were linked to Russia. Moreover, even Austria-Hungary and Italy, which traditionally backed the Albanians, insisted that the national movement function under their control. In the meantime, it was the intention of Sultan Abdul Hamid II to rely on the Albanians in order to sustain the Ottoman presence in the Balkans after the Eastern Crisis. Still, the Hamidian policy did not recognize a separate nationality as the Albanians desired, but awarded them the epithet of *the flower of the empire*,[219] meritorious for the state's achievements through centuries. Thereby, the theory held that the Albanians ought to continue to work for the empire, albeit not as a distinct nation, but under the oriole of "committed Islamists." Furthermore, this automatically presented the Albanians as religious missionaries in the most sensitive part of the old continent and in the precise fashion of the Serbian expansionist propaganda that sought to make the Albanians a target of a disastrous war between the East and the West.

It is noteworthy, nevertheless, that Abdul Hamid's proclamation, the first of its kind in Ottoman history, addressed "all the people of Albania" (Trk.: *umum Arnavudluk ahalisi*) with a sublime piety, praising their importance to the empire at a time when her grip on the European dominions

---

[219] See Abdul Hamid's 1880 letter to the Albanians in Buxhovi, *Kongresi i Berlinit 1878.*

weaken daily. Although the sultan refused Albanian demands for autonomy as dangerous and criticized Ali Pashë Tepelena's actions "in favor of the mutual enemy," the Ottoman sovereign acknowledged the ethnic integrity of the Albanians as a people (*umum*) and their strategic role in preserving the empire. In fact, when rejecting the requests for autonomy, Sultan Hamid created his so-called *Albanian policy* that, despite its reliance on a fragile equilibrium and pursuit of the monarch's narrow interests, permitted Albanianism to penetrate into the Ottoman administration and other social segments of the empire. The involvement became the greatest source of empowerement for the ethnic groups as was later reflected in key events. Thereby, the notion that of Ottoman-Albanian interdependence—that the Albanians were "the Empire's greatest supporters in Europe" and, likewise, the empire as "the savior of the Albanians before the apetites of the neighboring states"—gained support from both sides. Ottoman authorities and Albanian intellectuals used the concept of interdependence to harvest mutual benefits in the public life of the empire.

As evidenced in the *salnames* (official yearbooks), the effects of the Hamidian policy became increasingly pervasive in the vilayets of Rumelia.[220] The Albanians embraced the official concept of their "loyalty to Islam and the empire" to consolidate their position within the Ottoman state. The benefits were mutual—for the Albanians and the empire. The emphasis on Islamism presented Albanianism as a form of "Ottoman patriotism," which was a source of legitimacy for the Ottoman state even where the empire had previously been met with denial. For instance, as the *salnames* acknowledged the Albanian majority in the vilayets of Janina and Manastir, propaganda claims of a Greek and Bulgarian character of the two provinces were firmly rejected. Likewise, the data indicating an overwhelmingly Albanian makeup of the vilayets of Shkodër and Kosova supported the Albanian demands—of cultural, but primarily political motivations—for a unification of the four vilayets. The movement for a unified Albanian vilayet trumped all other causes, for unification alone could permit the Albanians to truly serve the empire and the latter to support the ethnic group. That a unified vilayet was the proper social and political treatment for the Albanians was a view shared even among Ottoman statesmen. Notably, Mehmed Esad Saffet Pasha, who had previously served as grand vizier (1878) and foreign minister (1879), wrote a memorandum in April 1880, recommending a series of reforms

---

[220] Nathalie Clayer, *Në fillimet e nacionalizmit shqiptar* (Tiranë: 2009), 238.

133

needed to earn the trust of the Albanians. The proposal called for greater economic growth, a reformed military consisting of a "service for defending the motherland" (Trk.: *hizmet-i muhafazat-i vataniyye*) and reserve troops (Trk.: *redif* or *muhtafiz*), and measures for improved education for Muslims in Rumelia.[221] In support of the plan, Saffet Pasha reiterated the important role of the Albanians, noting without hesitation that "nothing has been done for the Muslim Albanian *milet* [i.e., nationality]."[222]

Saffet Pasha's emphasis on the "Muslim Albanian *milet*" was of great importance for the Albanianism. For the first time, an Ottoman official acknowledged the Albanians as a distinct ethnic group or nationality of the empire. Furthermore, the former Ottoman prime minister recommended that primary schools (Trk.: *sibyan*) be opened in the rural areas and the provincial capitals be furnished with institutions of secondary education. Mehmed Esad Saffet Pasha introduced the idea of a "school of science" (*mekte-i fünün*) in Janina as a countermeasure against the influential *Zosimaia* gymnasium of the Greeks.[223]

Focusing on economic, military, and educational matters, the memorandum positive affected the Albanians, at least with respect to the armed forces and schools. Sultan Hamid's military reforms, as per Saffet Pasha's proposal, concentrated in the vilayes of Kosova and Shkodër, where the so-called *self-defense* corps was left entirely to the Albanians. Even though the measure intended to fortify the vilayets against "Slavic and Greek invasions," the Albanians improved their defensive capabilities to an extent that it proved fatal for the absolute reign of Sultan Hamid. The latter would finally collapse after the 1908 Young Turk Revolution, which had the support of the Albanians; later, during the anti-Ottoman uprisings of 1910-1912, the Albanians used their *self-defense* capacities against the Young Turks. The Hamidian policy, nevertheless, intended to assert control over the Albanians and to rely on their power for the needs of the sultan's despotic regime. For that purpose, in addition to the military reforms, Sultan Hamid relied on handout for certain landowning families in the vilayets of Kosova and Shkodër. In Kosova, the policy was highly divisive for it empowered the conservative *beys* (*Trk.*, lords)—Isa Boletini in the north, Bajram Curri in Gjakova, the Kryezis of Peja, etc.—to the expense of the rising middle class in the cities. The effect was

---

[221] Gawrych, *Gjysmëhëna dhe shqiponja*, 112-115.
[222] *Ibid.* 113.
[223] *Ibid.* 114.

intentional though, for the progressive city dwellers demanded social and political change in the country, including the reinstatement of the constitution that Sultan Hamid had suspended in favor of his despotic rule.

Besides Saffet Pasha and Sultan Hamid, another Ottoman statesman who became greatly involved in Albanian affairs was Dervish Pasha, the former commander of the imperial troops that quelled the Albanian uprisings of 1880 and 1881. The military officer wrote a letter to Sultan Hamid, petitioning the sovereign "to rely on Muslim Albanians for his rule in the Balkans." Like the sultan, Dervish Pasha also supported an Albanian policy based on Islam, "as a natural connection between the Empire and the Albanians."[224]

Aware that the Hamidian policy was an inevitably reality and hoping to avoid friction in their religiously-diverse ethnic community, Albanian intellectuals did not reject Islam as a basis of their ties with the empire. The leaders of the Albanian national movements—primarily, Sami Frashëri, Abdyl Frashëri, Pashko Vasa, and other members of *Shoqëria e të Shtypunit të Shkronjave Shqip* (Alb., the Albanian Print Press Society), and later *Komiteti për Bashkim and Përparim* (Alb., Committee for Unity and Progress)—supported the Islam-based theory with the hope of gaining social and political advantages for Albania.

In one of his early editorials, Sami Frashëri wrote that Albanianism and Islamism were not mutually exclusive; moreover, he held that Islam did not prohibit the empire's cultural diversity, concluding that ethnicity was an indispensable element. Under the circumstances, Ottoman officials did not deny the importance of the ethnic identity; in fact, they viewed it as a "factor of defense," as Dervish Pasha put it, "in an iron barricade against Serbia, Montenegro, and Greece." For that reason, Frashëri called for an emancipation of the Albanians through education at Ottoman schools and, in line with what he called "internal plural unity," the renowned writer also supported the teaching of the Albanian language. Furthermore, Frashëri also became a proponent of Ottoman patriotism, as a framework of Ottomanism (Trk.: *osmanlilik*), which he thought ought to be preserved and consolidated further. In that discussion, the Albanian writer paid attention to cultural, linguistic, and ethnic diversity, with a focus on the Albanians as an important pillar of the Ottoman Empire in Europe. Frashëri stimulated both an Ottoman conscience based on statehood and the national Albanian identity, built on common patriotism or the love for the *vatan*—i.e., homeland.

---

[224] *Ibid.* 114.

Frashëri unveiled his ideas in a drama, titled *Besa* (meaning faith, trust, or covenant in Albanian), which was well received by Albanians as well as other nationalities. Through his works, Sami Frashëri was able to infuse a notion of tolerance in the authoritarian regime of Abdul Hamid as the Albanians were able to articulate their demands for education in their own language.

A challenge to the Albanian school remained the Ottoman Empire's failure to recognize a distinct Albanian nationality, by having the ethnic group classified according to religion. Therefore, Muslim Albanians, officially registered as part of the Ottoman nationality, were entitled to an education in Ottoman Turkish. Christians, meanwhile, known as *Rums* (*i.e.*, Romans), were permitted to use religious schools in Greek or attend private institutions in Albanian as long as they were approved by the ever-watchful Ottoman authorities. Nevertheless, while many Albanians had retained their Christian faith, their "religious right" permitting education in the native tongue provided a unique opportunity. For that reason, Albanian schools, such as the secular Korça *Mësonjëtore* or the girls' school, were founded on the basis of the "religious right."

While Muslims were not allowed to express their national identity in their education system, Christian Albanians were also faced with a struggle within their religious communities. As the Albanians increased their efforts for education in their own language, the Greek and Bulgarian Orthodox churches vehemently opposed any expression of Albanian nationalism. Notably, the Greek Church used all means to halt any preaching or liturgy in the Albanian language. For this reason, the Hellenic ecclesiasts cooperated with the Ottoman authorities to control and persecute clergymen who used the Albanian tongue at church or in schools, even when education in the language was officially permitted after the Young Revolution.

Nonetheless, the Greek efforts did not halt the efforts of Orthodox Albanian preachers to promote their language in religious writings, despite the harsh measures, including the assassination of Papa Kristo Negovani and others by Hellenist nationalists. Indeed, the nationalist movements of the Orthodox peoples that, along with the Tanzimat reforms, spurred the Albanian national awakening. As a result, the Albanians took a defensive position to protect their lands and identity through a movement that resulted in their brief autonomy and final independence.

The successful uprisings of the Orthodox peoples were the first factor to instigate the Albnaian movement. The insurgencies of the early 19th century were of a peculiar nature, for as noted in the Greek War of Independence

(1820-1829), many Albanians were directly involved in combat. After the defeat of Ali Pashë Tepelena and the destruction of the Pashalik of Janina, Arvanites (*i.e.*, Albanians from central Greece) and Albanians from Epirus participated in the movement, for they believed to be fighting for their freedom and independence or because their religious and cultural identity succumbed to Hellenism that purported to include all Orthodox peoples.

In the meantime, an identity based on a common religion and culture with non-Greek speakers was widely promoted. The apostle of the Greek uprising, Rhigas Pheraios, called on Bulgarians, Albanians, Armenians, and Greeks indiscriminately to rise against the Ottoman Empire. The efforts inevitably shed led on the linguistic diversity of the Orthodox community without casting doubts on the common identity. The process strengthened further just as the individual languages gained momentum as the building blocks of distinct national identities.[225]

However, it was the Italo-Albanians, or the Arbëreshë of Italy, who moved to warn the Orthodox Albanians against the danger of the common Orthodox identity and other deceptive measures of the Hellenist propaganda. Noting the Orthodox rite the ancestors of Italo-Albanians brought from their homeland (mainly Morea, present-day Peloponesus, and the islands around Athens) and the émigré community had preserved all along, Arbëreshë writers spoke of their nationality, which they had kept even through the use of the Albanian language in Mass, liturgy, and the famous religious colleges. This way, Italo-Albanians not only opposed Hellenism and the hegemonic propaganda of Athens and the Patriarchate of Constantinople, which referred to Orthodox Albanians as *Albanian-speaking Greeks*; the Arbëreshë helped their Orthodox brethren to avoid becoming victims of deception and to promote further the Albanian cultural identity through education, as had previously been ever since the *New Academy* of Voskopoja.

The Italo-Albanian contribution to the national awareness, which would inevitably begin with the war on the Hellenization of Albanians, was followed by the involvement of other diaspora communities. The Albanians of Romania and Egypt, and later, the United States of America, raised their voice in favor of a powerful national movement, based on the common origin, homeland, and language.

In the contemporary spirit of European romantism, the Albanian nationalism relied on the glory of the past and the common language to rouse a

---

[225] Clayer, *Në fillimet e nacionalizmit shqiptar*, 165.

much-needed national pride. This then led to a common movement for national awakening, a process that began among the diaspora and inspired in the meantime the intellectuals and the masses at home, culminating to what is known as the Albanian National Renaissance or *Rilindja Kombëtare*.

The variety of influences from the diaspora, nevertheless, required domestic refinement, not only because the socio-cultural circumstances of the émigré communities differed from Albania's setting, but also due to the diversity within the Albanian people. A multitude of family, tribal, provincial, religious, and other attributes were to be incorporated into what was to appear as Albanianism, which would serve as the basis for the social and political platform for an autonomous state of Albania within the Ottoman Empire, as a steping stone to national independence.

The platform would also represent the project and later political concept of what could be termed as Ottoman Albania. Although the community's efforts often lacked adequate coordination, Ottoman Albania was the foundation of all political demands of the nationality, from the League of Prizren in 1878 up to the Memorandum of Shkup in August of 1912.

This project that was initially conceived among the Arbëreshë and later spread throughout the Albanian diaspora gained its greatest momentum when adopted by Albanian scholars in the Ottoman Empire. The majority of intellectuals lived in İstanbul, the Ottoman capital, from where they could spread their ideas to other parts of the empire. This centrifugal effect was highly elitist for it included high-level intellectuals, city dwellers, the upper-middle class that had begun to emerge, and later diffused to high-ranking employees of the imperial administration and certain military officers, whose role was later noted during the Young Turk Revolution. The elite group also included leaders of certain religious communities, such as the Bektashi Muslims, but also the Orthodox and Catholics, who played so crucial of a role as to be called partisans of Albanianism. Indeed, it was the religious leaders who provided the necessary bridge between the elite and the masses.

The wide spectrum of religious denominations spontaneously manifested that which turned into the motto of the Albanian national awakening—the idea that Albanianism as a conscience that encapsulated all other identities (religious, tribal, provincial, political, etc.), precisely as Pashko Vasa's poem articulated that *"the Faith of the Albanian is Albanianism."*

The metaphor met with increasing endorsement among Albanian intellectuals and the social class that followed them. As such, it constituted the first demonstration of Albanianism, helping to distinguish the Albanians from the *millet-i osman* in favor of modern Ottomanism. Later, the Albanians would break off with Ottomanism, too, after the Young Turks appropriated the ideology as a tool for their extreme nationalism, leading to the final dissolution of the Ottoman Empire.

In discussing Albanianism, a question arises on how the ideology became the *common faith* of the Albanians, serving as their common social and cultural denominator and providing for a general mobilization of the nation? Was the motto a magic formula needed to face an existential challenge at a time the Albanians could not be united otherwise? Or, did Pashko Vasa introduce a new political construction, which used the religious denominations and their coexistence as a unified foundation for any national program?

Indisputably, the answer ought to be found not in the analysis, but the synthesis of the phenomenon. In other words, one needs consider less of the way the ideology was created, and more of its unifying role and its goal of stimulating action. Therefore, Albanianism, or the reflection of the qualities of an Albanian, required that one's religious identity not define one's national identity, but that faith be taken as one important aspect, for it was the language, tradition, and ethnicity that united a group that also shared common political and social interests, which in fact proved decisive at the time.

Of course, it was not an easy task to set apart Albanianism from Islamism and Ottomanism (especially with regards to the former, whose worldviews had become solid clichés), because it was necessary to avoid confrontations, which were almost inevitable. As a result, the Albanians needed to follow a path of coexistence, for as much as possible, and avoid divisions. For this, a great deal of social audacity and political vision was required along with intellectual competence of the leadership. Fortunately, at the time, it was the Frashëri brothers (Sami, Naim, and Abdyl) who elevated Albanianism to the level of a national ideology, cultural conscience, and political concept of the Albanian *Rilindja Kombëtare*. As a target of orientation, *Rilindja* chose the western civilization. But turning to the West was not without difficulties and dangers. The project for an Ottoman Albania, as a precondition to national independence, had innumerous opponents, who would fight to prevent the Albanian plan. Keeping the Albanians away from the West gave such the nation's enemies the only opportunity to then exercise their "right" to annex more of the ethnic Albanian territory in pursuit of a "mission civilisatrice from the Christian West"!

Albanianism and Western Civilization

German scholars become increasingly interested in ancient Albanian history, serving as an important inspiration for the national cultural movement of the Arbëreshë. Jeronim de Rada and Dhimitër Kamarda become pioneers of Rilindja Kombëtare. The Italo-Albanian press serves as a spokesperson of the Albanian issue in Europe. Naum Veqilharxhi calls for an Albanian cultural awakening in an 1844 periodical. Activists spread awareness on the written language as a pass to the civilized way. Sami Frashëri speculates on the Pelasgian origin of the Albanians as an opportunity to break off from Islamism, Hellenism, and Turkism.

The İstanbul-based Albanian intellectuals made increasing demands for their national rights. First, they requested official recognition of their nationality to move on to calls for cultural tolerance; finally, the focus shifted to political demands for administrative and cultural autonomy within the Ottoman Empire, a goal for which the Albanians worked through legitimate means. But before the domestic movement was ever possible, there was the stimulation and tremendous assistance from abroad, specifically the Italo-Albanian community and later other diaspora groups. Their involvement initially pertained to cultural aspects, but it also became political later on. Arbëreshë scholars focused on the Western origin of the Albanians, as a people with its roots in antiquity, to construct a much-needed theory for the national awakening in İstanbul and other parts of the Ottoman Empire. Knowledge of Albanian history served to counter the Hamidian policy that identified the Albanians with Islamism and, on the other side, awareness of an ancient origin helped refute the hegemonic propaganda of the Orthodox nations, which had endeavored to anatomize the Albanians as non-Western to secure territorial claims.

The national cultural movement of the Arbëreshë, which began in the early decades of the 19th century and continued until the Albanian declaration of independence in 1912, was greatly inspired by the growing spirit of European romantism. Yet, the efforts of the émigré community would not have attained their vigor had it not been for the encouragement that German linguists provided with their works on the Albanian language, presenting the Albanians as an ancient and indigenous population of Europe. This general theory was precisely what the Arbëreshë scholars aimed to link the ancient origin of the Albanians with the beginnings of the European civilization. The works of German researchers were of a particular importance for they carried scientific competence from a nation with a growing political influence. The German unification had recently inspired the Italian movement for a unified state, motivating Italo-Albanians to also pursue a nationalist movement. The Arbëreshë felt a duty to inform the Italian and European circles on the truth about the Albanians as an ancient European people; meanwhile, the Apenine community's scholars also worked to awaken their brethren in the Ottoman Empire.

Germans played a vital role in discovering the origin of the Albanians. German studies became the major reference for the Arbëreshë who spread the message on the Albanian origin throughout Italy and beyond. Indeed, German writings on the Albanians dated back to the 15th century and are classified into two phases, denoting the time period and the content of the works. The first period includes the early writings on the Albanians by knights, crussaders, missionaries, and diplomats who visited the Albanian countries. The second phasis pertains to the scientific studies that began by mid-17th century and continued throughout the 20th century. During this time, high-profile linguists conducted authentic research that laid the foundations of Albanian studies, often termed Albanology.

The early German documents on the Albanians and medieval Albania come from a knight, Arnold von Harff. In 1496, he left his native Cologne in North Rhine-Westphalia for pilgrimage to Palestine, spending several days on the way in Albania. During his stay in Shkodër, Ulqin, and Lezha, von Harff compiled a glossary of fifty-two Albanian words and expressions that helped him communicate with the locals. In mid-17th century, von Harff's descendants published his memoirs that are preserved at the Cologne Library; the work includes the German knight's description on the Albanian lands and its inhabitants.[226]

Later, other European knights, missionaries, and diplomats also came into contact with the Albanians. The visitors journeyed through the Albanian lands, taking notes on the people and their language. Such were the efforts of the French consul in Janina, Poaqueville, who wrote a small dictionary along with grammatical observations on the Albanian language.[227] In the meantime, Englishman W.M. Leake left a short Albanian-Greek-English dictionary and a Albanian grammar.[228]

---

[226] Arnold von Harff, *Die Pilgerfahrt* (Köln: 1860).

[227] F. C. H. L. Pouaquevlle, *Voyage en Grece* (1820-1821).

[228] W. M. Leake, *Resarches in Greece* (1814).

The renowned German philosopher, G.W. Leibniz (1646-1716), was among the early erudites to observe the ancient origin of the Albanians. His knowledge of the language consisted of some hundred words, but referring to the Albanian tongue, Leibniz wrote that "it pertained to a people with ancient roots."[229]

After Leibniz's remarks, there was a continued preoccupation among German scholars with the origin of the Albanians and their language. The motivations were mainly of the scientific nature, but also cultural. Thereby, J. Thunmann defended the theory of the ancient origin of the people and the language, deriving them from the Thracians.[230]

Later, after the appearance of comparative linguistics, a noted scholar was J. Xylander. His works attracted the attention of scholars to the Albanian language and the discussion on the origin of the Albanians. Focusing on the ancient roots of the tongue, Xylander put the Albanian among the old languages.[231]

Xylander was followed by J.G.V. Hahn, the Austrian consul in Janina, who is duly considered as the father of Albanology. He published *Albanesischen Studien* (1853-1854), including historical notes, a description of Albania and the customs of its people, a grammar of the language and a rich dictionary.

As Albanian studies continued, a German physician serving in the Greek fleet, C.H.T. Rheinhold, published a collection of folk songs from the Arvanite (*i.e.*, Albanian) seamen of Poros and Hydra islands.[232] The songs reflected the extent of the ethnic Albanian presence throughout the Balkans and notably in Greece, where Albanians lived as far as the Aegean islands. This observation was of particular importance to counter the *Megali Idea* and the Hellenist chauvinism the project inspired, denying the linguistic and cultural reality of the Orthodox Albanians in favor of a Greek identity. In this regard, the work of another German linguist, F. Bopp, was crucial in that it classified the Albanian language as an independent branch of the Indo-European family.[233] In fact, Bopp's theory presented the Albanian as a distinct language, which further meant that the Albanians were a nation on their own.

---

[229] G. W. Leibniz, "L'opinone de Libniz sur la langua albanaise,"*Albania* 1(1897-1898): 41-43, cited in Skëndi, *Zgjimi kombëtar shqiptar*, 112.

[230] Leibniz, *Untersuchungen über die Geschihte der ostlichen europäischen Völker* (1774).

[231] J. Xylander: *"Die Schprahe der Alabanesen odrer Schipetaren"*, 1835.

[232] C. H. T Rheinhold, *Noctes Pelasgicae* ([Athens]: 1855).

[233] F. Bopp: *"Über das Albanische in seinen verwandschaflichen Bezihungen"*, 1854.

Intensified studies on the Albanian language were contucted in the last quarter of the 19th century. At this time, two German scholars appeared as representatives of the leading theories on the Albanian origin. A. Schleicher (1821-1868) supported the theory of Pelasgian roots of the Albanians and their language, while G. Meyer (1850-1900) maintained an Illyrian origin. According to Schleicher, the old European langauges, such as Greek, Latin, and Illyrian—as the predecessor of Albanian—stemmed from the ancient tongue of the Balkan Peninsula and the Mediteranean basin, that is, the language of the Pelasgians. Schleicher placed the Albanian language in a special, close relationship with Greek. Activists of *Rilindja Kombëtare* embraced the theory, for an ancient tongue served as argument to defend the rights of the Albanian nationality.[234] On the other hand, Gustav Meyer, one of the most prominent linguists of the time, opposed Schleicher's theory, contending that "the Albanian language was a dialect of ancient Illyrian."[235]

Inspired by the works of German linguists and the wave of early-19th century romantism, a number of Italo-Albanians began to write on the history, language, and folklore of Albania.[236] The Arbëreshë sought to rediscover the glory of the "Great Age," to elicit the pride that the Albanians would use in their struggle for national independence. In 1848, Vincenso Dorsa published his *Dagli Albanesi*, which he dedicated to "my divided and scattered, but one and only, nation, divided and scattered, but one."[237] This work unveiled the curtain to a great cultural movement in Italy, represented by the collection of folklore, language and history studies, and original literature.

The Albanians of Italy had always been dedicated to their native tongue and education; as early as 1791, the Albanian language was taught at the College of Saint Adrian in San Demetrio Corone, Calabria.[238] However, only by the second half of the 19th century, did the Arbëreshë begin to develop an

---

[234] Albanian writers such as Sami and Naim Frashëri defended the Pelasgian theory. See: S. Frashëri, *Shqipëria ç'ka qënë, ç'është dhe ç'do të bëhetë*; N. Frashëri, *Dëshirë e vërtetë e shqiptarit* (1886).

[235] For more from G. Meyer, see: *Albanensische Studien*; *Albanensiche Gramatik*; *Etimologiesches Wörtebuch albanensiechn Schprache* (published 1880-1890).

[236] Skëndi, *Zgjimi kombëtar shqiptar*, 114.

[237] *Ibid.* 114.

[238] For more on Albanian education in Italy, see A. Scura, *Gli Albanesi in Italia e i loro canti tradicionali*, (New-York: 1912), 75; A. Galeni: *L'Albania* (Roma: 1901), 134; cited in Skëndi, *op. cit.*, 115.

original literature with nationalist tendencies. As the movement could not begin in Albania proper because of the Ottoman occupation, Italy provided the venue for an authentic national literature:

Living in separate communities and having retained an Orthodox liturgy, the Arbëreshë had preserved the language, customs, and traditions of their fatherland. Since some [of the Arbëreshë] descended from the ruling families of Albania that fought against the Ottomans, they also recalled memories of victories and defeats of their ancestors. [The Arbëreshë] glorified in songs the Albanian resistance against the Ototman invaders and the deeds of Gjergj Kastrioti Skanderbeg, although such songs remained unsung in Ottoman-ruled Albania.[239]

Two of the masterminds of the Albanian movement in Italy, in the second half of the 19th century, were Jeronim De Rada (1814-1903) and Dhimitër Kamarda (1821-1882). As authors of an extensive corpus of fiction, scholarly articles, and editorial-political writings, the two intellectuals earned a distinguished place in the greater *Rilindja Kombëtare* that led to the independence of Albania. In his writings, De Rada glorified Albania's pre-Ottoman independence and Skanderbeg's war against the Ottomans, presenting the 15th century leader as a source of hope of the nation's revival. The Arbëreshë poet also reflects on the past in his *Serafina Topia*, depicting the fate of the Albanians who remained under Turkish rule. In addition to his literary ouevre, De Rada also published a political writings in his bilingual periodical *Fjamuri i Arbërit* (*Alb.*, The Flag of Albania). Issued in Albanian and Italian from 1883 to 1887, the publication served as an organ to increase public awareness of the Albanian national identity and the nation's aspirations for freedom and independence. Earlier, in 1848, De Rada founded and edited a Naples-based political and literary magazine, *L'Albanese d'Italia* (*Ital.*, The Albanian of Italy), which served as a tribune for the European nation. The Arbëreshë writings were generally in the spirit of the major changes that were taking place in Europe in light of the Italian unification and later the reunification of Germany—events that served as an inspiration for the Balkan peoples under Ottoman occupation. For many years, *L'Albanese d'Italia*, published in the Italian language, was highly influential among the inteletual and political circles of Italy in promoting the Albanian efforts for freedom and independence.

---

[239] *Ibid.* 114.

In addition to De Rada's legacy in literature and publications, another notable Arbëreshë, Dhimitër Kamarda, made great contributions in the academia. Focusing on the Albanian language and its ancient origin, Kamarda supported the Pelasgian theory and tried to describe the proximity of Greek and Albanian. In appendices to his work, Kamarda included prose excerpts as well as folk songs from Sicily and Calabria, Albania proper, and the Arvanite settlements in Greece. He was also a pioneer in the efforts for a unified written language, combining in his texts attributes of various Albanian dialects.[240]

Zef Skiroi (1865-1927) was another important name that joined the hall of prominent Italo-Albanian writers and scholars. Along with De Rada and Kamarda, Skiroi is praised for strengthening the ties between the Albanians on both sides of the Adriatic. In 1887, Skiroi began his publication of *Arbri i Ri* (*Alb.*, The New Albanian), which replaced De Rada's *Fjamuri i Arbrit*. Like his predecessors, Skiroi also drew from Albania's past to support the nation's right to independence.[241]

One must note that the Italo-Albanian movement benefited greatly from an ardent support and writer, Elena Gjika (*Rom.* Ghica or Ghika).[242] Using the pen-name Dora d'Istria, this Romanian princess of Albanian origin became a catalyst of Albanianism. In 1871, she wrote that "the time has arrived for our history to come out of the grave where the many Pharisees had buried it." Elena Gjika believed that greatest imperative was to prove the ancient origin of the Albanians so that they "be not mistaken for a . . . Slavic tribe, as many erudites, dictionary, encyclopedias, and papers continue to do."[243]

---

[240] Dhimitër Kamarda, *Saggi di grammatoligia comparata dell lingua albanese* (1864), cited in Skëndi, 115.

[241] *Ibid.* 115.

[242] *Elena Gjika* (Dora D'Istria) was born in 1828 in Bucharest to a noble family of Albanian descent. Her uncle, Grigore IV, ruled as Voivode of Wallachia between 1822 and 1828. Elena Gjika received her early education from a Greek mentor and later studied in Germany and Austria, where she lived with her parents. After marrying Prince Kol'tsov Masal'sky, she spent several years in Russia. In 1852, she separated from the Russian prince and lived in Switzerland for five years, before moved to Italy for the rest of her life. In Italy, she wrote fiction, non-fiction, and academic works. Many of her studies were published in journals such as *Revue des Deux Mondes*, *L'Illustration*, *La Rivista Europea*, *La Nuova Antologia*, *L'Internationale Revue* of Vienna, and Greek periodicals (*L'Independence hellenique*, *Neologos* and *Courrier d' Athenes*). Elena Gjika died in Florence in 1882.

[243] Clayer, *op. cit.*, 211.

Prior to this, she had studied Albanian folk songs dedicated to freedom for her renowned work *The Albanian Nationality According to Folk Songs*.[244] Using examples she excrated mainly from De Rada's rhapsodies about Skanderbeg, Dora d'Istria emphasized that, despite the religious diversity, the Albanians formed one nation and were entitled to enjoy their freedom and prosperity.[245] The writing was widely distributed as it was published in the French-language *Revue des deux mondes* (Review of Two Worlds) and was translated into many languages. In 1866, the study was rendered into Greek for a Trieste publication; an Italian translation came out in Cosenza in 1867, while 1878 publications in Livorno and Alexandria issued an Albanian version. In addition, Elena Gjika's work on the Albanian nationality was cited by Elisee Reclus in *Geographia.246* It is noteworthy that Hahn and Kamarda were the greatest influences in Dora D'Istria's take on the Albanian language. Like another contemporary, Theodro Mommsen, Gjika wrote of a common origin of the Albanian, Hellenic, and Italic "races." The Albanians were considered descendants of the Pelasgians, who once lived in Epirus, Macedonia, Illyria, Greece, and parts of Italy.[247]

Dora d'Istria focused on refuting misconceptions about the Albanians, attempting at a balanced discussion on religion and the national issue. For example, she held that Albanians had converted to Catholicism to emphasize their Albanian nationality vis-à-vis the Serbs, presenting a theory supported by experts of medieval theology.[248] On the other hand, Gjika also distinguished between Islam and the Turkish-Ottoman identity, contending that the unity of faith between Muslim Albanians and Ottoman Turks was not as strong as claimed by contemporary writings.[249] Here, Dora d'Istria's argument coincided with the Ottoman encyclopedia, *Kamus-i al A'Lam*, authored by Sami Frashëri decades later. To present an image that would

---

[244] *Ibid.* 211.

[245] Gawrych, *Gjysmëhëna dhe shqiponja*, 116.

[246] Clayer, *op. cit.*, 213.

[247] *Ibid.* 213.

[248] For more, see Georgie Ostrogorski, *Istoria Vizantije* (Beograd: 1969); J. Hoffman, *Rudimente der Territoralstaaten im byzntinischen Reiches* (München: 1974); B. Ferjanovic, *Tesalija u XIII i XIV veku* (Beograd: 1974); A. Hohlweg. *Beiträge zur Vervaltungsgeschichte des Oströmischen Reiches unter den Komnenen* (München: 1965); B. Rohberg. *Die Union zwischen der griechischen und der lateinischen Kirche auf dem II Konzil von Lyon 1274* (Bonn: 1964).

[249] Clayer, *op. cit.*, 213.

encompass all of the Albanians, regardless of religion, Gjika also published a lengthy study on Muslim Albanians in an Italian magazine. She gave a historical overview on how Albanians converted to Islam, refuting they had anything in common with the Ottomans, the "Porte's fanatics," or their version of Islam. Instead, Gjika insisted that Muslim Albanians remained commited to their "Arian race" and, as such, their European character.[250] To support her views, she drew a denominational line between the Tosks (*i.e.*, southern Albanians) and the Ottomans, noting that the former were not Orthodox Muslims (*sunnis*), but *shi'ites* like the Persians. Therefore, Gjika was of the opinion that Muslim Tosks preached a different type of Islam that favored the freedom of thought (here, she noted the mystic orders Ali Pasha was affiliated with) and, like the Persians, southern Albanians had chosen their form of Islam because of its compatibility with the "Arian race."[251] Gjika's views are similar to theories of the "European Islam" of Albanians and the notion of Bektashism as "protestant Islam" that some even proposed for a national religion. Nevertheless, Gjika's writings inspired the thought that accepting Islam was not just a matter of currying favors in a certain political environment; it also represented the philosophical concepts that the Albanians adapted to their spiritual needs.

Following Elena Gjika's writings, Albanians repeatedly noted the identity they had preserved despite the Ottoman occupation. However, references to the Albanian nation preceded Dora d'Istria. Naum Veqilharxhi (*born Naum Panajot Bardhi; 1797-1846*) wrote to his compatriots in 1846 on the importance of their mother tongue and education. Veqilharxhi believed that a nation without education was bound to slavery and that no people could ever prosper by other than its own language. "Culture may be earned in the mother tongue," wrote the Albanian activist.[252]

Veqilharxhi was born in Vithkuq, Korça, from where he moved to a sizable Albanian settlement in Wallachia (present-day Romania). In 1821, Naum joined other Albnaians in a great popular uprising that Wallachian frontrunners, Tudor Vladimirescu and Alexander Ypsilantis, led against the Ottoman Empire. Naum's experience in exile inspired him to think of the fate of his country. For his memorandum of 1846, Veqilharxhi seems to have cooperated with the Bulgarian illuminist, Ivan Selimeski, who was also exiled

---

[250] *Ibid.* 214.

[251] *Ibid.* 214.

[252] See N. Veqilharxhi, *E parthenme mbi djelmt e rinj shqiptarë*, reproduced in D. S. Shuteriqi, *Antologji e letërsisë shqipe* (Tiranë: 1955), 85-88.

in Bucharest. There, the Albanian writer became cognizant of the misery, in which the Albanian people had fallen, and reflected on the foreign invasions, political troubles, and ignorance as causes of the suffering. At the time, the Albanian people rose in consequent revolts but lacked the coordinated political programs for independence that other Balkan nations had begun to pursue. For that reason, Veqilharxhi noted: "The time has arrived to audaciously change [our] way, moving from now on [on the same direction] as the prosperous nations of the world . . . ."[253] Veqilharxhi's letter states further:

> Only nations that have a written language can join the way of the civilized nations, while others shall be punished [into slavery]. The Albanian nation has experienced a moral and political depression as a result of the various invasions, political turmoil, and . . . new religious dogmas. [The nation] has fallen in[to a state of] ignorance, barbarism, and slavery. Those who are educated are forced into emigration and do not work for their country. They no longer know the language of the nation; they abandon their friends and relatives. . . . they cooperate for the prosperity of other nations and are content to be called "Greeks," "Hellenes," or "Wallachians."[254]

The letter is the earliest known pragmatic document of the Albanian *Rilindja Kombëtare*. The movement's early efforts also included a unique alphabet that Naum created for his native tongue. Borrowing from earlier scripts, Veqilharxhi presented a set of characters for several Albanian publications he authored. In 1844, he published in Romania his *Evetar*, a concise primer book and the first of its kind in the Albanian language. A year later, Veqilharxhi published an expanded primer, *Fare i ri evetar shqip* (Alb.: Newly-Issued Albanian Primer), which also included a lengthy foreword.

Unlike prior isolated efforts to use the Albanian language in church books, Naum Veqilharxhi's works never fell into oblivion. In the second half of the 19th century, the Albanian national movement became increasingly powerful. Intellectuals endeavored to reestablish ties with the Western civilization, as a model for the political programs, including demands for an autonomous Ottoman Albania for a transition to an independent European state. Proponents of Albanianism promoted a national identity based on the common Albanian tongue. Thus, the language that had outlived four centu-

---

[253] H.P.Sh. 2 (Prishtinë), 47.

[254] See the Greek text, accompanied by an Albanian translation, in Pepo and Maslev, 1961, cited in Clayer, *op. cit.*, 167.

ries of Ottoman rule without any official use became an important factor of *Rilindja*. Sami Frashëri used the language to support his theory of the Pelasgian origin of his nation.[255] Meawhile, the Albanian national poet, and Sami's brother, Naim Frashëri, used the appellation *divine language*[256] to refer to his native tongue. Whether as a sacrosanct or by chance, Albanian survived to become a source of pride and inspiration, serving as the decisive factor to break the Albanians from the East.

---

[255] See Sami Frashëri, *Kamus-i al Al'am*, cited in Gawrych, *Gjysmëhena dhe shqiponja*, 143.
[256] Naim Frashëri, *Vepra* I (Prishtinë: 1986), 76.

Pan-Slavism and the Balkan National Movements

Ottomans continue their efforts to modernize in accordance with the requirements of major European powers; meanwhile, behind the scenes, Russia tries to turn the Ottoman Empire into plunder of war, reasoning that "the sick man of Bosphorus" should go soon. Russian Tsar Nicholas issues an ultimatum to the sultan, demanding the right of supervision over the Christian population of Jerusalem and the European part of the empire. Russia enters into war against the Ottoman Empire; Great Britain and France align on the Ottomans side. British and French troops disembark sail across the Black Sea, disembarking in Crimea; there, they lay siege on Sebastopol for a year. Ultimately, the Russian army capitulates in Sebastopol and the conflict concludes with the 1856 Treaty of Paris. Russia loses territory and privileges previously gained under the Treaty of Kuchuk-Kainarji in 1774, including the Azov port, free navigation in the Danube, and the right to maintain a fleet on the Black Sea. Europeans accept the Ottoman Empire among the continent's powers and its state sovereignty is guaranteed. The sultan promises new reforms favoring the Christian population of his realm.

Beginning with the Tanzimât reforms, which were brought by Sultan Abdul Mejid I (Trk.: Abdülmecid, 1839-1861), the Ottoman Empire strived for modernization in all fields, following the model of developed western countries. In this path, the Sublime Porte also had the support of Great Britain, whose influence in the region was increasingly evident. As the Republic of Venice dissolved after five centuries of domination on the Mediterranean water, the British Empire rose as a great naval power, with clear pretentions to oversee the Mediterranean as well as the sea routes that led towards India. For this purpose, the English were unlike other Great Powers of Europe, who were rather interested in the quantity of their future gains, when the Ottoman Empire failed to meet its commitments and would inevitably collapse; the British were intent on preserving the sultan's realm as to reap fruits from its continued existence rather than become involve in sharing the uncertain spoils of the Ottoman downfall. Apparently, the

English crown fell in direct conflict with its temporary "ally", Russia. The Eurasian empire sought to bring ruin to the Ottoman state to obtain the greatest advantage possible without engaging the Europeans, who always had their own interest in the matter. However, Russia was convinced that pitying Britain against other claimants, such as Austria-Hungary and France, would fulfill the Tsar's dream to egress into the Mediterranean Sea, permitting the Russians to fully occupy the Black Sea and assume permanent control of the Bosphorus Strait, and the Sea of Marmara. Accordingly, in January 1853, Tsar Nicholas I summoned the British ambassador to Saint Petersburg, advising that: "Before us, we have a sick man—a very sick man. It would be an apocalyptical wayward should he escape before we take the necessary measures." The metaphor about "the sick man of Bosphorus," originating in the Russian capital, gained specific diplomatic and political connotations from that time onwards until the Ottoman Empire really falls forever eighty and more years.[257]

Nicholas I succeeded in bringing Great Britain into this game by promising them that they got Crete and Egypt, which pleased their ambitions for naval power. However, even though the British cautioned that their interests required that the Ottoman Empire be reformed and preserved in the actual territory, the Russian Tsar did not hesitate to put pressure on the Porte, so that it would hinder its way of the reforms. Thus, in March 1853, Nicholas I sent an ultimatum to İstanbul, demanding that the Greek Church be granted rights over the Holy Land of Palestine and that Russia be recognized as the protector of all Christian Greeks in Turkish soil. The ultimatum was presented by Prince Menshikov, known for his disrespectful behavior as a military officer.[258]

The Sublime Porte promptly informed London, which offered immediate support for the troubled empire. Lord Stratford, British ambassador to Constantinople, personally assured the sultan that he would not lose his power over his subjects. As to custody of the Holy Land, the British diplomat suggested that the Porte honor the Russian request, for it only confronted the Tsar with other bidders and presented no danger to the Ottoman Empire. However, the British supported the Porte in categorically rejecting the Russian demands that had to do with the Greek Christian population, which by definition included all Orthodox Christians of the empire. Consequently,

---

[257] Ferdinand Schevill, *Ballkani: historia dhe qytetërimi* (Tiranë: 2002), 292.
[258] *Ibid.*

it did not take long before the Tsar and the sultan broke off diplomatic relations.

Indeed, the refusal of Russia's demands constituted the key differences between the British policy to maintain the Ottoman Empire and Saint Petersburg's efforts to destroy the troubled state. The political antagonism appeared as a worthy excuse for a new Russian war on the Ottoman Empire, the sixth conflict since 1695, when Peter the Great conquered the port of Azov, and four years later gained control of the northern Black Sea with the Treaty of Karlowitz. Unlike other agreements that often concluded wars the Russians had lost, the 1699 peace deal had conferred multiple benefits upon the Tsar, including free navigation on the Danube, on the Black Sea, and through the Bosphorus Strait, which led into the Mediterranean. Less than two centuries later, however, the Russians wished to bring the very end of the Ottoman Empire, through loopholes in the implementation of reforms to improve the position of the Christian population, especially in Ottoman Europe, where the Tsar had already laid his eyes on Bulgaria and Serbia, as main supporters for his expansionist policies.

Since no all European countries were opposed to the Ottoman Empire's dissolution for "proper cause" and, in fact, many of them viewed Britain's interest in support the sultan as a threat, the Russian declaration of war on the Ottomans was seen as inevitable. Moreover, the conflict would without doubt involve the British who had already given unreserved backing to the sultan to dismiss the Tsar's ultimatum.

Wishing to directly harass the Sublime Porte and to test the British readiness for war, in July of that year Russia ordered the army to cross the Prut River and invade the Danubian principalities in July 1853. The Ottoman Empire reacted and demanded an immediate withdrawal of the Russian troops, threatening with war. The British reluctance to send a note demanding the Russian retreat led the Tsar to believe that London had backed down on its promise to the Ottomans. He ordered the admiral of the Russian fleet at the Black Sea to amount a destructive attack on Ottoman ships anchored. The news, however, shook London, letting the British lion out of its cage amidst fears that the Tsar's ships could soon reach the Bosphorus.[259] The British hence realized they had no time to dawdle and rapidly mounted their arms against the Russians, marking the beginning of the Crimean War, a conflict for the preservation or the destruction of the Ottoman Empire.

---

[259] *Ibid.* 294.

The British had high confidence in Austrian and Prussian support, for the two German-speaking nations had their own interests to preserve the Ottoman Empire as a buffer against the Russians. However, Vienna and Berlin adhered to a policy of nonintervention. Support came in the meantime from France, since Napoleon III had multiple reasons for revenge against the Russians, but also saw the war as a good opportunity to increase his influence on Mediterranean Sea and the routes leading through Egypt to India and beyond. The war, in which Britain and France fought as allies of the Ottoman Empire, took its name after the Crimean peninsula, for it was Russia's southern coast, on the Black Sea, where the European powers undertook their attacks. The war lasted more than a year and French and British forces were deployed to the area to take Sevastopol, giving Russia an important lesson to respect the interests of the European powers. Sebastopol fell in March 1855 and, although the allies failed to bring about Russia's collapse as a military power, the Tsar agreed to a ceasefire and to peace talks. Carrying out what proved a political victory for the Ottomans and the Westerners, the European powers organized a peace congress in Paris, a year later. Austria and Prussia attended, too.

The Congress of Paris opened in March 1856 under the leadership of Great Britain, which had won the war and was able to dictate terms. The most important provisions striped Russia of its ambitions to decide the fate of the Ottoman Empire and the eastern part of the continent. As a result, the Europeans agreed to repeal the benefits Russia had obtained under the 1774 Treaty of Kuchuk Kainarji, after its previous victorious war against the Ottoman Empire. Specifically, the new Paris agreement forced the Tsar to give up all his claims to protect the Christian Greeks who lived in the territory of the Sultan, while Russia also lost the right to protection of the Serbian and Romanian principalities of Moldova and Wallachia. At last, Saint Petersburg was denied navigation on the Danube: Moldova gained Bessarabia, a territory the Russians had held since 1812, and the Danube Delta region was ceded to the Ottoman Empire, although the latter was denied the right to sail on the lower Danube and the treaty imposed international supervision over the river. Yet, Britain's greatest victory was taking away Russia's right to control the waters of the Black Sea. The Tsar was even deprived from having warships, arsenals and naval bases in the bay.

The Treaty of Paris was also beneficial to the Ottoman Empire, reassuring its territorial integrity and recognizing the triumphant ally as one of the European powers. The British supported the decision since the sultan had already granted his new rights to his subjects weeks before the congress began, in February 1856. The measures expanded the Tanzimât reforms of 1839, by abolishing the raya system, whereby the Christian population was treated differently under Ottoman law. Hence the imperial decree known as *Hatt-i Hümayun* provided for the equality of all Muslim and Christian subjects, while also assuming to place the entire Christian population under the protection of the sultan.[260]

On the other hand, Russia lost its right to look after Serbia, missing on the opportunity to expand the Tsar's influence in the region. However, the abolishment of the raya regime afforded the Russian a chance of revenge on the Europeans. While Christians no longer existed as a discriminated social category and the Ottoman Empire was on the way to becoming a European constitutional monarchy, Saint Petersburg used relied on the improved status of Balkan Slavs to further expansionist goals. Thereby, it incited Serbs and Bulgarians to fight for secede, while urging the Orthodox Slavic minority in Bosnia and Herzegovina and the Albanian vilayets to undermine the stability of the Ottoman Empire by provocative acts of violence.

On the European political scene, Russia gained an opportunity to reverse the damages suffered at Paris, after the German victory in the French war of 1870, when a unified German state arose as a new European empire, bringing a rapid shift in the balance of power. Britain, having lost France as its main partner, remained alone, while Austria-Hungary and later Italy forged the tripartite alliance with the new German Reich.

Under these circumstances, Austria and Russia developed increasingly closer ties as the two powers were determined to oversee the disintegration of the Ottoman Empire in the Balkan Peninsula, dictating not only the dynamics, but also the interests of the Great Powers. Meanwhile, depending on its friendship with the German-speaking nations, Russia grew less obligated under the Treaty of Paris and resorted once again to encouraging Balkan Slavs, primarily Serbia, to seek independence from the Porte. At the same time, the Tsar also elicited Slavs in other parts of the peninsula to join the Orthodox-based pan-Slavic movement. Therefore, in July 1875, the Orthodox population in Herzegovina rebelled, while the revolt quickly reached Bosnia. It was only the Orthodox who rebelled, while other Bosnian Slavs were opposed to the movement which relied on great support from Serbia and Montenegro. While the Ottomans subsequently intervened and crushed

---

[260] *Ibid.* 296.

the uprising, the Russian-fed lava accumulated underneath and was ready to erupt at any time. The occasion arrived the same Bulgaria also became the scene of uprising for liberation, which were crushed by the Porte, while another rebellion broke out in Bosnia Herzegovina a year later.

The suppression of the Bosian uprisings urged Russia to directly conduct the secessionist efforts in the Balkans. Thus, on June 30, 1876, Serbia declared war on the Ottoman Empire, and Montenegro followed suit on July 1st. In addition to the international support that the two Balkan countries received, the Tsar also aided his "Slavic-Orthodox brothers" with thousands of Russian volunteers, mostly heavily-armed soldiers, to fight in the war.

The Russian war through the Balkan proxies also prompted the secret projects of Vienna and Saint Petersburg to rearrange the political map of Eastern Europe. On July 8, 1876, Austria-Hungary and Russia reached a deal through separate notes exchanged in Reichsttadt, Bohemia, planning the new Balkan borders according to the interests of the parties. The two empires decided to refrain from military intervention in the interstate conflict that had begun over a week prior and agreed that, if the Ottoman Empire won the war, there would be no change in the political map. However, in case of a Serbian and Montenegrin victory, the Sublime Porte would be compelled to implement a few reforms in favor of the Slavic population. Austria-Hungary would annex most of Bosnia, and the rest would go to Serbia, which would also obtain northern Kosova, while Montenegro would be awarded a part of Herzegovina. Moreover, Bulgaria would become an autonomous state and Rumelia an autonomous vilayet. It is noteworthy that Vienna—under the constant pressure from Germany, urging against a large Slavic country in the Balkans—insisted for the agreement to prohibit Serbia to stretch to the Adriatic, while also preventing the inclusion of Macedonia within Bulgaria, for such an array would endanger endangered Austro-German interests in the Aegean Sea.[261]

The Austro-Hungarian note also affected the Albanian question, envisioning the creation of an autonomous state. Thus, at Reichsttadt, Albania entered for the first time the reel of European diplomacy as a political issue.[262] As known, the deal reached in Bohemia was supplemented with another secret agreement that Austria-Hungary and Russia signed in Budapest on May 15, 1877. The accord incorporated the platform approved six

---

[261] H.P.Sh. 2 (Tiranë), 134.
[262] *Ibid.* 134.

months prior in Reichsttadt as well as another agreement the empires signed on March 18th, 1877, providing for Austria-Hungary's promise of neutrality in the Russo-Turkish War in return for the right for the right of a military invasion of Bosnia and Herzegovina. The agreement in principle accepted the idea of an autonomous Albanian state, for it neutralized the model of local Christian autonomies such as the entity proclaimed by Prênk Bibë Doda who raised the flag of Mirdita and entered the war against the Ottoman Empire on Russia's side.

The Serbian and Montenegrin war against the Ottoman Empire was thoroughly fought with the support of Russia, which was interested to secure the benfits it had lost in the Crimea. Yet, the Serbs and Montenegrin were not only losing the conflict, Serbia in particular suffered heavy losses in its campaign to conquer the territories surrounding Prokuple and Kurshumlia. The Ottoman army was well on its march to Belgrade, but stopped after a Russian ultimatum threatened war if the Sublime Porte were not to halt its advance against Serbia. Thus, even though the Balkan country lost in the battlefield, the peace agreement that was achieved after four months of negotiations in İstanbul left Serbia unaffected by the defeat. In fact, even on the ground, the then Slavic principality had made progress during the initial incursions into areas rom Nish to Prokuple and Kurshumlia, where the Serbian army poured into Albanian-inhabited towns and villages and carried horrendous atrocities against the defenseless population. As a result, Serbia was able to ethnically cleanse the area as a part of the Albanian population that survived the Golgotha fled to Kosova and other parts of the Ottoman Empire. Despite the military defeat, Serbia had created the circumstances for an easy occupation the following year, when on April 24, Russia would declare war on the Ottoman state.

The Russo-Turkish War and the Treaty of San Stefano

Sultan Abdul Hamid enacts a new constitution and a second Ottoman parliament is convened. Europeans sign the Treaty of London provides for the autonomy of Christian peoples in a process supervised by the Great Powers. Preng Bibë Doda, the bajraktar of Mirdita, seeks autonomy on behalf of the Catholic population of his region; Russia supports the move, but Austria-Hungary rejects it, favoring an all-Albanian autonomous state, which could impede the Slavic-Orthodox expansionism. The Sub-

lime Porte renounces the Treaty of London as an infringement of sovereignty, while Russia rushes to threaten the Ottoman Empire with war. Following the 1870 Franco-Prussian war, the German Empire is founded, joining the club of the Great Powers of Europe. Serbia and Montenegro wage war against the Ottoman Empire in 1876; Serbia loses, but suffers no consequences, after the Russians warn the Porte against occupying Belgrade. Russia uses the Treaty of London to declare war on the Ottoman Empire in early 1878. Great Britain is unable to help the Ottomans, for it lacks the support of the French, while Germany and Austria-Hungary pursue their own special interests in the Balkans. The Albanians endeavor to enter into an alliance with the Greeks to prevent the penetration of Russian-Bulgarian coalition into Thrace and Macedonia. Abdyl Frashëri meets with government executives in Athens, proposing a joint Albanian-Hellenic, but the Greeks refuse to accept the Albanians as equal partners. The advancing Russian troops defeat the Ottoman army; Adrianople falls and the Porte is forced to sign the Treaty of San Stefano, which envisioned a Greater Bulgaria to the expense of Albanian lands.

The Russo-Turkish war began when it appeared that it was quite unnecessary. During the Conference of Constantinople, held in December 1876, the Ottoman Empire announced important changes in the country. The newly-crowned sultan, Abdul Hamid II, issued a decree instituting a new constitution, which gave an end to abuse and established an Ottoman parliament. A third of the seats in the new legislative body were reserved for Christians. Meanwhile, many Albanians, such as Abdyl Frashëri, Mehmet Ali Vrioni, and others, were also elected, but unlike Christian deputies who won on the basis of religious affiliation, the delegates of the ethnic group earned seats in accordance with regional representation.

The Ottoman Empire nonetheless provided convincing evidence that it had begun a course of sweeping reforms that would turn the country into a constitutional monarchy. The major European powers had long pushed for such changes, but for countries like Russia the padishah's recent measures were not enough. As a result, the Great Powers gathered the same year in London, where they signed a protocol, delineating a principle of nationalities of the Ottoman Empire and providing for their autonomy. The document named the several nationalities, all Christian peoples, that were to earn the right to self-government through a process to be supervised by the Europeans. The Albanians did not appear on the list, although Christian Albanians from the Mirdita highlands had already submitted their religion-based claims for home rule. With Russian instigation and Montenegrin support, Preng Bibë Doda, as *kapedan*, proclaimed the Autonomous Region of Mirdita not long before the London gathering. After Serbia and Montenegro declared war on the Ottoman Empire in 1876, Bibë Doda raised the flag of combat in Mirdita's capital Orosh, launching his efforts to secure the region's autonomy.[263]

The previous *kapedan* of Mirdita, Dodë Pasha, passed away in 1868. Yet, the Ottoman authorities held his son and successor, Preng Bibë Doda, in İstanbul under the pretext that the young man was still continuing his education. While in the Ottoman capital, nevertheless, Bibë Doda had several meetings with ambassadors of Russia, France, and Austria-Hungary, whom he informed of his desire to become prince of an autonomous Mirdita. While Paris and Vienna did not supported the idea—according to Austria-Hungary, the proposal extremely narrowed the Albanian question from the broader Habsburg focus on the entire ethnic group that could serve as a dam against pan-Slavism in the Balkans—Russia was supportive, albeit on certain conditions. Preng Bibë Doda was asked to form a military alliance with Montenegro and lead the clansmen of Mirdita to attack the Ottoman army, occupied with war along the Montenegrin border.[264]

The action, however, was not well received by the rest of Albanians, who feared the repercussions of Russia's interference. The major European powers, too, seem to have considered the effects of autonomy for Mirdita, as they refused to name the region as a self-governing entity in the Treaty of London. The agreement excluded the Albanians on the grounds that they were not recognized as a separate nationality in the Ottoman Empire.[265] Yet, not long afterwards, the idea of an all-ethnic Albanian state was acknowledged in another international diplomatic act when the Budapest agreement envisioned autonomy outside the boundaries of a feudal province such as Mirdita. The latter failed to gain any support from Europeans even after reappearing in the Congress of Berlin, for Austria-Hungary and Britain refused to recognize Mirdita's self-rule for the same motives.[266]

---

[263] H.P.Sh. 2 (Tiranë), 136.

[264] *Ibid.* 136.

[265] As noted earlier, the Porte continued to treat its population according religion; hence Muslim Albanians were a part of the *millet-i osman*, while others were classified as Greeks, Slavs, or Latins, depending on church affiliation.

[266] For more, see: Buxhovi, *Kongresi i Berlinit 1878*, 143-149.

The Mirdita question aside, the London plan—regardless of the Ottoman constitution—provided full European supervision of the reforms and the Sultan acknowledged the program. However, when Abdul Hamid declined to permit the loss of Ottoman sovereignty from the interference of big powers, Russia, which continuously worked to undermine the Ottoman state through the Slavic-Orthodox proxies, claimed the sultan's refusal as a pretext for an armed conflict. Thereby, on April 24, the tzar declared war on the Ottoman Empire.

As combat began, the Russian forces were on the brinks of defeat. Their initial attacks on Plevna (now Pleven), Bulgaria, was unsuccessful, while the Ottoman army, commanded by General Osman Pasha, maintained the upper hand in other battlefields. However, the turnaround for the Russians came when Prince Carol of Romania was put in charge of a joint Russian-Romanian army. After months of resistance, the Ottomans finally collapsed in Plevna, losing not only the city but seemingly also the morale to fight in subsequent battles. The sultan's army permitted the Russian-Romanian alliance to burst forth as they crossed the Balkan Mountains, arrived in Adrianople, and by January reached the Marmara Sea, approaching the very capital of the Ottoman Empire. It seems that the sultan had instructed the rapid retreat in hopes of provoking a military intervention of Western powers, similar to that of the Crimean war, in 1865. However, no one came to his aid this time and, so as to prevent a complete disaster, the sultan agreed to enter peace negotiations in the town of San Stefano.

The war had a major impact on the Balkan Christians who had allied with Russia and awaited the fruits of victory. The conflict also affected the Albanians and the Greeks who—with the exception of the *kapedan* of Mirdita, who sided with the Tsar—were greatly concerned about the epilogue of the peace talks. Whatever the negotiators agreed to at San Stefano, the outcome of the war confronted Albanians and Hellenes with the challenge of choosing between two zone of influence. If they submitted to the Russian block and the Slavic-Orthodox hegemony, the two peoples were excluded from the European sphere; if they decided to defend their territories from the Slavic-Orthodox invasions, Albanians and Greeks would be blamed for aiding the Ottomans against the "liberation war" of the Balkan peoples. Ultimately, in case of defeat, Albanian and Greek lands would become a target for annexation at the hands of the victors.

The dilemma of the two non-Slavic peoples provided an even greater opportunity for Russia, when on April 24, 1877, the Tsar issued a proclamation, calling on all Christian nationalities of the Balkan Peninsula to take up arms alongside the Russian army. The day had come, the Russian appeal said, for the Balkan peoples to be freed from the Ottoman yoke.

As trifling could provoke the Russian punishment, Albanian patriotic circles began to pay heed to the idea of a liberation uprising, for it had become clear that the Ottoman Empire was unable to defend the Albanian territories from the Slavic invasion. Thus, in May 1877, the Albanian Committee (also, the Janina Committee) was formed in southern Albania with the idea of organizing an anti-Ottoman liberation uprising. Members appointed Abdyl Frashëri, who had served as a deputy for Janina in the first Ottoman parliament, to lead the group. Although called the Albanian Committee, the group had a regional character, based in the Vilayet of Janina. Participants represented various parts of the vilayet; prominent figures included Mehmet Ali Vrioni as representative of Berat, Mustafa Nuri of Vlora, Sulejman Tahiri siting in for Tepelena, and Vesel Dino of Preveza. Undoubtedly, the Committee was in the interest the Ottoman Empire, which was concerned to mobilize the Albanian factor along the Greek border to fight against the Russian-led alliance. Since the Tsar had also come out against Greece, choosing to rely more heavily on Bulgaria, the Committee was formed as a defensive measure against the Slavic invasions, which threatened the interests of Albanians and Hellenes alike. The move would also benefit the Ottoman Empire, which could hope to obtain the support of anti-Russian European powers. As Abdyl Frashëri put it in communications to the European capitals, the only way to protect the continent's civilization from the Russian threat was to raise the Greek dam, but along with it, the Albanian factors was also necessary.[267] Frashëri hoped for an Albanian-Hellenic alliance against the Slavic block, but as would be proven shortly after, his plan was an aberration for the Albanian Committee as well as the Ottoman circles that believed the cooperation of the two peoples could prevent the calamity that later appeared in the Treaty of San Stefano.

The idea of a Greek-Albanian alliance also had the endorsement of nationalist Hellenic circles, which greatly feared that Russia's interest in the Balkans Slavs envisioned the inclusion of Thrace and Macedonia within the borders of a Greater Bulgaria. At the time, Greece had a population of only one million and, as a no match for the Tsarist army, contemplated the inclusion of Albanians in the war. Therefore, the Albanian Committee's

---

[267] H.P.Sh. 2 (Tiranë), 140.

proposal of an alliance with Greece was met with positive reception among state official in Athens and the Hellenic government agreed to negotiate with the Albanians.[268]

The talks were held "secretly" in Janina during the second half of July 1877,[269] when Abdyl Frashëri, accompanied by Mehmet Ali Vrioni, met with Epaminonda Mavromatis, an official of the Greek Foreign Ministry.[270] But the meeting was bound to failure from the beginning, since the parties had highly conflicting views. Abdyl Frashëri outlined the common interests against pan-Slavic invasions and proposed a military alliance on the condition that Greece support Albania's independence. The leader of the Janina Committee laid out a plan in which the Albanians would revolt and declare their independence from İstanbul, whereas Athens would declare war on the Ottomans and recognize an independent Albanian principality, consistent the ethnic boundaries that included Kosova in the north (all the way to Vranje in the east)), and Chameria in the south (with Preveza as the southernmost point). In return, the Albanians would help the Greek army to invade Thessaly and Macedonia. Since most officers in the Ottoman garrisons in the two regions were Albanians, they would obey the orders of the Janina Committee to surrender the towns without war. Although contemporary documents do not mention an "Albanian province," German and Austrian sources from İstanbul note that when the Greek representative asked for a wide Albanian participation in combat, he also demanded that the ethnic character of the movement be confined to the north of the Seman River. Furthermore, he conditioned that the limited areas then seek union with Greece in order to form an Albanian province under the sovereignty of the Hellenic king.[271] As the sources point out, however, the Greek government resorted to other means once it realized the reaction of southern Albanians, who sought to defend their territories while aspiring for an autonomous state within the Ottoman Empire. Accordingly, Athens pushed for immigrants and mercenaries in Corfu to form the so-called Epirus

---

[268] *Ibid.* 141.

[269] Documents of the Political Archive of the German Foreign Ministry indicate that the Ottoman Empire was aware of the negotiations, even though the Porte denied any knowledge. Previously, however, Abdyl Frashëri had consulted senior Ottoman officials about "the resistance front against Russia." See Dispatch of the German Embassy in İstanbul, no. 38/48, Aug. 2, 1877, PA AA, Türkei, band. 143.

[270] H.P.Sh. 2 (Tiranë), 141.

[271] PA AA, Türkei, band. 143, doc. no. 137-41.

Committee, seeking the unification fo the Vilayet of Janina with Greece. The organization, which included some Orthodox Albanian among its members, began operations in August 1877 with the aim of organizing an ethnic Albanian uprising, albeit for Hellenist purposes.[272]

The activity of the Epirus Committee invalidated the whole work of the Janina group, but did not preclude further Albanian contacts with Greeks about possible alliances. Several similar meetings were held in İstanbul between members of parliament when Abdyl Frashëri, elected to the Ottoman legislature in the 1877 fall elections, met with Stefanos Skuludos, a deputy of the Greek parliament. Abdyl Frasheri also represented the İstanbul Committee, formally called the Central Committee for the Protection of the Albanian Nationality Rights, as its chairman.[273] The negotiations yielded no result, aside from the Albanians' testing of their rapport with Greece and its claims on the Albanian territories.

Meanwhile, as the ominous prediction of a Russian occupation was becoming a reality, the leaders of the Albanian movement chose a different course. In early 1878, Russia turned the tide in the war and the Ottoman military collapse opened the way to the Serbia to expand southward. After Serbian troops took Pirot, Nish, Kurshumlia, Prokuple and Vranje, they marched on to Kosova, arriving in Gjilan in early January. Montenegro seized Tivar and Ulqin and reached the banks of the Buna River and its source in Lake Shkodër. And, as the Russians approached the very capital of the Ottoman Empire, the Albanian group known as the İstanbul Committee called off the planned war of liberation against the Porte, focusing rather on preventing the disintegration of Albania in the hands of the Slavic of alliance. As a result, the Albanians saw the Ottoman state as their only protector and, instead of rising against it, lined up on its side.

The Albanian siding with the padishah became even more forceful after the belligerents signed a hasted peace agreement on March 3, 1878. Named after the village where the deal was signed, the Treaty of San Stefano deprived the Ottoman Empire of around eighty percent of its Balkan territory. To satisfy the tsar's hegemonic intentions in Eastern Europe, the document provided for the creation of a large Slavic entity, making much of the acquired territory a part of a purported Greater Bulgaria, an autonomous principality with its own government, albeit nominally a tributary to the sultan. The proposed state would extend eastward to the Black Sea, south to

---

[272] *Ibid.*, dok 147/43,44.
[273] H.P.Sh. 2 (Tiranë), 142.

162

the Aegean Sea, north to the Danube and, in the West, to the mountains of Voskopoja. The rest of the territories ceded from the Ottoman Empire would be given to Romania, Serbia, and Montenegro, which were to be upgraded from autonomous principalities to independent states.[274] Thus, nearly half of Albanian lands were awarded to the Balkan Slavic states. The Treaty gave Bulgaria the areas including Korça, Blinisht, Pogradec, Struga, Dibër (Mac.: Debar), Kërçova (Mac.: Kičevo), Gostivar, Tetova (Mac.: Tetovo), Shkup, and Kaçanik. Serbia, expanding primarily to the southwest, would annex the northern and northeastern regions of Kosova, near Mitrovica. Montenegro, whose territory was trebled by the peace agreement, would include within its boundaries a range of Albanian provinces, such as Ulqin, Kraja, Anamal, Hot, Gruda, Tuz, Kelmend, Plava, Gucia, and Rugova.[275]

San Stefano and the Albanian Response in
the Contemporary German Press

The German press runs numerous reports on the Albanian response to the Treaty of San Stefano. The Albanians articulate their readiness to defend their territories. The German ambassador to İstanbul informs Chancellor Bismarck of the Albanian preparations to prepare a league that is going to animate political demands, such as the proposal for a unified Albanian vilayet within the Ottoman Empire. Germany and the Great Powers of Europe express an interest in the Albanian protests against San Stefano. The German ambassador encourages Albanian intellectuals for a powerful response through nationwide protests. Albanian activists form the Central Committee for the Defense of Albanian Nationality Rights, better known as the İstanbul Committee, after the Ottoman capital. The group proclaimed that it] "wish[es] no more than to live in peace with our neighbors . . . We do not desire and do not seek anything from them, but we are determined to defend that which belongs to us. All men should know that the Albanian lands shall belong to the Albanians."

As early as March of 1878, after the signing of the Treaty of San Stefano, the German opinion became aware of the Albanian discontent with the

---

[274] For more on the Treaty of San Stefano, see: Buxhovi, *Kongresi i Berlinit 1878*, 95.
[275] H.P.Sh. 2 (Tiranë), 148.

planned borders in the Balkans. A leading publication, *Hamburgischer Correspodent*, wrote on April 16[276] that the Albanians were greatly concerned with the announced partitioning of their country and are preparing to oppose the San Stefano terms by all means, including armed resistance. The newspaper gives an account of the situation in the Balkan Peninsula, noting the exacerbation anticipated if Europe were to ignore the Russian advance in the region. The harsh tone of the writing was nevertheless in line with the contemporary opinion in the German and European political circles, viewing Bulgaria's expansion as a *de facto* Russian occupation of the peninsula and a threat to the Western interests.[277] Therefore, the Hamburg-based daily shed light on the Albanian response as a means to garner support for the diplomatic offensive that Otto von Bismarck had so senationally began at the time. In cooperation with the Great Powers of Europe, the German chancellor devised a strategy to undermine the provisions of San Stefan, ultimately leading to a revision of the the peace treaty at a high-level meeting in the German capital. Diplomatic representatives in the Balkans, particularly the Reich's ambassador in İstanbul, Hasfield, and the consul in Athens, Brink, informed Bismarck and the German government of the Albanian activities ahead of the Congress of Berlin. The reports preserved in the Political Archive of the German Foreign Ministry in Bonn were most addressed to Bismarck personally, revealing that he was particularly interested to have the matter more widely publicized in the press, for the newspapers provided the only way of rationalizing—for domestic and foreign purposes—the slogan of "apparent war," on which the German leader hoped to rely on both ends. Imanuel Geis, an expect of the Bismarck era, notes that the chancellor was well-informed of developments in the most remote areas of the world and that he calculated political moves in accordance with the situation on the ground.[278] Most certainly, Bismarck had his loop on the Albanian response to the Treaty of San Stefano, too. As attested by archive documents, as early as April 6, he read an urgment note from Ambassador Hasfield, informing the chancellor that:

The Albanians have decided to unconditionally fight against the unjust decisions of San Stefano. It has been reported that prominent intellectuals in İstanbul and other parts of Europe drafted a comprehensive memorandum

---

[276] The article published in *Hamburgisher Correspodent* includes a brief historical narrative on the Albanians, noting that they are the oldest people of the Balkans and have inherited an ancient culture that has been buried by the century-long Ottoman occupation.

[277] Verner Knapp, *op. cit.*, 23.

[278] Imanuel Geis, 91.

to be delivered to the Great Powers of Europe once another decision is reached.[279]

Few days later, the German consul in Athens, Brink, also sent a secret telegram to the Reich's chancellor, informing him in details of the Albanian concerns about the San Stefano treaty and the possibility of an armed conflict. The communication, dated April 12, 1878, confirmed Hasfield's previous report, referring to engagements among Albanian circles in preparation of a decisive response to any claims against their ethnic territory. On the same day, Hasfield informed further that the Albanians were finalizing their preparations before forming local committees for territorial defense. Likewise, leaders of the movement demanded that the Porte recognize the Albanian nationality, a legal status that would also help prevent the partitioning of the country (for the Russian-backed neighbors could only annex Albanian lands as long as the ethnic group remained a part of the *millet-i osman*, which was seen as a foreign invader).[280]

---

[279] *Ibid.*

[280] Many authors contended that Bismarck, as host and presiding delegate at the Congress of Berlin, upon recepit of the numerous petitions the Albanians sent to the Congress, ostensibly asked, "Who are the Albanians when they represent only a geographic concept and nothing else?" Research, however, indicates no such statement or opinion in the protocols of the Congress of Berlin, including the originals and the reprint, Harald Bohold Verlag: Bopardt-Am-Rhein 1978, or Bismarck's selected works, *Die gesammeltern Verke*, vols. 1-12, Stolberg Verlag: Berlin 1924-32. The purported words were appeared in the works of Serbian and Greek historians for propaganda purposes; some Albanian writers have also accepted the assertion, using Serbian, Greek, or Russian literature, even though the complete protocols of the Congress of Berlin have been translated and published in Albanian. See: Buxhovi, Jusuf: *"Kongresi i Berlinit 1878"*, Prishtinë, 2008. Additionally, as quoted in an unverified political testatement attributed to the German chancellor, Bismarck stated, "There is no Albanian nationality, but a[n Albanian] millet" (Ger. *"Es gibt keine nationalität sondern nur Milet"*), which by no means could be interpreted as a denying the Albanians or politically disqualifying them. *See:* E. Fedler, "Bismarchs politisches Testament oder geheime preussisch-rurrische Vetrag" (Bismarck's Political Testament or the Secret Prusso-Russian Treaty), brochure, copy preserved at the Austrian National Library (ÖNB) in Vienna, cited in Eqrem Zenelaj, *Çështja shqiptare nga këndvështrimi i diplomacisë dhe gjeopolitikës së Austro-Hungarisë 1699-1918*, Prishtinë 2010, p. 171. The statement is simply an observation of the political reality, since at the time, the Albanians in the Ottoman Empire did not enjoy the status of a nationality, but were considered mostly as part of the *millet-i osman*. Although they continuously demanded that their nationality be recognized, the Porte refused to

In the meantime, German historian Peter Bartel cites a proclamation that the Central Committee for the Defense of Albanian Nationality Rights, better known as the İstanbul *Committee*, delivered to the Italian ambassador, Galioni:

> We wish no more than to live in peace with our neighbors—Serbs, Montenegrins, Bulgarians, Greeks, and others. We do not desire and do not seek anything from them, but we are determined to defend that which belongs to us. All men should know that the Albanian lands shall belong to the Albanians."[281]

Reporting on the Albanian activities ahead of the Congress of Berlin, *Kölnische Zeitung* warned that blood could once again flood the Balkans if the Great Powers were solely concerned with their own interests and failed to pay heed to those fighting for freedom and independence. "The recent events indicate what could become of the clashes and confrontations of the peoples who until yesterday fought against the common enemy—Turkey," says a newspaper article published in May. The item also appeals for aid to the Albanians that the Serbian army had forcibly expelled from their homes during the war.

Hasfield in İstanbul writes about the harsh conditions of the refugees. In a couple of reports on Albanians who had sought shelter in the eastern parts of the Ottoman Empire, the ambassador notes that the Porte was using the refuge crisis to pressure the Great Powers, not so much as to regain the lost territories but to defend Ottoman interests in the highly endangered European dominions of the state.

Despite such information from the German diplomatic services about the readiness of Albanians not to remain idle, and despite some dishonest writings on Albanians as victims of the Peace of San Stefano, published on the German Press of that time, from many archival and diplomatic sources it transpires that Bismarck's Germany would not do anything on the diplomatic and political campaign to review St Spehan, that Albanians in Berlin would would not be treated differently from the predetermined position, and that they would continue to be part of the Ottoman Empire.

Remaining within the Empire did not guarantee an autonomy, since this was in accordance with the interests of the Ottoman state and those of the then-spheres of interest. It was reasonable that Bismarck's Germany, which

---

do, fearing the move would lead to Albania's autonomy and ultimately independence from the empire.

[281] Peter Bartl, *Die Albanischen Muslime zur Zeit der Nationalen Unabhenigkeitsbewegund 1878-1912,* German translation cited in Galante, p. 117.

was aiming for a central position amongst the big powers, would not not care too much for Albania's autonomy, especially since the Reich did not see any particular interest in the Balkans. Bismarck as a mediator of peace was aiming for two things in Berlin: that Russia and its influence on the Balkans be removed as soon as possible, but without it having the impression of the loser on the peace table, and secondly, that Austria-Hungary's frontiers be widened further into the European territory of the Ottoman Empire, at a time when it was obvious that the latter was on the withdrawal. Bismarck was also thinking of Italy and its appetite as a new power, which would be kept away from the German spheres of interest, but which would hopefully be content with Africa and not the Balkans, even though it [Italy] would have liked to head towards Africa by "jumping" across the Adriatic and to Albania and the Dalmatian coast, which would touch upon Vienna's interests, and which Germany upheld with special care, since it viewed the Danubian monarchy as its first and closest ally.

Knowing that her time was also coming, Italy let Bismarck know that she was interested to win something in the Balkans, more concretely in Albania. During 1877 and 1878, Francesco Crispi, Head of the House of Italian deputies, responsible for matters of Balkan diplomacy, visited Berlin twice and met with Bismarck.[282]

In their first meeting, held on 17 September 1877 in Bad Gastein, while referring to a sort of Balkan balance, which would be acheived after Bosnia and Herzegovina would be given to Austria-Hungary, Bismarck said to Crispi that "perhaps a compromise could be achieved on Oriental matters, if you would throw yourself onto some Ottoman province in the Adriatic, as soon as Autria-Hungary took Bosnia."[283]

Crispi responds to Bismarck ironically: "A province in the Adriatic will not suffice for us. If we started this, we do not know where we will stop?"[301]

Also, the foreign minister of Italy, Tittoni, writes a telegram to the Italian ambassador to Berlin, Grof deLaunay, that:

The recent statements of Mr. Radovic, state secretary in the German Foreign Ministry in Berlin, that Italy, in case if Austria-Hungary takes Bosnia, will seek compensation in the form of Albania, are of great interest. It would be good if you could discover and find out the truth of these objectives, how sincere they

---

[282] Otto von Bismarck, *Die gesammelten Verke*, band. XI (Berlin: Stolberg Verlag, 1924-1932), 476.

[283] *Ibid.* 476.

are and to what degree they intend to prepare a quarrel between us and Vienna?[302]

Exactly at the time when the two countries were talking about the Adriatic, Francesco Crispi gave an interview to *Hamburgische Correspodent*, seeking the protection of the Albanians' interest. He would declare explicitly:

Albanians deserve, just like everyone else, the necessary degree of attention. In the European Turkey there are over 1.5 million Albanians, who never found a common language with the Gates. Also, Europe did not want to assist them in the fifteenth century to fight Turkey, and they pretty much remained alone in that endeavor. This must not be forgotten by us, because we left them to their own devices to fight off the Ottomans. So, they were amongst the first ones to fight, and their position in the last few centuries does not preclude them from deserving independence or national autonomy. The sunset of a people does not mean forgetting their rights. Italians should never forget who are the Albanians. Such forgetfulness would not be forgiven.

By wanting to justify its "neutrality," Bismarck's Germany officially tried to refuse the possibility of a secret sell-off with Italy, because this would devalue the authority of the peace broker, but would also harm certain interests in the wider context that [Germany] had with England and Turkey. The German Ambassador to Rome, Von Kendell, called Crispi's claims of conversations with Bismarck as untrue. "These are one-sided interpretations of the conversation and this remains a personal matter [of Crispi]," the Reich diplomat stated for the Italian press.

Precisely when some of Italy's hidden agendas began to emerge—and when Grof Andrássy, the eminent leader of the Austro-Hungarian diplomacy, made his objectives towards the Albanian issue,[284] Bismarck's cabinet received a confidential information from İstanbul. Hasfield wrote that:

---

[284] Andrássy's telegram to the Austro-Hungarian ambasador in Rome, Haymerle, dated April 26, 1878, best reflects Vienna's position on Albania, noting that:
We have neither the desire nor the money to annex Albania. It seems a much better solution for the province to become autonomous than to be occupied by a foreign country seeking to protect it from pan-Slavism. Thus, I wish to reiterate that we do not intend to annex Albania. To the contrary, we oppose the Montenegrin annexation of Tivar, for that threatens our trade on [the Adriatic] Sea. Likewise, we wish to protect the interests of Catholics in northern Albania and, in this aspect, we see eye to eye with Italy.

Albanians, regardless of religion, will get together to defend their lands and will allow noone to talk on their behalf. They will also try to get onto the tribunes of European speaker stands and wherever they are given an opportunity with the aim of defending their rights... from what I have learned from trusted people, Albanians will in this instance enjoy the support of the Gates, although it is not clear yet what this support will entail exactly.[285]

In regards to the warned actions of Albanians, Bismarck will be notified from the leaders of the national movement themselves. On 10 June, three days only before the commencement of the Berlin Congress, Albanians from İstanbul sent a telegram to the German Chancellor, expressing their dismay for not having been invited to this important European meeting like the rest:

Perhaps this is a mishap or lack of care, but we wish that this is rectified as soon as possible. Europe should know there is a place called Albania and there is an Albanian people that has its long and ancient traditions, culture and history. Therefore, we do not wish for our enemies to misinform the big powers that allegedly we are uncultured, barbarian and do not deserve attention. This is a big failure which was also done at the Peace of San Stefano and which we would not like to be repeated. We therefore hope that our cause will not be forgotten.[286]

The telegram holds the signature of Vaso Pasha, Omer Vrioni and others.

---

[285] PA AA, Türkei, band. 143.
[286] *Ibid.*, band. 134.

CHAPTER 5

THE ALBANIAN LEAGUE AND THE CONGRESS OF BERLIN

The Founding of the Albanian League of Prizren

The Albanians mobilize to defend the homeland, demanding autonomy. Three currents define the national movement: the radicals, calling for autonomy; moderates who support the defense of the Albanian lands but sought no self-governance, maintaining that the latter is a matter for the sultan to decide; and sultanists, opposing any type of autonomy or calls for an Albanian vilayet. The Ottoman Empire wishes to undermine the Treaty of San Stefano. Did the Ottoman Empire and the İstanbul Committee see eye to eye on the founding of the League and its demands? The constituent Convention of the League of Prizren is held on June 10, 1878; the body approves a basic act and a writ on the military and governing institutions.

The Albanians were the most heavily burdened from the Russo-Ottoman Peace Treaty of San Stefano. The situation created the urge for Albanians to act in unison regardless of their political beliefs or opinion on the future of the Ottoman Empire; the imperative was for the ethnic group to rise as a political factor vis-à-vis the Ottoman Empire and the international community. Despite the unfortunate peace agreement, the time was conducive, for the Albanians were not the only ones to oppose San Stefano. Besides the Albanians and the Ottoman Empire, the Great Powers of Europe also viewed the peace deal disapprovingly and insisted that it be nullified, even though they had remained indifferent to the Russo-Ottoman war the agreement concluded. Meanwhile, calls for military action became increasingly as Albanian prepared to fight against unfavorable decision the announced Congress of Berlin could take in review of the San Stefano document. Demands to create an All-Albanian organization also became very popular, since the move would also be in line with official policy of the Porte. The Ottoman Empire was interested to use the upcoming European congress to lighten the burden imposed by the peace treaty with the Russians. Moreover, the Porte hoped to rely on the Great Powers of Europe, whose rivalry with the Russians tipped the scale in favor of the Ottomans, determined to oppose the Treaty of San Stefano by all means and to the greatest extent. Therefore, any protest and any program, including the Albanian military plan for the defense of the homeland—here, *vatan*, the equivalent Ottoman term, could mean both, Albania, as the ethnic territory consisting of the four vilayets, and the entire Ottoman Empire in the broader sense. For the first time, nationalism and Ottomanism became compatible ideologies, providing an impetus for patriotism.

A sense of unity swept through despite its largely incongruent components. For example, many Albanians regarded defending the empire as a way to protect the Albanian lands from partitioning. This legitimized the so-called Ottoman or even Islamic patriotism, including nevertheless the *ethnic patriotism*. Sami Frashëri had viewed this latter element as a necessary expression of one's national identity within the empire, stimulating hence Ottoman identity for as long as this state identity allowed for the Albanian autonomy within the empire.[287]

Under the circumstances, Albanian patriots represented by the İstanbul Committee—the short-name for the Committee for Protecting the Rights of the Albanian Nationality—espoused the radical-wing ideas for an all-Albanian league. This political organization would mobilize the population in the name of the national rights of Albania and would lead a war to preserve the territorial integrity of the homeland. The plan included demands for an autonomous Albanian vilayet or, if international circumstances, an autonomous state that could be also called Ottoman Albania.[288] Proponents of these ideas further envisioned preparations for war not only against the neighboring states but, if need were to arise, the Ottoman Empire, too.[289]

In addition to the radical group, there was a second faction in the national movement. Known as moderates, this section included prominent patriots, such as Ali Pashë Gucia, Iliaz Pashë Dibra, Abedin Pashë Dino, Mahumd Pashë Biçoku, Omer Pashë Vrioni, and others. Like their radical counterparts, moderates insisted on a national character of the League. They

---

[287] For more on this topic, see Gawrych, *Gjysmëhëna . . .* , 11-17.
[288] H.P.Sh. 2 (Tiranë), 150.
[289] *Ibid.* 150.

agreed on principle on a united Albanian vilayet with administrative and cultural autonomy, but without a gateway to a sovereign state. The moderates were not inclined to oppose the Sublime Porte, because they hoped that the Albanian vilayet could be created with the sultan's approval. The centrist group believed that the sovereign would be willing to grant the Albanians their autonomy, for the creation of the autonomous vilayet was in favor of the Ottoman Empire itself.[290]

Besides radicals and moderates, there was a third group, known as the sultanists. This faction consisted of employees and senior official of the vilayet administrations, native landowners, and imams who self-identified as Turks. The faction views itself as part of the imperial ruling class, fully supported the policies of the Porte and served the imperial government's interests. The sultanists joined the Albanian movements under direct instructions from the sultan and demanded that the resistance organization be called the *Islamic League*.[291] In addition, the pro-sultan wing objected the idea of an Albanian vilayet, claiming that such an entity would divide Muslim Albanians from their Muslims "brothers" elsewhere in the Balkan Peninsula or the Ottoman Empire.[292] This creator of this political current was precisely Sultan Abdul Hamid II, who pursued a policy of "unity" for all Muslims. The head of state, furthermore, focused his plan on the Balkans and the Albanians, whom he presented as the *flower of the empire*.[293] Having earned this distinction from their emperor, Muslims Albanians were called upon to preserve the caliphate's presence in its European dominions. Indeed, Abdul Hamid's efforts reached a degree of success as the sultanist faction remained active throughout. Most notably, it was influential in introducing—at least in formal terms—declarations of loyalty to the sultan in Albanian political documents, from the *Kararname* (*i.e.*, basic act) of the Albanian League of Prizren in 1878 to a 14-point political program of August 1912.

To avoid factional strife, the İstanbul Committee decided to direct its efforts for an all-Albanian league under the calls against the Treaty of San Stefano. To oppose the peace agreement, the committee appealed on all groups without distinction to brace for war to halt the portioning of the homeland. This marked a great achievement in the internal plan since for the first time Albanianism and Ottomanism appeared as compatible ideologies.

---

[290] *Ibid.* 150.

[291] *Ibid.* 151.

[292] *Ibid.* 151.

[293] For more, see Buxhovi, *Nga Shqipëria Osmane te Shqipëria Evropiane.*

Albanian leaders brought the new values that gave their ethnic community social, political, and cultural credibility that lasted in the Ottoman state until the final withdrawal of the empire from the Balkans. Likewise, the Albanian unity sent the upcoming Berlin Congress a strong message in favor of nullifying the Stan Stefano agreement. Leaders of the İstanbul Committee used the European press to present their views. Abdyl Frashëri, for instance, wrote in the *Messager de Vienne* in support of the political rights of his people, stating that the Albanians desired no more that to live free, to come out of backwardness, and claim the place it deserves among the civilized nations of Europe.

Since there was limited time for preparation before the Congress of Berlin convened, the İstanbul Committee held a meeting to decide on the formation of a national league. The Committee reportedly gathered in a "top secret" fashion,[294] allegedly not to cause a reaction by the authorities. Mem-

---

[294] Many Albanian historians, including members of the History Institute of the Albanian Academy of Sciences, repeatedly note that the İstanbul Committee met "in conditions of compete secrecy" to decide on the formation of the League; see H.P.Sh. [History of the Albanian People], vol. 2 (Tiranë), 153. This position not only lacks a solid argumentation, but is disparate with the logic of events. The Ottoman Empire was highly interested in the Albanian response. Multiple sources refer to protest rallies held in towns, such as Prishtina, Shkup, and Shkodër, against the Treaty of San Stefano. The *valis* (*i.e.*, heads of vilayets) of Kosova and Shkodër held ongoing meetings with the leadership of the country and called for resistance committees. As a result, many volunteers had publicly signed up to defend the Albanian territories. The European press, and the German papers in particular, links the protests to the Ottoman authorities, since the Porte and the Albanians shared a common interest—that is, to defend the Ottoman territories from partitioning. Multiple authors—Bartl, *Die Albanishe Muslime zur Zeit der nacionale Unabhenigkeitsbewegung 1878-1912* (Wisbaden: 1968); Hans Diter Schanderl, *Die Albanienpolitik Österreich-Ungarns und Italien 1877-1902* (1950); Spiridon Gopčević, *Oberalbanien und seine Liga* (Leipzig: 1881); Ippen, "Beitrege zur innere Geschihte Albanien im XIX Jahrhundert," published in *Illyrisch-Albanische Firschungen* 1, (München-Leipzig: 1916); Skëndi, *Zgjimi kombëtar shqiptar*; Gawrych, *Gjysmëhëna dhe shqiponja*; Josef von Hamer, *Istorija Otomanskog Carstva* (Zagreb: 1968); et al.—assert that the İstanbul Committee maintained ongoing contacts with the Sublime Porte on the organization of the Albanian response, including the formation of the Albanian League of Prizren, which was far from being a "secret." The move came as an open manifestation and had the support of the Muslim clergy, which strongly propagated the League at all the time. The efforts also drew the attention of foreign diplomats. Documents from German, Austrian, and French consuls in Shkodër, Prizren, and Shkup are now preserved at the Political Archive of the German Foreign Ministry, in boxes labeled *Türkei*, 143 and 124, which also include reports from the contemporary press on Albania.

bers of the group agreed to call a constituent Convention, which would also finalize the Albanian position and the arguments to be presented before the Great Powers of Europe. But that the meeting was indeed clandestine has been disputed because overt and demonstrative efforts favored the Albanians and the Ottoman Empire as well as the European powers that were displeased with the Treaty of San Stefano. The Porte, in fact, was quite interested in an organized reaction among the Albanians. At the end of May 1878, the Ottoman government summoned to Constantinople notable leaders, such as Iliaz Pashë Dibra, Ali Pashë Gucia, Ymer Prizreni, Ahmet Korenica, Zija Prishtina, Mustafa Pashë Vlora, Sheh Mustafë Tetova, Vejsel Bej Dino, and dozens of others, including Abdyl Frashëri and Mehmet Ali Vrioni, as representatives of the İstanbul Committee, and members of the Ottoman parliament. German sources note that "the Sublime Porte and Albanian representatives, titularies of the vilayets of Kosova and Shkodër, agreed on a vigorous response in the affected territories."[295]

Therefore, it was not coincidental that Prizren was chosen to host the Convention. The Vilayet of Kosova, directly affected by the planned territorial cessions to Serbia and Montenegro, had for some time become the nucleus of protests from all social categories. Conservative landlords, moderate city dwellers, clergymen, and others had all embraced the patriotic slogan of "defending the *vatan*," which meant defending Albania and the Ottoman Empire simultaneously.

To organize the League's constituent Convention, the İstanbul Committee appointed a special commission, whose members were mainly from Prizren and Gjakova. Ymer Prizreni was chosen as chairman of the commission, while other

---

The idea of "clandestine" preparations for the Albanian League of Prizren, along with the "revolutionary" spirit of the League and other events of the Albanian movement leading to independence in 1912, is a remnant of the ideological clichés and the folkloric pathos that has overwhelmed the Albanian historiography (developed in Albania under the communist regime and partly in Kosova, then under the influence of the earlier). This position of Albanian historians survives to this day and appears in the revised 2002 edition of H.P.Sh. (see *supra*).

[295] See telegram to Chancellor Bismarck by German ambassador to İstanbul, no. 1276, Political Archive of the German Foreign Ministry, Türkei, band. 143, dated July 2, 1878. The communication was sent as a classified dépêche, giving details on the meetings of Porte officials with Albanian representatives from the Vilayet of Kosova and leaders of the İstanbul Committee, which the telegram says was formed with the permission of the Ottoman government as the Committee for Protecting the Rights of the Albanians.

prominent members included Ahmet Korenica and Ali Pashë Gucia. The latter, a popular landlord and patriot, at that time still known as Ali Bej Gucia, issued the first call for the constituent Convention by the end of April.

The constituent Convention or assembly of the League held its opening session on June 10, 1878, in the Mehmet Pasha Madrasa (*i.e.*, Islamic secondary school), located by the famous Bajrak Mosque in Prizren. Besides the venue, the date was not coincidental since the League founders rushed to meet before the opening of the Congress of Berlin, three days later on June 13. Sources on the first session of the Convention are scarce for only a part of the authentic protocols have survived. Nevertheless, it is established that 110 delegates of the several Albanian provinces were present in the meeting with two major exceptions: there were no representatives from the Vilayet of Shkodër (while it has been held that the Turkish *vali*, Hüseyin Pasha, conspired to prevent the delegates' participation, the absence is a more intricate subject) and Abdyl Frashëri was the only delegate for the Vilayet of Janina. From those present, the majority were from leading Tanzimât opponents the Vilayet of Kosova, such as Ali Pashë Gucia, Iliaz Pashë Dibra, Hasan Pashë Tetova, Ymer Prizreni, Abdullah Pashë Dreni, Ahmet Korenica, Shaban Bej Prizreni, Jashar Bej Shkupi, Shaban Bej Peja, Filip Doda, Sulejman Vokshi, Shuajip Spahiu, Ali Ibra, and others. Landlords from Bosnia-Hercegovina, and the Turkish mutessarif of Prizren, Kamil Bey, and sultanists also attended the Convention. Kamil Bey's active role, in particular, adds to reports by foreign diplomats about the events entirely disprove the contentions that the League was formed "clandestinely." It is practically impossible that the Ottoman government was unaware of the movement when agents of the Porte were involved as extensively as delegates of the League Convention.

Despite their limited content, surviving documents point out other inconsistencies in Albanian historiography. While Albanian authors emphasize that Abdyl Frashëri spoke at the Convention either as "president" or "presiding delegate" of the League, the noted activist actually spoke on behalf of the İstanbul Committee. In the opening session, the delegates elected Iliaz Pashë Dibra as President of the Convention.[296] Furthermore, it has been held that Abdyli Frashëri presented a political program in his speech, including his statement that "the goal of the Convention is to halt the advance of our soulless enemies by pledging the Albanian *besa* and swearing to defend with our

[296] See Rexhep Krasniqi, *Die Albanische Liga* (Wien: 1934), a doctorate dissertation at the University of Vienna, deposited at the library of Südost Institut in Munich, Germany; Ippen, "Beitrege zur innere Geschihte Albaniens im XIX jahrundert."

blood the lands [inherited] from our grand- and great-grandfathers."[297] A partial transcript of Frashëri's address at the assembly contradicts the mainstream position, reflecting rather a patriotic call similar to what the foreign consuls describe as the slogan of all participants, regardless of political orientation.[298]

The most important point, however, has to do with the decisions of the Convention. The delegates agreed to form a political-military organization, a League (Trk.: *İttifak*) for the defense of the country. The entity would have a central leadership in Prizren and affiliate offices in all the provinces of Albania. In accordance with the Albanian tradition, the delegates also declared a general *besa* (an Albanian word meaning trust, covenant, or faith), which instituted a moratorium on all blood-feuds in the provinces represented at the Prizren assembly.[299] On this occasion, the delegates also elected the governing bodies of the League. A Prizren-based General Council, under the leadership of Iliaz Pashë Dibra, was appointed to oversee the provincial structures. A Central Committee of the League was also founded, consisting of three specialized committees: Abdyl Frashëri headed a committee on the foreign affairs, Haxhi Shabani supervised internal or home affairs, and Sulejman Vokshi was put in charge of the finances.[300]

The first acts of the General Council included petitions to the Congress of Berlin and the Sublime Porte,[301] the *Kararname* (*Trk.*, literally "book of decisions"; often referred to as the "basic act" or the *Kanun* of the League)

---

[297] Xhafer Belegu, *Lidhja Shqiptare e Prizrenit dhe veprimtaria e saj 1878-1881* (Tiranë: 1939), 20.

[298] See reports of the German embassy in İstanbul sent to Berlin, PA AA, Türkei, band. 143, reports 26-31, July 1878. The reports contain information provided by the embassy's informants in Prizren during the Convention.

[299] H.P.Sh. 2 (Tiranë), 155.

[300] *Ibid.* 156.

[301] Albanian historians—see: H.P.Sh. 2 (Tiranë), p. 156—note that the League sent a petition to the Sublime Porte, requesting the unification of the Albanian lands in a single, unified vilayet (*Tevhidi vilayet*), which would have a "unified assembly" serving the vilayet's government, a unified administration, a separate budget and military—hence a demand for administrative and cultural autonomy—is nowhere located in the documents of the League. It is likely that the petition was sent by the İstanbul Committee to representatives of the Great Powers in Constantinople, but without a reference to the Convention of Prizren. Such a document is found in the Political Archive of the German Foreign Ministry, among petitions and letters sent to the Congress of Berlin (Türkei, 143).

and the *Talimât* (*Trk.*, writ, ordinance).[302] The *Kararname* consisted of sixteen articles, sanctioning the formation of the League as an Albanian political organization (Art. 16) and describing its most urgent responsibilities. Article 1 specified the League's defensive character vis-à-vis any government, except for the Sublime Porte, and endorsed the active defense and by all means of the country's integrity.[303] Through Article 4, the delegates agreed, "pursuant to the sublime laws of the Sharia, we shall defend the lives and honor of non-Muslim loyal friends as we protect our own."[304] This apparently gives the League an Islamic character, which was an inevitable element under the circumstances. However, the religious stipulation did cause for the League to abandon its Albanian essence. During its existence, particularly after 1880, the League pursued a policy of tolerance and national unity in line with the thoughts of *Rilindja* intellectuals, defining hence the national program that led to Albania's independence decades later.

Indeed, the League was deprived of its national in the June Convention. Delegates present approved no demands for the unification of the four vilayets, which would enable a type of autonomy for Albania and afford it protection in light of the threatened partitioning from all sides. The tide shifted on July 1, however, as the General Council of the League held its first session with ninety-six delegates representing Kosova, twenty-six from the Vilayet of Shkodër, and twenty from Janina. The General Council approved a resolution or the New Kanun, taking important steps in refining the national program of the League. The new document defined the organization as an *Albanian League* and re-named the central governing body to *National Committee*.[305]

The New Kanun or basic act was void of the religious formulas and provisions declaring loyalty to the Ottoman Empire, which were included in the *Kararname*. The new instrument explicitly stated that the League would fight for the Albanian national rights and limited the organization's activity to the Albanian lands. The New Kanun delegates the National Committee the right to form subcommittees of the League in the administrative centers of Albanian sanjaks, to organize an armed force for the defense of Albania, and to declare military mobilization of all men fit for service. The National Committee was also given the power to levy various taxes to cover its needs and to

---

[302] *Ibid.* 156.

[303] See *Kararname*, reproduced in its entirety in Pollo, Pulaha, eds., *Akte të Rilindjes Kombëtare Shqiptare 1878-1912* (Tiranë: 1878), 40-41.

[304] *Ibid.* 41.

[305] H.P.Sh. 2, 160.

mandate criminal penalties for those who deserted from the Albanian League. In other words, the scope of the New Kanun virtually created the conditions for the League to assume the functions of a national government.[306]

The General Council passed the New Kanun on July 2, 1878, marking a great victory for the Albanian national movement within the League of Prizren. In reality, the rights provided in the document set the legal foundation for Albania to gradually become a state within the Ottoman Empire.[307]

Congress of Berlin: A European Response to Slavic Hegemonism in the Balkans

The Treaty of San Stefano threatens the international equilibrium in favor of Russian Pan-Slavism with a Greater Bulgaria to serve as Russia's right-hand man in the Balkans. While all of the Great Powers of Europe object to the Treaty, Great Britain expresses the most radical dissent, threatening war against Russia. Germany avails itself as a mediator between the exacerbated Great Powers. Bismarck undertakes a mission to Russia, convincing Saint Petersburg to agree on a new congress in Berlin. Twenty sessions are held from June 13 to July 13, 1878 in the Reich Chancellor building on Wilhelmstrasse. Bismarck presides over the Congress, while the Marquess of Salisbury leads the English delegation, Shuvalov and Gorchakov head the Russians, the Ottomans are led by Sadullah Bey and Mehmed Ali Pasha (Magyar Pasha), and the Austro-Hungarians appoint Foreign Minister Andrássy as their chief negotiator; France and Italy send their teams, too. Peoples seeking autonomy or independence are invited to send representatives to observe at the Congress, but Bismarck bypasses the Albanians on the pretense that they were part of the Ottoman nationality. At the 13th session of the Congress, held on July 5, participants discuss the local autonomy of the Catholic population of Mirdita; after a lengthy exchange of opinions with the French and English diplomats, Sadullah Bey proposes a compromise solution, including the Porte's commitment not alter what he calls Mirdita's "privileged" status. The Congress recognizes Serbia's independence and annexation of Albanian territories occupied during the Russo-Ottoman war. Montenegro is also awarded Plava, Gucia, and Tivar.

---

[306] See: The *Talimat* of the League, mandating the organization of the administration and the military, reproduced in *"Akte të Rilindjes Kombëtare Shqiptare 1878-1912"*, p. 40.

[307] H.P.Sh. 2, 161.

For the peoples of Europe, the Congress of Berlin of 1878 marks the great historic event that defined the political landscape for many decades. Until then, "the ongoing decline of the Ottoman Empire, on the brink of its inevitable collapse and the rise of Germany and Italy as new powers provided for a continued international balance."[308] The equilibrium fell through after Russia reached a victory over Turkey in 1877 and the parties hastily signed the Treaty of San Stefano, in March 1878. The terms of the agreement provided for a state of Bulgaria, whereas Russia was designated to oversee the state-forming process. But the Greater Bulgaria envisioned at San Stefano was evidently tailored to be Russia's right-hand man in the Balkans, giving the czar control over the most sensitive part of the peninsula, securing also an outlet to the Mediterranean Sea, the historical confluence of the East and the West.[309] This had been an ancient desire of the Russians, for the region was essentially the world's geostrategic nerve. But just as the San Stefano agreement was a cause for jubilation at Saint Petersburg, so it was an urge for categorical protest among other European capitals. The British Empire, so deeply involved in the Middle East and in pursuit of new naval routes to India, was severely concerned of a Russian fleet in Mediterranean waters.[310] Meanwhile, Austria-Hungary and Italy felt the Pan-Slavic victory as an end to their hopes of influence in the Balkans.[311]

The peoples of the peninsula, thus, were not alone in their disappointment with the Treaty of San Stefano, as the Great Powers also voiced their objections. So vigorous was European opposition such that England vowed to fight the Russians over the peace deal, threatening to bring other states into combat, too.[312] Fear of war urged European leaders to insist on an international meeting, where the Great Powers could discuss at length on the pressing issues. German diplomacy became the most active, mediating in almost all cases from efforts to ease tensions to preparations of a high-level congress of the Great Powers. In addition to the delegations of Russia, the Ottoman Empire, England, Austria-Hungary, Italy, and France, the event would gather the representatives of peoples fighting for national independence. The

[308] Karl Otmar, *Bismarcks Aussenpolitik und der Berliner Kongres* (Wiesbaden: 1978), 7.

[309] Verner Knap, *Der Berliner Kongres* (Wiesbaden: 1978), 13.

[310] *Ibid.* 15.

[311] Karl Otmar, *Bismarcks . . .*, 19.

[312] Klaus-Detlev Gothusen, "Die Oreintalische Frage als Problem der europeische Geschiht," *Südosteuropa Mitteilungen* 4-78: p. 4.

latter, nevertheless, would not be at the Congress as decision-makers, but as observers of the decision-making process. Bismarck, who had until then contributed so much for the unity and prosperity of the new German Empire, was now faced with a difficult task. The primary challenge was to reconcile, to the greatest extent possible, the emerging disagreements and conflict between the Great Powers. Meanwhile, it also fell on the German chancellor to ruthlessly undermine the Treaty of San Stefano. Bismarck was determined to keep Russia from Europe while keeping the Great Powers from war and unrest.[313]

Metaphorically, Bismarck's plan has been compared to "grilling the perfect steak" for the high flames of tensions among the Great Powers threatened to burn any hopes for an agreement. Through the chancellor's swift mediations, Germany assumed the role of an *ehrlicher Makler* (*Ger.*, honest broker) between the Powers. The German strongman explained:

> The Germans had no direct interest in the Balkans or further, at a time when we still had domestic problems, but we were nevertheless worried about what was taking place around and could affect us. Russia was deeply involved in the Balkans, causing Austria-Hungary to protest repeatedly and to begin pushing England to form an alliance against the Russians. Italy, constantly observing the developments and ready to create trouble at any moment, was also distressed. France, albeit somehow impacted by the recent events, paid attention to the developing situation and did not approve of the new status quo being so one-sidedly slanted in Russia's favor. Thus, indications were clear that the Great Powers could horrendously clash among themselves and the conflict would, willingly or unwillingly, include Germany, which was not interested in entering into any conflicts. Therefore, who else besides us would assume the role of a reconciliatory? We were the only [power] that had no involvement in the Balkans of the Near East. Hence, the burden fell on us to prepare such a meeting, where for the first time talks would be held so that a conflict among the Great Powers would not happen.[314]

As such, Germany was indeed the best-situated country to help maintain the balance, while Bismarck, as the most energetic of the leaders, was well suited to mediate talks between the frenzied Powers.[315] Of course, assuming

---

[313] Otmar, *Bismacks . . .*, 21.

[314] Emil Ludwig, *Bismarck* (Wilhelm Goldman Verlag, 1926), 27.

[315] In June 1878, an international symposium was held in Meinz, Germany, to discuss "The Congress of Berlin and the Eastern Crisis." The scholarly event gathered over sixty experts from Europe and Asia, who viewed Bismarck's Germany as the most favorable venue for the

the role was not an light decision for the Germans. Emil Ludwig, a prominent expert on Bismarck and the Berlin Congress, Emil Ludwig, notes "the circumstances at the time were such as to require a powerful personality, who could diplomatically subdue Russia and shift the balance of power in favor of Russian opponents. This task required excellence in diplomacy and Bismarck was the only who would carry it."[316]

From March to June 1878, as Europe was gripped by a diplomatic fever leading to the Congress of Berlin, Bismarck became the central figure of the preliminary talks between the Great Powers. Using diplomatic channels, the German chancellor attempted to clarify and harmonize the positions of the parties well before the high-level meeting.[317] History sources speak of success. After the Treaty of San Stefano was signed in late March, the Russians categorically refused all British requests for a revision of the agreement. As England threatened war, other Powers, including Austria-Hungary and France, suggested their own resolutions to the crisis. One notable proposal came from Vienna on March 26. Previously, the Austro-Hungarians had ratified two important documents relating to Russia: a Reichstadt Agreement in 1876 and a Convention signed with the Russians on January 15, 1877. The Convention provided, *inter alia*, that in case the Ottoman Empire withdrew from the Balkans, three independent countries—Bulgaria, Rumelia, and Albania—be created in the peninsula. German sources are not clear on the Albanian issue because the Russian-Austrian agreement uses *self-governance* and *autonomy*, terms also employed by foreign ministers Gulya Andrássy and Alexander Gorchakov.[318] In other words, the Powers worked to undo the San Stefano deal. However, recognizing that the Russians could not be taken back to their antebellum position, the European states did not seek to deny the Slavic gains, but endeavored to limit the extent and strategic influence of the new czarist expansion. Ultimately, fearing that war against a potential Austro-Hungarian, French, and British alliance, Saint Petersburg did give in to pressure for direct talks. Indicating its willingness to negotiate the Treaty of San Stefano, Russia nevertheless claimed an important role in the European diplomatic

symposium. Following the victory over the Ottoman Empire, the Russians agreed to come to Berlin because they believed that Germany, while not an ally, was certainly not against them. This was the opinion of many scholars, including Verner Knopp, Teodor Schider, and Looar Gall.

[316] Ludwig, *op. cit.*, 36.

[317] Detlev Albers, *Reichstag und Aussenpolitik 1871-1879*, 101.

[318] For more, see Bartl, *Die Albanische Muslims* . . . and Schanderl, *Die albanienpolitik* . . . .

scene. In May, Prime Minister Pyotr Shuvalov travelled to Berlin twice within two weeks. There, he entrusted Bismarck to organize the international meeting that would revise the post-war affairs.[319] Days later, Count Shuvalov received a British delegation in Saint Petersburg, reassuring Queen Victoria's envoys of the upcoming congress. By the end of the month, Austria-Hungary, too, announced its proposal on the final settlement of the Eastern Question.[320]

Diplomacy was having its say. The Great Powers of Europe were able to rely on mediation and talks, facing off the threat of war with the willingness to curtail their demands well in advance of the Congress of Berlin. As the Europeans reach an understanding, the agenda for the high-level meeting narrowed down to the actual signing of the agreements and discussions on lateral matters that, regardless of their consequences, would not hinder the negotiations. The essence of the deal was this: Russia agreed to give up its planned presence in the Balkans and to keep the Ottoman Empire in Europe. The underpinning concern, however, was to buy some time before the Europeans finally decided on how to split the dominions that for five centuries had belonged to the Bosphorus sultanate. The British were particularly active in the weeks leading to the Congress. London insisted in resolving major issues in its relations with Saint Petersburg and İstanbul, while also seeking to clarify the situation in the Balkans. On May 30, after several mediations by the German, French, and (to a lesser extent) Italian diplomats, Shuvalov met the British foreign secretary, Lord Salisbury. At this historic summit, the Russians surrendered to the British demands to revise the Peace of San Stefano,[321] shunning the menace of a war between the two empires.[322] Now that the Powers opened way to understanding, subsequent events became more of a formality, but the Congress of Berlin would be remembered in history for, like never before, European leaders met face-to-face to define the affairs of the age.

On June 3, the German hosts invited the five other Great Powers of Europe and the Ottoman Empire to attend the Congress of Berlin, due to begin

---

[319] Otmar, *Bismarcks . . .*, 10.

[320] According to Graf Andrássy, foreign minister of Austria-Hungary, Bulgaria was to receive only a small portion of the territory awarded by the Treaty of San Stefano; Russia was obligated to withdraw from that part of Bulgaria, whose borders would be determined by the Congress of Berlin, while Serbia and Montenegro would be allowed minor territorial expansions. See *Berliner Kongres 1878* (Wiesbaden: Harald Bohland Verlag, 1978), 15.

[321] *Ibid.* 16.

[322] *Ibid.* 16.

in ten days.[323] Invitations to the gathering were also sent to representatives of many Balkan and Middle Eastern peoples fighting for independence[324] to appear at the Congress as observers. The organizers of the historic occasion, however, did not summon any representatives of the Albanian people. Indeed, such a move was not excepted because the Ottoman Empire considered the Albanians as part of the Ottoman nationality, not as a distinct ethnic community. The treatment persisted even though a group of İstanbul-based intellectuals had begun to press on the issue, for the Ottoman government insisted that any recognition of an Albanian nationality. Meanwhile, the League of Prizren also failed to make any calls on behalf of the Albanian nationality during the early days of the organization. Formed only three days before the Congress, the League was determined to prevent the partitioning of the Albanian lands, but made no demands for autonomy within the Ottoman Empire. It was not until later into the Congress that the League confronted both the European Powers and the Ottomans.[325]

The lack of an invitation to Berlin makes it worth noting an ambiguity or intentional misinformation that appears in modern Albanian publications. The 2002 edition of *Historia e Popullit Shqiptar II*—a comprehensive history of the Albanian people, authored by the History Institute of the Albanian Academy of Sciences—remarks:

> The Albanian delegation, headed by Abdyl Frashëri, who had travelled [to Berlin] to present before the Great Powers assembled in Congress the petition with the demands of the Assembly of the League of Prizren, had returned from Berlin [and was now attending] the session of the League's General Council on July 1, 1878.[326]

---

[323] *Ibid.* 17.

[324] *Ibid.* 17.

[325] Bartl, *Die Albanischen Muslime . . .*, 116.

[326] This misinformation could not be a mistake due to ignorance of the facts; likely, the false statement was made to strengthen the "anti-European and anti-German spirit" that a part of the Albanian historiography has cultivated for ideological purposes, relying heavily on the intentional fabrications of Serbian historians, such as Hađi-Vasiljević and Gopčević. It is well established that Abdyl Frashëri and Mehmet Ali Vrioni travelled to Berlin in May 1879 (hence a year after); while at the Roma Hotel, the two leaders mailed the Albanian Memorandum to State Secretary Bülow, who received it two days later. Thus, Frashëri and Vrioni did not even meet with a German officials who honored the Ottoman ambassador's

Despite the manipulative insinuations that continue to this day, the League eventually pursued efforts for a unified vilayet and the autonomy of Albania to an extent that cannot be ignored. Meanwhile, as the Ottoman Empire counted its final days in the old continent, the Albanians were to become an inevitable factor in the political plans of the European Powers.

For instance, England instructed Lord Edmond Fitzmaurice to demand that the Porte unite the Albanian vilayets into a single entity. Pursuant to the Berlin agreement, the British plan was to create an autonomous Albanian territory under the suzerainty of the sultan. In 1880, the so-called International Commission for the Reforms, overseeing the implementation of domestic changes the Porte had committed to, held a gathering in the Ottoman capital. Speaking at the Constantinople conference on April 20, Lord Fitzmaurice conveyed a message from Lord Beaconsfield that it was in Europe's best interest to see Albania as a strong autonomous entity. Hanns Dieter Schanderl, author of a book on the Austro-Hungarian and Italian involvement in Albanian affairs from 1877 to 1908, emphasizes the British statement as an important signal on the way to Albania's statehood.[327] Citing a document of the London Foreign Office, dated May 26, 1880, Schanderl notes that Lord Fitzmaurice reiterated the British position once more in a meeting with the Ottoman foreign minister, Sava Pasha, handing him a memorandum on an autonomous Albanian vilayet.[328]

Nonetheless, Ottoman diplomats also spoke on behalf of the Albanians as Ottoman nationals. The protocols of several séances[329] of the Congress indicate the role of Alexander Karatheodori Pasha and Mehmed Ali Pasha during talks on the Serbian and Montenegrin annexations of Albanian-inhabited lands and the Greek claims on Epirus and Thessaly. The Porte's delegates presented the Albanian concerns as those of other Ottoman subjects—i.e., members of the *millet-i osman*, who did not wish to become a bargaining chip between foreign states. Notably, on day tenth of the Congress, Karatheodori Pasha refused to cede the city of Tivar to Montenegro, warning the Powers not to alter the border of Albania. He explained that "[t]he Porte has no objections over Spica, but insists that Tivar is Albanian [and] that

---

request that Albanians representatives be paid no official attention. For more on the topic, see Buxhovi, *Kongresi . . .*, 58-59.

[327] Schanderl, *Die Albanienpolitik . . .*, 47.

[328] *Ibid.*

[329] The protocols pertain to the seventh, eighth, tenth, twelfth, and thirteenth meetings of the Congress of Berlin.

the Montenegrin may remain there only by violence and against the will of the Albanian population." Karatheodori further noted that the Ottoman government had received disturbing telegrams on ongoing clashes between Albanians and Montenegrins. Furthermore, on the twelfth session, Mehmed Ali Pasha requests that the Albanian areas of Plava, Gucia, and Tivar be kept within their ethnic compound, asking the delegates whether it would not be a better solution to prevent peoples of different races and cultures from unnecessarily under the rule of a foreign race. For that reason, Mehmed Ali recommended that, instead of being awarded Albanian lands, Montenegro annex territories whose population is of the same race and mainly of the same religion with the Montenegrins. The Ottoman representative suggested ceding the communities of Kuçi and Drekalović and the Moraça (Srb.: Morača) basin all the way to Lake Scutari. But he insisted that the Albanian areas of Plava and Gucia as well as the city of Podgorica be retained under Turkish rule, along with a sufficient territory for defense purposes. Mehmed Ali applied the same argument in rejecting demands that the city of Tivar be cut off from Albania. Similarly, in the thirteenth meeting, Karatheodori Pasha reminded the participants that the population of Epirus and Thessaly was not made of Greeks alone as Hellenic, French, and Russian delegates had contended. At the meeting, Karatheodori cited three petitions from the local population of the contested areas.[330] In the register of communications sent to the Congress, the three petitions are described as Albanian responses against the partitioning of their land.[331]

While participants of the Congress spoke of the Albanians, the references still considered the ethnic group as part of the *millet-i osman*. This had led a German historian, Peter Bartle, to conclude that "not only were the Albanians not invited to the Congress of Berlin, which decided on their fate; they had no advocate to speak the least on their behalf." This indicates that the Ottoman representatives were mandated to defend the Albanian vilayets in order to cede less of their territory; to do so, they emphasized *Albania* as an ethnic entity, but avoided any implications of an autonomous status for the unrecognized nationality.[332]

The Congress of Berlin formally opened on June 13, 1878 and lasted until the 13th of the next month.[333] During this time frame, participants held 20

---

[330] Petitions no. 15, 19, and 23.

[331] See Buxhovi, "Protokollet origjinale të Kongresit të Berlinit" (*i.e.*, original protocols of the Congress of Berlin), *Kongresi . . .*, 101-262.

[332] Bartl, *Die Albanischen Muslime . . .*, 116.

[333] Buxhovi, *Kongresi . . .*, 13.

sessions at the Reichschancellor's building on Wilhelmstrasse. Under the leadership of Bismarck, several delegations sat at the negotiating table: the British, led by the Marquess of Salisbury; the Russians, headed by Gorchakov and Shuvalov; Sadullah Bey and Mehmed Ali Pasha (Magyar Pasha) as the top Ottoman envoys; and Andrássy leading the Austro-Hungarians; France and Italy sent their delegations, too. At the Congress, there were correspondents of the contemporary press, observers, and politicians from Germany and the neighboring countries.[334] The public opinion and the participants paid particular attention to the appearance of high-level leaders, including the Russian and British prime ministers, Count Shuvalov and Benjamin Disraeli, Earl of Beaconsfield, and the French foreign minister, William Henry Waddington.[335] The makeup of the delegations is a strong indicator of the tensions on the brink of war and Britain and Russia had come to Berlin to also demonstrate their political and diplomatic power. This made it obvious that, despite the preparatory negotiations throughout April and May, Berlin was to become the main arena of historic talks.

On the original protocols, a heated argument between the English and Russian delegations appears as early as day two of the Congress. British Prime Minister Disraeli protested in the English language against the czarist warships stationed in proximity to Constantinople, to which Prince Gorchakov replied that it had been precisely the English presence in the area that had convinced the Russians not to withdraw.[336] Bismarck, presiding at the meetings, demanded that the parties cease accusations and avoid distractions that could hamper the Congress. To maintain the participants' focus on the agenda, the chancellor largely ignored other events, including an assassination attempt on the German emperor, Wilhelm I.[337]

It was, in fact, impossible for negotiations to run without animated exchanges, considering the gravity of the matters. Quarrels were most notable at the fourth and sixth sessions, during the debates on Russia's presence and indirect influence in the Balkans, even though the parties had reached a principal agreement during the pre-Congress mediations. Then, at the fifth and sixth session, participants approved the Austro-Hungarian proposal that Russia withdraw from Eastern Rumelia within six months, including nine- and twelve-month term to retreat from Bulgaria and Romania, respectively.

---

[334] *Ibid.* 14.

[335] *Ibid.* 15.

[336] Buxhovi, *Kongresi . . .*, 18.

[337] *Ibid.*, protocol no. 1, p. 101.

On the eighth gathering, the parties deliberated on Bosnia and Herzegovina, one of the most sensitive issues on the agenda. At the proposal of the British delegation, the Congress approved the Austro-Hungarian annexation of the province. Foreign Minister Andrássy had been instrumental for the gain well before the Congress, relying on his diplomatic skills to ensure that the dual monarchy would receive the territory.[338]

With the Bosnian issue resolved, participants then moved on to recognize Serbia as an independent country. Formally, the Congress required the new state to respect the religious and ethnic identity of non-Serb nationalities within its borders. Upon insistence by Mehmed Ali and Andrássy, Serbia committed to the demands on June 26, promising fair treatment of the non-Serb population in the newly-acquired territory in the south. The Serbian government vowed to not take any actions to force the inhabitants of those areas to leave their homes. Serbian Prime Minister Ristić, speaking on behalf of Prince Milan, read a declaration, assuming to protect the rights of the non-Serb population, including its freedom of religion and the sanctity of private property. Thereafter, Serbia was granted the Kurshumlia (*Srb.* Kuršumlija) area and a part of the Vranje province, including the eponymous city.[339]

At the thirteenth session, held on July 5, the Congress discussed the local autonomy of Mirdita. Representatives of Austria-Hungary and France proposed that "the privileges the Mirdita [Catholic] highlanders have enjoyed all the time . . . be guaranteed in the future."[340] Mehmed Ali Pasha rejected the proposal, stating that he could not speak of any privileges, for that could have a domino effect through the empire. He assured participants, however, that the Porte would consider special cases as part of the promised reforms. After an exchange of views with representatives of England and France, Sadullah Bay proposed a compromise solution under which the Porte would not change the status of Mirdita, meaning that the highlanders were to retain the so-called "privileges." This seems to have further honored the concession Europeans had made to Russia and the South Slavic people that the Congress would not discuss autonomy except for Bulgaria, reasoning that any similar requests had to be resolved as part of the domestic reforms the Ottoman Empire committed to at the Congress.[341]

---

[338] *Ibid.*, prot. co. 1, p. 103.

[339] *Ibid.*, prot. co. 8, p. 160

[340] *Ibid.*, prot. co. 8, p. 166.

[341] Geis, *op. cit.*, p. 91.

Even though treated as bartering items, entire kazas and cities—including Ulqin, Tivar, Prokuple, and Kurshumlia—were referred to and registered in the protocols as Albanian settlements. This indicates an acceptance of the Albanians as living and insurmountable factor in the region's affairs. The Albanian ethnicity as tied to its homeland also appeared on maps reviewed at the Congress. Ultimately, the final map of the high-level meeting even contained *Albanien* (*Ger.*, Albania) as a label over the four Albanian vilayets.

However, the multitude of contemporary documents stored in German archives[342] points to a different treatment of the Albanian issue outside of the negotiating table. While considered as part of the *millet-i osman* at the Congress, the German press was increasingly attentive to the Albanians as a distinct nationality. Contemporary newspapers contained news reports as well as analyses and editorials on the Albanian issue during the Congress of Berlin and throughout the period leading to the country's independence. The attitude of the press in such vital moments was to be expected in light of the interest the Germans had maintained on the Albanians since the two peoples first came into contact in the 12th century. As noted, German missionaries, diplomats, and chroniclers authored important documents about the Albanians in the Middle Ages and beyond. Later, German scholars studied the Albanian tongue, concluding that it originated from the ancient European civilization as a descendant of the Illyrian language. Individuals like Arnold von Harf, Xylander, Hahn, and Lamberz, among many others, had contributed a great deal to Albanian studies; meanwhile, the prominent German linguist, Gustav Mayer, published his monumental *Etymological Dictionary of the Albanian Language* at the time of the Berlin Congress.

Thus, the German press made a great honor and service to an almost forgotten people, whose opponents wanted to keep it as far away from the space of European civilization (some of them, like Serbia, Russia and Greece, did not even hesitate to vilify the Albanian people, among other slanders, as destroyers of civilization).

In general, the Congress of Berlin in 1878 managed to invalidate the Treaty of San Stefano that Russia imposed on Turkey after winning the eighth chapter in the series of wars between the two countries. The decisions of the Great Powers spared the life of Ottoman Europe for some time, but provided neither the sustainable peace nor the stability that the Europeans

---

[342] The German Foreign Ministry Archives (PA AA) in Bonn and other archives in Berlin, Koblenz, and Aachen.

claimed.[343] To the contrary, Austria-Hungary's annexation of Bosnia and Herzegovina, on the pretext that the move would help prevent a misbalance among the old rivals Powers, opened the way to future crisis for the developments in the following decades preceded the Balkans wars as well as the First World War. Politically and strategically, the peninsula became an unstable polygon where the Great Powers delineated their irreconcilable interests.

The Congress of Berlin and the Albanian Issue

The first Albanian telegram to reach Berlin is sent by Daut Effendi, a theology teacher from Tivar, protesting the announced political changes in the region. The series of letters, petitions, and telegrams sent to the Congress of Berlin notes the willingness of the Albanians to defend their territories from partitioning; the documents also evidence the demands for autonomy within the Ottoman Empire. In Shkodër, 451 people sign a petition British Prime Minister Disraeli, demanding the autonomy for Albania. On June 16, Preng Bibë Doda requests autonomy for Mirdita. On June 20, the İstanbul Committee submits to the Congress a prayer for an autonomous vilayet. The German ambassador to Turkey informs Bismarck of the Albanian demands and national program. The leadership of the Vilayet of Kosova sends a telegram to the Congress on June 25. The mufti of Prishtina, Zenel Abedini, informs of the humanitarian crisis and the harsh conditions of the refugees after the ethnic cleansing of Kurshumlia and Prokupa. The German press publishes sensational reports on Mehmed Ali Pasha's assassination in Gjakova and supports the Albanian calls for autonomy. The Ottoman foreign minister, Abedin Pasha, sends a letter to the Albanians, promising that the sultan would not abandon Albania.

The Albanians had no allies or representatives to support them at the Congress of Berlin. Since the Porte did not recognize an Albanian nationality, the situation was expected. However, cognizant that the Berlin gathering was going decide their fate, the Albanians—in addition to their domestic activities through the League of Prizren—addressed the Congress via numerous letters, petitions, and telegrams. Owing to an extensive diaspora, Albanians sent such communications from all over the world such that their

---

[343] *Bismarcks Aussenpolitik und der Berliner Kongres* (Wiesbaden: 1978), 36.

protests were more vigorous than those of other Balkan peoples. That stands even though other nations of the peninsula had their representatives at the Congress, for the Great Powers gathered primarily for their own interests.[344]

The Albanian telegrams and memoranda sent to the Congress of Berlin and the subsequent Commission of the Congress, which carried its mission for another three years at the ambassadorial level, could be classified into two categories: the first pertains to demands that Albania's territorial integrity be preserved; meanwhile, the second group contains documents calling for autonomy, including warnings of an armed struggle for self-governance.

Preserving the territorial integrity
The demands in favor of Albania's territorial integrity were a natural priority in the milieu of the San Stefano decisions and the state terror the Albanians faced in the northeastern regions during the incursion of the Serbian army in the winter of 1877-1878. The main goal of the Serbian state was to ethnically cleanse the area of Albanians, as prescribed by the *Načertanije* project (an approach that appears in later projects of the Serbian state, too). Therefore, the telegrams and letters that arrived at the Congress of Berlin conveyed the Albanian protest against the unjust terms of the San Stefano treaty. The Albanians feared that Europe might continue to ignore their cause. The concern was founded for the nation's representatives had not been invited to attend the Berlin meeting. On the other hand, the Albanians were also alarmed by the Serbian, Greek, and Russian propaganda, which labeled the ethnic group as incompatible with European interests, holding it belonged instead in the Ottoman Empire.

Formally, the first telegram that arrived at the Congress was that of Daut Efendia, a theology teacher from Tivar, on the very first day of the meetings. In a few words, the document calls on the Great Powers not to implement the Treaty of San Stefano. Efendia hopes that the "majesties . . . may act in accordance with divine justice and you will not forget us or sell us off at all."[345]

---

[344] The Political Archive of the German Foreign Ministry contains around a hundred letters, telegrams, memoranda, and petitions from the Albanians and others regarding the Albanian issue. The majority of the documents are addressed to the Congress; many are written to Bismarck personally, while others to English, Austro-Hungarian, French, and Italian representatives.

[345] PA AA, Türkei, band. 143, doc. no. 214.

The Tivar telegram contains no additional and numerous signatures, as was often the case with other documents of this nature. It is a personal telegram that opens the book of communiqués from different countries and peoples, among which the Albanians sent the most and the longest letters. Thus, on June 13, the Shkodër representatives of the Albanian League sent the Earl of Beaconsfield (Benjamin Disraeli) a memorandum, stating, *inter alia*:

> Albania [is] the only among the Balkan countries having no representative in Berlin. She has no government of her own, but is not represented by the Turkish delegation either.
>
> The Albanians have their own national attributes, rich and diverse traditions, and their own language. Our ancient history as well as [the modern] from Skanderbeg to Marko Boçari [i.e., Markos Botsaris], is heroic.[346]

The Shkodrans then pray the British prime minister for his state to defend the Albanians, since "defending the Albanian lands would halt the advance and consolidation of pan-Slavism," which had become Russia's main preoccupation in the Balkans, seriously threatening British interests at the time.

On June 20, the Congress of Berlin received another telegram from Shkodër, informing that the Albanians have decided to resist the San Stefano terms by arms, and would do the same if Berlin did reach a different agreement. The telegram states:

> As of the 16th of this month, we had the honor, your majesties, to send to the honored Congress of Berlin a letter expressing our sincerest desires for a successful meeting. We, the Muslim and non-Muslim Albanians of the Shkodër region, decided to gather in the name of our rights hundreds and hundreds of signatures and that you, excellencies, may become familiar with the content of [the petition] beforehand, we shall briefly inform you in this telegram . . . noting that we Albanians desire to protect the integrity our lands under the Majesty of Sultan.

The lengthy letter of the Shkodrans, which is announced in the June 20 telegram, arrives a week later, on the 27th.[347] The letter contains a total of 451 signatures and, as the longest petition, presents a master document of the

---

[346] *Ibid.*, no. 216.

[347] PA AA, Türkei, 143, doc. no. 128.

Congress. Page one contains the signatures of Daut Efendia, the theology teacher, and of Selino Gurezi and Filip Muzani. Like the telegram, the letter also demands that the Albanian lands be kept under the Porte.

A similar telegram, but without any references to the sultan, was sent by representatives of southern Albania from Janina.[348] The documents states, among others, that "[the Albanians] categorically protest against the partitioning of our lands. We hope that you will give heed to our issue." Abdyl Frashëri was among the signatories of the telegram, who also included two pashas, Mustafa and Mehmedali, in addition to other political leaders (Abedin Bej, Omer Bej, Xhelal Bej, Hasan Bej, Sabri Bej, Mehemed Bej, Mehmedali Vrioni, Osman Tahiri, Muslim Vasini, Xhelosh Osmani, Ali Leskoviku, Sylejman Bej, and Tefik Bej).

Another telegram that deserves attention came from representatives of the Vilayet of Kosova on June 25. The signatories of this lengthy document include a Roman Catholic, Tadea Latini of Prizren, in addition to Mufti Zenel Abedini from Prishtina and Musim landlords from other parts of the vilayet (Zija Bej of Gjilan, Hysen Aga of Gjakova, Abdurrahim Aga of Peja, Halil Bej of Tetova, Zenel Efendia from Shkup, and Hasan Aga of Vranje). They inform the Congress on the humanitarian crisis following the ethnic cleansing in Kurshumlia and Vranje:

> Thousands and thousands of innocent of our countrymen were violently expelled from their homes and treated like animals from the invaders. Women, children and elderly were thrown out on the streets and treated in the most brutal ways. They are now at a merciless mercy. Left homeless, they have lost all what they had for centuries. Many of our brothers who insisted by all means to remain on their lands were brutally murdered and many others were arrested and nothing is known of their fate. Be aware that the majority of the population in our lands is Albanian and only a small portion comprises Greeks, Bulgarians, or Latins, and now, as a majority, we are to be ignored at the behest of the minority. On behalf of justice and humanity, on behalf of civilization, we pray for your support and protection so that we may not remain at the merciless mercy.[349]

The harsh condition of the refugees who were in Kosova since they were driven out of their homes during the Serbian theater of the Russo-Turkish

---

[348] *Ibid.*
[349] *Ibid.*

war of 1877-1878, was addressed in yet another telegram. Mufti Abedini of Prishtina sent a second message to the Congress with a humanitarian appeal on the Great Powers to care for the numerous Albanians that had become double victims—of the war and of the unjust treaties, such as San Stefano. Similar pleas came from the Albanians, whose lands were awarded to the proposed Greater Bulgaria by the San Stefano agreement. Notably, Iliaz Pasha, and other Albanians representatives from Dibër and Manastir, sent a telegram from Janina on June 26; the mufti of Shkup sent a telegram on the 24th; another, dated June 20, was sent by Rrustem Pasha. There were also letters, signed June 20, such as that of Mirimon Hoti and others from Manastir and Dibër and another communication from the Albanians of İstanbul, all calling against the partitioning of the Albanian lands.[350]

The pile of letters and telegrams, which initially requested the Congress to be mindful of the Albanian territorial integrity, was later augmented by more extensive requests. On June 16, the Congress received a letter from the *kapedan* of Mirdita, Prenk Bibë Doda. With *kapedan*'s signature preceding those of fifty-one *bayraktars* of the province,[351] the letter demands that Mirdita's privileges of self-government be preserved by recognizing the region's autonomous status under the Porte.[352]

The protocols of the Congress indicate that the letter had to some extent piqued the interest of participants, notably the Austro-Hungarian and French representatives. At the 13th meeting, the delegates of the two Powers presented the issue for discussion, but the outcome was null other than having the Albanian demand profiled in the official protocols. The same occurred to other requests for autonomy, such as the June 20 letter from İstanbul. This plea sought to unify the four Albanian vilayets into one, under the supervision of the Porte—a condition that Albanians viewed as transitional, for the Ottoman Empire would remain only for as long as the Great Powers were interested in keeping the Turks in Europe.[353]

Demands for autonomy

The June 20 message of the İstanbul community, in the series of protest letters and telegrams from different parts of the world, gives the impression that of frustrated and uncoordinated grassroot efforts to fill in for an inexistent

---

[350] *Ibid.*, doc. no. 33.

[351] *Ibid.*, doc. no. 20.

[352] *Ibid.*

[353] *Ibid.*

central authority, which could lead and supervise the periphery on the basis of a program with well-defined political demands. While certain goals were stipulated with the founding of the Albanian League, the Prizren authorities never relayed them as such to the Congress of Berlin. Without dwelling on the League's failure to send an official communication to the German capital, one may note that the letter from İstanbul was in a way a restatement of decisions taken at Prizren. The document, signed by Pashko Vasa among other representatives,[354] offers a nine-page description of the history of the Albanian people along with contemporary political demands of the nation.[355]

The authors addressed the letter directly to Bismarck. It seems that the İstanbul Albanians were aware that, in addition to presiding over the Congress, the German chancellor exerted insuperable influence over the decision-making process. They decided hence to brief him on Albanian history from Pyrrhus to Skanderbeg as a way of proving that the Albanians were a European people. Notably, they wrote:

> We are the oldest people of the Balkans . . . Our history is sensational and utterly marked with dramatic events. We were the only to fight by ourselves the Ottoman Empire at the height of its power and when we all feared her like the devil. And today, we forget. Intentionally, someone ignores us as if we had never fought for our independence.[356]

The message notes, as did most of the letters and telegrams to the Congress, that:

> The Albanians are one regardless of religion and, when it comes to defending their homeland, they forget of their religious affiliation. For their only religion is the defense of the homeland. [Thus], we have decided to not give our lands. At the present, we seek autonomy under the reign of His Majesty, the Sultan, since this is currently the most appropriate solution for us.[357]

Then, the document gives details on the *Albanian autonomy* and the territories taht would be included, mentioning the four vilayets—Shkodër, Kosova, Manastir, and Janina. At the end, expressing hope that Bismarck himself may read the letter with due attention as if he were standing before

---

[354] In addition to Pashko Vasa, signatories include Omer Vrioni, Omer Shefkiu, S. Toptani, Hajredin Tekitani, I. Husamedini, A. Dinoshi, and G. Samiu.

[355] PA AA, Telegram lists 8-9, telegrams no. 33-35, 40.

[356] *Ibid.*, no. 40.

[357] *Ibid.*

the whole Albanian people, the signatories reiterate that autonomy under the sultanic crown and the willingness to oppose any decisions the Congress may take against the Albanians.

Secretaries in Berlin carefully registered all letters, telegrams, memoranda, and protests sent to the Congress. Many of the communications were addressed to the presiding officer, Bismarck. Nevertheless, the protocols do not indicate whether or to what extent participants of the Congress considered the outside correspondence at the actual meetings. There is only one passus from the 13th meeting, at which the Ottoman foreign minister, Karateodori Pasha, argues with the Russian and Hellenic representatives over the territories Greece demanded in the Epirus region. To object to ceding any Albanian lands, Karateodori refers to the petitions Albanians had sent from Janina and Preveza and specifically cites the register of Congressional correspondence, emphasizing numbers fifteen to twenty-three.

In the meantime, Bismarck was likely informed about all requests addressed to the Congress. As indicated in chancellery documents, the German strongman held separate meeting with members of the delegations, asking them of details, including requests or complaints from abroad.[358] Then, he also relied on supplementary information he requested from ambassadors, consuls, and other diplomatic sources. In October 1878, Ambassador Hasfield sent from İstanbul additional remarks on the idea of Albanian autonomy, which Sami Frashëri had announced a month earlier in the Ottoman newspaper *Tercüman-ı Şark*. The diplomatic report, classified by the German *kanzleramt* as "specially ordered to supplement prior information,"[359] notes that the Albanians are discontent with the Congressional decisions and have formed a Revolutionary Committee and announced a program for autonomy. The specific demands include:

1. That the Albanian vilayets be unified into a single vilayet;
2. That [the administration of] those vilayets hire clerks who know the Albanian language;
3. That the Assembly of the Albanian Vilayet convene twice a year;
4. That the Albanian language serve for daily use and in education, while Turkish be used only to communicate with the central authorities in İstanbul;
5. That a police force be formed from the inhabitants of the vilayet.

---

[358] See: Notes of the German chancellery during the Congress of Berlin, archived along the main documents of the Congress, band. 145, file no. 3.

[359] PA AA, Türkei, 143, doc. no. 23.

The list concludes with the demand that Ohër be chosen as capital of the Albanian autonomous entity and that tax revenue remain within the vilayet.[360] Hasfield reports that "in all likelihood, the Albanians enjoy the support of the Turkish government for such [autonomy] proposals," noting firther that Ottoman authorities encouraged the Albanians to sabotage the Berlin decisions.[361]

Albanian autonomy presented a transitory phase, which would be in the best interest of the Europeans, who wished to keep Balkans free of Russian influence. The Congress permitted the creation of Southern Slavic states, but the czar was expected to exert control, since the Balkan Slavs leaned closer to Russia rather than the West. Therefore, some of the daily papers, which did not agree with the decisions of the Congress, vastly focued on the Albanian issue. After Mehmed Ali Pasha was killed in Gjakova on September 6, 1878, *Hamburgische Correspodent* ran a frontpage report on the event. The article, appearing on the October 1 issue, notes further that:

> The Albanians are determined and, as they have announced before, will fight by all means for their rights and a fruit of their pledge is the assassination of Mehemed Ali Pasha, the chief of the Ottoman diplomacy, who went [to Albania] to convince the Albanians to give up their lands. This event will not be without consequences for later developments, especially since it is already apparent that the decisions of the Berlin Congress will not be implemented through diplomacy, as some expected, but by blood, for no one will agree to voluntarily leave one's own home.[362]

The report recalls that the Albanians were ignored in Berlin, but this was returning as a boomerang to those who thought that the interests of the small nation could be overlooked as if they had not existed. *Hamburgische Correspodent* then asks, "Why should [the Albanians] not have their autonomy? . . . What do they have in common with the Orient when it is known that they are the oldest people of the Balkans?"[363] Considering autonomy as the only solution that could bring peace to the peninsula, the German paper calls on the Great Powers to make wise use of their time to correct the previous decisions.

---

[360] *Ibid.*

[361] *Ibid.*

[362] *Hamburgische Correspondent*, Oct. 15, 1878.

[363] *Ibid.*

At the end of the high-level meeting in Berlin, the Europeans set up commissions of the Congress, which continued to work at an ambassadorial and experts level for another three years at the German capital. The signatories of the 1878 agreements vowed to carry out every provision of the deal. However, the Albanian issue remained unsolved, warning of major trouble for the commissions such that certain articles of the agreements had to be amended. The implementation process dragged on and seriously threatened the decisions of the Congress. In fact, the Albanians decided not to accept the terms and, in doing so, they surfaced to the foreground, highlighting the fundamental problems of the Berlin agreements. These had the blessing of the decision-making powers, but did not conform to the reality they created. As a result of the agreements, the Balkans faced tremendous crises, which ultimately affected even those who vested peace efforts in unilateral agreements rather than the equal rights for all nations.

The members of the post-Congressional commissions were among the first to face the consequences of the unjust decisions of Berlin. As European diplomats were increasingly unable to meet the scheduled deadlines, even what had been though of simple matters became serious impediments. This largely occurred because the Albanians objected to the Berlin terms. Original documents of the event illustrate the challenge, noting the "Albanian oppositions to the decisions of the Congress." At least 147 reports, notes, and other documents from diplomats and special border commissions pertain to the Albanian issue.

The key events that are described in the archive documents began with the assassination of Mehmet Ali Pasha in September 1878 to continue through the end of 1881, when the Albanian League surrendered the city of Ulqin (*Mont.* Ulcinj, *Ital.* Dulcigno). The Congress initially decided to give Montenegro Plava and Gucia; later, a post-Congressional commission altered the plan, awarding the small Balkan state an alternative territory. Since the Montenegrin army was unable to gain any of the lands by force, Europe decided to hand the city of Ulqin as "compensation" to Montenegro. However, when the Albanians refused to lay down their arms, the Great Powers resorted to a show of naval force in the Adriatic. Ultimately, this enabled the Turkish military to force the League troops to give up the city's defense. Documents also describe other military confrontations between the Albanians and their neighbors. After an initial combat with the Montenegrins, there are references to an Albanian war against the Greeks in the vicinity of Janina and other towns in the south. The Congress had left it to the Ottoman and Greek governments to set the border in the south through bilateral agreements that provoked the Albanian dissent.

The Berlin-based Control Commission received the first report on the Albanian resistance as early as the first half of 1879. Montenegro requested from the Commission that Plava and Gucia be handed over by the scheduled deadline.[364] The Ottoman Empire also agreed to surrender the northern territories. However, in November, the Albanians informed the Commission that they disagreed with the planned Montenegrin annexation and that they would resort to arms to defend their homes.[365] On this occasion, Ambassador Hasfield notified his government that "Turkey is in control of the Albanian stubbornness and is inciting [the Albanians] to an armed resistance. Thus, the sultan will be able to drag matters as much as possible and will do this through the Albanians."[366] In addition, Hasfield reports that confidential sources have informed him that "the Albanian League has quite a strong military and that, in the military aspect, Montenegro is unable to obtain control of the lands awarded by the Congress of Berlin." By the same token, the Austrian consul in Shkodër, Ippen, confirms the military superiority of the Albanians. This information was later relayed to the Control Commision by Vienna's representative. "The Albanians in control of Plava and Gucia," he stated, "are under the command of Ali Pashë Gucia and the Montenegrins have no business with him."

Ali Pashë Gucia, as evidenced in the reports of the Control Commission, led the Albanian League's toops, when on December 4, 1879, the Montenegrins endeavored to invade Plava and Gucia. After serveral attempts to take the Berlin gifts by force, on January 8, 1880, Montenegro ultimately gave up on military confrontations with the Albanian League.

In an attempt likely to circumvent the Albanian resistance, the Italian representative proposed an alternative solution. Instead of Plava of Gucia, the Commission decided to give Montenegro a section of the Cem River that included the Hot, Gruda, and Kelmend districts.[367] The Italian proposal, which was approved by the Commission, was labeled the *Corsti Plan*, after the Rome delegate to the international body.[368] Yet, like the compatriots in Plava and Gucia, the inhabitants of Hot, Gruda, and Kelmend refused to

---

[364] PA AA, Türkei, band. 143.

[365] *Ibid.*

[366] *Ibid.*, doc. no. 190.

[367] PA AA, band. 143, doc. no. 190.

[368] *Ibid.*, doc. no. 16.

yield to the decision of the Great Powers. On April 4, 1880, representatives of the three provinces sent an unlenient letter to the Berlin Commission, vowing the Albanians would "fight until the last man and we will not abandon our lands. Why are we being treated this way? Are we not like the others?"[369] The highlanders threatened to defend themselves by arms.

The Corsti Plan was greatly publicized in the Cologne newspaper *Kölnische Zeitung*. A report in May 1880 notes:

Threats of war continue. The front broadens increasingly. The Albanians achieved victories in Plava and Gucia, hence it is anticipated they will continue to defend their homeland. Hot and Gruda have no intentions of surrendering either and no one would expect that to happen.[370]

The newspaper calls the crisis a Balkan tragedy and an unscrupulous game of the Great Powers at the expense of the smaller peoples.

That the Corsti Plan would also suffer the fate of Plava and Gucia was a widespread concern. In a letter to Bismarck, Ambassador Hasfield informs his superior that a new border change agreement, which Turkey and Montenegro executed on April 12, may fail. The German representative in İstanbul suspected that:

Turkey is playing a double game: on the one hand, it signs international agreement on the territories that are to be given to the Montenegrins; on the hand, it encourages the Albanians to oppose and even fight, assisting them with military preparations, too. This behavior is already evident and how long it will last is not known.[371]

Hasfield repeatedly calls attention to the "Turkish aid" and reliance on the Albanians to circumvent the Berlin agreements. Virtually in every report, the German ambasador emphasizes that "the Turks benefit from the Albanian resistence and that they will again use that card in the future." Hasfield maintains the same opinion, even after the Great Powers sent Turkey a note on June 26, 1880. The Europeans demanded the Porte, in case the Cem basin could not be ceded to Montenegro, to come up with an acceptable proposal for immediate implementation.[372] On this occasion, Hasfield remarks:

The Porte intentionally proposed on August 19 to give Ulqin to Montenegro, even though the town's inhabitants are one hundred percent Albanians and

---

[369] *Ibid.*

[370] *Kölnische Zeitung*, May 15, 1880.

[371] PA AA, Türkei, band. 16.

[372] PA AA, report no. 277.

they will not agree to surrender to Montenegro. This is a demonic plan, for the Porte is convinced that the Albanians will not give up Ulqin.[373]

On August 20, 1880, the Ambassadors' Conference in Berlin agreed for the Great Powers to stage a show of force before the Albanians. The parties also arranged for the Porte to pursue direct military action against the League, assuming to carry out the task by all means.[374] In details, an allied fleet—comprising of three French warships, two British and two Austro-Hungarian, and one from each, Germany and Russia—would be anchored in the Adriatic shores of Ulqin in early September. The Conference appointed British Admiral Seymour to command the European forces.[375]

Reporting on the military undertaking, *Hamburgische Correspondent* wrote:

> Europe has declared war on the Albanians! A small Balkan people has not surrended for two years now and is persistently seeking to protect its rights! Recently, to vanquish [the Albanians], after neither Turks nor Montenegrin were able to do so, the fleet of the Great Powers had to join to attack as needed if the Turkish army was unable to subdue [the Albanians] and to hand Ulqin over to the Montenegrins.

Ulqin fell on November 26, 1880, after a powerful Turkish army, commanded by a famed general, Dervish Pasha, attacked the Albanian defenders. As the city was handed over to the Montenegrins, the Hamburg newspaper wrote:

> After a heroic war against an entire army, the Albanians were defeated, but they were defeated because they had no alternative [as they were] faced with the risk of annihilation that, if not at the hands of the Turkish general, then inevitably from the European fleet.[376]

After Ulqin surrendered, the Europeans removed the so-called "northern Albanian problem" from the agenda. But, before the Ambassadors' Conference in Berlin, lay another major issue—the South. At the Congress, the Great Powers generalla agreed that the southern border would run from Salaryrias to the Aegean Sea and from the Kalamas River to the Ioanian Sea. However, the final, detailed settlement of the border remained an open issue

---

[373] *Ibid.*

[374] Bartl, *Die Albanische Muslime . . .*, 121.

[375] *Ibid.* 121.

[376] *Hamburgische Correspondent*, Oct. 12, 1880.

for direct talks between the Porte and the Greek government.[377] For that reason, the local branches of the League, appearing well-organized, immediately began a diplomatic campaign to protect the Albanian territories from the planned Greek invasion. On January 28, 1879, Berlin received a letter from southern Albanians.[378] The communication carries, among other, the signature of Abdyl Frashëri.[379] The opening of the letter states:

> We have the honor to inform Your Excellency that Turkish and Greek commissioners have come to Preveza to discuss the border issue. Since the border today raises the issue of our very existence, our gravely important concerns deserve to be heard. On the one hand, our existence under Ottoman rule for four centuries and, on the other, our bad experience with the Greeks convince us that, in case our people fall under the Greeks, [our people] will be ruined mercilessly and their identity effaced. Therefore, we are bound to defend ourselves should you decide that we are to fall under Greece. But, we rest our hopes in your philanthropic sentiment and that you may spare us from resorting to arms to defend our lands. Our people, otherwise, have no way but to defend themselves. And this would then have severe consequences for us and others.

In the meantime, Greek and Ottoman negotiations also had vast disagreement as to the boundary line. The Ottomans were hesitant to honor the Greek aspirations to incur deeper into Albanian lands, even beyond the general contours set by the Congress of Berlin. Th German consul in Athens, Brink, informed:

> Muhtar Pasha and General Soutzos do not agree on the new border line. The Greeks demand the Albanian lands, Janina, Aidonat, Preveza, Arta, and Lous, while the Turks wish to give less. It is also reported that the Albanians in those areas will wage an armed struggle to defend their provinces.[380]

Hasfield also notified Berlin of manifold difficulties over the southern border. The German ambassador reasoned that the disagreements "had to do

---

[377] Protocol of the Congress, Article XXIV.

[378] The signatories represent the constituencies of Janina, Preveza, Gjirokastra, Delvina, Përmet, Vlora, Margarit, Filat, Parga, Arta, Tepelena, and Korça.

[379] Other representatives who signed the letter include Mustafa Nuriu, Sabri Veseli, Çerkin Selimi, Fehmi Sylejmani, Jasin Mehmedi, Nexhip Muhamedi, Jusuf Sadiku, Abedin Proga, Xhelal Shehu, Ibrahim Skënderi, Islam Vrioni, Ali Mehmedi, and Xhejlon Jakupi; PA AA, Türkei, 143, band. 23.

[380] *Ibid.*

with areas inhabited by Albanians," whom he sometimes called "established Albanian ethnicity." While this acknowledgment would imply the right of the population not be treated as a bartering item, Hasfield had doubts that the Albanians were fighting for their existence. At least in official correspondence, the ambassador reported that "Turkey desires to push the Albanians by all means into an armed conflict with the Greeks.[381]

To support the view, Hasfield relied on a memorandum that the Ottoman minister of foreign affairs, Abedin Pasha, himself of Albanian nationality, sent to the leaders of the Albanian League in May 1880. The ambassador's report, dated June 2, informs Bismarck on the possibility that, according to Hasfield, the Sublime Porte may use the Albanians for its own purposes, without giving the ethnic group the united vilayet or the autonomy as had recently been claimed.[382] Hasfield notes:

> The memorandum Abedin Pasha sent to the heads of the Albanian League has authenticity. Many of my colleagues take the matter seriously and as a move against the decisions approved by the Congress of Berlin. I have received notice that the English ambassador has spoken with Abedin Pasha in person about this matter and told him that he is inciting the Albanians for an uprising.[383] Abedin Pasha rejected the accusations and stated that after his appointment to the high position, he did not even accept any letters of congratulations from his fellow [Albanians] only so that he would cause any suspicion. The English ambassador did not find Abedin Pasha's words convincing.

Along with the report, on June 29, the German ambassador sent Bismarck a supplementary report, which includes Abedin Pasha's memorandum in its entirety. The text arrived in Berlin translated into German and contains an additional notes stating:

> This text has evoked great interest and curiosity among the diplomatic circles and İstanbul and it is by all means clear that Abedin Pasha, who is Albanian, wants to gain his compatriots' trust and to support them. My adviser who translated the text is of the opinion that if the text's authenticity is verified and it is concluded that he has indeed sent it to the heads of the Albanian League, which he denies, then Abedin Pasha ought to resign.[384]

---

[381] *Ibid.*
[382] PA AA, Türkei, report no. 214.
[383] *Ibid.*
[384] *Ibid.*

The memorandum became prone to various speculations. Many diplomats viewed it as "an attempt of the Porte to manipulate and misuse the Albanians against the decisions of the Great Powers and the neighbor[ing countries]." In the meatime, other decision-makers interpreted the document as a warning of Albanian statehood. Convinced that the Albanian issue could not be circumvented, Austro-Hungarian Foreign Minister Andrássy suggested that a state be erected on a substantial portion of the the four vilayets. The diplomat viewed believed the move would offer a balance to the Slavic states already formed in the Balkans.

Meanwhile, the debated memorandum itself contained generally favorable language for the Albanians, stating among others that:

> Turkey's existence in Europe is closely linked to Albania's existence. This is a vital matter, the same for both sides, Albania as well as the Porte. All the intentions and positions of the Porte are for Albania to remain strong and important. This is also the wish of the Great Powers, which have an interest in the Ottoman [presence] in Europe.[385]

Of course, the German ambassador to İstanbul considered the letter as supportive of the Albanians, even though the promises made were never delivered. Abedin Pasha was incorrect in assuring the Albanians that Montenegro would not succeed with its territorial claims and Hasfield was aware of the epilogue. Moreover, the foreign minister's prognosis was inaccurate in regards to southern Albania, too, when he promised that the Ottoman Empire would not yield to the Greek demands. As early as the fall of 1880, the Ambassadors' Conference in Berlin approved a French proposal for the border line to annex Janina, Aidonat, Margarit, Lura, and Preveza to the Greek state.[386]

Responding to a note of the Great Powers, the Sublime Porte agreed to cede the territories, except for Janina and Meçova (Metsovo).[387] However, after lengthy debates and the intervention of European Powers before the sultan, Turkey permitted Greece to seize Volo, Arta, and Larissa; the empire held on to Janina and its vicinity, albeit not for much longer. Thus, the Great Powers resolved the "southern problem" more easily than the northern crisis, which remained in the center of attention for two years marked by war, renegotiations, and the deployment of European warships in the Albanian

---

[385] A translation of the letter attributed to the Ottoman minister of foreign affairs, Abedin Pasha, has been included in the Appendix to this volume.

[386] *Ibid.*

[387] *Ibid.*

waters. On May 24, 1881, Turkey signed an agreement with the Great Powers over the Greek border, awarding the Hellenic state 13,400 square kilometers of land. Of the 300,000 inhabits, the majority were Albanian.[388]

The Diplomatic Activities of the Albanian League

The Albanian League of Prizren has no organized diplomacy, but zealous activists help maintain the organization's external relations. The League initially maintains a cautious relationship with the Ottoman government and often silently complies with the Porte; the ties later escalate into disagreements and armed conflict. The League's envoy to Prizren, Qemal Bej, is entrusted to animate the imperial decision-makers in favor of the Albanian autonomy. The League delegates, Abdyl Frashëri and Mehmet Ali Vrioni, travel to European capitals—Rome, Paris, London, and Berlin—a year after the Congress. In their Albanian Memorandum, Frashëri and Vrioni agree to give up the defense of the Kosovar territories awarded to Serbia and Montenegro in exchange for the southern territories. No German official receives the Albanian representatives in Berlin.

The Albanians did not carry out their diplomatic activities as part of the institutional efforts. But while external relations lacked coordination and often failed to move beyond informal and personal contacts, they were nevertheless part of the Albanian League's overall exertions in pursuit of autonomy and national independence. Contemporary German documents and other history sources reflect widely on the activities, which could be grouped into two categories: (1) relations with the Porte; and (2) Europe diplomacy.

As a formal association, the League endeavored to demonstrate a high level of organization, representing the goals and the desires of a people found at a historic crossroad. The policies of the Porte and the Western governments had placed the Albanians before an existential challenge, but it was precisely the powerful states that the representatives of the small nation had to lobby for support. Notably, the British and the Austro-Hungarian empires appeared as the greatest opponents of Russia's hegemonic intentions in the Balkans, while relations with the Ottoman Empire were also an inevitable process.

---

[388] Bartl, *Die Albanische Muslime . . .*, 125.

Relations with the Ottoman Empire

Contemporary documents from the German Empire indicate increasing efforts of the Albanian League of Prizren to establish direct ties with the West. Originally, the organization declared its loyalty to the sultan and the Porte, including a specific provision for this purpose in the *Kararname* of 1878. Having accepted the authority of the Ottoman government, the League initially acted only to defend Albania's territorial integrity; only later did demands for autonomy begin as part of a plan to unify the four vilayets into a single a unit. The League's position was thought at the time to be the most beneficial under the circumstances, as the Albanians hoped for the Berlin Congress to revise the onerous Treaty of San Stefano. The League worked to minimize the impact of the peace agreement at a time when neighboring Slavic countries, whose national movements and ongoing wars, instigated and supported by Russia, had brought a new reality to the region. Of course, this cautious and dualist approach of the Albanians was not entirely easy or without consequences, since the League was tied to rely on the imperial authorities for domestic as well as foreign policy goals, which required a necessary balance and constant vigilance.

Nevertheless, in order to preserve the essential balance and to earn room for its own activities, the League made certain efforts that, under different conditions, resembled but failed to reach the level of a proper functional diplomacy. In fact, it was certain actions in pursuit of foreign relations that were later viewed as the League's weaknesses.[389]

Since inception, the League had to follow a balanced and cautious path to the ultimate goal of Albanian statehood. This would be a natural outcome for, during five centuries of Ottoman rule, the Albanian identity had been preserved as distinct and reflected in administrative units, such as the sanjaks and the kazas called *Arnavud* (*i.e.*, Albanian) in the Elayet of Rumelia,[390] the pashaliks, and later the four vilayets of Shkodër, Manastir, Janina, and Kosova; finally, in 1912, Albania reappeared as an independent nation. But considering the difficulties presented by the hostile neighbors, the League cautiously pursued its mission with gradual steps. The Prizren-based organi-

---

[389] PA AA, Türkei, band. 143, doc. no. 222.

[390] For more on the *Arnavud* (Albanian) Sanjak in the 15th century, see: Halil Inalcık, "*Arnavutluk*: History," *The Encyclopaedia of Islam*, vol. I, iss. 11 (London: 1958); Rizaj, *Kosova gjatë shekujve. . . .*; H.P.Sh. (Prishtinë); Pulaha, *Lufta shqiptaro-turke në shekullin XV: Burime Osmane* (Tiranë: 1968); K. Frashëri, *Skënderbeu . . . .*

zation resembled an embryo government with its own administration and military,[391] yet a balanced foreign policy was also required. The League had to seek stable ties with the Porte and West to ensure that the Albanians would have the necessary preparations to stand on their own in the future.

For this reason, the League called for autonomy. Such an internal independence within the Ottoman Empire would in fact be mutually beneficial for the Albanians and the Porte. On the one hand, Albania would unity the four vilayets into a single autonomous unit, prepared to stand as fully sovereign in case the Ottomans withdrew from the Balkans; on the other hand, the Porte would also lengthen its presence in the region for, as Abedin Pasha put it, "Turkey's existence in Europe [was] closely linked to Albania's existence."[392]

The concept of autonomy, nonetheless, caused difficulties and even friction between the Albanians and the Porte. A part of the international conjunctures, such as Russia and her allies, were never relenting to either, Albanian statehood or Ottoman presence in Europe. Western powers, such as the British and Austro-Hungarian empires, had pursued the friendship of the southern Slavic states with the hope of excluding Russia's influence over them. The Balkan Slavs felt much closer to their fellow Orthodox in Saint Petersburg than Western Europe to begin with; but to make matters worse, the peninsula's young nations were resolutely opposed to an autonomous Albania, inciting fears among Western powers that any support for the idea could impair their ability to decrease Russian sway over the region.

It is likely that after the Treaty of San Stefano, the Albanian community and the Porte viewed each other as a partner in reaching their respective goals—continued Ottoman presence in Europe and autonomy in preparation for statehood. This has led many historians to conclude that the Porte instigated the League for the benefit of the empire. While not overlooking the Ottoman crackdown on the Albanian League of Prizren, Peter Bartel suggests "a possibility that [the latter] was formed with the knowledge of the sultan."[393] However, the German scholar rejects that the League saw the Ottoman territorial integrity as the only concern. As the Congress of Berlin extended the Ottoman presence in the Balkans, the Albanians saw this as an opportunity for internal consolidation by obtaining their autonomy. Since

---

[391] See *Akte të Rilindjes Kombëtare Shqiptare 1878-1912* (Tiranë: 1978), 40.

[392] See letter of Abedin Pasha to the Albanian people, reproduced in Buxhovi, *Kongresi . . .*, 83-85.

[393] See Bartl, *Die Albanische Muslime . . .*; Schanderl, *Die Albanienpolitik . . . .*

the continued Ottoman rule was considered only a "transitional state," the *status quo* would enable the Albanians to eventually stand as a sovereign nation—even with the approval, and for the benefit, of the Porte. Furthermore, Albania's path to independence was seen as advantageous to Western powers. After the San Stefano fiasco, Britain continuously sought to maintain a stable ally, which would protect the queen's interests in the East. In fact, Bartel sees a partnership with the British as a target of the Albanian movement, especially in the early stages of the League, when the organization's *Kararname* expressed its alliance to the sultan and affirmed the imperial Sharia law. The German historian opines that the content of the League's basic act was reasonable because—if the Great Powers succeeded in saving the Ottoman rule, which was not expected to last long, either way—it assured the West that, in case of a Turkish withdrawal, the Albanians could serve as a new reference point in the attempts to curb Russian influence in the region. Bartel notes further that the League pursued a cautious, step-by-step campaign for autonomy even through the second phase of the activities, which remained in accordance with the organization's aspirations for closer ties with the West.[394]

The cautious approach is witnessed in a proclamation on April 10, 1880, by representatives of the northern highlands in the League's General Council. In addition to entreating the sultan for autonomy, the petition included requests for a prince chosen by the Albanians and the withdrawal of Turkish troops from Albania. Likewise, the highlanders called for non-Albanian employees to be replaced with Albanians in the administration and that the Albanians elect their own representatives to İstanbul. Meanwhile, the sultan would retain wartime powers to draft Albanian troops for the imperial military.[395]

The highlanders' demands were followed by similar petitions that came out of the General Council's session in June and July that year. The League decided to demand the Porte to grant an Albanian autonomous province with Manastir or Ohër as capital. The move presents a new, advanced phase of the League's plan to achieve autonomy by dialogue, avoiding confrontations with the Porte for that would be a tragedy for both sides. With that in mind, in October 1880, the League appointed an emissary to İstanbul, naming Qemal Bej, son of Iliaz Pashë Dibra, to petition the sultan for a

---

[394] Bartel, *Die Albanische Muslime . . .* , 126.
[395] *Ibid.* 127.

208

unified, autonomous vilayet.[396] The move clearly represents the most important stage of the League's communication with the Porte. Since the Albanians were to serve as the empire's defenders, they reminded the Ottoman government that their service comes at a price—that is, home rule for Albania. Thus, the Albanians demanded a guaranty, not only a formal nature, but practical and already enforceable through the institutions of the Ottoman Empire.

On the other end, the sultan felt the need to show the Albanians that he remained heedful of their cause and has now made it an imperial priority because it concerned what was called "the left wing of the empire." To do so, the Ottoman padshah chose for his minister of foreign affairs Abedin Pasha, an ethnic Albanian who openly identified with his nationality and its interests.[397]

League members received the appointment as the initial sign that their policy of mutual Ottoman-Albanian benefits was destined to fail. However, the Albanians maintained their calm and continued their peaceful efforts[398] for as long as the Porte did not explicitly reject the demands for autonomy. The situation took for the worse when the Ottomans deployed an army under Field Marshal Dervish Pasha to quell the Albanian forces in successive campaigns, in Ulqin and the Vilayet of Kosova.

Until then, the League had behaved cautiously and wholly embraced the idea that the Albanians are the empire's foothold in the Balkans while the empire is the protector of the ethnic group (albeit contending that the latter be recognized as a distinct nationality outside the *millet-i osman* that had greatly hindered the impact of progressive reforms on the Albanians). However, the expulsion of Turks from the vilayet administration and the Albanian takeover of Kosova in 1881 is considered to be the final dissolution of any ties or mutual cooperation with the Sublime Porte.[399] The radical breakoff was unfortunately detrimental to the Albanians because they were left without a protective umbrella, becoming easy prey for the hostile neighbors. This failed to become a lesson learned for the Porte's protection was needed even in the final stages of the Albanian war of independence, when upon Turkish retreat, the Balkan countries devoured on Albania's territory.

Remarkably, that the double-edged policy of the Albanian League was failure-bound was a sentiment proclaimed well in advance in the German

---

[396] *Ibid.*

[397] *Ibid.*

[398] *Ibid.* 128.

[399] PA AA, Türkei, 143, doc. no. 184.

press. The Albanians did not succeed because of a conflict of interests. The struggle for autonomy was righteous and quite similar to the movements that culminated with the freedom of other nations in the region. However, the Albanians could not attain their autonomy through the Porte, for they did not agree with what neither the empire's commitment for reforms nor the government itself sought by labeling the predominantly-Muslim ethnic group as the *flower of Islam*. The Porte's intention was to rely on the Albanians, whom it viewed "as a property" of the empire, to perpetuate the Ottoman dominions in Europe. Whereas the Albanians not only were displeased with the one-sided treatment; they were ready to fight against it, as actually happened.

Hamburgische Correspondent states:

> The Albanians knew that siding with Turkey meant standing on ice under the sun; but, they also knew that, at that stage, when they had no friends and protectors like the other peoples, a definite break-off from Turkey would be a merciless suicide.[400]

Therefore, at the very beginning, they announced that they desired to remain under the Sultan in order to buy time and, depending on what terms and how long [the empire] will remain in the European areas, project its own future, which appeared outside of [the empire].[401]

Hasfield, the German ambassador to İstanbul who insisted that the Porte relied on the Albanians and their League to sabotage the decisions of the Berlin Congress, noted the following when the Albanian conflict with the Ottomans broke out:

> The Albanians endeavored to keep the sultan on their side and the sultan [tried to keep them]—as much as the situation permitted. When words depleted, the conflict became inevitable and it was well clear who would suffer.[402]

While describing the League's policy towards the Porte as "special diplomatic approach" may seem buoyant use of the phrase, it is nonetheless appropriate. As contemporary European press notes, "although many things seem to have begun with an agreement between the Albanians and the Porte, later developments proved that their ways stood predictably apart."[403]

---

[400] *Hamburgische Correspodent*, 1881.

[401] *Ibid.*

[402] PA AA, Türkei, 143, doc. no. 223.

[403] See: *Hamburgische Correspodent, Kölnische Zeitung, Neue Presse*, etc., stored at PA AA, Türkei, band. 143, file: "Presse," no. 18-32.

Relations with Europe

Leaders of the Albanian League and the intellectual elite were well aware that the movement's success rested upon ties with Western Europe. Whether through personal connections with decision-makers or newspaper articles that reflected on the Albanian issue, officers of the League became increasingly active in publicizing their national movement. At a time when the propaganda machines of neighboring countries ballyhooed all types of prejudices against the Albanians, the League undertook to present the idea of autonomy and the importance of the ethnic identity as a natural, homogenous building block for the future state of Albania.

The Albanian League of Prizren, appearing for the first time as the leading body of the threatened nationality, was faced with two possible scenarios: the Albanians were to maintain close ties with both, the Porte and Western Europe, while the earlier could even adopt the character of a European government as proposed by some (even though this seemed an illusion); or the Ottoman Empire was to dissolve altogether, in which case an already autonomous Albania would have higher chances of survival as an independent state.

The Porte did not expressly reject the autonomy option at the beginning. Even though there had been no affirmation of the Albanian proposal, the Ottoman government was fond of the calls for defending the homeland that the League made in conjunction with its autonomy demands. That meant that the Porte was tolerant to the idea for Albanian self-governance and the League had act on it quickly for the autonomy plan could help save the troubled empire, too. Therefore, beginning with the first phase of activities, the League began to promulgate its main concerns for the territorial integrity and demands for autonomy. The organization's representatives in İstanbul and contacts with foreign diplomats stationed in the Albanian towns proved a useful means to lobby the Porte as well as the Western powers for their support, which was indispensable to the Albanian demands.

By the same token, the League decided to send a delegation to Europe for meetings with political representatives, intellectuals, and members of the press. The League's envoys were entrusted with the historic task of presenting the existential struggle of the Albanian people, while maintaining that there is hope for peace in the region even though the line dividing the East and West civilizations cuts through that part of the world. In addition to delivering memoranda, letters, and other support for the Albanian demands, there was a growing need to rebut the various misconceptions that hostile propaganda groups had spread about the struggling ethnic community. Particularly, Serbian and Greek state officials and diplomats had distributed numerous foreign-language publications that vilified the Albanians as the Porte's right-hand men in the Balkans, accusing them of violence against Christians, and other malevolent defamations. They denied the Albanians any right to statehood, which they had especially enjoyed under Skanderbeg and the medieval princes when they alone fought against the Ottoman Empire.

In a time crunch of this nature, a separate chapter in the League's foreign relations covers the close ties with the consuls and other diplomatic representatives that some of the important European countries maintained in Albanian and other Balkan towns; for it was such contacts that proved the most beneficial of all diplomatic activities of the Prizren League. They were important because they served as a means for the Albanians to announce their intentions and receive direct advice. But most importantly, the foreign diplomats helped the Albanians send quick and safe messages to high-level decision-makers in the West. Instead of relying on the snail mail of the watchful Ottoman government, important Albanian letters cut corners through the diplomatic pouch. This likely made it possible for the League's local branches in the north to remain active and well-informed, since the Austro-Hungarian, French, English, and Italian consuls in the city of Shkodër held their doors opened for contact. Notably, the memorandum that the Shkodrans addressed to Benjamin Disraeli in 1878 was delivered to foreign diplomats in town the day the Congress of Berlin began; the communication was then telegraphed to the British prime minister that very day.[404]

Among the Shkodër-based diplomats who developed close relations with the Albanians was the Austro-Hungarian general consul, Lippich. Through his contacts, the dual monarchy's representative became a linking bridge between Albania and Vienna, but also Berlin, after the two German-speaking countries formed the famous Zweibund alliance (or Dreibund, after Italy joined group). Therefore, it comes as no surprise that Count Andrássy was well-informed on Albania throughout the Congress; together with British representatives, the Austro-Hungarian foreign minister ensured that all delegations were briefed on the Albanian demands. Furthermore, many foreign diplomats in Albanian towns began to write for the contemporary

---

[404] Bartl, *Die Albanische Muslime . . .*, 117.

press about the Albanian movement as an influential elements in regional politics. The French representative, Hugonet, and the Italian diplomat, Galanti, stood out for their sincere writings on the issue.[405]

It is also likely that the same diplomats residing in Shkodër maintained ongoing contacts with some of the leading European newspapers, providing them with fresh, sensational news from Albania. In the press excerpts stored in the Political Archive of the German Foreign Ministry in Bonn, German, Italian, and French publications cite European consuls as a source. Remarkably, Galanti gave a crucial interview in which he spoke at length about the Albanian movement and political program.

Besides permanent contacts with European diplomats, League placed much of their focus on the Congress. Many of the letters, memoranda, and other documents that the Albanians mailed to Berlin were addressed to Bismarck personally, as the presider of the meetings. The communications were important since, even if they did not wind up on the Berlin agenda, they kept the European decision-makers in the loop of Albanian affairs. Attempted contacts with the Congressional delegations and prudent behavior during the European summit were hence a recommended course for the League as its members hoped in a just revision of the San Stefano terms. Although the Albanians were ignored at the very beginning, the letters and telegrams they sent nonetheless expressed high expectations. Such communications include the telegram sent from Shkodër on the very first day of the Congress, the letter of the Mirdita highlanders, the memorandum of İstanbul Albanians,[406] the Shkodër petition containing hundreds of signatures, and a letter from southern Albania. League activists continued their efforts even after the Congress ended and ambassadorial commissions were set up to finalize the details of the Berlin agreements. One monumental document is a lengthy letter that southern representatives, including Abdyl Frashëri and forty-one others, sent on February 28, 1879, remonstrating against an unfavorable redrawing of the Greek border. Meanwhile, the certain Memorandum that Abdyl Frashëri and Mehmet Ali Vrioni addressed to the German government during a visit to Berlin later in the year presents another historic attempt to solicit European support for Albania.

---

[405] For more on the letter dated July 20, 1878, that İstanbul Albanians sent to the Congress, see Schanderl, *Die albanienpolitik . . .*, 46. The German historian states that the document was sent to Count Andrássy. Archived materials, however, reveal that the letter was rather addressed to the Congress in general. See PA AA, Türkei, band. 143, doc. no. 86.

[406] PA AA, Türkei, band. 143, doc. no. 86.

From the myriad of letters sent to the Congress and the subsequent commissions, numerous documents give the impression of hasted, uncoordinated draftsmanship that often makes the Albanian positions unclear and confusing (this, moreover, raises doubts that many letters may have been written by others on behalf of the Albanians; by the time, Serbia and Greece had developed thriving counter-propaganda agencies). Still, the Albanians sent several communiqués that successfully conveyed the underpinning concerns of the national movement.

Noticeably, the League did not disclose all matters of interest during the first phase of activities when activists began to make pronouncements on the European origin and identity of the Albanian people. The caution may reflect the League's wait-and-see approach on the Congress and the Ottoman government for it was expected to retain its presence in Albania. The situation changed, however, after the Berlin gathering. While the European powers spared much of the Balkan dominions the Porte was due to cede under the San Stefano agreement and the Ottoman Empire committed to internal reforms, the decisions were not as favorable for the Albanians. In addition to awarding Albanian territory to the neighboring countries, the Congress failed to treat the ethnic group as a separate community and, except for the discussions on the Mirdita Catholics, delegates spoke of the Albanians as part of the Ottoman nationality. Under the new conditions, when the justice the League had hoped for was not instituted, demands for autonomy were the anticipated stride of the national movement. Unable to change the decisions that now lay in the past, the Albanians launched their campaign for self-governance as a look to the future.

European historians, including Bartel and Schanderl, hold that the 1879 Frashëri-Vrioni memoradum presents a turning point for the League. The document that the Albanian diplomats mailed to the German government and the Ambassadors' Commission came in the new mise en scène that the Berlin Congress created. The Ottoman Empire retained its presence, even though temporarily, in the Balkans, giving the Albanians an opportunity to assume the reigns of its fate. Meanwhile, the changes in the region--Serbia's independence and southward expansion, Montenegrin annexation of northern Albanian territories; Bulgaria's autonomy, and the augmented border of the Hellenic realm--left Albania and Macedonia as the only regions of the peninsula that were yet to attain their statehood. The plan seemed plausible in that an Albanian state was in the interest of the Ottoman Empire as well as Western Europe, which were greatly affected by Russia's influence in the region. Even though the Treaty of San Stefano did not take effect, the newly-formed Slavic states were conducive to czarist advance on the peninsula. The Albanians, however, could help halt the Russian impingement, and such a role was a political asset in the hands of the Prizren League. Despite the risk of exacerbating Slavic hostility against them, the Albanians relied on their anti-Russian card to make offers of partnership to the Western powers. Ultimately, it was the dread of the vast Eurasian empire that led Britain, Austria-Hungary, Germany, and Italy to support the independent, albeit partitioned, state of Albania after 1912.

Notwithstanding the quandary of the independence movement, the masterminds of the Albanian League of Prizren had their eye on statehood. It was hence not fortuitous that stalwarts of the cause would serve in diplomatic expeditions. Overdue by a year, the League assigned Abdyl Frashëri and Mehmet Ali Vrioni to travel to European capitals to present the Albanian issue as key to peace and stability in the Balkans. The representatives delivered memoranda demurring at the planned incorporation of Albnaian lands into the Greece. Meanwhile, the League's delegates also addressed the autonomy issue in meeting with officials in Rome, Paris, London, and Vienna. But no such meeting was conducted in Berlin, where the German authorities refused to pay heed to the Albanian diplomats.

Had Bismarck received the Albanian delegates, they would have likely proposed a compromise solution. Despite the position expressed in their Memorandum, they were willing to suggest that the border issue be suspended temporarily until such time when the people would be on an equal footing to resolve the matter on their own (implying therefore Albania's independence). This plan was revealed on May 15, 1879, by the *Kölnische Zeitung* in a lengthy article about Frashëri and Vrioni, whom the newspaper commended as fine Westerners with a proper intellectual and political background. The Cologne-based daily appealed to Bismarck to meet the two diplomats and discuss with them thoroughly so that the Ambassadors' Commission supervising the drawing of the new southern border could consider the Albanian proposals. Moreover, the article insisted that the dialogue could help prevent a conflict between the two peoples, which had no reason to go to war with each other. *Kölnische Zeitung* illustrated its anti-war position with the common ancient roots of Albanians and Greeks, also mentioning the joint war against the Ottomans. Arvanites of Beotia, Suli, and Athens had participated in the Greek War of Independence and many of them had become heroes of the new Hellenic state, which would not have enjoyed its freedom without the sacrifices and the contribution of Albanians.[407]

Perhaps, the newspaper's announcement of an Albanian package "with interesting and tolerant proposals to resolve the southern crisis" prompted German officials to ignore Frashëri and Vrioni. They, too, expected the same scenario. They arrived in Berlin on May 15, 1879, and checked in at the luxury Roma hotel,[408] from where they mailed their Memorandum to the German government. Instead of delivering the document in person, the two diplomats sent the ten-page letter through the mail and enclosed a request for a conference with Bismarck. However, in lieu of an appointment with the chancellor, then-Foreign Secretary (and future chancellor) Bernhard Von Bülow wrote: "Gentlemen, I had the honor of receiving your letter, dated May 19, 1879, sent from Roma Hotel along with the Memorandum and an appendix. I thank you cordially for the notice and express my regards."[409]

Since Frashëri and Vrioni had already left Berlin, they never received Bülow's response. The letter was returned to the German Foreign Ministry with a note from the hotel management that "the two gentlemen have departed as of two days ago to Vienna via Dresden."[410]

As one may infer from the documents, neither Bismarck nor another senior official of the Reich received the Albanian delegation. Frashëri and Vrioni stayed in Berlin for two days and sent their Memorandum through the postal service. Such a flow of events rejects the contention of Hadi-Vasiljević that "Bismarck welcomed the League's delegation in Berlin."[411] The Serbian scholar has also influenced some Albanian historians to relay the mistake, saying that Bismarck "unofficially" met with the Albanian representatives. Such an event is not supported by any meritorious German document and moreover it is unlikely that the meeting could possibly take place. The Albanians were unable to meet with the foreign secretary, Bülow, who was responsible for the Balkans, or another lower ranking official of the department. That this was to occur is foretold by a letter the Ottoman ambassador in Berlin, Abdullah Bey, sent to German foreign ministry. On behalf of his foreign minister Karatheodori Pasha, Abdullah requested the German officials to not accept any Albanian representatives with the pretext

---

[407] *Kölnische Zeitung*, May 15, 1879.

[408] PA AA, Türkei, 143, nr. 43.

[409] *Ibid.*, doc. no. 43.

[410] *Ibid.*, doc. no. 43.

[411] Jovan Hađi-Vasiljević, *Arbanaska liga . . .*, 39-44.

that the Ottoman Empire alone was responsible for the matters the Albanians wished to raise. Hađi-Vasiljević's assertion, nevertheless, is likely intentional. When Germany and Austria-Hungary declared war on Serbia in 1914, the propaganda apparatus of the Balkan state accused its enemies of being pro-Albanian. Hađi-Vasiljević alluded to Germany's ostensibly secret friendship with Albania as early as the Congress of Berlin, but in doing so legitimized an inaccurate theory, which—meanwhile the original documents were unknown—earned wide support among scholars. The group of misled writers also includes the German historian, Schanderl, who cites the Serbian author.[412]

The Memorandum encompasses a distinct chapter of the national movement's history. Likewise, the content of the document differs from the usual communications that Albanians sent to the European powers. Yet, despite the numerous citations to it, the Memorandum remains largely unknown, hence warranting a presentation and an analysis of the integral text.[413]

Bearing the date May 19, 1879 and handwritten in French, the ten-page original is found in the Political Archive of the German Foreign Ministry in Bonn. In recent years, German archivists have included the document in the pile of "same materials secured from different sources," a classification indicating that Albanians sent the same content in multiple letters to the several delegations in Berlin, although quite frequently, the text would vary according to the addressee. The content is important in revealing the circumstances, under which the documents were written, while the lack of coordination that is evident in some of the letters may as well be the product of foreign hands seeking to distract the Albanian movement. Thus, in the Bonn archive, there are three to four versions of the same letter, causing confusion as to their classification. In the meantime, the text of the Memorandum that Frashëri and Vrioni delivered to Bismarck is not entirely identical with the Austro-Hungarian version stored in Vienna archives, making it worthy of providing the German version in the notes.[414]

If the unique document is to be considered as truly representative of the League, it follows that, by May 1879, the strategic focus of the Albanian organization had largely shifted to the south:

---

[412] *Ibid.*

[413] PA AA, Türkei, band. 143, doc. no. 2876.

[414] For the English rendition of the 1879 Albanian Memorandum to the German government, see Appendix, "The Frashëri-Vrioni Memoradum."

Even though Serbia and Montenegro were given entire districts, such as Shpu-za, Podgorica, and Vranje, we, the Albanians, believe that we ought to refrain from action for that would endanger the respect of the Congress of Berlin, which we value so highly. The loss of those territories is not of the same gravity and value as the present Greek claims. These would be catastrophic for us. One must by no means forget that the Serbian and Montenegrin annexation of the said territories has brought great difficulties and turmoil that continue to this day. The decisions broke the perpetual harmony that the two people had en-joyed until then. This was hence a mistake.

The letter describes the endangered districts, including Janina, Parga and Preveza, as the heart of Albania:

The value of Epirus cannot be compared to the territories lost in the north. The importance of Epirus is much greater since key Albanian ports, including Pre-veza, Narta, and Parga, are situated there. Albania has no other harbors that could rival [those of Epirus]. Moreover, the areas are of vital strategic im-portance, among the most valuable in Albania.

Should those areas be given to the Greek, as he now persistently demands, [the decision] would touch the hearts of every patriot willing to defend his country above all. If the keys to Albania are handed to another people, this would serve as a starting point to seize all of Albania. Thereby, the most strate-gic areas would be given to a state, which has for a long time taken a hostile stance against us. This would bring us such a diminishment that no people gripped by patriotic feelings could endure.

It is well-known that the Albanian farmers subsist on their arid, mountain-ous pastures. In wintertime, the flocks graze in Preveza, Parga, Margariti, and all the way to Janina. If those areas are to be given to Greece, the Albanians would have no place to overwinter their livestock and would be forced to sell it. Has any thought been given to such a situation? This would inflict a people with having no basis to subsist. The said areas that the Greeks demand are the only in the region that provide food for the Epirus population.

This is the truth and the reason behind the territorial claims since the Greeks are well aware of the said benefits. . . .

This rightly raises the question as to why the League braced for a diplo-matic campaign for the south when activists had vowed to defend all Albani-an lands. Concurrently, the discussion necessitates a comparison of the northern territories ceded to Serbia and Montenegro with the southern districts, questioning whether the latter were indeed of a greater importance.

Ultimately, would wisdom require that the Albanians give up a part of the homeland, arguing they had to defend another more significant piece of their territory? Did the imbalanced focus come as a sign of deference to the decisions of the Congress or because the Albanians hoped to concentrate on a battle they had not yet lost?

Of course, the Albanians had not given up from a part of their counry to defend another and neither had the League of Prizren officially proclaimed such a policy. However, under particular circumstnaces, the Albanian organization was forced to defend that which could be defended. Although this standpoint remains debateable, the League redefined its approach in accordance with the situation. The Albanians pursued an armed resistance in the north, where their military victories compelled the Great Powers to revise their decisions, and the Ottomans had to attack by land, while the Europeans threatened at sea, to force the League to back down on its positions. To defend the southern border, in the meantime, the League decided to exhaust the diplomatic resources.

For the Albanians to change their way was a natural choice since the Berlin decisions on the borders were not uniform. The northern line was final; the protocols set the Montenegrin border and defined the status of Yeni Pazar (Alb.: Jenipazar, or Tregu i Ri; Srb.: Novi Pazar) in detail,[415] leaving no room for dilemma,[416] for the Great Powers expected the Ottoman Empire to fully comply with the decisions and the Porte could not dodge the terriorial losses. However, the matter stood differently for the south as the Congress permitted Greece and the Ottoman state to determine the border on their own and only prescribed Hellenic gains in Thessal and Epirus. Although the Berlin decisions did not name the lands that Greece was to annex,[417] the protocol of the 13th séance provided for an international commission to resolve disputes regarding the territorial conveyances between the two countries. Based on the foregoing, the League could have well chosen to fight against the final border in the north, but opted instead for diplomacy in the negotiable southern matter.[418] Albanians hoped to influence the final solution or to prevent unfavorable irreversible decisions that could make diplomacy defunct, recognizing that if arms had to be substituted, they

---

[415] Decisions of the Congress of Berlin, Articles XXVIII-XXXIV.

[416] Buxhovi, Kongresi . . ., 658.

[417] Specifically, Article XXIV deals with the Greek border.

[418] Ibid. 659.

would open a front against a significantly better prepared opponent than Montenegro.

For that reason, the League resorted to diplomatic means in its dealings with the Porte and Europe. The strategy was expected to yield great results, because the Ottomans were greatly interested in prolonging the border settlement in order to use the Albanians for the Porte's own goals. In the meantime, the Albanians also agreed with the Ottoman government for as long as they were able to defend their own lands. The German ambassador to İstanbul thought that "the Porte is trying to use the Albanians and their movement in all respects, but the Albanians also seek to achieve the same from [the Porte]. This type of cooperation is not coincidiental."[419]

The Porte's strategy here seems to have been perfidious, seeking to fulfill all the obligations to the Great Powers in order to provide the empire with a chance to recover its state authority. In the meantime, the Ottoman government professed to be a protector of the Albanians, but pointing out what the Porte presented as its limitations vis-à-vis the the European powers that appeared as enemies of the League of Prizren. The 1880 memorandum of Abedin Pasha, for instance, could qualify as evidence of such a hypocritical behavior by the Porte.[420]

Thus, even after the Ottomans had given in on the Greek border, the İstanbul authorities promised another thing to the Albanians. The Porte used Abedin Pasha, who openly admitted his Albanian nationality, to call on the League leaders "to refrain from any action that could contradict our goals," suggesting peaceful means as the only solution. Furthermore, the imperial minister of foreign affairs assured his fellow Albanians that the Porte would oppose the Greek claims and "protect you from the greed of your neighbors." Such promises were made to the Albanians not long before the disappointing epilogue of March 24, 1881, when the Ottoman Empire signed the new border agreement, ceding the town of Volas, Margariti, Aidon, and Lura and other districts in Thessaly and Epirus that greatly added to the east and west of the Greek coast. Indeed, Janina and Larissa remained Ottoman territories, but this was not a success of İstanbul's diplomacy, as the Porte tried to portray the border deal. It was the Italian and Austrian intervention that spared the towns the two powers had long held in contemplation. This came as Italy desired to include Epirus within its sphere of influence and Vienna as

---

[419] PA AA, Türkei, band. 143, doc. no. 184.
[420] *Ibid.,*

well as Berlin agreed to the move as a compensation for Rome's support of the Austro-Hungarian annexation of Bosnia.

While the League reminded the Porte to be persistent in the talks with Greece, the Prizren-based organization entreated Europe for reason and justice. Here, Albanian activists noted the ancient past of their people, its culture and ethnic compactness, preserved in the same territory since the early times of history. For example, to oppose the so-called "linguistic argument" of the Greek claims, the Frashëri-Vrioni 1879 memorandum presented a theory on the interaction of state and language that retains its value in international law and relations. Thus, when Greeks demands a part of Epirus because of the Hellenic-speaking population, Albanians revealed the weaknesses of the argument, recalling that:

> [I]f the language spoken must determine to which state a territory will belong, we ought to change the maps of Asia, Europe, and the world at large. Should we define citizenship on a linguistic basis, we would have to begin with Greece, annexing the 210,000 of its inhabitants who today speak Albanian within the present Greek borders; then, we ought to take 160,000 Albanians from Italy, 150,000 from Serbia, Montenegro, Bulgaria, and Dalmatia [Zadar (Alb.: Zara); then part of Austria-Hungary], and so on. This is the logic that Greece relies on today. One may wonder where it would take us.

The memorandum made a particular reference to Germany and Bismarck, not because they hosted the Congress, but because the Reich was seen as a state "erected on justice and reason." It is hence not perchanced that the document demanded for the Albanians to be allowed into "the path of reforms and progress." If the Porte did not permit the Albanian autonomy, the reforms would be rendered meaningless. Therefore, the League petitioned Berlin, as direct supervisor of the changes in the Ottoman Empire, to push the Ottoman government to recognize the Balkan people's right to self-government.

The diplomatic activities of the Albanian League of Prizren scored no political marks. First, they began noticeably late and with much unclarity, and failed to secure the status of a nationality for the Albanians or promote the League as a legitimate representative of the people. However, in the contacts with the external world, activists succeeded in increasing awareness on their national question and Albania's importance for peace and stability in the region. A great source of help came from the leading German newspapers, which took the role of a protector for the small European ethnic group, during and after the Congress of Berlin. Even as the Great Powers sidelines the Albanians, the press remained attentive. Highlighting facts from history, Western publications returned the Albanian place in Europe, wherefrom others sought to expel the defenseless community.

The League Forms a Provisional Government, Restores the Albanian State

Following the loss of Ulqin, the League focuses on the southern border and the campaign for autonomy. An extraordinary session of the General Council decides to supplant the Ottoman administration with an autonomous, native structure. The League's National Committee is declared a Provision Government with Ymer Prizreni as its president. The Albanian government extends its authority over many sanjaks of the Vilayet of Kosova. Resumed negotiations on an Albanian-Greek alliance against the Ottomans fail; Hellenic nationalists conceal their intentions, deceiving their Albanian to-be partners. Dervish Pasha leads the Ottoman expedition against the Albanian government, retaking the city of Shkup. The League issues a call to arms and a major battle occurs at Slivova. Dervish Pasha marches against Suhareka and Prizren; Ottomans quell the Albanian resistance in the main towns. The Turkish pasha makes a deal with moderate Albanian leaders who condemned the idea of an Albanian vilayet. Sultan pardons the Albanian leaders and appoints them to high posts in the vilayet administration of Kosova and Manastir. Sulejman Vokshi holds out in the Gjakova Highlands as the Ottomans dissolve the Albanian League of Prizren.

Through the armed resistance to defend the lands the Congress of Berlin awarded to Serbia and Montenegro, the Albanian League of Prizren proved its political and military significance. In October 1879 and January 1880, the League forces defended Plava and Gucia and, in the spring, mobilized to guard Hot and Gruda. The Albanians were willing to face even the Ottomans, when on September 6, 1878, Mehmed Ali Pasha was assassinated in Gjakova, where he had travelled to persuade the League to respect the commitments the empire had made to the Great Powers in Berlin.

When the Albanians prepared to defend Ulqin, the League stood, in addition to Montenegro, in front of two powerful opponents, the Ottoman army and the international fleet. The national movement was challenged with radical decisions: to fight the Ottomans in defense of lands in the north and south, but to also carry out plans for Albania's autonomy. Therefore, at the end of December 1880, Albanian leaders called an extraordinary convention of the League. Prominent members, including Ymer Prizreni, Sulejman Vokshi, Abdyl Frashëri, Shuaip Spahiu, and Ali Ibra, were present at the meeting held in Prizren. In his address, Frashëri noted, *inter alia*, that:

> The Sublime Porte wishes to do nothing for Albania. It treats with great contempt our requests as well as our persons . . . . Let us thing and work for ourselves and let there be no difference between the Tosks and the Ghegs. Let us all be Albanians and form a united Albania.[421]

At the closing of the session, the extraordinary convention replaced a few members of the League's National Committee. As a more important step, meanwhile, the convention decided to substitute an autonomous Albanian government for the Ottoman administration. Thereby, the extraordinary meeting upgraded the National Committee to a Provisional Albanian Government, with Ymer Prizreni serving as president and Shuaip Spahiu as vice-president. The cabinet comprised of ten members, including Abdyl Frashëri, charged with foreign affairs, and Sulejman Vokshi, overseeing the military.[422]

During the formation of the government and its armed forces, the League authorities undertook to take the Albnaian lands under control. Therefore, on January 4, Sulejman Vokshi led his forces to take over Shkup after a brief skirmish with the Ottomans. On the 18th, the Albanians captured Prishtina without war and, a week later, seized Mitrovica. As a result, most of the Vilayet of Kosova accepted the authority of the Provisional Albanian Government. In other towns, such as Peja, Ferizaj, and Vuçitërn, the League ousted the senior Ottoman official, replacing them with Albanians. Likewise, the armed forces of Provisional Government restrained the movement of the Ottoman troops, ordering them to remain unarmed in certain garrisons under the League's supervision. Ottomans could leave only without their weapons and on the condition that they returned home. In this regard, Albanian military officers took care to ensure the Ottoman soldiers were safe and were being treated properly.

---

[421] H.P.Sh. 2 (Tiranë), 217.
[422] *Ibid.* 218.

The Provisional Albanian Government extended its power to Tetova, Gostivar, and Dibër. By mid-February, Prizren authorities sent Abdyl Frashëri to Dibër to prevent sultanist landlords from opposing the Albanian government. Subsequently, the local population expelled the town's Turkish mutessarif and landlords who followed him.

By the same token, the Provisional Government installed its authority in all of the sanjaks of the Kosova Vilayet, except for Yeni Pazar. Meanwhile, the Albanians also gained control of some areas of the Vilayet of Manastir, but encountered difficulties in the Vilayet of Shkodër and central Albania. The autonomist expansion wilted after the Sublime Porte began heavy punitive measures against the local League committees. Another impediment came from pro-Turkish landlords and sultanists who exerted great influence in the areas.

Despite the alarming situation and the military activities, the Provisional Government attended to the state-building process. Thus, the Prizren cabinet purged the administration in the liberated territories from Turkish functionaries and Albanian sultanists, while also taking measures against leaders of the pro-Ottoman reaction that undermined the new regime. However, such actions were a part of the regular efforts to establish law and order in the country. Reporting from Shkodër in March 1881, the chief Austro-Hungarian consul wrote:

> Even the most inferior clerks were appointed by the League: the judge is a resident of Prizren; the taxes collected from the population are paid into the League's treasury; government employees receive their pays regularly. The League takes care to keep order in the city as well the countryside. Public safety is in a much better state that it was under the administration of the sultan's functionaries.[423]

In addition to the limited territorial expansion and the internal problems, the Albanian government was also faced with the stringent response of the Ottoman Empire. After concluding the treaty with Athens over the new boundary—which detached 35,000 square kilometers and about 800,000 people of Albanian origin from the rest of the country—the Porte returned to the Albanian League and its Provisional Government. Besides the urge of domestic politics that necessitated the empire to act against the Albanians, pressure also came from abroad. The Great Powers as well as the regional

---

[423] Ippen, "Beitrege zur innere geschihte Alanbaniens im XIX Jahrhundert," 117.

countries pushed for the Ottomans to react. Notably, Serbia, Montenegro, Greece, and Bulgaria were aware that the Provisional Albanian Government endangered their expansionist plans at a time when the neighbors had not ceased, but sought to snatch in the future all of the Albanian territories, which the Berlin Congress had retained under the Ottomans.

Aiming at a raucous "patriotic" campaign that would please the domestic needs, the Sublime Porte ordered Marshal Dervish Pasha to begin an expedition against Kosova and the autonomous government. Ymer Prizreni's cabinet was the first state mechanism the Albanians had had since the era of Skanderbeg, over four hundred years prior. However, in contrast to State of Arbër in 15th century, when Europeans prayed in Notre Dame de Paris for their bastion's victories over the Turks, the Provisional Albanian Government was all alone, facing the Ottoman revenge as well as the Western pressure. Thus, Ottoman troops managed their first strike on the Albanian League's local committee in Shkup. The operation succeeded easily since the Albanian leaders of the town, Jashar Bej Shkupi, had left the Ottoman administration, along with the mutessarif and the garrison, intact. The imperial structures in the city had accepted the request of the League's representative to recognize the authority of the Provisional Government. After the Porte ordered the expedition, Shkup Ottomans changed their mind and the imperial forces took the city on February 27, 1881, encountering no resistance. Meanwhile, Ibrahim Pasha, as the town's commander, summoned Jashar Bej Shkupi along with ten other members of the League's local committee and treacherously arrested.[424]

After the fall of Shkup, the Albanian League issued a call for mobilization throughout Kosova. The Provisional Government formed its defense staff, composed of twenty-five members, with Sulejman Vokshi serving as commander; other prominent members of the military body included Mic Sokoli, celebrated as a hero among the Albanians.[425] The autonomous government had only 5,000 soldiers at its disposal and, despite the willingness of the population to serve, the number of troops failed to increase. Ottoman forces had encircled the Vilayet of Kosova. Dervish Pasha had twenty battalions and 30,000 soldiers at his command. The defeat at Ulqin and the Greek annexation of the southern territories had depleted the morale of the population in areas outside of the League's control. Moreover, loyalist

---

[424] H.P.Sh. 2 (Tiranë), 221.

[425] Other members of the staff included Ali Ibra, Mic Sokoli, Binak Alija, Sefë Kosharja, Halim Efendiu, Zeqirja Aga, Mullah Hyseni, Mustafa Aga, and Halil Efendia.

landlords did not view the Albanian regime favorably and awaited the moment to reclaim the influence they had lost after the formation of the autonomous government.

Meanwhile the military preparations did not yield much hope, the League of Prizren sent a memorandum to the ambassadors of the Great Powers in İstanbul. The document, dated April 15, explains the reasons why the Albanians formed the Provisional Government. Speaking of autonomy, the letter insists on Albanian self-governance, in line with the ethnic, social, cultural, and political realities. While the Albanians had already demanded their autonomy, the Great Powers ignored the calls, leaving the matter to the Ottoman Empire. In this regard, the April memorandum reminds the Europeans that the Porte wishes to keep the Albanians as pawns for its continued presence in the Balkans. Therefore, the League opposed the treatment of the Albanians as part of the *millet-i osman*, which denied them their nationality and hindered the autonomous Albanian state.[426]

The letter was the last diplomatic act of the Albanian League of Prizren and the Provisional Government in relation with the international community. There was no time left for other communications, for the League soon faced the fatal Ottoman offensive. Dervish Pasha marched to the Kaçanik Canyon, near the town of Ferizaj in the southeast, to then move on to the central parts of the vilayet. However, the army of the Albanian League refused to surrender without war, as had been the case in Shkup. Thus, at the Kaçanik Canyon, the Albanians staged an enormous resistance, but failed to stop the advance of the Ottoman battalions. Accompanied by mountain cannons, which bombarded the surrounding villages, the Ottomans took Ferizaj on April 7. Their commander, Dervish Pasha, moved with his staff to the town, where he issued an ultimatum on the League fighters to lay down their arms, threatening with a stern punishment.

Dervish Pasha's warning resonated with certain landowning leaders of the League. Among them, Ali Pashë Gucia appeared before the Turkish officer, affirming his and his men's allegiance to the sultan. On this occasion, he reportedly condemned the creation of the Provisional Albanian Government and the expulsion of the Ottoman officials from the Vilayet of Kosova.[427] The pasha of Gucia, one of the first leaders to organize the armed defense against Montenegro two years before, reflected the various currents

---

[426] See: Letter to Berlin of the German ambassador to İstanbul, Apr. 20, 1881; PA AA, Türkei, band. 143, doc. no. 120.

[427] H.P.Sh. 2 (Tiranë), 222.

that had existed within the Albanian movement. In harmony with the interests of the Ottoman Empire, the League leaders had endeavored to defy the international factor in order to halt the partitioning of the country. In the meantime, activists of the *Rilindja Kombëtare* insisted that the Albanian League become the standard-bearer for the formation of the national state.

The epilogue of the Albanian League of Prizren and its Provisional Government, however tragic, elucidated the ideological splits among the Albanians. Nonetheless, this fact finds no room in the Albanian historiography as a result of its ideological clichés and the folkloric pathos. Possibly, Albanian scholars did not wish to specify the various interests within the Albanian movement, let alone the belief that any political change ought to take place in coordination with the Ottoman Empire. For a layer of the contemporary leaders, the Sublime Porte was the only defender against the territorial amputations and the Slavic occupation. Such a thought survived through the year 1912, on the brink of the Balkan wars and as the Ottoman Empire was in the throes of death.

Following the surrender of the landlords, the Ottoman army faced the Albanian forces through the beginning of May. On April 20, heavy combat took place in Slivova; another battle was staged in Shtimje, two days later. On the morrow, the Ottomans defeated the Albanians in the Carraleva Canyon near Prizren and the same day, on April 23, entered the city with 14 battalions. Although the battles were expected to end in Ottoman victory, the Albanian endeavored to resist heroically in defense of their autonomy and the provisional government that temporarily restored the Albanian state after almost five hundred years. After the fall of Prizren, Sulejman Vokshi retreated to the highlands, where he continued his defiance until the fall.

Having moved his staff to the city, Dervish Pasha called former heads of League committees. On April 30, the local leaders of the sanjaks previously held by the Provisional Government attended, except for Vokshi who, as representative of Gjakova and the Highlands, continued his armed resistance. In the presence of the native sultanists, the Ottoman marshal ordered the Albanian leaders to sign a declaration, condemning the activities of the Albanian League and the demands for the unification of the vilayets, which Dervish Pasha called an "inimical act."[428] The declaration was signed by the "moderate leaders," Ali Pashë Gucia, Iliaz Pashë Dibra, Hasan Pashë Dërralla, and Esat Pashë Tetova. As a result, the sultan granted their pardon

---

[428] *Ibid.* 224.

and promoted some of them, such as Ali Pashë Gucia, to important posts in the administration of the vilayets of Kosova and Manastir.[429]

However, a different fate followed those who remained loyal to the Albanian state through the end. Sulejman Vokshi, the commander of the Provisional Government's armed forces, was imprisoned along with many of his soldiers. Liekwise, the Ottomans arrested Abdyl Frashëri, as he tried to escape to continue his activities abroad. The authorities returned the former foreign minister of Albania to Prizren, where he served three years in the city castle penitentiary. Subsequently, Frashëri and his family were deported to the Marmara area, nearby İstanbul. The Ottomans arrested meanwhile other leaders of the Albanian League of Prizren, including Shuaip Spahiu, Zija Prishtina, Omar Efendi Narta, Jusuf Duhoshishi, who were convicted to long-time imprisonmnet and severe internments.

The League of Prizren—A Legitimate Representative of the Albanian People

In Germany, three positions prevail on the Albanian question: the press defends the Albanians and the activity of the League of Prizren, recognizing its legitimate role in representing the people; the government does not deny the Albanians, but defends the conclusions of the Congress of Berlin, insisting that the Ottoman Empire fulfill its commitments, regardless of the Albanian response; moderates call for humanitarian aid for combatants and war victims, despite the political decisions.

The battles that the armed forces of the Albanian League of Prizren waged resonated throughout Europe and almost ruined the "harmony" that dominated among the Great Powers so firmly convinced in the Berlin resolutions. Although, well before the Congress, the Albanians had indicated that they would not dither and dawdle before the European decisions, few people, if any, expected the small people to cause much trouble for the Great Powers. In the next two to three years, the League was so resolute in its objections such that the Europeans saw no alternative but to amend their

---

[429] *Ibid.* 224.

decisions several times before any Albanian land could be annexed to the neighboring countries.[430]

The Albanian resistance gave cause for different opinions that developed in the political sphere and among the media in Europe. Germany was particularly active as it also served as mediator for peace in what became the new Reich's first major appearance in the diplomatic arena of the continent. The empire was seeking to find its place in the lodge of the powerful, but without creating the impression that the German nation was willing to give up from justice and equality as universal values proclaimed by the country's political class.

Meanwhile, many contemporary documents pertain to Albania. The German government received various notifications and reports from diplomatic representatives. Another source was the "itinerant consuls" who were involved in the work of the many commissions, including the Control body that supervised the new border lines. Simultaneously, multiple writings appeared on German newspapers that received wires from special reporters travelling in the area. Archived materials, more or less, point out to two conflicting views: a pro-Albanian stance called for the ethnic group to be treated like others in the border drawing that the Great Powers assumed to impose on the Balkan Peninsula; meanwhile, another position defended the decisions of the Berlin Congress, dominated by political realism regardless of the compromises at the expense of the smaller and defenseless peoples. A third, middle way also manifested as an embodiment of moral principles, calling for humanitarian aid for victims of unjust politics, urging the opinion to provide relief.

The first, pro-Albanian position was that of the press. In addition to reports on current events, German newspapers often published editorials and political analyses in an effort to increase awareness in the public opinion and among the political class about the Albanians. Notably, writings touched on history and the ancient origin of the ethnic group, providing a countermeasure to the Serbian and Russian nationalist propaganda that stigmatized the Albanians as "savages" void of culture and as enemies of Christianity and the West. Meanwhile, the German government had its position, whose most distinguished proponents included political leaders and diplomats, especially those stationed in Turkey, Greece, and Russia. The German representative in İstanbul, Hasfield, nearly at all times made sure to provide his own opinion on the Albanians, adding a *post scriptum* even to reports purported as solely

---

[430] PA AA, Türkei, band. 143, doc. no. 121.

informative. In letters that he mostly addressed to Bismarck personally, ambassador Hasfield insisted by all means to create supporting arguments for Germany's foreign policy even when there were little or no grounds to rely on.

The attention of the press for the Albanian question intended, in addition to presenting the injustice done to a defenseless people, to encourage the public opinion against Bismarck's take on Southeastern Europe. German newspapers did not wish for their country to coalesce with unjust and unsustainable solutions that opened the way for new conflicts ultimately affecting the Great Powers. Thus, authoritative publications, such as *Hamburgische Correspodent, Kölnische Zeitung*, and *Neue Presse*, as well as local papers in the German-speaking countries, followed almost every move of the Albanian response, from the peaceful actions to the armed resistance. The German press seems to have relied principally on independent and diplomatic sources on the ground, including the abundance of consuls and missionaries present in Albania, such the Austro-Hungarian, Italian, and French consulates in Shkodër, Prizren, Shkup, and some southern towns. German newspapers were hence predisposed to cover the northern crisis, which escalated into open war between the Albanians and Montenegro and later, from 1879 to 1881, between the League and the Ottoman Empire itself. *Kölnische Zeitung* wrote in August 1880 that northern and southern representatives of the Albanian League have decided to fight, should any neighboring country attempt to take their lands.[431] The same news item reports that the ethnic-based organization has sent a delegation to İstanbul to petition the sultan for autonomy within the Ottoman Empire.

Ambassador Hasfield also sent a notice of the Albanian initiative, adding that "in October, representatives of all Albanian provinces gathered in Dibër to oppose Europe. They demand autonomy."[432] Later, when the League's relations with the Porte soured, the same ambassador—who had previously clamored of the ostensible "anti-European spirit of the Albanians," shown in the opposition to the Berlin resolutions—noted:

> Turkey was forced to attack the Albanians, realizing it is impossible to keep them as allies after they began to undermine the agreements. They created trouble every time they realized that [the Porte could not fulfill its obligations properly].[433]

[431] *Kölnische Zeitung*, Sept. 20, 1881.
[432] *Ibid.*
[433] PA AA, Türkei, band. 143, doc. no. 129/2.

Disgruntled with the Albanian decision to take over the Vilayet of Kosova, the German ambassador expressed great concern that in Prishtina, Shkup, Dibër, and other towns, the rebels ousted the Turkish mutessarrifs. Hasfield recommended that the Great Powers must insist to enable Turkey return its authority over Kosova. Otherwise, he feared that the Albanian secession would set a precedent for other unsatisfied vilayets to split off from the Ottoman government. He urged for the Sublime Porte to put down the movement for autonomy, for if Albania's statehood were permitted, the European concept for "sustainable peace in the Balkans" would be at stake.[434]

The Porte acted accordingly seeking to please the European powers, but also to prevent the further dismemberment of the empire. The Ottoman government sought to maintain its authority in the Balkans, even though the Congress of Berlin called for internal reforms, including autonomies for the nationalities—that is, Albania was also expected to be a self-governing entity. *Kölnische Zeitung* and *Neue Presse* reported on the developments, which also had the approval of the powerful Western governments. The Cologne-based newspaper wrote that it was the turn for the Europeans, after they took the Albanians' land, to now crush the small people. "They are forced to fight all alone against the Anatolian regiments only so that the protocols of the Berlin Congress commissions are put off once and for all," said *Kölnische Zeitung*.[435] *Neue Presse* conveyed similar pessimism, as the Balkan developments centered on the Albanians as the main victim of the crisis. The small people had a difficult battle ahead, said the newspaper, noting the Albanian relations with Europeans, Ottomans, and particularly the neighboring countries. In addition to the territory already annexed, the regional states were planning to seize the last remaining of the Albanian lands, leaving the nation without a state. The Russian bloc "see any Albanian state in the Balkans as a fatal wound," wrote *Neue Presse*.[436]

The German consul in Athens also notified Bismarck that the Ottomans had sent an army led by Dervish Pasha to quell the Albanian movement. Months later, Ambassador Hasfield, as if he were bringing glad tidings, wrote to Berlin that "Dervish Pasha successfully routed the Albanians . . . lastly giving them the proper punishment."[437] Hasfield reported on the definat Albanian resistance, taking into account days of heavy casualties among the

---

[434] *Ibid.*, doc. 129/3.

[435] *Ibid.*

[436] *Neue Presse*, at PA AA, Türkei, band. 143, doc. no. 78.

[437] PA AA, Türkei, 143, doc. no. 21.

Ottoman forces, whose eventual victory and revenge was worthwhile "because it was all in service of peace and tranquility in this part of Europe."

Yet, to what extent could one claim that peace and tranquility had been secured, as did the German ambassador in his joyous announcement of the Ottoman triumph? On October 11, 1881, Hasfield was forced to back off his words, notifying his superiors that "nevertheless, calm was not secured in the Albanian vilayet neither after the latest military expedition, since the Porte admits that the rebels remain strong in many areas." For that reason, Dervish Pasha was stationed with the army in northern Albania and, according to the Reich's diplomat:

> The pasha says that full control of Albania has not been achieved, and he has to remain further in the area. He demands that martial law remain in effect to enable him free hands to undertake military action to punish the rebels. For that purpose, he informs that he ordered days ago a military expedition against Prizren and Dibër to pacify the rebels who continue to fight and to also force the local population to pay taxes, which were long overdue.[438]

Hasfield informed that the Austro-Hungarian ambassador in İstanbul had protested before the sultan, expressing concerns about regional security. The Vienna diplomat warned that the military operation in northern Albania could also threaten Austria-Hungary, whose new border now lay in the nearby sanjak of Yeni Pazar.[439]

The German opinion received the news of the Albanian League's defeat with concern and regret. The press expressed its indignation that "the Albanians are the most extreme victims of the diplomatic games of the powerful Europeans." In the meantime, the government attempted to easen the frustration, justifying the actions as "indispensable for the implementation of the Berlin Congress decisions." Nevertheless, the German leaders did not conceal their fear that the Balkans could be prone to unexpected developments while the Berlin agreement relied on unsecure grounds. The dynamic movements of the Albanians and other peoples against the European verdicts likely raised enough cause for concern.[440]

---

[438] *Ibid.*

[439] *Ibid.*, doc. no. 35.

[440] *Kölnische Zeitung*, Sept. 20, 1881.

The War for Autonomy Echoes in the German Press

The German press, for the most part, becomes the spokesperson for the Albanian demands. Newspapers publish many writings on the Albanian autonomy and the defensive wars. The media report on the severe conditions of the Albanian people in the areas occupied by Serbia and Montenegro, while the Great Powers remain silent. In summer 1882, Hamburgische Correspodent *runs a series of articles on the Albanians, presenting them as an ancient people and a center of civilization; the writings speak of the role of the Albanians, under the Byzantine Empire and later during the Skanderbeg era, for the protection of the European civilization. Many editorials in the German press argue with the hegemonic Slavic propaganda, which stigmatized the Albanians as a primitive people without a historic past; meanwhile, the Serbian propaganda lays claims on Kosova as a "Serbian spiritual center." German newspapers warn that the lack of a solution for the Albanian question, in line with the historic and ethnic rights, could destabilize the region and cause profound crises.*

While the German government formally regarded the Albanian issue as a domestic matter of the Ottoman Empire, the contemporary German press, for the most part, spoke of Albania as a European question. Newspapers demanded that the issue not be negated and that a solution be found in accordance with the importance of the matter. From this standpoint, the German press of the time was highly active through profound and dedicated editorial writings. These were of such distinct quality such that even if the Albanians had had an institution of their own would hardly be able to treat their national issue with the same level of competence. German writers pursued an open and direct polemic with the policies of the German government and all of the Great Powers, which at the Congress of Berlin ignored justice in favor of their narrow interests.

In the archives, several newspapers of influence in the German-speaking world covered the Albanian question; the group includes *Kölnische Zeitung, Hamburgische Correspondent, Politische Correspondent, Die Post, Neue Presse, Frankfurter Correspondent*, and Vienna's *Die Presse*.[441] Between 1878 and 1885, the newspapers published over forty different articles, from news items, extended reports, and notes to important commentaries and analyses.

---

[441] PA AA and German Newspapers State Archive in Aachen.

The editorial approach exemplifies to this day an effective method of presenting issues that certain interest groups intentionally ignore. Such was the case with the Albanian question with respect to the South Slavic people, whom the European gave advantage despite the unreliable nature of the new Balkan states, so heavily inclined towards the Russian-led Orthodox alliance. Almost half of the newspaper articles deal with the Albanian autonomy and statehood, as an important development for the region and the continent. The analyses were, most of the time, dedicated to the historical and ethnic aspects of the Albanian world, constantly highlighting the facts that the Albanians are an ancient people, one of the oldest in Europe, and that they have a distinct language, tradition, and history. Such writings presented a counterbalance to the quasi-scientific and incorrect theses that the Slavic-Orthodox propaganda placed before the German opinion as part of an attempt to justify the Congress of Berlin and defend even violent actions against the Albanians.

The political commentaries and the informative entries did not die out with the military defeat of the Albanian League and the fall of its Provisional Government in 1881. To the contrary, German dailies and periodicals continued to cover the Albanian question with an unwavering dedication, riveted by the same concern that the unjust decisions of the Berlin Congress had turned the Balkans into a source of distressing news.

Several newspapers—such as *Kölnische Zeitung, Hamburgische Correspodent*, and *Frankfurter Correspondent*—someway assumed the role of the spokesperson for the Albanian League and in general for the national question and the Albanians as an ancient European people. With this stance, the German press appeared as an opposition not only to the German government, which endeavored to justify its position as political pragmatism, but stood, on cultural and intellectual grounds, as a direct opponent of the European policy on Albania.

Kölnische Zeitung published on May 15, 1879, a lengthy article, "Albanians Knock on Europe's Doors," on the diplomatic voyage of Abdyl Frashëri and Mehmet Ali Vrioni as the League's representative. Focusing on the envoys' visit to Berlin, the paper wrote:

> The Congress of Berlin did not find it reasonable to consider hundreds of letter that Albanians sent from all over the world; [the Great Powers] did not wish to pay attention to thousands and thousands of refugees, who were violently expelled from their homes by the Serbian military terror used for that purpose; thus, [the Albanians] today wish to speak directly with the representatives of

Europe so that [the Albanian] demands are considered before a decision is reached on the southern border with Greece.

Another entry, "Albanians and Europe," dated June 9, reported on the dissatisfaction of the Albanians with the Congressional decisions, giving detailed descriptions of the League and its political and military structures. As to the Ottoman military campaign, *Kölnische Zeitung* wrote:

> Not even the slightest has the way of peace in Europe been secured, as the architects of the Berlin agreements hold. Thousands and thousands of Albanians, as victims of the last war with Turkey, to save their own lands, are the best example of how the Congress of Berlin left many matters unsolved, including the most miserable—that of the Albanians, who have now been abandoned and left at the mercy of the merciless Ottomans and neighbors who seek to snatch their lands.

The daily drew parallels to the past, too:

> When the Albanians alone are facing a mighty military such as the Ottoman army, Europe remains silent. This is the second time that the Albanians find themselves in a woeful situation: once, some four hundred years ago, at the time of Skanderbeg (then Europe was weak and feared Turkey), while today, when [Europe] is strong, it still wishes to encourage Turkey to fight against the Albanians![442]

Unleashing heavy criticism on the European powers for condoning and even supporting the Sublime Porte, the article ends with a warning that inciting war and bloodshed in defense of unjust decisions means neither peace nor justice, as it was clamored elsewhere. To the contrary, the newspaper emphasizes that the Ottoman Empire would fail to resolve the Albanian question through arms or to earn the population's obedience to the Porte because:

> [The Albanians] have never laid down their arms and will not do so now either. The highlanders of the Albanian tribes of Gruda, Hot, Kuç, and Shkrel vow not to give up their weapons and would rather die for their sacred cause than live in slavery.[443]

---

[442] PA AA, Türkei, band. 143, file: "Presse," no. 37.
[443] *Ibid.*

Hamburgerische Corespondent also informed on measures of the "Ottoman Empire to implement the decisions of the Congress of Berlin."[444] The newspaper feared that as long as the Albanian question was not resolved, peace in Europe would remain fragile. Calling for justice, the article reminded the German government that:

> The Albanians are an ancient people, one of the oldest in Europe, and it makes no sense in our age for them to live under Asians and for this to be done on the pretext of setting peace. This is shameful! The highest justice would entail for them to break off from Annatolia. But how? They cannot do this on their own, because now they have two opponents: the Ottomans and Europe. One cannot find against both at the time same time. The case of Ulqin illustrates this best.

In concluding the calls for the matter to be revised, the newspaper holds that justice would prevent conflicts in the Balkans. "But, perhaps," the writing noted, "someone likes such clashes and turmoil."

Besides the political commentary on the complex matter, the press also covered the activities and the situation on the ground. German newspapers paid heed to the developments in Albania well after the Albanian League and the Provisional Government were defeated and their main leaders detained, awaiting punishment with or without trial. The loss was disastrous, but the national movement did not cease. This is reflected in the Porte's restlessness when its forces were being attacked by all sides, even after victory was declared over the insurgents. In the meantime, the state administration was also disintegrating.

This is well illustrated by *Hamburg Correspondent* on December 15, 1882, noting:

> Sings of concern and unrest have appeared for a while among Christian and Muslim Albanians. They are discontent with the events of last year and insist by all means to remind the new Turkish administration that they are not defeated and do not permit to have their arms taken, as the Shkodër command announced. Notably stubborn in this regard appear the Muslims, who accept any terms but to surrender their weapons. Although the pasha of Shkodër promised there would be no punitive or retributive measures against the bearers if they surrender their arms, they are nonetheless are against [the request].

---

[444] *Hamburgische Correspondent,* PA AA, Türkei, 143, file: "Presse," doc. no. 14.

The article reports further how two Albanians of different religions became part of an assassination of an Ottoman official, warning of repercussions from the act. The newspaper describes the event:

> Two days ago, the situation worsened further in Albania after two Albanians of the Shkrel tribe (one Muslim and another Christian) killed in the city of Shkodër the commander of the Turkish militia, Salih Agha, one of the most prominent men in the hierarchy of Turkish power in the province. While the vali said he would not revenge for the killing and that the assassins would be brought before the justice, there is belief that the conflict will take wider proportions once the military undertake actions against the highlanders. For this reason, the Albanians have delivered a petition to the commission of the Great Powers in Shkodër, expressing dissatisfaction. The [Albanian] representatives told the European envoys that [the Albanians] will continue to fight against their rights. Thus, there will be war again.[445]

Accordingly, the newspapers seek to attract Europe's attention to the Balkans and Albania. The German press labored continuously for the matter, even after the defeat of the League, covering all of the Albanian activities as an offshoot of the movement that began in 1878. The articles indicate that the yearning for freedom was quelled by neither violence nor the scorching that Dervish Pasha's battalions carried out in Albania. In the meantime, the Ottoman blazoning of military power undermined rather than consolidated peace, as some circles believed. *Politische Correspondentz* illustrated the matter on June 8, 1883, in a report from Shkodër:

> News from Albania is again distressing. The Albanian tribes of the northern highlands are attacking the Ottoman garrisons in order to take their weapons and ammunition. In Tuz, war broke out between the Ottoman garrison and the Albanians and there is no information that the fighting has ceased.

The article attributes the Albanian move to the outstanding border issue with Montenegro. The small Balkan principality had been due to receive another strip of land around Lake Shkodër and, hoping to avoid war with the Albanians, had asked the Ottoman authorities to provide for a peaceful transfer of the territory. For this reason, *Politische Correspondentz* reports, the governor of Shkodër, Mustafa Pasha, met with the highlanders, urging to "avoid trouble" and carry out the plan "as a favor to the Porte and the

---

[445] *Ibid.*

sultan." But the Albanians resolutely rejected the appeal, reminding the Turkish official that they would obey any order from the sultan "but for the one commanding us to leave our lands." The newspaper then informs that:

[T]he northern Albanian tribes, led by the Kastratis, who seem to be the most concerned, have united and sent a message to the Shkodër commander of the army, Hafiz Pasha, to not surrender the territories without war. Thus, the governor of Shkodër and the commander of the Turkish army thereof are in a difficult situation. The Turks fear a reenactment of the 1880 situation when Dervish Pasha was forced to fight against the Albanians in Ulqin and, later, after a bloody war, to "peacefully" hand [the town] over to the Montenegrins. The current situation is in fact much worse than in 1880, because the Albanians have vowed to not give up. Montenegro, on its part, has no intentions of measuring its military power against the Albanians. [Montenegrins] demand that the Sublime Porte force the Albanians to surrender the territories. This, for the Montenegrins, is a wise and very beneficial move.[446]

A day later, July 9, 1883, *Kölnische Zeitung* revisited the same problem, placing emphasis on the question of autonomy. The paper notes that, regardless what had taken place two years ago, the Albanians did not forget the movement for self-government:

The high number of victims that came as a result of the clashes between Albanians and Ottomans reminds Europe once again that the Albanian question hangs unresolved. Briefly, it occurred as if the new governor was apt to pacify the rebellious Albanians. The Turkish government . . . attempted to suppress the revolt of the Kuçi tribe by atrocious means. The *bajraktars* of the Hoti, Gruda, and Kastrati tribes reminded the new governor of Shkodër that for some four hundred years now they had proved great loyalty to [the sultan]. Thus, why did they now have to surrender to another sovereign? . . . Therefore, they inform the governor that they have decided to find against the new borders if Turkey takes the matter in its own hands.

The highlanders noted, as the newspaper reports, that they would mobilize all men of military age and, if needed, women would participate in combat. The governor responded that "the border issue was not his responsibility" and that:

---

[446] *Politische Correspondentz*, Dec. 15, 1882, PA AA, file: "Presse."

He has to regretfully carry out the orders and if the orders are not obeyed, then he will be compelled to use force, regardless of the consequences.

After the open threats [of the governor], Albanian representatives held another meeting in Shkodër and reiterated their previous positions, this time sending a message to the general *vali* [i.e., head of the vilayet]. Taking their determination seriously, the governor then sent them another communiqué, informing them that the border remained an issue for the international commission to decide, according to the decisions of the Congress of Berlin. Meanwhile, the Albanians were guaranteed their freedom of religion and national identity, regardless of the sovereign they were under!

After this message, the sons of the Albanian mountains are even more determined to demand autonomy and respect for their rights. They have now made an irrevocable request and, without a doubt about their own beings, for they are aware that Turkey's time is running out and that, to satisfy its interests, Turkey is ready to sell them multiple times.[447]

The two articles indicate the prevailing subject in the Albanian-Ottoman reports of the time: the unresolved border issues and the question of autonomy that began to reemerge even though, after the capitulation of the League, the wounds of combat had not yet healed for the parties to reach an agreement on the matter. Thereby, the press contradicted the German government's claim that the treat of Albanian rebellions no longer existed "after Dervish Pasha's campaign throughout the vilayet of Kosova." The newspapers, however, had contrasting information and sought to convince the political leadership to change its course, which proclaimed the Berlin decisions as "in service of peace and a new order in the Balkans and elsewhere."

This spirit defines yet a major series in *Hamburgische Correspodent*. The lengthy article becomes more striking due to the introductory note of the editor, informing that the Hamburg newspaper has decided to bring a series of articles on Albania , since the country was a victim of the Berlin Congress and:

> The recent events called everyone's attention to Albania. The events in the Greek-Turkish border and the Albanian opposition is to be noted. This people is becoming increasingly political, inciting a great interest of the European press. The newspaper, on this occasion, will offer, in a series of articles, an opinion on the ethnic group, as seen by a German, who has spent a long time among them and remains neutral.

---

[447] *Hamburgishe Correspodent*, July 9, 1883, PA AA, Türkei 143, file: "Presse," doc. no. 158.

The anonymous work gives the impression of a prolific research writings published in the contemporary daily press. This demonstrates that the author must have been a refined connoisseur of the Albanian question. Furthermore, based on the content of the series, the writer may have been a "itinerant" missionary in the area, since there were many of them in northern Albania. Another possibility is for the author to have been a German diplomat in the Balkans who had followed developments in Albania for a long time. Particularly, the writing begins with an authoritative explanation on the etymology of the Albanian demonym, *shqiptar* (*i.e.*, Albanian). Then, the author moves on to the ethnographic definition of the territory, its ancient and history, from the Pelasgians to the Ottomans, to conclude with the Albanian League of Prizren. The series includes references to the fundamental characteristics of the Albanian nation, including its language, ethnos, and homeland. Describing the Albanian League and its genesis, the author makes an interesting remark:

> The League was a great historic event of the Albanian people, which came out stronger and more organized, despite the military defeat, because it remained perpetually determined to seek its national rights, initially through a transitional autonomy at a time when the empire's future is highly unclear, while its European territory is returned to the people who live there, where the Albanians have their share and cannot be left without a state.

The anonymous author also observes the phases of the League's activities: the first stage, when the Albanians demanded protection for their lands; and the second, when the people sought autonomy, leading to the armed conflict with the sultan. As for the "loyalty" to the sultan, the writer opines that "at the time, and in those circumstances, it would be suicidal to seek from the very beginning to secede from the Ottoman Empire or [to look for] another ally."

When one considers the content and the discussions of the series, questions inevitably arise about the goal and the ramifications of the work. Of course, one of the motivations for the article was to increase awareness on Albania, as an unattended issue and zone of crisis. Another goal is to oppose some of the diplomatic intrigues of the Balkan countries, which led a rampant campaign against the Albanian people, influencing the policies of the Great Powers at the expense of the Albanians. Such efforts were well suited for contemporary propaganda machines, for there were no Albanian diplomats or representatives in European saloons to refute intrigues and defama-

240

tions and to speak on behalf of the Albanian people. Given that Germany—allegedly neutral in the developments that so greatly affected the Albanian people—carried a heavy burden of responsibility, German newspapers would reasonably assume to represent the Albanians. The German press would appear as an opposition to Bismarck, but would remain faithful to its pursuit of the truth and justice, especially on behalf of those who were victims of the stronger. Therefore, it is not by chance that many dailies and periodicals disagreed with the policy of the Reich's government, especially after the alliance with Austria-Hungary and Italy that entrenched the German Empire amidst the warmongering clique, opening the way for crises and world conflicts.

One of the key facts that needed to be highlighted at the time was the religious identity. As a people of three faiths—Islam, Catholicism, and the Orthodoxy—the Albanians cultivated mutual tolerance and the various religions did not create rivalries and enmities, as had occurred in other nations. To the contrary, the Albanians were able to nurture understanding among one another. The Slavic propaganda had infested the opinion with fabrications presenting the Albanians as Muslim fundamentalists who had moreover embraced the interests of the invaders and derived favors against others (Serbs and Greeks). From this standpoint, Serbian, Greek, and Russian nationalists sought to vilify the Albanians as enemies of Christendom and Europe at a time when such accusations were politically important in light of the anticipated Ottoman withdrawal from the continent.

Through its coverage of the problem, the German press was constantly at work to remove the veil of deception from the Slavic propaganda. Emphasizing numerous examples, newspapers demonstrate, among other matters, that not only have the Albanians not destroyed Christian temples; they have, in fact, defended them with their lives. For instance, the media make reference to the two most important Orthodox sites in Kosova—the Patriarchate of Peja and the Monastery of Deçan—that influential Albanian families, as voivodes, have assumed to protect the holy places for hundreds of years. A German writing notes that "Albanians have done this because initially they were Christians . . . so they protect [the sites] because they take them for their own temples, which they built themselves and respect them." Meanwhile, *Hamburgische Correspondent* adds that "when it comes to defending the homeland, then the Albanians, Muslims and Christians alike, are united under one slogan: the faith of the Albanians is Albanianism."[448] Writings

---

[448] *Ibid.*

note that the League of Prizren manifested the same spirit, which became a part of all letters, telegrams, and petitions sent to the Great Powers and prominent individuals anywhere in Europe so that no religious differences be made, because the Albanian question appeared as a national issue of a people with three religion and not as a religious issue.

In this regard, an observation of *Hamburgische Correspondent* in the series of writings on the Albanians appears emblematic, noting that:

> The Albanian demands failed to change the position of the Great Powers and [others]. This is regretful because the same prejudice will cause future crises. The Albanians, however, were able to articulate the truth on their existence as a nation and their identity based on ethnicity rather than religion, as was speculated from the outside . . . [449]

As the Hamburg-based paper states, conscious efforts were made to divide the Albanians along religious lines, hence making the ethnic group a target of clashes between the East and the West while sidelining the national issue.[450]

The Historic Significance of the League

Historians distinguish three phases of the Albanian League of Prizren: (1) efforts to defend the Albanian lands; (2) the demands for autonomy; and (3) the confrontation with the Ottoman Empire and the establishment of the Provisional Government in control of the Vilayet of Kosova and parts of the province of Manastir. The three stages represent the first test of Albanian national movement towards creating conditions for secession from the Ottoman Empire. The historical mission of the League is launching an ongoing political process as a result of a pro-Western intellectual project, embraced by different strata of patriots who sought to implement it. However, not all leaders have the sense of responsibility to accept separation from the dated Ottoman Empire; while some local landowners abandon the Ottoman state, others become a barrier to the national movement in the most crucial moments. Still, the opposition fails to put a stop to a process that begins with the League and will end with national independence.

---

[449] *Ibid.*
[450] *Ibid.*

Archival sources and scholarly research present the Albanian League of Prizren as a broad movement that intended to protect the ethnic Albanian territory and later to create an autonomous state, which idea was in line with internal reforms of the empire, but also predicted the possible scenario of the dissolution of the Ottoman state. The organization was neither a clandestine nor a revolutionary, but an overt group with a clear political program. Moreover, the program was national not only by definition but by nature, because it planned that the Albanians gradually and naturally secede from the Ottoman Empire and return to the European civilization, where they belonged. The formation of the Provisional Government in 1880 and the expansion of its authority in most of Kosova and parts of the Vilayet of Manastir were the best proof of the League's vision.

This assessment remains despite the negative views, which saw the League as a right hand of the Ottoman Empire, as the Porte's "deceptive creature" purposefully induced to later to vegetate outside government scrutiny and undermine the European peace.

The activity of the League took place in several stages, between which is difficult to draw clear lines of definition. Some German historians, Peter Bartel and Hans Dieter Schanderl, estimate that, in the first phase of development, the League was almost entirely a Muslim organization and merely promised anything but to serve the needs of the Ottoman Empire. Relying on the opinion of Spiridon Gopčević, a Serbian historian educated in Vienna, Bartel says that "for Albanians, at that time, it was extremely important to defend their lands and, in order to do that, protecting the sultan was more than necessary."[451] The same author says that the first phase continued until the autumn of 1879, when the League was mainly concerned to protect their lands from Montenegro. "Autonomy is barely mentioned and, even if it is, it happens casually and without any clear concept."[452]

The second phase traversed the activities from late 1879 to June 1880, when Albanians sent a letter of seven points to the sultan, including the demand for autonomy. Developments after June 1880 were called "the solid turns," which defined the League as an organization promoting home rule for Albania, with its own capital city, revenue and any element that a self-administered state may need, ranging from a general *vali* (*i.e.*, governor)

---

[451] Gopčević, *Oberalbanien und seine Liga*, 99.
[452] *Ibid.* 101.

elected among ethnic Albanians, local officials, and the supervision of taxation.[453]

The last phase covers the war that League forces waged beginning in 1880. At this time, unable to resist the Turkish army, superior in numbers and armaments, Albanians withdrew from the defense lines at Ulqin. The Turks surrendered the city to Montenegro in accordance with the obligations they assumed at the Congress of Berlin. But then, the League formed the Provisional Government, which for several months spread its authority in most of the Vilayet of Kosova and parts of Manastir, from where the Albanians sent a clear message that they have not forgotten their country, and that sooner or later they would achieve their national independence.[454]

Bartel believes that, even after the military defeat in 1881, the national movement did not die out. However, efforts were then more sporadic and did not involve any coordinated action for all vilayets as had been the case prior to the League's dissolution.[455]

Apart from the dilemma of whether the League was originally "a pure Islamic movement," Bartel concludes that:

> The League of Prizren, regardless of the interests that had to do with its creation, began, continued, and ended as a national movement, whose main burden was carried by the Albanian Muslims, joined by Catholic Albanians of the North. Formed as a necessity to protect foreign larceny (though the partitioning of the land), through time, the League transformed into a national movement, which demanded the autonomy of the Albanian vilayets under the umbrella of the Porte. Moreover, its radical wing wanted autonomy to lead further—to full independence.[456]

"Three years of League activities make up a bright and distinct chapter in the history of the Albanian people," says Schanderl. It demonstrated a homogeneous military plan and managed to abrogate some of the decisions of the Congress of Berlin. In particular, Albanians defeated paragraph 28 of the agreements, which gave Montenegro Plava and Gucia, and paragraph 34, which recommended that Janina and Larisa pass under Greek rule.[457]

---

[453] Bartle, Peter, *op. cit.*, p. 187.

[454] *Ibid.* 188.

[455] *Ibid.* 190.

[456] *Ibid.*

[457] Schanderl, *Die Albanienpolitik . . .*, 124.

Therefore, the German author believes that, for the first time after a long Ottoman rule, the League greatly encouraged the people to strive for their national freedom, which was eventually achieved thirty-four years later, albeit two-thirds of the ethnic Albanian territory, along with half of Albania's population, remained under occupied by Serbia, Montenegro, and Greece after the Balkan wars of 1912.

A slightly more cautious approach, in terms of minimizing the League's significance, comes from Georg Stadtmüller, who estimates that "the League did not achieve the character of a great popular movement, because its leaders were constantly struck by external influences, such that their beliefs were not unique."[458]

Yet, outside influences were not only inevitable in the circumstances; they were even necessary. Since the beginning of the Eastern Crisis, as a result of wars, the sultan's reign was coming to an end and the final departure was only a matter of time and international factor. And, the Ottoman withdrawal would also draw the lines for the new entities, the autonomous or independent states that would complete a new mosaic on the Balkan map. Of course, under the conditions, external influences were evident throughout the region, including Albania. Foreign impact initially made the League show its loyalty to the Porte, while later inspired the efforts for autonomy in the context of domestic reforms. Ultimately, the Albanians were forced to resort to arms in hopes of achieving their right to self-government.

Albanians experienced extreme hardship in trying to fit in the contemporary mold for they carried the label of "the Empire's supporters" at all times alike: when they agreed with the reforms under foreign pressure, as happened with the Congress of Berlin, or when they waged an armed struggle. Trials of time prompted excessive caution among Albanians such that, even when they finally acted, their moves were often viewed as belated. For Albania itself did not become a state until the last moments of the empire when, through the whiffs of war, the nation's leaders approved the historic declaration of independence.

The tribulations of history were best reflected in the spirit of the Congress of Berlin. The sidelining of Albanians led the contemporary German press as well as the subsequent history studies to criticize the attitude of the Great Powers as unprincipled and even immoral. The condemnation was especially directed at the German government, which ruled out any consid-

---

[458] Stadtmüller, "Volkstumechichte," *Albanische Forschungen*, 376.

eration for the Albanian demands, insisting in the agreement Berlin reached with Russia and France in preparation for the Congress to have the Albanian question from the agenda, no matter the depositions of the small nation. The exclusion of the matter was the condition that the tsar imposed, while aiming to come to the aid of his Balkan supporters, namely the Serbs, Montenegrins, and Bulgarians. Simultaneously, Russia wanted to shut any route leading to an Albanian state, an eventuality seen as harmful to the Slavic interests in the peninsula, particularly because through Albania, "Westerners and Easterners would one day come to terms against the Russian interests."[459]

Purposefully then, the Slavic propaganda presented the Albanians as "defenders of Turks in Europe," vilifying the ethnic group as an opponent of the West; yet, when Albanians fought against the Ottomans, they became "peace wreckers, destroyers of European agreements and interests."[460] As attested in German documents, this label followed the Albanians at all times. German ambassadors in İstanbul, Hasfield and later Radulin, employed the harshest polemic, depicting the League either as an "Ottoman creature" and "camouflage of the Porte" at the early stages, or—after the Albanians came into conflict with the imperial government—as "slayers of the peace, slayers of the agreements of the Congress of Berlin."[461]

Radulin, who succeeded Hasfield in office, exceeded his predecessor's vile rhetoric. In frequent reports to the Bismarck, the new ambassador degraded any efforts of Albanians for autonomy, accusing them of "working against European interests." Accordingly, he suggested the German government that "it is in the interest of Europe that, despite the current turmoil in the Balkans, caused by the Albanian, Bulgarian, and Vlach uprisings, Turkish rule be preserved further in Europe."[462] Moreover, the diplomat reminded his superiors that "the opponents of the Berlin agreements were opponents of Europe's strategic interests," asserting that:

> Albanians are looting throughout the Balkans; they are irresponsible; they at-
> tack Ottoman garrisons; they have no respect for the Ottoman authorities and
> it was they who killed Mehmed Ali Pasha in 1878 at Gjakova and had the least
> concern for anything! They can only serve the Ottoman Empire to carry out
> violence against Armenians and other nations in [Ottoman] Asia fighting for

---

[459] *Hamburgische Correspodent*, July 1882.
[460] *Ibid.*
[461] Report of the German Ambassador to İstanbul, PA AA, Türkei, band. 143, doc. no. 70.
[462] PA AA, Türkei, 143, doc. no. 78.

independence, which would have long ago broken off [from the Porte] had it not been for the dreadful Albanian officers, who wherever they go raze all things to the ground.[463]

The report contains extensive contradictions, even absurdities, such how the Albanians irresponsibly attack Ottoman garrisons and disobey the law of the Ottoman Empire, but serve at high ranks in the imperial military, suppressing Armenian and other independence movements in the East. In assessing the Albanians, the German diplomats in the East expressed political biases and prejudice of the kind ingrained in the very Slavic propaganda.

In other words, despite the crises and wars the Berlin Congress caused, the Europeans did not change their attitude, insisting in the *status quo* and in preserving even the most volatile regimes such as the Ottoman presence in the Balkans. Radulin said that the Congressional decisions should be implemented for the sake of Europe, although it was readily apparent that the Porte's authority could no longer be maintained, let alone strengthened. The prolonged changes in the Balkans were surely in favor of the Russian bloc as during the next few years when most of Albanian territories (except for the partitioned, modern state of Albania) fell completely under the Greek and Slavic rule. For thirty-four years after the revision of the Treaty of San Stefano, Russia managed to regain the positions lost in Berlin and harvested even greater benefits.

The League of Prizren was formed and operated in difficult times, when the Russian-backed neighboring Slavs and Greeks were not the only enemy; the organization was also faced with the Ottoman Empire, even though the latter was initially seen as a protector that shared in the Albanian struggle. The Porte ignored the demands for autonomy, insisting instead in the anachronistic concept of the Albanians as "the flower of Islam." For that reason, the empire eventually lost the one and only case, which the Berlin Congress gave the Ottoman state to preserve the European holdings, accrued over the centuries.

Notwithstanding the foreign contention that the 19th-century organization served foreign interests that were not in favor of the Albanians, the League of Prizren appears as the first movement and the most organized for the national autonomy and independence in the long and laborious road of the Albanian population for national independence. The League's formation challenged two main strands of prejudice that threatened to turn into a

---

[463] *Ibid.*

permanent political cliché: (1) the categorization of Albanians as a part of the Ottoman nationality, which would exclude them from the European family; and (2) the labeling of the Albanians as the last sponsors and pillar of the Ottoman presence in the continent.

Launched as a movement to protect Albanian lands from the partitioning that the Treaty of San Stefano envisioned and the Berlin Congress in a way justified, the League became an important political, military, and administrative mechanism, culminating with the establishment of the Provisional Government in early 1881. Although the efforts ended in a military defeat after the Ottoman Empire undertook a ferocious campaign against the League, the developments turned into a moral victory, in an unrelenting verve that continued until the Albanian declaration of independence on November 28, 1912. Despite the shortcomings, the Albanian national movement channeled the mentality and energy of the people towards a great historic victory. The movement was seen as such by all sides—by those who supported it, by those who neither opposed nor supported it, as well as by those who opposed it.

CHAPTER 6
THE STRUGGLE FOR NATIONALITY RIGHTS

Ethnic Identity, National Identity, and Emancipation

In light of emerging national movements in the Balkans, the Albanians relate their ethnic identity, based on a common language and traditions, to their national identity. The Ottoman Empire counteracts with plans for an Islamic emancipation for the Albanians; Islamic Albanianism, a theory furthering the Ottoman aspirations, insists that the Arabic script be adopted for the Albanian language. Ottoman statesman Midhat Pasha calls for schools to be opened throughout Albania to facilitate the emancipation of the people; Albanian activists lend their support to the idea, albeit motivated by national goals. Sami Frashëri stresses the need for new schools, demanding also that the Albanian language be taught in Albanian towns and villages. Moreover, Frashëri views cultural diversity and the Albanian national identity as a prerequisite to a civic Ottoman patriotism celebrating the equality of all citizens of the empire.

Naum Veqilharxhi's memorandum calling on his Orthodox compatriots to seek national awakening through education was neither unexpected nor outside the norm of contemporary events. On the one hand, it continued on the old Albanian efforts to oust the Ottoman Empire with external help, including Pjetër Budi's 1619 call for a Western crusade as well as the Austrian wars against the Ottomans between 1689 and 1730. On the other hand, the Veqilharxhi memorandum initiated the internal battle for national emancipation.

The progress that was sought for the Albanian people was to serve the national movement in light of the unavoidable changes the Ottoman Empire had to embrace. The Slavic-Orthodox peoples of the region—Serbs, Montenegrin, and Greeks—began their own national movements, inevitably

249

catching the attention of Albanians at home and abroad. Internally, in the Ottoman Empire, the Albanians were distressed with the Slavic-Orthodox national movements, for many of them threatened the territorial integrity of the Albanian people. Among the diaspora communities, however, the wave of Balkan nationalism sparked hope as the expats believed their fellow countrymen had no choice but to join a region-wide struggle for national independence. Nevertheless, the internal concerns and the diaspora's hope inevitably placed the Albanian people in a new position. Whether emphasizing the defense needs, nurturing inspiration, or calling for any action, this new situation obviated the need for a unified ideology, a platform based on the national identity and territory.

Albanian communities outside of the Ottoman Empire became instrumental in erecting a national platform. The Arbëreshë in Italy and the Arvanites and Orthodox Albanians in newly-independent Greece projected a Western civilizing platform onto their brethren in mainland Albania. The bulk of ethnic Albanians, living under the Ottoman Empire and predominantly of the Muslim religion, were called to celebrate their national identity, whose attributes—the ancient language, traditions, and ethnic heritage— were deeply rooted in the foundations of the Western civilization.

The focus on the national identity was prompted nonetheless by wider social and political developments in Europe as well as within the Ottoman Empire. The Crimean War of 1856, in which British and French armies for the first time allies with the Ottomans to defeat the Russians, and the subsequent Conference of Paris the same year, where the Ottoman Empire was welcomes among the Great Powers of the continent, exerted great effect on the smaller ethnic groups. In addition, the sultan announced the *Hatt-ı Hümayun* imperial decree, setting the stage to a new political era for the Sublime Porte. The Ottoman entry among the Great Powers did away with the external threats—precisely with the Russian threat—to the empire's territorial integrity and provided the security needed for internal reforms. However, the domestic changes that were proclaimed in the imperial decree faced the Porte with new challenges that arose from the nationalist and separatist movements, which gained momentum following Greece's independence; Serbia had already become autonomous and Romania was increasingly consolidating its home rule, while the Bulgarians and especially the Albanians remained a growing concern that the empire wished to prevent from following any breakaway tendencies.

Contrary to the Slavic-Orthodox peoples, which possessed the key to the fragile balance between the West and the East, in the new shifting dynamics, the Albanians suddenly appeared with a new role for the stability of the Ottoman Empire. The Porte's hopes to continue its presence in Europe could be projected on the Albanians and their century-long loyalty, especially since the ethnic group needed the imperial protection against the expansionist tendencies of the neighbors. The Albanians, however, sought that the loyalty to the Ottoman Empire prompt in return their recognition as a distinct nationality, with the right to self-government and equal treatment against other nations. Such a step forward would secure the future of the Albanian people amidst developments that could—and had already begun to—bring the Ottoman Empire to the verge of collapse.

The new relationship between the Albanians and the empire, nevertheless, remained one-sided. It was so desired by the Ottoman state that the Albanians be not considered outside the scope of the *millet-i osman*, which also included the eastern ethnic groups. It was the sole option, in the eyes of the Ottomans, for maintaining the empire's presence in the European continent. Thus, when the Ottoman Empire announced the *Tanzimât* reforms for all peoples alike, the Albanians had reasons to oppose as much as to support the new policies of the imperial government. Prior to the reforms, the Albanians had enjoyed certain privileges, including self-governance according to the Kanun, the right to bear arms, and tax cuts. While the ethnic group had remained isolated from the rest of Europe, the Albanians had also maintained their distinct identity from the *millet-i osman*, the formal group in which they partook. As the reforms threatened to take away all the benefits of the old regime without granting the Albanians the very autonomy that was announced for other ethnic groups, there was reason for resentment against the central authorities. Therefore, the Albanian people were faced with an absurd situation: their loyalty to the empire (which could be said to have been the subject of a "contract" for it provided for the political advantages that preserved their ethnic, linguistic, and social identity) awarded them with punishment, whereas the opponents of the empire gained cultural and social rights that reached the level of autonomy.

The Ottoman Empire had already begun to feel the Albanian pressure and was aware of a long-lasting challenge with the ethnic group. At the same time, it was also cognizant of the political reality the Albanians were facing. The Porte and the sultan knew that the Albanians' sole remedy against the expansion of their neighbors was in submitting to the imperial umbrella and

251

by no means in abandoning it. Therefore, the empire attempted at directing the Albanian affairs in favor of strengthening Ottomanism as a unifying conscience, where the Islamic identity would continue to serve as the common denominator. The Ottoman Empire hence became attentive to the Albanian demands for national emancipation, but redirected the efforts to an Islamic spirit. The calls for schools, publications, and cultural associations were tied to Islam as an inevitable premise that could provide for defense against the Slavic-Orthodox threat and, furthermore, allow for the Albanians to consolidate as an ethnic group with a strong Islamic sentiment. In 1864, the *vali* of Shkodër, Midhad Pasha, issued a memorandum calling on the Ottoman Empire to support a process of civilization for the Albanians, by opening schools and providing for mandatory education in all parts of the country, even in areas where the autonomous Kanun tradition was in effect. The reform-minded administrator was aware of the pressing need for education among the Albanians in order to separate them from the unsustainable feudal structures. These were believed to present an obstacle to the reforms in the Albanian provinces or *vilayets*, then a newly-implemented unit of administrative division in the Ottoman Empire. Midhad Pasha together with another Ottoman official, Cevdet Pasha, sought to introduce the modern concept of civilization through an organized, Islam-based educational system with the ultimate purpose of dismantling the Kanun-based norms and the local autonomy, a phenomenon which had provided for the mutual trust between Albanians and the central authorities during centuries of existence under Ottoman sovereignty.

Emancipation through education was also the goal of Albanian activists—or the *rilindas*, the term used in the Albanian language to refer to the protagonists of *Rilindja Kombëtare*, the great period of national awakening that began in the 1800s. Sami Frashëri's demands, in his early years of activities, for state schools in all of the Albanian vilayets are well known. "Wherever there is ignorance," he wrote, "there can be no development." Frashëri called on the Ottoman Empire to include in the compulsory primary education and to provide the facilities for secondary education. The celebrated activist also requested for the Albanian language to be taught as a subject in state schools, further supporting permits for private Albanian schools, in the same manner Greek and Serbian, and lately Romanian and Bulgarian, institutions had been allowed by the Porte.[464]

---

[464] See Sami Frashëri's writings in *Tercümeni-i Hakikat*.

Around the same time, state schools known as *rujdiye* opened in some major towns of the Albanian vilayets (Shkodër, Prizren, Shkup, Manastir, and Janina).[465] Albanians also attended. Lessons, however, were taught in Turkish and purported to give an Islamist education. In the meantime, Greek schools also began to operate in Albanian towns. Institutions such as the Zosimea Gymnasium in Janina provided a high level of education and served a civilizing mission that benefited many Albanians. Almost all of the leading *rilindas* were educated at Zosimea, including the Frashëri brothers (Abdyl, Naim, and Sami), Konstandin Kristoforidhi, Ismail Qemali, and many others.

The exposure of Albanians to education, regardless of the type of schools or the language of instruction, proved one fundamental issue of contemporary politics. Proponents of an Islamist education, such as Ahmed Cevdet Pasha who petitioned the sultan for religious schools in Albania, had hoped that the calls for a national Albanian education would wane as more Albanians entered the Islamist classrooms. The effect, however, was quite the contrary and Albanians became increasingly vocal in their demands for national schools. Those who received an education were able to witness the surge of nationalism among the Slavic-Orthodox peoples and the related separatist trends. As a result, educated Albanians were alerted of the need for the cultural and social emancipation of their compatriots to recognize the ethnic peculiarities. This was not only a pre-condition for the reform spirit to include all parts of the country and all socio-economic groups alike, but also a shield against the separatist and expansionist tendencies of the Slavic-Orthodox. The latter could not be countered by concepts such as Islamism and Ottomanism, for they lacked the much-needed vigor to unify the people; an ethnic-based national identity was the sole means that could prevail under the circumstances.

Islamism as a social and political concept that united *din* (faith) and *vatan* (homeland) was severely affected by the 1856 *Hatt-ı Hümayun* decree. The Ottoman Empire effectively lost its power not only over its European subjects; imperial authority weakened also with respect to non-Europeans, including Arabs, other ethnic groups native to Asia, as well as the Turks as the titular nation of the empire itself. Ultimately, this was the result of a new

---

[465] Clayer, *Në fillimet e nacionalizmit shqiptar*, 197. In 1869, the law on public education provided for the development of primary education. Kindergartens (*ibtidaiye*) opened in 1872, but they did not appear in the Albanian provinces until the 1880s.

ideology that came as part of the reorganization under the *Tanzimât* reforms. An official program adopted by the state, Ottomanism, known in Turkish as *Osmanlılık*, proclaimed as its core value the equality of all citizens of the empire, regardless of origin, religion, or ethnic identity. The *Tanzimât* reformers hence aimed at instituting a new Ottoman identity and sense of civic loyalty within the existing borders of the empire. While there were aspirations for *a new supranational Ottoman identity*,[466] the reformers were aware of the values and responsibilities that arose from the ethnic, religious, and linguistic diversity of the Ottoman state. With a focus on diversity, therefore, Ottomanism sought a clear policy that accepted and engaged the cultural pluralism in the empire.

The spirit of *cultural pluralism*, as embraced by the reformers, was not unknown or foreign to the Ottoman Empire.[467] Ahmet Cevdet Pasha, a prominent historian and reformist politician, attributed the power of the Ottoman state to its very diverse cultural heritage. In an overview of the empire's history, he explained how the "Ottoman community" came to be what he called a great society, owing to its diverse background. The community, he wrote, was formed of people who spoke many languages and who chose the best traditions and customs of the various ethnic groups to which they belonged.[468] On the basis of the cultural diversity, the Ottomans had revived the Islamic nation, and it is with the Islamist ideology in mind, that the Ottoman writer dwells on the notion of *cultural pluralism*.[469]

Pluralism in the era of reform and constitutional monarchy was no longer a matter of ethnic diversity, which the empire tolerated and, to a certain degree, used to maintain the state's integrity within the framework of the religion-based homeland. The modern understanding of cultural pluralism sought social and political dividends on the basis of the proclamation that all citizens were equal, regardless of language of religion, language, or

---

[466] Gawrych, *Gjysmëhëna dhe shqiptarizmi*, 23.

[467] In a certain way, even when ignored, pluralism had existed in the Ottoman Empire. Different peoples, such as the Albanians, embraced Islam, but nonetheless saved their language, traditions, and certain political convictions. In fact, even the urban higher class— those who had integrated with the Ottoman society, reaching the higher levels of state hierarchy or serving in the local administration—demonstrated the prevalence of the Albanian identity. Not only did the urban elites continue to speak their native tongue; they became in fact the leading force of Albanianism and the Albanian national movement.

[468] *Ibid.* 23.

[469] *Ibid.* 24.

race. Known as the platform of Ottomanism, this promise of equality trumpeted the rise of the so-called *Ottoman patriotism* honoring the one common state that belonged to all citizens. Notably, the modern state would not do away with the distinct characteristics of the various communities, but would raise them to the level of shared and accepted values of the Ottoman society.

While political and ideological constraints made the Ottomanism aspirations very unrealistic, some change did occur. The influential, old-fashioned military order of the janissaries was abolished. The Ottomans began to modernize the armed forces. Trade and business were modeled after contemporary European practices. Foreign capital also poured into the country such that the Sublime Porte grew increasingly dependent on Western banks. Notably, the country opened to the emancipating ideas of the French Revolution. A process of Westernization hence had begun and there was welcomed by various groups in the country. The Ottomans themselves viewed the change as an inevitable destiny, and the other ethnic groups of the empire saw it as the beginning of a "historic turn." Nevertheless, it was the perception of modernization that led the reform process to its downfall. The inevitable destiny of progress alluded at the consolidation of the Ottoman state, while the "historic turn" meant the path to independence of the Balkan nations, a different vision on the future of the empire.

To further complicate matters, the role of the sultan and religion were rendered ineffective for serving in preserving the state's unity. Sultan Selim III, followed by Mahmud II and lastly Abdul-Rashid, personally oversaw the reforms. Due to the opposition of the privileged elite, reluctant to surrender to relinquish its influence, reforms had to be imposed from the very top of the imperial hierarchy and, as a result, stroke at the outset the corroded system of feudal landlords. The process necessarily evolved into a struggle against regional despots and in favor of a modern centralized state. However, the centralization did not just shift the political balance in the country; it affected the very ideological foundations of the states. Islamism, which originally served as the cornerstone of the empire, became controversial as much as anachronistic as the reforms continued. The concept of a modern, constitutional monarchy seized from the sultan the power of Islam. In turn, the reform automatically effaced despotism, the constitutional arrangement that enabled the foundation and rise of the Ottoman Empire.

The opposition to the reforms remained strong throughout as the conservative circles refused to abandon the faith-based notion of the *vatan*. The threat to the reform efforts increased particularly after secular courts (Trk.: *nizamiyye*) were established in the country pursuant to new legal codes. Ultimately, following the decade-long reign of several reform-minded sultans, a change in the leadership brought the westernization process to an end. While initially dedicated to furthering the *Tanzimât* policies of his predecessors, Sultan Abdul Hamid II (reigned 1876-1909) broke off with the tradition soon after his accession to the Ottoman throne. With the ideological shift, he not only gave up on the reforms, but reverted to hardline Islamism with such vigor as to emphasize the Islamic caliphate and engage in staunch anti-Western rhetoric. As the leader of the Muslim world, Abdul Hamid II even warned that *jihad* or *holy war* would ensue in event that the West endangered the caliphate.[470]

In the meantime, Abdul Hamid came up with his own version of Islamism, one that sought to also incorporate Ottomanism to facilitate the centralization of power. However, not only was Islamism incompatible with Ottomanism in this regard; the faith-based ideology ran counter to the modern European concept of a nation that had inspired the emergence of Ottomanism. In Italy, Germany, and elsewhere in the West, nationalism appeared victorious and it had greatly inspired the breakaway peoples of the Balkans in seeking independence from the Ottoman Empire. Serbs, Romanians, and Bulgarians were already in pursuit of their secession from the Ottoman state. Even the more cautious groups, such as the Albanians, who initially had hopes of prosperity within the Ottoman Empire, were soon found at odds with Abdul Hamid's policies. Seeking a centralized government, Hamid's Islamism ultimately endangered the cultural pluralism that for centuries had permitted ethnic communities to preserve their language, customs, and traditions, and had kept the empire together.

Albanianism appeared as a platform on which the Albanians could support their demands for full equality in the Ottoman Empire, including territorial autonomy and cultural identity. However, early Albanianism avoided conflict with Islam. In fact, emphasizing Islam as the bridge between the ethnic group and the empire, there appeared for a while a concept of Islamic or Muslim Albanianism.[471] This was thought of as a compromise solution that could provide for ethno-cultural autonomy although under the

---

[470] For more on the sultan's position, see Sulltan Abdylhamiti, *Kujtimet e mia nga politika* (Shkup, 2010).

[471] Gawrych, *Gjysmëhëna dhe shqiponja . . .*, 97.

mantra of a "Muslim Albania," which favored Islam over Christianity. But the likelihood of a Muslim Albania coming to life was practically inexistent, for Abdul Hamid II firmly rejected ethnically-nuanced expression of Islam as a threat to the integrity of the empires.

Sultan Abdul Hamid ignored even those demands by Albanians declared as Islamic militants who wished to write their native language for the needs of the believers. Similarly, efforts by proponents of Muslim Albanianism to introduce Albanian in public schools also failed. Daut Shyqri Efendi, also known as Daut Boriçi, a native of Shkodër and graduate of the Zosimeia high school of Janina, petitioned the Ottoman government in 1882 for permission to teach Albanian in his hometown. Boriçi had previouslys written an Albanian primer using Arabic letters,[472] justifying his choice as follows: "Since Albanians learn the Arabic alphabet used by Muslims, I did not consider it necessary to create other letters for the Albanian alphabet, and so, in developing this script, I was based on the Arabic alphabet, with some modifications as required by the nature of the Albanian."[473] Boriçi was not granted permission to teach Albanian, but he continued to write the language using Arabic letters until his death in 1886.

Albanianism grew at a time at a time when the Turks in the Ottoman Empire were also rediscovering their ethnic identity. By late1860s, the concept of a Turkish nation emerged, seen as separate from the empire and the ruling dynasty.[474] And among the leading figures who contributed to the concept of the Turkish nation is Sami Frashëri.[475] Sultan Hamid, however, suppressed Turkish nationalism as well as Albanianism, ruling as a despot for over three decades on the basis of the Islamist ideology.

---

[472] Gawrych, *Gjysmëhëna . . .*, 131.

[473] Clayer, *Në fillet . . .*, 201.

[474] *Ibid.* 119.

[475] Frashëri showed a great interest in the Turkish language, recommending that the common spoken language replace the official Ottoman standard, which was not suited to the needs of the people. He published the first Turkish dictionary in two volumes (Trk.: *Kamus-ı Türki*) as well as the first encyclopedia (*Kamûs-ül Â'lâm*). Notably, in his dictionary, he included the words for the Albanian people and language, while defining Albania as both a nation or nationality (*cinsiyet*) and a country (*memleket*), which consisted of the four vilayets (Kosova, Shkodër, Manastir, and Janina). Gawrych, *Gjysmëhëna . . .*, 195-96.

Politics and Diplomacy for Nationality Rights

The first Ottoman constitution opens the way to Albanian demands for nationality rights. Albanian deputies elected to the first imperial parliament present a project for Albania's administrative autonomy. The Russo-Ottoman War interrupts the democratic progress; Sultan Abdul Hamid II suspends the constitution and dissolves the parliament. The Albanians focus on defending their territories from invading neighbors, but plans for autonomy continue. Albanian intellectuals and public officials form the İstanbul Committee to serve their national interests. The Ottomans refuse to recognize an Albanian nationality or permit self-governance. The Committee establishes ties with the Great Powers, while seeking to maintain friendly relations with the Porte. Albanian intellectuals call for friendship with Europe. A French-language publication by Pashko Vasa presents a positive image of the Albanian people to the Western world.

The early years of Abdul Hamid's reign—in stark contrast to his decades-long absolute rule—marked the pinnacle of the modernization efforts that had begun under his predecessors. In 1876 the Ottoman Empire scored an easy victory in a brief war against Serbia, but at the insistence of the Great Powers submitted to an international conference in İstanbul. Commencing in December, the event sought to facilitate reforms and find solutions that would improve the status of the various ethnic and social groups of the empire.[476]

In particular, Germany was interested in helping the Ottomans. It was also aware of the struggle for equality of the nationalities, but had to take a realistic approach to cope with pressure that the Great Powers exerted in furthering their own interests in the region. Therefore, the German Empire focused on direct cooperation with the Porte, while the Ottoman leadership at the time was also interested in furthering the reforms. Reformist Grand Vizier Ahmed Şefik Mithat Pasha (1822-1884), who was in friendly terms with Europeans, used the foreign assistance to turn the Ottoman state into a constitutional monarchy. On December 23, 1876, the empire adopted its basic law, *Kanun-i Esasi*, which became the country's first constitution, providing for a parliament and the equality of citizens. The legislature was to

---

[476] *Ibid.* 58.

258

consist of two chambers—a chamber of deputies and a chamber of nobles—while one deputy in the lower chamber was elected to represent about 50,000 men of Ottoman nationality. The parliament opened officially on March 19, 1877.[477]

With the adoption of the constitution, Ottomanism became the official ideology of the state, marking a major victory for ethnic groups that sought recognition and inclusion in the empire's public life. Article 8 of the document stated: "All citizens of the Empire shall be called Ottomans, whatever their religion or denomination may be." The Albanians were particularly hopeful of achieving equal treatment as a nationality by presenting their goals through the state's institutions. Indeed, there were Albanian feudalists influenced by Islamist fundamentalists in Kosova and Shkodër who opposed the demands for national identity, but the constitution did not prevent others from furthering the nationality agenda, including autonomy.

A turning point that prompted quick reaction of Albanian leaders was the worsening of Ottoman relations with Russia and its Balkan allies, Serbia and Montenegro. Members of parliament sensing a threat for their native land seek to save and strengthen the empire by calling for administrative autonomy.[478] Deputies Abdyl Frashëri and Mehmet Ali Vrioni as representatives of the Vilayet of Janina introduced a plan that specifically called for ethnic Albanians in the administration, the opening of Albanian schools, and the restriction of military service for Albanian men to their territories. The two leaders had embraced the aspirations the *rilindas* had nurtured since the 1840s, hoping for a national education that would promote an identity beyond the regional and local interests.

The proposal resonated with Arab and Armenian deputies, who believed that administrative reform would strengthen the empire. The plan for self-government provided the foundation of the political concept that would later become known as *Ottoman Albania*. Granted, while it had the support of Albanian intellectuals, it pitied Islamist fanatics against Albanianism, but more importantly the Ottoman Empire, the Slavic-Orthodox neighbors, and Albanians all came into conflict with one another. The constitution and parliament had provided the first opportunity for the Albanians to present their demands through democratic institutions, but the demands would provoke Russia to instigate a new war.

---

[477] *Ibid.* 58.
[478] *Ibid.* 59.

Russia declared war on the Ottoman Empire using the slow reforms as a pretext. But in reality, the tsar had no interest in the reforms and was in fact against them, since any liberalization in the Ottoman Empire would lead to Albania's autonomy and prevent Russian hegemony in the Balkans. Soon, Russia would try to create powerful satellite states in the region, requesting the formation of a Great Bulgaria in the Treaty of San Stefano. Russia's goals were clear and Sultan Abdul Hamid was ironically willing to fulfill them. On February 14, 1878, the Ottoman monarch played his Islamist card to dissolve and suspend the parliament, claiming that it harmed the interests of the country. Among the actual threats, Albania's autonomy was seen as the worst, for it ruined the Islamist absolutism and set a precedent for other peoples—such as Arabs, Armenians, and Kurds—to seek their own right to self-government.

The Ottoman Empire reaped no benefits from the suspension of the parliament. Without an effective venue to defend their rights and influence the government, the Albanians lost considerable portions of their territory under the international agreements that followed the war. It is likely, however, that the sultan had sensed Europe's inevitable involvement, where the Western powers would condone his despotic rule as they struggled to curb Russian influence and urge reforms in the Ottoman Empire. Abdul Hamid II abolished the parliament at such an inconvenient moment as to elicit accusations that of a flirt with Russia against the Europe.

The Albanians nevertheless became a political factor after the Treaty of San Stefano when their founded their own League of Prizren. The Ottoman Empire failed to defend the Albanians, and the ethnic group faced the threat of extinction. But Britain and Austria indirectly saved the Albanians by refusing to accept the terms of San Stefano. The Albanians used the involvement of the Great Powers in the region to also work for autonomy and nationality rights.

As the revision of San Stefano began in Berlin, the Albanians were supportive of the Ottoman Empire, expressing their loyalty to the sultan and caliph on numerous occasions, including a memorandum in which they promise to die for the state, nation, and homeland.[479] The motives were clear: to protect Albania's territorial integrity. But to this goal, the Albanians also added the demands for autonomy, and this led to a straining of relations with the Sublime Porte. Thus, it was not because of the Ottoman

---

[479] S. Pollo and S. Pulaha, *Akte të Rilindjes Kombëtare Shqiptare 1817-1921*, pp. 40-42.

failure to defend the Albanians that the latter abandoned their loyalty to the empire; it was the refusal of autonomy that instigated the two sides into a disputes and fights. Notably, in 1880, the Albanians formed their provisional government seated at Prizren and ruled parts of Albania independently until they were defeated by the Ottoman military. The Albanian determination to tie territorial defense with the demands for autonomy had the Albanians fighting in two fronts, internally against the central government, and externally against the expansionist neighboring countries.

To coordinate the efforts for autonomy, Albanian leaders formed in 1878 the Central Committee for Defending the Rights of the Albanian Nationality (*Komiteti Qendror për Mbrojtjen e të Drejtave të Kombësisë Shqiptare*) at the imperial capital. Commonly known as the İstanbul Committee, this organization demanded that local Albanians be hired in the local and vilayet administration and that a portion of the tax revenue remain in Albania. Further, the group called for the development of agriculture and trade as well as some form of emancipation that included Albanian-language education, cultural associations, and press. In its founding manifesto, the İstanbul Committee proclaimed that it sought for the Albanians the rights and freedoms that other peoples in the Balkans already had.

Denying the Albanians their nationality rights did not only entail discrimination an inequality to other ethnic groups; it undermined the very stability of the Ottoman Empire. All forms of Albanian autonomy that were proposed following the Frashëri-Vrioni model provided for the internal unity the empire needed to cope with the external pressures. The İstanbul Committee had brought together Albanians of different religions—for instance, Sami Frashëri was Muslim, Konstandin Kristoforidhi was Orthodox, and Pashko Vasa was Catholic—to work for their homeland's autonomy. Yet, the sultan declined to capitalize on the opportunity to secure his European dominions by honoring the Albanian demands. Instead, Abdul Hamid II chose to adhere to Islamism and copiously resorted to centralized rule, even though the political risks warned against it. So fixated was the monarch to the religious ideology that he disregarded even the obvious results of the liberal reforms (primarily in the military and economic fields) of his predecessors. His Islamist seal particularly targeted the Albanians on the verge of the war with Serbia and Montenegro in 1877-78, when Abdul Hamid proclaimed that Islamic patriotism and faith were the way to defend one's native land.

Albanian leaders, too, were keen not to press for autonomy at the outset of the political campaign for territorial integrity, although likely due to other motives. The İstanbul Committee joined the European powers in opposing the San Stefano agreement. Western diplomats accredited in Constantinople, in particular British and Austro-Hungarian envoys, who met with Albanian representatives expressed sympathy for the Albanian demands and promised them that Russia would not gain control of the Balkans. British Ambassador A. H. Liard encouraged Vaso Pasha to continue with the protests against the territorial cessions, for the West would listen.[480] The German government as the host of the Berlin Congress was also interested in the Albanian protests as it hoped to exert greater pressure on Russia.[481]

The Ottoman Empire on its part worked for the protests to expand as much as possible in the vilayets of Kosova and Shkodër, which lay on the defense line against Slavic expansion. Ottoman officials in Prishtina and Shkodër had received clear instructions to instigate the Albanians to demonstrate against the Bulgarian, Serbian, and Montenegrin invasions. As British consul Kirbin Grueen transmitted to London at the time, the *vali* of Shkodër, Hüseyin Pasha, established contact with his Kosovar counterpart, Nazif Pasha, to ensure that massive demonstrations took place in Kosova, too.[482]

Even when disparaging decisions were reached at Berlin, the İstanbul Committee refrained from the anti-European rhetoric observed in petitions and protests from Albania itself. Albanian leaders in Constantinople, particularly Sami Frashëri who authored extensive columns in *Tercüman-i Hakikat*, were attentive of the relations with the Porte and Europe:

> The Albanians, who have the Slavic neighbors and Russia for enemies, ought not to add to the circle of foes by falling out with the Empire, let alone fall out with the European countries, which should be kept very close and, if they had to make a concession to prevent Russia from piercing through the Balkans, we should be considerate.

Frashëri believed it was important to convince the Ottoman Empire of the strategic significance of a united Albanian vilayet, while he viewed European support as indispensable in obtaining nationality rights in through the reform process.[483]

---

[480] *Ibid.* 66.

[481] See Buxhovi, *Kongresi i Berlinit 1878.*

[482] Gawrych, *Gjysmëhena dhe shqiponja*, 67.

[483] *Ibid.* 83.

Pashko Vasa (Vaso Pashë Shkodrani) also focused on political Albanianism as a reaction in defense of the territorial integrity. He sought the support of the Great European Powers, but also tried to create closer ties with the Ottoman Empire. In 1879, Pashko Vasa published in French *La vérité sur l'Albanie et les Albanais* (Fr., The Truth on Albania and the Albanians), which was later translated into German, English, Albanian, and Greek. This book, written by a senior Ottoman official of the Albanian Catholic community, portrayed the Albanians as an ancient European people of three faiths and whose identity depended on ethnicity and not religious affiliation. Vasa wrote about the ancient history of Albanians and their later wars against the Ottomans, including the celebrated era of Skanderbeg. The Albanian writer presented to Europe a people with a pre-defined cultural identity and needed help in reclaiming its roots in the West. Eight years later, an abridged edition (portion confronting Albanians with the Ottomans were redacted) was published in Ottoman Turkish.

Pashko Vasa, Sami Frashëri, and other activists continued to work on improve Albania's image in Europe and set the stage for an independent state in the future. Neighboring countries had greatly succeeded in convincing many European circles that peace in the Balkans could be achieved only by excluding—even if through violence—Albania from the map of the continent. The Albanians had to make their own case instead.

The National Literature and Emancipation

The İstanbul Committee creates a standard Albanian alphabet. Writers and intellectuals found the Albanian print-press society. The Drita *newspaper in Bucharest spearheads the emancipation and national awakening of Albanians. Activists engage in polemic with Greek and Slavic chauvinists; Albanians defend their distinct national identity, origin, and right to statehood. The first secular Albanian school opens in Korça in 1887.*

Albanianism took its first important challenge towards a national program when the Central Committee for Defending the Rights of the Albanian Nationality began its work on a standardizing the writing of the Albanian language. This society, created in the beginning of 1878 during the Russo-Ottoman War, had enough resources to assume the responsibility and used those resources in the best possible way. Passionate supporters of Albanianism who had previously labored to preserve the territorial integrity began their efforts at developing a national Albanian literature. The İstanbul Committee appointed a commission—consisting of Sami Frashëri, Pashko Vasa, Jani Vreto, and Hoxha Tahsin—with the task of creating a unified alphabet.

Sami Frashëri wrote that the Albanians needed a standardized alphabet so they could become an enlightened nation (Trk.: *millet-i ilmiye*). In an article published in *Tercüman-i Hakikat*, he explained that his brethren possessed two languages—Albanian as *milli* or national tongue, and Ottoman as *resmi* or official language. Frashëri argued hence that the Albanians needed to also study their national language and write it in their own letters. On March 19, 1879, the alphabet commission accepted a set of thirty-six letters and characters proposed by Frashëri. This alphabet consisted of twenty-five Latin, five Greek, and six Cyrillic characters.

Observing the political and social context—at a time when Albanians were determined to prevent the implementation of the unfavorable decisions made in the Berlin Congress and while the Ottoman Empire had an obligation to recognize the rights of nationalities—the Sublime Porte began to view Albania as a social and political factor. The Ottoman Empire was under supervision by the Great Powers and did not have the ability to stop the cultural emancipation of Albanians. Therefore, the Ottomans chose to support the process, at least temporarily, in order to turn it in their favor.

The alphabet became the first writing system based on Latin that was also used by Muslim Albanians. This represented the first important step the Albanians took in reclaiming their Western identity. On the other hand, it was also beneficial to the West as Europeans would use cultural and social ties with Albania for political gains, which included a pro-Western autonomous state.

The alphabet would help Albanians develop a literature in their native language. To facilitate the efforts, Albanian intellectuals founded on October 12, 1879, the Albanian Print-Press Society (primarily known as the İstanbul Society, or as in the original, *Shoqëria e të Shtypurit Shkronja Shqip*). Sami Frashëri, his brother Naim, and Pashko Vasa were the most prominent of the founding members.

The Ottoman government tolerated the early activities of the group. In doing so, the Porte hoped to keep Albanians on its side as they struggled against the decision of Berlin. Furthermore, the imperial government aspired to nurture a unity of Albanians with the Ottoman nation. But the alphabet and publications made it clear that the Albanians had turned their back on Islamism and cast their vision on their national identity and the Western civilization. It was for this reason that the Porte banned *Shoqëria*, fearing that the society's impact would be too disruptive for the empire.

The ban on the İstanbul Society and Albanian publications did not put an end to the national emancipation process. Albanians abroad picked up the activities of the İstanbul intellectuals and took steps further. Books in the Albanian language continued to be published in Romania, Egypt, and Italy (Rome and Naples). Newspapers also became very important for the spread of Albanianism among Albanians in various parts of the world. The process of emancipation had thus begun, and would not stop despite the difficulties.

Skeptics who had calculated that religious pluralism will divide the Albanians were proven wrong and were disappointed to see that the development of a written language would inspire the ethnic group to embrace its national identity. Accordingly, the content of the publications was secular. The *Drita* (*Alb.*, Light) and later *Dituria* (*Alb.*, Knowledge) newspaper became a leading medium. Before the government had instituted its ban, an Orthodox Albanian activist, Petro Poga, succeeded in obtaining permission for publication. Writers included Sami Frashëri who submitted entries about human development, while Naim Frashëri argued for the importance of education. Jani Vreto wrote about moral values, and Pandeli Sotiri commented on various statistical data. The editors also added excerpts of world literature translated into Albanian as well as selected proverbs of a secular nature. None of the content had religious underpinnings.

After *Dituria*'s twelfth issue, the government outlawed both, the newspaper and its publisher, *Shoqëria e të Shtypurit Shkronja Shqip*. The reasons were straightforward: the newspaper was not based on religion, but on a national identity, hence challenging Sultan Abdul Hamid's objective of maintaining the Albanians as part of the Ottoman nation.

The only books printed in the empire after the dissolution of the İstanbul Society were Christian publications. The Ottoman Empire had promised Britain and France to permit Protestant and Catholic missionaries to publish religious literature. The British and Foreign Bible Society specifically worked on providing an Albanian translation of the Christian Holy Book. The Bible Society began its operations in İstanbul and later expanded to Manastir and Elbasan, where it hired Konstandin Kristoforidhi to translate religious book into Albanian. Kristoforidhi began his efforts promptly and provided original works as well, including an Albanian-Greek dictionary and some literary pieces. Using its Albanian-language publications, the Bible Society played a crucial role that went beyond religious matters, as Protestant missionaries preached mostly to Orthodox Albanians who had been suffering from the political oppression under the Greek Church.

The British as well as Jesuit missionaries served as an impetus for cultural emancipation and education as activists associated with the religious groups worked to set up schools in the Albanian language. On March 7, 1887, Pandeli Sotiri opened the first secular Albanian school in Korça. In collaboration with Albanian patriots in İstanbul, he petitioned the Ottoman ministry of education for permission, which was easily obtained as the senior official approving the request happened to be Naim Frashëri. The school struggled, however, in Korça, because of the hostility of the local authorities and the fear incited among parents who were reluctant to enroll their children in the institution.

Another notable example of Protestant converts is the Qiriazi family. A mission of the American Board was established in 1873 in Manastir, where Gjerasim Qiriazi became one of the first to embrace the evangelic message. He was later sent to the protestant seminar in Bulgaria, where he graduated in 1882. Upon returning to Albania, Gjerasim joined the Bible Society, since this organization focused more heavily on translations and publications in the Albanian language. Besides his religious service, Gjerasim focused on promoting the Albanian language and education. While in İstanbul, he developed his own alphabet for the language, and managed to convince Alexander Thompson, the leader of the Bible Society in the city, to publish the works of Albanian authors. As a result, in 1889, two books were printed in Bucharest. Two years later, Qiriazi opened a girls' school in Korça, where Naim Frashëri once again played a decisive role in securing the government's permission.

The activity of protestant missionaries in Albania specially focused on the struggle against Hellenism and its propaganda. This engagement was very important for the future of Albania, because ever since the Eastern Crisis had begun, Greek nationalist had become increasingly intrusive in Albanian affairs. On the one hand, Hellenists lay territorial claims on some important regions on Albania, and on the other, they sought to keep the Albanian national movement under Greek influence. For instance, Greek writers had already cherished the theory that the Greeks and Albanians belonged to the same race. In the beginning, Hellenism affected Albanians in a positive way towards emancipation, while Greek nationalists showed no

266

tendency for religious discrimination. Soon, however, it became apparent that Hellenism would prevent the prosperity of Orthodox Albanians. The Greek Church denied their right to a native language and national identity (an Albanian priest, Papa Kristo Negovani, was assassinated for his support of his mother tongue), and argued instead that all the Orthodox were Greek.

As the Hellenist influence grew, Albanian activists devoted much of their writing to refuting the "one race" theory of Greek authors. Sami Frashëri portrayed the Albanians as descendants of the Pelasgians, the ancient inhabitants of the Balkans Peninsula, who preceded the Greek arrival for some two thousand years. The Albanian intellectual engaged in a longstanding polemic with the Greek newspaper *Neologos* and wrote extensively about the distinct between one's national and one's religious identity.

Sami Frashëri further defined what he viewed as Albanian lands and used official statistics on Balkan demographics to refute some of the territorial claims of neighboring nations. Specifically, Sami contested the ethnic makeup of Serbia, which was recognized as an independent state at the Congress of Berlin, after the Serbs had annexed and ethnically cleansed large Albanian-populated areas. Serbia had forcibly removed nearly 200,000 Muslims, mainly ethnic Albanians, from the region between Nish and Kosova. Sami criticized the Serbian assertion that Kosova was a medieval Slavic center, dismissing the notion as a propaganda tool that Belgrade hoped to use for future territorial expansion.[484]

Sami's brother, Naim, also wrote in defense of an Albanian identity and right to statehood. In a Greek-language poem, Naim expressed the "true desire of the Albanians" to live in peace and mutual respect with their neighbors.[485] For this reason, he was critical of the Greek view that all Christians were Hellenes:

> All Europeans Christians are indeed,
> But they are Greek the least nor Greek do they feel."[486]

Orthodox Albanians who had initially been attracted by Hellenism were often the most vocal opponents of the Greek nationalist ideology. Notably, Thimi Mitko called for unity among ethnic Albanians,[487] whose only viable

---

[484] *Ibid.*, "Arnavutluk", 149-153.

[485] Naim Frashëri: *Vepra* I (Prishtinë: 1986), 143.

[486] See N. Frashëri, *Dëshir' e vërtetë e Shqiptarëve* in *Vepra* I, 138.

[487] Thimi Mitko, *Vepra* (Tiranë: 1981), 26.

path was to create a state of their own.[488] Mitko is celebrated primarily for his work in folklore. In 1878, he published *Bleta shqipëtare* (*Alb.*, The Albanian Bee), a collection of 505 popular songs and 39 tales from different parts of Albania. The common themes present in the folklore were emphasized as an indication of an Albanian identity that went beyond the local and regional kinships.

Meanwhile, an Arvanite publisher, Anastar Kullurioti (*Grk.*: Anastassios Kouloriotis), who had converted to Protestant Christianity, contributed important Greek-language publications pertaining to the Albanian question.[489] Writing for his own newspaper, *Foni tis Alvanios* (*Grk.*, Voice of the Albanians), he called on Europe to create an autonomous or independent Albania in the way other states had been formed in the region.[490] Kullurioti, also an education activist, was imprisoned for attempting to distribute an Albanian primer in Gjirokastër, and reportedly died in his cell after due to poisoning.[491]

Despite the various efforts to cooperate with Athens, Hellenism remained a precarious route for the national movement. Jeronim De Rada warned against a unification with Greece in his newspaper *Fiamuri i Arbërit/La Bandiera dell'Albania* (*Alb./Itl.*, The Flag of Albania). The Arbëreshë author preferred to maintain Ottoman sovereignty or creating an Ottoman-led Balkan federation rather than engage in dangerous adventures.[492] It was at a time of distrust towards Greece, that another road to cooperation opened for the Albanians. Friendship between Albanians and Romanian-akin Vlachs (Aromanians) appeared as a necessity as more Albanians migrated to Romania and as the two peoples formed the majority in Albania and Macedonia.[493]

---

[488] *Ibid.* 30.

[489] The *Pelasgos o promitheos* newspaper, owned by Anastas Pykaios, was published only once. Three weeks after the Treaty of Berlin, the publication wrote for the Greek opinion about the Albanian struggle for territorial integrity. For more on *Foni tis Alvanias* of Kullurioti, see: Skoulidas (1992), Liço (1983), and Konitza, "Memoire sur le mouvement national albanais" (1899), HHStA, PA XIV/18, Liasse XII/2, 15-16; Clayer, *Në fillimet . . .*, 262-64.

[490] Clayer, *Në fillimet . . .*, 264.

[491] *Ibid.*

[492] For more on De Rada's views on the future relations with Greece, see: Skëndi, *Zgjimi kombëtar shqiptar*, 201-221.

[493] Max Demeter Peyfuss, *Di aromunische Frage. Ihre Entwicklung von Ursprüngen bis zur Frieden von Bukarest (1913) und die Haltung Österreich-Ungarns* (Wien/Bohlau: 1974), 38.

The diaspora in Romania took hold in the early 19th century, when Orthodox Albanians from Korça began to seek jobs with Albanian craftsmen and business who had already established themselves in the country. As the émigré community grew, it gained political significance as well, with many members such as Naum Veqilharxhi participating in the Romanian Revolution. The immigrants also contributed to education in their homeland by providing Albanian-language textbooks. [494]

The community nevertheless remained fragile and vulnerable to the divisive activities of Greek and Ottoman agents.[495] Yet, attesting to the capacity of the immigrants and the Romanian government's interest in encouraging the Albanian identity, Sami Frashëri endeavored to provide the community with the needed guidance and coordination. Frashëri advised activists to form a branch of *Shoqëria e të Shtypurit Shkronja Shqip*, and, soon, prominent immigrants, including Thimi Mitko, established *Deg' e shoqërisë së Stambollit për vivlla shqipe* (*Alb.*, Branch of the İstanbul Society for Albanian Books). The group developed a network of supporters throughout the Albania diaspora, in countries such as Italy, Egypt, Bulgaria, and the United States.

Bucharest Albanians would later, in 1884, form the *Drita* society. Wealthy businessmen such as Anastas Avramidhi Lakçe and Konstandin Eftimi were chosen to lead this organization, which focused on promoting education and publishing Albanian textbooks drafted by İstanbul Society. Affluent patriots donated to a fund that *Drita* used to purchase a print-press. Most of the works published were authored by the Frashëri brothers and Jani Vreto. The Bucharest society printed eight textbooks in 1886, including a primer, grammar, reading, and history books, two poetry collections, an adoption of a Greek-language mathematics workbook, and a compilation for moral education.[496] Two years later, then the renamed *Dituria* society, issued another four publications: a new edition of the primer, geography and

---

[494] An Albanian primer, *Pelasgika: shqip apla alfavitar*, using a Greek-based alphabet with additional Romanian characters was published by Korça-born Vasil Dimitri Ruso in Bucharest in 1877.

[495] Ibrahim Temo, *Ittihad ve Terakki Cemyiyetinin Tesekkülü ve Hidemaati vatyniye ve inkilabi milliye dair Hatiratim Mecidiye* (1939), 53-54, cited in Clayer, *Në fillimet . . .*, 268.

[496] The works included: Sami *e gjuhësë shqip* (78 pages); *Shkronjëtore e gjuhësë shqip* (133 p.); Naim Frashëri, *E këndimit çunave Këndonjëtoreja* 1 (59 p.); *Historia e përgjithshme* (për mësonjëtoret e para) (116 p.); *Vjersha për mësonjëtoret e para* (96 pages); *Bagëti e Bujqësia* (23 p.); Jani Vreto, *Numeroteja* (167 p.); *Mirëvajta* (176 p.).

science textbooks, and another poetry anthology.[497] Three new titles, including a discourse on sciences and a folklore compilation, came out in 1889, but none were school textbooks.[498] Naim Frashëri had several of his poems published in a book the following.[499] Lastly, two textbooks were printed in Bucharest in 1894 and 1895, but since the society was in the process of dissolution, it did not include its name or emblem.[500]

The Bucharest society journeyed through a difficult path during its years of existence. Indeed, *Drita* or *Dituria* achieved its success partly by taking advantage of, and at the same time serving, the interests of the Romanian government. In addition to the common struggle against Hellenism and pan-Slavism, Bucharest had an incentive in cooperating with Albanians to promote the Vlach or Aromanian issues. The largest concentration of Vlachs was in Macedonia, and a minority lived in Albania, too, inspiring projects for a joint political agenda. One major plan was to create a dual state of Albania-Macedonia, where Albanians and Aromanians would form the majority of the population. A bilingual Albanian-Romanian newspaper in the late 1880s, *Shqipëtari/Albanezul* (*Alb./Rom.*, The Albanian), explored theories of a common origin of the two peoples as descendants of the Pelasgians.[501]

Yet, the Albanian community in Romania was able to score two achievements of historic significance that outlived the challenges of the time. The activities of the Bucharest society encouraged the cultural and spiritual unification of Albanians and paved the way to political unity. Meanwhile, the Hellenist campaign of the Greek Church to assimilate the Orthodox Albanians also suffered a blow and weakened noticeably.

---

[497] Muhamet Çami's *Erveheja*, completed by Hajdar of Gjirokastër and purified of foreign words by Jani Vreto, 40 pages; Sami Frashëri, *Dituritë, për mësonjëtoret e para.*

[498] Jani Vreto, *Radhuashkronjë* (158 p.); *Ungjilli sipas Mattheut* (154 p.); *Të bërëtë* (253 p.).

[499] Naim Frashëri, *Luletë e verësë* (80 p.).

[500] Naim Frashëri, *Mësime* (125 p.); *Gjithësia* (140 p.); *Will of Anastas Avramidhi Lakçe*, brochure in Greek, Romanian, and French.

[501] Clayer, *Në fillimet . . .*, 274.

CHAPTER 7
THE ALBANIANS AND THE YOUNG TURKS

The *Jeunes Turcs* Movement and the Albanian Involvement

In the struggle against Abdul Hamid's despotic rule based on fanatic Islamism as well as in the overall efforts to gain greater elbowroom for its activities, the Albanian national movement finds an important domestic ally in the Young Turk movement, where many Albanians, including founding members such as Ibrahim Temo, played a vital role. Ottomanism, as a new model of patriotism based on the unity and equality of all subjects, regardless of religion, language, and race, stands in compatibility with Albanianism. Albanians contribute greatly to the consolidation of the Committee of Unity and Progress and the efforts for a comprehensively diverse opposition. Although the Young Turks announce the idea of the Ottoman supra-nation as tied to citizenship, Sami Frashëri maintains that "being an Ottoman means being an Albanian, too," calling on his countrymen to support and cooperate with the movement, on the condition that the Young Turks make the Albanian question a priority, protecting the Albanian-inhabited territory from further partitioning and respecting the group's national identity. Ismail Qemali successfully pushes at the 1907 Congress of Paris for the Young Turks to accept the new Albanian factor in the empire and to consider the demands of the ethnic group. Abdyl Frashëri writes to Arbëreshë Prime Minister of Italy, Francesco Crispi, on the autonomy of Albania.

The Albanians had no alternative but to pursue an ethnic-based political program. Cooperation with other national movements and ideologies seemed impossible. Great confrontations broke out between Albanianism and Islamism on political grounds, while social and cultural aspects spurred

271

disagreements with Hellenism and Slavicism. An ethnic-based platform was hence a viable option since the language provided the common denominator that surpassed the religious and provincial divisions. External support, however, was also required. Therefore, the Albanians had to strike a balance between ethnic identity and the preservation of the Ottoman Empire by seeking a special status, such as an autonomous state or a similar entity, within the imperial framework. Self-government as a matter complied with the reforms that the Ottoman state had committed to at the Congress of Berlin in exchange for the European guarantee of the empire's territorial integrity.

Autonomy was not an easy task to achieve. So far, demands for self-government had led to quarrels with the Hamidian regime, which utilized the Albanians ever since the Congress of Berlin. Presenting them as the "flower of the empire," Sultan Abdul Hamid II turned them into a dike against the expansionist neighbors, while also lengthening the life of Ottoman rule in the region without granting the Albanians the status of a nationality or their right to self-government. The sultan rejected the demands of the ethnic group, which he not only acknowledged but highly valued for its "Islamic piety."

In the struggle against Abdul Hamid's despotic rule and Islamist fanaticism, the Albanian national movement found a powerful ally within the empire. The Young Turks (Trk.: *Jönturkler*, from Fr.: *Jeunes Turcs*) began to emerge in the Ottoman political scene as an opposition force, which soon adopted Ottomanism as its ideology, promoting a state-based patriotism that called for change in the empire. The new political movement despised the Hamidian despotism, feudal oligarchy, and the fundamentalist Islamic clergy that impeded progress by depriving the Ottoman society of the right to structural change. Since the Tanzimât reforms, moreover, the political establishment had also incited violence, which greatly affected the Albanians.

The Young Turks were a broad opposition force that was sparked by Abdul Hamid's tight grip on power. The driving force behind the movement were students and youth who despised the abrogation of the parliament, while many Ottomans who were sent to France for training that would assist the Tanzimât reforms called for a modern state. Inspired by the illuminist and revolutionary ideas of the time, Western-educated intellectuals, including many Albanians,[502] gathered around an elitist social platform that later

---

[502] Among them was also Hoxha Tahsini, one of the pioneers of modern education in the Ottoman Empire and a leader of the Albanian national movement. He was also a member of the *Shoqëria e Shkronjave Shqip* of İstanbul.

developed a political arm concerned with the modernization of the Ottoman Empire. The movement wished for the troubled monarchy to compete with the European progress in social, cultural, and political spheres, blaming Islamism and religious obscurantism for the setbacks. Therefore, the Young Turks offered as an alternative the principles of freedom and equality without regards to race and religion, where all subjects of the empire would be equal citizens enjoying equal rights. The intellectual elite, adhering to Turkish nationalism, regarded Ottomanism as a new wave of patriotism that the empire need for its revival. In the meantime, the concept was also devised as a measure against the dictate of the Great Powers, which wielded excessive influence on the empire ever since the Eastern Crisis had begun. Sultan Abdul Hamid II greatly yielded to European control in the economic and political matters, but used his despotic rule at home to camouflage the regime's weakness abroad.

Considered from this perspective, the Young Turk opposition was well attractive to the Albanians, who had already become estranged from Abdul Hamid II. While the sultan had propagated the Albanian role as "an Islamist pillar of the empire," he was not only unable to defend the ethnic group's land, but had repeatedly conceded to the Russian-backed neighbors on demands for disadvantageous reforms (of which more will be said later).

Many of the proponents of Albanianism were also key figures in the Young movement at all times. Ibrahim Temo was one of the cofounders of the leading opposition group, Njazi Resnja became a hero of the Young Turk Revolution, while Mehmet Rauf Leskoviku and many others founded the local branches of the movement. Other important participants in the Ottoman opposition included Ismail Qemali, Dervish Hima, Shahin Kolonja, Hasan Prishtina, Nexhip Draga, and others, who helped the Young Turks in the yearlong struggle for regime change, which decisively occurred after the Albanian uprising in Ferizaj in the summer of 1908.

The clandestine opposition movement came to live in 1889 when four medical school students—an Albanian from Ohër, Ibrahim Temo, a Circassian from the Caucasus, Mehmet Reşit, and two Kurds, Abdullah Cevdet and Ishak Sukk^uti—formed the Ottoman Society for Unity (İttihad-ı Osmanı Cemiyeti). The group, better known by its later name, the Committee for Unity and Progress (CUP),[503] attracted many intellectuals in the Ottoman

---

[503] Although the organization was formally called the Committee for Unity and Progress only in September 1907, after the merger of the Free Ottomans Society and the Progress and Unity Society, it will be referred to as the CUP here indiscriminately.

273

capital and soon expanded to the European part of the empire, including Albania. Temo, whose Albanian name was Ibrahim Starova, brought many of his compatriots to the movement, believing that the Albanians would greatly benefit from a constitutional monarchy in the Ottoman Empire, where they would be able to fulfill their cultural, social, and political interests. In the early days of the CUP, Temo recruited Nexhip Draga, a prominent aristocrat from Kosova and other Albanian activists from the Kosova vilayet and southern Albania.[504]

Thereby, Albanians and Young Turks united around two main goals: (1) the reinstatement of the constitution and the parliament, suspended by Sultan Abdul Hamid II in 1878 during the Russo-Turkish war; and (2) to continue the social reforms through which the Ottoman Empire sought modernization by focusing on economic development and giving up on the corroded Islamist structures that kept the country backwards. The Young Turks appears with the alternative of a functional state, based on Turkish nationalism and with the Ottoman principle uniting all subjects, regardless of religion, race, and language. In other words, the movement desired a revolutionary turn, since Islamism (the combination of the Muslim faith with patriotism) was to be replaced by Ottomanism, a social and state framework that initially followed the French Revolution principles of liberty, equality, and unity, in which the Albanians saw an opportunity to appear as an independent nation. Here, equality—in that it respected cultural and national identity—was seen as a precondition to the Albanian support for the Ottoman platform.

The most significant occasion for the Albanian cooperation with the Young Turks came after a peace treaty the Ottoman Empire signed with Greece on December 4, 1897. The agreement concluded a war that the Ottomans had won, but the Sublime Porte, under the dictate of the Great Powers, lost Crete. The island was declared autonomous and "neutral," ruled by a Christian governor, in reality an ethnic Greek; the Great Powers undertook to supervise the Cretan administration.[505]

The "peace" imposed on the Ottomans had other great ramifications, including the severe concession that Sultan Abdul Hamid made to Serbia, Greece, and Bulgaria. The compromise definitely brought the Young Turks and Albanians together on the year-long platform. Ultimately, this led to the

---

[504] Gawrych, *Gjysmëhëna dhe shqiponja* (Tiranë: 2007), 214.
[505] H.P.Sh. 2 (Tiranë), 266.

victory of the Young Turk Revolution in summer 1908, whose epilogue was determined by the successful Albanian uprising in Ferizaj. Among the concessions that were most troubling to the Albanians was the restoration of the Serbian Patriarchate in Peja, where the Serbian Orthodox Church had last maintained its seat in 1767, and the inclusion of Dibër and Manastir under the jurisdiction of the Bulgarian exarchate. In summer 1897, the Sublime Gate appointed a Serbian metropolitan in Shkup and the same day announced the opening of Serbian schools in the vilayets of Kosova, Manastir, and Selanik. At the beginning of the following year, the Ottoman government appointed two Bulgarian despots (exarchists) for Dibër and Manastir. The concessions exacerbated the contradictions between Bulgaria, Serbia, and Greece, leading gangs of the three states to bloody clashes over parts of the Albanian lands and the Macedonia region. In the meantime, the political situation in Albania worsened, as the Albanians became increasingly discontent with the threatened annexation of their territories by neighboring countries.[506]

As the empire continued to make political concessions and suffer territorial losses, Albanian confidence in the Hamidian rule was on the rise. To maintain its grip, the regime relied heavily on a heavy crackdown of Albanian activists and the growing opposition, demanding the reinstatement of the constitutional order. After the Albanians organized an uprising in order to halt the expanding Serbian and Greek influence in their lands, the Ottoman government ordered a military operation under the command of Tefik Pasha. In the meantime, the Porte unleashed its reprisals against the Young Turks, group around their newly-formed political organization, the CUP, which included Albanians in the leadership. On this occasion, many of the CUP leaders were imprisoned or interned to various parts of the empire, while several others escaped abroad to continue their activities with even greater dedication. One of the founding members, Ibrahim Temo, migrated to Bucharest, where he also focused on the Albanian national question, which he viewed as closely tied to the Young Turk opposition.

However, the ban on CUP activities and Albanian clubs and the closure of the Normal School of Elbasan and Albanian newspaper that had begun to emerge in İstanbul and in Albanian towns did not extinguish the Young Turk movement or the spreading of Albanianism. To the contrary, both ideological groups resorted to underground movements within the country,

---

[506] *Ibid.* 267.

while exiled branches flourished, turning into promoters of crucial developments that toppled the despotic regime of Sultan Abdul Hamid. The Young Turk movement was centered in Paris, while branches were founded in Geneva, Cairo, and other cities, strengthening the opposition platform with the European model of governance, including secularism. Consequently, Hamidian despotism consolidated its feudal and Islamist support base, which demanded even tougher Sharia-based measures against the opposition. Meanwhile, the exiled Young Turks began with the publication of newspapers and other propaganda materials that were then easily smuggled into the country. Among the most popular media was *La Jeune Turquie* (Fr., New Turkey), published by Khalil Gunemi, Lebanese Catholic and former member of the first Ottoman parliament.

Three opposition groups coexisted in the expat movement: the faction of Ahmed Riza, a follower of Count Auguste and his positivist philosophy, called for a constitution but opposed foreign interference; Ottoman leaders Murad Bey, Damad Mahmud Pasha, and Ismail Qemali, headed a group of mostly high-ranking officials who demanded a consultative council and called the great powers, especially Britain, to intervene; meanwhile, a flock of medical students constituted their own faction.

In addition, two other groups were formed: the partisans of deed and the so-called Balkan network. The latter was led by Ibrahim Temo who, operating in Romania and Bulgaria, urged for solidarity among the Balkan Muslims. In the meantime, activists founded CUP subsidiaries within the Ottoman realm, too. Albanians were extensively involved in the activities: a religious leader and some Albanian officers formed the branch of Adrianople, Mehmet Rauf Leskoviku formed the representative office in Thessaloniki, Dervish Hima began his mission in Durrës, while other branches were formed in Manastir and Tirana.[507]

In these circumstances, the prominent Albanian leader, Ismail Qemali, was also forced to leave İstanbul along with the majority of CUP activists. In exile, the renowned politician considered the national question a priority, although he did not ignore the Ottoman opposition movement, for he knew that the solution for Albania was dependent on the turn the empire would take. In December 1899, Damad Mahmud Pasha, a son-in-law of the sultan, also fled from Turkey. The defection changed the configuration of Young

---

[507] *Ibid.* 267.

Turk movement, giving priority to the pro-English group of London, while activists urged Ismail Qemali to take the leadership of CUP.[508]

With the justification that he will be devoted to the Albanian issue, Ismail Qemali refused the post of the CUP president, but promised to remain faithful to the principles of movement and vouch for its success. At the 1902 CUP Congress in Paris, where partisans gained a majority in the organization's leadership, Ismail Qemali entreated the Great Powers to intervene against the Hamidian dictatorship, while also promising to elicit support from Armenians and Albanians. However, realizing the shortcomings of his political plan, he conspired with a powerful ethnic Albanian in the Ottoman ranks to overthrow Abdul Hamid by force. While Qemali and the governor of Tripoli, Marshal Rexhep Pashë Mati, gained the moral support of the British for a military coup, the efforts failed because no other major power was interested in the radical twist that could follow if two Albanian leaders, a marshal and a politician, were to oversee the overthrow of the absolute monarchy. Certainly, the failure was prompted by the possibility of the Albanian issue becoming a dominant factor, which would endanger the balance of power in the region and beyond, bringing the Great Powers into an inevitable conflict. Likely, it was precisely the fear of an Albanian and Armenian empowerment that promoted Turkish nationalism within the movement. The titular community of the empire, yet a minority within the Young Turk movement, ethnic Turks towards turned towards nationalism and centralization of power. Under the leadership of Ahmed Riza, the CUP became an anti-separatist and anti-imperialist organization, resorting even to Islam and other rhetorical elements to attract various opposition groups to their cause.[509]

The political developments and the theoretical reflections on a post-Hamidian Ottoman Empire did not impede the Turkish-Albanian cooperation, which appeared as a necessity for both sides. In fact, Albanians played a role on both ends: as Albanians and as Ottomans. The foreign policy and the reforms of Abdul Hamid, having disfavored the Albanians and endangered the integrity of the empire, added to the joint dedication of the two ethnic groups to replace the absolute monarchy with a constitutional order. Activists attempted at reconciling Ottomanism and Albanianism on major issues, while trying to promote tolerance so that issues that proved irresoluble for

---

[508] Ismail Qemal Vlora, *Kujtime*, 294.
[509] *Ibid.* 296.

the moment could be addressed later at an auspicious time. Since the main concern was the reinstatement of the constitution and the reopening of the parliament, on principle, most Albanians accepted Ottomanism as a state framework for the empire. Promises of equality, unity, and freedom for all, as propagated by the opposition movement, were deemed adequate for ethnic communities to cooperate as they hoped for liberty to express their own national identity. This way, circumstances arose for parties to speak openly and on common interests about other pending issues, where the structure of government remained of foremost importance. The Young Turks had now unveiled their concept of an Ottoman *supranation* as a state-based identity, while Sami Frashëri believed that "to be an Ottoman also means to be an Albanian." The motto placed the line of potential conciliation, as had once the idea of a common *vatan* supported the coexistence of Islamism and Albanianism, prompting a decisive position that members of the ethnic group took in crucial moments, such as the events leading to the June Revolution of 1908, acting acted both as Ottomans and as Albanians.

Nevertheless, the relation between the two ideologies was of an immense complexity, for Albanians were primarily concerned with attaining the status of a nationality within what appeared as a joint state framework. Likewise, they were reasonably preoccupied with the response the Young Turk Revolution would give to the Balkan countries seeking to partition Albania. If for both Young Turks and Albanians the constitution was a matter of priority, defending their ethnicity and the recognition of their nationality for the Albanians was a matter of their existence that also defined the ethnic group's stance on the common goal and the fate of the empire.

Therefore, grave and irreconcilable differences existed between the Young Turk and the Albanians. But for the sake of the common interest, the two currents tried to conceal their incompatibilities for as years as the opposition life continued in exile and the Hamidian persecution of dissent persisted in the Ottoman Empire. However, once the Revolution triumphed, disputes manifested themselves, marking the beginning of the end for the Ottoman Empire.

Nevertheless, Albanians made no attempts at ruining the unity of the Young Turk movement, just as they did not seek the dissolution of the Ottoman state. Divisions ensued after factions broke off from the mainstream orientation, promoting instead centralization of power and Islamist rhetoric, as noted after the first 1902 Congress, when Ahmed Riza assumed the leadership of the CUP. Yet, neither then did the Albanians work to undermine the support for the Young Turk movement or to impede its activities in the Albanian vilayets. Instead, Albanian activists involved in the CUP leadership called on their compatriots to not give up the opposition movement, regardless of its direction. Frontrunners such as Ismail Qemali, Hasan Pristina, Ibrahim Temo, Nexhip Draga, and others feared indifference to the political developments in the empire could leave the Albanians secluded. For that reasons, the leaders urged their ethnic community to return to a catalyst for the opposition, for they believed that to be the only way to advance their interests.

At this stage, Albanian members of the CUP saw the reinstatement of the constitution as an opportunity for people to realize their goals through democracy. Moreover, even when the Young Turks adapted the centralization of power as part of their political platform, Ismail Qemali—who was the closest with CUP leader Ahmet Riza and helped the movement find a common language with all the trends that appeared in imperial political spectrum—was convinced that if the Albanians became the right hand of the opposition with the goal of toppling of Abdul Hamid's regime, then all the roads will be open for them. During his stay in Greece and Belgium and some other European countries, Qemali behaved primarily as a partisan of liberal reforms and decentralization under the protection of the Great Powers, such as Britain, because it was only through their support that he could work for Albania's autonomy or independence. (At this time, national leaders also thought for *other solutions*, such as that of creating a Greek-Albanian federation.[510] This long-time option, which was first considered in 1878 during at a meeting between Abdyl Frashëri and Mehmet Ali Vrioni with Greek prime minister,[511] was re-instated in other negotiations of Ismail Qemali with Greeks, between 1904 and 1907, and according to some sources remained on the table well until the eve of national independence.[512])

That proponents of Albania's statehood embarked on a complex journey with the Young Turk movement is exemplified in the political activity of Ibrahim Temo. As cofounder of the CUP, Temo at all times tried to keep Albanianism related to the Young Turk ideals. When he first met Ahmet Riza in Paris, where the two leaders decided to unite various groups of the movement into a single organization, the Albanian-born activist also ex-

---

[510] H.P.Sh. 2 (Tiranë), 141.

[511] *Ibid.* 142.

[512] *Ibid.* 143.

279

pressed concern about the fate of his people and demanded that the CUP attend to the question. While Temo committed to the movement's aspirations for a constitutional monarchy, he also insisted that the Albanian issue be addressed in order to the ethnic group to lend its support to the Young Turks.[513]

Temo's role best illustrates the weight that Albanians had for all opposition forces of the empire. So the common interests of Young Turkism and Albanianism interacted, while Temo with his compatriots played a dual role: as Ottomans and Albanians. This liaison was present almost at all Albanians that they were in that boat, but Temo's case was stronger and more emblematic, since he was a leading founder of Young Turkism, yet he never ceased in his efforts to unite Albanians on the national basis. As cofounder of the CUP, Temo was involved in Albanian movement, presenting a program for reform and emancipation on a nationality basis. . While in exile in Romania, he became vice-president of an Albanian society named *Bashkimi* (*Alb.*, Unity), which he helped create in Constanta. For this purpose, he drafted several memoranda, in which he emphasized the Albanian linguistic and cultural rights as a balance against the risk of Serbian, Greek, and Latin impingement. According to him, the *Rum* (*i.e.*, Greek) district in İstanbul, a symbol of Hellenic power and wealth, was a "nest of intrigues," and called for an immediate end to its influence on the Ottoman Empire. He even urged the imperial palace to change the way it took the census by admixing nationality with religion, in order to prevent Christian Albanians from registering as Bulgarians, Serbs, or Greeks. The proposed reform would delegitimize the neighboring countries' claims that other ethnic groups and not the Albanians allegedly constituted the majority in the Albanian vilayets of the empire. Temo advised the use of the terms *Orthodox* or *Catholic* to show the religious affiliation on the census, while he also called for the introduction of the native language in churches and schools, where students could also learn Turkish.[514] He urged Orthodox Albanians to cooperate with the Vlachs,

---

[513] Gawrych, *Gjysmëhëna dhe shqiponja*, 216.

[514] For more on Ibrahim Temo, see his memoirs, *İttihad ve Terakki Cemiyetinin Teşekkülü ve Hidemat-ı Vataniye ve İnkılâbı Milliye Dair Hatıratım* (Mecidiye: 1939); Kristaq Prifti, *Doktor Ibrahim Temo: Jeta dhe vepra* (Prishtinë: 1996); Hasan Kaleshi, "Dr. Ibrahim Temo – osnivać mladoturskog komiteta ujedinjenje i napredak," *Prilozi osvjetljenja uloge Albanaca u mladoturskom pokretu* in *Prilozi za Orijentalnu Filologuiju* (Sarajevo: 1972); Şükrü Hanioğlu, *The Yung Turks in Opposition* (Oxford UP: 2001); Clayer, *Në fillet e nacionalizmit shqiptar*; Gavrych, *Gjysmëhëna dhe shqiponja*.

believing that the two groups that shared the same religious had other common interests and could further strengthen the movement. He called for the two communities to step up efforts for schools and churches in their respective native tongues, which were not permitted by the Greek and Bulgarian ecclesiastic establishments.[515]

As an Ottoman, Temo thought of Albanians along ethnic lines and not on religious divides. His concomitant engagement for Albania and the empire proves the great mutuality between Ottomanism and Albanianism in such circumstances, although there were external efforts to split the two ideologies. The demands for national rights, at least in the first phase, as Temo said, were not only a personal issue of one of the leaders of the opposition movement; they were a contribution to the political program of CUP. This is proved by the appeal that Ishak Sükûti, a member of the Kurdish nationality and cofounder of the Young Turk movement, made in the article "Albanians and Kurds." The article published in *Osmanli*, a CUP organ in Geneva, urged two ethnic groups to join the Turks, regardless of "special interests."[516] According to the author, both nationalities (Trk.: *millet*) served as a "point of support" for the Ottoman Empire: the Kurds in the east and Albanians in western frontier. After mentioning the ancient history of the Albanians and their merits for the empire, Sükûti mentioned the nationality's demands for *"bir idare-i mümtaz"* (*Trk.*, "for an autonomous government"). He advised the people not to rebel on their own, warning them of a similar fate to Bosnia-Herzegovina (*i.e.*, foreign occupation). Instead of isolated rebellion, the Kurdish writer invited the Albanians to join forces with the CUP to fight together against the Serbs, Greeks, and Italians and prevent them from realizing their territorial claims on the empire. "Unity guarantees peace," he wrote, "while its absence causes a disaster."[517]

Sükûti's call for the "unity [that] guarantees peace" was not all that convincing for most of Albanian CUP members, especially those in exile. Activists feared that if Turkish nationalism under the guise of the Ottomanism continued to deal with the Albanians on religious grounds, it would remain an obstacle as much as Abdul Hamid's regime. Owing to these doubts, which later proved to be right, Albanian expats were less supportive of the nationalists, including Ahmet Riza, who constantly avoided the

---

[515] Gawrych, *op.cit.*, 216.

[516] *Ibid.* 215.

[517] *Ibid.* 218.

demands for autonomy with indirect statements that "the purpose of the Young Turks was to overthrow the regime of Sultan Hamid and the return of parliamentarism." Moreover, the Albanian newspaper *Drita e Sofies* (*Trk.*, The Light of Sofia) sharply criticized the CUP, uttering that "for the Albanians, it is necessary to fight for Albania, the Albanians and their language and not for Turkey, Sivas and Adrianople."

Purporting to convey the same message, Dervish Hima also wrote an editorial in the first issue of *Arnavudluk Sadası* (*Trk.*, Voice of Albania), a Turkish-language newspaper published in Rome. The Albanian writer recalled that:

> The existence of Turkey in Rumelia [i.e., the European part of the empire] depended on the existence of Albania and the Albanian existence depended on the existence of Turkey . . . Hence, we want to govern our own country as a united Albania, but still under the guidance and protection of the Ottoman Empire, and want to purge our land from the officers who came from Arabia and Anatolia.[518]

Hima envisioned a unified Albanian vilayet, a plan that Abdyl Frashëri had unsuccessfully presented to Sultan Abdul Hamid. Frashëri himself had been convicted for his involvement in the Provisional Government of 1881, but he never gave up his activities. Immediately after he was released from internment in Anatolia, he wrote to European leaders to demand support for his home country. He sent three letters to Francesco Crispi, an Arbëreshë who at the time had become prime minister of Italy.[519] The former foreign minister of Albania sent his first letter in November 1887, and in September next year he mailed a second memorandum together with Mehmet Ali Vrioni, informing Crispi of the Albanian determination to preserve their

---

[518] *Ibid.* 219.

[519] *Francesco Crispi* (1819-1901), an Arbëreshë, participated in the 1848 Revolution, becoming a member of the parliament of the Kingdom of the Two Sicilies. After the popular movement was suppressed, he spent several years in hiding in the Italian state of Piedmont, from where he was expelled in 1853. He then sought refuge in Malta, later moved to Paris, and lastly to London. In 1860, he inspired Garibaldi's *Expedition of the Thousand* to conquer Naples, leading to the irredentist victory over Sicily and the proclamation of the unified Kingdom of Italy. Crispi was a liberal politician and an ardent support of the Tripartite Alliance with Germany and Austria-Hungary, while he vehemently opposed France. Later, he pushed for Italy to become a colonial power.

territory and to achieve statehood.[520] After mentioning the ongoing resistance of his compatriots, the former diplomats of the League of Prizren wrote that "consequently, Albania deserves independence more than any other nation in the Balkans. We hope it will be the most worthy for European support and most able to govern themself."[521] Later, in a letter sent in 1890, Frashëri reiterated his well-known opinion that "the Eastern Question will never be solved if Europe does not consider the fate of Albania, which occupies a very important place in the Balkan Peninsula." He also expressed the conviction that the Albanians were willing to give their lives to protect their lands and national identity, seeking for that reason the Italian support for Albania's statehood.[522]

Although Frashëri never abandoned the principles of administrative autonomy, he was also willing to accept other forms of government that would save the country. Thus, he pointed out that the Albanians could become part of a Balkan Confederation or recognize the supremacy of a larger state with the condition that they be granted administrative autonomy and allowed to preserve the natural and ethnographic borders of their homeland.[523] In the 1890 letter, the former member of the Provisional Government wrote about the possibility of a dual state of Macedonia and Albania, which could dwell together under the same prince, should Europe decide to give both regions a similar level of autonomy.[524] Furthermore, by outlining the territory that he believed to belong to Albania, Frashëri specified that autonomous Macedonia may include vilayet of Selanik and southern sanjaks of the Manastir province, and that Albanians would not object would not object to such a boundary if land on both sides of the line were included within the dual state.[525]

The Albanian diplomat had two reasons to the Italian prime minister: on the one hand, considering Crispi's own heritage, Frashëri wanted to link the national movement with the Arbëreshë of Italy, who had raised their voice for Albania since the beginning of the Tanzimat reforms; and, on the other hand, Crispi led one of the European powers that, together with

---

[520] H.P.Sh. 2 (Tiranë), 235.

[521] Ibid. 236.

[522] Ibid.

[523] See Abdyl Frashëri, Letter to Francesco Crispi (Constantinople: 16 Sept. 1890), archived in ASMAE, fsh. 1495, cited in Skëndi, Zgjimi kombëtar shqiptar (Tiranë: 2000), 159.

[524] Ibid.

[525] Ibid.

Germany and Austria-Hungary, was part of the influential Tripartite Pact. The second issue was also important for the fact that Vienna and Rome already maintained an interest in Albania that countered the predatory plans of Serbs, Montenegrins, and Greeks on the nation's territory. Yet, Frashëri's contact with Italy also created the dilemma of choosing between two major powers, an issue that inevitably brought internal consequences. Although the Tripartite Pact dictated harmonized actions, Vienna and Rome each had its own plans for Albania, not excluding their protectorate over the small country. Furthermore, it was exactly Crispi (shortly after Frashëri's third letter) who called for Italy to establish its protectorate of Albania, launching a campaign that began with simultaneous political and economic actions.[526]

In fact, Crispi's plan came after May 20, 1882, when Austria-Hungary and Germany in a way recognized Italy's right for a new role in the Balkans as the three countries to protect each other against French and Russian expansion in the southeastern peninsula.[527] During the negotiations for the pact, Vienna stated that it would not object to increased Italian influence in the Mediterranean, for as long as Rome would strictly abide by the *status quo* in the Adriatic. The treaty was renewed five years later along with the vows to maintain the existing balance of power. However, the increasing tensions in the Balkans, especially after the Turkish-Greek war, indirectly revealed the Italian ambitions on Albania. The Apennine aspirations, in the meantime, were paralleled by the dual monarchy, which had its own plan.[528] This way, Rome and Vienna had an ongoing rivalry over Albania that shed positive light on the country, regardless of what the two powers intended. In addition to ruling out the possibility of Serbia and Greece engulfing the Albanian area, the two powerful monarchies projected Albania's future as part of Europe. This brought immense encouragement for the national movement to turn to the West with solid hopes that Italy and Austria-Hungary would be instrumental in Albania's independence.

---

[526] Skëndi, *Zgjimi kombëtar shqiptar* (Tiranë: 2000), 224.

[527] L. v Chlumesky, *Österreich-Ungarn und Italien* (Leipzig-Wien: 1907), 6.

[528] Buxhovi, *Kongresi i . . .*, 21-24.

The Austrian-Italian Rivalry over Albania and
Support for the National Movement

Vienna's interests in Albania reach beyond the sphere of religious mentorship, aiming at creating an independent state within the Albanian ethnic borders. Meanwhile, the Italian plans are of an expansionist nature. The Arbëreshë of Italy support the national movement, publicizing the Albanian question at an international level, even as the Italian government signs secret deals with the Slavic states to the expense of Albania. The Austrian consul in Shkodër, Lippich, authors a memorandum, concluding that the formation of a state within the ethnic Albanian territory is in Vienna's, as well as Europe's, best interest. Popular leader Ismail Qemali debates with writer Faik Konitza over foreign alliances; the former seeks friendship with Italy, while the latter insists on closer ties with the German-speaking nations, which he considers natural and historical allies of the Albanians. The competition between Rome and Vienna, nevertheless, causes no major effect other than providing greater impulses for the national movement.

The Young Turk Revolution opened the final chapter of the Albanian separation from the Ottoman Empire and the ethnic group's turn to the West. Initially, the new regime did so by remaining faithful to the promises, opening the way for the Albanian national awakening to continue among the masses. Later, however, the Young Turks turned their revolutionary coats and ignored the given word, resorting to centralization of power, shutting down Albanian schools, and taking a series of other measures that infringed on the notion of equality of the different nationalities. Nevertheless, the regime change carried the political focus of the Albanians to the West, even though the hurdle of the Ottoman heritage remained in the spiritual and cultural aspect, for many Albanians retained their Muslim faith, which the Slavic-Orthodox propaganda trumpeted as the danger of a "continued Islamist expansionism" in the old continent.

The label of Islamism was purported to serve foreign interests, whose support or hindrance of Albania's statehood affected the stability of the region up to modern days. The Albanians came to the spotlight of Western powers the moment the Congress of Berlin decided to maintain the *status quo* in the Balkans. Of course, the Europeans did not believe that keeping the Ottoman state in the peninsula would prove a lasting deal, but the decision enabled Western oversight in the empire's dissolution, minimizing the risk of unpleasant surprise alternatives could bring.

From that point onward, Europe effectively maintained two conflicting positions on the Ottoman Empire: the official policy in support of the troubled state's territorial integrity and the separate diplomatic agenda, including secret and overt preparations for a post-Ottoman Balkans. As part of the latter efforts, the West also induced regional actors in service of European interests. The Western agenda was significant in that the Albanians were an indispensable element when treated as a subject on their own right as well as when European powers viewed them as an object of political bargains.

It is noteworthy that the interests and positions of Western monarchies did not remain constant. Nevertheless, Austria and Italy were the most active powers in the Albanian question and greatly affected the political and diplomatic currents that delineated the future of the Balkan country. Both Rome and Vienna were highly influential, even though their involvement was not of the same nature. While earlier came into the picture relatively late, appearing only in the second half of the 19th century after the Italian unification, the Habsburg-led monarchy had continuously maintained ties with the Albanians since the 1400s. Later, the Austrians were particularly important during the thirty-year Ottoman war that lasted with minor interruptions from 1685 to 1715.

The earliest Austrian presence in Kosovo came with General Piccolomini's penetration following the 1686 Battle of Nish. The military officer later arrived in Prishtina and then marched south to Prizren and Shkup. During the four years of the Habsburg campaign in parts of Kosovo and northern Albania gave the Austrian-Albanian relations a unique significance, since the two sides were united in a common anti-Ottoman struggle; thousands of Albanians took part in the war, and their prelate, Pjetër Bogdani, carried a crucial a role.[529] Therefore, the defeat brought severe consequences to the Albanians, whose cooperation with the Austrian army made them a target of revenge upon the Ottoman return. Scores of Albanians were forced to follow the retreating troops to the north on a route of no return.

While the Austrian presence in the country was brief, Albanians were bound to Vienna through another link that remained. That is Austria's

---

[529] See Odette Marquet, *Pjetër Bogdani – letra dhe dokumente* (Tiranë: 1997); H.P.Sh. 1 (Prishtinë); Petrika Thëngjilli, *Shqiptarët midis Lindjes dhe Perëndimit* (Tiranë: 2003).

spiritual caretaking of Roman Catholics in the European dominions of the Ottoman Empire, a role the Western monarchy had acquired sometime in mid-1600s and continued to play throughout the padishah's rule. It was through its official right of religious protection that Austria diminished the Vatican's impact, which nevertheless began to revive by mid-18th century and onward. When the Ottoman Empire announced the Tanzimat reforms, Jesuit and Franciscan orders appeared in northern and central Albania, greatly assisting with the spiritual emancipation of Catholic Albanians.

By mid-1800s, the unified kingdom of Italy as a rising political factor on the continental scene developed a pivotal interest in the Balkans, while Austria promoted the so-called concept of *Kultursprotektorat* (*Ger.* Cultural Protectorate). This way, the Vienna-Rome competition over Albania took on greater proportions for the two powers were already hedging their bets on the eventual withdrawal of the Ottoman Empire. Realizing the plans of the European monarchies, the Albanians also began to brace for their political future. It is noteworthy that Albania's potential as a dike against the Slavic expansion became the common denominator of what may be viewed as Italy's and Austria's "shared interest" in the Balkan ethnic group. While Vienna and Rome contemplated an Albanian state conducive by its size and influence to the interests of one or the other power, but they would never permit that the small nation be endangered by Serbian, Montenegrin, or Greek hegemonism.

Nevertheless, the "shared interests" did not preclude the "several interests" of the two monarchies of the Adriatic coast. As a longtime rival of the Ottoman Empire, Vienna held an "advantage," that is the spiritual caretaking for Balkan Catholics, including a sizeable community in the northern portions of the ethnic Albanian territory. Since the Eastern Crisis, specifically when the Russo-Ottoman War of 1877 broke out, the dual monarchy had decided to include the Albanian question in what it identified as its *Orient-politik* (*Ger.* Policy on the East). Thereby, the Austro-Hungarian Foreign Ministry instructed its consul in Shkodër, F. Lippich, to draft a *Denktschrift über Albanien* (*Ger.* Memorandum on Albania).

Since the Habsburg diplomat was a fine connoisseur of the Balkans and the Albanian questions, it was expected that the dual monarchy would request his services in the strategic planning for the region. According to him, the Albanians and their territory deserved special attention; hence he proposed that Austria-Hungary undertake concrete steps, in light of what Lippich saw as the trend leading to the Ottoman withdrawal from the area, to turn the ethnic group into a valued ally. For this, he noted that "Not only are they a strong people with a firm anti-Slavic determination; they also possess a territory that extends, on the one hand, up to the borders of Serbia and, on the other, all the way to the Bulgarian Morava." The Austrian diplomat adds that "Albanians would significantly refrain the Serbian and Bulgarian desires for expansions, and in the monarchy's hands, they would earn a position that would make it impossible for the Russian-protected Slavism to wage a war in the Western Balkans that belongs to the Austro-Hungarian sphere of interest."[530]

In addition to Lippich and his memorandum, which influenced Vienna's agenda on the Albanians, other documents of varying recognition also caught the eyes of Austrian policymakers. Notably, the empire's ambassador to Thessaloniki, Count Greneville, gave crucial recommendations. Unlike his colleague in Shkodër who highlighted the Catholic factor in Albania, Greneville called on his government to engage Muslims and focus on eastern Albania (*i.e.*, present-day Kosovo and Macedonia) and the South. The areas were so fundamental, because "friendship with a strong eastern Albania secured our plans as to an end-bound Turkish rule, and an autonomous Albania is a powerful bastion against the extravagant desires of Serbia and Bulgaria."[531]

As the dual monarchy broadened its scope of involvement with Vienna-educated Albanian intellectuals conducting scholarly research at the imperial capital or running Austrian-funded publications in other European towns (*e.g.*, Faik Konitza's *Albania*), Italians were compelled to resort to similar means. Gripped by a sense of supremacy, Italy persistently sought to formulate its own policy on Albania. Intent on a share of the Ottoman remnants, the Apennine monarchy claimed its right to lay roots on the eastern shores of the Adriatic, alongside the Austro-Hungarian Empire.

Francesco Crispi, a famous Italo-Albanian who reached the post of Italy's prime minister, was the creator of this policy. In March 1880, he declared in the Italian parliament that "with the treaty of Berlin, Austria gained territory, creating with Bosnia-Herzegovina an inviolable border against the

---

[530] F. Lippich, *Denkcshrift über Albanien* (Wien: June 20, 1877), archived in HHStA, PA XII/256, Türkei 1pv. See also Skëndi, *Zgjimi kombëtar shqiptar*, 221-223; Zavalani, *Histori e Shqipnis*; H.P.Sh. 2 (Prishtinë); N. Jorga, *Geschichte des osmanichen Reiches*, vols. I-II (Gotha: 1908-09).

[531] V. Greneville, *Ostalbaniens Bedeutung* (Wien: Aug. 25, 1881), HHStA, PA XII/263, Türkei VIII B.

East, and it should be content for this. While we shall not envy the unjustly-acquired possessions, we ought to demand that they remain there and seek no more than what they treaty gives them. It is in our interest and in accordance with the principle of our great revolution that we be the protectors and friends of the small Balkan states."[532]

As an Arbëreshë, Crispi was among the first individuals to illustrate the importance of his community for Italy's foreign policy. As the newly-unified kingdom began to vie for influence in Albania, the Arbëreshë added a historical dimension to the Italian strategy, recalling the close relations the state of Skanderbeg had enjoyed with Naples and Genoa centuries ago. Moreover, the Albanian prince was directly involved in Neapolitan politics when he helped King Alphonse regain his lost throne. The European monarch then showed his gratitude by offering shelter to tens of thousands of refugees, including the Kastrioti family, who fled Albania following the Ottoman takeover and settled permanently in the Italian countries.[533] Additionally, Skanderbeg and the Albanians in general had intense relations with the papacy as well as cultural and trade ties with the Italian cities even after the Ottoman conquest. Particularly, Venice held many of the Albanian coastal towns, including Shkodër, the birthplace of many Renaissance humanists who significantly contributed to the intellectual ties between the two peoples.

The Arbëreshë continued to exert their influence in the relations between Italy and Albania well into the modern era. The émigré community's direct participation had fostered the national awakening in Ottoman-occupied Albania, while the Arbëreshë involvement in politics was naturally within the scope of the Italian state interests. Nevertheless, one ought to a draw a line between the cultural and social aspects of the Arbëreshë influence in the Albanian question. Culturally, national awakening began with the Italo-Albanians themselves, as an internal mission with an emphasis on the folklore, literature, and history.[534] Politically, the Arbëreshë nurtured a

---

[532] G. Salvemini, *La politica estera di Francesco Crispi* (Roma: 1919), 35, as cited in Skëndi, *Zgjimi kombëtar shqiptar*, 223.

[533] For more on the topic, see H.P.Sh. 1 (Prishtinë), 249-301.

[534] The Albanian national renaissance literature began with the Arbëreshë. Jeronim de Rada (1814-1903) and Zef Skiroi (1865-1927) opened the way to Albanian romanticism, which later included the national poet, Naim Frashëri, and other prominent writers. As to de Rada's role in evoking the Albanian national conscience, one ought to note *Fjamuri i Arbërit*, a bilingual Albanian and Italian periodical, which promoted the existence of the

patriotic sentiment to their ancestral land, Albania, and were ready to offer tremendous sacrifices for its freedom, including their participation in a liberation war. However, much of the Arbëreshë political activity also supported the Italian state interests that at times displayed imperialist tendencies that were well attested not long afterwards when Italy joined the very Balkan forces that invaded and partitioned the Albanian lands.

Here, the patriotic morality failed to overcome the state interests and many Arbëreshë served the Italian politics even to the expense of the Albanian question. The most notable was Francesco Crispi himself who, as head of the Italian government, participated in a secret deal with Belgrade and Athens. Although he later refused to honor the treaty, the Italo-Albanian prime minister agreed to dividing up the ethnic Albanian territory in three parts—Serbian, Italian, and Greek zones of influence.[535]

Under such circumstances, many Arbëreshë maintained their patriotic orientation and opposed the policies of the state. Prominent writers of the community not only criticized the unfavorable trends of Italian politics, but also called on their compatriots to avoid what they viewed as government ploys. Through correspondence and personal contacts, Jeronim de Rada, Zef Skiroi, and other Arbëreshë intellectuals approached the activists in the Ottoman Empire and the diaspora. Both sides endeavored to strengthen ties and create a unified national platform in the struggle for freedom and national independence.

The competition between Vienna and Rome did not remain within the boundaries of the regional politics; it reflected well into the domestic social landscape, dividing the Albanians into *pro-Italians* and *pro-Austrians*, a split that was not wholly without consequences within the ethnic group and between Albanians and the two powers. As the filters of Italian and Austrian interests lay on the path of any major undertaking in the national movement, the European rivalry gave rise to irreconcilable factions among Albanians.

Of the two groups, however, pro-Austrians seem to have been greater in number and influence. This may be explained with the Danubian monar-

---

Albanian nation, whose traditions warranted its aspiration for freedom and independence. Meanwhile, Dhimitër Kamarda (1821-1882) published his *Saggio di grammatologia comparata della lingua albanese* (1864), in which he presented a scholarly study of the Albanian language and its ancient origin. Relying on the Pelasgian theory, he attempted to show the close relationship between Greek and Albanian.

[535] Zwiendek's report, Wien, Dec. 1901, Secret acts of the Austrian State Archive, HHStA, p. 15.

chy's view of the Albanians as a patriarchal society, where the absence of public opinion had permitted noted individuals to wield great influence in their communities. Therefore, Vienna's official policy was directed at establishing ties with such authorities as well as the heads of the national movement, while also assisting with the intellectual development and the material wellbeing of the people. Yet, besides the trust the Albanians traditionally had in the Germans, it is important that both Austria and Hungary were opponents of Serbia and by no means had an interest in seeing the South Slavic state increase its regional influence. On the other hand, Italians appeared more inclined for a friendship with Slavs and Greeks, while the very ruling Savoy family took a Slavic princess, daughter of Prince Nicholas I of Montenegro, to be the wife of future king Victor Emmanuel III.

At the peak of the Albanian struggle for statehood, Austria-Hungary was in favorable terms with a considerable part of Albanian intellectuals and leaders of the national movement in Albania, İstanbul, and Europe. In Albania, Vienna's influence had long extended to the north of the country in areas from Shkodër and Mirdita to Kosovo. As an unwavering supporter of the Austrian policy was the abbot of Mirdita, Monsignor Doçi, a highly influential leader among the Catholic clergy, and Faik Konitza (also Faik Konica), a young intellectual from the south but whose fame as a proponent of the national conscience had already begun to grow.[536]

Both public figures believed that their country's needs coincided with the Austrian interest. Doçi gave this explanation: "The only power that is not trying to annex Albania is Austria. She wants of Albania not a subordinate, but a friend and ally . . . It is in Austria's interest that Albania become powerful and independent just as it is in Albania's interest to have trust in Austria and secure her support, because only she could defend Albania from her enemies."[537]

Meanwhile, Faik Konitza reached further in his pro-Austrian writings. He believed that Albania needed time for what he viewed as becoming properly civilized and for that reason he insisted in the friendship of Austria-Hungary. Konitza expressed his opinion openly to Austrians, because he considered them the only power that effectively supported the Albanians in scientific, cultural, and social aspects. Commending the dual monarchy for an adequate promotion the national identity and the language of the Albani-

---

[536] Skëndi, *Zgjimi kombëtar shqiptar*, 244.

[537] See Monsignore Primo Dochi, "Über Albanien," pp. 7-8, HHStA. Ges. Arch. Konstantinopel, Fasz 422.

ans, he even held as fortunate a prospect that—should full political autonomy were impossible to attain—his country were to enjoy an administrative autonomy under a political and military union with Austria.[538]

After the Italo-Albanian newspaper, *La Nuova Albania*, criticized Konitza for his amity with Vienna, he defended his pro-Austrian stance, noting: "that Austria has for a long time defended the Catholics of Albania, who have fought to preserve the Albanian nationality; that if it were not for the fear of an [Austrian] intervention, Greeks and Slavs would seize Albanian within twenty-four hours; that Austria has proved it wishes for the Albanians to learn their national language and to become enlightened; and that Austria has subsidized schools teaching in the Albanian language, while schools supported by Italy teach only Italian."[539]

Besides Konitza, other intellectuals also joined the Austrian camps. Shahin Kolonja, Sotir Peçi, Kristo Luarasi, and Dervish Hima were fundamentally of the same opinion with Doçi and Konitza. They all distinguished the Austrian assistance as the most beneficial and convenient of the foreign help that Albania could receive. Moreover, the modern historian, Savro Skendi, speculates that Naim Frashëri would have also supported the Austrian foreign policy, had the national poet lived longer than 1900. Skendi bases his observation on a letter that Frashëri wrote to Konitza. "That which might be well-heeled for the Albanian nation," said the poet, "is for Austria to annex Albania—all of Albania."[540]

Italy, nevertheless, insisted in offering parity to Vienna's influence, focusing on education and cultural development outside the scope of the Catholic Church. While the Austro-Hungarian *Kultursprotektorat* program relied heavily on the Catholic clergy and was concentrated in the north, Italians earned a significant advantage through schools they opened throughout the country. Moreover, these institutions also taught the Albanian language and, as secular schools (*It. regia scuola*, civil school) were highly attractive for the time as they provided a non-religious, general curriculum, while also preparing students for their vocation. Cognizant of the Italian success, Vienna attempted to apply the same model at least in Shkodër. However, Italians had by this time begun their social and humanitarian activities in other walks of life, working to improve healthcare, offering

[538] See Konica, Letter to Ippen, Brussels, 18 Aug. 1897, HHStA, PA XIV/18 Albanien XII/2.
[539] *Albania* II (1989), 137-138.
[540] *Albania* XII/2.

evening classes to adults, opening kindergartens, and tending to the elderly and the disabled. The Arbëreshë communities, already active in fostering ties with their ancestral land, joined forces with scholarship funds designated for graduate of Italian schools in Albania who wished to continue their higher learning in Italy at the College of Saint Adrian, home to one of the oldest Albanian-language cathedrae in all of Europe.

The Austrian-Italian competition in education had its own benefits for Albania, for the newly-founded schools created opportunities for a greater emancipation of the people who, regardless of whether they leaned towards Vienna or Rome, rediscovered the Western culture. In fact, the Albanian bonds with Europe were the greatest benefit of the rivalry between the two powers; while the final destination carried an address in one or the other European capital, the effect was such that the Albanians turned to the West.

Italy began to also make political strides, earning the commendation of many influential Albanians. These were not from the ranks of the Catholic clergy, as was expected, for Austrians held a monopoly on the church; support for Rome came from among Albanian intellectuals, who believed that Vienna was insincere in the promises made to their people. Their doubts heightened significantly after Austria-Hungary annexed Bosnia-Herzegovina in 1908 and pushed for Bulgaria to declare its independence the same year. Realistically, Vienna's moves in both instances had set off a terminal enmity with Serbia that even triggered the events leading to World War I. However, many Albanians grew distrustful of Vienna when Russia endorsed the Austrian takeover of Bosnia, eliciting speculations over a secret deal between the two empires that may have reserved certain concessions for the Slavic countries in the region. This way, skeptics suspected of a plan to give Serbia Albanian territories in Kosovo and Macedonia. Likewise, some feared that the Habsburg and Romanov emperors would also honor certain Montene-grin claims over northern Albania in a move to undermine Italian plans efforts to turn the tiny Balkan principality into anti-Austrian outpost.

The skepticism began to receive much publicity in the Italian press and among the Arbëreshë, leading to turn many Albanian intellectuals away from Vienna, if not fully towards Rome. Vacillations of such nature reached a high point when one of the leading figures of the national movement, Ismail Qemali, contemplated an Italian role in Albania. In the meantime, he also explored an agreement with Greece as a realistic option, which could also favor Italy's heightened influence on the eastern coast of the Adriatic. The exiled Albanian leader expressed his position during his stay in Italy in 1907, evoking the disparagement of Faik Konitza, who had already criticized Qemali after the two met in Brussels to discuss the future of Albania. Konitza wrote that his collocutor had indicated "signs of pro-Greek politics."[541]

One must note here the striking difference between Konitza as a public intellectual and Ismail Qemali as a career diplomat and politician. While the earlier sought traditional supporters for his people, he thought outside the boundaries of political sagacity. Meanwhile, Qemali acted pragmatically, reasoning in accordance with the spheres of interest, where the more power-ful entities determined the lines and the lesser actors served the bargains of the stronger that would inevitably affect Albania and its people.

Albanians had many reasons for caution, which implied responsible be-havior before all factors in the international arena. Inevitably, the Albanian leadership had to consider all possible partners in accordance with the shifting dynamics and interests, where Austria-Hungary appeared as a key influential factor in the Balkans. Yet, despite the support for Albania, Vienna was subject to such international conjunctures that could also include secret deals with the Russians at the expense of the Albanians. Therefore, as Ismail Qemali emphatically threw the Italian card into the Balkan poker, his inten-tion was to add new bates and by no means eliminate the existing stack, as it may have occurred to Faik Konitza.

Nevertheless, Italy's contestation of the Austrian influence in Albania does not seem to have weakened the Albanian position, as it is sometimes thought, or to have endangered the nation in that it could end up as a simple object of political bargain between the powers or with respect to other actors.

In fact, ever since Italy signed the Tripartite Pact with Germany and Austria-Hungary in 1879, a treaty that was reconfirmed another four times until 1914, Vienna and Rome had pursued no action that damaged the Albanians. This observation remains even though the two European powers had often entered into unilateral agreement with a third party such as when Austria reached a deal with Russia ahead of the annexation of Bosnia and Herzegovina or earlier, in 1903, when Italy held secret talks with Greece over the Macedonian Crisis, discussing a possible division of spheres of interest if Macedonia were to break off from Turkey (in that case, the Hellenes would give up Epirus, while Italy planned to disembark on the Albanian coast). Moreover, from a strategic standpoint, despite the internal disagreements as to whether to align with Austria-Hungary or Italy, Albanians enjoyed equal

---

[541] *Ibid.*

acceptance from both powers as a factor in the Balkan political scene. As to the Ottoman Empire, both Vienna and Rome supported Albania's autonomy under the sultan, but they also supported the contention that, in case of a violent collapse of Ottoman authority in Europe, the Albanians were to have their own nation-state. Furthermore, with the formation of the Tripartite Alliance, the troika had also internally agreed to not permit the partitioning of Albanian lands by and among the Balkan countries. Instead, the three empires agreed to protect the Albanian state from foreign invasions (*i.e.*, from Serbia and Montenegro) and contemplated multilateral efforts to resolve relevant matters.

Although Austria as well as Italy were naturally following their several interests on Albania—Rome in particular was determined to reject any Austrian invasion of the area, even as pretexts became available for such a scenario—Vienna was increasingly supportive of autonomy. This was repeatedly attested in diplomatic meetings, which the two countries intensified after the Macedonia Crisis. Fearing the *status quo* spelled out at the Congress of Berlin could prove unsustainable, Austria emphasized the need for a self-governing Albanian entity.

Vienna's stance was first announced during the Ottoman-Greek War of 1897, when Austro-Hungarian Emperor Francis Joseph met with Russian Czar Nicholas II to discuss the situation in the Balkans. It was reported that during the meeting, the dual-crowned monarch had proposed an independent *Principality of Albania* with a territory running from Janina in the south to Lake Shkodër in the north and to a "reasonable" border in the east. The lands that would remain afterwards would be awarded to the small Balkans states in order to maintain the existing equilibrium. The secret Austrian project envisioned the Albanian state as a protectorate of the empire, while also providing, if circumstances permitted, for a partial occupation of Albania, primarily of the coastal towns of Durrës and Vlora. Military presence in those areas would enable Austria-Hungary to control the Otranto Straits and the Adriatic Sea right across from Italy.[542]

---

[542] H.P.Sh. 2 (Tiranë), 266.

In Search of a New Albanian League

Sultan Abdul Hamid II's attempted reforms in favor of the Slavic-Orthodox population of Rumelia are met with resistance from the Albanians. Accepting the changes, which included guaranteed quotas for Christians in the police force, judiciary, and administration, even where their participations did not proportionally match the ethnic makeup of the land, where the Albanians were in greater numbers, created an opportunity for the Christian minority to destabilize the affairs as directed from Serbia, Greece, or Montenegro. Belgrade plans to rely on Serbian enclaves to instigate a crisis in Kosovo; this would create a pretext for a Slavic-Orthodox intervention to protect Serbs from what they call the "Arnaut outrage." The Albanians form the League of Peja and reiterate the demands for internal unification and autonomy. The İstanbul Committee supports the new organization and its calls against the despotic regime of Abdul Hamid, who had until then enjoyed the support of a sizeable portion of Kosovo landowners. Intellectuals appeal for a new national political program.

As time went by, the Balkan crisis deepened with the Ottoman concessions to the Christian subjects, particularly Serbs, Greeks, and Bulgarians. Meanwhile, a wing of the formerly secular Young Turk opposition began to embrace Islamist rhetoric to support the spirit of Ottoman patriotism, leading Albanian members of the Committee for Unity and Progress to rethink their strategy for their national struggle. Numerous officers who from the CUP branches in the Albanian towns (including Manastir, Shkup, Tirana, and Elbasan) imposed a military spirit in their ethnic community's movement, emphasizing the Ottoman Empire's own vows to defend every corner of its territory. Thereby, some of the Albanian officers in the imperial units in Selanik, Manastir, and Shkup joined the Albanian bands in the south of the country to fight against the Greek gangs, as well as Bulgarian and Serbian formations, which terrorized the local Albanian population. Meanwhile, with the support of Serbia, Bulgaria, and Greece, the gangs comported as a national liberation movement, even though their activity was known to be purported at destabilizing the Albanian vilayets of Kosova, Manastir, and Janina.

This development is worthy of greater clarification, for it marks an additional stage of the Albanian consolidation as a political factor in the Ottoman

Empire and beyond. Internally, the events demonstrated that the Ottoman survival in the Balkans was closely tied to defending the Albanian ethnicity from the partitioning of its territory and by granting their self-government. On the other hand, the Albanians had an external impact for, as key supporters of the opposition and the following regime change, the new Ottoman government owed them the status of autonomy as a reward for their contribution to the Young Turk Revolution. However, the post-Hamidian government failed to accept what was projected as an Ottoman Albania, but the continued demands for autonomy became a catalyst of the future Balkan crisis. And, the calamity that ensued reached a magnitude so disastrous as to shake and tumble all of the fragile pillars that had buttressed the European *status quo* for thirty-four years since the Congress of Berlin.

Nevertheless, the factorization of the Albanians and their demands for recognition of their nationality and autonomy, and particularly their role during the last leg of the Hamidian regime, could be said to have brought provocations on both ends. On the one side, the Russian-backed neighboring countries, eying Albania's territory for annexation as a remnant of the Ottoman dominions, objected any move for an Albanian state (the barrage to pan-Slavism that Austria-Hungary and Italy planned to erect). On the other end, the Sublime Porte also provoked the Albanians, not only refusing to grant their autonomy all while their demands became increasingly more vocal, but also seeking to carry out a series of reforms to maintain the international support for the empire's presence in the Balkans. The primary target of the planned changes was the Albanians as the Porte continued to make concessions to Russia and the Balkan Slavs. Furthermore, the Ottomans continued to pour gas on fire and increasingly prompted foreign intervention as the imperial government unrelentingly celebrated the Albanians as "the flower of Islam," while equally rejecting their demands for autonomy.

By the turn of the century, Abdul Hamid undertook certain measures in the Balkans that, although were thought to improve relations with the Albanians, had the countervailing effect of irritating the ethnic community, the Young Turk opposition, as well as the region's Slavic countries. Tensions heightened as the sultan issued his 1896 Decree on Reforms in the Elayet of Rumelia and the empire lost Crete in the Greek war of 1897, while the ultimate setback came in 1903 with the Treaty of Mürzsteg on the reforms in Macedonia. The agreement gave Austria-Hungary and Russia nearly complete mandate to supervise the critical part of the peninsula, pushing the

Balkan crisis into a precarious stage that, instead of stabilizing the *status quo*, triggered the ultimate catastrophe—the First Balkan War and the end of Ottoman rule in the region.

Sultan Abdul Hamid II justified his reforms in Rumelia with paragraph 23 of the 1878 Berlin agreement, which required the Ottoman Empire to provide for the equality of Christian subjects and regulate other matters pertaining to the participation of ethnic communities in local government. In practice, the controversial 1896 decree came to the expense of the Albanians and considerably worsened the Balkan crisis. As to the Albanians, the Ottoman Empire rejected the demands for autonomy that, under a broad construction of the Berlin agreement, were warranted by paragraph 23. However, the sultan decided to institute "equal" treatment for the Christian population, including the appointment of ethnic Bulgarians, Serbs, and Greeks as deputy *valis* and members of the administrative councils (Trk.: *meclis*) in the vilayets of Edirne, Selanik, Manastir, and Kosova. Moreover, the 1896 reforms reserved ten percent of the police force in the vilayets for the said Slavic or Hellenic nationalities, diminishing the position of the Albanian majority. The new measures empowered the minorities with tools they could use to complicate the country's political situation to a level that had been unattainable before. Therefore, the sultan's proclamation of the reforms in April 1896 incited the opposition of Albanian political factions. Various groups put their differences aside and joined their forces to prevent the announced changes in the vilayets of Manastir and Kosova. Despite the incongruent ethnic reality on the ground, where the Albanians formed the majority,[543] the reforms designate the two imperial provinces as Slavic Macedonian, thereby creating the risk for Manastir and Kosova to break off from the other Albanian vilayets, Shkodër and Janina. The sultan's 1896 effectively opened the gate for the neighboring countries to intervene and obtain the land they had long planned for prey.

The series of territorial claims on Albania, including the 1844 Serbian expansionist project, *Načertanije*, and the Greek *Megali Idea*, was later augmented with the plans of another Slavic nation. Recognizing the Bulgarian Exarchate in 1870 for the vilayets of Manastir and Selanik, the Ottoman government activated a national propaganda with hegemonist claims to the area. Thus, emulating the Greek efforts, Bulgarians also deployed their own

---

[543] *Ibid.* 262.

agents to set up "liberation bands," which increasingly disturbed the Albanian population and undermined public safety and security in the region.

The proclamation of the 1896 Decree had the greatest impact on the Vilayet of Kosova, making its Slavic minority a privileged class. But in the province, where the Albanian population ranged from sixty to ninety percent in all sanjaks, Serbs and Bulgarians had already enjoyed their religious freedom, worshipping in their own national churches, and the right of education in their native tongues with the continued caretaking of Serbia and Russia. It was hence anticipated that the people of the vilayet would view the reforms with great distrust. For that reason, the Ottoman government postponed the implementation of changes in Kosova until November 1896, but this did not defer the opposition to the reforms. In Prizren, Peja, Gjakova, Gjilan, Shkup, and other towns, local Albanians protested against the imperial decree, while a revolt also broke out with demands for special reforms in Albania aimed at the country's autonomy. As the popular resistance grew and in many instances took on the form of an armed uprising, a renowned patriot from Peja, Haxhi Zeka, appeared as the leader of the Albanian movement.[544]

Prior to the armed resistance that ultimately defeated the reform efforts, Albanians held demonstrations throughout the Albanian provinces, for which they received broad support from the contemporary press and the nation's diaspora. By then, Albanians in exile had created a successful propaganda network for not only was the Ottoman Empire unable to protect the interests of the Albanians or the state's own presence in the Balkans, as the Porte promised; it was acting to the opposite, prompting activists to respond. Among letters sent to the sultan and senior officials of the Porte, a document bearing the signature of Dervish Hima is noted for its harsh criticism of the monarch for his failure to protect Albanian interests. Among other requests, the communication calls on the Ottoman government to put an end to the propaganda, to close the foreign schools and expel their teachers from Albania. Instead, the letter demands that the government provide for educational institutions where both Muslim and Christian Albanians teach the children in their native tongue. The Albanian schools were said to contribute to the consolidation of the Albanian nation, protect its identity, uproot the foreign influences, and lead the Porte and the European powers to recognize a distinct Albanian nationality.[545]

---

[544] *Ibid.* 262.

[545] *Ibid.* 263.

Similar demands also appeared in another letter that activists sent from Bucharest. Signing "on behalf of the Albanian people," Ibrahim Temo, Nikolla Naço, and Faik Konitza referred to Article XXIII of the Berlin decisions, demanding reforms in Albania. The memorandum called on the Porte to release all Albanians imprisoned or interned for political motivations and to ban the Greek and Slavic propaganda in schools and churches. In addition to education in the national language, the diaspora group requested that the Ottomans permit an Albanian church as well as the use of the Albanian language in the Greek and Slavic churches.[546]

Another document, written in French, was sent as a petition to the Great Powers. It incorporated much of the content of the Bucharest memorandum, but provided additional information on the history on the Albanians as part of an appeal for Europe's support and protection. Specifically, the petition suggested a series of radical reforms, which would culminate with the formation of an autonomous Albanian statoid. The plan was to unify the four Albanian vilayets into a single unit with its capital at Manastir and an ethnic Albanian as governor-general (*vali*) at the head of the administration. The letter also proposed a Council of Elders as a legislative body for the unified vilayet, where twenty-four representatives would be proportionally elected from among Muslims and Christians of Albania.[547]

In the meantime, the Albanians endeavored to organize a unified resistance against the foreign interventions, founding for the purpose a group modeled after the League of Prizren.[548] A prominent activist, Haxhi Zeka,[549]

---

[546] *Ibid.* 263.

[547] The idea of a *Pleqësi* (*Alb.*, council of elders, senate) as a collegial head of state appeared in Sami Frashëri's *Shqipëria: ç'ka qënë, ç'është e ç'do të bëhetë* (roughly, Albania: The Past, Present, and Future). The noted writer urged for Albania to steer away from monarchy, favoring democracy with regional representation, where the traditional tribal structures, such as the *bajraks* and communities, would play a role in the new government system.

[548] H.P.Sh. 2 (Tiranë), 264.

[549] Haxhi Zeka was a veteran of the Albanian League of Prizren. He participated in combat as a member of the League's armed forces, served in the Central Council, and worked with Sulejman Vokshi, then commander of the Albanian troops. Zeka remained faithful to the League's ideals even after its dissolution. Due to his political activities, Ottoman authorities took him to İstanbul where they kept him under arrest for three years. After his release from prison, he returned to Albania and continued his patriotic activities, which culminated with the establishment of the *Besëlidhja Shqiptare* and the League of Peja. At all times, Zeka called for a nationwide movement to defend the Albanian lands from the neighboring countries

took the initiative to mobilize the Albanian population. At the end of October 1896, he summoned in Prishtina some of the heads of the national movements to discuss measures against the Ottoman reforms and to find a solution for the country's autonomy. In a certain way, the Albanian reinstated the League of Prizren, since once they demanded autonomy while referring to Article XXIII of the contemporaneous Berlin decisions.

Relying on the provision of the European congress almost two decades after its conclusion, the Albanian faced somewhat of an absurdity. While they opposed the reform process because as detrimental, they also called for changes while they claimed their self-government as a reform measure. This exacerbated the relations with the Ottoman Empire and the international factor, which labeled the Albanians opponents of the reforms and "defenders of the old feudal-despotic order" who objected to the Christian population enjoying equality to the Muslims. The ethnic group owed this image mainly to Sultan Abdul Hamid II and his policy of utilizing the Albanians every time the empire faced pressure from the Great Powers to make concessions to the Slavic and Greek peoples. For example, the Ottoman monarch agreed to Crete's autonomy after the Greek war and permitted the Serbian and Bulgarian Orthodox churches to extend their presence and open schools in the vilayets of Kosova and Manastir, while he banned the private institutions of learning the Albanians labored so tediously to build. To add to the negative image of the Albanians, neighboring Serbia and Greece also decried the Albanian demands for autonomy as an "Islamist course of the Albanians" in defense of the caliphate.

This brought extreme hardship to the Albanian movement, which was forced to struggle in two fronts alike. The label of Islamist anti-reformers occurred credible to many foreign eyes. After war broke with Greece in 1897, Albanians rose up in protests in the Vilayet of Kosova, beginning with Gjakova and Peja and then spreading to Prishtina and other towns, which united to form a new ethnic-based league baptized *Besëlidhja Shqiptare* (*Alb.*, Albanian Covenant or League). Yet, the Ottoman Empire did not hesitate to present the Albanian movement as an expression of "loyalty to the sultan and the caliphate." Sultan Abdul Hamid II was successful in using his slogan to

---

and to create an autonomous state wihitn the Ottoman Empire. He was assassinated in Peja, on February 21, 1902. The perpetrator was the captain of the gendarmerie, Adem Zajmi from Gjakova. It is speculated that the killing of the Albanian patriot was the fruit of Ottoman collaboration with Serbian nationalist circles, which under the circumstances found much ground in common and cooperated closely.

mobilize a sizeable number of Albanians from the vilayets of Kosova and Manastir in the Greek war. Moreover, *Besëlidhja Shqiptare*'s manifesto (which emphasized the defense of the Albanian territories from the expansionist neighbors) was attributed to "the loyalty of the Albanians to defending the territorial integrity of the Ottoman Empire."[550]

In reality, the matter deserves some attention. The anti-reform and autonomy movements juxtaposed two factors: the pro-sultan and pro-caliphate conservatives (mainly in the vilayets of Kosova and Shkodër) and the supporters of the Young Turk opposition who viewed parliamentarism and modern Ottomanism as a necessity. The two groups marked another internal division: with a group accepting the sultan's centralized government and another seeking change, the national movement suffered from discordance and failures. The same fate followed *Besëlidhja Shqiptare* to continue with important events up to the Memorandum of August 1912 that failed to implement Albania's autonomy.

To avoid factionalism, leaders of the national movement, mainly members of the İstanbul Committee and exiled activists took preventative steps. They hurriedly proposed a political platform and spoke on behalf of the commotion in Kosova in their attempt to undermine the sultan's readiness to utilize the Albanians for his own needs. A Vienna-based activist, Preng Doçi, delivered a memorandum to the Austro-Hungarian government, presenting the demands of *Besëlidhja Shqiptare* with an emphasis on autonomy.[551]

In the meantime, the İstanbul Committee, which at had been reorganized as the Albanian Committee under the leadership of Sami Frashëri, came to the support of *Besëlidhja Shqiptare*. In spring 1897, the İstanbul group published the manifesto *Ç'duan Shqiptarët* (*Alb.*, What Do the Albanians Seek), approving of *Besëlidhja*'s activity and reiterating its adherence to Albania's territorial integrity and autonomy.[552] Meanwhile, the Kosova-based organization began to lay roots in central Albania and the Manastir Vilayet, but the growth suffered from a lack of coordination among the local groups.

Yet, the İstanbul Committee urged for the Albanians to unite in a struggle against the sultan's government. This was a clear indication that the leaders of the national movement had begun to follow a set course against

---

[550] H.P.Sh. 2 (Tiranë), 268.

[551] *Ibid.* 269.

[552] *Ibid.* 269.

Abdul Hamid II. They held the same position even when discussing matters that implied coordination with the Sublime Porte, such as defense. The İstanbul intellectuals no longer insisted on autonomy under the Ottoman umbrella, but contemplated the prospects of an independent state in the event the empire was unable to hold onto its European territories. The Frashëri-led committee stated in manifesto that:

> Should Europe continue to respect the [territorial] integrity of the Ottoman Empire, then the Albanians shall work to secure the autonomy of Albania, to unite her vilayets into a single self-governing vilayet, with Albanian as [the official] language and a general governor administering the country under the supervision of a national assembly consisting of Albanian members. If Europe decides to bring an end to the Ottoman Empire, then Albania shall become a free and independent state, completely seceding from [the empire].[553]

Both variants envisioned Albania as a modern democratic state. Sami Frashëri and other patriots of the İstanbul Committee believed that a republican system that took into account the specific conditions and national traditions was most suitable to their homeland.[554]

The committee's call for war against the sultan was in line with the position of Albanian patriots who had become involved in the Young Turk movement. However, the anti-Hamidian cry was not received with equally well in Kosova, where the absolute monarchy had great support among members of the privileged feudal establishment. The threatened landlords were allied with the fanatic Islamic clergy whose frightening slogans decried "the Young Turks and the Albanian autonomists seek the fall of Islam and return Christendom." However, the Vilayet of Kosova was also home to a vibrant Albanianist movement. Hailing the tradition of the League of Prizren, many Kosovars had not abandoned their ideal, even though compared to the wealthy and powerful sultanists, the Albanian patriots were not only fewer in number; ever since the creation of Albania's Provision Government in 1881, they suffered persecution and torture at the hand of the regime.

One of the dedicated patriots who accepted the guidelines of the İstanbul Committee was Haxhi Zeka. His opponent Riza Kryeziu led a large group of loyalists who believed the sultan and the caliph were the "shield" of the

---

[553] *Ibid.* 269.

[554] For more on the proposed constitution of the state of Albania, see S. Frashëri, *Shqipëria ç'ka qënë, ç'është e ç'do të bëhet* (Bukuresht: 1899).

Albanians, even though it was abundantly clear that the monarch's policies had endangered the country in relation to the expansionist Balkan neighbors. During the 1897 Ottoman-Greek war, the differences between the two wings were did not greatly hinder the military orientation of the national movement, since defending the homeland trumped all other matters. With such a devotion to their country, a considerable number of Albanian volunteers helped the Ottoman victory which they believed would minimize the Greek threat to southern Albania.

Following the Ottoman triumph in the war, which nevertheless ended with Crete's autonomy, the Hamidian establishment rapidly returned to compliance with the European requirements. Requesting an end to the Albanian anti-reform revolt, the Great Powers argued that the ethnic movement exacerbated the Porte's rapport with the Bakan Slavic nations as well as Greece. Faced with the pressure, the Ottoman government resorted to its double-standard strategy against the Albanians. The Porte undertook additional punitive measures, using the military to crush the revolt when the latter continued to conflict with imperial interests. Concomitantly, the regime also continued to reward those who were willing to switch sides. To achieve its goals, it promised high offices to Albanian leaders in the same manner it employed to undermine the Albanian Provisional Government in 1881.

Haxhi Zeka was aware of this problem and worked to ensure it would not reoccur without the Albanians gaining their autonomy. On the other hand, Kryeziu's wing oriented to the sultan, entering into talks with the mission that Abdul Hamid sent to Kosova. The delegation headed by Is'han Bey was accompanied by imams who proclaimed "the sultan's determination for Albania to remain part of the caliphate" and threatened that without the Islamic state, the small Balkan nation would become prey of its Russian-backed neighbors. After striking a deal with the monarch's representatives, Kryeziu was invited to İstanbul where he was received by Abdul Hamid and decorated for his loyalty. The sultan appointed Kryeziu as a member of the presidency of the Council of State, while other members of the mission were promoted in the civil and military ranks and received numerous honors and gifts from the sovereign.[555]

The rapprochement of the Kryeziu faction with the sultan and the imam's calls seemingly brought some type of "pacification" to the Kosova

---

[555] H.P.Sh. 2 (Tiranë), 273.

movement. However, this did not last too long. The Sublime Porte, in pursuit of its commitments to the Great Powers, set out to quell all focal points of crisis in Kosova as well as other Albanian vilayets, wherever impediments to the reforms arose.

At the time when the İstanbul Committee and the Albanian clubs intensified their activity, trumpeting autonomy as the only solution that could provide peace and keep the empire in the Balkans, the Sublime Porte came up with its *Project for Albania*, mandating that "the empire's salvation is secured only with the complete centralization of power in the Albanian vilayets." The reform project, drafted by the *valis* of Kosova and Manastir and the interior and war minister presented in 1898, demanded military measures against a revolt opposing tax collection. Marshall Et'hem Pasha, commander of the Ottoman forces in Kosova, insisted in a general disarmament of the Albanians for the reason that "arms were the main tool of [the Albanian] insurgent actions."[556] In addition to being subject to gun collection, the Albanian vilayets had the highest concentration of the 150,000 troops were stationed in the European part. Sultan Abdul Hamid II hence reconfirmed his commitment to a military solution for the Albanian question. The actions were justified before the Great Powers as attempts at "implementing the reforms," while at home the sovereign claimed credit for preventing autonomy or that which the Russian bloc called Ottoman Albania.

The measures not only failed to reach the intended effects, but they worsened the crisis, giving it regional proportions. The Albanians continued to resist and worked towards creating a new league that would lead the people in the war for territorial defense and autonomy.

A driving force behind the movement was the flare-up of the Macedonia question that led to disturbances in the Balkans. At the end of 1899 and the begging of the following year, Bulgaria, Serbia, Greece, and Montenegro increased their interventions in the Ottoman European territories in an action that greatly provoked the Albanians for it was their land that was being targeted for annexation. The appetites of neighboring nations hindered the plan for autonomy, which remained a real possibility and had the backing of Austria-Hungary and Italy as well as Britain. Russia and her Balkan protégés were aware of the Western support for Albania and worked to prevent the autonomous state from ever coming into existence even if doing

---

[556] *Ibid.* 274.

so meant going to war with the Ottoman Empire. As was later seen, the Slavic commotion was not just one of the tactical threats that so often appeared at the time from all sides. The Russian-backed Balkan countries had reached their optimal objectives and were not in pursuit of their maximum goals of a hemenogic nature, seeking to occupy and divide the sultan's European possessions, which—with the exception of the Vilayet of Selanik— had been mostly inhabited by Albanians since the beginning of Ottoman rule.

Given the chances that Albanians and Young Turks had to jointly overthrow Abdul Hamid, the Great Powers feared that the Albanian question could reach new proportions, not excluding autonomy, which could lead the Balkan nations to war. Therefore, the Europeans pressured the Sublime Porte to carry out the reforms in Macedonia pursuant to the decree the sultan had proclaimed three years prior. Just as initial attempts to implement the plan had led to the formation of *Besëlidhja Shqiptare*, the Porte again faced a ferocious opposition when trying to honor the word given to the Western powers.

Major trouble appeared as Bulgarian bands began to roam in the sanjaks of Dibër and Ohër and, shortly after, Greek *komitas* also penetrated into the Manastir region and Epirus. The gangs had the support of Sofia and Athens to cause a sense of insecurity among Albanians and to disturb their plans for autonomy. In the meantime, Serbian bands also began to descend in the northern parts, maneuvering around Mitrovica and Yeni Pazar with calls for resurrecting Old Serbia.

Despite the intensified threats of attacks, the Ottoman Empire did not cease to hand out gifts to Serbs, Bulgarians, and Greeks, granting them privileges over the Albanian population. So strongly did the Porte favor the Orthodox people such that they began to appear as masters in the lands that until recently had been known as Albania. Therefore, the Albanian leaders realized no other way but to resume the activity of *Besëlidhja Shqiptare*. Having stumbled once in the middle of the road, they now took care to disregard the sultan as the movement's objectives. The sultan had for a while relied own loyal beys who helped him suppress the Albanian movement, even though many of the landowners had also sought to strengthen ties with Belgrade and Cetinje to ensure an exit strategy in case the Young Turks threatened the interests of the upper class after the expected regime change. The Albanian lords, moreover, spoke with Serbia and Montenegro about a "joint war," where the beys would keep their lands even after the Ottoman Empire had withdrawn.

Haxhi once again travelled through different parts of the country to solicit support among all groups, particularly the landowners and the influential families. In doing so, he sought to create a wide movement for territorial
defense and Albania's autonomy. The fruit of the efforts was a convention
held in Peja between January 23 to 29, 1899, with the participation of popular
leaders from the Vilayet of Kosova.[557] Representatives of the Manastir and
Janina vilayets also took part in the meeting founding a new Albanian
organization that, following the example of the League of Prizren, was called
the League of Peja. The participants elected Haxhi Zeka chairman of the
convention and the executive committee.[558]

Considering the documents that the organization ratified, it was nearly
analogous to the League of Prizren. The main difference was that the League
of Peja lacked representatives from all four Albanian vilayets. The convention approved a basic act (*Kararname*) consisting of 11 articles and a covenant with 12 points. As observed at Prizren two decades ago, the Peja gathering also expressed its loyalty to the sultan and Islam, these being unavoidable
mottos, precisely because they alone enabled the much-needed internal
unity. Likewise, the *Kararname* failed to include any provisions on autonomy or a similar plans, but the document contemplated an administration
comprised of native employees.

The Austrian consul in Shkodër, Ippen, paid close attention to the developments himself or received adequate information from an internal
source. The diplomat reported to his government that the Albanians had
revived the political program of the League of Prizren, noting that Islam and
"loyalty to the sultan and the caliphate" had "dominated the Peja convention." The consul's observations, however, do not necessarily reflect the
actual situation, since the Albanians were aware of what the sultan was able
to do for them.[559]

The expression of loyalty to the sultan, nevertheless, weighed consequences on the Albanians. Influenced by Serbian and Greek propaganda,
many Europeans viewed the League of Peja outside the political context,

---

[557] Representatives included Halil Hasan Pashë Begolli, Myderriz Ismaili, Myderriz
Abdullahu, Myfti Salihu, Bajram Curri, Myderriz Mehmet Hamdiu, Mehmet Aqifi, Zenel
Bey, Ali Pashë Draga from Rozhaja, Ismail Haki Pashë Tetova, Abdyl Halimi, Mehmet
Sherifi, Myderiz Abdyli, Naxhi Mehmet Sulejmani, Mehmet Sherifi, Mehmet Aqifi, Mehmet
Tahiri, and Mehmet Murati of Senica.

[558] *Ibid.* 276.

[559] HHStA, Ippen's letter to Goluchowski (Shkodër: Feb. 1899), nr. 21 B.

calling the organization "an Islamic religious congress."[560] Abdul Hamid's official view was also on par with Belgrade such that the success in portraying the League as an Islamic organization was nearly guaranteed.

It was, however, Faik Konitza the one who furnished the Europeans with a different take on the League of Peja. Writing for his *Albania* magazine, the young intellectual called the January convention "a national assembly, held in Albania, where discussions were held in the Albanian language on the means of defending the Albanian territory."[561]

Konitza's writings were accompanied by an article in the Turkish language—Dervish Hima's "The Road of Salvation for the Fatherland is in the Besa-Besën [*i.e.*, the League]."[562] The contentions of the Albanian authors had in fact to do with the necessity of the internal unity on the autonomy question, which continued to appear as an objective of a part of Albanians rather than a common goal of the entire nation. The differences and divisions pro and contra the sultan—while Belgrade and other centers had also begun to sponsor the disunity—undermined the ability of Albanians to work together for their national cause.

In the meantime, the Balkan countries continued to threaten the Albanians. Geography played a role as the vilayets of Kosova bordered Serbia, while Manastir lay next to Bulgaria and Greece. The reasons for the conflict, however, also stem from the historical confrontations between Albanians and Serbs. Since the medieval times, especially during the Byzantine period after the fall of the empire, when independent principalities were formed in the region, the two peoples clashed with one another. The rivalry was marked with continuous wars that intensified in from the 12th to the end of the 14th century when halted by the Ottoman conquest. During the three centuries, the Albanian principalities, from Progon to the Balsha dynasty, was faced with continuous Slavic incursions from Rascia, which sought to occupy the Albanian territories—particularly Dardania, Shkodër, and Durrës. The Ottoman invasion brought an end to the lengthy Slavic-Albanian wars after which—one might say—the Albanians stabilized their presence in their historical territories. An new era, however, started after Serbia gained its autonomy in 1815 and announced its national program *Načertanije* in 1844. Ever since, Albanian lands were exposed to an ongoing threat from Serbia and Montenegro. Ancient Dardania, which was renamed

---

[560] H.P.Sh. 2 (Tiranë), 278.

[561] F. Konica, *Memoire sur le movement nacional albanais*, 15-16.

[562] H.P.Sh. 2 (Tiranë), 278.

Kosovo in the 19th century, and the northern parts of the Vilayet of Shkodër became the target of the Slavic claims. The northern neighbors carried out several military attacks and invaded Albanian lands that the Great Powers often officially awarded to Serbia and Montenegro. For instance, in addition to Toplica and Kurshumlia that Serbia occupied during the Russo-Turkish war of 1877-78, the Congress of Berlin granted the Slavic state additional Albanian territories towards Prokupa and Leskovc.

One the other end, the Ottoman Empire was unable to face the expansionist tendencies of the Balkan countries. For that reason, the imperial government left to the Albanians to defend the *vatan*, but did so under the oriole of defending the caliphate, and Islam. Doing so, the Porte argued, meant the Albanians were defending themselves. Meanwhile, to prop up the loyalty to the empire, the regime relied heavily on handouts that the local population of the "outer" vilayets had traditionally enjoyed. The privileges inspired a continuity of conservatism and Islamism that combined religion with the task of defending the homeland.

Sultan Abdul Hamid's strategy to preserve his European dominions relied for the most part on the Albanians. Using the epithet of "the flower of Islam," the padishah assigned them a defensive role and excessively empowered them.[563] The measure seems to have pitied the neighbors further against the Albanians, not only because the latter hindered the hegemonic ambitions but because they supported the Ottoman Empire, too.

The role, even though viewed one-sidedly from the angle of Ottoman interests, was decisive in the emergence of the Albanian patriotic consciousness and that which is called Albanianism. This new current flew in two segments: (1) tied to Islamism and Ottomanism and in service of imperial patriotism; and (2) as a national awakening and a movement for autonomy within the empire. Therefore, it was a natural result for the oath by *din ve dövlet* (*Trk.*, faith and state) to also incorporate the *vatan*. Although Islamism was the cornerstone of the state, the *vatan* inevitably added the aspect of

---

[563] See Sultan Abdul Hamid's 1880 address to "all the people of Albania" (Trk.: *umum Arnavudluk ahalisi*). In his proclamation, the padishah rejected the demands for a unified Albanian vilayet (consisting of the four then extant vilayets), calling it a "disruptive idea" (Trk.: *fikr-i fesad*) supported by certain individuals that "intended to put the state in danger." "An autonomous Albania," the sultan stated, "would serve to diminish the Ottoman state and would consequently leave the Albanians defenseless before the predatory ambitions of the neighbors." Then, the Ottoman head of state addressed the Albanians "as [their] father" and promised his full protection and support.

patriotism that could not exclude what Sami Frashëri called "special homeland," which for the Albanians was Albania. This principle also guided the first Albanian mobilization on a national basis—the League of Prizren in 1878. Although the Ottoman authorities were affectionate to the idea of defending the imperial *vatan*, the flow of events soon took a sharp turn. The sultan did not view the League favorably and turned against it because he feared that Albanians would subordinate Islamism and Ottomanism to their national identity.

As a result, the sultan worked on maintaining a loyal support base in Albania, beginning with the Kosova and Janina vilayets, and later including Manastir. The Albanians in fact never cut their ties with the monarch, but their support dwindled as the regime continued to make concessions in favor of the Slavic Orthodox. As a result, the ethnic group resorted to Albanianism and conditioned the loyalty to the sultan with the recognition of the Albanian nationality and autonomy or a similar solution. After the 1903 Peace Treaty of Mürzsteg compelled new reforms in Macedonia, the movement for Albania's autonomy gained even greater support. The agreement between Austria-Hungary and Russia forced the Ottoman Empire to give up its authority over main state functions in the vilayets of Kosova, Manastir, and parts of Janina. Seeing the police, judiciary, and education being affected by the reforms, even the landowning conservative Albanians equated their allegiance to the sultan with their country's autonomy. Seen from this perspective, the League of Peja (1899-1900) did not achieve its goals but made noteworthy progress in promoting Albania's political and cultural autonomy. It was not until after the sultan agreed to the reforms in Macedonia that the sultanists embraced the idea of self-government; however, the turn would have been nearly impossible without the impact of the League of Peja in mobilizing the population around the autonomist cause.

Sami Frashëri's Treatise on Albania: A Political Program for National Revival

The renowned thinker, Sami Frashëri, publishes his recommendations for the Albanian movement in light of the dissolution of the Ottoman Empire. He urges his compatriots to follow the road to national independence and the European civilization. Writing on his country's future, Frashëri promotes religious freedom and a secular regime for the country, calling on all Albanians to unite in brotherhood as nature has decided and as they once lived in the ancient times.

The League of Peja and the efforts to overcome divisions came as Albanianism broadened its reach and different social strata became increasingly aware of the existential test facing the nation. The cultural and patriotic activities of various clubs and associations certainly contributed to the spread of Albanianism. The İstanbul Committee as a leading group included most of the prominent figures of the *Rilindja Kombëtare* and served as a hub linking the nation with the expats, particularly the Arbëreshë communities in Italy and immigrants in Romania, Bulgaria, Egypt, Austria, and the United States. The diaspora played a crucial role in the Albanian publications, including literary works, textbooks, newspapers, encouraging the national awakening in plans for the future, beyond the urging fear of the empire's dissolution.

Meanwhile, Sultan Abdul Hamid II continued at all times to make concessions to expansionist neighbors to a degree that threatened the very being of the Albanians. The Ottoman sovereign incessantly used the predominantly-Muslim population to safeguard the empire's dominions, but he failed to legitimize the ethnic dimensions through a mutually-beneficial autonomy. Moreover, while Albanians rebelled against the state of affairs, such efforts remained uncoordinated or were often used by the sultan himself for his own needs. The revivalists (Alb.: *rilindas*), as the *Rilindja* activists were called, focused on mobilizing the people and materializing their potential by means of a clearly-devised political platform. In 1899, activists had already formed a new organization, the League of Peja, which soon spread to other cities of Albania. In March, as the organization prepared to hold a general convention, a migrant society of Bucharest, *Drita* (*Alb.*, the Light), published a political treatise entitled *Shqipëria ç'ka qënë,ç'është dhe ç'do të bëhetë?* (roughly, Albania: Yesterday, Today, and Tomorrow).

While printed anonymously, the work was authored by the renowned scholar, Sami Frashëri, and presented a national program for the establishment of the Albanian state, outlining the people's position vis-a-vis the Ottoman Empire and envisioned the nation's future within the European family. In historic times, Frashëri's work helped the idea for an independent, European Albania in gaining the support of the people from all walks of life.

Frashëri saw the formation of the League of Peja as an important event, expressing hope that the organization would unite the Albanians people and guarantee their territorial integrity. "The League, the gathering, and the covenant that are being established today in Albania will lead to the salvation of the country," he said.[564] Further, the writer argued for the League to expand its geographic presence and called on Albanian Muslims, Orthodox, and Catholics to unite. "Above all," he wrote, "Albanians must give their word of honor and form a covenant and a union, which will spread throughout Albania."[565]

The Albanian writer also called for self-government, urging Albanian patriots to transform the League into a permanent state authority that would defend and administer the country. Recalling "that the Turkish government is a destructive rather than a constructive government," Frashëri suggested that the League assume control over Albania, whether by implementing on its own or by forcing the Porte to put into effect the demands of the national movement.[566] He also laid out the organizational structure of the new Albanian League: for every sanjak, he suggested a permanent local council, functioning at the behest of the General Council, which would convene once a year or when needed. The proposed legislative body would subsequently appoint the League's executive organ, carrying out the duties of a national government.[567]

S. Frashëri's treatise as a platform for the new League and the growing participation of Albanians, including supporters of the sultan from among the feudal and nobles, prompted the Sublime Porte to halt the planned convention of Albanians. The meeting, scheduled for late May 1899, was not held because the Ottoman government feared the mobilization of Albanians on a national basis, which was at the core of Frashëri's manifesto. After all the misconceptions and divisions that the Ottoman state had caused among the Albanians, *Shqipëria: Ç'ka qënë . . .* showed the people a clear path, calling on them to secede from the Ottoman Empire. Although a former supporter of an Ottoman Albania, Frashëri urged his countrymen to work on creating an independent state, as the only way for national salvation in face of the threatened portioning.

The Albanian author regarded secession as essential since:

> European Turkey has a short life. Albania has laid no roots and bedrock of its own; it lives on Turkey's rotten foundations . . . Upon the demise of this unsustainable, gargantuan creature, Albania will fall, too, and it will be trodden underneath the heavy ruins . . .[568]

---

[564] S. Frashëri, *Shqipëria ç'ka qënë . . .* (Bukuresht: 1899), 4.

[565] *Ibid.* 4.

[566] *Ibid.* 5.

[567] *Ibid.* 5.

[568] *Ibid.* 6.

If the Albanians continued to endure Ottoman tyranny, living divided into the four infamous vilayets and rising for no rights or freedom of their own, they ran the risk of being identified with the Turks.[569] When the empire collapsed, Albania could then be treated as part of the Ottoman remnants to be divided between the monarchies. The fight against Ottoman rule was hence essential, "for Albania to secede from the Ottoman Empire, to be spared of the destruction and the catastrophe whither the empire is bound."[570]

S. Frashëri urged for Albania to have its own government before the dissolution of the Ottoman Empire. "It is a priority," he wrote, "for the Albanians to petition the sultan and the European states that Albania be separated from the Turkish trunk, for Albania to soon secede and for its borders to be defined. Our country shall be known as Albania, and Europe shall recognize it as Albania."[571]

Even when discussing autonomy within the Ottoman Empire, Frashëri contemplated secession as an inevitable occurrence. He wrote that the "Albanian government may for the time being be under Turkey, but on the condition that, in the event of Turkey's demise, Albania may stand as it is."[572]

To achieve secession and statehood, the writer suggested armed action in addition to the political process:

> Albanians ought to achieve their goals against the will [of the Porte]; they must utter their demands through words, yet keep a loaded rifle [ready for war] . . . Turkey yields nothing out of love and kindness . . . Albanians are able to maintain and seek their rights even through their guns. Justice interwoven with power obtains such strength that none could ever withstand.[573]

Owing to his calls for well-planed military action, S. Frashëri partially abandoned his previous evolutionary approach, which he defended in the prior years, particularly in the correspondence with the Arbëreshë writer, Jeronim de Rada.[574] Among the letters the two figures exchanged, it is worth mentioning a Frashëri's reply to the Arbëreshë poet, when the latter suggest-

---

[569] H.P.Sh. 2 (Tiranë), 291.

[570] S. Frashëri, *Shqipëria ç'ka qënë* . . . (Bukuresht: 1899), 34.

[571] *Ibid.* 35.

[572] *Ibid.* 35.

[573] *Ibid.* 36.

[574] See S. Frashëri's correspondence with Jeronim de Rada in *Buletini për Shkencat Shoqërore* II (Tiranë: 1954), 114-118.

ed in 1881 that Albania be organized as a confederate state, divided into three religion-based entities. For Sami, who preferred greater unity among the people, De Rada's plan was neither palatable nor feasible; for Albania was not geographically divided by religion and (except for the South where there were no Catholics) Albanians of different faiths did not live in separate areas, but were mixed with each another. There were tribes that consisted of Christians and Muslims and a Christian felt closer to a Muslim tribesman than to a Christian of a different origin.[575] Frashëri wrote that despite efforts by Turks, Greeks, and Slavs to divide the Albanians, the links of brotherhood remained unbroken, warranting against any separation on account of religion. "Creeds ought to be left to churches and mosques and Albanians should all become brothers as nature has intended and as it once was in the ancient times."[576]

Frashëri also touched on the subject matter in the treatise *Shqipëria Ç'ka qënë...*, repeatedly emphasizing that religion does not divide Albanians, and that the presence of three faiths among the people was the best evidence. This provided an answer to an issue that was seen as a problem externally rather than domestically. Particularly, foreign interests wanted the Albanians identified on religious grounds rather than united on the basis of their national identity, which Frashëri placed above religion while *Rilindja Kombëtare* adopted Albanianism as the "creed of the Albanians."

Although the Bucharest edition of *Shqipëria ç'ka qënë, ç'është dhe ç'do të bëhetë* was published anonymously (and only later publications, including the posthumous German translation, properly credited the writer),[577] the author's name remained no secret. The Ottoman-Albanian patriot, writer, philologist, and philosopher, Sami Frashëri or Şemsettin Sami, was one of the greatest of polymaths of the time. He had made historic contributions to the Turkish language and Ottoman nationalism and had built bridges between the peoples of the Ottoman Empire, using Islam as a binding force. However, his past merits were not enough to keep the Porte from placing him under house arrest and the constant surveillance of government minders. A judicial process was never held for the authorities feared that an influential Ottoman-Albanian figure such as Sami Frashëri could endanger the very existence of the empire. The future of the tri-continental state could dependent on the

---

[575] Skëndi, *Zgjimi kombëtar shqiptar*, 160.

[576] *Buletini për Shkencat Shoqërore* II (Tiranë: 1954), 114-118.

[577] Semsettin Sami, *Was war Albanien, was ist es, was wierd werden* (Wien: 1913).

Albanian question: Frashëri could save the empire by accepting, on behalf of his people, an Ottoman Albania; but, were he to insist on secession, the Ottoman Empire risked its collapse.

Sami Frashëri died four years later (1904), in isolation and confinement, but his works and ideas disseminated through Albanian communities worldwide. *Shqipëria ç'ka qënë*... became the guidebook for one of the most important undertakings of the Albanian people, nurturing their national consciousness with a vision that led to unification and national independence.

The regime and Sultan Abdul Hamid himself were aware of the views the Albanian writer had proclaimed in the leading publications of the time. Exemplifying qualities of a linguist, scholar, and prolific author, Frashëri composed the six volumes of the Ottoman encyclopedia *Kamus al-Al'am* (1889-99) and a modern Turkish dictionary in two volumes. He was also distinguished in social sciences with his *Medeniyet-i İslamiyye* (*Trk.*, The Islamic Civilization), *İnsan* (*Trk.*, The Human Being), and *Kadınlar* (*Trk.*, Women) in a series of sensational works. In addition to his views on the Ottoman Empire, Islam, and civilization in general, Frashëri also wrote about the Albanians and their history, placing the ethnic group within the Western civilization while also highlighting the character of the historic ties with the East, particularly with Islam, which he presented under a positive light.

Maintaining his viewpoint on his people, Frashëri created the platform to separate the Albanians from the *millet-i osman*, under which they were forcibly identified. Instead, he categorized the ethnic group as an independent nation (Trk.: *kavma*) and called for its political recognition and autonomy. Frashëri tried to foster a spirit of conciliation and cooperation between Albanianism and Islamism, arguing that the unity of religion and state did not prevent cultural and ethnic pluralism while faith and the national identity both helped strengthen the state. As a proponent of Islamism, Sami acknowledged the merits and the role of Islam, but also defended the national identity, holding it above religion. "An Albanian," he wrote, "even as a Muslim remains Albanian just as much as he would as a Christian."[578]

This was the most effective clarification on the relationship between national identity and religion and became the political platform of Albanianism at a time when the Albanians were denied their ethnic identity and the right of self-government as a nation, which non-Muslim populations enjoyed.

---

[578] [Sami Frashëri], *Shqipëria ç'ka qënë, ç'është dhe ç'do të bëhetë?* (Bukuresht: 1899), 35.

315

Frashëri entered a major contribution in this aspect, because he managed to affirm Albanianism without confronting it with Islamism and Ottomanism. Noting the differences and links between the state and the nation (Trk.: *dövlet ve millet*), he provided a unifying formula, where nationality was a "unique identity" within what he called a "shared identity" based on the imperial homeland. Thus, as he presented the Albanian context within the Ottoman establishment, Frashëri gave his countrymen the opportunity to link the cultural and ethnic identity with the political identity without confronting them with religion, which was the same for all people. Nurturing this view, Frashëri made his first reference to the Albanian question in a play, *Besa*, and progressed into more profound editorial writings in Turkish and Albanian newspapers, some of which he directed himself. As early as December 1878, Frashëri declared that "Albania [is] my special homeland." The article published in the *Tercümen-i Hakikat* (*Trk.*, Interpreter of the Truth) newspaper argued that "nothing stands higher for man than the *vatan* [*i.e.*, homeland] and *cinsiyet* [*Trk.*, race, ethnicity]." Meanwhile, the *Sabah* newspaper published Frashëri's letter in which he reasoned that the words *Muslim* and *Albanian* were not synonymous, recalling that the whole nation did not have the same religion and not all Muslims were Albanians. Without denying the influence of religion, which he held as crucial primarily in the East, the Albanians writer saw nationality as a more important identity. Accordingly, he illustrated the significance of national identity for the state, noting that the Albanian demonym "is not just a part of modern geographic terminology, but is also of great importance for the Ottoman state."[579]

Sami Frashëri hoped for the Albanians to keep their ties to Ottomanism, because he was aware that his people needed the Ottoman Empire for some more time just as the empire needed an Ottoman Albania—*i.e.*, an autonomous Albania. He saw the transition as a useful period for the Albanians to clarify their identity from within, but also in relation to others, especially with Islamism and Ottomanism. In his writings between 1879-1889, the years during which he served as head of the İstanbul Committee, Frashëri always aspired for his people to reach a social awareness and political maturity to find a common language with the Ottoman Empire. Thus, he called for internal autonomy in accordance with the ethnic and cultural boundaries of the Albanians. In the same writing, he called on his people for maturity and

---

[579] Nathalie Clayer, *Në fillimet e nacionalizmit shqiptar*, 253.

responsible behavior, since neighboring Serbs and Greeks presented double threats: the perils of military action as well as the cultural menace, which were once a danger to the Ottoman Empire. He propagated the Albanian autonomy and cultural emancipation as an Ottoman interest such that they provided a supporting pillar for the sultan's domination in the Balkans. Frashëri saw human development as necessary so that his people were able to give adequate answers to pan-Slavism and Hellenism, which exploited the lack of an Albanian national education to assimilate the population and use them as a premise of hegemonic claims on Albanian lands.

Frashëri's previous ideas, some of which required interaction with the Ottoman Empire, could be explained with the author's hope that Sultan Abdul Hamid II, whom he supported at the beginning, would change his policy toward the Albanians, recognizing them as a nation and granting them autonomy. But in *Shqipëria ç'ka qënë . . .*, Frashëri nearly denied the necessity of cooperation with the Ottomans when he urged his countrymen to arms if so needed to prevent Albania from being identified as part of the Ottoman legacy. Accordingly, he allured the Albanian eyes towards Europe and the western civilization. Unsurprisingly, he even called on the Albanians to do everything in order for Europe to discover and learn about Albania before recognizing it as a nation.

In reality, many educated Albanians had begun to turn to Europe. These men, especially those educated in the West, inevitably fell into contact with Albanianism, which in various ways—in Albanian societies, clubs, and newspapers—was present in Vienna, Brussels, Rome, and Paris. However, Albanian Muslims, who had greatly embraced Albanianism, saw their European identity as a means to legitimize their presence in the continent after the Ottoman Empire was eventually forced to retreat from the Balkans. Thus, *Shqipëria ç'ka qënë, ç'është dhe ç'do të bëhetë* became a great source of encouragement in the pursuit of the European identity as well as statehood.

If Sami Frashëri as an academic is to be credit for defining the vision for a free Albania, Ismail Qemali was the leader whose diplomatic and political activities provided the practical basis for the creation of the state. Thus, it is not a matter of coincidence that history entrusted Qemali with the responsibility of declaring Albania's independence in November 1912 during the tumultuous times that threatened the very existence of the nation.

Ismail Qemali, as many Albanians who joined the national movement, belonged to the intellectual elite and came from an aristocratic family well-established in the Ottoman state hierarchy. Born in Vlora on May 24, 1844,

317

to the prominent landowning Sinanaj family, he received his secondary education at the renowned Zosimea gymnasium in Janina, a school where the Frashëri brothers had also attended. Qemali began his career once he moved to İstanbul, where in 1859 he was hired as an interpreter at the Ministry of Foreign Affairs, while he also enrolled in his higher studies in law.[580] Later, he embarked on his perennial career as a politician and diplomat, who lived through all of the twists and turns the Ottoman Empire experienced at the time—from the opening of the first parliament and its subsequent suspension from Sultan Abdul Hamid II to the Young Turk Revolution and the Balkan Wars, which ended with the Ottoman defeat, but also prompted Albania's declaration of independence.

Nevertheless, Ismail Qemali's long career carries the brand of his dedication to two important matters: the modernization of the Ottoman Empire and the Albanian efforts for autonomy as a nation within the empire. With respect to the latter, Qemali was one of the Albanian activists in İstanbul who between 1864 and 1867 endeavored to create a unified alphabet for the Albanian language and to form an Albanian cultural society. The Vlora-born diplomat opposed the use of the Arabic script for his native language, joining Pashko Vasa, Konstandin Kristoforidhi, and other literati who supported the Latin alphabet.[581]

From that time, Qemali remain more or less tied to the national movement, although he never abandoned his political activities as an Ottoman, whether in the government or in opposition, at home or abroad. In fact, even when he was in service of the sultan, as governor in remove provinces, lastly in Tripoli (1900), from where he defected to Europe, Ismail Qemali was constantly devoted to the Albanian cause. In the meantime, after the fall of the absolutist regime of Sultan Abdul Hamid II and Ismail Qemali's return to the Ottoman parliament as representative for Vlora, the liberal politician became the leader of the national movement, since this role was imposed on him by the new state of affairs that arose after a profound conflict broke out between the Albanians and the Young Turks. He strived for a political balance in order to keep the Albanian demands for the status of a nationality and autonomy in line with the spirit of reforms in the empire (the Ottoman state was specifically obligated to undertake reforms under international

---

[580] For more on Ismail Qemali, see *The Memoirs of Ismail Kemal Bey*, London, 1920, published in Albanian as *Kujtime* (Tiranë: 1997).
[581] H.P.Sh. 2 (Tiranë), 293.

agreements, in particular Article XXIII of the Berlin resolutions). Although Qemali viewed autonomy as a transition, for he was aware that the *status quo* could eventually change, he did not rule out other possibilities, such as a federation with Greece or a protectorate under the Great Powers.

Despite the contemplated alternatives, Ismail Qemali remained loyal to the idea of self-government within the empire until the First Balkan War broke out. He was relieved of the autonomy cliché only after the Balkan allies defeated the Ottoman Empire and occupied Albania. During a meeting in Bucharest on November 17, 1912, Austro-Hungarian Foreign Minister Berthold reminded the Albanian leader that the era of autonomous principalities had ended and that it was the time for his people to declare their national independence.

The struggle for statehood was in line with Sami Frashëri's *Shqipëria ç'ka qënë . . .*, which had gained universal acceptance in the national movement. Despite the rhetoric that Ismail Qemali used in certain situations, he followed the fundamental guidelines that Frashëri emphasized, such as the creation of an Albanian state, even if autonomous in the initial stages, while the country made a comeback to the European civilization.

I. Qemali began his work to implement the Frashëri platform after he left Turkey in April 1900, staying initially to Athens, from where he later moved to Naples, Rome, Lausanne, Paris, and Brussels, to finally find shelter in London, where he remained the longest. This route, in fact, marked the first phase of the national movement's active lobbying in the Western capitals through prominent individuals such as Qemali. The Great Powers could not avoid him, for he was also a representative of the Ottoman opposition. Hence, using the status of an Ottoman leader, Qemali presented the Albanian autonomy, cultural emancipation, and education as part of the reforms that the Ottoman Empire had begun a century prior, but the Hamidian dictatorship had nearly quashed.

The Albanian leader made his public debut with comments on his homeland in a 1900 interview to a leading Italian newspaper during his stay in Rome. The news published on May 21 spurred a boundless sensation, since *La Tribuna* remarked positively on Qemali, considering him "sincerely benevolent to the Ottoman Empire and a cautious spokesman for the Albanian question." Further, the article emphasized that he sought no "secession from the empire, but a political autonomy" as an achievement for both sides and with mutual benefits. Meanwhile, on October 15, Qemali published in the *Albania* magazine a call titled "To the Albanian Brothers," in which laid out the main objectives of the national movement.

In both documents, the Albanian leader urges for the recognition of the Albanians as a "nation that lives together in Shkodër, Kosova, Manastir, and Janina, and throughout other territories of European Turkey."[582] Ismail Qemali further explained his people's desire for the "unity of our Albanian race, its intellectual and economic progress so as to be able to defy those who seek to annex us," and articulated a dedication to the West, noting that the Albanians "have always remained Europeans in their hearts."[583] He also focused on autonomy and national education, two themes that were carefully addressed in Sami Frashëri's works. Qemali believed that Albanian schools would help the people improve their self-government, which he argued was provided by Article XXIII of the 1878 Treaty of Berlin. Based on the document, Ismail Bej called on the Great Powers to grant Albania the same type of autonomy that was awarded to Crete in 1897 by the European states. Cautious not to disturb the spirit of the *status quo*, since doing so could banish him from the political scene, the Albanian leader did not call for his homeland to secede from the Ottoman Empire, but required a state framework where his people enjoyed their right to self-government.[584] Speaking to Rome's *La Tribuna*, the career politician expressed his wish for good neighborly relations with Greeks, Italians, and others, viewing the friendly ties as beneficial to all. Qemali also referred to another Greek-Albanian agreement, arguing that "the understanding between Greeks and Albanians should be based on parallel development within their national spheres."[585] While supporting the *status quo*, he insisted in reforms that could diminish the potential for crises in the region.

Ismail Qemali reiterated much of his views in the *Selamet* (*Trk.*, Salvation) newspaper, published in Turkish, Greek, and Albanian. He defended the interests of the Albanian people as identical in certain aspects with the interests of Greece.[586] It was this statement, however, that led most many contemporary patriots to cast their doubts, going as far as to call Qemali a stooge of Greek politics. One of the arduous critics was Faik Konica, who

---

[582] *Ibid.* 296.

[583] *Ibid.* 296.

[584] *Ibid.* 296.

[585] See Ismail Qemali interview by Lalis Paternostro, *La Tribuna* (July 27, 1907), cited in S. Skëndo, *Zgjimi kombëtar shqiptar*, 173.

[586] See *Kujtime* (Tiranë: 1997), 229-249.

repudiated the Albanian-Ottoman leader's pro-Hellenic stance as detrimental to the national cause.[587]

Through his contemplated alliance with the Greeks, however, Qemali did not necessarily oscillate from Frashëri's platform; the Albanian leader rather maintained a realistic approach in politics, as he carried the task of testing out political maneuvers that nonetheless were often risky (for instance, negotiations with Greece and later Italy failed, leaving the Albanians only with the Austro-Hungarian support, crucial for Albania's independence).

Ismail Qemali's activity, as an Albanian and Ottoman leader, is likely to have evoked the suspicion that the Albanians wished to preserve the Ottoman Empire while they sought their own autonomous state. This aspect, however speculative, led to further deepening of the Balkan crisis, since the neighbors were finalizing their strategy for the annexation of Albania, while the Great Powers, primarily Austria-Hungary, also motioned to prevent such developments. The European empires devised their own plans for Albania, as an autonomous state under the supervision of the Great Powers. The plan to keep Albania temporarily under the Ottomans risked turning the country into a battlefield, as indeed happened with the outbreak of the First Balkan War. Yet, Europe had no choice but to give an answer, even if unfair, to the Albanian cause, which had embarked on a route of no-return toward statehood and Europe, despite the difficulties and the injustice.

The Beginning of the Macedonia Crisis

Albanian leaders nurture illusions of regional cooperation, pursuing failed projects for an alliance with Greece. The join Austro-Hungarian and Russian plan for reforms in Macedonia caused disadvantages the Albanians, causing discontent among them. The Russian consul in Mitrovica is shot dead on August 3, 1903; the Albanian revolt spreads in Kosova. Bulgaria intervenes in the vilayets of Manastir and Selanik and reaches a deal with Serbia on splitting the Albanian territories. Sultan Abdul Hamid II proposes a vilayet of Rumelia incorporating three existing Albanian vilayets as an ostensible step towards the unification of the Albanians in a single administrative unit; in reality, the Ottoman sovereign uses his

---

[587] *Albania*, VII (1902).

plan for further concessions to the Christian population at the expense of Albanians. The 1903 agreement between Vienna and Saint Petersburg provides for an international supervision of Macedonia. Serbian and Bulgarian intelligence and military services deploy bandit groups into the vilayets of Kosova and Manastir on the pretext of defending Christians from the "Arnaut crimes."

One may note that the Great Powers, including Russia, were well aware that an Albanian question existed and was becoming increasingly pressing regardless of the treatment it received in the international arena. Likewise, the Great Powers, including Russia, were aware that the matter required an answer even though that was no easy task to undertake, for Albania had fallen into a vicious cycle where strategic interests of the more powerful clashed. Moreover, even when the Great Powers ignored the Albanian question in principle, such as at the Congress of Berlin in 1878, they were all the time more convinced for the urgency of the matter as the Albanians became catalysts for international crises—regardless of whether they were considered by the European states. Therefore, the continental powers tried to avoid the Albanian question by preserving the *status quo*. While unsustainable in the long run, the current state of affairs opened the way to the European ambitions, ranging from annexation to partitioning and including a variety of possible compromises (*e.g.*, autonomy or similar solutions).

The influence in the Balkan and European crises made the Albanian question highly complex and perilous alike. Owing to their activities, the Albanians were now affecting regional affairs on themselves. While the demands for autonomy did not directly bring an end to the *status quo*, external factors were noticeably impacted. Neighboring Serbia, Montenegro, Greece, and Bulgaria acted to suppress the prospects of a self-governing Albania, even threatening to go to war against the Ottoman Empire as they finally did in 1912. Therefore, the consolidation of the autonomy movement on the one hand and the neighbors' objection on the other laid ignited the visible and the invisible rivalries between the Great Powers.

In general, those who supported the Albanians engaged in completion that was cultural and economic nature, whereas those who opposed the independence of the small nation disagreed with one another over their hopes for invasion. The Austrian-Italian rivalry over Albania was conducive to the national awakening of the people, while the neighboring countries pursued their national plans for territorial expansion at the expense of the

Albanians. Serbian ad Greek programs such as *Načertanije* and *Megali idea* also had their "benefits," because the Albanians were compelled to think of their fate as a nation in light of the threatened occupation by their neighbors. This served as a promoter of the national awakening before it became too late. At certain points, Serbs and Greeks seemingly expressed an interest in supporting the Albanian involvement in the regional anti-Ottoman movement. However, the strategy of the Balkan states was that of divide and rule—at all times they sought to weaken the Albanians and the Ottomans so that they could subsequently prey on both.

Guided by this strategy, Serbia and Montenegro poured weapons into the northern parts of the vilayets of Shkodër and Kosova and reached several agreements with local landlords and *bajraktars*, who assumed to protect the properties of Serbs and Orthodox monasteries. Importantly, the two Slavic countries also insisted that they were placed in charge of the anti-Ottoman uprisings.[588] Belgrade and Cetinje undoubtedly tried to portray themselves as friends and protectors, promising the Albanians that their faith, heritage, and property would remain intact.

In this regard, the Greeks were more perfidious, attracting many Albanians into the Hellenist movement. After Ali Pashë Tepelena failed to secede from the Ottoman Empire, Arvanites and Orthodox Albanians fought vigorously for Greece's independence. Even when the Eastern Crisis broke out, Greeks endeavored to engage the Albanians in joint projects. An example is the first negotiations of Abdyl Frashëri and Mehmet Ali Vrioni with the Greek prime minister in 1878: during the Russo-Ottoman war, a Greek-Albanian alliance was contemplated against the Ottoman Empire. The Albanians suggested a federated state for the two peoples, but Athens refused out of fear that Greeks would be a minority in the proposed entity. In fact, authentic Hellenism—as a cultural movement rather than a tool for assimilation—found wide support among Arvanite, Orthodox Albanian, and Ar-

---

[588] For more on the cooperation of some Albanian landowners with Serbs, arms supplied received from Serbia, and some one-sided agreements between the two groups with respect to the 1908-1912 uprisings (where Isa Boletini is on the focus), see Branko Perunović, *Pisma srpskih konzula iz Prištine 1890-1900* (Beograd: 1985), 366-368; Tahir Abdyli, *Hasan Prishtina: monografi* (Prishtinë: 1990); Zekeria Cana, *Lëvizja kombëtare shqiptare në Kosovë 1908-1912* (Prishtinë: 1979); Tajar Zavalani, *Historia e Shqipnisë* (Tiranë: 1998); Stavro Skendi, *Zgjimi kombëtar shqiptar* (Tiranë: 2000); Nathalie Clayer, *Në fillim të nacionalizmit shqiptar* (Tiranë: 2009); Edwin Jacques, *Shqiptarët* (1995); Misha Glenny, *Histori e Ballkanit 1804-1999* (Tiranë: 2007).

bëreshë intellectuals who thought that the two nations could join forces to liberate themselves from the Ottoman Empire. However, when the Greek monarchy adopted the *Megali idea* expansionist project in mid-19th century, sincere efforts for cooperation could no longer lead to success.

As the Albanian national movement consolidated with Frashëri's manifesto and the instrumental role of the diaspora and the Arbëreshë community, the Balkan countries changed their approach toward Albania. They began to ramp up their pressure on the Ottoman Empire for reforms, mainly in favor of Christians (*i.e.*, Serbs and Bulgarians). The changes directly provoked the Albanians to react from both ends: as opponents of the reforms and enemies of the Ottoman Empire. In the meantime, the neighboring countries also began to infiltrate into the troubling region of Macedonia, an action that threatened to rule out any option for Albania's autonomy. Thus, from the Greek-Ottoman War of 1896-97 to the 1908 Young Turk Revolution, all parties focused on Macedonia. Given the threats of an invasion, the historical Aegean province enabled Slavs and Greeks to continuously pressure the Porte for reforms and against any autonomy plan for Albania.

Owing to its influence over the Balkan countries, it was Russia that ultimately held the key to the developments in the region. The tsar, however, knew that using the Slavic and Orthodox nations could induce the Tripartite Alliance. Austria-Hungary, Germany, and Italy could directly intervene in the Balkans and such action could best serve the Albanians. As a result, the Russians worked to separate the Austro-Hungarian interest from the Italian aspirations, elevating the earlier to a "special interest" between the two empires. As noted earlier, the 1881 agreement between Vienna, Petersburg, and Berlin already recognized the parties' positions in the Balkans and reaffirmed the *status quo*, which could only be altered with mutual assent.[589]

However, the Ottoman-Greek war over Crete caused Austrians and Russians to fear a misbalance of power. As a result, the two empires agreed on a fifty-fifty solution to the Albanian question: that is, the maximalist Albanian demands to unify the four vilayets were no longer viable, but the Slavic and Greek ambitions to split all of Albania among them would no longer be on the table. This formula, which reflected after Albania's independence when Europeans set the borders of the new state, first appeared in April of 1897. Austrian and Russian foreign ministers, Galuhovski and Muraviev, seeking

---

[589] See section II of the treaty; A. F. Pribram, *The Secret Treaties of Austria-Hungary 1879-1914*, vol. I (Cambridge, Mass.: 1920), 39, cited in Skëndi, *Zgjimi kombëtar shqiptar*, 265.

to avoid "the risk of a catastrophic rivalry," agreed on a scenario in case the *status quo* could no longer be maintained in the Balkans.[590] On a note dated May 8, 1897, Vienna indicated its desire to annex Bosnia and Herzegovina and the sanjak of Yeni Pazar. Likewise, the Habsburg empire also supported the creation of an independent Albanian state and specifically excluded "any foreign rule" over the entity that would "span from Janina to Shkodër" and sufficiently extend to the east.[591] Austria-Hungary also objected to the partitioning of the then-Ottoman possessions among the Balkan states and the Russian raised no objections in their response. However, the tsar's government sought to postpone a deal on Albania's independence in the proposed borders, arguing that "it is difficult to reach an agreement at the present."[592]

The statement may have well been an effort to calm Italy rather than as an objection to the Austro-Hungarian plan for Albania. In the European scene, the tsar's agreement in principle with the dual monarchy sparked a regional competition over Macedonia. As Serbia, Greece, and Bulgaria laid claims on the province, Britain and Germany were also concerned. While they had no direct interests in the Balkans, the two powers feared that what seemed as "local" rivalries could become a cause for wider problems. In addition to the contentions over Macedonia, Italy had also engaged Montenegro in an effort turn the tiny principality into a Rome ally.

Germany sided with Austria-Hungary and Russia in seeking the stability of the Ottoman Empire and an expanded economic partnership with the Porte. The English were against this and hoped to see the decline of the eastern empire, even if that would entail an end to the *status quo*, which London had so vigorously defended in the past and continued to support in rhetoric. But, before the British and German rivalry led to a major crisis, Austria-Hungary and Russia use their mandate as great powers to take the cautionary measures. As they had done before, they pressured the Ottoman Empire for reforms in the European parts, in particular in Macedonia.

The focus on the province was not coincidental, because Macedonia was the center of the crisis that affected all other unresolved issues in the Balkans. The Ottoman Empire, since 1897 when reforms were first announced, struggled with its own limitations. The Albanians objected to the changes.

---

[590] See W. M. Corlegren, *Iswolsky und Aerhenthal vor der bosnischen Annexionskrise* (Wien: 1955), 14.

[591] *Ibid.* 14.

[592] Skëndi, *Zgjimi kombëtar shqiptar*, 266.

The Young Turk opposition, which found common grounds with the Albanians, was also against the reforms. The situation worsened further when neighboring countries tried to utilize they had received within the Ottoman Empire. The Porte had recently empowered the Serbian and Bulgarian churches in the European parts, permitted Slavic schools in Kosova and Manastir, and most importantly given the green light to Serbian consulates in Prishtina and Shkup. Owing to such benefits, Serbia and Bulgaria gained great influence that they hoped would advance their expansionist goals. Belgrade portrayed Kosovo and Macedonia as the "Serbian spiritual cradle," while Sofia depicted Macedonia as "the center of Tsar Samuel's Bulgaria," and both pressured the Great Powers to consider their claims in determining future borders.

Faced with the internal decline and the aggressive behavior of the neighbors, the Ottoman Empire was compelled to go beyond reforms and concessions to the Slavs. Abdul Hamid II resorted to oppressing the Albanians, while working to maintain his friendship with Austria-Hungary, Russia, and notably Germany. The latter had developed expansive ties with the sultan in all fields, providing a boost for the modernization of the Ottoman economy as well as the empire's position on the international arena as a bridge linking the West and the East. Therefore, Abdul Hamid II whipped those whom he affectionately called the "flower of Islam" and the empire's European "bastion" for they threatened the reforms. In addition to the crackdown on Albanians, the authorities also approved military action against the Slavic revolt in Macedonia.

Since the instatement of the exarchate, Bulgaria had increased its presence in the vilayets of Manastir and Selanik with a clear intention of territorial expansion. Sofia had already proclaimed a project for a Greater Bulgaria, gaining as well the approval of Austria-Hungary and Russia. As a result, Bulgaria deployed *komitas*, military groups that, alongside the Serbian and Greek bands, destabilized the region. By the end of 1890, the Bulgarian agitation in Macedonia entered a new phase with frequent attacks of the newly-formed Internal Revolutionary Macedonian Organization (VMRO). The group had already adopted a unified platform, announced a year earlier at the Congress of Macedonians and Bulgarians in Geneva, Switzerland, with the demand for an autonomous Macedonia consisting of the Manastir and Kosova vilayets.[593] The Slavic-Macedonian population in the two vilayets had

---

[593] K. Prifti, *Le Mouvement nacional albanais de 1869 à 1900: La Ligue de Pejë* (Tiranë: 1989), 149-50.

begun to organize in the "internal" committees. Local leaders such as Gotse Delchev and Jane Sandanski called for cooperation with Albanians to face the Serbian and Greek aims. For its own cause, Bulgaria had formed "external" comities with essentially megalo-Bulgarian orientation. Sofia recruits came from "the other side of border and included militias and members of state police services. Their leader, Yankov ordered sabotage acts and assassination plots with of destabilizing Macedonia. Russian logistics provided the main assistance in these affairs. In the meantime, Bulgaria had already begun secret talks with Belgrade and Athens on how to split the Macedonian territory. In this way, the three states used their guerilla groups to foster the partitioning of the province, deepening further the calamity in the Balkans.

The great powers of Europe feared the developments. Austria-Hungary and Russia previously agreed to not allow any changes without a new agreement between the two powers. Therefore, Vienna requested energetic measures from the Sublime Porte to prevent unexpected turns. The same way, Russia was interested to preserve Abdul Hamid's position against the Young Turks as well as the Europeans. The tsar supported the sultan, viewing him as a guarantor of Slavic interests in the East. As a result, Russia intervened at the Porte, asking for rough measures against the Albanians, whom Saint Petersburg blamed as the culprits for the calamity. On this occasion, Russia emphasized that the Albanians' "anti-Slavic" activity was connected to the Ottoman authorities that were not interested in implementing the reforms and hence played a double game with the Balkan people.

On the other hand, the regional countries increased their armed interventions every time the Sublime Porte mounted military campaigns in Kosova. Beside the Manastir and Selanik vilayets, in the spring of 1902, bands began their activity in the northern part of Kosova, too. This expansion followed the secret agreement between Belgrade and Sofia on dividing the region into zones of Serbian and Bulgarian bands that, according to them, "were defending the Christian population from *Arnaut* outrage.

The opening of a Russian consulate in Mitrovica only added gas on an existing fire. The Albanians viewed the events as preparations for a new Slavic-Orthodox expansion. They did conceal their frustration with Sublime Porte that allowed foreign offices in Kosova and Macedonia. In the northern part of Kosova, Albanians revolted to stop the activity of the consulates. They insurgents were led by Isa Boletini, who in fact had very good relations with the sultan.

The revolt persisted throughout September and October and was limited around Mitrovica and Isa Boletini's domains. Its scope and lack of a likely expansion created doubts that the Porte was circumventing the commitments to Great Powers, by blaming the Albanian unrest. The likelihood of a conspiracy is supported by the role of Şemsi Pasha who, instead of oppressing the revolt, entered into direct negotiations with Isa Boletini. Although deployed to suppress the Albanians militarily, the pasha convinced spoke with their leader and convinced him to leave Mitrovica. By the end of November 1902, Abdul Hamid brought the Albanian lord to İstanbul, and appointed him guard (Trk.: *tüfenci*) of Royal Palace. Boletini remained in the Ottoman capital until 1906 and then returned to Kosova with a substantial land grant from the monarch and an officer position in the regional police.[594]

The Albanian withdrawal allowed the Sublime Porte to turns to the bands that created the turmoil in Macedonia. Throughout September and October, the Ottoman military suppressed with great rage the armed groups in the province. This action received in a way the Albanian approval of Albanians who suffered at the hands of the Slavic and Greek bands that committed crimes against the defenseless population.

While the Great Powers also permitted the use of force, they demanded reforms in Macedonia. In December 1902, the Ottoman authorities announced the so-called "Guidance for the Rumelia Vilayets." Thereby, Abdul Hamid II united the three vilayets—Selanik, Manastir, and Kosova—into a single, larger unit named the *Three Vilayets* (Ottoman Trk.: *Vilayet-i Selase*). The Ottoman monarch claimed that this entity, and not the Albanian vilayets, would constitute the empire's pillar in Europe. He planned to achieve this goal through his seven-point plan, which provided that:

1. The police force shall include Muslims and Christians in proportion to local demographics and needs;
2. The *valis* shall oversee the development of agriculture and commerce and road construction;
3. Civil courts consisting of Muslims and Christians shall be established;
4. A commission of four members shall be nominated to control the activity of the *vali* and of inspectors overseeing the reforms;
5. A kaymekam for administrative affairs shall be nominated to serve under the *vali*;

---

[594] Gawrych, *Gjysmëhëna dhe shqiponja*, 203.

6. A chief inspector shall be nominated for all Turkish provinces of Europe; and

7. The tax system shall not modified.[595]

These reforms, ridiculed as the "Rumelia hoax," were a robust strike against the Albanian aspirations to unite the four vilayets in one autonomous unit. As a plan that did not contradict the calculations of Great Powers, self-government already had the indirect support of Europe. When in 1880, as we previously mentioned, the British raised the issue of an Albanian vilayet, the Ottomans objected, claiming that the idea would negatively affect the state unity.[596] Nevertheless, Albanian statehood remained an open and current issue at all times.

With the proclamation of the *Three Vilayets*, the sultan denied the Albanian demands once more with the same motivations. At the same time, he made all the efforts to stop the partitioning of Macedonia among Serbia, Bulgaria and Greece. But, treating the two questions as a single matter, Abdul Hamid received no benefits for his government. Although he avoided the Albanian autonomy, he was unable to halt the wrecking of the state since the Albanian question and Macedonian crisis proved fatal for the Ottoman Empire.

The "Rumelia hoax" failed to restore calm, let alone resolve the problem. Previous projects on Rumelia had also proposed economic development and administrative reforms, but such ideas always remained on paper. The situation was only exacerbated because the measures never received the support of the landlords or the clergy. This way, the reorganization of law enforcement, judicial and financial systems, and the appointment of a general inspector (a position that had the powers of a government minister) were never favorably received by the local population. Albanians viewed the changes as efforts to toughen state control and to provide privileges to the Slavic and Greek Christians. After the sultan nominated Hüseyin Hilmi Pasha as general inspector, with his headquarters in Shkup, the government's representative laid a tight grip on the local government. *Valis* and *mutesarrifs* reported all developments in their jurisdictions and the inspector constantly relayed the information to the imperial palace and the Sublime Porte.[597]

---

[595] Pllana, *Kosova dhe reformat në Turqi*, 170.

[596] For more, see Buxhovi, *Kongresi i . . . .*

[597] Gawrych, *Gjysmëhëna dhe shqiponja*, 203.

The Great Powers were dissatisfied with the incomplete implementation of the reforms and the interethnic tension caused by the unpopular measures. Another great eruption, Europeans feared, could lead to war throughout the Balkans. The *status quo*, which Austria-Hungary and Russia had been entrusted to safeguard, was in danger. With the approval of Britain, France, and Germany, Vienna and Saint Petersburg, sent a special request to Sublime Porte: on February 21, 1903, a reform project on the *Three Vilayets* of Macedonia was delivered to the Ottoman government. The sultan initially objected, but was later compelled to accept the European suggestions for the Kosova, Manastir, and Selanik vilayets.[598]

By means of reforms, the Great Powers hoped to preserve the *status quo* in southeastern Europe. Through rights extended to Christian Slavs and Greeks, the European states wished to prevent insurgencies and the reappearance of armed groups that could possibly lead to a military intervention of Balkan countries against the Ottoman Empire.[599]

The proclamation of the project caused great dissatisfaction among the Albanian population worried of a further partitioning of the country. The selective implementation of reforms was a practical endorsement of division: the Kosova and Manastir vilayets were being separated from Shkodër and Janina. For this reason, the Albanians opposed the Austro-Russian plan. Revolts erupted in many Kosovar towns. On March 31, 1903, an Albanian soldier shot a Russian consul near Mitrovica. The diplomat died from the wounds ten days later. On August 3, another Russian representative was killed by an Albanian in Manastir. The two assassinations within four months were part of the reason that Vienna and Petersburg relinquished their plan in districts where the Albanian formed the majority.[600]

The Albanian diaspora press greatly resonated with their compatriots. The Sofia-based *Drita*, another *Drita* of Bucharest, and the *Albania* magazine objected the European plan and demanded that Great Powers reconsider the Albanian autonomy as the only solution. The press attempted to inspire a new national league, realizing that the Albanian resistance was limited to the Kosova and Manastir vilayets. *Drita* of Bucharest encouraged Albanians to force the sultan to grant them autonomy. The newspaper suggested the self-government of Albania as a condition that the Ottoman monarch could

---

[598] H.P.Sh. 2 (Tiranë), 308.

[599] *Ibid.* 308.

[600] Gawrych, *Gjysmëhëna dhe shqiponja*, 205.

present to the Great Powers for the reforms in Macedonia. As the diaspora insisted that the autonomy would stop the Slavic attacks stabilize regional situation, pressure mounted on the sultan, who was already facing the growing opposition of the Young Turks. As a result, Abdul Hamid did not remain silent for too long. He issued a communication calling upon Albanians to subdue and refrain from revolt, and by the end of February 1903, he send special commissions to promote reforms in Kosova. Sultan's commissioners arrived in Peja, Gjakova, Reka, and other communities, advocating that Albanians would also profit from tax collection, rule of law, and education. The head of the Ottoman government, Said Pasha, meanwhile, attempted to minimize the Albanian opposition to the reforms. "Except for a few leaders," the grand vizier declared, "the majority of Albanians and the wealthy seek tranquility."[601]

In fact, it was the upper class that opposed the reforms. The planned changes threatened the interests of noble and commoner Albanians alike. This was made clear to Rumelia's chief inspector, Hilmi Pasha, during a meeting with Kosova landowners and leaders of the anti-reform movement. The local strongmen demanded measures of an ethnic character in the Albanian vilayets, including the recognition of the Albanian nationality and the right to use the native language in schools and religious establishments. Other demands related to the hiring of Albanian employees in the administration, the allocation of regional revenues for constructing schools, the release of political prisoners, and disallowing foreigners to interfere in the affairs of for Albanian vilayets.[602] The foreign interference was the most aggravating and the most unacceptable of all issues raised in the meeting with the Porte's representative. The Albanians feared that the empire was ready to give up Albania and that it remained in the hands of the people to fight against foreign presence in Kosova and the other vilayets. Through their activity on the Albanian territories, Serbia, Bulgaria and Greece were setting the stage to oust the Ottoman Empire from the region. The greatest for the Albanians was the presence of Serbian and Russian consulates working as open agents to destabilize the region. Diplomatic representatives pitied local Slavs to operate against Albanians to allegedly gain the rights granted by the Congress of Berlin. Slavs in the region complained of being victims of the so-called "*Arnaut* ourtage," alarming thereby the Great Powers of the

---

[601] *Ibid.* 309.
[602] *Ibid.* 309.

"unspeakable situation of Christians." In consideration of the picture they were presented with, the Europeans pressured the Sublime Porte to take measures against Albanians and make further concessions to the Christian population. The one to profit were, first and foremost, the Serbs; they did not cease their nationalist activities even after Abdul Hamid officially recognized them as a nation, granting the full status of a *millet*.[603]

The *Ilinden* Uprising and its Impact on the Albanian Question

The Ilinden Uprising or the Macedonian revolt hurts the Albanian question, denying the Albanian ethnic and political integrity. Albanians embrace clandestine warfare in the model of Slavic-Orthodox bands, although this strategy is incompatible with the Albanian national movement. Albanians join Bulgarian and Greek bands; the political platform of Rilindja Kombëtare suffers from the appearance of a clandestine revolutionary movement, a chimera of Russian secret services. The Mürzsteg Agreement of 1903 marks the end of Ottoman sovereignty over the main Balkan vilayets. Vienna proposes an "Albanian sanjak" in Kosova asa zone excluded from the reforms; Belgrade objects, fearing the creation of an "ethnic Albania." Albanian landlords concur with Serbia, sabotaging the Austrian-planned Vienna-Sarajevo-Mitrovica line of the European railway, which would further link the ethnic Albanian territories with Selanik.

The Porte's concessions and the presence of gangs in the Kosova and Manastir vilayets not only bolstered the position of the Balkan countries, but turned them into contenders for greater influence in the historic region of Macedonia. Bulgaria supported the Slavic-Macedonian population and Belgrade and Athens turned to their respective ethnic groups in a rivalry that also aimed Albanian territory. However, the three Balkan countries differed as to strategy. While Serbia and Greece agreed on partitioning Macedonia, they sought the approval of the Great Powers. Therefore, the two nations did

---

[603] See the Imperial Decree (*İrade*) of 1903 granting the Serbs in the Ottoman Empire the status of a nation. Two years later, the same right was granted to the Vlachs. Meanwhile, when Sultan Abdul Hamid II decreed the opening of Serbian- and Vlach-language schools in the vilayets of Kosova and Manastir, he issued an order prohibiting American missionaries from teaching in the Albanian language.

not oppose the *status quo* and came to terms an autonomous Macedonia as an interim solution. But Sofia was more precautious, attempting to seek Europe's involvement in the Macedonia issue with hopes that the province would ultimately unite with Bulgaria. As a result, Bulgarian services attempted to destabilize the region. VMRO committees invited Albanians and Vlachs to join the movement for Macedonia as a state of all peoples. The slogan "Macedonia for Macedonians" did indeed entice Albanians and Vlachs looking for protection from Serbian and Greek ambitions. However, two non-Slavic peoples fell into the Bulgarian trap, since Sofia used the inter-ethnic alliance to hinder plans for an independent Albanian state.

Bringing into play the discontent with reforms, Bulgaria spurred numerous Bulgarian-Macedonian comities to revolt for "freedom or death." After they received the blessing of Bulgarian priests, committees from the regions of Ohër, Kostur, and Serres attacked Ottoman garrisons in the spring of 1903. Then on Saint Elias Day, on August 2, a major uprising broke out in Manastir. The same day the rebels took over the town of Krushevo (Mac.: Kruševo; Alb.: Krusheva; Trk.: Kuruşova), where they proclaimed the so called Krushevo Republic. The commander of the town's rebel forces, Nikola Karev, became the head of the republic.

Soon afterwards, the movement progressed into Thrace, in the Vilayet of Selanik, and continued for three months, until the end of October, when the Sublime Porte intervened against the movement. Ottoman forces quashed the uprising and ruthlessly revenged against the population of the affected regions.

Albanian historiography holds that the *Ilinden* uprising had the support of Albanians residing in the eastern regions. Albanian authors contend that activists from Manastir, Prespa, Struga, and Pogradec, and other regions supplied arms and ammunition to Macedonian troops.[604] Additionally, they note that Albanian troops also began to cooperate with Macedonian insurgents. Themistokli Germenji, an activist who lived in the city of Manastir, assisted the rebels and maintained connections with their formations.[605] Because of the contribution they gave to the *Iliden* uprising, Albanians received important positions in the governing structures that were founded during the time. Of the sixty members of the council of the Krushevo Republic that was established in the town, twenty or one-third were Macedonian

---

[604] H.P.Sh. 2 (Tiranë), 311.
[605] Shukri Rrahimi, *Vilajeti i Kosovës*, 201.

Slavs, another third were Albanians, and the rest were Vlachs. The executive branch of the provisional government consisted of two Slavs, two Albanians (Gjergji Çaçi and Nikolla Balo) and two Vlachs. The chairman, Vangjel Dino, was Albanian.[606] Furthermore, the Krushevo Manifesto, which was proclaimed at the beginning of August, called on all nationalities, and primarily on Albanians to join the uprising, and fight against the common enemy—the Ottomans.[607]

The conclusions of Albanian historians in the 2002 edition of the anthological *Historia e Popullit Shqiptar*, volume II, are not in accordance with the other authors from the region. Slavic-Macedonians do not deny the participation of Albanians in the *Illiden* uprising.[608] However, they consider the role to have been marginal, outside of leading structures. Likewise, Slavic connections with Albanian insurgents from Manastir are not mentioned. Meanwhile, Serbian, Greek, and Ottoman sources seem to complete ignore the presence of Albanians. International publications barely mention the Albanians, describing their role in uprising at best as secondary.[609]

Mistakes and manipulations are numerous in history texts in the Balkans. Nevertheless, they do not deny the common interests of Albanians, Bulgarians, and Vlach in the *Illiden* uprising. The revolt was an effort of the three groups to unite against Serbian and Greek hegemony; separately, all three peoples had the same objectives, too. The Albanians, whose ethnic

---

[606] Shukri Rrahimi, "Format e rezistencës së popullit shqiptar kundër sundimit turk gjatë viteve 1900-1903 dhe karakteri i tyre," *Përparimi* 4 (Prishtinë: 1962), 212.

[607] H.P.Sh. 2 (Tiranë), 312.

[608] Todor Simonovski, "Za učevstvoto na malcinstvoto vo Ilindenskoto vostanie," *Zbornik Ilinden 1903-1905* (Skopje: 1953), 15; Gligor Todorovski, "Sredbi na zblizavanje po Bistra," *Nova Makedonija* (Skopje: 27 July 1959).

[609] For more on the Ilinden Uprising, see: Fikret Adanir, *Die Makedonische Frage: Ihre Entstehung und Entwieklung bis 1908* (Wiesbaden: 1979); Žika Avramovski, *Ratni ciljevi Bugarske i centralne sile* (Beograd: 1985); H. N. Brailsford, *Macedonia: Its Races and their Future* (London: 1906); Richard Cramton, *Bulgaria 1878-1918: A History* (Boulder: 1983); Doglsa Dakin, *The Greek Straggle in Macedonia* 1897-1923 (London: 1971); Alfred Dietrich, *Weltkriegsende an der mazedonischen Front* (Berlin: 1926); Angel Diniev, *Ilindenskata epopeja* [2 volumes] (Bitola: 1987); Ljubiša Doklesti, *Kroz Historiju Makedonie* (Zagreb: 1964); Gustav Hubka, *Die österreichisch-ungarische Offiziermission in Makedonien 1903-1909* (Wien: 1910); Hubka, *Istoria na Makedonskiot Narod* (Skopje: Institut za Nacionalna Istorija, 1969); Ivan Katadjiev, *Sto godina ot formiranjeto na VMRO: Sto godina revolucionerna tradicija* (Skopje: 1993).

territory had always been the target of Serbian occupation, had more motives to cooperate. Yet, the cooperation was not always genuine. Bulgarians talked to Albanians on several occasions on joining forces together, while Sofia's representatives at the same time concluded secret agreements with Serbia on dividing the Albanian territories.

Nevertheless, neither the *Illiden* uprising nor the way the Macedonian question was treated internationally was in the interest of Albanians. Instead, *Illiden* hurt the Albanian cause, especially when Orthodox Albanians embraced the movement. Accepting the revolutionary strategy of the Russian-led Slavic-Orthodox bloc, Albanians suffered two harsh consequences: on the one side, they lost the territorial integrity of what was until then was known as Albania; and on the other side, the Albanian question ceased to be treated as a single issue among the Great Powers.

Beginning with the League of Prizren, the Albanian movement had soought the unification of four vilayets, but such demands were no longer attainable. In the meantime, the Albanian question itself—marked by the disharmony among Albanians—was treated collectively with other national issues (Bulgarian, Serbian, and Greek); and this continued in different forms until present times.

That said, one cannot contend that Albanians had at any point denied the Macedonian cause (in Eastern Rumelia inhabited by Bulgarians and in the southern part of Thessaloniki Vilayet, inhabited by Slavic-Macedonians and Vlachs). To the contrary, the requirement for the unification of the four vilayets was based on the principle of ethnic composition. The Albanian national movement considered Ottoman official statistics that mostly concurred with the data compiled by the Orthodox or the Catholic Church. As Sami Frashëri proclaimed, *Rilindja* leaders demanded to include only the sanjaks where Albanians comprised an absolute majority—more than two-thirds of the population. This principle excluded sanjaks where a third of the inhabitants were Albanians; the national movement relinquished any claims to districts (*kazas*) with an Albanian majority but situated within a sanjak with mixed population as well.

Even though limited, the Albanian participation in the *Ilinden* uprising shed led on three important phenomena: (1) The Albanian national movement had begun to shatter and break apart, while its activists took on serving other movements; (2) Albanians started to abandon *Rilindja*'s political concept of obtaining statehood through a legitimate political process; and (3)

Albanians became predisposed to be used and manipulated by other factors, especially Serbs and Bulgarians.

The tendency of national movement to break apart was not new. Albanians become part of the Greek liberation movement in 1822-1830, turning into a resilient force in the struggle for the Hellenic state. It is well-known that Albanians suffered from their good deed because they entered into the war without any agreement with the Greeks, where the parties could at least formally define their position. It did not last long and Albanians witnessed the betrayal. But this initiated the other extreme, where Albanians from Epirus and Thessaly joined the Ottoman army in the Greek war of 1896-97. Even though the Ottoman Empire returned victorious from the battlefield, Greece was able to achieve autonomy for Crete and was making preparations to revenge against Albanians. Soon, before and during the Balkan wars, the Hellenic state invaded southern Albania and committed atrocities against defenseless population.

Despite the conclusions of Albanian historians, the *Illiden* uprising benefited the idea of Great Bulgaria. Breaking away from their national movement, Albanians suffered on religious divisions as well. Orthodox Albanians participated in the uprising, while Muslim Albanians refused to join. In fact, they viewed the movement as Slavic-Macedonian, pro-Bulgarian and damaging to the Albanian question, and they were right. Regional countries subsidized armed groups to cause a calamity and to draw international attention to the region. Thereby, Serbia, Bulgaria and Greece tried to promote their own solutions in disregard of the Albanian cause. The Balkan monarchies never thought of creating a multiethnic Macedonian state—even when they were discussing about piece and coexistence. In fact, the Bulgarian slogan, "Macedonia to Macedonians," was designed for the benefit of the plurality; in other words, it aimed for a Macedonian state to belong to the Slavic people as the largest group in territory.

The "revolutionary" approach of *chetas, komits,* and bands that Albanians accepted was not in harmony with the strategy of *Rilindja Kombëtare.* Albanian historiography continues to praise the Albanian *chetas* established during that time. This point of view presents the Albanian state as the outcome of clandestine combatants, denying the political and diplomatic activity and the regular armed resistance.[610] Such a view concurs with neither reality nor historical truth. Albanian national movement was determined to

---

[610] For more see H.P.Sh. 3.

pursue a transparent and legal activity from the beginning, but without excluding popular protests or uprisings (that is, the revolts of 1908, 1910, and the general uprising of 1912). *Rilindja* did not seek to create an Albanian state by destroying Ottoman Empire: to the contrary, Albanians desired their autonomy within the Ottoman state and the with endorsement of Great Powers.

The clandestine method concurred with the Slavic-Orthodox strategy of sabotaging the legitimate Albanian demands. Many groups that Albanians established (either with the hope of defending the Albanian population from Slavic and Greek groups or for the purpose of participating in the "Balkan revolution") were in the favor of other neighboring countries. On certain occasions, the Sublime Porte also reaped benefits, but the Albanian cause was damaged under all circumstances. The greatest setback occurred between 1904 and 1908, when the Albanian national movement virtually split into two parallels: the all-popular movement for autonomy and the concerted activities of the clandestine bands.

Soon, the clandestine faction faced the opposition of the mainstream leadership. Moreover, the illegal bands strengthened the position of land-lords and fanatical Islamic in the Kosova and Shkodër vilayets, where the oppressive ruling class entered into secret deals with Serbia "for common war of liberation against the Ottoman invader." This affected even the most powerful supporters of Albania. Until then, Austria-Hungary and Germany thought that armed groups were the exclusive means of pro-Russian states to create calamity. Observing that Albanians began to pursue this activity as well, Berlin endorsed the government of Abdul Hamid, who used the foreign support to oppose Albanian autonomy.

The *Ilinden* Uprising, nevertheless, disclosed another development that, at least for some time, annulled the unjust agreement of the Balkan monarchies to divide Macedonia and broke the equilibrium among those countries. This came about as a result of Ottoman efforts to use Greek *andars*[611] to pacify the Slavs, particularly the Bulgarians. The Sublime Porte initially sent its *başıbozuk* units against the Bulgarian *komitis*. Once the Ottoman units finished their work, plundering the area and causing vast destruction throughout, Rumelia's chief inspector allowed Hellenic militants to enter western Macedonia. Thereafter, Greek *andars* assumed responsibility for

---

[611] The andars were armed Greek units, which were paid for their services. For a period, the Ottoman Empire was tolerant of these groups.

security in the region that had been under the jurisdiction of the Bulgarian Exarchate since 1870. They obligated those regional churches to return to Greek-speaking Constantinople Patriarchate, restoring the Hellenic domination in the area. The Greeks behaved as vengeful tyrant, executing the alleged rebels whenever the locals did not accept the İstanbul church. Greek andars used arms to impose their way of religious ceremonies, when the priests and believers did not agree to conduct services according to the Greek version.[612] The despot of Kostur, Germanos Karavangelis, who was convinced that the fight between the patriarchate and exarchate was not for religious reasons, personally led vicious masses. He openly asserted that the only cause for Macedonia was the future map of Balkan states, after the Ottomans would be purged.[613]

With the suppression of Bulgarian *komits* in Macedonia, the Serbian approach changed significantly. Belgrade had previously vouched for a federated Macedonia, an idea of a Slavic character. But now, Serbs resorted to armed activities with a focus on increasing the influence of the national church. Therefore, they fought not only against Greeks and Bulgarians, but against Albanians and Turks. At the same time, Serbia called for the friendship of Austria-Hungary and Russia, and would continuously strengthen ties with whoever offered greater support for the Serbian goals. In order to connect with one of the powerful monarchies, Belgrade accepted the reforms of the Great Powers for Macedonia. Meanwhile, Serbs continue to deploy armed bands to spur the conflict with Albanians and other ethnic groups. In doing so, Serbia hopped to undermine the plans for Albanian autonomy, diverting the international attention to the issue of protecting ethnic Serbs in the Ottoman Empire. Sultan Abdul Hamid had recently granted them the status of nation, permitting the use of the native language and the appointment of Orthodox metropolitans in Prizren and Shkup.[614] But the Serbian monarchy sought to further its territorial claims, by defining Kosova as the center of medieval Old Serbia.

---

[612] Misha Glenny, *Historia e Ballkanit 1804-1999*, p. 206.

[613] *Ibid.* 206.

[614] The sultan awarded Ottoman Serbs the status of a *millet* by imperial decree (*irade*) in 1903. Then, the use of the Serbian language in education and the restoration of Serbian Orthodox metropolitans in Prizren and Shkup had already been approved (by imperial decree in 1886).

This goal is best revealed by an order that Serbian Prime Minister Nikola Pašić transmitted to diplomatic representatives abroad, directing them, in addition to performing other duties:

> To defend our compatriots from the harmful of the monopoly of Patriarchate institutions, which serve Hellenization at the expense of the non-Greek followers of Patriarchate; and to work against the activities of the Exarchate, whose armed committees have appeared in areas of our interest—Poreç, Kërçova, Drimkol, Dibër, and Qyprili.[615]

The suppression of the *Illiden* Uprising was unable to put an end to the nationalist war; instead, the situation worsened further. The war began to spread, but now with a different equilibrium among the parties. Like Despot Karavangelis, the İstanbul government considered the Bulgarian insurgents as the greatest threat. Bulgarians and Albanians became the main target of Greek and Serbian *komitis*, which also fought against one another but without engaging the Ottoman forces. Their activity became so widespread such that Christian *komitis* almost assumed the role of the state within the territory where they operated.[616]

In a certain way, the Porte's approach favored Serbia's position. When the Ottomans restored the Greek religious authority in the area that in the recent decades had been under Bulgarian control, Belgrade was better situated to increase its own influence. The Slavic population in Macedonia was more inclined to side with the Serbs if choices were reduced to Greece and Serbia. Thereby, Belgrade profited from closer linguistic and religious ties with the Slavic-Macedonians to lead them away from Greeks.

However, the violence in Macedonia soon alarmed the Great Powers, especially Austria-Hungary and Russia, which had the international mandate on the Balkans. After preparations and discussions during September and October 1903, the two empires agreed to demand reforms for the troubled Balkan region. The Mürzsteg Agreement, known after the royal residence near Vienna where parties signed the treaty, provided for a reorganization of the gendarmerie along with other measurements in Macedonia. The Austro-Russian plan called on the Great Powers to deploy professional police officers to establish and command the new law enforcement troops. Im-

---

[615] Glenny, *Historia e Ballkanit . . .*, 207.
[616] *Ibid.* 208.

portantly, Christians would be included in the gendarmerie,[617] and the local population would be disarmed.

The treaty required also that Vienna and San Petersburg appoint two high-ranking civilian officers to serve alongside the Ottoman general inspector in Rumelia. Thereby, Hüseyin Hilmi Pasha would be working together with a Russian and an Austrian, whom would oversee the general situation and implementation of reforms in Macedonia. For major questions the two European officers held the final word such that Austria-Hungary and Russia effectively assumed control over the so-called "Macedonian" vilayets of Kosova, Manastir, and Selanik. The reform territory was divided into five areas, to avoid divergences among Great Powers: Serres, Drama, Thessalonikki, Shkup, and Manastir. Foreign officers, respectively French, English, Russian, Austrians and Italians were appointed for each zone.[618]

The Austro-Russian plan included additional other provisions that called on the Ottoman government to make certain changes, such as reforming the administrative division of Ottoman Europe in such a way as to enable the different nationalities to live within the same administrative boundaries. The agreement defined local autonomy as the principle of the reformation. At the same time, Ottomans were required to guaranty the equal participation of Christians alongside Muslims in courts. Main administrative courts would be supplemented by mixed commissions (with an equal participation of Muslims and Christians), as institutions that reviewed political errors under Russians and Austro-Hungarian control. A crucial requirement was for the Ottoman government to pay for damages caused during the suppression of Albanian and Macedonian insurgents. Compensation would be determined by mixed commissions. In the meantime, Christians would be exempted from taxation for a year, while the Porte would work to encourage refugees and emigrants to return and would rebuild their houses in the countryside. Finally, the Ottomans were requested to disband certain irregular forces in the Balkans and to accept and implement the European demands without delay.[619]

This was the first time that an "international force" with members from Great Powers was appointed to quiet internal calamities in the Balkans and

---

[617] *Ibid.* 206.

[618] H.P.Sh. 2 (Tiranë), 313.

[619] L. Bittner, Chronologisches Verzeichnis der Österreichischen Staatsverträge III (Wien: 1914), 526.

to further the interests of European states.[620] The Mürzsteg Agreement infringed the Sultan's authority in the peninsula. But by this time, Abdul Hamid had already turned in a quasi-vassal of Europe, and for this he was convinced when Vienna and San Petersburg confronted him with their demands. The sultan had no choice: to accept the reforms or to face the wrath of Great Powers. The Russian representative, Goluhovski, agreed that the plan meddled with the internal affairs of the Ottoman Empire, but he considered it indispensable to preserve the *status quo* in the Balkans and to secure a peaceful resolution. The Austrian foreign minister, meanwhile, declared that the two powers did not intend to set up their domination over the region, but would not permit another force to do the same either.

Abdul Hamid accepted the European demands on November 25, 1903. Consequently, the Europeans established two supervisory commissions, one to oversee reform implementation and the other to reorganize the gendarmerie. Austria-Hungary and Russia appointed their agents as well (Austrian representatives Henry Riter and Müller von Roghei and Russian appointee Nikola Demernik).[621] The sultan accepted and decreed the European nominee, General De Gergis, as commander of gendarmerie, on December 30, 1903.[622] Germany also approved of the appointments.[623]

As it will be seen, this mission was the precedent of a long tradition of unsuccessful intervention of the Great Powers in the European part of the Ottoman Empire. As far as the Albanian question is concerned, such interventions have continued until present days, in different forms. The foreign intervention incited uprisings in Albania from the very beginning, especially in the Kosova and Manastir vilayets. Albanians rose again against reforms, because they were associated with new taxes that the Sublime Porte imposed for to sustain the great expenses. At the same time, the Mürzsteg Agreement provided for the disarmament of the highlander population, doubling the incentive for anger. Uprisings began in different parts of Kosova, but th insurgents failed to coordinate their action. In the meantime, the Albanian movement in the Manastir vilayet adapted to the circumstances, applying clandestine strategy of the Slavic and Greek bands. This was a new oppor-

---

[620] Glenny, *Histori e Ballkanit . . .,* 206.

[621] Jacob Ruchti, *Die Reformaktion Österreich-Ungarns und Russlands in Mazedonien 1903-1908* (Gotha: 1918), 2.

[622] *Ibid.* 3.

[623] A. Geschke, *Die Deutsche Politik in Macedonischen Frage bis zur Tükischen Revolution von 1908* (Danzing: 1932), 77.

tunity for the Albanians to act wisely, but the establishment of Albanian *chetas* nonetheless hurt the unity of the national movement and the legitimate requirements for autonomy. In this manner, the national movement became entangled with the "liberation" activity of neighboring states even though the "liberation" war of Slavic and Greek bands meant nothing but the forced annexation of Albanian territories by the region's monarchies (as in fact happened after the First Balkan War).

Nevertheless, the movement in Kosova continued according to the principles of *Rilindja Kombëtare*—by means of a popular uprising. Gjakova was the epicenter this time. A local leader, Sulejman Batusha, directed hundreds of insurgents in an assault against Ottoman garrison, but failed to gain control of the town. Nevertheless, the uprising spread to Peja, Luma, Reka, and even to Mitrovica. With ups and downs, the movement continued throughout spring and summer that year. However, in September, Şemsi Pasha, well-experienced with his expeditions in Kosova, lead Ottoman forces in an intense offensive against the Albanians. In the meantime, the *vali* of Kosovo, Şakir Pasha, concluded an agreement with some of the rebel leaders. As a result, the popular movement was quenched, although some of the resistance centers remained opened, indicating the Albanian disapproval of the reforms.

In general, the 1903-1904 uprisings were limited in space and power. As a result, they did not present difficulties for the Ottoman forces, which were stationed in Albanian territories in greater numbers to assist with the reformation. Nevertheless, Albanians remained an important factor even after internationals arrived in the region to supervise the reform process. The European presence was a direct indication of the spheres of influence. Austria-Hungary concentrated in the Albanian parts, while Russia focused in the Slavic-Macedonian part. For the first time, Italian interests appeared here, too, and they complied with the Russian tsar as far as diminishing Vienna's influence in Albania was concerned. French interests with a pro-Serbian nuance and British ones with a pro-Greek leaning were also detected in the meantime. Berlin maintained its "integrity": in the name of the *status quo*, the German Reich expressed an interest for the stability of the Ottoman Empire. Nevertheless, Germans had their economical story with Ottoman state, and wished for their ally Austria-Hungary to be able to expand its influence.

To spare the Albanians from the reforms, Austria endeavored to create an Albanian sanjak in the Vilayet of Kosova. The entity would include lands with an Albanian majority, from Kaçanik in the south to Kollashin in the north, and would detour then towards Yenipazar and Pleve to the northwest. Nevertheless, after the Austrian military attaché, Baron Gizel, presented the idea to the International Military Commission,[624] Serbia and Russia stood adamantly opposed to the proposal. As a result, owing also to Italian support, the Russian were able to defeat the Austrian motion for an Albanian sanjak.[625]

The Russian-Italian approach in the International Commission did not cause Austro-Hungary to give up. Vienna instantly demanded a suspension of reforms not only in the Shkodër and Janina vilayets, but also in the Albanian areas of Kosova and Manastir. This created unexpected disharmony among the Great Powers, but the Austrians were determined to contain the Italian influence. Thus, in February 1904, the Commission accepted Vienna's request.[626] Accordingly, on April 5, the Military Commission produced set the final borders of the zones where reforms were to be implemented. Austria-Hungary took control of the Sanjak of Shkup, Russia was put in charge of Salonica, the British were stationed in Ohër, the French in Serres, and Italy assumed responsibility for the Sanjak of Manastir.[627]

General De Gergis demanded that the regions of Prishtina and Prizren be included in the reforms. However, Austria-Hungary objected, refusing to make any concessions to the Italians on Albanian territories. The Italian general argued that the Mürzsteg Agreement did not foresee the exclusion of certain areas from the process. He maintained that Russia would not have agreed to such a scenario, given that reforms were necessary to "preserve the Serbian character" of the vilayet.[628]

The Ottoman Empire also demanded reforms in Kosova. The Porte distrusted Austria-Hungary, and therefore proposed to the Great Powers that the Albanian areas be included in the reformation process. Likewise, the

---

[624] *Diplomatische Aktenstücke* (Wien: 1906), 27.

[625] Ruchti, *op. cit.*, 6.

[626] Namely the following lands in the vilayets of Kosova and Manastir were exempted from the reforms: the sanjak of Korça (except for the Kostur kaza therein), the sanjak of Elbasan, the western part of the kaza of Ohër, sanjaks of Dibër, Prizren, and Prishtina, the southern and southwestern parts of the sanjak of Peja, and the kazas of Plevle and Senica in the sanjak of Yenipazar.

[627] *Diplomatische Aktenstücke* (Wien: 1906), 36.

[628] *Die Grosse Politik der Europäischen Kabinette 1871-1914*, Collection of Diplomatic Acts of the German Foreign Ministry, vol. 22, nr. 7390.

Ottoman government demanded that representatives of all Great Powers oversee the process.[629] From the standpoint of the imperial interest, this seems paradoxical given that the international presence had caused the Ottoman Empire to lose its authority in the region. However, the Ottoman feared that Austria-Hungary planned to create an autonomous vilayet of Albania, on the border of Bosnia-Herzegovina. Such a development would enable Vienna to create a long corridor from Sarajevo to Shkodër, Prishtina, Shkup, Manastir, and all the way to Janina.

The dual monarchy easily managed to suspend the reformation in the Albanian areas, since Russia was already occupied with the Japanese war. Saint Petersburg tried in a way to console Serbia, promising continued support for its interests in Kosova.[630] Under such circumstances, however, the Russian words lacked much significance, and Belgrade continued to protest. It insisted that reforms were implemented in all of Kosova, requesting further that Italian and French officers oversee the process.[631]

The non-implementation of reforms in the Albanian areas demonstrated their ethnic makeup (the Great Powers acknowledged this fact, even though they did not implicitly mention it). Likewise, this presented a great victory for the Albanian national movement, but was unable to extinguish the threat of an invasion from the expansionist neighbors. To the contrary, Belgrade, Sofia, and Athens, with the support and under the tutelage of Russia, did the utmost to impede the Albanian movement. Particularly, the Balkan monarchies had their eyes on Kosova, since they knew that the vilayet could become the birthplace of the Albanian state, and this had already appeared briefly with the Provisional Albanian Government in Prizren in 1881.

The Albanian Dilemmas on the Eve of Revolution

The Mürzsteg Agreement envisions a reorganization of administrative divisions; Serbia, Bulgaria, and Greece rush to create "new facts" by violence that would favor their state objectives. Albanians form their own chetas; the Committee for the Freedom of Albania adopts the Slavic-Macedonian

---

[629] M. B., *Stara Srbija i reforme* (Beograd: 1906), 7, cited in Emin Pllana, *Kosova dhe reformat në Turqi*, 195.

[630] Vladimir Čorović, *Odnosi Srbije i Austro-Ugarske u XX veku* (Beograd: 1936), 31.

[631] *Ibid.* 36.

model, becoming thereby part of the Balkan chaos. Kosova is divided into "reform" and "exempt" zones, while Albanians undermine the reform efforts in the vilayet. The Great Powers split on the issue of the Yenipazar and Baghdad railways, given by concession to Austria-Hungary and Germany. Ismail Qemali fails in efforts to ally with Greece. Vienna demands and end to the clandestine movement; Romania and Bulgaria hope to get Albanians involved in plans against Serbia and Greece. Young Turks obtain the support of Albanian chetas for the anti-Hamidian revolution; Albanian "revolutionaries" substitute regime change in the empire for their oath to liberate Albania by war; instead, they resume the plans of Rilindja Kombëtare for autonomy within the Ottoman state.

The Treaty of Mürzsteg, in addition reaffirming the current balance of power in the Balkans, had some side effects that grew increasingly significant over the years.[632] If, for the Great Powers, Mürzsteg was practical exercise in administering crises, Greece, Serbia, and Bulgaria misinterpreted the agreement, mainly in accordance with their expansionist ambitions. Balkan states hoped to benefit from Article C of the agreement, which permitted administrative borders "to be revised to create sustainable groupings of different nations."[633]

The regional monarchies perceived the treaty provision on border change as a geopolitical test to finally partition Macedonia among them. When the Great Powers later decided not to implement the Mürzsteg reforms in several Albanian counties of Kosovo, the Balkan countries objected, relying on statistics and other publications on Kosova's demographics. But the picture provided in the publications was not accurate: neighboring states lay claims of a mixed population, with a slight Serbian or Greek majority. To achieve their intentions, they presented redacted documents and medieval land deeds based on manipulated registers of churches and other Christian monuments, which also belonged to Albanians. The fabricated data intended to convince the Great Powers to implement the reforms in the exempt areas, too, by denying their ethnic Albanian population.[634] However, Austria-Hungary insisted that the planned changes would not be implemented in the

---

[632] Glenny, *Histori e Ballkanit . . .*, 208.

[633] *Ibid.* 208.

[634] For more on manipulation with census registers and the fabrication of demographic statistics, see vol. 1 of the series, chapter on Albanians and Slavic invaders on the 13th and 14th centuries.

central part of Kosova and the Shkodër Vilayet. The dual monarchy, being the initial proponent of the reforms and the ultimate authority in determining the territories involved in the process, prevailed in keeping certain Albanian areas exempt. Vienna had its own statistics, diplomatic means, and the press propaganda, which proved that the majority of the population in the disputed regions.[635] Moreover, taking advantage of the international situation, with Russia at war with Japan, Austria-Hungary assumed the supervision of the reform process in the communities subject to the Mürzsteg Agreement. The Austrian mandate included the areas from Yenipazar and Albania's northern border to the Kriva Palanka and Kratovo.[636] The Sanjak of Shkup was also under Vienna's direct supervision. This district, which separated Macedonia with Serbia, included the predominantly-Albanian *Kaza* of Kaçanik, an important strategic territory that enabled Austria to penetrate to the east.

Since Bulgaria was already defeated in the *Ilinden* Uprising, the main competition was now between Serbia and Greece. To prove the presence of ethnic Serbs and Greeks, Belgrade and Athens used their bands. Some armed groups were organized in native Serb and Greek communities, but others came from Serbia and Greece from time to time, with the main purpose of ethnic cleansing the region through murders and tortures. The two Orthodox nations sought to decrease the number of Albanians for strategic purposes. Bands acted in regions that the Belgrade and Athens propaganda claimed as Slavic or Hellenic territories. With this in mind, Serbia and Greece delivered fabricated data to the International Commission and European governments to convince them of the ethnic nature of the land. Serbia claimed the disputed areas as "medieval Serb territories," that even though "reduced by the *Arnaut* violence through the centuries," proved the Serb character of Kosova. Athens similarly that local Greeks in Albanian districts had difficult conditions of life. Both Balkan countries claimed that the ethnic minorities were in the hands of the merciless and they needed to defend themselves by recruiting guards for the communities and monasteries. In fact, the guards were not defensive formations of desperate people faced with no alternative, as claimed by propaganda; they were well-organized *chetas* created by Belgrade and Athens. Moreover, the armed

---

[635] Emin Pllana, *Kosova dhe reformat në Turqi*, 198.
[636] *Ibid.* 199.

groups included in their ranks military officers from both Serbia and Greece, who served the expansionist goals of their states.[637]

Furthermore, the *chetas* had already begun to act in regions where there were no Serbs at all. Their aim was to provoke the Albanians to revenge against Serbs in surrounding areas, so that the propaganda could then accuse the Albanians of crimes against other ethnic groups. For this purpose, Serbian bands went as far as vandalizing the Orthodox churches. Serbia then would point its finger at the Albanians, utterly disregarding that the medieval churches and other religious monuments in Kosova also belonged to majority ethnic group (most Albanians were Christians and belonged to Orthodox Church prior to Ottoman rule). They protected Orthodox sites even when there were no Serbs or they were only a small minority in Kosova. Albanians look after monasteries and churches when the Serb Patriarchate relocated outside Kosova in the 17th century. During this time, it was Albanian voivodes (*i.e.*, custodians) that made great sacrifices to guard the cultural heritage (including prominent monasteries in Deçan, Peja, and Deviq), for they considered them part of their ancient spiritual tradition.[638]

For their efforts at destabilizing the Albanian Vilayets to succeed, the regional countries were compelled to cooperate with one another. Serbia, intending to keep Bulgaria away from the vilayets of Kosova and Manastir, resumed collaboration with Sofia. This was a deliberate move in Belgrade's attempts to prevent an alliance between Bulgarians and Albanians. Serbia suspected that Austria-Hungary and Germany, which maintained an interest in the ethnic groups, could encourage Albanians and Bulgarians to cooperate.

Belgrade hence resorted to bilateral relations and, on April 30, 1904, signed a treaty with Sofia. While the document recited the parties' "support for the reform actions," the true intent was to encourage the implementation of changes in the entire Vilayet of Kosova.[639] This agreement was followed a month later by another treaty. The Slavic states agreed that Serbia would take the Vilayet of Kosova as a compensation for Bulgaria's expansion in East

---

[637] For more on Belgrade's sabotage acitvities through *chetas* in Kosova and their infiltration in Serbian enclaves, churches, and monasteries, see Branko Perunović, *Pisma srpskih konzula iz Prištine 1890-1900* (1985).

[638] For more on the topic, see: Skënder Rizaj, *Kosova gjatë shekujve . . .*; Gaspër Gjini, *Raško Prizrenska Biskupija* (Zagreb: 1968); Odette Marquet, *Pjetër Bogdani – letra dhe dokumente* (Shkodër: 1997); Noel Malcom, *Kosova: një histori e shkurtër* (Prishtinë: 2001).

[639] Vladimir Čorović, *Borba za nezavisntost Balkana* (Beograd), 126.

Rumelia.[640] Prior to that, Belgrade also reached an agreement with Cetinje on dividing the Albanian territories with Montenegro. On February 2, 1904, parties agreed that Serbia would annex the Vilayet of Kosova, including the Sanjak of Yenipazar, and a part of the Vilayet of Manastir.[641]

The actions taken by the Balkan countries provoked Austria's response. Because the Slavic states were under Russian influence, Vienna compelled Russia to send a joint protest note to Belgrade and Sofia; a note was also delivered to Athens. The empires demanded that the Balkan states cease the guerrilla actions, which endangered the *status quo* that the Great Powers wished to preserve further.[642]

In its response, Belgrade promised to create favorable conditions for the reforms, but also reiterated its demand that all of Kosova be included in the process. Serbia claimed that "the *chetas* were not formed by the neighboring countries, but by local Serbs and Christians to defend themselves from the Albanian violence." Further, the response reminded the Great Powers that they should take the Albanians into consideration if they wanted stability in the region.[643]

In the meantime, the Sublime Porte appointed a commission, headed by Ali Riza Pasha, to reorganize police forces in Kosova (in the exempt areas). According to a plan devised by Hilmi Pasha, the vilayet's gendarmerie would comprise of 2,800 members; two percent or 202 officers would be Christians. Meanwhile, a campaign for tax collection would also begin and the population would be disarmed.[644]

As a result, the partial exemption from the Mürzsteg reforms did not spare Kosova of multiple difficulties: on the one side, Serb, Greek, and Bulgarian bands had already infiltrated the vilayet and, on the other, the Sublime Porte tried to implement the previous, equally unpopular reforms that Abdul Hamid announced in his infamous "Rumelia hoax" decree.

These measures, particularly the confiscation of weapons, provoked massive protests and uprisings among the Albanian population in most parts of Kosova. In Peja, crowds attacked the city prison and called for the mutesa-

---

[640] Liljana Aleksić, "O srpsko-Crnogorskim pregovorima o savezu 1904-1905," *Istoria XX veka: Zbornik radova I* (Beograd: 1959), 338, cited in Emin Pllana, *Kosova dhe reformat në Turqi*, 199.

[641] *Ibid.* 199.

[642] Jovan Jovanović, *Borba za narodno ujedinjenja 1903-1908* (Beograd: 1938), 147.

[643] *Ibid.* 148.

[644] Emin Pllana, *Kosova dhe reformat në Turqi*, 200.

rif to leave. In Vushtrri, rebels murdered the kaymekam and ousted the non-native administrative employees and similar actions occurred in other parts of Kosova, too.

The Sublime Porte ordered Omer Pasha to mount a counterattack. As a commander of nine battalions, he attacked Prizren and other parts of Dukagjin, where twenty-five rebel leaders were arrested and sent to Anatolia.[645] In the meantime, the Ottomans interned 150 rebels from Peja and 153 from Gjakova and its vicinity.[646]

In the non-Mürzsteg areas of Kosova, where the Ottoman held its authority and promised to undertake reforms, the situation began to worsen due to the intrusions of Serbian consuls. The diplomats came to Prishtina, where they collaborated with Russian consuls to clearly mobilize the Serb population, even though the Serbs were just a privileged minority in Kosova. Following the consuls' instruction, local Serbs formed the *National Council* that, in addition to opposing taxes, insisted on *self-defense chetas*, claiming the people needed to provide for their own safety and security because the Ottoman authorities had failed. In the *kazas* of Sjenica and Yenipazar, the Slav population, refused to pay taxes and supported the actions of *chetas*. In fact, Austria-Hungary blamed the turmoil directly on a Shkup-based Russian consul and the Serb consuls in Prishtina. Vienna contended that the Slavic diplomats did not keep an eye on their own assigned areas, but paid attention to Peja and Sjenica, where they encouraged local Serbs to join insurgent groups.[647]

The reform areas under Austrian control (notably the Sanjak of Shkup) were also troubled. On nine *kazas* of the Kosova Vilayet, the reorganization of the gendarmerie did not occur according to the plan because of the local reaction. Albanians believed that the new measures did not intend to improve the condition for all inhabitants, but that their main aim was to bestow great privileges upon Christians and to help partition Albania. For example, the dissatisfied population complained that Ottoman government exempted Christians from taxes for a full year, while it continued to confiscate weapons from the majority. This angered the Albanians since they were the only target of the disarmament campaign, whereas Serbs were unaffected even when they joined *chetas* acting in the Karadak of Shkup and the Presheva Valley.

---

[645] Hasan Kaleshi, Hans Jürgen, "Vilajeti i Prizrenit," *Përparimi* 2-3 (Prishtinë: 1967), 187, cited in Pllana, *Kosova dhe reformat në Turqi*, 201.

[646] *Ibid.* 201.

[647] *Ibid.* 206.

The Ottoman Empire presented trouble for both the Albanians as well the Great Powers. With exception of military campaigns, the Porte was uninterested in undertaking any action to implement the economic and judicial reforms to which it had committed. Indeed, the economic package was not clearly defined and the existing provisions were insufficient to create a tax system that could serve the reforms. However, disadvantages did not warrant the Porte's failure to pursue the right way for making crucial changes, which would initially help regain the trust of the people, whose opinion was a precondition to success. The Great Powers—even though they had their own interests in the region—knew that only changes in the economic plan could improve the living condition, but such progress would not be possible without the sincere and determined cooperation of the Ottoman Empire. Therefore, as early as January 1905, ambassadors of Austria-Hungary and Russia in İstanbul drafted a project about financial reforms for the vilayets of Kosova, Manastir, and Salonica, envisioning immediate measures to be taken in agreement with the Porte Sublime and the Ottoman Bank.[648]

The Austrian-Russian project stipulated that every sanjak and *kaza* was to have its own budget. Revenue from the three vilayets and the Thessaloniki customs would be deposited in local branches of the Ottoman Bank in Thessaloniki, Manastir, and Shkup. These banks would handle all official transactions, including salary payments for the administration, army, gendarmerie, reform officers, and other government employees. The general inspector and the civil agents were assigned the responsibility to control the vilayet budgets.

When the two ambassadors presented the project for the Ottoman approval, however, the Porte Sublime conditioned the proposed reforms with an agreement to increase import tariffs from eight to eleven percent.[649] Austria-Hungary and Russia initially refused the trade imposts, but later coalesced as Britain expressed an interest to become involved in the process. London was not pleased that only Vienna and Saint Petersburg were to supervise the economic reforms and asked for more comprehensive oversight by the international community—with representatives of all six Great Powers. The British proposal did not see the light, but it greatly encouraged

---

[648] Radoslav Popov, *Austro-Ungarija i reformite v Evropskejska Turcija 1903-1908* (Sofia: 1974), 110, cited in Emin Pllana, *Kosova dhe reformat në Turqi*, 211.
[649] *Ibid.* 212.

the Porte to stand its grounds as much as possible. Italy, which disliked the Austro-Hungarian domination, also favored the English approach in a way. If Vienna were able to put Albania under its influence, Rome would have no means of penetrating in the Balkans, as it intended for a long time. But Italy eventually accepted the compromise reached after an international financial commission consisting of civil agents and members from all Great Powers was formed to assist the Ottoman reforms.

In March 1905, the Great Powers set the commission's rules, mandating a two-year term with headquarters based in Thessaloniki. Six members were appointed to the commission: J.P. Grizinger represented Germany; France sent L. Steeg; F. Maissa was the Italian delegate; Harvey sat in for Britain, Openheimer for Austria-Hungary, and N. Demernik for Russia. The Ottoman Empire, which also had a seat in the body, appointed Cemal Bey. The commission's duty was to observe the situation in the vilayets and supervise the administration in tax collection. The financial reform package included fifteen points, with the most important relating to the Porte's commitment to implement new laws on mines, customs, and tax revenue allocation to ensure that the vilayets of Rumelia received a greater share to sustain development opportunities. The Great Powers, meanwhile, agreed to the increased import tariffs.

The harmony about the reforms did not sustain and the process fell apart along the way, when The Porte Sublime gave certain advantages to Austria-Hungary and Germany. The two German-speaking empires received important concessions for constructing railways. Vienna gained the right to build the route from Yenipazar to Mitrovica, which linked Kosova with Bosnia and Herzegovina in the north and Thessaloniki in the south, while Berlin earned the permit to work on the Baghdad line.

The railway projects opened way to a rearrangement of the spheres of interest and disagreements among the Great Powers that eventually led to the Balkans wars and World War I. Italy was not satisfied with the Balkan line, because the railway granted Austria-Hungary unrestricted access to the Aegean Sea. Meanwhile, Britain opposed the Baghdad railway, which gave Germans the upper hand over the affluent energy resources of the Middle East. This was a good opportunity for the British to withdraw from the European consensus on maintain the *status quo*, and Russia would likely support London in such a move. But the tsar's power had greatly declined after his defeat in the Japanese war and the once powerful Russian empire had completely fallen under the influence of Austria-Hungary and especially Germany.

That is in fact how the Sublime Porte had benefited from the Russian decline and the British limitations in order to act on its own, furthering the cooperation with the German-speaking countries. Investments from Vienna and Berlin helped the Ottomans regain the lost power, by modernizing the country in accordance with the German development concepts, among the most dynamic in the West. Yet, this also highlighted the ideological inconsistency of Abdul Hamid's regime. One of the one hand, he sought to strengthen the Islamic caliphate and continue his absolutist rule and, on the other, he tried to reform the country economically and financially after the German system; in other words, the sultan aspired for a well-organized western state, governed by an eastern despotic government. In this spirit, the sultan permitted the new railway lines. Within five years, Abdul Hamid had two friendly meetings with the German head of state, Keiser Wilhelm II, and reached several long-term trade and economic agreements, permitting Germans to invest in the east. In the meantime, Germany also earned a four-year deal to modernize the Ottoman army with a focus on military technology and organization. Adding the Baghdad railway to the abundance of Ottoman-German initiatives, Berlin became İstanbul's main ally in the efforts to modernize the Ottoman Empire.

The railway concessions caused concern even among the Balkan countries, especially Serbia. Belgrade complained to the Russians, and later to Italy, that the Yenipazar line threatened the regional balances, while it assisted in "the peaceful invasion of Kosova" and created "transportation links with Bosnia and Herzegovina and, ultimately, with German Europe."[650]

Paradoxically, Serbia received the greatest support against the Austrian railway from among Albanian landowners in Kosova. The opposition of a few noblemen indeed became a main reason for this project to fail. But, Albanians were the greatest victims of the failure, because the railway would have ruled out Serbia's invasion of Albanian territories. Clearly, had the Yenipazar-Thessaloniki line been completed, Kosova would have a crucial node to Austrian interests an Vienna would not permit Serbia to invade Kosova in 1912, let alone, agree to the 1913 decision of the Ambassadors' Conference that awarded the vilayet to Belgrade.

While Belgrade sought by all means to undermine the project it decried as a "German plot against strategic Serb interests,"[651] local landowners and

---

[650] Jovan Jovanović, *Borba za narodna ujedinjenja 1903-1908* (Beograd: 1938), 148.
[651] *Ibid.* 149.

Islamist clergymen in Kosova prompted Albanians to protest and revolt against the European railway. Large numbers of rebels headed from Mitrovica to Prishtina demanding that the Austrian plan be abandoned. Albanian conservatives opposed the railway with the reasoning that "Germans were ruining the empire from within" and were hence affecting Albanian interests at the same time. On the other hand, the Porte Sublime and the sultan himself regarded the project as a possibility to foster development in the vilayets and benefit from improved communication links with the rest of the empire, with the railway being the fastest means to transport commodities.[652]

The opposition to the railway and reforms pushed the Albanians further into the limelight of Italy, which was in most aspects compatible with the intentions of Serbia and Greece. The Balkan countries also had the backing of France and Great Britain, two powers aiming to hinder the Ottoman ties with Vienna and Berlin, even more so when Russia was supportive of such relations. The foreign influence consequently led to further disagreements among Albanians. Italians supported landowners and the Islamist clerics who were also in good terms with Serbia and Greece. On the other end were the reformists, consisting mainly of intellectuals and members of the emerging middle class, tied to Austria-Hungary and Germany. Nevertheless, the Albanian cooperation with the German powers was not an easy pursuit, for the wealthy conservatives and Islamist imams—influenced by Slavic-Orthodox around Bosnia and Herzegovina—increasingly vilified Vienna and Berlin as "devourers on the Ottoman Empire."

Regional developments following the Mürzsteg Agreement affected the position of the Albanian national movement. Namely, the demands for equality and autonomy within the Ottoman Empire were relegated to the second plan or replaced by calls for "national liberation." This motto demanding secession from the Ottoman state emerged more like a populist slogan rather than as a result of a clear political platform. Supporters of the new approach were a significant number of radical patriots, mainly members of the middle class, including teachers at Turkish schools, employees of the state administration, journalists, and well-educated youth. Among the activists, there were also Ottoman military officers dissatisfied with the turmoil and bloodshed that Serb, Greek and Bulgarian *chetas* were causing in the country, mainly against the Muslims. As a result, Albanian radicals

---

[652] For more on the protests and uprisings against the northern railway, see H.P.Sh. 2 (Tiranë), 312-316.

initiated the formation of secret organization purporting to lead a guerilla war through native *chetas*.[653]

In Macedonia, the Great Powers as well as the Ottoman Empire focused on improving the lives of Christian peoples (*i.e.*, Serbs, Greeks and Bulgarians), and hence ignored the Albanians (Muslims and Christians alike). The latter were treated in accordance with the interests of Christian peoples, which nonetheless were a minority in the troubled vilayets. The situation warranted concern and reaction, as was indeed the case with the ongoing protests and uprisings, especially in Kosova. But, the popular movements in vilayet—in exempt as well as reform areas—not only failed to improve the circumstances, but also deepened the dissatisfaction of the people who were under the impression that the greater the chaos caused by the *chetas*, the more numerous the concessions to the Serbs, Bulgarians, and Greeks would become.

While Balkan states were developing a relentless propaganda in sanjaks already were proclaimed "Macedonian," Albanian nationalists were necessarily influenced by the Slavic-Macedonian movements that fought a guerrilla war through their *chetas*. The Austrian vice-consul in Manastir, Kral, observed the Slavic-Macedonian influence on Albanians, especially among government employees and military officers.[654] Later, the diplomat reported to Vienna that Albanian Christians were approaching the Slavic-Macedonians, becoming increasingly involved with foreign clubs in the country rather than developing an Albanian national propaganda. Kral warned that the Albanians would also organize secret committees, entirely under Slavic-Macedonian influence and supervision.[655] And, it did not take long and the model of *chetas* and *komitis*—already employed by Serbia, Greece, and Bulgaria with the aim of gaining lands in Macedonia—found its way among a group of Albanians from the Vilayet of Manastir.

It is likely that a faction of radical Young Turks adopted the *cheta* warfare, too. Many of the sultan's opponents looked forward to an uprising that would lead to regime change, and they may have encouraged the Albanians to react. Many Albanian officers in the imperial army were already discontent with Abdul Hamid and could lend a hand to the Young Turk Movement. Indeed, as it will be discussed later, high ranking officers soon came into contact with the Albanian *chetas*.

---

[653] H.P.Sh. 2 (Tiranë), 317.

[654] *See* HHStA, PA XII/ 312, Kral, Manastir, 3/2/1899.

[655] *Ibid.*

Although the Albanian armed groups called for "national liberation," their activity was not in accordance with the political program of the *Rilindja Kombëtare*, which sought autonomy within the Ottoman Empire. By adopting the clandestine war, best fitted to the Slavic-Orthodox interests, Albanians were the main victims of this war. The illegal movement of *chetas* and unknown *komits* aimed to create an atmosphere of insecurity and that was precisely what Serbia, Bulgaria, and Greece desired, even though Albanian activists believed they were performing a patriotic sacrifice.

The neighboring countries had already laid their claims on the Albanian vilayets. To achieve their goals, the Balkan monarchies used guerrilla war so that Macedonia could turn into a "typical Balkan saloon," where murder is rampant and murderers are unknown. The only strand of clarity in this obscure picture was the shared intention of the neighbors to prevent Albanians from forming an autonomous state. With or without notice of their unneighborly vicinity, many Albanians also joined the Balkan conspiracy.

Certainly, it was difficult for Albanians to avoid the provocations of the "Balkan saloon," in light of the violence of Serbian, Bulgarian, and Greek *chetas* and ongoing killings and mistreatment compelled Albanian patriots to create their own armed units.[656] The Albanian response was hence a necessary counteraction to the destructive external pressure of the neighboring states.

More significant, however, was that the reaction introduced a new strategy in the Albanian movement, abandoning plans for autonomy in favor of a liberation war against the Ottoman Empire. The national movement reverted to illegality and lost coordination. The İstanbul Committee did not approve of the *cheta* actions, while regional divisions were also threatened. The Ghegs, as Albanians in the north, differed from many of their southern counterparts, the Tosks, as to the methods used. The vilayets of Shkodër and Kosova preserved the course of an open popular movement, relying on protests but also overt uprisings. The vilayets of Manastir and Janina, on the other hand, had adopted the clandestine revolutionary model of the Slavic-Macedonian gangs, whose goal was to bring down the Ottoman Empire by internal strife and—to the detriment of Albanians—to prevent any plans for Albania's autonomy.

---

[656] Official documents between 1905 and 1907 note that various armed gangs in the eastern parts of the Albanian vilayets, from Shkup in the north to the Greek border in the south, killed over 3,800 people, or one in every 1,500 inhabitants.

The underground model was approved when Albanian activists formed their first secret organization in November 1905. The Manastir Committee, formally the Committee of the Freedom of Albania (Alb: *Komiteti "Për Lirinë e Shqipërisë"*), was formed in Manastir under the initiative of Bajram "Bajo" Topulli, principal at the Turkish gymnasium in the city. Other founders included Colonel Halil Bërzeshta, head of the pharmaceutical service of the Third Ottoman Army Corps; Fehmi Zavalani, businessman; Sejfi Vllamasi Novosella, city veterinary; Gjergj Qiriazi, interpreter/translator at the Austrian consulate in Manastir; and, Jashar Bitincka, teacher at the Manastir gymnasium. The men, all local patriots, admitted they did not consult the İstanbul Committee on forming the clandestine group.[657]

The Manastir Committee approved its program called *Kanonizma*, relying on armed patriotic *chetas* to liberate Albania from the Ottoman Empire. The group, nonetheless, did not renounce demands for education in the Albanian language and related cultural matters that would require an agreement with the Ottoman authorities.

The clandestine organization tried to expand its activity, deploying representatives who established ties with scores of patriots throughout Albania. The committee also built relations with societies abroad, particularly with immigrants in Bucharest and Sofia. The diaspora communities were highly supportive, given that the countries where they lived hoped to utilize the Albanians to further state policies. Both Romania and Bulgaria encouraged Albanians to follow the type of program outlined at Manastir.

Given the involvement of the Balkan states, Austria-Hungary condemned much of the committee's work. Vienna did not wish to allow Slavic and Orthodox nations (especially Serbia) to take advantage of the Albanian people. In guidelines provided in April 1906, Foreign Minister Goluhovski requested Austrian diplomats in Albania to reject the revolutionary goals of the Manastir Committee and insisted that the group "do not abandon the objective of the peaceful movement and do not use means of violence."[658] Vienna, nevertheless, supported the cultural aspects of the Manastir organization. The dual monarchy promised financial assistance to build Albanian schools, pay teachers, and publish textbooks. Notably, Albanians received commitments to sustain the girls' school in Korça and help increase its capacity.

---

[657] *Ibid.* 317.
[658] *Ibid.* 318.

In contrast to the Manastir Committee, the national movement in Kosova continued to rely on popular protests and uprisings, now directed against the reforms adopted by the Porte. Besides reiterating their persistent political demands, Kosovars also objected the tax collection efforts and the plan to disarm the local population. In fall 1905, revolts erupted, as a result, in Gjakova, Peja, and Prizren. The Porte was able to return calm by declaring an amnesty for the political deportees, most of whom were from the affected areas. In the spring, however, turmoil broke out again. When the government levied new taxes on livestock to generate revenue for education and arms purchases for the military, the local population rose up again. In the initial encounter with rebels in the Dukagjin area, Ottoman forces lost fifty men and had over 200 wounded. However, as the uprising then spread east to the Sanjak of Prishtina, Albanians loyal to the sultan intervened at high levels of government to reclaim peace in Kosova. Isa Boletini, who at the time served as chief guard of the imperial palace, successfully lobbied at the Porte to have new taxes suspended in the exempt zones.[659]

The imperial government kept its promise and fragile peace was maintained in Kosova, lasting through the year. But the Serb and Bulgarian *chetas* active in the vilayet once again provoked a conflict and Belgrade had it both ways: in the eye of the world, it supported the reforms and called for the changes to be implemented throughout the vilayet, but secretly, it deployed armed groups to destabilize Kosova. The situation worsened around Mitrovica and Sjenica, when bandits attacked police stations and private property of local residents, but Belgrade blamed the Albanians instead.

Nevertheless, there were obvious changes between exempt and reform areas. In the lands excluded from the Mürzsteg reforms, the Ottoman Empire maintained the order, whereas in the zones under Austrian, Russian, or Italian supervision. There, the situation became increasingly unclear as the population reacted (according to instructions by Balkan governments). The European representatives authorized with implementing the reforms were also faced with a rising activity among *chetas*, which already were fighting more among themselves than against the Ottoman Empire or the foreigner powers.

In such circumstances, the Committee for the Freedom of Albania also announced its decision to form what the founding instrument called "armed troops." These *chetas* would mainly operate in the mountains, but would also

---

[659] *Ibid.* 318.

have their covert units in the countryside. The first *cheta* was formed in April 1906, in Kolonja, near Korça; the group consisted of twenty members with Bajo Topulli as their commander. Another *cheta* headed by Fehmi Zavalani and Sali Butka was also formed in Kolonja.[660]

The radius of Albanian *chetas* initially included the areas from Kolonja to Gora and Leskovik, but later expanded further into other parts of southern Albania. The first actions took place in these areas, including the assassination of the Greek metropolitan bishop of Korça, Photon. Bajo Topulli's *cheta* killed the church leader to revenge against the Greek chauvinists, who massacred the patriot Papa Kristo Negovani and his followers.

The Ottoman government reacted to the violence, taking strong and efficient measures against the Albanian *chetas*. After reserve units from the Manastir garrison took part in several skirmishes with the guerrilla groups, the Porte managed to neutralize the armed branch of the Manastir Committee. The organization lacked the foreign support enjoyed by the Slavic and Greek *chetas* that, whenever threatened from the Ottomans, retreated into Serbia, Bulgaria, or Greece and recovered with the help of the respective governments. To begin with, Albanian *komitis* lacked universal support of their own people. In Kosova, for instance, the population identified *chetas* with Serbian and Bulgarian groups; for the Slavic gangs, commanded by Belgrade and hosted by the Serb Orthodox Church, had indeed brought an awful experience to Kosovars.

Ottoman authorities, therefore, managed to imprison a good portion of members and supporters of the Manastir Committee. Among those arrested members in July 1906 were many officers of the Manastir garrison and government employees who joined the Committee. In January 1907, the official newspapers of the Vilayet of Manastir published a list with names of activists wanted by the authorities; patriots on the lam included Bajo and Çerçiz Topulli, Beqir and Sali Butka, Islam Anfi, Ahmet Zylfiqari, Dervish Ismaili, Fejzo Bej, and Mersin Abdyli.

Following the crackdown, many of the leaders of the *chetas* the Manastir Committee left the country. The Topulli brothers fled to Sofia and Bucharest. They stayed in the Balkans until 1907, and then moved to Paris and shortly after to the United States. Other fighters, such as Idriz effendi Gjakova, also sought refuge in Bulgaria.[661]

---

[660] *Ibid.* 320.

[661] *Ibid.* 320.

As revolutionary leaders wound up in jail or in exile, the weaknesses and inadequacy of the clandestine war as opposed the traditional war became clear. The Albanian *chetas*, which launched an ill-planned war for liberation without a national consensus, not only failed to secure foreign support, but elicited suspicion that the whole movement was organized by hostile neighbors.

The Albanian national movement apparently ran the risk of an internal rivalry over the extent of cooperation with the other Balkan nations. Local warlords joined forces with Bulgarians and Greeks under the banner of "national liberation" in a move that threatened the position of national leaders, such as Ismail Qemali and Hasan Prishtina, who remained loyal to the legitimate, peaceful demands for autonomy within the empire.

The Manastir Committee also presented the first confrontation between the concept of a nation state formed by means of political and diplomatic tools, but without excluding popular resistance, and the goal of liberation from Ottoman rule through a guerrilla war. The *cheta* activities were detrimental to Albanians, because as a strategy they did not conform to the policy of the Great Powers, but assisted the plans of neighboring countries that had territorial claims on Albania.

The Great Powers, however, hindered this salto mortale. In particular, Austria-Hungary, which maintained clear strategic interests and had greatly invested to increase its influence among Albanians, feared that members of the ethnic group were becoming a prey of Slavic-Russian objectives.

Bulgaria and Romania were increasingly at disaccord with Serbia and Greece as to Sofia's share in Macedonia. The two eastern Balkans countries had now taken measures, including plans to instigate Albanian *chetas* in the Manastir and Kosova vilayets to act against Serbs and Hellenes, even though Sofia had agreed that Belgrade would take the two Ottoman provinces (while Bulgaria itself would receive a large portion of the Salonika vilayet).[662]

Sofia did not conceal its appetite, as was noticed when Foreign Minister Nikola Genadiev proposed to Bajo Topulli for Albanian *chetas* to cooperate with Bulgarians in exchange for arms supplies from the Bulgarian principality. In the meantime, Vlachs, a group that piqued Romania's interest, also supported the alliance. The Albanian colonies in Sofia and Bucharest like-

[662] For more on the treaties between Serbia, Bulgaria, and Montenegro, see Vladimir Čorović, *Borba za nezavisnost Balkana* (Beograd: 1936), 112-127; Jovan M. Jovanović, *Borba za narodno ujedinjanja 1903-1908* (Beograd: 1938); Liljana P. Aleksić, *O srsko-crnogorskom programu o savezu 1904-1905* (Beograd: 1965).

wise wished for their compatriots in the home country to cooperate with the two Orthodox states.

The Sofia-based *Drita*, with Shahin Kolonja as its editor, became the most voracious mouthpiece of the proposed Albanian-Bulgarian alliance. Emphasizing Bulgaria's interest in sharing Macedonia with the Albanians, the diaspora newspaper served as an organ of the Committee for the Freedom of Albania. Guerilla commander Çerçiz Topulli wrote his own editorial, titled "The Feelings of a Patriot" (Alb.: "Ndjenjat e një mëmëdhetari"), calling upon "Tosks and Ghegs, Christians and Mohamedans, to take to the mountains, to fight until death, and to let the voice of the uprising be heard from Preveza to the borders of Serbia and Montenegro."[663]

Other publications, including Boston-based *Kombi* and *Shpnesa e Shqypnís*, issued in Ragusa, Trieste, and Rome, also covered on the activities of the Albanian chetas. However, the commentaries were not always positive for not all Albanian patriots supported the guerilla war, given the risky nature of the strategy and the heavy involvement of the Russian block. Many activists at the time were aware of the Albanians' limited capacity to wage a successful war on the Ottoman Empire. Yet, even assuming that the people could defeat the Porte, hopes of creating an independent state were slim as neighboring countries remained on stand-by to devour on Albanian lands the moment the Ottomans withdrew from the region; and, that indeed happened shortly after during the First Balkan War.

Faik Konitza, as editor of *Albania*, also ran several editorials against the *chetas*. In entries such as "Bajo Topulli and the assassinator's politics" (Alb: "Bajo Topulli dhe politika e asasinatëve"), Konitza called the clandestine war "useless and harmful." Demonstrating his sagacity in discerning diplomatic trickery, he wrote: "The fastest and most propitious path to liberating Albania is the spread of literacy and science among the people."[664]

The Albanian *chetas* evoked Greece's interest, too. This was expected since Athens incessantly repeated its claims on Albanian territories. To achieve its goals, it played its Arvanite card (relying on Albanians in Attica, Morea, and the Aegean islands) as well as Orthodox Albanians, mostly residing in the Vilayet of Janina (throughout southern and central Albania). During the assiduous struggle between the Greek Patriarchate and the Bulgarian Exarchate, Orthodox Albanians had sought to avoid any identifi-

---

[663] *Drita* (Sofie: Dec. 1906).

[664] *Albania*, issues 8 and 11 (1906).

cation with the Macedonian Slavs, seeking refuge instead with the Hellenic church, the very gateway to embracing the Greek national interests.

While Athens had already failed to harvest on the idea of a "dual Hellenic-Albanian monarchy," the assimilationist Greek policy continued to plant the seeds of an alliance between the two peoples. Trumpeted for its mutual benefits, the proposal was actively promoted by Arvanite organizations. In addition to the Albanian-Greek League, another Athens-based group came to life to hearten "the two people to cooperate for shared interests." With this purpose in mind, Neoklis Kazazis (Alb.: Nikolla Kazazi), a renowned Arvanite professor in Greece, formed the *O Ellēnismos* (*Grk.*, Hellenism) Society, which notably published a written appeal "to the Albanian brothers." The authors of the document, Sekos, Boçari (Grk.: Botsaris), and Xhavella (Grk.: Tzavelas), came from prominent Arvanite families that had greatly contributed to the foundation of modern Greece.

Issued as a brochure, the document praised the Albanians as "sons of Alexander the Great and Scanderbeg," but recounting further that they were unable to live independently and form their own state, for they were ridden by poverty and had no literature or a single national religion. To cope with the difficulties, *O Ellēnismos* rekindled the shared history of Hellenes and Albanians; the Arvanites had liberated Greece, the document said, adding that "the Greek, before he became Greek, was Albanian, *i.e.*, Pelasgian." The brochure hence argued that the two peoples had a viable common future, even reviving the idea of a joint Hellenic-Albanian kingdom modeled after Austria-Hungary. A straightforward conclusion commended Albanian brothers to "see . . . how many important reasons we have to unite with the Greeks and for none of us to support the Italian, Austrian, [Romanian], Montenegrin, Serbian, or Bulgarian yoke."[665]

The Arvanite contention about foreign occupation seems to have initially attracted prominent names of the Albanian movement. Ismail Qemali, who was well aware of the Greek envy for Albanian lands, nevertheless agreed to cooperate with Athens against the common threat of a Slavic invasion.[666] The Albanian leader conducted his first negotiations during his stay in the Greek capital in 1900, shortly after he left the Ottoman Empire. It is als reported that, during his eight-year exile, Greece regularly subsidized Qemali in his activities.[667]

---

[665] "Prokirixi tou Arvanitikou sindesmou tis Athinas pros tus Aderfous arvanaites tis Arvanitias," (Athens: Etarireia "O Ellēnismos"), p. 19 in HHStA, PA XXXVIII/443.
[666] H.P.Sh. 2 (Tiranë), 328.
[667] Clayer, *Në fillimet e nacionalizmit shqiptar*, 449.

In 1906, Qemali met with Nikolla Kazazi, the president of *O Ellēnismos*, to discuss the proposed binational cooperation. The exiled leaders also met with other Greek personalities and, by February 1907, he forged an Albanian-Hellenic alliance in the form of a league organization. This group's main objectives were proclaimed in a manifesto published on April 4. Meanwhile, Athenian newspapers reproduced a separate press release made on behalf the "Committee of the Hellenic-Albanian League."[668]

Both documents emphasized the mutual interest of Greeks and Albanians, as two ancient peoples of the Balkan Peninsula, to defend themselves from a future Slavic aggression. The manifesto and the press release expressed a commitment of both nations to the *status quo* in the East and favored the reforms spelled out by the Great Powers but with on condition that the process would be intensified and include all ethnic groups in the Ottoman Empire.[669]

According to B. Kondis, the Greek government enticed Ismail Qemali with the hope of reaching a favorable deal on the future border between the two nations in exchange for Greece's support to Albanian independence. At the same time, according to the Greek consul in Shkodër, the Hellenic government had also contemplated establishing an Albanian language cathedra at the University of Athens to enable the publication of a bilingual newspaper. This medium would promote an agreement that would secure the Albanian trust in Greece's political leadership and support for the language was indispensable in achieving this goal.[670]

But before the ink could ever dry on Qemali's agreement with the Greeks on the binational league, Prime Minister Teodokis openly expressed the Hellenic claims on Epirus (southern Albania) during a meeting with Austria's representative in Athens. This action proved once again that the Greek government saw the Albanians only as a means to its own ends.[671]

Ismail Qemali's deal with Greece was largely illegitimate; Qemali acted in his own personal capacity and under the auspices or with the support of no Albanian organization. Moreover, the contemplated alliance was vehemently opposed by prominent Albanian circles. The editor of *Albania*, Faik Konitza, was likely the most protuberant, alongside the Arbëreshë press in Italy and the pro-Bulgarian Albanian immigrants in Sofia and Bucharest.

---

[668] H.P.Sh. 2 (Tiranë), 328.

[669] *Ibid.* 328.

[670] Clayer, *Në fillimet . . .*, 450.

[671] H.P.Sh. 2 (Tiranë), 328.

The *Drita* newspaper of Shahin Kolonja heavily criticized any cooperation with Greece, fearing the involvement of Serbian interests that opposed the Albanian cause.

Nevertheless, Ismail Qemali soon realized that the alliance with Greece did not serve the Albanians. As an experienced diplomat and politician, Qemali sought to find a common interest between the Great Powers and the Balkan nations, viewing a Greek-Albanian alliance as favorable to Britain and Italy. These states had already contemplated the possibility and in a way supported the cooperation of the two peoples. However, Greece was reluctant to recognize any rights for the Albanians and, even when faced with the Slavic threat, Greece would rather concede to Serbs or Bulgarians and sacrifice its Albanian allies. This situation led Qemali away from Athens and permanently turned him to Austria-Hungary, the only empire that under the circumstances could protect the Albanians from becoming victims of their expansionist neighbors.

There were other leaders who understood their naïvité, too. After years in exile, Bajo Topulli declared in 1907 to Vienna's representatives that "the situation in Albania has not yet matured for a general uprising." He did add that the affiliate groups of the Committee for the Freedom of Albania would work towards an insurgency, but that they would refrain from terrorist acts and would instead contribute to the spreading of Albanian national ideas.[672]

As a result, the Albanians were able to overcome the threat of internal divisions along the lines of regional alliances with neighboring countries. Yet, since obstacles on Albania's road to statehood remained, the national movement contemplated further action and inevitably turned to the Young Turks seeking to overthrow Abdul Hamid. Hence the Albanian opposition sought an end only to the sultan's despotic rule, which prevented the plans for autonomy, and not the breakup of the Ottoman Empire, as desired for by Serbs, Greeks, and Bulgarians.

Since the Macedonian crisis had created conducive grounds for secret committees, the appearance of the CUP was a natural epilogue. The Young Turk committee played a threefold role, fighting: to overthrow the Hamidian regime and to restore the constitution; to suppress the Serbian, Greek, and Bulgarian *chetas*; and to protect the Ottoman Empire from disintegrating altogether. The CUP had long ago adopted this platform and, once the various factions united at the 1907 congress, it launched its efforts to secure

---

[672] *Ibid.* 323.

the Albanian support. The Young Turks were well aware that the Albanians, who comprised of a considerable part of the Muslim population in the European provinces, were indispensable for the movement to success.[673]

The Albanians, in fact, were in line with the Young Turks since their inception in 1889. At the Congress of Paris in December 1907, the Young Turks reconfirmed their position on the Albanians and did so by issuing a communication in the Albanian language. Such a significant move convinced the ethnic group that a Young Turk victory would provide for equality with other nationalities, which remained a principal Albanian demand in the struggle for autonomy. While Abdul Hamid was appreciate of the strategic importance of the Albanians, he discriminated against the Albanians in denying the rights to a national identity and education that other groups enjoyed in the empire. The Young Turks, however, using the Albanian language in official communication with the ethnic group marked a great turn that created the trust that allowed the Albanians to join the opposition movement and coordinate their political, social, and cultural demands with the same. At Paris, likewise, the CUP proclaimed its support for armed resistace against the oppressive policies of the government. In order to overthrow Abdul Hamid, the organization also permitted revolutionary activities, which had until then been prohibited. This was of importance for the Albanians, particularly those with revolutionary inclinations who served in the *chetas* and had already become part of this development. Moreover, the course of cooperation with the Young Turks in favor of preserving the caliphate and the calls for an executive appointed by the parliament, which would replace the despotic regime,[674] separated the Albanians from becoming a tool in the hands of Serbs, Bulgarians, and Greeks. Religious fanatics were also relieved of their fear that the constitution would bring an end to the monarchy and caliphate and institute a secular regime. Indeed, the conciliatory tone on preserving the sultanate while reinstating the constitution reconciled the Albanians themselves divided into a loyalist faction and the opposition.

A high number of Muslim Albanians joined forces with the Youg Turks. Most of the volunteers came from the Kosova vilayet and the Macedonian sanjaks, but also from the Vilayet of Janina and, to a lesser degree, the Vilayet of Shkodër. In particular, military officers and government employees

---

[673] Gawrych, *Gjysmëhëna dhe shqiponja*, 222.
[674] *Ibid.* 222.

became members of various branches of the CUP that began to spring up throughout the country. This class of people in service of the state was directly involved in the war against the *chetas*, and was well aware that the Albanians would continue to be the victims of the clandestine activities. In Shkup, a young member of the CUP and former student of the notable *Mülkiye* school of İstanbul, Nexhip Draga, became one of the main activists of the Young Turk movement. In Mitrovica, Sylejman Kylçe (Trk.: Süleyman Külçe), a young officer originally from Tetova, also joined the local CUP cell.[675]

On this occasion, it is noteworthy that Bektashis throughout Kosova joined the CUP and propagated its message. The religious order became an important factor in promoting Albanian cooperation with the Young Turk opposition, for the Bektashis were already supportive of the Albanian national movement and its efforts to gain autonomy within the Ottoman Empire.

On the other hand, the part of the national movement that had taken on to waging a guerilla war was faced with the dilemma of cooperating with the neighboring countries or joining the Young Turks. In the summer of 1906, a Thessaloniki-based CUP began to operate, becoming very influential in Balkan affairs and the Albanian guerillas were challenged to break off their ties with the Slavic *komitis* and to moreover turn against them. Had the *chetas* decided to fight against the CUP, they would also be fighting against other Albanians, because the very Young Turk movement was cofounded by Albanians such as Ibrahim Temo. Furthermore, other members of the ethnic group, such as Ismail Qemali and Hasan Prishtina, continued to serve the opposition and sought to achieve the goals of the national movement by working together with the Young Turks. The escalation of the Macedonian crisis threatened a Balkan-wide conflict that would have brought the end of the Ottoman Empire in Europe and the regional monarchies would have divided the remaining territory among them. The cooperation of Albanian "revolutionaries" with Serbs, Bulgarians, and Greeks would indeed be an obscure path that threatened the existence of the nation following the disintegration of the Ottoman Empire. However, the Albanians decisively chose to side with the Young Turks and what the mainstream leaders of the time saw as conducive to the Albanian interest.

---

[675] Clayer, *Në fillimet . . .*, 514.

This dilemma was cast aside in December 1907, after the Second Young Turk Congress. Gathered at Paris, the CUP adopted the armed uprising as the *sole* strategy to provide for regime change.[676] Consequently, the Balkan *chetas* were given the option to further exercise their "revolutionarism," although this time the fight would not serve the goal of "liberation" from the Ottoman Empire (as desired by the Russian-led Balkan block), but the end of Abdul Hamid's despotic rule and the return of parliamentarism. In other words, it was an opportunity for a "democratic revolution."

This new orientation, in addition to the promises the CUP made at Paris to the Albanians, Macedonians, and others, that the constitution would bring them "freedom, equality, brotherhood, and justice," earned the Young Turk leadership the support of the people, and of the Albanians in particular.[677]

In the spring of 1908, in many Albanian towns, including Ohër, Prespa, Struga, Manastir, Shkup, Gjirokastër, Shkodër, Prizren, Ferizaj, Mitrovica, and others, Young Turk committees for "Unity and Progress" (local CUPs) were formed in addition to the regional branches of the national committees "For the Freedom of Albania." The local CUPs brought together Albanian intellectuals and military officers in a successful effort for the maintstream opposition to attract and recruit the illegal "revolutionary" opposition groups to the cause of the "democratic revolution." The Young Turk movement laid its eyes not only on the Albanian and Slavic-Macedonian *chetas* and the *komitis*, but also on what began to emerge as an open mutiny of Ottoman officers disillusioned with the disarray in Macedonia. The greatest success of the CUP was hence in the Ottoman military, especially among Albanian soldiers and officers who were conscious of the need for a rebellion to restore the constitutional order and not to break the empire apart. The majority of Albanian officers in the Shkup garrison backed the Young Turk movement. A similar scenario followed suit in many garrisons of the Salonica Second Army, hen considered as the best-trained and in charge of defense of the European part of the empire.

The opportune moment came in the early days of July, when an Albanian colonel by the name of Ahmet Njaziu (Trk.: Ahmed Niyazi Bey) took to the mountains and issued a proclamation calling for the constitution. Resonating Njaziu's cry, CUP members in the city and the countryside announced that their goal was to reinstate the constitution and thereby "secure

---

[676] H.P.Sh. 2 (Tiranë), 373.

[677] *Ibid.* 375.

freedom, equality, brotherhood, and justice for all peoples of the Empire, regardless of religion,"[678] while also promising the Albanians tax cuts and an end to the arbitrary bureaucracy. It was at this moment that the Albanian revolutionaries in honoring the needs of the "democratic revolutions" began to separate from the Balkan network of *chetas* fighting a clandestine war in the Slavic and Greek model and joined instead the waves of an overt uprising for regime change. In other words, it was another important turn of those who had for so long vowed to liberate Albania from the Ottoman Empire by their arms, but now pledged to use their guns only against Abdul Hamid's despotism and to reinstate the constitution after thirty-two years of suspension.

The Manastir-based Committee for the Freedom of Albania accepted CUP's offer for cooperation and hence returned to the authentic principles of the Albanian national movement—that is, using legitimate means to further the goals of autonomy in the Ottoman Empire. In doing so, the Albanians—who since the 1903 *Ilinden* Uprising risked being marginalized due to internal rivalries and the influence of regional countries—became once again an actor in the Balkan political scene.

---

[678] Colonel Ahmet Njaziu was a military officer of Albanian origin who became a hero of the 1908 Revolution. Born in the Resnje region, to the southwest of Manastir, he studied in the military idadiye of Manastir, where he was exposed to the emerging ideals of Ottoman patriotism. Later, he attended the military school in İstanbul. In 1897, he participated in the Turkish-Greek war. Later, he was stationed in Ohër and from 1904 he served in the third battalion fight the Slavic and Greek bands. On the eve of the Young Turk Revolution, colonel Njaziu moved to the mountains where he united the Albanian chetas, which he called Çerçizi's Tosk Committee, and kept them from cooperating with the Slavic or Greek units. He hence helped unite the Albanians around their national cause few days before the proclamation of the 1908 constitution.

CHAPTER 8
THE KOSOVA UPRISING AND THE ALBANIAN INDEPENDENCE

The Young Turk Revolution and the Albanian Role

The interaction with the Young Turks represents the first, most important "contract" of the Albanians with opposition in the crucial struggle for constitutional monarchy. Bektashism plays a prominent role in strengthening Albanianism, helping foster the changes leading to the overthrow of Sultan Abdul Hamid II. The Ottoman constitution and the imperial parliament are reinstated after Albanians gathered at Ferizaj issue an ultimatum to the sultan.

Albanians played an important, if not the principal, role in the Young Turk Revolution of July 1908. They took part in the revolution as both Ottomans and as Albanians. This dualism is of special importance, since it explains the success, but also the subsequent failure of the revolution. Furthermore, it explains the initial agreements and disputes between Albanians and Young Turks that would later lead to conflict and induce the Balkan Crisis along with the collapse of the Ottoman Empire.

While participating in the revolution, the Albanians asserted a clear position on Ottomanism, just as they had done previously with Islamism. In other words, the Albanians indicated their status as a nation and political factor, a consequence of the national awakening process. When the national movements of the Balkan peoples began in early 19th century, the Albanians had to decide: to remain within the *millet-i osman* with the Islamic identity that forever tied them to the East, or to separate from it, even though doing so required promoting a national, cultural, and civilizational identity that pointed to the West. It was this first challenge of the historical importance that the Albanians seriously faced after more than four centuries under Ottoman rule. Its significance was even greater, primarily because it passed through an internal confrontation: most Albanians had already embraced Islam and, regardless of their spiritual attachment to the religion, they had become a part of the Islamic civilization.

As seen and explained above, the Albanians clarified their position on Islamism in terms of their national identity. Here, they also benefited from Islam, given that religion in the imperial circumstances did not deny cultural and ethnic identities, but could be the ultimate identity in an amalgam state as was the Ottoman Empire. After the Tanzimât reforms were announced, however, a wave of national patriotism—that is, Ottomanism—began to replace Islamism. A great help for the Albanians came through Bektashism, a religious order that helped the people avoid conflicts with Islam and in the crucial moments encourage them to side with the Young Turks against Abdul Hamid's absolutist regime.

Nevertheless, if one may assert that the relationship with Islamism based on the *vatan* permitted the Albanians to foster their national identity and work for their autonomy, the same cannot be said of Ottomanism. As an idea of civil patriotism, Ottomanism raised centralization of power to a cult, excluding even the century-long tradition of local government that Albanians had enjoyed. The local autonomy had in fact served the Ottoman Empire, too, fostering a sense of loyalty to the monarchy. This was noted particularly in the Vilayet of Kosova, where various political organizations, beginning with the Albanian League of Prizren in 1878, reaffirmed their loyalty to the sultan and the Sharia. By doing so, the Albanians hoped to achieve their autonomy within the Ottoman Empire, while also protecting their lands for expansionist neighbors.

The Albanian declarations of allegiance to the Ottoman Empire—beginning with the Eastern Crisis and on, and especially after the Berlin Congress, when Albania became a target of neighboring Serbia, Montenegro, Greece, and Bulgaria—was by no means a carte blanche. This is because the Albanians conditioned their loyalty to the sultan on the protection of their lands. Even when Abdul Hamid entreated the Albanians with epithets such as the "flower of Islam," defense and autonomy remained the sole measure of confidence in the empire. The justifications that unifying the Albanian lands in a common province would "undermine internal unity" and "clear the way for the divisions that the enemies sought,"[679] were not convincing or accepta-

---

[679] See letter of Abedin Pasha to the Albanian League of Prizren, dated 1880, in the Appendix. See also Buxhovi, *Kongresi i Berlinit 1878*, 83-85.

ble in face of ongoing concessions that the sultan made to the neighboring nations.

With the Macedonian crisis (particularly after the 1903 Mürzsteg agreement, when the Ottoman Empire practically gave up its sovereignty in the European parts), the political situation in the region lead towards the fragmentation of Albanian territories. Waning confidence in the sultan and the empire's ability to defend itself led the Albanians to ally with the Young Turks against Abdul Hamid's regime. The opposition movement also gained the backing of the conservative clergy, even though the fanatic imams objected to constitutional monarchy and the secular parliament, which they saw as the root cause of the empire's decline. At the Paris Congress, the Committee for Unity and Progress pledged to preserve the sultanate and caliphate, hence attracting many conservative Albanians (landlords and Islamists) to abandon the Hamidian regime and support the opposition. The sultan had privileged the conservatives as a means to prop up his reign for decades, but the recent concessions to the Great Powers, the regional states, and the local Christian population pitied many of the ruling elite against the monarch.

This turn, nevertheless, would have probably not been possible without the open determination of the Bektashi on the side of the Young Turks opposition. His *tariqah* (from *Arb.*, [Islamic] order), which included most of southern Albania (Toskëria) and a part of Kosova and central Albania, became a crucial supporter to Albanianism as well as the revolution. Since 1826, when Sultan Mahmud II issued his famous decree abolishing the janissary corps, the Sunni majority and the Shi'ite minority in the Vilayet of Kosova appeared to be in "state of war" and the Bektashis seemed to have found the opportune moment to retaliate as if revenging for the historical Battle of Karbala. However, the rising Slavic-Orthodox peril had already begun to show its devastating power against the Albanians, leaving the Sunnis with no choice but to accept that the Bektashis as the frontrunners of national defense. It was the Bektashi's role in the national movement and the Ottoman opposition that inspired the notion that the Albanians practiced a "different Islam," that is in accordance with their European identity.[680] Aimed at Albanians and other European peoples of the Ottoman Empire, the idea was believed to extend the life of Ottoman rule in the Balkans.

---

[680] For more details, see Dora d'Istria, "Albanian nationality according to popular songs," *Revue des deux mondes* (1886).

The issue, however, turns to the role of Bektashism in the development of Albanian nationalism. Bektashi involvement was not a mere coincidence nor was it outside of social, cultural, and political contexts that favored various models for an Ottoman Albania, a country with ties to the two worlds, standing as a bridge between East and West, not only politically but also spiritually. This observation, if properly explained, points also to the social processes and historical circumstances that highlighted Bektashism as an important factor, related not only to the historical success of the Ottoman Empire, but also with the penetration and acceptance of Islam in Europe, especially among Albanians. Bektashism was of great importance from a military standpoint: the order was the spiritual foundation of the janissaries, the imperial elite where Albanians had been highly influential, owing to the recruitment through the *devşirme* process. Meanwhile, Bektashism was seen a sect with a liberal and humanistic nature within Islam, which was acceptable to Albanians. Since the rise of Albanians in the military and administrative structure in the Ottoman Empire was tightly linked with the janissary order, acceptance of Islam also was encouraged by Bektashism and its liberal and humanist nature, reconciling Islam with oriental mysticism, but also in some respects with the West. From the Eastern Crisis onward, when Albanianism appeared as a necessity to preserve the Albanian territories and ethnic identity, while Ottomanism will become an indispensable substitute for Islamism as the imperial ideology, it was Bektashism that enabled the Albanians an alternative to Islamist fanaticism. Additionally, the liberal religious order provided the opposition movement, where many Albanians participated, with the thrust to combat the Hamidian despotism and restore the constitutional monarchy.

The convergence of Bektashism with Albanian nationalism and the Young Turk movement was a product of the sect's own character. Socially, culturally and politically, the Bektashis were open to change, and accepted different ways of thinking, often adopting and reconciling opposing views. Meanwhile, Sunni Islam had become synonymous with fanaticism and despotism. Targeted by the sultan as supporters of the janissaries, the Bektashis were subject to persecution from the regime.[681] After the massacres that took place in most of the Ottoman Empire, Bektashis remained un-

---

[681] There is much speculation about the number of victims in the massacres Sultan Mahmud II committed during the suppression of Janissaries and the Bektashi order. Figures range from several thousand to 200,000. Some reputable sources estimate 60,000 Bektashi pashas, clerics, dervishes, and followers were slaughtered mercilessly.

touched in Albania. Hence many members of the religious community found refuge and support in the country, especially in southern Albania and the main cities of Kosova (Tetova, Prizren, and Gjakova). It was not a mere coincidence that the Bektashi network was one of the main supporters of Albanianism, appearing since the inception of *Rilindja Kombëtare* in the works of intellectuals such as the Frashëri brothers.

Abdyl Frashëri was the first to explore his family's affiliation with the Bektashi *tariqah*. He decided to use faith to support the movement against the partitioning of Albania (*i.e.*, accession of Albanian territory to Greece) and to promote his country's autonomy. In May of 1878, Abdyl Frashëri organized a meeting with the governors of southern Albania in the Frashëri *tekke*. The participants openly declared the demands of the national movement for the first time and requested that the Sublime Porte give its consideration.[682]

While Abdyl relied on Bektashism for political influence in Toskëria, his brothers, Sami and, above all, Naim, were able to transform the *tariqah*'s theology into an ideology that best suited Albanianism.[683] In 1880, Sami noted the existence of Bektashis and Sunnis as two groups of Muslims among Albanians as he attempted to prove cultural pluralism and present the Albanians as a civilized nation. For the Frashëri brothers, Bektashism did not deny one's cultural and national identity. This hence explains the prevalence of the *tariqah* among Albanians at a time when other sects of Islam denied secular identities, placing religion above all. Naim took the Albanian-Bektashi harmony even further. He linked the Bektashi doctrine about the martyrdom of Imam Hussein in the 7th-century Battle of Karbala with the honor the Albanians paid to Abbas Ali at Mount Tomor. He combined the national identity with the divine spirit, holding that the two were forever intertwined ever since man began to contemplate about the creation of the universe and his relationship with the Creator.[684]

As political developments of 1890 unfolded, Naim tried to inject nationalist proportions to Bektashism.[685] His literary works hence became a powerful source of inspiration for the masses to embrace Albanianism. In *Fletor' e*

---

[682] HHStA, PA XIV/18 Liasse XII/2: "Memoire sur le mouvement national albanais," *Albania* (Brussels: 1899); 8-9.

[683] Clayer, *Në fillimet e nacionalizmit shqiptar*, 430.

[684] *Ibid.* 431.

[685] *Ibid.*

Bektashinjve (*Alb.*, Book of the Bektashis),[686] first published in 1896, he reformulated the order's doctrine, addressing not only the masses but also the Bektashi spiritual leaders.[687] In the last part of the text, Naim Frashëri called:

> Let us strive day and night for the nation that we call Father; let us work together with our leadership and the elders for the salvation of Albania and the Albanians, for knowledge and for the civilization of the Nation and the Motherland, for their language, and for progress and prosperity . . . Let us foster . . . love and brotherhood, friendship and unity among all Albanians, and resist divisions; let Christians and Muslims be together and let us work productively so that the Albanians may not be scorned today, for they have forever been praised throughout the world.[688]

Naim also introduced an Albanian, nationalistic component in the Bektashi catechism, thoroughly transforming the concepts of love, knowledge, and enlightenment, which he viewed as *divine*. Fraternity and mystical love could allow for compatriots to join one another in brotherhood well beyond religious differences:

> With one another and all men alike, the Bektashis are brothers and souls . . .
> They love other Muslims and Christians as they love their own souls . . .
> But they love the most their motherland and their countrymen . . .
> True Bektashis honor others regardless of faith and they never consider their brothers and beloved ones foreigners.[689]

Naim also managed to transform the epic poem *Qerbelaja* (*Alb.*, the Karbala Battle),[690] inspired by the Persian *Hadiqatu's-su'ada* (Persian, Garden of the Blessed), into a nationalist poem. In the final verses, the poem calls on Bektashi Albanians not only to remember the Battle of Karbala, but to also realize that all Albanians belonged to the same family and that,

---

[686] This booklet was reprinted in 1908 in Sofia, in 1910 in Thessaloniki, in 1921 in Korça, and in 1996 in Tirana. It has also been translated several times: in part by Faik Konitza (published in *Albania*, vol. A: 174-176, 193, 212-213), by F. W. Haulsuck (into English), by H. Burgeois (into French, 1920), and Norbert Jokl (into German).

[687] [John Kingsley] Birge, *The Bektashi Order of Dervishes* (London: 1965), cited in Clayer, *Në fillimet . . .*, 431.

[688] N. Frashëri, *Fletor' e Bektashinjet* (1896), 14.

[689] Clayer, *Në fillimet . . .*, 432.

[690] *Qerbelaja* (1898).

although divided into different religious beliefs, they were still one nation. The author ends with a prayer to God that the Albanians may be enlightened and love their country:

> In virtue knowing no restrain,
> So may the Albanian remain,
> And wisdom may he always gain,
> To love Albania, die for her name,
> As did Muhtar fall for Hussein.[691]

The Frashëri brothers were not the only *Rilindja* activists who used and transformed Bektashism for the benefit of Albanianism. They certainly paved the way to more progressive thinking in the Albanian national movement that affected the *Rilindja*'s views on the spiritual, intellectual, and overall political issue. Many other writers with ties to the religious order also explored the benefits of Bektashism.

Faik Konitza, as editor of the *Albania* magazine, wrote on the connection between Bektashism and Albanian nationalism.[692] In 1897, having already founded his own magazine, Konitza tried to build a certain image of the Bektashis while writing for both domestic and foreign audiences. He took Bektashism as an Islamic schism that evolved to such an extent that it could be appropriately qualified as a "'body of pantheistic principles' rather than a religion with a ceremonial cult."[693]

The Bektashi factor as a "different Islam" and its important role in the national awakening helped foreigners gain a perspective of Albania as a religiously diverse nation, where faith not only does not impede the national identity, but in fact strengthens it. This phenomenon caught the attention of some Westerners who emphasized it repeatedly in countering the Slavic-Orthodox propaganda that depicted Albanians as pro-Ottoman Islamist fanatics. Scholars, diplomats, politicians exploited the Albanian connections

---

[691] *Shqiptari trim me fletë,*
si ka qenë, le të jetë,
ta ketë gjith' urtësinë,
e ta dojë Shqipërinë,
të vdesë për Mëmëdhenë,
si Myhtari për Hysenë.
N. Frashëri, *Vepra 4* (Prishtinë: 1986), 289.

[692] Clayer, *Në fillimet . . .*, 436.

[693] *Albania* A: 88 (Brussels : 1897).

with Bektashis and the believers support for Albania's statehood (at least as an autonomous entity, if national independence were not politically feasible). The Austro-Hungarian consul in Shkodër, Ippen, who was one of the best connoisseurs of the Albanian people and their national question, recommended his government to support the Bektashis, because "as liberals, [they] accept Christians and to have good relations with them."[694]

The idea of a tolerant practice of "liberal Islam," contrary to Sunni Islam, was also a way of making the Bektashis "non-Turks." The order's followers hence could also serve as a bridge connecting two civilizations in places where the East and the West seemed incompatible and were constantly at war. even European in a way in which they can connect civilization in places where it was seen as incompatible and in a mutual war/struggle. This shift is noticed in lectures of Brailsford,[695] who viewed the Albanians as "medieval Europeans" left in a "frozen" state that nevertheless caused for their practice of Islam not to reach the fanaticism observed among Asiatic Turks. Brailsford also said that the majority of Albanians, like all Indo-European peoples that had embraces Islam, were "not rigid Muslims."[696] Indeed, in Brailsford's eyes, Bektashism was a liberal and heretical form of Islam adapted to Europeans, some of whom even found comfort in the religion because of the profound mystical aspects that dwelled on secrets of the soul. Finally, the image of a Europeanized Islam would be sealed with the compatibility that Bektashism was thought to have with Christianity.[697]

Bektashism aligned with Albanianism in critical moments. Bektashi clergymen became militants of the national movement along with many Albanian Orthodox priests, promoting the motto of *Rilindja Kombëtare* that "the faith of the Albanian is Albanianism." This opened the road to national independence the return of the Albanians to the heart of the Western civilization. In addition to the contribution to the national cause, Bektashis also played a significant role in encouraging the Albanian participation in the Young Turk Revolution.

---

[694] For more, see: Ippen, "Beiträge zur inneren Geschihte Albaniens im XIX Jahrhundert," *Illyrische-albanische Forschungen* 1, 342-385; *Skutari und die Nordalbanische Künstenebene* (Sarajevo: 1907).

[695] See: [H. N.] Brailsford, *Macedonia: Its races and their Future* (London: Mathew & Co., 1906), 235-247.

[696] *Ibid.* 235-247.

[697] *Ibid.* 235-247.

Supporting the movement that toppled the absolutist regime of Abdul Hamid, the Albanians carried a double quality. Acting as Ottomans and as Albanians, the ethnic group hoped to preserve the Ottoman Empire but to also prepare for the eventual dissolution, were the state unable to maintain its European dominions. This formula was part of a wise political judgment, since it prepared the Albanians for their independence while also allowing for them to exploit the options of remaining a part of the empire.

At the Second Congress in Paris, the Young Turk's CUP approved a declaration that all subjects of the empire were to be fully equal, under a concept of national patriotism based on the Ottoman identity. Ottomanism, which the CUP argued would keep the empire from falling apart, had the support of Albanians. The latter even achieved leadership positions in the Young Turk movement. The idea that all subjects were to cooperate in the name of an "Ottoman nation" pooled the interests of various groups together. However, the Albanians saw Ottomanism only as a means to an end; for they hoped that the restoration of the parliament would enable them to realize their aspirations through legal political institutions. This effort was part of a consciousness embraced by most Albanians intellectuals, not only during the Young Turk Revolution, but throughout the period of *Rilindja Kombëtare*.

The Albanian interaction with the Young Turks was undoubtedly the first, major political "contract" of the Albanians with the opposition in a crucial process for the future of the empire. Contemplating the removal of the absolutist government and the return of constitutional order, the agreement was of historic significance since the Albanians became a decisive factor that could determine the fate of political events of the time. In the end, Albanians needed the Ottoman parliament more than others because the legislative body provided the only way in which the ethnic group could gain political power in proportion with its size and geographic extent (a factor that neighboring countries had begun to manipulate since the emergence of the Macedonia Crisis, hoping to increase their numbers by means of religious identification). During the first parliamentary period (1876-1878), the Albanians clearly laid out for the first time their demands for autonomy within the Ottoman Empire and for the recognition of the Albanian nationality. Although Abdul Hamid had categorically rejected the demands, the Albanians did not give up their aspirations for a nation state even under the threat of annihilation.

To achieve their goals, the Albanians had to join the Ottoman opposition against the absolutist regime and pledge to preserve the Ottoman Empire. These two requirements were interrelated and interdependent. The latter was the main element because only a continued Ottoman presence in the Balkans could protect the Albanians against the claims of their expansionist neighbors who became increasingly vocal in their aspirations of dividing the Albanian territory among them.

Under the circumstances, the Albanian national movement had to maintain its grounds during the Macedonian crisis, the calamity that the Balkan states created for their own the great powers became involved in the situation; the ethnic group had to remind the Europeans of the Albanian interest. While the Balkan monarchies sought to divide and annex Macedonia, the Albanians wished to keep the province intact Dictates that that was the only way they could remain within the same political entity and preserve their ethnic territories. Therefore, the Albanians desired for the territorial integrity of the Ottoman Empire to be preserved. The ethnic group had to refrain from any armed action, such as forming bands in the Slavic-Greek model. The Albanians hence hoped to gain the support of the Great Powers that were interested in propping up the Ottoman Empire and could provide a peaceful political solution to the Albanian question.

However, there was apparently no easy solution because the likelihood of an Albanian state was affected by a cluster of relationships. The matter depended on ottoman reports with the Great Powers but also with the European ties to the Balkan countries. As a result, the Albanians had to compete for the attention of the Great Powers, so that the Albanian question was not altogether ignored. But since the European involvement in Macedonia proved to be a failure, the Albanians became even more vulnerable to the shifting dynamics among regional factors.

The reasons why the reforms were aborted when believed to be on track for implementation lay in a new agreement that Austro-Hungary made with the Sublime Port for the construction of a railway. The line began in Yenipazar, ran south to Mitrovica, and then, through Prishtina and Shkup, was linked with Salonika in the south; northward, the planned railway led to Vienna. In the meantime, the Ottomans also reached a deal with Germany on a railway to Baghdad. Thus, Vienna and Berlin, according to some negotiations with the Sublime Port, offered it a secret military convention to protect it together from the aggression of Balkan states and any other military interventions.[698]

---

[698] See: *Die Grosse Politik der Europeischen Kabinette 1871-1914*, no. 22; W. M. Carigren, "Iswolsky und Aerenthal von bosnischen anexionskrise," *Russische und Österreichisch-ungarische Balkanpolitik 1906-1908* (Uppsala: 1995), 206.

The Yenipazar-Shkup railway in particular was one of the most important Austro-Hungarian projects affecting the Albanian vilayets. Thus, Albania was projected to gain strategic importance, but it also became a target not only of the Great Powers, but also of the Balkan countries, which were well aware of the significance of a railroad linking the Albanian vilayets with Central Europe and Austro-Hungary with the Southeast. This and other projects put forward between 1907 and 1908 clearly indicated a competition among European states, which began to unite around two blocks: the Central Powers (Austro-Hungary, Germany, and Italy) and the Entente (Britain and France); Russia at the time sat back and watched for the opportune moment for a greater advantage of picking sides.

The Austrian railway project, which featured an Austrian-German-Ottoman pact that was also in the interest of the Albanians, inspired other railroad plans for the Balkans. Through such endeavors, the Great Powers competed among themselves, causing the Albanian lands to lose their strategic importance. Russia, having concluded a war with Japan, presented a project for the Adriatic railway. The road would pass through Romania and Serbia, linking the enormous empire with the Adriatic coast of Montenegro. The project received the green light from England and France, which were also interested in hindering a further penetration of Austria-Hungary and Germany in the Balkans, a region that enabled the German-speaking countries to reach the Middle East. Austro-Hungary would of course reject the Russian proposal. Instead, the dual monarchy announced that, in accordance with the decisions of the Congress of Berlin, Montenegro could be entitled to communications links with Shkodër or any part of Albania, but not to roads leading northward to Serbia. The Russian project, however, only failed after London withdrew their support.

Once the British conquered Egypt, they opted for preserving the *status quo* in the Ottoman Empire. The rivalry over the railway plans, Britons thought, could bring the German-speaking nations even closer to the Ottoman Empire. As a result, London chose to return to the planned reforms for Macedonia and sought Russian backing for the matter, too. But despite the tsar's disagreement with Austria over the railways and his hopes to see the reforms take place, he refused to withdraw his support for certain interests of Austro-Hungary. Therefore, Russia continued to back Vienna's claims over Bosnia and Herzegovina hoping to receive, in return, unfettered access to the Mediterranean Sea through the Bosphorus and the Dardanelle straits (right at the heart of the Ottoman Empire).[699] Eventually, the tsar joined Britain in the plans for a new reform package that appeared in June 1908 at a summit of the two countries' leaders in Reval, Russia. However, St. Petersburg's special ties to Vienna remained intact. Italy also agreed with the Austro-Russian agreement over Bosnia and the Mediterranean, provided that the Apennine monarchy was allowed to obtain Tripoli and Cyrenaica from the Ottoman Empire.[700]

The Austro-Hungarian withdrawal from the reforms caused great concern for the Albanians. As known, the Vilayet of Shkodër and most parts of Kosova had already been exempted from the reforms, while sanjaks with an Albanian majority fell under Vienna's supervision. Now, seeing the Austrians back off from their mission, the Albanians feared that Britain and Russia were attempting to include all Albanian territories into the reform area. Such a move heightened the risk of neighboring countries dividing Albania among them. However, fears also spread that Austro-Hungary was planning to occupy parts of the Albanian territories through an agreement with the Sublime Porte.

The Young Turks, in fact, viewed the sultan's approval of the Austrian railway as the beginning of the end of the Ottoman Empire in Europe. They blamed Abdul Hamid of having acceded to pre-arranged scenarios against the Ottoman state. The Young Turks criticized the agreements with Austro-Hungary and Germany, arguing that the railroad projects leading all the way to Baghdad strengthen the influence of the two German-speaking empires from the Balkans to the Middle East. Likewise, the opposition group expressed concerned about the British, fearing that London could retaliate against the Ottoman Empire because of the Austro-German economic pact. This was seen as a possible scenario with the help of the Russians, who were always able to induce their Balkan satellites into favor of St. Petersburg. This implied a deterioration of the regional crisis to the point that foreign powers could intervene. In this case, the British were more likely to do so and that could consequently bring Austro-Hungarian and German involvement.

Given such speculations, which rightly upset the Albanians and the Ottoman opposition, it was expected for the Young Turks to consider an armed uprising to overthrow Abdul Hamid. The Young Turks began to use the

---

[699] Vasilj Popović, *Istočno pitanje* (Belgrade: 1946), 198.

[700] I.S. Galkin, *Diplomacija evropejskih država v svajazi s osvoboditelnim dvizeniem narodov Evropejskoj Turcii 1905-1912* (Moskva: 1960), 220, cited in Pllana, *Kosova dhe reformat në Turqi*, 228.

railway project as a pretext to accuse the sultan that he sold the country's interests to Austria and Germany. Although, in reality, the European railway was seen as an economic and political interest for the Albanians, who would be able strengthen their position on the playground of European rivalries over the Balkans. The railway would turn the Albanians into a strategic interest of Austria-Hungary, which was more likely to protect the ethnic group from the predatory tendencies of neighboring countries. But the Young Turks resorted to frightening the Albanians that the railway was making them a "target of the Austrian-German invasion," a slogan that provided a useful justification for the violent overthrow of Abdul Hamid. In this action, the Young Turks exploited with great perfidiousness both the anti-European and, in particular, anti-German sentiments, that Islamist fanatics and a part of the landowners had planted in the vilayets of Kosova and Shkodër. They were greatly assisted with money and propaganda efforts by Serbia, which through numerous, dispersed agents throughout Kosova, had begun to gain the support of the nobility that had been loyal to Abdul Hamid. Since some Young Turk committees had already established ties with the Albanian Committee for the Freedom of Albania (Alb.: *Për Lirinë e Shqipërisë*), led by the Committee of Manastir, it was expected that Albanians would soon join the planned anti-Hamidian uprising.

The circumstances for a joint action arose in the first days of July 1908, when two young officers ordered, almost at the same time, the beginning of the uprising. Initially, Ahmet Njazi Bej (Trk.: Ahmed Niyazi Bey; 1873-1913), a great captain (Trk.: *kolağasi*) of Albanian origin, attacked the military depot in Resen. With two hundred people at his command, including the mayor of the city, Ahmet Njazi Bej escaped to the mountains, where he issued a proclamation, calling for restoration of the 1876 constitution. At about the same time, a member of the CUP, major İsmail Enver Bey (later Pasha), fled to the mountains near Resen.[701]

Ahmet Njazi and İsmail Enver issued a war cry for the uprising. Other officers followed their example and went up the hills and mountains forming their own bands. Njazi easily managed to gather the Albanians around the cause because he, an Albanian himself, had already reached an agreement with Bajo Topulli, described in Njazi's memoirs "chief of the Albanian Tosk Committee."[702]

---

[701] Gawrych, *Gjysmëhëna . . .*, 228.

[702] See memories of Ahmet Njaziu (Ahmet Niyazi), *Balkanlarda bir gerillaci* (İstanbul: 1975).

Certainly, the agreement of Colonel Njazi with Bajo Topulli and the Albanian bands, which were included in the uprising and generally connected with Bulgarian groups, was achieved before the uprising began. *Baba* Hysen, head of the Melmepan Bektashi *Tekke* in the Korça region, served as mediator. At the time, Topulli had realized that clandestine (illegitimate) warfare through *chetas* was not helpful to the Albanian question as initially thought but instead favored opponents, such as Serbs and Bulgarians, who increasingly hoped to include Albanians in their revolutionary bands. Father Hysen, as a Bektashi leader determined to assist the Young Turks in overthrowing the absolutist regime, helped find common ground between the Albanian bands and the Ottoman opposition. A good portion of Albanian fighters turned their back on Bulgarian and Greek bands, which used the slogan of "liberation war" to create chaos in Albania with the hope of obtaining territorial gains.

The revolt that began in Resen found suitable ground to spread to the Vilayet of Kosova by mid-June, when a great portion of the population rose at the call of the landlords and influential leaders, after having received the news that construction of the planned Yenipazar-Mitrovica railway had begun. This was followed by rumors that the Austro-Hungarian army, allegedly after an agreement with Russia, was also preparing to invade Kosova.

Indeed, the uprisings against railroad constructions had begun by mid-April in Mitrovica, in the domains of Isa Boletini, to expand little by little in other areas as well. Soon, other towns of vilayet were included in the revolt, with Ferizaj becoming the focus of the events. Rumors spread that the Sublime Porte intended to sell the lands in the Ferizaj area to Austro-Hungary for the construction of military bases. To exacerbate the matter, cadets from the German military school in Salonika visited the area while on vacation. This was sufficient for Young Turk and Serb agents to instigate uninformed Albanian masses to take up their arms and join insurgent groups "to prevent the German invasion of Kosova."

To place the situation under control, Sultan Abdul Hamid ordered his trusted general, Şemsi Pasha, to Resen to suppress Njazi and İsmail Enver and then move on to Kosova. On July 7, on the road to Resen with two battalions of regular troops, Şemsi Pasha stopped in the town of Manastir to send a telegram to the imperial palace. He recommended that the sultan mobilize the privileged class of Albanian leaders to oppose the rebellious officers. As the Ottoman general emerged from the telegraph office and approached his carriage, a young officer shot Şemsi Pasha in front of his Albanian bodyguards, leaving him dead on the spot. His death was a major blow to the Hamidian regime.[703]

The killing along with the increasing propaganda inspired a great movement among rebel forces in Ferizaj. From July 5 to 23, the town became an arena of hostility to what was described as "German intervention." At this point, the Albanian propaganda of fanatical Muslims in a way joined ranks with Young Turks and Serbs, although in reality the three groups were extremely incompatible as they diverged in their goals. But, in those circumstances, creating commotion was important to them. Thus, Albanian fanatics protected Abdul Hamid, Serbs wanted to fight the Austro-Hungarian and German impact, and for this to join with whomever agreed to oppose Vienna; the Young Turks, meanwhile, aimed at the downfall of Abdul Hamid and preventing the penetration of Austria-Hungary, but Serbia was also their opponent, given Belgrade's hopes to occupy Albanian territories.

The different actors, who despite their diametrically opposed interests played similar roles, elicited in Ferizaj one of the largest demonstrations that Ottoman Europe. The Young Turk Revolution prevailed. On July 24, Sultan Abdul Hamid decreed the Restoration of the 1876 Constitution. This highlighted that it was not the masses, but the ability to use them, that determined political changes.

Yet, the Ferizaj insurgency was subject to conflicting demands. On one hand, General Mahmut Şevket Pasha, the governor and commander of Kosova, denounced what he called "foreign interference" and called on the privileged Albanian landowners to support the sultan. Prominent landowners (including Isa Boletini from the north, Bajram Curri and Sulejman Agë Batusha from Gjakova, Qerim Mahmut Begolli from Peja, and Jahja Bey and Rasim Aga from Prizren) hence sided with the sovereign "to defend their homeland from their neighbors." On the other hand, however, insurgents yielded to Mirliva Galib Bey, the commander of the Gendarmerie Regiment of Shkup. As a member of the CUP, he used his superior position to garner support for the revolution. He relied on the people's fear of a foreign intervention and offered the restoration of the constitutional monarchy as a solution. A constitutional government, he claimed, would prevent foreign meddling in the internal affairs of the empire.[704]

---

[703] Gawrych, *Gjysmëhëna . . .*, 230.

[704] Gawrych, *Gjysmëhëna . . .*, 230.

The split among Ottoman state officials had an impact on the Albanians, who themselves were divided into opposite camps: the educated elite, which had mostly begun to side with the Young Turks, and the landowners who still defended the sultan and the caliphate. However, the support seemed largely dependent on the evolving circumstances. Some activists insisted that the gathering of Ferizaj take a reconciliatory approach so that all parties join forces to protect the country from what they called "Austrian occupation." For instance, Nexhip Draga, who led the Young Turks in the Shkup branch, supported the promulgation of a constitution, but he agreed to maintain the monarchy with Sultan Abdul Hamid as the head of state. Isa Boletini, a deputy chief of the police, equaled the calls for a constitution with disloyalty to the monarch (Boletini remain a supporter of Abdul Hamid on later occasions as well). Nevertheless, in meetings held in mid-July, Albanian leaders from Kosova agreed to avoid divisions. They decided that, in absence of an alternative, constitutional monarchy ought to be the compromise for the sake of the *vatan*. Among the participants, Hasan Prishtina seemed the most active in trying to bring about reconciliation of the factions. During the July meetings, the focus hence shifted to preparations needed against the reforms that could endanger the integrity of the Albanian lands and a potential foreign invasion. The activists alluded to Austro-Hungarian intervention,[705] even though it was very unlikely given the sultan's excellent relations with Vienna and Berlin. In addition to the railway project, Abdul Hamid has signed on to a secret military pact with the German-speaking empires, which would be obligated to protect the Ottoman Empire in case of a foreign invasion, especially from the Balkan countries.[706]

The Young Turks were well aware of the sultan's friendship with the Central European empires, but they wished to gain momentum by speculating with the sentiment against the railway. The demands for autonomy, however, were not mentioned anywhere. In the Ferizaj meeting, self-government was ignored, but not because doing so helped defend the country against the propagated foreign invasion, but because the Young Turks opposed Albania's autonomy. However, unlike Abdul Hamid who rejected the Albanian demands as "jeopardiz[ing] the unity of the Ottoman Empire," the Young Turks adopted the slogan "that all citizens of the Empire, as Ottomans, lived in equality, brotherhood, and liberty" guaranteed under the

---

[705] H.P.Sh. 2 (2002), 376.

[706] See: *Die Grosse Politik der Europäischen Kabinette 1871-1914* (Samlung der diplomatischen Akten des Auswärtigen Amtes, Berlin, 1915-1927, volume 25, 2. p. 870.

constitution and the parliamentary government. Owing to their fears of an Austrian invasion, Albanians of all political views as well as the clergy found no alternative but to join arms with the Young Turks who agreed to retain the sultan as head of state and caliph in accordance with Islamic law.

The Young Turks were not reluctant to compromise over the sultan for they knew that constitutional monarchy would strip Abdul Hamid of his absolute power and the influence of the hardline clergy would be curtailed. Thus, on July 20, insurgents gathered at the Ferizaj meeting sent a telegram to the sultan, requiring the immediate restoration of the 1876 Constitution and the convocation of the parliament. Two days later, rebel leaders at Ferizaj transmitted another telegram, advising the monarch that if the constitution was not immediately announced, "the people will march with their guns to İstanbul."[707]

The ultimatum tone was the message of the Young Turks, who were now well prepared to compel the changes. They managed to fully infiltrate the Ferizaj gathering, even though Kosovar Albanian leaders in Ferizaj pronounced a *besa* (*Alb.*, word of honor) as a patriotic pledge of allegiance to the sultan and the homeland, noting that "faith and religion" (Trk.: *din ve iman*) as their motivation.[708] Moreover, they defined the constitution as a document guaranteeing "the sacred rights of the padishah and the general safety of the *vatan*."[709] It is the wording, however, that seems to have encouraged conservatives to sign the communication to the sultan; the mufti of Shkup also added his name to the proclamation of *besa* by the 194 "imams, *shehs*, beys, and tribal chieftains of all Kosova" gathered at Ferizaj.[710]

The demands undoubtedly came as a shock and great disappointment to Abdul Hamid. The telegram was a major blow to the sultan's policy of relying on Albanians to prop up his thirty-two year old regime while refusing to grant the ethnic group the status of a nationality in the empire. Yet, the reinstatement of the constitution seemed imminent after the Ferizaj demands. It is likely that Grand Vizier Mehmet Ferit Pasha, himself an Albanian, urged the sultan to concede in an effort to spare the country from bloodshed. On July 23, attempting to find a scapegoat, Abdul Hamid sacked his prime minister, citing his failure to maintain the loyalty of fellow Albanians; Mehmed Said Pasha was subsequently appointed to the office. However, on

---

[707] H.P.Sh. 2 (2002), 377.

[708] Gawrych, *Gjysmëhëna . . .*, 232.

[709] *Ibid.* 233.

[710] *Ibid.*

July 24, the sultan announced his decision to restore the constitution, ending thirty-two years of his absolute rule in the empire.

For over three decades, Abdul Hamid had presided over a government with two faces; progressive from the outside and hardliner from within, the Hamidian regime was unable to adopt European military and economic advancement, while still retaining the despotic oriental mentality and the dated social order. The Ferizaj Convention put an end to the autocratic rule, while the Albanians proved a key factor, no matter how much they were aware of their influence. The Revolution succeeded by uniting all masses, but it remained to be seen how sincere the unity was. Above all, what remained to be seen was whether the Young Turks would keep their promises to those who paved the road to victory—that is, the Albanians.

The popular jubilation for the constitutional monarchy was well-founded. The constitution guaranteed the life, liberty, and sanctity of property to all subjects—or the Ottomans, as they were called—regardless of religion and race. The euphoria of solidarity and joy swept across the empire and triumphant crowds staged huge rallies in almost every town in Kosova and others parts of Rumelia. The proclamation of the constitution, or *hürriyet* (*Trk.*, freedom), enthused the Albanians in their exaltation of the Young Turk slogan of "liberty, equality, fraternity, and justice." Only a handful of conservative landowners and clerics from the privileged Hamidian elite welcomed the constitution in somber self-restraint.[711]

The Albanians were not the only ones to celebrate. The Young Turk call for "freedom and equality" appealed to many Macedonian Slavs in the vilayets of Manastir, Selanik, and Janina as well as to Kosova Serbs. The new regime sought to appeal to all groups, particularly to Christian peoples. It was an attempt to demonstrate that Ottomanism was a formula that reconciled and united all subjects of the Ottoman Empire indiscriminately. The CUP, standing at the forefront of all events, took a proactive role with statements that conveyed an image of unity, progress, and brotherhood.

"We are all equal; we are all proud to be Ottomans," said İsmail Enver Bey, the Turkish officer from the Resen uprising who had now been promoted to the rank of a major along with his Albanian comrade, Ahmet Njazi. A hero of the Revolution, İsmail Enver urged religious minorities to join the CUP, where in which a number of Greeks, Bulgarians and Serbs had already began to adhere. Accordingly, over a thousand Greek, Slavic, and Albanian

---

[711] H.P.Sh. 2 (2002), 377.

committees symbolically handed over any unnecessary arms to the authorities. When the VMRO leader, Jane Sandanski, threw his weapons away, he gained immediate popularity among the Young Turks and received wide attention in the press. In an interview to *Tanin* (*Trk.*, Echo), a CUP organ, the Slavic-Macedonian leader praised the Revolution. He stated that the regime change was the right answer to the very causes of the guerrilla war and announced that his organization had concluded its armed activities.[712] Serbian and Greek committees followed Sandanski's example soon after.

Nonetheless, Slavic and Hellenic bands did not renounce guerilla war because, as the Young Turks claimed, the constitutional liberties had made the *chetas* unnecessary; the *komitis* gave up their activities at the orders of their true masters—Serbia, Bulgaria, and Greece. In the following days, major developments were to take place in the region: Austria-Hungary annexed Bosnia-Herzegovina, Greece assumed Crete, and Bulgaria gained full independence, ending Ottoman suzerainty. Thus, the Balkan states, some of which would receive other benefits, waived, at least temporarily, their efforts to destabilize Ottoman Europe. Their fear was that continued *cheta* activities could lead the Young Turks to adopt a radical pro-Albanian approach. The new regime was expected to revenge on Austria-Hungary and Bulgaria by reorganizing the remaining Ottoman territory in Europe (*i.e.*, the Albanian provinces and the Vilayet of Selanik). The options included the creation of a self-governing Albanian entity and restructuring of the Vilayet of Selanik in accordance with its Slavic and Vlah ethnic makeup and in a way to prevent Bulgarian interference in the future. Yet, in doing so, the Young Turks would violate the principles of Ottomanism, which they increasingly relied on to rebuke any regional autonomy.

The likelihood of an Albanian state was Serbia's nightmare, too. Seeing the Bulgarians reach their historic goal and the Greeks take over Crete, Belgrade anticipated Albania to be the next beneficiary following the reinstatement of the Ottoman constitution. The Slavic state also feared European support its southern neighbors. Austria-Hungary was a traditional supporter of Albania and Russia could also play along with Vienna in exchange for free passage through the Marmara Sea. On the other hand, Britain could also have an interest in Albania, and both Russia and Italy would lend their approval, in hopes to curb the Austrian influence in the region. However, Vienna could have also decided to annex Albania, provoking an uprising to

---

[712] Gawrych, *Gjysmëhëna . . .*, 234.

387

warrant intervention and, more importantly, assuaging Serbia with parts of the Kosova and Manastir vilayets.

Such possible scenarios explain the nonbelligerent position that the revolutionary organizations took in Macedonia. As instruments of the Balkan governments, the *chetas* were there to further the masters' interests on the Albanian vilayets, by generating disorder and imposing the outstanding issue of the Macedonian Slav minority. Thus, if the strategy were to aid Albania's statehood, it would be counterproductive for secret groups to carry out attacks in Ottoman Europe.

From Common Interests to Disagreements with the Young Turks

Albanians form clubs and open schools in a historic leap of the national awakening. Two political factions emerge: institutionalists calls for Albanians to use their constitutional freedoms for political and cultural emancipation; autonomists seek self-government. Parliamentary elections are held for the first time after the reinstatement of the constitution; Albanians win seats in the assembly and raise their voice for the national question. The Congress of Manastir sanctions the use of Latin alphabet for the Albanian language, marking the nation's ultimate return to its roots, in the Western civilization. The Young Turks, however, insist on the Arabic script; in retaliation to the Congress of Manastir, the authorities turn against Albanian education and cultural life. Grand Vizier Hakki Pasha declares in the Ottoman parliament that the Latin letters signified the Albanian secession from the empire. A handful of pro-Ottoman Albanians in Kosova and Shkodër also rally for the Arabic abjad. In 1910, the Ottoman government banned the use of Albanian language in schools and shut down newspapers and magazines in the language. The empire's chief theologian orders Kosova muftis to not use the Albanian letters. An Islamist organization is founded in İstanbul, demanding the Ottoman-Arabic alphabet for the Albanian language. At the same time, the Albanian Youth Society at İstanbul University defends the Latin alphabet.

The constitution brought hope of social and political change that would relieve the Albanians of discrimination based on religion or nationality. They embraced Ottomanism as a new form of government and expression of patriotism that united all Ottoman subjects on the principles of equality and liberty. While persecution of dissidents had been so rampant under the Hamidian regime, the Young Turks reversed the trend: not only did they release thousands of prisoners throughout the empire; they also amnestied and gave preferential treatment in the new administration to those who had opposed the absolutist monarchy. Local Young Turk committees assumed control of all levels of government; they began to reach to people of all backgrounds.

The positive climate was felt even among Albanians. Since the 1878 League of Prizren, activists of the national movement had suffered greatly under the Hamidian regime. Many were persecuted, tortured, imprisoned, or deported. Over 5,000 Albanians—only from Kosova, Manastir, and Janina—were released from imprisonment and internment. Many of them regained their property and wealth confiscated by the regime; some even received took compensations from local Young Turk committees and became affiliated with such entities. Prominent Albanian leaders, such as Ismail Qemali, Ibrahim Temo, and Dervish Hima, returned home from nearly a decade in exile.

There was also concern that in the euphoric moments following the victory, the Ottoman Empire could face external reaction. On October 5, Bulgaria surprisingly declared its independence. A day later, Austria-Hungary announced the annexation of Bosnia-Herzegovina, fully severing the region's ties with İstanbul. Crete, then an autonomous province, proclaimed its unification with Greece. None of the Great Powers came to the aid of the Ottomans, and the Young Turk government found itself in diplomatic isolation.

This came as no wonder given the CUP's determination to halt foreign interference in domestic affairs, particularly with respect to Macedonia, where the European involvement had led the Young Turks to accuse the Great Powers of seeking to occupy the troubled parts of the empire. From April to June 1908, during the campaign preceding the revolution, the Young Turks became unduly hostile to Austria-Hungary and Germany, countries that were friendly to Abdul Hamid. Ahmet Njazi's declaration during the uprising highlighted "the risk of the invasion from Austria-Hungary," and called on the people to fight Vienna's interests and for the Ottoman Empire to severe economic ties with the Austrians. be fought in this part, and to break all economic ties with them.

And indeed, the annexation of Bosnia-Herzegovina and the fallout with the Young Turk government quickly destroyed all the long ties that the Danubian monarchy had with the emperor at Bosphorus. The Young Turk leaders, though, intended the precise consequences when they instructed the Albanians to rise against Vienna and boycott Austrian goods. The result was such that it discontinued all economic and commercial ties and caused the removal of all students and intellectuals residing in the Austro-Hungarian Empire. Now, Young Turks were convinced that Vienna also had its hands in the sudden declaration of independence of Bulgaria and Crete's unification with Greece. Secret deals were purportedly stricken, the new government thought, to urge the CUP leadership to abandon its attacks on Austrian interests.[713]

Albanian support, in the meantime, became even more important for the empire. Under such circumstances, Ismail Qemali led residents in his hometown of Vlora to sign a petition promising support for the Ottoman Empire during this diplomatic crisis. The Austrian vice-consul, Taha, reported from Manastir of a wave of Ottoman as well as Albanian patriotic sentiment sweeping across the country.[714] Austrian documents do not indicate that Qemali employed anti-Austrian rhetoric, as the Young Turks required of him. The Albanian leader was likely cautious, knowing that Vienna remained an influential factor among the Great Powers.[715]

Despite the diplomatic standoff, the people of Kosova and Shkodër vilayet perceived the constitution as a declaration of freedom and the right of self-government of Albania. Since the first days after the revolution, Young Turk committees in towns such as Shkup, Prizren, Gjakova, Peja, Gjilan, and Kaçanik, began to replace the old administration. The new regime exiled many mutessarifs, kaymekams, judges, gendarmerie commanders, and police officers, who had served under Abdul Hamid. Caretaker councils were formed to provide for a local government. A campaign to reconcile blood feuds among local families was also noticed.[716]

However, as the old administration unraveled rapidly in Albania, a substitute was not adequately provided, leading many areas to show signs of anarchy. Thus, Young Turks formed local committees, also called CUP, which began to take over the local government, instituting a responsible administration and justice system. At all times during this transition, the local committees took the Albanians into account and worked with them

---

[713] *Ibid.* 236.

[714] *Ibid.*

[715] See the Austrian-Hungarian, Kral from Manastir, to Aerenthal, on November 23, 1908, nr 73, HHStA, PA XIV/15, Albanien XI/6.

[716] H.P.Sh. 2 (2002), 378.

closely throughout the country. The Young Turk committees in many cities showed greater interest in the Albanian population and this was to be expected given the Albanians held a leading role in the local groups and served as a bridge connecting the people with the new government.

In the Vilayet of Kosova, the political situation remained tense such that the Young Turks were able to establish their own local committees only in larger towns such as Shkup and Ferizaj. In many other cities the Young Turks formed mixed committees with representatives of the local noblemen and members of the Ottoman CUP. Nevertheless, the Shkup-based CUP became an important body of governance for the whole vilayet, hence placing the Young Turks at the forefront of the Kosovar leadership.[717]

The greatest advance that the Revolution secured was the freedom for political organization, the free press, and the rights of the Albanians to seek cultural emancipation through a national education. Almost all Albanian political forces embraced the idea of a national movement friendly to the new liberal regime. Activists aimed at pursuing national and political interests in legal means through state institutions and the parliament, seeking equality and civil rights for the Albanians. This premise ended the illegal political activity and the related violence that emerged since the Macedonia crisis, where Slavic and Greek model of armed bands had succeeded in having Albanian groups, too, join their cause.

The political freedom and the pluralistic nature of parliamentary democracy also necessitated efforts at clarifying the national demands of the Albanians. Two aspirations defined the national movement—the struggle for statehood and cultural emancipation. But under the new circumstances, the question arose on how to reach the goals of the Albanians. Were they to insist on an autonomous state or were they to temporarily suspend plans for self-governance and focus on cultural issues and education first as not to risk the very political freedoms that afforded such progress?

At the very least, it was during this period that Albanian schools opened throughout the country, assisting in the teaching of the Albanian language and strengthening the national consciousness and unity of the ethnic group. On the other hand, the demands for autonomy certainly led to an unavoidable strictness with the Young Turks, who had already embraced the Ottomanist doctrine, announced in the 1876 Constitution (Article 8). This was later included in the program the CUP adopted at the meeting held in

---

[717] *Ibid.*

Thessaloniki in the first days of September of 1908, declaring Turkish the official language of education and state administration.[718]

This, nevertheless, did not exclude the Albanian nationality rights. In parliament, deputies could raise the question of their future status as a nation and ethnicity. Moreover, the constitution approved by the Young Turks was not unchangeable: it could be supplemented or amended accordingly with the approval of the parliament and chances of an amendment were very high in light of propositions by all sides. The *Kombi* newspaper, days after the promulgation of the constitution, wrote that "the desire and the means of every Albanian should be self-government and adopting a national constitution, that of an Albanian state. All of our actions should turn there."[719]

The second demand pertained to national and cultural emancipation, which would require the opening of Albanian schools and would take at least ten to twenty years to reach a satisfactory stage. The bulk of Albanians supported the idea; in cities, in particular, citizens sought to create some preconditions for education. The *Shkopi* newspaper called for the opening of Albanian schools, but also appealed for political rights: the recognition of the Albanian nationality by the Ottoman government and self-government for Albania.[720]

A great proponent of education was the son of Abdyl Frashëri, Mit'hat Frashëri, who between 1908 and 1910 ran the *Lirija* (*Alb.*, Freedom) newspaper in Thessaloniki. After the Revolution, the young intellectual stated that the Albanians would see their cultural and educational demands fulfilled and "will enjoy the fruits of modern culture if they entered in the com\munity with the Turks" and "will cooperate with [the CUP], because nothing separates the Young Turks and the Albanians."[721]

The cooperation with the Turks, propagated by Frashëri, could provide an opportunity for emancipation. But this was not without a price. Soon, the Albanian demands, whether cultural or political, conflicted with the principles of Ottomanism and the concept of an *Osmanlı* (*i.e.*, Ottoman) nation that the Young Turks emphasized especially in their program for national emancipation. The government began to view the Albanian demands with suspicious and even accused them of separatist tendencies.

---

[718] *Ibid.* 380.

[719] *Kombi* (July, 31, 1908).

[720] *Shkopi* (Nov. 15, 1908).

[721] *Liria* (Thessaloniki: July 17 – Aug. 18, 1908).

Despite these differences and suspicions, nevertheless, the new regime provided room for an organized political and cultural movement that would further serve to strengthen the national conscience and to unite the people. For this purpose, immediately after the Revolution, cultural clubs were established in various Albanian towns and other parts of the Ottoman Empire where Albanians lived. Many Albanian schools were also built in the country; foreign schools began to teach native students their mother tongue; and attempts to adopt a unified Albanian alphabet were made during this time.[722]

In the wake of these events, on July 31, 1908, patriots in Manastir formed the *Bashkimi* (*Alb.*, Union) Club. Fehmi Zavalani, who had just been released from internment as president, was elected president, Gjergj Qiriazi served as vice-president, and Naum Naçi became the group's secretary. The *Bashkimi* Club soon became the largest and most important organization in Albania. Renowned for its contribution to the national movement, the Manastir-based group encouraged and assisted the formation of other sister clubs. Just through August and September 1908, clubs were founded in Korça, Vlora, Elbasan, Shkodër, Shkup (The Albanian Educational School), Kumanova (Mac.: Kumanovo), Tetova, Berat, Pogradec, Filat, and Janina. Well over forty groups were formed throughout Albania, while notable activities also took part in other parts of the empire, particularly in Selanik and İstanbul.[723]

The clubs were broad, pro-democracy organizations with a diverse membership. Intellectuals and state officials were most often elected club leaders. The groups adopted almost identical statutes with mission statements therein calling for the Albanians to enjoy their constitutionally-guaranteed rights. First and foremost, the right of education in the native language was an imperative for the Albanian clubs. To foster progress, they called for "the enlightenment [of the nation] through education," for Albanian schools, the development of the national language, publication of books and newspapers, and cultural advancement of the people.[724]

During this period, the nation saw an unprecedented outburst of *Rilindja*'s illuminist spirit that helped the Albanians make critical strides for the time. Club leaders demonstrated outstanding wisdom in declaring that they would "not interfere with politics"; instead, they took advantage of the

---

[722] H.P.Sh. 2 (2002), 381.

[723] *Ibid.* 381.

[724] *Ibid.*

favorable climate after the revolution to promote social progress in the country. Circumstances were conducive, and the clubs greatly contributed to, the national emancipation of Albanians of all backgrounds.

Noticeably, in the aftermath of the Revolution, the Young Turks did not oppose the activity of Albanian clubs. Representatives of the Young Turk committees agreed in many aspects with the cultural and educational movement of Albanians and considered it useful to strengthen Ottomanism. Local Turks and the hardline clergy, on the other hand, having lost power with the restoration of the constitution, sought to suppress the Albanian activists in the name of Ottomanism. In Elbasan, it was only after a major confrontation between Albanians and Turks that local activists were able to establish the *Bashkimi* Club. Similar objections arose in Vlora as well, when local Albanians gathered to form the *Labëria* Club. In Shkodër, local Turks and fundamentalist clergymen disbanded the city's Albanian club, arresting Dervish Hima, a patriot who called for a free and independent Albania. Hima had recently returned from exile prompted by his rejection of the Young Turk notion that the Albanians were Ottomans.[725]

The increasing pressure on Albanian clubs and patriotic activists to "lighten" their opposition to Ottomanism did not remain without consequences. Gradually, some clubs withdrew from genuine activities, while others were subjected to Young Turk control, as was the case of the Thessaloniki club, which attracted criticism from many patriots. However, some groups quickly adapted to the circumstances, creating "special committees" within the legal clubs to pursue the campaign in support of Albania's autonomy. The special committees, while described in some instances as "secrets,"[726] cannot be compared with the clandestine activity of the *chetas* that appeared during the Macedonian crisis. The turmoil in Macedonia embraced the slogan of the "liberation war" against the Ottoman Empire, based on a well-known Slavic-Orthodox model and political aspirations. The special units, on the other hand, were under the supervision of the İstanbul Committee and served as an intensification of the war for Albanian autonomy within the Ottoman Empire. Its service was to oppose the centralized Young Turk government and, for this reason, open (not clandestine) protests were expected. The protests ultimately lead to rebellions and large-scale armed uprisings, leading to the very declaration of independence in 1912.

---

[725] *Ibid.* 383.
[726] *Ibid.*

Before the Young Turk repression began, the clubs played an important role in organizing the national movement through peaceful activities. At their initiative, Albanian-language newspapers were published for the first time in Albania and the Ottoman Empire. Notably, the *Shkupi* newspaper, named after the place of publication, was issued at the capital of the Kosova Vilayet under the directorship of Jashar Erebara. [727] The Albanian press developed quickly throughout Albania, with towns such as Korça, Manastir, Janina, and Elbasan, maintain regular publications. In metropolitan centers of the Ottoman Empire, Mid'hat Frashëri edited the Thessaloniki-based *Liria* (1908-1910), while Dervish Hima oversaw the publication of *Shqipëtari* (1909-1911) in İstanbul. In the meantime, the diaspora publications continued, particularly in Sofia, Bulgaria, in Egypt, and the United States. Between 1908 and 1912, in Albania and abroad, more than thirty-five newspapers were published in the Albanian language.[728]

In addition to the founding of clubs and publications that sprung rapidly throughout, Albanian activists remained devoted to the cause of national education. While the new constitution recognized a right to education for all citizens, regardless of religious affiliation, it nonetheless declared them to be all "Ottomans" with Turkish as their language, which precluded non-Turkish speakers from receiving a public education in their own tongue. The opening of Albanian schools and the spread of education in the native language, therefore, continued to dominate the agenda of the Albanian national movement. In particular, the campaign for education remained a duty for the clubs and patriotic societies.

The opening of Albanian schools was a serious challenge for the religiously-diverse ethnic group. Until 1908, the schools in Albania had been organized in accordance with religious lines—Muslim, Orthodox, and Catholic. As Albanian patriots sought to unite the people and nurture their national consciousness, secular schools became a necessity. [729] Indeed, most new schools were irreligious, consistent with the recommendation of *Rilindja* activists, including Veqilharxhi and the Frashëri brothers.

Based on the *Rilindja* principles, the first secular elementary school opened on August 2, 1908, in the city of Elbasan. During September, Albanian schools were established in Tirana, Berat, Gjirokastër, and Korça. Similar

---

[727] *Ibid.* 384.

[728] *Ibid.*

[729] Skëndi, *Zgjimi kombëtar shqiptar*, 334.

institutions were also launched in Manastir and the Nistova village in the vicinity of Dibër, while an existing school in Prizren continued to serve its students.

The education campaign attracted foreign support as well. The Austrian ambassador to İstanbul, Johann von Pallavicini, presented the Sublime Porte with Vienna's request for the introduction of the Albanian language in all state schools in rural Albania.[730]

The pressure on the Porte by Albanian leaders who were also senior activists of the CUP led to an order by the Ministry of Education in October of 1908 mandating the teaching of the Albanian language as a subject in national Turkish primary and secondary schools. At the end of October, the *Bashkimi* Club of Janina decided to introduce the Albanian language in all Turkish schools and develop an Albanian school for the training of Albanian language teachers for the whole Janina Vilayet.[731]

Albanian was taught even in Kosova. Nexhip Draga, one of the leaders of the Shkup Club, opened several schools in rural Kosova. Observing this expansion, citizens from Prishtina and other towns of the vilayet petitioned the Sublime Porte to allow the teaching of the Albanian language in public schools, especially in high schools. These demands were accepted, even though pro-Turk forces and fanatical Islamists in parts of Kosova requested the contrary and protested against the decision, claiming it weakened the empire and the Islamic culture.

In addition to the introduction of the Albanian language in Turkish schools, another great success was for the national education was the founding of the Normal School in Elbasan. The school began operating on December 1, 1909, and was the first national Albanian high school. Its first teachers were well-known patriots and intellectuals, including Aleksandër Xhuvani, a philologist educated in Greece, distinguished in the field of literature, and Sotir Peci, who also studied in Greece for mathematics and physics and served as director of *Kombi* newspaper in the United States. Luigj Gurakuqi was appointed as the first director of the school.[732] In the first year, 160 students from all over the country enrolled at the school; 50 came from Kosova. Albanian clubs, such as the ones in Shkup and Dibër, sent many of

---

[730] Vienna's reliable memorandum no. 77 on October 8, 1908, HHStA, PA XIV/15, Albanien XI/6.
[731] H.P.Sh. 2 (2002), 389.
[732] *Ibid.* 418.

the students, while other attended under the supervision of the patriots, including Hasan Prishtina, Bajram Curri, and Nexhip Draga.[733]

Owing to the efforts of the Education Club of Shkup, and particularly to Hasan Prishtina and other patriots from Kosova, Albanian schools opened in the vilayet. Gjilan and Pozharan, towns in the Morava region, had their own schools in fall 1909. Schools had previously opened in Prizren, Gjakova, Peja, and Vuçitërn. In January of 1910, the Shkup club established a private Albanian school in this city, while in February another institution began to operate in Mitrovica.[734]

The growing focus on education and the eventual calls for the state to financially support Albanian schools prompted the objections of Islamic fundamentalists in parts of the Kosova and Shkodër vilayets. Young Turk clubs and some Albanian feudalist supporters of Sultan Abdul Hamid protested for the introduction of the Albanian language in Turkish schools and the opening of private Albanian schools in general. In grievances to the central government, the opponents of Albanian education stated that the schools were not expressions of the Muslim willpower, but instead of foreign agents. In some cities of the Kosova and Shkodër vilayets, there were open protests and demonstrations against Albanian schools.

The propaganda against Albanian education intensified as Albanian activists presented their demands in İstanbul and sought to realize their goals by exercising the political rights guaranteed under the constitution. The propaganda was now supported also by the Greek Church, which openly threatened Albanian Orthodox students seeking to learn their native tongue with excommunication.[735] Such was the situation as to create the impression of a conspiracy to provoke the masses into refusing Albanian education after the government had permitted it. Soon, after the opposition surged in the Kosova and Shkodër vilayets, the Young Turks changed their position on the use and teaching of the Albanian language, because "this will help create a separatist awareness."

Other difficulties in promoting Albanian education were textbooks and the alphabet. Because Albania was unable to print textbooks, the majority came from abroad, especially from Romania. Upon the promulgation of the constitution, the *Bashkimi* Society of Bucharest sent, in care of the Manastir

---

[733] *Ibid.*

[734] *Ibid.*

[735] K. Kral report directed to Aerenthal from Shkodër, January 20, 1909, including the documents of the State Archive of Austria, HHStA, PA XIV/15, Albanien XI/6.

Club, about 20,000 primers and other Albanian books. The Bucharest group remained the leading supplier of books for the Albanian schools, this being one of the greatest contributions the society gave for the consolidation of national education. The books, however, were not written with a unique alphabet; three different scripts were prevalent in the country. In the north, two scripts, promoted by the literary societies based in Shkodër, *Bashkimi* and *Agimi* (*Alb.* Dawn), were used; the İstanbul or Frashëri alphabet dominated in the south. However, all writing systems were based on the Latin script and some included additional characters borrowed from other alphabets. The only difference was that the *Agimi* and İstanbul alphabets used one character per sound, while *Bashkimi* employed digraphs for sounds not covered by the basic Latin letters.

The standardization of the alphabet was not only a cultural issue; under the circumstances, it also appeared as a political debate that threatened the internal unity and the dilemma of the East and West that reemerged in the final years of Ottoman rule. The use of Latin letters was now already a resolved matter for the Albanians and had created the preconditions for national unity. This determination would announce once more another important victory of the Western civilization to redeem the space lost five centuries ago, for which loss the Serbs, Greeks, Russians would blame the Albanians who supposedly sided with the Ottomans against the Christians in return for privileges.[736]

Albanian patriots demonstrated a high sense of responsibility on the matter of the East-and-West divide. An important factor in this regard was the foundation of *Shoqëria e të shtypurit shkronja shqip* (*Alb.*, the Albanian Print-Press Society) in İstanbul, a year after the Albanian League of Prizren was formed.[737] The founding document of the society stated the need for emancipation through the native language:

---

[736] For more on the issue, see the Serbian Memorandum of the Orthodox Church in 1909, directed to French, German, British, Austro-Hungarian, and Italian governments. The documents, which complains about the "danger to the Christian civilization from Albanian Islamists and their efforts to ruin European Christianity, is found at the Political Archive of the German Foreign Ministry in Bonn, document no. 13667, Türkei, band. 136.

[737] *Shoqëria e të Shtypurit Shkronja Shqip* was established in İstanbul on September 30, 1879. Sami Frashëri served as its leader. Other members incuded Mehmet Ali Vrioni, Ibrahim Dino, Abdyl Frashëri, Pashko Vasa, Nikollë Banoti Shkodrani, Koto Hoxhi, Anastas Konstandin Frashëri, and Jani Vreto Postenani.

All educated nations have been civilized with the writings of their language. A nation that does not write its own language and does not have publications in its language is in darkness and barbarity. And the Albanians who do not write their own language and who do not have contemporary publications in their language are in the same situation . . . As a result, those who reflect and witness this great catastrophe are also aware of the great need to write and read in their own language.[738]

Many writers feared that without a written language, the Albanians would cease to exist as a nation. In 1878, Konstantin Kristoforidhi expressed the same concerns when writing on a partial translation of the Bible, which was aided by a newly-founded branch of the British Bible Society in Elbasan.[739] Meanwhile, Sami Frashëri wrote to the Arbëreshë author, Jeronim de Rada, that "the Albanian language should be one and undivided, exactly as Albania should be.[740]

The work of the activists in developing the Albanian language culminated at the Congress of the Alphabet, which convened in Manastir between the 14th and 22nd of October 1908. The historic event followed decades of activities that had begun in the 1840s. Then, the *Tanzimât* reforms at least formally recognized the right of Christian peoples to public education in their native tongue.[741] The Albanians, who were denied recognition as a nationality and could have no schools in their own tongue, intensified their endeavors for political rights. Obtaining the status of a nationality and the introduction of the Albanian language in schools and churches became even more urgent as schools and churches in other languages began to gain a foothold among Albanian Christians.[742]

The first and major effort was undertaken by Naum Veqilharxhi (born Naum Panajot Bredhi), a pioneer of the *Rilindja Kombëtare*. He received his

---

[738] See "Shoqëria e Stambollit," *Dituria* II (1926).

[739] For more on the activities of the British Bible Society and the efforts to introduce Albanian as a liturgical language, see Chapter 3.

[740] See parts of the correspondence between S. Frasheri and De Rada in Skëndi, *Zgjimi kombëtar shqiptar*, 117.

[741] Buxhovi, *Kthesa historike 3*, 142.

[742] After the announcement of the *Tanzimât* decree, there was an expansion of Greek and Serbian schools. New Greek-language schools were opened in towns such as Korça and Berat, and despite the secular curriculum, the schools were under the supervision of Greek bishops and marked by an intolerant religious and national spirit.

education abroad and participated in the Romanian rebellion against Turkish rule, where he drew the inspiration to call on his Albanian brethren that "[t]he time has arrived to audaciously change [our] way, moving from now on [on the same direction] as the prosperous nations of the world . . . ."[743]

In this spirit, his efforts to design a special Albanian alphabet ought to be recognized. He thought that Latin, Greek, or Arabic alphabets that were used until then to write Albanian were not only unable to represent all the sounds of the language, but they would also fail to be accepted by all Albanians, because of religious reasons. Borrowing elements from previous alphabets, Veqilharxhi created a new alphabet, which he used in several Albanian texts, including the first primer, *Evetari*, in 1844, and a revised edition, *Fare i ri evetar shqip*, a year later. Veqilharxhi also focused on cultural and scientific terminology, by standardizing and coining new Albanian words to facilitate education.[744]

In addition to Veqilharxhi and his compatriots in the Albanian diaspora in Romania, Bulgaria, and Egypt, powerful impulses emanated also from the Arbëreshë community in Italy. Observing the influence of romanticism and the interest of European linguists in the Albanian language in the first half of the 1800s, Italo-Albanian scholars became increasingly involved in the study of their history, folklore, and the national language they inherited from their former homeland. Notably, the Arbëreshë became proponents of the Pelasgian thesis of Albanian origin, holding that the Albanian people and language descendent from the most ancient inhabitants of the Balkans and the forefathers of the European civilization.[745] Jeronim De Rada called on his compatriots to discover and embrace their heritage, by reclaiming their place in the Western world.

Significant efforts for the Albanian language and its creation of the alphabet were noted after the establishment of *Shoqëria e të shtypurit shkronja shqip* in İstanbul in 1879. Under the supervision of Sami Frashëri, a committee adopted a Latin-based script with additional special characters to be used in textbooks. Known as the İstanbul alphabet, the writing convention first appeared in books published in Bucharest by the *Drita* society together with the literary works of Naim Frashëri and other prominent *Rilindja* writers. The publications issued abroad represented the spiritual and cultural wealth

---

[743] Buxhovi, *Kthesa historike 3*, 144.

[744] *Ibid.* 144.

[745] *Ibid.* 145.

in support of a Latin-based Albanian alphabet, which was further justified on the basis of early books dating back to Buzuku's *Meshari* in 1555. But as other alphabets continued to be used, the time had come for writers to standardize the letters.

The Congress of the Alphabet in Manastir was organized by the Albanian club of the city. Thirty-two delegates from Albanian clubs, societies, and schools arrived from all parts of the country and immigrant colonies. An additional eighteen men attended without the right to vote. Some of the most prominent participants included Mid'hat Frashëri, president of the Thessaloniki club and publisher of the *Lirija* newspaper, the two Catholic priests, Father Gjergj Fishta and Dom Ndre Mjeda, representing the Shkodër-based *Bashkimi* and *Agimi* clubs, and Sotir Peçi, the published of *Kombi* in the United States. Many other prominent activists of the national movement also attended.[746]

The Congress was headed by Mid'had Frasheri as president and vice presidents were Luigj Gurakuqi and Gjergj Qirazi. Meanwhile, two of the delegates who contributed to the working atmosphere and the deepening of the brotherhood were the two religious leaders, Gjergj Fishta and Afiz Ibrahimi, an imam representing Shkup at the Congress. On one occasion, after Fishta delivered an emotional speech, the tearful imam clasped the priest in the arms, fraternally and literally embracing him. This left a vivid impression on the audience of over 300 men, three quarters of whom were Muslims.[747]

The overall work of Congress and its decisions left good impressions. The Congress chose a committee for the alphabet, consisting of eleven of the most educated delegates, who for three days straight maintained a great spirit of collaboration. The committee was headed by Gjergj Fishta.

From the three proposals, the Congress focused on the variant of *Bashkimi* and that of İstanbul. Finally, the commission decided that two scripts— a modified İstanbul alphabet and the new Latin alphabet—would be the only ones used and that all Albanian schools were required to teach both alphabets.

---

[746] Participants also included Shahin Kolonja, Gjergj and Shahin Qiriazi, Dom Nikollë Kaçorri, Hilë Mosi, Mati Logoreci, Thomas Avrami, Luigj Gurakuqi, Adem Shkaba, Bajram and Çerçiz Topulli, Mihail Grameno, Fehmi Zavalani, Dhimitër Mole, Nyzhet Vrioni, Rrok Berisha, Leonidha Naço, Dhimitraq Buda, Akil Etemi, Shefqet Frashëri, Refik Toptani, Grigor Cilika, Emin Bej of Shkup, Hafiz Ibrahim Efendi of Shkup, Ramiz Daci, Xhemal Bej of Ohër, Fahri Frashëri of Resnja, et al.

[747] Skëndi, *Zgjimi kombëtar shqiptar*, 337.

The resolution on the alphabet was an important step towards the unification of education and strengthening national unity. Although it was not an ideal solution, as a single alphabet would be, it was still a wise choice. The İstanbul Alphabet could not be abolished because of its long tradition. However, eliminating all other alphabets, the Manastir decision made it easier for the Albanians to communicate in writing. A paper or a book published in the south now could also be read in the north of the country, or the other way around. This would also help make the Albanians of the Muslim and Christian faiths more aware of their common heritage.[748]

Although the question of the alphabet was the most important in the proceedings, the Manastir Congress was not a simple linguistic meeting, but a political event also.[749] Along the open sessions, closed meetings were also organized to discuss political issues, including relations with the Young Turk government, the struggle for Albanian national rights, cultural and economic development, as well as the relationship with European countries.[750] Finally, a program of eighteen points was developed and handed to the deputy of Korça, Shahin Kolonja, for presentment to the parliament on behalf of the Albanians. The program is an important document of the Congress of Manastir, reflecting the aspirations for the Albanian territorial and administrative autonomy.[751] In the eyes of the Albanians and some European countries among the Great Powers, the project for an Ottoman Albania was in preparation for independence, once the Ottoman Empire were to depart from the continent.

The main points of the program demanded the *"official recognition of Albanian nationality and the Albanian language."* An independent Albanian school system was also sought, by implementing Albanian as the language of instruction in all state schools, while maintaining Turkish as a subject to be taught beginning in the fourth grade in elementary schools. Closely related were proposals for Greek-language schools attended by Christian Albanians. By turning them into Albanian-language state schools, the program also hoped to remove the Greek schools from the influence of the Hellenic clergy.[752] One of the most important demands yet in the education field was

---

[748] *Ibid.* 339.

[749] H.P.Sh. 2 (2002), 394.

[750] *Ibid.* 394.

[751] *Ibid.* 394.

[752] *Ibid.* 395.

the establishment of an Albanian university, which had been an early aspiration of *Rilindja*.

The Young Turks and Islamic fundamentalists feared they were in no position to reach an agreement with educated Albanians that would allow the empire to maintain its presence in Europe. They hence resorted to Islamist propaganda against the alphabet and the Albanian language, seeking to attract the Albanian Muslims to their side even through mass intimidation. The rejection of the Latin alphabet was called a "sin" against the Quran, and it was further said that the holy scriptures would be completely misinterpreted if written and read in Latin letters from left to right and that doing so was against the "rules of the prophet."[753]

The heresy accusations opened the final phase of the struggle for spiritual secession from the Ottoman Empire and the return to Western civilization. While in political discourse the struggle was attributed to autonomy and equality, this was nothing but a useful strategy to achieve national independence while always taking into account the circumstances and the consequences of any action.

With the attitude that the Albanian language be written in Arabic characters, which would shortly turn into an official government request and be followed by a bitter campaign involving most of the fanatic society and the head of the Islamic clergy, the Porte further provoked the Albanian commitment to the Latin alphabet and the protection of the Albanian language and schools. Thus, the national sentiment prevailed over the religious teachings, centuries after the Ottoman conquest was thought to have resolved such dilemmas in favor of Islam.

The furious campaign against the Albanian language and its alphabet resorted to unscrupulous use of the Quran for its polemic, warning of jihad with the unbelievers. However, it should be noted that not all Albanian clergymen accepted the language of İstanbul scholars, and that not all Ottomans thought that the Albanian identity had to be sacrificed for Islam. Instead, there were Albanians who thought that Ottomanism should not be weighed against the Albanian national sentiment, but rather focused on the protection of the Ottoman state and its presence in the European part as their common interest. It was believed that this was the only way to face the hegemonic aspirations of the neighbors and pan-Slavic trends directed by Russia and its allies. Therefore, it was not by chance that many of the repre-

---

[753] See *Liria* (Nov. 15, 1908).

sentatives of the Muslim clergy in Albania supported the Latin alphabet with special characters and that would later be in compliance with the historical tradition of Albanian writing.

Even though the Sublime Porte tried to conceal the patriotic activities of Albanian clerics, there were many imams who supported the Congress of Manastir and the national movement for independence. A notable cleric, Vildan Efendia, a member of the Advisory Committee of the Congress of Manastir, not only opposed the attitude of the Turkish officials, but will also defend the alphabet choice. He criticized the despotic rule of Sultan Abdul Hamid and emphasized the importance of unity for the Albanians, because only united could they protect themselves and the empire. "Albania is now happy," he said, "because it is united through the alphabet, which is a powerful tool for its progress. Any nation has the right to choose the alphabet that suits its language as the Albanians chose the Latin alphabet.[754]

The imam stated that the Turks also had no letters to write their language; they had adopted those of the Arabs. Moreover, he spoke in all the areas that the Commission of İstanbul visited. He stressed that it was wrong to believe that the Quran permitted the writing of the Albanian language only in Arabic letters and argued that the letters did not have a divine origin, but were the creation of man. In his view, "[i]t could not be said that Arabic was the only language that God liked, since there were many religious books written in Turkish. Consequently, there is no obstacle to using Latin characters for the Albanian language."[755]

Imam Vildan Efendia's position was vital to the alphabet issue. He and Colonel Riza, as delegates of the "Albanian Club" of İstanbul, then largely controlled by the Young Turks, had arrived late at the Congress of Manastir and were suspected as missionaries of the CPU. But the two participants of the Congress devoted themselves to the Latin alphabet as a choice purported to best serve the Albanian interests.

In the meantime, even the Bektashis who were key supporters of the Young Turk Revolution refused to join the CPU campaign for Arabic letters. Bektashi representatives in all parts of the country defended the Congress of Manastir and the rights of Albanians for their alphabet. Some clerics even joined militant groups defending the alphabet and were ready to take up

---

[754] Skëndi, *Zgjimi kombëtar shqiptar*, 340.
[755] Kral's report to Aerenthal, Shkodër, Dec. 31, 1908, no. 166, HHStA, PA XIV/15, Albanien XI/6.

arms for this cause.[756] The Bektashis had long supported preaching of faith in the Albanian language and called for an East-and-West conciliation. They also became proponents of the national identity and contributed greatly in the struggle for emancipation. As noted prior, the *tekkes* turned into Albanian schools and clubs, where the national identity was expressed. It is not by chance that the prominent Frashëri brothers came from a Bektashi family, while Naim Frashëri himself would greatly influence Bektashi views on the soul.[757] His theological and literary works would be preached in *tekkes* throughout the country, becoming a source of patriotic inspiration for the illiterate masses.

Although the central authorities of the CUP had declared that they would not be involved in the selection of the alphabet, they soon mobilized against the Albanian national movement and against Albanian schools and clubs throughout the state administration—central and local—and fanatic Muslim clergymen, and the expeditions of the Ottoman generals.[758] In doing so, the Young Turks relied on the so-called "Law on Gangs" and "Law on Societies," statutes which prohibited organizations of all nationalities, except for the Ottoman one. The laws were enacted by the Ottoman parliament in the autumn of 1909, despite the vehement opposition of the non-Turk nationalities, where a part of Albanian deputies were more vocal and warned about the consequences for the stability of the country.

Thereafter, the Young Turks began to take measures that escalated into hostility with the Albanians, turning the latter into protagonists of the Ottoman Empire's collapse. In attempts to pique a conflict with the Albanians, in September 1909, the authorities closed the Albanian school in Peja. In January the following year, another school was closed in Gjilan. And in February, the *vali* of Kosova ordered that all private Albanian schools be closed and that Albanian language classes in public schools be discontinued.

At the beginning of the year, the minister of education stated that "*the [central] Ottoman government will remain neutral in the affairs of the alphabet, but in national schools the Arabic alphabet will be placed.*"[759] The government, however, did not remain "impartial." Rather, it banned the Albanian language from state schools, and mobilized religious, national, and political factors in the matter. These factors worked to undermine the

---

[756] For the expansion of Bektashism in Albania beginning in the 15th century, see Stephen Schwartz, *Islami tjetër* (Prishtinë: 2009).

[757] Naim Frashëri, *Vepra* I (Prishtinë: 1986), 26.

[758] H.P.Sh. 2 (2002), 419.

[759] *Ibid.* 420.

legitimacy of the Latin alphabet. In parts of the Kosova and Shkodër vilayets, some Muslim clerics and fanatics protested against the Albanian schools and the Latin alphabet. This would even encourage some of the Albanian deputies with pro-Turk tendencies to join in the cause for Arabic letters. A deputy from Peja, Mahmut Bedri, Fuat Pasha from Prishtina, and Sait Efendi Idrizi from Shkup were among the six members of parliament, who in "expressing the feelings of the Albanian people," petitioned the Ottoman prime minister in January 1910 to order the use of Arabic letters in Albanian writing and ban the Latin alphabet.[760]

As a response, patriotic deputies, including Ismail Qemali, Hasan Prishtina, Nexhip Draga, and Shahin Kolonja, sent a letter of protest to the prime minister. They called for the legitimate rights of the Albanians to be respected and that the people be allowed to use the alphabet of their choice without government intervention.[761] A Second Congress of Manastir was held between April 2-3, 1910, where the majority of Albanians reaffirmed their preference for the Latin or a modified Latin alphabet.[762]

---

[760] *Ibid.* 420.

[761] *Ibid.* 420.

[762] *The Second Congress of Manastir* convened at the initiative of the town's *Bashkimi* club. Twenty delegates represented thirty-four clubs and societies of the four vilayets as well as the Albanian associations in İstanbul and Thessaloniki. Unlike the previous congress, this gathering included a large number of delegates from the vilayet of Kosova and Manastir. There were representatives from Peja, Gjakova, Gjilan, Mitrovica, Vuçitërn, Shkup, Tetova, and Dibër, among other cities. Among participants were Dervish Hima, Fehmi Zavalani, Petro Nini Luarasi, Hysni Curri, Ferit Ypi, Bedri Pejani, Qamil Shkupi, Gjergj Qiriazi, Bejtullah Gjilani, Themistokli Germenji, Tefik Panariti, Hajdar Billoshmi, Abdyllah Efendiu (Struga), Qazim Iliaz Dibra, Rexhep Mitrovica, and Xhafer Kolonja. Bedri Pejani was elected president of the Congress, while Ferit Ypi and Petro Nini Luarasi served as secretaries. The main acts of the second Congress of Manastir were a Ten-Point Program and a Four-Point Memorandum addressed to the Ottoman government. These documents provided for important measures for the development of national education, protection of the Albanian alphabet with Latin letters, and the publication of textbooks and general literature. For this purpose, an educational-cultural committee called the Academy was established and put in charge in charge of preparing and publishing textbooks, literary works, and an Albanian-Turkish dictionary. Discussions were held about a large school with dormitories to be opened in Shkup, similar to the Normal School of Elbasan, while delegates also explored the possiblities of a bilingual Albanian-Turkish newspaper that would help inform the Albanian and European public opinions of events taking place in the country.

The complete rejection of the Arabic letters at Manastir angered the İstanbul government, which turned to repressive measures against the growing Albanian movement, but eventually failed to curb its momentum. The İstanbul government issued a unilateral decree banning the Albanian press and associations, closing private Albanian schools, and shutting down the publishing houses in Manastir and Thessaloniki. At the same time, the Albanian language was also removed from the curriculum in state schools.

This vandal act, which would lead the Albanians to irreconcilable differences with the Young Turks, would even become the reason for the latter's removal from power shortly after. In advance, this lead to a harsh statement from Ibrahim Haki Pasha, who declared in parliament that:

> The government considers the desire for the adoption of Latin characters (from the Albanian's side) as the first step of secession from Turkey. The government must do its best and will do everything to prevent the adoption of the Latin alphabet.[763]

On April 5, 1910, with the encouragement of the Turkish government, the *Shaikh ul-Islam*, the chief Muslim cleric, wrote to the Albanian leaders:

> [Prior to this], we sent an official letter to the Ministry of Education, warning it not to accept the Latin alphabet for the Albanian language and to have in mind that its use in schools is strictly forbidden. That is why we are addressing this letter to all of the Albanian provinces so that they act as ordered.[764]

Thus, the last efforts against the Latin script were also those of the Young Turks. On April 1910, founded a club in İstanbul called *Arnavud mahfit-u merifi* (*Trk.*, The circle of educated Albanians) in support of Arabic letters. The club was headed, among others, by the cleric and Senator Haxhi Ali Elbasani, and Mahmut Bedriu, a deputy of the Peja district. In addition, the first and last Albanian newspapers ever printed in Arabic letters were issued in İstanbul.[765] This activity did not expand in the Kosova Vilayet as predicted, while opposition arose in the imperial capital itself. Albanian students at the University of İstanbul founded the *Friendship of Youth Albanian Intellectuals*, standing in favor of the Latin script and ultimately defeating the Young Turks and Islamist fanatics at the heart of the empire.[766]

---

[763] HHStA, PA XIV/24, Albanien XIV.

[764] *Ibid.*

[765] *Ibid.*

[766] See *Leka* XII (Shkodër: 1940), documents no, 36, 377, pp. 39-42, 45-47.

From Disagreements to Conflict with the Young Turks

Twenty-six Albanian deputies are elected to the Ottoman parliament in 1908. However, the Young Turks deny a seat to the CUP's co-founder, Ibrahim Temo, for he insists on granting rights to the Albanian nationality. Ismail Qemali creates an opposition party—Ahrar (Liberals)—in the imperial parliament; he is joined by other Albanian deputies opposed to the Young Turks. The CUP's nationalist policies and the unrestrained power of the local Young Turk committees provoke landowners loyal to Abdul Hamid to seek the reinstatement of his absolute monarchy; after the failure of the 1909 Counter-Revolution, the Young Turks take measures against the Albanian people. Albanian schools and publications are banned and activists persecuted. The Ottoman state becomes heavily militarized, as the Young Turks rely increasingly on the armed forces to maintain order; Minister of War Mahmut Şevket Pasha becomes the empire's strongman. The so-called "Law against Gangs" enables the military to take repressive campaigns against Albania; Cavit Pasha leads a series of devastating expeditions against Isa Boletini and other Hamidian landowners in Kosova and in pursuit of highlanders in northern Albania. Following the uprising of 1910, many Kosovars and highlanders seek refuge in Montenegro, where King Nicholas pressures them to serve his political agenda. The highlanders organize another uprising in 1911; the Ottomans mount another campaign against Albania. The Assembly of Greçe demands Albania's autonomy. In early 1912, the increasing influence of the Albanian deputies leads the Young Turks to dissolve the parliament.

Albanians played an important role in the July Revolution. In Ferizaj, tribal chiefs and aristocrats took the commitment to start an uprising, urged the restoration of the constitution, and maintained loyalty to Sultan Abdul Hamid and the empire.[767] Unlike the League of Prizren of 1878, which focused on territorial preservation and creating a vilayet that would be governed by Albanians within the Ottoman Empire, the 1908 movement instead put in a greater effort to replace the Ottoman despotic regime with the constitutional government. Therefore, it can be said that the Revolution found the Albanians more nationally conscious as well as more politically combative. The second constitutional period created a new context for the

---

[767] Gawrych, *Gjysmëhëna dhe shqiponja*, 256.

public discourse. In 1878, Sultan Abdul Hamid closed the Parliament before the creation of the League of Prizren and before the emergence of the Albanian issue, which was required a solution through political means. In 1908, a dynamic Albanianism appeared before the commencement of parliament, ready to continue where it left off thirty years ago.[768]

Albanian deputies, many from a new generation of leaders that emerged from the League of Prizren, won a public forum to debate on government policies. However, the Young Turk Committee brought to power a new, politically-determined leadership that acted quickly "to suppress the system of towers on the outskirts of the empire."[769] This opened interior "fronts" (as opposed to the external, foreign wars), mainly with Albanians who were the most deserving factor for the Young Turks' rise to power and the return of the parliament.

In spite of the difficulties, inconsistencies, and finally the open confrontation with Young Turks, Albanians would take advantage during the four years of the second parliamentary and the constitution (1908-1912). Albanians worked to make the most of the state institutions. Parliamentary life did not force Albanians to give up their demands for cultural, social, and national emancipation. In fact, they continued to work for recognition as a nationality and administrative and political autonomy within the Ottoman Empire. Even though it was met with fierce opposition, Albania's political class attempted to behave responsibly and in accordance with the confidence gained by the voters.

Twenty-six deputies were elected from Albanian vilayets in the Ottoman Empire, but only some of them, such as Ismail Qemali, Hasan Prishtina, Nexhip Draga, Shahin Kolonja, Bedri Pejani, represented the patriotic Albanian forces that acted in parliament as the opponents of the Young Turks' anti-Albanian policies.

However, the trust that Albanian deputies gained passed through very discriminatory circumstances. The electoral law passed by the Young Turks on September 15, 1908 did not recognize any nationality besides that of the Turks and declared all inhabitants of the Ottoman Empire as "Ottomans." In order to run for deputy, one had to accept the Ottoman nationality as their own, know the Turkish language, and possess a large amount of wealth; this excluded a large portion of the city population. Because of this provision

---

[768] *Ibid.* 257.
[769] *Ibid.* 258.

of electoral law, the Catholic population of Shkodër boycotted the elections, and so did the people of Mitrovica, where Isa Boletini, a great friend of Sultan Abdul Hamid, had his own lands and enjoyed the support of a good part of the population. The Young Turks used all their means to persuade voters to vote for Turk and pro-Turk deputies, who stood as candidates for the CUP.[770]

The discriminatory campaign of the Young Turks did not spare the founders of the party itself, even those who had done the most to establish and strengthen the party. Despite the fact that Ibrahim Temo was the founder of the CUP and simultaneously one of the most deserving members of the largest opposition movement, he did not have the support of his own party, since he refused to side with Ottomanism against Albanian interests. Ismail Qemali encountered similar difficulties in Vlora, Hasan Prishtina in Pristina, and other Albanian patriots, respectively. These leaders managed to win through hard work—they were not only regarded as the opponents of the Young Turks, but also as opponents of their local committees who did not hesitate to use police and military forces for campaign purposes.

A good number of Albanian patriots succeeded in joining the Ottoman parliament. Ismail Qemali was elected as a leader of the Albanian caucus and was simultaneously in charge of the liberal opposition, which in December 1908 formed a separate party named *Ahrar* ("Liberals"). *Ahrar* also collaborated with members of other nations of the Ottoman Empire—Kurds, Armenians, and Arabs—that appeared with demands for decentralization of the Ottoman administration and self-governing national provinces.[771]

Ahrar drafted demands for self-government and national education in Albania and Macedonia, but this was followed by fierce nationalist demonstration by Young Turks who warned against undermining the Ottoman centralization. The Albanian vilayets were labeled as supportive to the absolutist government of Sultan Hamid. In light of this assertion, the Young Turks began a campaign against Isa Boletini after the latter declined to join the CUP.[772]

Isa Boletini maintained respect for Abdul Hamid and tried to motivate his supporters against the Young Turks. He first attempted to avoid a conflict, but was quickly declared an "opponent" of the constitution. A

---

[770] H.P.Sh. 2 (2002), 396.

[771] *Ibid.* 397

[772] *Ibid.* 398.

campaign of 1,500 heavy-armed soldiers was deployed against him, and after the first clashes, Isa Boletini retreated to the surrounding villages and later found refuge in Isniq of Peja.[773]

The punitive military forces of the 18th Division of Mitrovica, commanded by Cavit Pasha, set out to find him in March 1909. The Ottomans surrounded Isniq and sought Boletini's surrender. The Albanian nobleman withdrew, but Isniq and several surrounding villages were not spared from the Turkish cannons.[774]

The campaign against Isa Boletini and the measures taken by Cavit Pasha in Kosova, such as taxation and enforcement of mandatory military service, greatly aggravated the situation in the country. In various parts of the country protests and armed confrontations increased noticeably, starting from Mitrovica, Peja, Prizren, Prishtina, and as far as Dibër. Armed clashes with the Ottoman army also took place in several parts of central Albania and made their way to the south. The Ottomans enforced strict penalties against those who refused to serve in the military. To break the resistance to the army, the authorities executed eighty-one Albanian soldiers in Janina in March 1909.[775]

The Young Turks' nationalist course rapidly trumped the promises of "liberty, equality, and brotherhood without distinction of religion and ethnicity," which had attracted the many different nations of the Ottoman Empire to the struggle for the constitution. This disappointed not only the Albanians who had done the most for the Revolution but also many of its initiators who had imagined a different role in the development. *Ahrar* also cooperated with the clergy in Kosova and other parts of Albania to provoke the pro-Hamidian base and inspire an uprising against the Young Turks.[776] Most Albanians, however, did not join the call of *Ahrar*, since Sultan Abdul Hamid II was unable to protect their interests.

Several Albanian officers led by Hamdi Çaushi and feudalists such as Isa Boletini supported what would later be called the military's Counter-Revolution of 1909, which enabled the reemergence of pro-Hamidian elements.[777] It has been theorized that Ismail Qemali played a role in the first

---

[773] *Ibid.*

[774] *Ibid.*

[775] *Ibid.* 399.

[776] Gawrych, *Gjysmëhëna . . ,* 255.

[777] *Ibid.*

uprising by persuading the lower house to accept the new government formed by Abdul Hamid.[778]

The First Army played a crucial role in the escalation of the rebellion. The key stakeholders were mostly Albanians guarding the sultan and the palace, who refused the orders of the war minister. At the time, the minister intended to send these troops to Yemen, where they would have lost some of the privileges they enjoyed in the capital city. Nevertheless, the Young Turks continued to take other measures to deprive Abdul Hamid and the palace from any power after the departure of two Albanian battalions to Manastir. Units from the First Army loyal to the sultan quickly reacted and were joined by theology students as well as other residents of the city. Together they marched to the Hagia Sophia Mosque, demanding the implementation of the sacred Islamic law of Sharia.[779]

As a result of the protests Hüseyin Hilmi, the grandvizier, resigned and, on April 14, Sultan chose another successor. During the turmoil, demonstrators killed a number of army officers and torched several CUP office buildings.

This course of the events, however, did not favor the counter-revolution as the Young Turks quickly gained the support of Mahmut Şevket Pasha. The pasha was already the commander of the Third Army stationed in Thessaloniki when he accepted the call to eliminate the insurgency. Supported by the commander of the Second Army headquartered in Edirne, Mahmut Şevket formed the so-called *Hareket Ordusu* (The Army or the Horde of Action), a military formation consisting of 25,000 regular troops and 15,000 volunteers, including 4,000 Bulgarians, 2,000 Greeks, and 700 Jews. Bajram Curri and Çerçiz Topulli brought 8,000 Albanians with them; Njazi Bey recruited another 1,800 troops from Resnje. On April 24, this multiethnic force easily entered İstanbul and occupied part the city.[780]

The Young Turks decided to use the counter-revolution as a pretext to oust Sultan Abdul Hamid II, and on April 27, four CUP members warned the monarch of his impending end of his reign. This group consisted of two Muslim leaders, a Jew, and an Armenian. One of the Muslim leaders, Esad

---

[778] About the Albanian role in the first uprising, see: Gawrych, *ibid.*; Ismail Qemal Vlora, *Kujtime* (Tiranë); Eqrem Bej Vlora, *Kujtime* (Tiranë); Peter Bartl, *Die Albanischen Muslime zur Zeit der Nationalen Unabhängigkeitsbewegung 1878-1912* (Wisbaden: 1968); Clayer, *Në fillimet e nacionalizmit shqiptar* (Tiranë: 2009).
[779] Gawrych, *Gjysmëhëna . . ,* 254.
[780] *Ibid.*

Pashë Toptani, presented the sultan with a declaration, which included an allegation that the "nation" had removed him from the throne.[781]

Reshat Effendi (1848-1918), Abdul Hamid's brother, took over as sultan. Also known as Mehmed V, the new monarch ruled until his assassination in 1918. Abdul Hamid was deported to Thessaloniki, where he remained under house arrest until the First Balkan War, which brought him back to İstanbul.

After the oppression of the counter-revolution, the CUP and Mahmut Şevket Pasha emerged as the two leading factors in the Ottoman political scene. Mahmut Şevket was put in charge of the army owing to claims that he had saved the Revolution. He first took over the inspector-general's post of the first three armies, and in January 1910, he became minister of war, a position he held until his resignation on July 9, 1912.

In order to "save the country," the CUP and the army both responded with heavily centralized and ruthless policies. For Albania, this meant a military campaign to establish security, and the price that had to be paid was the loss of many privileges, including the right to local government according to the Kanun, the right to bear arms, and the exemption from heavy taxation—the privileges Albania had enjoyed during the last three centuries. Serbian-Orthodox propaganda was used to label Albania as a "lawless country" that supposedly defied the Ottomanist "vision of order and progress" that emphasized unity at the expense of diversity.[782]

This would lead to the approval of a law "against gangs," which gave the military the right to intervene in collecting arms in the name of the national interest. The law provided that the Young Turks could control Albanian lands without exception, hence breaking off with the tradition of "privileges." In assuming the new role, the Ottoman forces surpassed even the janissaries, who despite of their enormous power respected the "armed Albanian," and considered him a patriot and defender of the motherland.[783]

---

[781] *Ibid.* 255.

[782] *Ibid.* 259.

[783] About the Albanian "privilege" to bear arms and its role in the social and political life, see: H.P.Sh. 2 (2002); Skënder Rizaj, *Kosova gjatë shekujve XV,XVI dhe XVII* (Prishtinë: 1982); Gawrych, *Gjysmëhëna . . ,*; Jürgen Faensen, *Die Albanische Nationalbewegung* (Wiesbaden: 1980); Peter Bartl, *Die albanische Muslime zur Zeit der Nationalen Unabhängigkeitsbewegung 1878-1912* (Wiesbaden: 1968); Paul Siebertz, *Albanien und die Albanesen* (Wien: 1910); Marie Amelie von Godin, *Aus dem neuen Albanien* (Wien: 1914); Edith Durham, *The Burden of the Balkans* (London: 1905).

After eliminating the counter-revolutionaries, Mahmut Şevket Pasha held the military above other state institutions. The armed forces already prided themselves as *Nigah-ban-ı Meşrutiyet* (Guardian of the Constitution), and the CUP relied heavily on them to maintain public safety and security.[784] So pervasive was the spirit of militarism in the Young Turk party that main bodies of the organization adopted names of a martial nature, such as *Silah* (weapon), *Süngü* (bayonet), *Bıçak* (knife), *Kursum* (bullet), and *Bomba*. Political militarism was in accordance with the nationalist, Ottoman doctrine that entitled the state to restore order by direct military action.

This confronted the Albanians with military expeditions that led to widespread frustration in the country. To further aggravate matters, Mahmut Şevket Pasha proclaimed that "the only solution for the Albanian issue is the stick."[785] The new governor of Kosovo, Macar Bey, was also once a member of the CUP. He received instructions to implement a tough line against Kosovo, relying on martial law. Besides the fierce campaign for tax collection and enforcement of mandatory military service, he strictly supervised a thorough census of the population, property, and household equipment. He also appointed military courts that had authority to act quickly and harshly against the people.

This behavior led Albanian deputies to address the issue in parliament and demand accountability. In the House of Deputies, Mehmet Ferid Pasha, recently appointed as the internal minister, defended the politics of Kosova's government, arguing that it was in accordance with *"establishing order."* However, Albanian deputies, led by Said Bej and Hysein Fuat Pasha, expressly criticized the methods employed by General Cavit Pasha, who had resorted to copious use of artillery and razed many civilian homes. Albanian deputies were also enraged with the retribution against the insurgents, who they believed were only reacting to the government oppression.[786]

Hasan Prishtina also took part in fierce debates in the Ottoman parliament, criticizing the government for a preemptive, contentious campaign aimed at forcing the Albanians to give up their legitimate political demands.[787] The *Tanin* newspaper reported on Prishtina's speech, which called on the authorities to follow the example of Midhat Pasha, a reformer gover-

---

[784] Gawrych, *Gjysmëhëna . . .*, 260.

[785] *Ibid.* 261

[786] *Ibid.* 267.

[787] Tahir Abdyli, *Hasan Prishtina: një lëvizje kombëtare e demokratike shqiptare 1908-1912* (Prishtinë: 2003), 40.

nor of Danube who had brought much prosperity to his province.[788] Hasan Prishtina warned that military reprisals and violence could not restore normality in Kosova; that had to be done through negotiations with Albanians on their self-governant.

The autonomy issue was set forth by Ismail Qemali in a manifesto published in the Italian newspaper, *La Nazione Albanese*.[789] The writing, which was distributed throughout Albania, castigated the CUP ambitions for a centralized state, and praised autonomy as the only way to save the nation from the "desires of foreigners." The Albanian leader appealed to his compatriots to embrace "self-government for Albania in the shade of the Ottoman Empire."[790]

Qemali further laid out a political platform on key issues regarding the creation of an autonomous state. Firstly, he called for the unification of all Albanian lands into a single *Arnavutluk Vilayeti* (Albanian vilayet) with Ohër or Elbasan as its capital. He also drew approximate borders of the Albanian state, including areas from all four vilayets: he specifically named towns such as Janina, Preveza, Manastir, Dibër, Shkup, Prishtina, Peja, and Prizren as part of the proposed autonomous entity.[791] He suggested that a governor appointed by İstanbul could serve as head of state, while civil servants and military personnel would be of Albanian ethnicity. He further demanded that the Albanian language be used along Turkish for instruction in public schools and that military service be confined to the territory of Albania.[792]

The Ottoman government failed to notice the Albanian demands. Instead, it ordered Cavit Pasha to continue his use of force. As Cavit told *Le Progrès de Salonique* (*Fr.*, The Progress of Salonica), his campaign had no purpose but "to eliminate some Albanian rebels."[793]

Albanian activists in İstanbul and abroad continued to protest, arguing that the actions the Young Turks were taking would ruin the Ottoman Empire. On September 21, 1909, Albanian leaders, Ibrahim Temo and Zenel Abedini from Gjilan, wrote to the minister of internal affairs, Talat Bey,

---

[788] Gawrych, *Gjysmëhëna . . .*, 267.

[789] See "Shpresa jonë, jeta jonë të jetë vetëurdhrimi i Shqipërisë," *La Nazione Albanese* (July 15, 1909).

[790] *Ibid.*

[791] H.P.Sh. 2 (2002), 406.

[792] *Ibid.* 406.

[793] *Le Progrès de Salonique* (Sept. 20, 1909), cited in H.P.Sh. 2 (2002), 408.

calling on him to fight ignorance and substitute education for the arms.[794] In late October, a caucus of Albanian deputies in İstanbul formed a national committee that vouched for an end to the military campaign and a peaceful solution to the Albanian question. The committee proposed that the Sublime Porte send a delegation to northern Albania to investigate the causes of turmoil. The deputies insisted that wrongdoers be punished with due process under the law, and that compulsory military service be restricted to the vilayets of Shkodër, Kosova, and Manastir. Finally, the committee called for measures to promote economic development. These demands were laid out in a memorandum that was accepted and signed by all of the Albanian deputies in the Ottoman parliament.

The Albanian protests and the international pressure, particularly from Austria-Hungary and Italy, compelled the Young Turk government to promise a solution through dialogue. The Porte hence instructed Cavit Pasha to talk with the Albanians in order to restore order in the area. Cavit sat on the table with the people of the Luma highlands and promised that he would withdraw his troops if the Albanians accepted the government's authority. But the retreat has little practical effect, as Cavit Pasha's army remained in Rumelia as a check on future disobedience. The military presence only caused further rebellions in the Kosova vilayet, making it clear to the Turkish government that force was not a solution to the Albanian issue. Interior minister Talat Bey was forced to consider the Albanian demands for Cavit Pasha's withdrawal from Rumelia and his prosecution for initiating the conflict in Kosova.

Violence committed by Cavit Pasha's troop widened the gap between the Albanians and the Young Turks. This is best presented in a report from Shkup, published in the U.S.-based *Dielli* newspaper on November 26, 1909. "The Nation is entitle," stated the article, "to great compensation because of the behavior of some Young Turks ... The ideas and desires for the self-governance of Albania have grown so much, but we have not be able to achieve it even after twenty years of campaigning.[795] The oppressive measures led to a revival of the national movement in Kosova. On April 5, 1910, the Young Turks banned all Albanian schools and clubs, and a harsh military campaign ensued in the vilayet as Cavit Pasha sought to implement government policies by force.

---

[794] H.P.Sh. 2 (2002), 409.
[795] Cited in H.P.Sh. 2 (2002), 411.

Hoping to put an end to the violence, Albanian deputies and senators were tremendously active in the imperial institutions. Albanian leaders worked to restore peace, preserve the territorial integrity, and secure development and progress for their nation. By the end of 1909, a special commission was formed in İstanbul to regulate Albanian relations, serving as a representative of the ethnic group or "an unofficial Albanian government."[796] Among others, Senator Sylejman Pasha, Aziz Pasha, representative of Berat, Hasan Prishtina, General Mehmet Pasha, and Rexhep Efendi, mufti of Manastir, were part of the commission.[797] But the more the political and diplomatic activity of Albanian parliamentarians increased, the more ruthlessly would Cavit Pasha strike against the people of Kosova. This was certainly aided by the collapse of Hilmi Pasha's government in April 1909. The succeeding grand vizier, Haki Pasha, did not appoint even a single ethnic Albanian to his cabinet. In fact, he expressed his anti-Albanian stance in the very first meeting of the new council of ministers, stating that: "The greatest threat to Turkey, from all nations who live in our empire, are the Albanians; it is a great fear that they may be awakened from the deep slumber, recover, and gain knowledge their its own language; for that would be the end of European Turkey."[798]

Observing this situation, the Albanians soon expressed their dissatisfaction by rushing to arms in the early days of spring. Many young people took to the mountains when the Young Turk government instated mandatory military service.

Under pressure by the military, Sultan Mehmed Reshad declared a state of emergency in Kosova and ordered the insurgent forces dispersed. Mehmed also mandated that the organizers of the uprising be arrested and tried in military courts. A census of the population and financial income, compulsory military conscription, and tax collection were also imposed on the people of Kosova. The Porte instructed the minister of war to prepare a punitive campaign as quickly as possible, and Şevket Turgut Pasha, as one of the most eminent generals of the empire, was chosen to carry out the mission.[799]

Leaders such as Isa Boletini, Sulejman Batusha, and Shaban Binaku called an assembly in mid-April to discuss Albanian actions. A meeting was

---

[796] Abdyli, *Hasan Prishtina*, 41.

[797] *Ibid*. 41.

[798] *Leka*, VIII-XII, bl. I (1937): 338, cited in Abdyli, *Hasan Prishtina*, 42.

[799] H.P.Sh. 2 (2002), 427.

held near the town of Deçan at a locality called Verrat e Llukës. But it was not until the gathering of Ferizaj in 1912 that the Albanians would unite for a general uprising against the Young Turks.

Albanian leaders in the Ottoman parliament sought to prevent the escalation of the conflict. In a statement on behalf of the Albanian deputies on April 10, Kosova representative Nexhip Draga called the imposition of the state of emergency unjust and deserving of punishment. Ismail Qemali, Myfit Libohova, and other Albanian deputies presented evidence that the events in Kosova were the result of a weak administration and the primitive measures of the Young Turk government.[800] Hasan Prishtina, furthermore, reminded Grand Vizier Haki Pasha that "if true constitutional regime is established, you will stand in front of the high court." Prishtina asked for the prime minister's resignation, warning that the empire was headed to a catastrophe.[801]

General Turgut Pasha also pretended adopt a peaceful approach. He travelled to the capital of Kosova, Shkup, stating that he was there not to cause more bloodshed, but to establish peace and punish those who motivated conflict. He declared that the government wished to secure the constitutional rights for the Albanian population, and that the rebel's surrender would be beneficial to both, the ethnic group and the empire.[802]

However, Albanian insurgents led by local landowners, Isa Boletini, Hasan Hysen Budakova, and Idriz Seferi, had already prepared for action and disregarded Turgut's call for surrender. Isa Boletini focused on Carraleva and the Ferizaj-Shtime-Prizren line; Hasan Hyseni Budakova on the western part of Ferizaj all the way to Carraleva, and Idriz Seferi on defending Kaçanik and the Tetova-Shkup highway. Initially, the Ottoman army attempted to test and scout on the Albanian forces, by applying minimal strikes, even though many Albanian historians have assessed the course of fighting as indicating a powerful resistance.[803] Thus, by mid-April the command of the Ottoman forces concentrated on the outskirts of Shkup drove small formations into action, and this did not weaken the Albanian defense of Ka-

---

[800] *Ibid.* 429.

[801] Hasan Prishtina, *Dokumente*, extracted from the parliament record the record in parliament, 38-39, cited in Abdyli, *Hasan Prishtina*, 48.

[802] H.P.Sh. 2 (2002), 427.

[803] Albanian academics contradict themselves in presenting the resistance as a large-scale war, and yet blaming the defeat on the limited scope and lack of coordination of the defensive efforts. See H.P.Sh. 2 (2002), 429-438.

çanik. On the last day of April, after the creation of a comprehensive report on the number of Albanian insurgents, Turgut Pasha commenced his attack on Kaçanik with ground troops assisted by cannons that shelled the surrounding villages. Idriz Seferi's fighters resisted, but days later were forced to retreat to Kaçanik. This aided the advancement of Ottoman troops towards Shtime and Ferizaj. There, Isa Boletini endeavored to halt the Ottoman penetration through Carraleva into Prizren and the Dukagjin area. Boletini resisted until mid-May, but could no longer match the superior imperial army. Turgut Pasha acted in accordance with the plan to keep the Albanian rebels divided, and every time they attempted to retreat, they had no choice but to surrender.

The violent repression spread further to other parts of Albania. Even though there was no resistance like in Kosova, Turgut Pasha insisted on "placing order" in the disobedient Albanian vilayets, indicating through acts of terror that the era of local autonomy had forever ended. Moreover, he used several ambushes by members of the Shosh and Shala tribes, to intensify his retaliation against the population. The Ottomans acted in a similar fashion all the way to Shkodër, where they visited solely to establish military courts. After a short stay in Mirdita, the Ottoman general headers to Tirana and Elbasan, where the military courts had sentenced many people to long prison terms for participating in the illegal activities of Albanian clubs.

The military campaign enforced the abrogation of the Kanun in the formerly self-governing areas of Albania and put an end to the ethnic group's cultural movement. The army effectively ceased all Albanian schools as well as publications in the Albanian language. Owners and editors of newspapers were accused as "instigators of revolt," arrested, and imprisoned. In Manastir, imperial troops arrested Fehmi Zavalani, the publisher of *Bashkimi i Kombit*, along with many of his associates, because of an article that exposed the Ottoman atrocities in Kosova. Editors of other newspapers, including Mihail Grameno from Korça and Lef Nosi from Elbasan, were also detained.[804] Similar measures were taken against Albanian language teachers and officials who participated in the cultural movement; notably, Imam Hafiz Alia was interned for ten years for his Islamic lectures in Albanian at the Normal School of Elbasan.[805]

---

[804] See HHStA, PA XIV/24, Albanien.
[805] *Ibid.*

The uprising in Kosova revealed a pessimistic situation in Albania. The Young Turks were determined to increase the role of the military in politics, and for this they enjoyed external support, all the while Albanians lost their willingness to resist the oppression. Hoping to eliminate the risk of an Albanian movement in Kosova, Russia also provided unfettered assistance, including financial handouts, to the Porte to undertake certain reforms in the vilayet. Serbia and Montenegro encouraged Albanian landowners to rise against the empire, and even supplied arms for that purpose. But at the same time, Belgrade diplomats urged the Porte to punish the "Albanian bandits." An organization known as the Serbian National Council operated in Orthodox monasteries, and followed Belgrade's advice to assist the Ottoman government and military agents with intelligence on Albanian insurgents.[806] Meanwhile, Albanians themselves were plagued by internal factions. While the landlords were keen on pursuing their resistance against the Young Turks, many Albanians who served in the Ottoman parliament as members of the CUP were not as distressed by the defeat of the Kosovar feudalists. It is sufficient to mention here a dispute between Isa Boletini and Nexhip Draga over the ownership of forestlands in northern Kosova. Boletini held a grant from the sultan, while Draga had received title from the Young Turks, embittering the relations between prominent leaders of Kosova Albanians.[807]

Turgut Pasha's campaign severely weakened the Albanian movement and forced many insurgents to seek refuge in Serbia and Montenegro. But Serbia agreed to accommodate only a small group of insurgents, mainly leaders such as Hysen Budakova, Zejnel Bej of Gjilan, and Shaqir Çavdar-basha of Peja. In the meantime, rebels from northwestern Kosova at first remained in the Albanian Alps; only as wintertime approached and their food supplies were slashed did they seek shelter in Montenegro.

Isa Boletini requested to move to Cetinje with his comrades and their families. Montenegro conceded the request, and the Albanian refugees

---

[806] About the cooperation between Kosova Serbs and Ottoman authorities, especially during the 1910 uprising, see: Branko Perunović, *Pisma srpskih konsula iz Prištine* (Beograd: 1985); Tahir Abdyli, *Hasan Prishtina në lëvizjen kombëtare demokratike 1908-1933* (Prishtinë: 2003); Zekeria Cana, *Lëvizja kombëtare shqiptare në Kosovë 1908-1912* (Prishtinë: 1979); Milan R. Radovanović, *Sokolsko društvo u Prištini od 1909-1912* (1969); Jovan Hadži-Vasiljević, *Četnička akcija u Staroj Srbiji i Makedoniji* (Beograd: 1928).

[807] Widely about the conflict of interests between Boletini and Draga family see Gawrych, *Gjysmëhëna . . .*, 246-248.

settled in Cetinje, Podgorica, Shpuza, Nikšić, and Ulqin.[808] The migration incited other insurgent leaders to move to Montenegro, too. Dedë Gjo Luli, Mehmet Shpendi, Sulejman Batusha, Mirash Ndou, among others from Malësia and Shkodër, sought refuge in the small Balkan principality. According to Montenegrin government records, around 800 Albanian families entered the country with approximately 3,000 people in 1910. This figure soon doubled as a result of the Ottoman reprisals throughout Kosova and northern Albania that spurred an exodus of the population.

While King Nicholas claimed humanitarian motives for accepting the Albanian refugees, he was quick to begin promoting his own political agenda. This became apparent when Cetinje urged the Catholic tribes from Shkodër to protest against the Ottoman Empire. Nicholas hoped to spark an uprising that would depend on Montenegro for support and would further the monarch's goal to annex northern Albania. Even though Russia had clearly instructed him to avoid using the Albanian for such purposes, Nicholas promised his assistance for an uprising when Albanian refugees rallied for war.

Montenegrins and their collaborators demanded military action and armed uprisings in Kosova and northern Albania. Various committees, operating mainly in Italy, Romania, Bulgaria, and Greece, were all called to organize an uprising, which would begin in the north and quickly encompass central and southern Albania. The Bari Committee in Italy, formed by Nikollë Ivanaj, aspired to coordinate all activities among diaspora groups. Ivanaj hoped to expand the uprising beyond Albania and promised weapons and other forms of aid. The Bari Committee was further encouraged by wider Italian efforts to increase the nation's influence in Albania. Activists of all backgrounds joined the newly-formed *Pro Albania* Committee in hopes of halting Austria-Hungary increasing presence in the Balkan country.

This pro-Albanian trend, although motivated by Italy's foreign policy orientation, inspired many Arbëreshë who expressed their readiness to fight in Albania. The case of Italian volunteers in the small Balkan country became well publicized and turned into a major campaign headed by the son of Giuseppe Garibaldi, Riccioti. The main goal of the campaign would be to spread the anti-Ottoman uprising in Albania, but around the same time Italy commenced preparations to attack Tripoli, Riccioti Garibaldi resigned his position and the project collapsed.

---

[808] H.P.Sh. 2 (2002), 438.

After Albanians from Kosova and northern highlands were defeated by Turgut Pasha, many were forced to seek refuge in Montenegro where they were pressured to continue the fight. Despite the unfavorable circumstances, Austro-Hungary and Great Britain requested the Sublime Porte to pursue political compromise with the Albanians, including granting the refugees safe return to their homes. Vienna warned Cetinje to not take advantage the Albanians and their difficulties for political purposes. Austrian diplomats in İstanbul, as well as Shkodër, Shkup and Manastir, worked to convince Albanian leaders to relinquish their "intrusion into foreign adventures" and pursue a solution to the crisis through dialogue with the Porte. The message to the Albanians was clear: with the weakening of Kosova, diplomats saw the strengthening of the pan-Slavism.[809]

Driven by international pressure and the risk of a Kosovar-Albanian uprising, Cetinje took the role of the mediator. King Nicholas implored the Ottoman representative in Cetinje, Sadredin Bey, and the Albanian refugees to find a solution. The Albanians requested the return of their weapons, exemption from the latest taxes, road constructions, and the reinstatement of national schools.[810] Sadredin Bey found the requirements unacceptable and advised his government to abandon the immigrants. This intensified the situation as more and more Albanians sought refuge in Montenegro. Their numbers doubled in a short amount of time, further complicating matters in Cetinje. Unable to lead an uprising against the Ottoman Empire—as Russia and Serbia had warned him against such action—King Nicholas took the role of a peacemaker. He called fourteen Albanian patriots from Montenegro, proposing terms for their return. The Montenegrin monarch suggested a general amnesty, restriction of military service to one's home vilayet, admission of ethnic Albanians, including Catholics, for service in the local administration, and compensation for previously confiscated arms and property.[811]

The representative of the Ottoman government on principle found the proposal agreeable and recommended them to the Porte. On November 18, 1910, the Ottoman government conceded to the demands with minor exceptions: money would not be provided for confiscated weapons, but families who had their houses destroyed would be compensated. After the

---

[809] The secret report directed to Aehrenthal from Giesl, 12 HHStA, PA XIV/28, Albanien XX/10.

[810] Skëndi, *Zgjimi kombëtar shqiptar*, 370.

[811] Coded wire to Ritter von Zambaur in Shkodër, Vienna, Nov. 19, 1910, HHStA, PA XIV/33, Albanien XXXIV.

Montenegrin government received İstanbul's confirmation, King Nicholas gathered the Albanian leaders and ordered them to return home with their people. The *vali* of Shkodër, Bedri Pasha, awaited them in Tuz and coordinated their return.[812]

After many refugees return to Kosova and northern Albania, a conflict arose in Shkodër between highlanders and the Ottoman military. In March of 1911, in Mbi-Shkodër highlands, Dedë Gjo Luli and his men attacked the Turkish patrol along the border with Montenegro.[813]

Prior to the attacks, a number of refugees refused to return out of fear that the Turkish government would betray them again. Instead, they formed a committee in Podgorica and explored the possibility to organize an armed war. This group was also assisted by the Albanian patriots such as Risto Siliqi, Nikollë Ivanaj, Hilë Mosi, as well as Luigj Gurakuqi. The committee sought to secure Montenegro's assistance and, hoping to soothe the political difficulties, choose Sokol Baci, who was considered King Nicholas's right-hand, as its leader.[814] But the efforts failed to yield any protection against Ottoman reprisals, as Bedri Pasha mobilized forces against the insurgent groups of Dedë Gjo Luli and Gjekë Marash Gjeloshi.

To break the uprising, Bedri resorted to divisive politics on religious grounds. He sought to alarm Muslim Albanians of a Catholic-Montenegrin alliance against Albania.[815] Meanwhile, Şevket Turgut Pasha also sent reinforcements through the sea from Thessaloniki to join the Albanian volunteers on the ground. As the attacks on the predominantly Catholic border region became imminent, the insurgent commanders and leaders exiled in Montenegro feared a civil war across religious lines.

To avoid this dangerous course, insurgent leaders gathered on March 30 in Cetinje to broaden the scope of their demands. They prepared a memorandum petitioning the Great Powers to protect all Albanian lands. The terms included the use of Albanian as the official language in all four vilayets, in state offices, courts, and schools. The insurgents also demanded that the local administration hire domestic workers and that the Albanian nationality

---

[812] See Giesel's letter to Aehrenthal, Cetinje, Nov. 20, 1910, no. 102, cited according to Skëndi, *Zgjimi kombëtar shqiptar*, 372.

[813] Zambau, Report to Aehrenthal, Shkodër, Mar. 27, 1911, no. 27. HHStA, PA XIV/33, Albanien, XXXIV.

[814] H.P.Sh. 2 (2002), 443.

[815] Zambau, Report to Aerenthal, Shkodër, March 27, 1911, no. 24, HHStA, PA IV/33, Albanien, XXXIV.

be recognized by law. Other points called for government revenues to be spent for the benefit of the population and for Albanian soldiers to be allowed to complete military service in their native territory.

The memorandum was signed by Muharrem Bushati, Isa Boletini, Sokol Baci, Dedë Gjo Luli, Abdullah Aga, Preng Kola, and Mehmet Shendi. It has been speculated that it was written with the assistance of an Austro-Hungarian envoy. Vienna's role would help keep the Albanians from falling under Montenegrin or Italian influence and would prevent divisions motivated by religious differences.[816]

Montenegro and Italy nevertheless exerted influence on Albanian affairs. On April 27, 1911, an Arbëreshë lawyer and nationalist, Dr. Terenc Toçi (Itl.: Terenzio Tocci), gathered the Catholic leaders of Mirdita and Dukagjin and the Muslim chiefs of Dibër and Mat, and raised the Albanian flag in the Kimëz (Gimis) village of Mirdita. Prior to the event, Toçi had visited the exiled insurgency leaders in Podgorica and had worked closely with the committee of Riccioti Garibaldi. At Kimëz, the delegates declared Albania's independence, and appointed a short-lived provisional government with Toçi as president.[817]

Faced with a growing Albanian uprising, along with the possibility of foreign interference (by Montenegro and Italy), the Sublime Porte turned again to military measures, appointing Şevket Turgut Pasha and Preng Bibë Doda to quell the rebellion. As the Ottoman generals arrived in Albania, the insurgents issued a proclamation on May 1, 1911. The document, written in Albanian, French, German, and Italian, called for an autonomous government, national education, and the restriction of military service to Albania.[818]

The diaspora also voiced its support for the highlanders. Fan S. Noli, who at the time lived among the Albanian community in the United States, worked on securing the backing of the Greek state, but Athens insisted on an Albanian border along the Shkumbin River.[819] In spite of this attitude, Albanian patriots such as Nikollë Ivanaj, Themistokli Gërmenji, Ismail Qemali, Pandeli Cale, Stefan Kondillari, and Spiro Bellkameni gathered in

---

[816] *Ibid.*

[817] See also: P. Pal Dodaj, "Shqypnija e Shqyptarve e Qeverisë së Përkohshme," *Hylli i Dritës* X (Shkodër: 1934): 245-255; the text of the declaration, *ibid.*, 514-515; C. Libardi, *ibid.*, II, 37-49, 52-53; Krajewski, Report to Gruppi, Shkodër, June 4 1911, no. 99. AMAE, Turquie, Politique Interieure, Albanie, Jan.-June 1911, vol. IX.

[818] H.P.Sh. 2 (2002), 446.

[819] *Ibid.* 447.

the Greek island Corfu in May to create a branch of the Albanian Committee of Bari. As a result, efforts for an uprising in southern Albania also increased.[820]

In May, Şevket Turgut Pasha called on rebel leaders to surrender to the military courts. In addition, he also announced that whoever fired at an Ottoman solider would be sentenced along with one of the village elders. After he waited for four days, the Ottoman general launched his military campaign towards Deçiq. He placed most of his forces along the Tuz-Deçiq-Kastrat line, while directing Ethem Pasha to send additional troops towards Gucia. Meanwhile, the actions added to the humanitarian crisis. As the number of highlanders displaced increased because of the war, so did their dependence on Cetinje for aid. By supporting the refugees in preparation for an anti-Ottoman uprising, King Nicholas hoped to lay the ground for the annexation of northern Albania, where he envisioned a puppet principality ruled by his son, Mirko.[821]

On June 10, 1911, in fear of Austrian intervention, the Ottoman government announced through the press that the rebels had been defeated and that Sultan Mehmed V Reshad would visit Kosova to grant a general amnesty[822] The theme of reconciliation permeated the monarch's entire visit through the vilayet, as Kosovar leaders declared their allegiance and the sultan repeatedly praised the Albanian loyalty to the empire. Mehmed began his tour in Shkup on June 11, where local leaders pledged eternal fidelity to the Ottoman state. Four days later, the sultan arrived in Prishtina, where he signed a general amnesty for all of the participants of the revolts of 1910 and 1911. Although Kosova had traditionally been loyal to the sultan, the reception was unimpressive. At the nearby site of the historic 1389 battle, where a great turnout was expected, only people from the suburbs and surrounding villages appeared to greet the caliph. Cities like Peja, Gjakova, and Prizren did not send representatives.[823] On June 18, Şevket Turgut Pasha announced the imperial amnesty, which gave rebels ten days to surrender their weapons. In addition, the sultan offered them a gift of 10,000 Turkish liras for reparations.

To avoid an impression that the Ottoman amnesty had pacified the Albanians, Ismail Qemali gathered the leaders of the national movement who were residing in Cetinje to prepare for action. Qemali was joined by Luigj

---

[820] *Ibid.* 447.

[821] Skëndi, *Zgjimi kombëtar shqiptar*, 374.

[822] *Ibid.* 375.

[823] *Ibid.* 377.

Gurakuqi and the Podgorica Committee to prepare a general assembly for June 23rd. That day, the insurgent leaders convened on the Greçe plateau of Malësia e Madhe, adopting a principal document for Albania's autonomy. The *Greçe Memorandum,* which is also known as the *Red Book* after the color of the booklet in which it was later printed, was written by Ismail Qemali and Luigj Gurakuqi and presented to the assembly.[824] Following its approval, the Red Book was handed to the Ottoman ambassador of the Ottoman Empire, Sadredin Bey. An Albanian delegation, consisting of Luigj Gurakuqi, Dedë Gjo Luli, and Sokol Bacaj, presented the Memorandum to the representatives of the Great Powers in Cetinje, too.

The Memorandum laid out detailed terms on Albania's autonomy and measures to prevent the reoccurrence of violence. Notably, the document called for free elections and the unification of the four vilayets and for the Albanian people to enjoy the same rights as other nationalities in the empire. In addition, the Red Book insisted that ethnic Albanian serve in the administration and that Albanian be used for official business and as a language of instruction in schools. Like other similar documents, the Greçe Memorandum set terms on military service, taxation and spending, infrastructural projects, compensation for property damages, and the return of confiscated weapons.[825]

On July 30, 1911, Sadredin Bey announced in Podgorica a counter-proposal, limiting Albanian autonomy to the insurgent zones. The Ottoman government promised full amnesty to all rebels who agreed to surrender their arms and agreed to restrict military service to the Vilayet of Shkodër, except for a twelve-month assignment in İstanbul. The Porte would also permit the Albanians to defer their tax payments, while two state-funded elementary schools were promised for the highlanders. Possession of weapons would be allowed under special permits, while the state would also work on constructing roads and bridges in the affected areas.[826]

At first, the highlanders opposed the deal, insisting on the terms of the Greçe Memorandum. But as the Ottomans refused to honor the demands of nationality rights, and Cetinje increased its pressure following Russia's instruction to not support the Albanian struggle, the highlanders and the Young Turk representatives signed an agreement on August 2, 1911. On August 5, highlanders began to return in groups.

---

[824] H.P.Sh. 2 (2002), 450.

[825] *Ibid.* 451.

[826] *Ibid.* 457.

The return followed a difficult period of Albanian confrontations with the Young Turks. A year prior, Şevket Turgut Pasha's military actions broke the resistance of the Kosovar landlords loyal to Abdul Hamid II. In 1911, the interference of Montenegro and Italy left the highlanders' uprising detached from the Albanian national movement. Cetinje had its eye on northern Albania, hoping to create a satellite state under the pretext of a "Catholic autonomy." Albanians were supplied with weapons during the Kosova uprising in summer 1910, but the armed conflict only weakened both Kosova and the empire to the benefit of Serbia and Montenegro. King Nicholas sought to pity Catholic tribes against Muslims for a fratricidal war on religious grounds. Therefore, the Greçe Memorandum significantly reduced the threat of foreign inversion, although it did not completely do away with external influence.

Despite the difficulties, the armed resistance paved the way for Albanians to successfully rise against the Young Turks the following year. The CUP-led government was forced to accept the first signs of this development following the endorsement of the agreement of Podgorica. On September 29, Italy declared war on the Ottoman Empire and later attacked Tripoli. In these circumstances, the Turkish government began to reopen the Albanian schools that had been closed for a year. Similar actions were taken by permitting the operation of several banned Albanian newspapers and Albanian cultural clubs. Many political prisoners were freed and many leaders of the uprising released from their long internments. Although Shkodër's *vali* did not meet many of the demands of the Podgorica Committee and the Albanians had lost their trust in the Young Turks, the "reconciliatory spirit" reflected through measures that affected the political scenery.

The war with Italy and other development created opportunities for a new political movement. Thus, an opposition party known as *Hürriyet ve İtilaf Fırkası* (Freedom and Accord) was formed in November 1911. Important features of the party's program were the decentralization of government and constitutionally-guaranteed rights for the nationalities. Albanians played an active role in the party—Hasan Prishtina was one of the eleven founders; Basri from Dibër and Mid'hat Frashëri also joined the party, which entered into an agreement with the Albanian leadership and, in December of 1911, became a powerful voice in the lower chamber of the Ottoman parliament. However, faced with a growing challenge to their Ottomanist policies and centralized governance, the Young Turks resorted to extreme measures and dissolved the parliament on January 18, 1912. The goal was to ensure an absolute majority in early elections, which would deprive the Albanians among others of a forum to promote decentralization.[827]

The Kosova Uprising and the Great Historical Turn

The Young Turks dissolve the parliament, leading to major political measures. A covenant of Albanian leaders, known as the Taksim Agreement, plans for a general uprising. Ismail Qemali and Hasan Prishtina begin diplomatic efforts to secure support from abroad. Albanians hold an assembly in Junik, Kosova, demanding autonomy. The Albanian uprising marks its initial success; Prime Minister Mahmud Şevket Pasha resigns on July 9, 1912. Negotiations begin in August between General Ibrahim Pasha and Albanian rebels on terms set in a memorandum by Hasan Prishtina. Albanians disagree on whether to continue the uprising; Hasan Prishtina argues that his Fourteen Points would open the way to an Ottoman Albania and eventual independence. H. Prishtina's program prevails, although many participants of the Taksim Agreement not only failed to perform their duties, but worked against the Kosova uprising.

In early 1912, the Young Turks decided to dissolve the Ottoman parliament and call for early elections. The dissolution benefited the ruling CUP amidst several crises for the empire—the Albanian crisis being the most severe. Meanwhile, there were external troubles, including the war with Italy, which ended with the loss of Tripoli. The dissolution gave the CUP an absolute majority after the new elections and enabled them to create a government with the full confidence of the legislature, a significant achievement considering the circumstances and the far-reaching goals of the Young Turks.

Hasan Prishtina along with other Albanian deputies warned of the dangers of the Young Turk scenario and the serious consequences for the Ottoman Empire and its stability. Prishtina spoke in the last parliamentary session (held on January 11, 1912—only a week before the dissolution), reminding his fellow deputies that:

---

[827] See Kral's report to Aehrenthal, Thessaloniki, Jan. 5, 1912, no. 6 (secret documents), HHStA, PA XIV/33, Albanien XXXIV.

If the government does not change its policy and administration in Albania, and if the Albanians do not enjoy their political rights[828] . . . [then] this country will face an uprising and a revolution will take place. Perhaps one of the first people to raise the flag of the revolution will be I.[829]

As expected, the Young Turks would not consider Hasan Prishtina's warning or many of the other statements made by the Albanian parliamentarians. For the CUP, it was important to achieve a complete victory in the upcoming extraordinary elections; it was believed it would "create [the] inner unity" needed to overcome numerous challenges, particularly in foreign relations. The former Hamidian regime had contended that "brotherhood" with the West, especially Germany and Austria-Hungary, was appropriate for the empire since the West defended the Ottomans against Russia and its allies. However, the Young Turks, at least during their years in opposition, had lost all or their foreign allies with the slogan that "The whole world [was] against the Ottoman Empire." The consequences were dire, especially when Austria-Hungary used the unfriendliness of the Young Turks to attack from all sides, annexing Bosnia and Herzegovina, signaling Bulgaria to declare independence, and remaining indifferent towards the unification of Crete with Greece. A few years later, the Young Turks found themselves at war with Italy, which put an end to Ottoman rule in the northern African region of Tripoli (present-day Libya).

While left without foreign friends, the Young Turks also gained internal enemies among the ones who had the greatest merits for the Revolution, such as the Albanians. The CUP, aware of their true power, endeavored to include in its ranks some "moderate" Albanian representatives, mainly Ottomanists, who would run in elections against the leaders of the Albanian national movement. The CUP candidates were extensively supported by local committees, the national administration, and military officers under Young Turk influence.

As a result of a tough CUP campaign, most Albanian leaders lost the elections. Hasan Prishtina, kept his seat owing to the great authority he enjoyed in the Vilayet of Kosova. The elections, however, did not favor Ismail Qemali, who was defeated by the governor of Janina, Mehmet Avni, the candidate of the Young Turks. On April 18, during the convention of the

---

[828] Hasan Prishtina, *Nji shkurtim kujtimesh mbi kryengritjen shqiptare të vjetit 1912* (Bari: 1925), 7.
[829] *Ibid.*

new Ottoman parliament, the Young Turks occupied 215 of 222 seats. However, this was to be a victory the Young Turks would not forget. Because of the parliamentary farce and constitutional violations by the CUP, the Albanians were forced to join forces for a general uprising against the Young Turk government. The Young Turks had come to power four years earlier with the help of the Albanians and their uprising that forced Sultan Abdul Hamid II to restore the parliament and the Constitution of 1876. It was now the same Albanians who, in a similar action, would force the Young Turk government to resign; in order to do so they needed a great uprising that was well-coordinated as well as all-inclusive in order to achieve its goal.

The decision for a general uprising was made in a meeting held in the Taksim quarter in the European part of İstanbul, on January 12, 1912. Prior to the event, Hasan Prishtina and Ismail Qemali had discussed the response to the dissolution of the parliament as well as the response to an agreement by the Balkan League (consisting of Serbia, Montenegro, Bulgaria, and Greece) for war against the Ottoman Empire as soon as Russia called for war. The two principal leaders of the Albanian movement hence agreed to a meeting in Taksim with the aim of working on a strategy aimed at two fundamental objectives—administrative autonomy within the Ottoman Empire and official recognition of an Albanian nation. Prishtina and Qemali felt that the Albanian uprising should not permit the collapse of the Ottoman Empire, but were also unwilling to condone the centralized regime of the Young Turks. Thus, the two politicians called for the Taksim meeting so that prominent leaders and activists would join forces and assume responsibilities accordingly.

In addition to Qemali and Prishtina as the organizers, Syrja Bej, Myfit Bej Libohova, Esad Pashë Toptani, and Aziz Vrioni took part in the discussions at the house of Syrja Bej Vlora. Bedri Pejani and Mustafë Aziz Kruja recorded the minutes. Heading the discussions was Ismail Qemali, whereas Hasan Prishtina outlined the platform and planned actions. After a unanimous approval of the platform and other matters pertaining to the tasks of each participant, the group agreed that "in order to put an end to the Turk policy on the issues of national culture and to protect several political privileges for Albania, there are no means but to begin a general uprising."[830]

The crucial role in the uprising was assigned to Kosova, whose actions would be followed by other Albanian territories in accordance with the

---

[830] *Ibid.* 10.

duties outlined at the meeting. Hasan Prishtina was therefore responsible for leading the uprising in Kosova. Meanwhile, Qemali assumed the responsibility of travelling to Europe and, through negotiations with politicians and diplomats of the Great Powers, to secure 15,000 rifles and 10,000 golden napoleons for the uprising. Esad Pashë Toptani promised to organize the rebellion in central Albania and in the Vilayet of Shkodër, while Myfit Bej Libohova, Aziz Vrioni, and Syrja Bey Vlora were assigned to the vilayets of Manastir and Janina. As it would be observed, Hasan Prishtina was the sole individual who would perform the duties assumed in Taksim.

The agreement required quick action at home and abroad. Ismail Qemali and Hasan Prishtina, the heads of the national movement, decided to negotiate with the diplomatic representatives of the Great Powers accredited in İstanbul. They were also to meet with the representatives of the Balkan countries, since these nations had now come together for a common war against the Ottoman Empire. Given that the neighboring countries considered the war against European Turkey as their way of invading Albanian lands, this alliance held great importance. The territorial expansion had become a national priority for the region's nations, whose maps designated Kosova as "Old Serbia," the Vilayet of Manastir as "Bulgarian Macedonia," while the Janina Vilayet was called "Northern Epirus."

Indeed, the first conversation of Ismail Qemali with Johann von Pallavicini, the Austro-Hungarian ambassador in İstanbul, began with the same concern. Qemali was interested about the position Vienna would take if the Albanians reached an agreement on their autonomy. Would this motivate the Balkan countries (Serbia, Montenegro, Greece, and Bulgaria) to enter into war with the Ottoman Empire to prevent Albania's self-governance? In that scenario, the ambassador was informed that the Albanians were determined for independence with their territorial integrity intact if the conflict led to the collapse of the Ottoman Empire.[831]

Pallavicini's report to the foreign minister of the dual monarchy did not mention the answer given to Ismail Qemali; the document only states that "[the Albanians] were aware of the attitude favoring the *status quo*."[832] However, Qemali expressed the same concern to Count Szecsen, the Austro-Hungarian ambassador in Paris during the Albanian leader's tour in European cities. Qemali petitioned for Austro-Hungarian assistance, especially in

---

[831] See Pallavicini's report to Foreign Minister Aehrenthal from İstanbul, classified as "top secret," HHStA, PA XIV/9, Albanien V/6.
[832] *Ibid.*

preventing an invasion by the neighboring countries. He told the ambassador that the only defense the Albanians would have was Austria-Hungary. In addition, Ismail Qemali spoke of the Albanian plans and the objectives of the general uprising set to begin in the spring. The conclusion was as follows:

We do not seek the destruction of the Ottoman Empire; we desire that it remain powerful. However, we insist that power be kept by restoring the trust of the citizens when their demands are met. For the Albanians, this means administrative autonomy and recognition equal to that of other nations.[833]

Vienna's ambassador in Paris was cautious, but he asserted that his country would not allow Serbia or Montenegro's expansion at the expense of Albania. He made it clear that Vienna had formally warned Belgrade to not take any action against the Albanian territories. He also spoke of Russian contacts who could help keep Petersburg's allies from threatening peace in the Balkans.[834]

Hasan Prishtina received the same response in a meeting with general consul Kral in Thessaloniki. During the discussions, Prishtina expressed concerns about the risk of invasion by neighboring Slavs and Greeks, who were in the final stages of preparations for war with the Ottoman Empire.[835]

As the Balkan crisis worsened, and war became almost inevitable, Albanians had their eyes on Austria-Hungary. The important matter was that Albanians of all classes saw Vienna as their only protection, since security against a Slavic invasion was closely tied with Albania's role after the collapse of the Ottoman Empire. Regardless of its status (whether autonomy supervised by a foreign power, international protectorate, or some other form), Albania would serve as a barrier against the Russian-led Slavic-Orthodox hegemony. This role was mentioned at the Congress of Berlin in 1878, when the British representative, Lord Beaconsfield, objected the Russian demand that Albanian lands be given Serbia and Montenegro. He opposed the Slavic takeover of another people with the excuse that the "Slavs appeared as oppressive and uncivilized." Lord Salisbury would later explain the British attitude was based on Albania's strategic role against Russia.[836] In this regard, Germany was more or less supportive of Albania. Italy somewhat

---

[833] See letter from Szecsen to Aehrenthal, no. 38-D, HHStA, PA XIV, Albanien, V/6.

[834] Buxhovi, *Kthesa historike* 3, 188.

[835] *Ibid.*

[836] Buxhovi, *Kongresi . . .*, Protocol VI, 147.

agreed as well and could accept any demands for an Albanian state as long as it were not under Vienna's complete influence.

For Albanians it did not matter on what basis Albania and its existence were portrayed abroad; what mattered was support since it was the only means to securing an independent state, which had to be declared before the collapse of the Ottoman Empire. Petitions to Austria-Hungary from different parts of Albania reiterate the pleas for protection. Father Ndre Mjeda and Don Luigj Bumçi made an appeal to the Austrian heir, Franz Ferdinand, arguing that Albanians were weak and unprotected against the Slavic invasion. Sometime later, a similar request, but with an emphasis on military aspects, was sent to Vienna by the archbishop of Shkodër, Zef Seregji.[837]

It seemed that Vienna, despite its obligations as a member of the Triple Alliance, did not rule out a unilateral military intervention in northern Albania. Austria-Hungary would appear as the "authorized protector" of Catholics in the Balkans. In a reliable report to the emperor, the chief of staff of the imperial army, General Schemua, proposed to immediately invade Kosova if the Ottomans lost the war. This would secure the connection with northern Albania, which he considered "without any condition" within the sphere of Austrian influence.[838]

Even Ismail Qemali, acting as chief Albanian diplomat, did not rule out Austria's intervention, which could turn Albania into a temporary protectorate. These options were presented to Ambassador Szecsen, after Qemali ensured him that Albanians did not plan to establish special ties with Italy or any other nation.[839]

Qemali's assurances were meaningful because of his prior, unfavorable engagements to Austria-Hungary and Germany. He was indeed more than an opponent to Vienna. However, he was unavoidable as a leader of the Albanian national movement, which made him crucial to Austria's interests in the Balkans. In the familiar zigzags with Greece and Italy, Qemali had acted as a diplomat and politician, but now he beseeched the Austrians for help as a man who needed rescue. Vienna was aware and used the situation to direct Qemali's actions in every step leading to Albania's independence.

On the other hand, Hasan Prishtina acted consistently in favor of Vienna. He had personally taken the leadership of the insurgency to avoid any of

---

[837] Buxhovi, *Kthesa historike* 3, 190.

[838] See *Österaich-Ungarns Aussenpolitik 1908-1912* (Vienna: 1917).

[839] Skëndi, *Zgjimi kombëtar shqiptar*, 402.

the internal contradictions that took place in prior uprisings. In his conversation with Consul Kral, Prishtina explained that he had severed all ties with the Young Turks since their pan-Turkist orientation was destructive and offered no consideration for the Albanian demands; hence he called for a general revolt in Albania. The Kosovar leader emphasized that the national sentiment had grown in Kosova and the vilayet's leaders were tirelessly working to reach an agreement with other parts of Albania for a great uprising. Additionally, he reiterated the position for an Albanian state within a strong Ottoman Empire, but doubted its possibility. "On the one hand," he said, "Turkey is unable to stand for long because it is being dismantled. On the other hand, Turkey will not consider the reasonable Albanian requests and does not want to let them prepare [for statehood]."[840]

Besides the efforts to ensure the support of a strong ally such as Austria-Hungary, which had an interest in the ethnic Albanian territory, Ismail Qemali and Hasan Prishtina also paid attention to the Balkan countries, regardless of their position.

Prishtina tried to ensure the cooperation with the Bulgarian-Macedonian movement in eastern Albania.[841] For this purpose, he met with the former representative of Shkup in the Ottoman parliament, Todor Pavlov, and proposed the organization of a joint uprising without excluding the possibility of an autonomous Albanian-Macedonian state.[842] After consulting with the center of the Macedonian-Bulgarian movement in Sofia, Pavlov replied that "the Bulgarians could not possibly take part in the uprising."[843] Indeed, Sofia had its own plans to occupy parts of the Albanian lands during the concerted actions of the Balkan League against the Ottoman Empire.

Unlike Bulgaria, Serbia showed interest in the uprising, but from the outset, Serbs refused to speak with Ismail Qemali, Hasan Prishtina, and other members of the Albanian national movement who had served in the Ottoman parliament or partaken in the Young Turk Revolution. Instead, Belgrade sought interlocutors among the local chiefs, feudalists, and the remaining supporters of Sultan Abdul Hamid II who still hoped for the monarch's restoration. Serbia had already been working in this direction and had

---

[840] See letter from Kral to Aehrenthal, Thessaloniki, Jan. 5, 1912, no. 6. Sekrete. HHStA, PA XIV/33, Albanien XXXIV.

[841] H.P.Sh. 2 (2002), 463.

[842] *Ibid.* 464.

[843] *Ibid.* 464.

succeeded in establishing connections with some Kosovar leaders. During the 1910 uprising, some of those leaders were given refuge in Serbia after being defeated by the Ottoman military. Belgrade again began negotiations with such figures as Isa Boletini, Hasan Hysen Budakova, Iliaz Agushi, Mahmut Zajmi, Bajram Daklani, Sadik Rama of Gjurgjevik, Ramadan Shabani, and many others.[844]

Some of the Kosovars went to Belgrade, where they were received by Prime Minister Nikola Pašič and his foreign minister. Belgrade conditioned its support for the uprising with the *renunciation of any plans for the administrative autonomy* and also requested to set the time for the beginning. However, Serbia promised to supply weapons and other materials and allow the smuggling of arms to Albania, which on the eve of the uprising expanded enormously.[845]

Sofia's refusal to cooperate and the constraints from Belgrade did not prevent action in accordance with the Taksim Agreement. The new elections for the Ottoman parliament where most of the Albanian leaders lost, the failed promises to the northern Albanian refugees who agreed to return home after the uprising, and other weaknesses of the Young Turk government created a favorable environment for the Albanian uprising. Seeing that this was inevitable, the Young Turk authorities resorted to some concessions such as the reopening of some Albanian schools and road constructions so as to give signs of reconciliation but without renouncing Ottoman centralism and nationalism.

For this purpose, the Turkish government created a governmental commission headed by Interior Minister Haci Adil Bey who visited Albania and negotiated with local. The commission began its visit to Kosova, knowing that preparations had already begun for a new insurrection. He had the opportunity to witness this. In Prishtina, the government delegation was warmly welcomed, but on the way to Peja and Gjakova, it was attacked by the rebel forces of Mahmut Zajmi. Officials were similarly received even in northern and central Albania and all the way to Manastir and Janina. The minister devoted a good portion of his attention to the manipulation of polling stations, which were aiming towards a deep victory for the CUP candidates in the Albanian territories, a scenario that created even more suitable conditions for the uprising.

---

[844] *Ibid.* 465.
[845] *Ibid.* 465.

The failure of the government commission and the declaration of an almost absolute victory of the Young Turks candidates in all Albanian centers, while eliminating most of the Albanian leaders, gave way to the uprising of Kosova, which according to the Taksim Agreement would include the entire country without exceptions.

Following a decision the Central Committee of the Uprising took in April of 1912, and in line with his warnings to the Ottoman parliament in January, Hasan Prishtina finally abandoned İstanbul and returned to Kosova, which was to become the center of the Albanian insurgency.[846]

In accordance with the decision, Hasan Prishtina went to Kosova and made his first contacts in Shkup and Prishtina with some of the local nobles and feudalists who were long in conflict with the Young Turk government. He would then begin to make connections with the insurgent leaders in the regions of Gjakova and Peja.[847] Hasan Prishtina also went to Drenica where he was supported by Ahmet Delia in Prekaz and Sadik Ramë Gjurgjeviku from the outskirts of Peja. Shortly after, Hasan Prishtina was joined by Isa Boletini and several comrades. This was reasonable since the hostility with the Young Turks made Isa Boletini distrustful even among Albanian leaders who had supported the Young Turk movement. Boletini wanted not only to bring down the Young Turk government, but to also restore Sultan Abdul Hamid II to power. The attitude opened the dilemma of interdependence or the connection of the leaders from Kosova with different interests that were engaged in conducting the Albanian movement in accordance with their interests. These interests were well masked "with the support of brotherly assistance" and similar slogans that were persuasive to loyal Albanians.

Regardless of Isa Boletini's intent, his appearance on the side of the uprising was necessary because of his important authority in the Shala region of northern Kosova. Nexhip Draga also managed to convince the leaders of the Shala region to join the uprising at an assembly where the leaders expressed their commitment to the cause. Draga, however, did not join the uprising due to claims that he suffered from poor health, but used all means for the uprising to succeed. The reasons he did not physically join the uprising had to do with a property dispute with Isa Boletini. Knowing the importance of one and the other, Hasan Prishtina did his best to utilize the military force of

---

[846] See I. G. Senkevich, *Osvoditel'noe dvizhenie albanskogo narodo v 1905-1912* (Moskva: 1959), 217, cited in Skëndi, *Zgjimi . . .*, 384.

[847] The insurgent leaders included Mahmut Zajmi, Zefi i Vogël, Ali Binaku, Qerim Binaku, Bajram Mani, Zog Avdyli, Bajram Deklani, and others.

Isa Boletini and the diplomatic-political skills of Draga for the needs of the uprising. Thus, even without Nexhip Draga's presence, his name would be used publicly to help keep him personally connected to the national movement.[848]

In early May, after they agreed on the structure of the operation and the liaison with a commanding center, the Dukagjini groups, led by Zajmi and Zefi i Vogël, attacked the Ottoman forces on the outskirts of Peja and which resulted in considerable losses. As a result this impaired the movement of Ottoman troops towards Mitrovica, where there were also hostilities taking place.

Faced with the attacks, the Porte continued to concentrate new forces in Kosova. By the end of May, the division of Nizam, capable of special tasks and equipped with modern weaponry and combat vehicles was placed in Ferizaj. Corps VII of Shkup, under General Ismail Fadil Pasha, were in preparations, but it seemed that the Young Turk government was not initially interested for a punitive campaign similar with that of Derviş Turgut Pasha.[849]

The initial military success of the insurgents in different parts of Kosova posed as a pressing task for the coordination and organization of the uprising on the national scale in accordance with political programs. The return of Hasan Prishtina to Kosova, along with other activists, was conducive to the uprising and its role as a beacon of an all-Albanian struggle. During initial meetings with the local leaders and heads of *chetas*, Hasan Prishtina requested that the uprising have as a motto the *administrative freedom of Albania*, and an agreement on the issue was signed by Mahmut Zajmi, Bajram Daklani, Zef i Vogël, Pjetër Çeli, Halil Mehmeti, Idriz Jaha, Hasan Bllaca, and Sali Hoxhë Elbasani.[850]

This and the successful expansion of the uprising showed the need to unite all forces around a national political program. Hasan Prishtina took the initiative to call for a general assembly in Junik. Prishtina preliminarily held numerous meetings with some of Kosovar leaders who had different ambitions, swayed by agreement with Belgrade and Cetinje, or other centers interested that the Albanian movement lack leadership and unity in order to remain vulnerable to external influences.

---

[848] See Prishtina, *Nji shkurtim kujtimesh . .* (Bari), for more on Nexhip Draga's role in the uprising.

[849] Gawrych, *Gjysmëhëna . . .*, 293.

[850] H.P.Sh. 2 (2002), 470.

The assembly gathered in Junik on May 21-25 of 1912 with 250 delegates from the Kosova Vilayet as well as the sanjaks of Dibër, Shkodër, and El-basan. There were most likely representatives of the southern provinces, too,[851] although this cannot be documented due to the lack of records.

In the Junik Assembly, Hasan Prishtina, Isa Boletini, Bajram Curri, Riza Kryeziu, Nexhip Draga and others vowed to fight against the CUP and the Young Turk government. The key to the unification of all Albanians was here. This especially attracted the feudal forces that had plenty of reasons to avenge the Young Turks for the campaign they had taken against them a year ago. Because of this, *Besa* (commitment) was made.

A *besa* (covenant) was reached to fight the CUP after a powerful confrontation with the pro-Turks, who were present in the assembly and claimed that war would damage the Ottoman Empire and the Albanian interests. The mutessarrif had sent a "peace" mission to the assembly, calling for talks with the Young Turk government, in lieu of arms. But the autonomy bloc was stronger and won, while the assembly adopted a political program aimed at the following:
- The recognition of the autonomy of Albania;
- The establishment of an Albanian administration;
- The adoption of the Albanian language written in its own alphabet as an official language;
- Raising the Albanian flag in the entire country;
- The appointment of a descendant of Albanian princely families as governor-general; and
- A guarantee of the Great Powers for the fulfillment of the demands.[852]

These requests were delivered to the government in İstanbul and distributed in assemblies and committees of other areas of Albania, which also lent their support.

Hasan Prishtina soon began to work on implementing the decisions of the "Assembly of Junik." He issued a proclamation to the *"freedom-loving Albanians and the civilized world,"* presenting the struggle for autonomy as a war against malicious oppression and anti-Albanian administration of the Young Turks. He invited all those who desired freedom and prosperity in

---

[851] *Ibid.* 470.
[852] *Ibid.* 471.

the empire to support the Albanians because the "*Fatherland expects unity from us. The day and minutes are near for us to be saved from the evils of the Young Turks.*" The statement ended with the call "*Survival or death!*"[853]

Since the Ottoman government did not grant any of the requests of Junik, the insurgents took to action. By mid-May, operations began in the Dukagjin Plateau under Hasan Prishtina and Bajram Curri.[854] Military actions then expanded Peja. On May 31, forces led by Isa Boletini, Bajram Daklani, Sadik Rama, Mahmut Zajmi and Zefi i Vogël attacked the city, destroying military positions and gendarmerie posts in the suburbs. On June 6, the insurgents broke into Peja but did not remain there long. The Ottoman forces were aided by the Nizam XIX Division from Mitrovica, and Albanians had to retreat towards Gucia where they remained during further operations.[855]

The insurgents continued to attack the Ottoman forces in other parts towards Prush and Përdrin. The forces of Bajram Curri operated successfully in Has, Gash, and Bytyç. They managed to break the government forces in Prush, confiscating ammunitions, guns, machine guns, and cannons, which were used to arm the insurgents. During the fighting, 300 people were killed and many were wounded. For the first time, the uprising forces captured war prisoners.[856]

Since the early days, the uprising of Gjakova and Peja was supported also by the Albanian population of the Catholic highlanders of Mërturi and Nikaj, and Mirdita quickly joined them. The Ottoman efforts to use religious differences to put Mirdita between the Muslims of Shkodër and Kruja did not succeed.[857]

Kruja and Tirana each joined the uprising in the end of June. There was also support in Shkodër, where an uprising committee was formed. Thus, Muslim and Catholic towns were united. The revolt then intensified in Dibra and in the southwestern provinces of Albania.[858]

The Bucharest colony sent a representative Pandeli Cale, from Korça, to southern Albania, to persuade Orthodox Muslim Albanians to join the uprising that had already begun in Kosova and was expanding day after day.[859]

---

[853] Prishtina, *Nji shkurtim kujtimesh . . .* (Bari), 28.

[854] H.P.Sh. 2 (2002), 472.

[855] *Ibid.* 472.

[856] *Ibid.* 472.

[857] Skëndi, *Zgjimi . . .*, 384.

[858] *Ibid.* 384.

[859] Kral, Report to Berchtold, Thessaloniki, June 23, 1912, no. 102 (secret), HHStA, PA XIV/39, Albanien XXXIV.

In light of the successful uprising, opposition circles within the Ottoman army showed their displeasure with the Young Turk government. Instead of focusing on the war against Italy in Tripoli, the Young Turk government added armed forces in Kosova and other Albanian territories by opening domestic fronts with great risks for the empire, especially when the Balkan League was preparing for a war against the Ottoman Empire. In late May, a group of officers (mostly Turks) formed a secret society in İstanbul called The Group of Savior Officers (*Halaskar Zabitan Gurubu*), seeking an end of the CUP and the military intervention of the Young Turks in Albania. They also drafted a political program for this purpose.[860]

Albanians established connections with the opposition officers as well as the opposition party, *Hürriyet ve itilaf* (Freedom and Accord). The communication was successful especially with the military opposition, since most of the Albanian officers and soldiers in Rumelia now belonged to the Savior Officers and awaited the opportunity to peel its accounts with the anti-Albanian stance of the Young Turks. By June 21, 1912, eight officers and 140 soldiers of the first battalion of the 49th Regiment of Infantry, led by an Albanian officer, Tajar Tetova, who had participated in the 1908 Revolution, left the camp near the Manastir and took to the mountains. Other wards, such as the battalion which was commanded by Major Xhenabi Adil Gjakova, also joined the uprising.[861] The desertion of Albanian and Turkish soldiers from the Ottoman military formations continued in other places. In Dibër, the uprising committee led by Dan Cami, welcomed officers Ismail Haki Devaja, Ismail Haki Libohova, and Ibrahim Gjakova.[862]

The officers issued a communiqué on June 21 explaining the reasons for their defeat. They accused the Young Turk regime of destroying the empire and constitutional order thru a government that instituted the injustice and terror that was being practiced for years in Albania. In further announcements, they claimed solidarity with their Albanian compatriots who had risen up against all who brought the country to this tragic position.[863] The military defectors demanded the immediate resignation of the government, dissolution of the parliament, new elections, and the prosecution of the highest government officials, such as Ibrahim Haki, Mehmet Şevket, Said and Rifat Pasha, Talat Bey, Cavit Bey, and the chief of the general staff. The

---

[860] Gawrych, *Gjysmëhëna dhe shqiponja*, 294.

[861] H.P.Sh. 2 (2002), 474.

[862] *Ibid.* 474.

[863] *Ibid.* 474.

officers declared that they would not let go of their weapons if their demands were not met.[864]

Opposition officers debated on their position on the Albanian political demands, especially the calls for autonomy. Albanian officers demanded that the military opposition to support the request of Albanians for political autonomy because it was also for the benefit of the country. Most of Turkish soldiers, however, remained loyal of the *itilaf* (*i.e.*, accord) era, hence only calling for the replacement of the "evil" government with a "good" one, which had to come from new elections, but without changing the Ottomanist spirit.

Despite the differences, there were no confrontations in the Group of Savior Officers. The Turkish opposition and military sought to benefit from the Albanian uprising overthrowing the Young Turks. While Albanian leaders had agreed at Junik on a struggle for autonomy, the developing situation and the alarming threat of an invasion by the Balkan League, convinced the heads of the uprising to change course. They did so by harmonizing some of their positions with the Savior Officers and temporarily withdrawing from the plans for self-government.

In late June, the newspaper *İkdam* published a declaration signed by Hasan Prishtina, Isa Boletini, Riza Gjakova and Jahja Prizreni, which was formulated in the spirit of the opposition's demands. After emphasizing their ties with the Ottoman Empire and the caliphate, Albanians declared that they had risen to protect the "true constitution," which was the common goal of all the opposition forces of the Ottoman Empire.[865] The statement also explained that the Albanians had rushed to arms because of the need the country had to laws that conformed to its unique nature. These laws implied the fulfillment of national rights. However, Albanian autonomy was not specifically mentioned in the declaration.[866]

The "tactical" withdrawal from the requests for autonomy brought Albanian insurgents even closer to the opposition and the military defectors. In addition to desertion, the military factor gained responsibilities in the war front. The officers of the Sixth Army in Manastir demanded the government's resignation and new elections—steps which were justified by the uprising of Kosova.[867] The pressure from the officers expanded each day and

---

[864] *Ibid.* 474.

[865] *Ibid.* 476.

[866] *Ibid.* 476.

[867] See Halla, Report to Bertchtold, Manastir, June 27, 1912, no. 65, HHStA, PA XIV/39, Albanien XXXIV.

many of them took to the mountains. The Albanian insurgents increasingly grew, giving the war national dimensions. Southern groups also took military actions against the Ottoman forces. As a result, on July 9, the minister of war, Mahmut Şevket Pasha, who had ruled with an iron fist since the Counter-Revolution of 1909, was forced to resign.

On July 22, Sultan Mehmed V assigned Gazi Ahmet Muhtar Pasha, the president of the Senate, the task of forming a new government. The monarch also chose Mehmet Feridi from Vlora and Hüseyin Nazım Pasha, two independent candidates of the Young Turk committee. One of them was announced foreign minister and the other as the minister of war.[868] In the first meeting of the cabinet, the newly-appointed grand vizier told his ministers in a ghastly manner, that the CUP "had only about three or four days left to live."[869] He also made it clear that his cabinet would not be in the service of the Young Turks, but would work to save the Ottoman Empire from their poor leadership. He pointed out to specific tasks, of which the most urgent was to make peace with the Albanians.[870]

On July 24, 1912, the government formed a commission to responsibly investigate the situation and to create a possibility of reconciliation with the Albanians.[871] Three officials—Danush bej Prishtina, former *vali* of Selanik; General Sylejman Kolonja, senator and governor of Plevle; and Esad Pashë Toptani, deputy of Shkodër—were appointed to serve in the *ad hoc* entity. It is noteworthy that the committee was formed at the request of the sultan, who on July 22, 1912, directed his government "to end the inequities and injustices" in Albania.[872] On the grounds that Albanians were "the strongest and most important part of the Ottoman nation besides Rumelia," and Albania, which consisted of the four vilayets, an "important part of this great leftover," the government instructions specifically called for the Albanian demands to be addressed "within the legality of the Constitution."[873]

The principal task of the government commission was to travel to Prishtina to meet with the insurgent leaders. However, Esad Pashë Toptani declined to travel to Kosova. Likely, he did not do so because he had failed to

---

[868] Gawrych, *Gjysmëhëna . . .*, 295.

[869] *Ibid.* 295.

[870] Skëndi, *Zgjimi . . .*, 386.

[871] *Ibid.* 119.

[872] For the prime minister's instructions to the governmental commission, see *Leka* (special issue), cited in Tahir Abdyli, *Hasan Prishtina*, 119.

[873] Abdyli, *ibid.*

perform in accordance to the Taksim agreement, which entrusted him with organizing the uprising in central Albania and the Vilayet of Shkodër. Likewise, Myfid bej Libohova also failed with the task of preparing the rebellion in the vilayet of Janina.[874] To fill the gap, the Ottoman Council of Ministers chose another Albanian, Rashid Akif Pasha, but he also claimed poor health, and had to be replaced by Marshal Ibrahim Pasha from Manastir. Avni Gjinali, a respected patriot, was appointed secretary of commission.

Gazi Ahmet Muhtar Pasha oriented the commission towards an agreement through negotiations with the Albanian insurgents. The governmental body arrived in Prishtina on July 27, 1912. The rebels, who had gained control of many areas of Kosova, had taken the city as of July 21 without encountering any resistance of the Ottoman army. The military advantage enabled the insurgents to demand the dissolution of the parliament as a precondition for further negotiations. If the government failed to meet this demand within forty-eight hours, Albanians would resume the attacks. This was a well-measured ultimatum which reveals the Albanian position vis-à-vis the Sublime Porte, following the fall of the Young Turk government and the appointment of Muhtar Pasha as grand vizier. Yet, it is noteworthy that the ultimatum was preceded by the first meeting of the Porte's envoy, Ibrahim Pasha, with Hasan Prishtina, whose main requests sought:
- To formally recognize the borders of Albania;
- To institute civilian and military authorities of Albanian nationality;
- For Albanians to perform military service in Albania and under Albanian commanders; and
- For all official business to be conducted in the Albanian language.[875]

The General at first attempted to treat the Albanian uprising as a local movement that belonged only to Kosova, but was flatly told that the rebellion was part of the Albanian national movement. Hasan Prishtina explained that Kosova was deliberately set as the center of the uprising, just as Albanians had done during the League of Prizren decades ago, while other parts of the country waited for the epilogue and, if needed, the call for action.[876] Subse-

---

[874] For more on the failure of parties to the Taksim Agreement to fulfill their duties, see Prishtina, *Nji shkurtim kujtimesh* . . . (Bari); Abdyli, *Hasan Prishtina*; Zekeria Cana, *Lëvizja kombëtare shqiptare në Kosovë 1908-1912* (Prishtinë: 1979); Pllana, *Kosova dhe reformat në Turqi* (Prishtinë: 1978).

[875] Prishtina, *Nji shkurtim kujtimesh* . . (Prishtinë: 2009), 30.

[876] See Prishtina, *Nji shkurtim kujtimesh* . . (Bari), 30-31.

quently, Ibrahim Pasha reasoned that the demands were risky since the Balkan League countries had threatened to go to war if Albania became autonomous. Yet, he also accused Hasan Prishtina of separatism and stated that the demands "would not look good for Albania because the people are Muslim."[877] After responding that "religion has nothing to do with nationality," Hasan Prishtina shifted his focus to the Young Turk regime. Counting numerous acts of violence committed by the Young Turks against his country and stressing the destruction they had brought about, he noted as a last point the recent elections. He made it clear that Albania as a united entity demanded the immediate dissolution of the parliament because it did not have the mandate of the people.[878] Ibrahim Pasha told the insurgents that the sultan had sent the special commission to hear their grievances and that reasonable demands would be taken into account.

Soon after the meeting, Hasan Prishtina moved the center of the uprising from Prishtina to Ferizaj and called representatives from all provinces of Albania to the National Assembly in Ferizaj in order to avoid the pressures by the governmental commission and get away from the divisive efforts of various Serb envoys and diplomats in Kosova.[879]

The Ottoman government, then experiencing parliamentary difficulties, was forced to bow to the Albanian pressure and, on August 5, 1912, in spite of the CUP's great disappointment, dissolved the parliament by imperial decree. This decision was a hefty defeat for the omnipotent Young Turks, and greatly strengthened the position of Muhtar Pasha's cabinet. During the time of the Albanian League of Prizren, Abdyl Frashëri and other members of the organization had expressed their desire for Ahmet Muhtar Pasha to become the head of a united province in Albania. Thirty years later, the same official was chief of the imperial cabinet that would give the Albanians their nationality rights.[880]

The dissolution of the parliament satisfied only a part of the insurgents, the followers of the opposition group Freedom and Accord—the so-called *itilafists*—who were relatively strong in Kosova and came from the ranks of the pro-Turks. In Kosova, however, there were two streams with different

---

[877] *Ibid.* 30.

[878] Tahy, Report to Berchtold, classified as "top secret," Mitrovica, Aug. 4, 1912, no. 45, HHStA, PA XIV/39, Albanien XXXIV. See also Prishtina, *Nji shkurtim kujtimesh . . .* (Prishtinë, 2009), 30.

[879] H.P.Sh. 2 (2002), 490.

[880] Gawrych, *Gjysmëhëna . . .*, 296.

interests: the *autonomists*, directed by Hasan Prishtina, Nexhip Draga, part of Albanian aristocrats, and that of *Hamidist conservatives* pursued by feudalists such as Isa Buletini, Idriz Seferi, Bajram Curri, Riza Bej Gjakova, and others. Autonomists had the support of central and south Albania, despite the failure of some participants of the Taksim meeting to complete their share of the job. Noticeably, a common national spirit was pervading the country from north to south, and calls for autonomy were present throughout. Elbasan and Shpat sent joint greetings to the new cabinet, reiterating demands common for both Tosks and Ghegs. An Albanian convention in Fier requested from the Great Vizier to be represented by two delegates in the negotiations that were taking place in Kosova, since discussions there would affect the north and the south alike.[881] Influential figures such as Ismail Qemali, Omer Pashë Vrioni, Aziz Pashë Vrioni, Colonel Haki Tatzati, and Izet Bej Zavalani, who took part in the Fier meeting, sent a telegram to Hasan Prishtina, authorizing him to speak and decide on behalf of southern Albania.[882] The Fier convention decided that Ismail Qemali would not be sent to Kosova, but would instead return to İstanbul to negotiate with the new government.[883]

Qemali's absence in Kosova impacted Hasan Prishtina's position with respect to the political factors in the talks with Ibrahim Pasha. With little elbow room to contain the Hamidian stream that demanded the restoration of the previous monarch, Prishtina was soon forced into a compromise that nonetheless helped sustain national unity. This empowered the former member of the Ottoman parliament, who assumed the role of chief negotiator for all of Albania. Hasan Prishtina hence emerged as the single leader facing one of the greatest historical challenges of the Albanian people, and he overcame the challenge successfully and owing to a mandate he won in all parts of the country. Manastir assigned a delegation to present its demands to Prishtina, while Elbasan also sent its representatives, including patriots such as Lef Nosi and Ahmet Dakli. Meetings were held in Preveza, Leskovik, and Gjirokasër, while leaders of the Janina vilayet telegraphed the grand vizier with similar demands to those of other Albanians.[884]

---

[881] Report to Foreign Ministry, Vlora, Aug. 7, 1912, HHStA, PA XIV/41, Albanien, XXXIV.

[882] H.P.Sh. 2 (2002), 490.

[883] *Ibid.* 490.

[884] Halle, Report to Berchtold, Manastir, Aug. 8, 1912, no. 89, and Aug. 15, 1912, no. 95; Bilinski, Report to Berchtold, Janina, Aug. 15, 1912, no. 61, all in HHStA, PA XIV/41, Albanien XXXIV.

After difficult negotiations on the brink of the Balkan wars, Hasan Prishtina and other leaders of the uprising presented a revised list of Albanian demands. This provided for a moderate program that Prishtina hoped would avoid divisions in the Albanian leadership and would also receive the blessing of the Sublime Porte. On August 6, the program known as *The Fourteen Points of Hasan Prishtina* was adopted from the representatives of the uprising at an assembly held in Ferizaj, and the demands were presented in writing to the Ottomans.

At Isa Boletini's request, a copy of the final memorandum was given beforehand to representatives of the Serb elements in Kosova, namely Belgrade's envoys who did their best to impede autonomy proponents and promote the extension of the uprising to Thessaloniki. Serb expansionists hoped that the rebellion would wear out Albanians and Ottomans alike, and that Serbia would eventually find it much easier to realize its aspirations on the Albanian lands.[885]

Facing such risks and with the determination that the agreement between the Albanians and the Ottoman government be of mutual interest, on August 9, 1912, Hasan Prishtina presented Ibrahim Pasha with the following demands:

1. The implementation of justice in certain Albanian areas under the "Law of the Highlands";
2. The restriction of military service in Rumelia, except in case of war or in extraordinary conditions in the country;
3. The return of confiscated weapons;
4. The appointment of officials who know the local language and customs;
5. The opening of high schools and agricultural schools in the provincial capitals of Janina, Shkodër, Manastir, and Kosova, and for lessons to be taught exclusively in Albanian;
6. Additional primary schools;
7. The freedom to open private schools;
8. The introduction of the native tongue as a subject in public schools;
9. The improvement and expansion of roads;
10. The creation of additional *nahiyes*;
11. Honor and respect for the moral principles of Islam and the constitution and laws of the empire;

---

[885] Prishtina, *Nji shkurtim kujtimesh* . . . (Prishtinë), 32-33.

12. The prosecution of Ibrahim Haki and Said Pasha;

13. A general amnesty; and

14. Reparations for property damages.[886]

As seen here, the issue of autonomy was not mentioned. This was the main point that emerged in the Assembly of Junik in various forms and had presented the core of political requests of Albanians ever since the Albanian League of Prizren. The need to protect the Ottoman Empire as a shield for the Albanians against the neighboring countries also highlighted the different political streams: the conservatives, who demanded the return of earlier privileges, the Kanun, and the restoration of aristocracy; the intellectuals, demanding autonomy within a modern country; and members of the Ottoman opposition party, Freedom and Accord.

The Ottoman government did not respond to the Fourteen Points within forty-eight hours. Ibrahim Pasha made an impression that he still wanted to divide Albanians, even though in principle the government of Muhtar Pasha wished to prevent any disorder. Those who sought to continue the rebellion were already a minority compared to the autonomists and *itilafists*, but would be greatly emboldened by Serbia and its allies to deepen the crisis between the Albanians and the Sublime Porte. This prompted some leaders of the uprising to call for a march to Shkup and issue even harsher ultimatums. Isa Boletini, Idriz Seferi, Bajram Curri, and Riza Bej Gjakova agreed to order their troops to march on to the vilayet's capital for the reason that "our people cannot wait any longer."

Between August 12 and 15, Albanians entered Shkup without encountering any resistance. The first group of insurgents that entered this city was that of Bajram Daklani and Zef i Vogël, who raised the Albanian national flag.[887] The last one to enter was Bajram Curri with his main forces of the uprising with about 6,000 people. As soon as he arrived in Shkup, Curri opened the prison and freed hundreds of prisoners. It was assessed that about 30,000 Albanians peacefully entered Shkup within three days. Some units were directed towards Tetova, Kumanova, and Presheva, where they also entered without any resistance. The Ottoman army remained in barracks and did not oppose the Albanian march onto Shkup and other nearby cities. They had a decisive order to not subject to provocations.

---

[886] Gawrych, *Gjysmëhëna . . .*, 298.
[887] H.P.Sh. 2 (2002), 491.

The passive attitude of the Ottoman army clearly showed the determination of Muhtar Pasha for an agreement with the Albanians. The increasing pressure only helped him convince his opponents to accept Hasan Prishtina's proposal. Faced with the new developments, as insurgents took over Shkup and other rebel leaders threatened to continue towards Thessaloniki and restore Abdul Hamid to power, on August 18, the Ottoman government approved all but two of the Fourteen Points. Specifically, the cabinet claimed that the return of weapons and the prosecution of Young Turk officials were issues on which the parliament alone had the power to act.[888]

There are many signs that Muhtar Pasha had the deal discussed with the Austro-Hungarian diplomats in İstanbul and agreed with them on a project for Albanian autonomy. Vienna's attitude about this agreement and the energetic withdrawal of Russia and the Balkan League's objections clearly indicated that the Fourteen Points had the blessing of Vienna and the Tripartite Alliance. Without it, Albania's independence would not have had the support of the Great Powers in the Ambassador's Conference of London later that year when European representatives recognized the small Balkan state.

The insurgent leaders declared they would accept the agreement and announced the termination of the uprising. Hasan Prishtina also informed the representatives of central and southern Albania to cease armed actions against government troops, even though they had not been as disturbed by the conflict. In this case, he reported that the demands of the uprising had been accepted for all of Albania and the uprising had ended. Albanians hence reached a historical victory and could hope that the nationality rights would lead the way to autonomy. But the triumph soon alarmed their neighbors. Serbia, Greece, Montenegro, and Bulgaria realized that Albania had embarked on a journey to statehood, and acted to prevent it at any cost.

The Balkan War and Albania's Declaration of Independence

Neighboring countries object to the Albanian agreement with the Ottoman government. Austria-Hungary supports the Albanian demands. The First Balkan War begins as a regional alliance invades the Ottoman Empire. Neighboring countries occupy Albania. Ismail Qemali travels to Vi-

---

[888] *Ibid.* 494.

enna and Budapest to seek Austria-Hungary's support. A national assembly declares the independence of Albania from the Ottoman Empire.

For the Balkan countries, the political influence that the Albanians had gained was more disturbing than the content of Hasan Prishtina's Fourteen Points. In 1908 they were instrumental to the Young Turk Revolution; four years later, they again forced the resignation of the government. Therefore, the Albanians had reached political maturity that could lead only to independence. Additionally, while the Fourteen Points made no mention of autonomy, they inevitably hinted at statehood within the ethnic Albanian domains. The tide had turned in Albania's favor, and the expansionist neighbors had to act before it had become too late.

Indeed, the active movement of the Balkan countries (Serbia, Montenegro, Greece and Bulgaria) against the possible Albanian autonomy began as soon as Italy went to war with the Ottomans in Tripoli. Serbia and Russia begin to renew their efforts for a Serbian-Bulgarian alliance, convinced that the Ottoman rule in the Balkans was coming to an end.[889] After the Balkan countries sought war against the Ottoman Empire, and more so with Albania, the repeated Albanian demands had deeply shaken them.

The concern for the Albanian autonomy started to manifest more openly when the Balkan countries attested to the extent of the Kosova Uprising and the solidarity from other parts of Albania. The Bulgarian envoy to İstanbul recounted to Austrian Ambassador Pallavicini that the news about a potential unification of the four Albanian vilayets was appalling. He stated, "Such a move will give the Albanian element absolute dominance and will threaten the vital interests of the Bulgarian, Serb, and Greek elements living in those vilayets."[890]

The possibility of the Balkan countries going to war with the Ottomans over Albania disturbed Austro-Hungary. Vienna believed the collapse of the *status quo* would render the region uncontrollable.

Vienna was certainly prepared for the development, especially considering the Austrian support given to the government of Ahmet Muhtar Pasha. The Ottoman prime minister believed that the conciliatory attitude toward the Albanians and the fulfillment of their requests were favorable for the

---

[889] E. G. Helmreich, *The Diplomacy of the Balkan Wars, 1912-1913* (Cambridge: 1938), 47, cited in Skëndi, *Zgjimi Kombëtar shqiptar*, 402.

[890] Pallavicini, Report to Berchtold, Aug. 5, 1912, no. 66, HHStA, PA/39 Albanien XXXIV.

stability of the empire. Yet, the empire's rule in its European part was subject to the ultimatums and threats of the Slavic countries, which planned to partition the Albanian lands and prevent the emergence of any political entity from the Albanian people.

The Slavic plans highlighted one major aspect—Albania's role as a dam against pan-Slavism. Nonetheless Vienna was interested in the Albanians initially achieving recognition of their nationality in order to gradually attain their autonomy. For that reason, Austro-Hungary's joint foreign minister, Count Leopold Berchtold, hoped that if the Great Powers exerted pressure on the Balkan countries to refrain from action against the Ottomans, the Sublime Porte could incite decentralization and equal rights for the Albanians in a manner that would not threaten the *status quo*.[891]

Fueled by Vienna's position, the Russians, who sensed the possibility of an Albanian state, went as far as to warn Italy that "Berchtold's real objective is to create an Albania ruled by the dual monarchy."[892] To Russia it seemed that Austria-Hungary would exert enormous influence on Albania but would fall short of formal annexation; this would unnecessarily produce a rivalry with Italy. Many Albanian intellectuals also sought Austria's tutelage, knowing they had no experience with autonomy. Prior to independence, the Balkan countries had all gone through a transitional period of autonomy, ranging from seven years for Romania to thirty years for Bulgaria. Albania therefore needed foreign guidance to assist with the state building opportunity within the Ottoman Empire.

Russia continued to oppose Vienna, even when Albania's autonomy appeared to be the only option to save the *status quo* in the Balkans. In response to this option, St. Petersburg initiated the following series of pacts among the Balkan countries: (1) the Serbian-Bulgarian agreement of March 13, 1912; (2) the pact between Bulgarians and Greeks of May 29, 1912; and (3) the treaty between Serbia and Montenegro on October 6, 1912 (only two days before Cetinje would declare war on the Ottoman Empire).

The Serbian–Bulgarian pact was the most influential for Russia's interests since it gave the tsar hegemony over the Balkans on the basis of the Slavic-Orthodox platform. The agreement contained a secret clause in which Bulgaria recognized not only Serbian lands populated by Serbs, but also the

---

[891] Kr. T. v. Sosnonsky, *Die Balkanpolitik Östereich-Ungarns seit 1866*, vol. II (Stuttgart/Berlin: 1914), 276-281.

[892] L. Salvatorelli, *La Triplice Alleanza, storia diplomatica, 1887-1912* (Milano: 1939), 445-446, cited in Skëndi, *Zgjimi kombëtar shqiptar*, 404.

annexation of the Albanian land to the north and the west of the Sharr Mountains, including central, northeastern, and northern Albania. On the other hand, Serbia acknowledged all lands east of the Rhodopes and the Struma River as Bulgarian territories. The territory between the Sharr Mountains, Struma River, and Lake Ohër—encompassing the cities of Dibër, Kërçova, Gostivar, Manastir, Tetova, Kumanova, and Shkup—was defined as a questionable zone, and the arbitrator chosen to resolve the issue was Russia.[893]

The pact between Serbia and Montenegro was more so a formality since two countries had determined their future borders as early 1903—during the crisis of Macedonia. Montenegro would annex Shkodër and the northern Albanian highlands, in addition to a part of Dukagjin encompassing Peja all the way to Gjakova. Serbia would take the bulk of the Vilayet of Kosova and more than half of Manastir. An important provision of the agreement, however, was Montenegro's assumed role in inciting Albanian Catholics to rise against the Ottomans. Owing to its geographic proximity and prior developments, Cetinje had several ties with Catholic tribes from Malësia e Madhe to Podgorica. Notably, Sokol Baci openly sided with the Montenegrins.[894]

Supported by Russia, Serbia continued to pressure the Ottoman Empire to decline Albanian demands for autonomy. Belgrade had previously given money and weapons to Albanian feudalists to fight the Ottoman Empire, yet repeatedly protested against İstanbul, demanding use of military force instead of engaging in dialogue with the Albanians, whom Serbia accused as "agents of Austro-Hungary [seeking] to shove a knife on the empire and the region."[895] Belgrade warned the Ottoman government that, unless the Albanian requests were suppressed, the empire would face harsh military action. Additionally, Belgrade and Sofia persistently demanded that Russia and England firmly intervene against the Albanian autonomy.[896]

Threats from Serbia along with Russia's dissatisfaction with the Fourteen Points forced the Ottoman government to take palliative measures, claiming that the rights given to the Albanians would also be given to non-Albanians of the vilayets of Kosova, Manastir, and Janina. The Ottoman

---

[893] H.P.Sh. 2 (2002), 492.

[894] *Ibid.* 502.

[895] For more on the Serbian propaganda and its anti-Albanian attitudes during the Balkan War, see Branko Perunović, *Pisma srpskih konzula sa Prištine* (Belgrade: 1985).

[896] *Ibid.* 502.

foreign ministry also insisted that the empire would not negotiate on decentralization or nationality rights for the Albanians, as Berchtold had pressed, since these were internal matters for the Porte. This, however, didn't satisfy the Balkan countries. Furthermore, they showed no interest in the Ottoman government's decision on September 24 to extend the "privileges" the Albanians enjoyed to the non-Albanian people of the Rumelia vilayets. The regional bloc was already prepared for war and refused to back down; they solely awaited Russia's signal to begin. Aware of the situation, the Porte hoped that Austrian or German intervention to protect the Albanians would also save the Ottoman Empire.

In late September, the Ottomans and the Balkan countries mobilized their armed forces. Montenegro ordered general mobilization on September 30; Bulgaria followed suit on October 1, and Serbia did so two days later. Austria-Hungary and Russia, as the main supervisors of the Balkan countries, observed that war had become inevitable, and on September 7 declared on behalf of the Great Powers that they would not permit any change in the territorial *status quo* of the Balkans.

At a time when the end of the war was nowhere in sight, Vienna hoped the declaration would succeed. On the other hand, Russia ensured the protection of the Balkan allies in case of defeat.[897] Vienna would give the same assurances to Ismail Qemali in Budapest on November 17, when Foreign Minister Berchtold promised that "*occupied Albanian territories will be subject to international review.*"[898] The Austrian statement was important in that it portrayed the Balkan War as an invasion and not as a liberation war as the Balkan countries claimed it to be (Serbia, Montenegro, Greece, and Bulgaria claimed they were freeing their own lands from Turkish occupation based on the Slavic and Greek minorities that lived in the Albanian vilayets). Moreover, the promise of international review was of utmost significance, assuring the Albanians that there would be no unilateral fracture of the *status quo* at a time when neighboring countries planned to annihilate them.

Despite Vienna and Russia's attitudes, Montenegro declared war on the Ottoman Empire on October 8, marking the beginning of the First Balkan War. On October 17, Serbia, Bulgaria and, the following day, Greece, would join Montenegro. Notably, Serbia and Montenegro would make a "brotherly call" to the Albanians to join them in the "liberation war."

---

[897] *Ibid.* 503.

[898] Buxhovi, *Kthesa historike* 3, 200.

King Nicholas of Montenegro would invade the Ottoman Empire sending his units towards Shkodër. The Montenegrin army itself boasted over six thousand Catholic Albanians of the Mbishkodër Highlands, who had been promised an autonomous Albania, and were left to fight with the Albanian national flag. Yet, when the war started, many of the Albanian units were trapped into the hands of Montenegrins, and the flag of the Slavic kingdom replaced the Albanian one.[899] By the time the highlanders realized the deception, it had already become too late. The same fate followed some 1,000 Albanian highlanders in the brigade of General Vasojević invading Peja and Gjakova. The Montenegrin army placed them in the front lines, but soon they found out they were not fighting the Ottomans, but their own people from Kosova.

Serbian King Peter, too, in his declaration of war, promised to bring freedom, brotherhood, and equality the Albanians. On the day the his military attacked the border at Merdar, the commander of Serbian forces, General Božidar Janković, issues a proclamation in Albanian written in the Cyrillic alphabet announcing to Albanian tribes that the Serbs were coming "[i]n the name and with the help of Allah" to end the Ottoman oppression.[900] He further called on the people to:

> Have no doubts, brothers; for the faith of God, we are not coming to do you harm; we are coming with the honor of the highlands and with good intentions. Have no doubts that it will be otherwise; you will have your own faith, your traditions, and self-government as you please and as Albania has had since Leka [Dukagjini].[901]

---

[899] H.P.Sh. 2 (2002), 504.

[900] Abdyli, *Hasan Prishtina* (Prishtinë: 2003), 166-167. The author also discusses a deal that Isa Boletini reached with the Serbs in regards to "the united war against Ottomans" in Kosova. The agreement provided that Serbia would furnish Boletini with arms and financial assistance, and additionally laid the groundwork for the political landscape in the post-Ottoman era. The Albanians were given promises that they would be independent, but those plans disappeared after Serbia invaded Kosova and unleashed a wave of terror against the local Albanian population. For more on this issue, see also: Hasan Prishtina, *Nji shkurtim kujtimesh* (Bari: 1925); H.P.Sh. 2 (2002); Zekeria Cana, *Lëvizja kombëtare shqiptare në Kosovë 1908-1912* (Prishtinë: 1979), 208-251; Tajar Zavalani, *Histori e Shqipnis* (Tiranë: 1998), 222; Skëndi, *Zgjimi kombëtar shqiptar*; Gawrych, *Gjymëhëna dhe shqiponja*; Pllana, *Kosova dhe reformat në Turqi*; Edwin Jacques, *Shqiptarët* (Tiranë: 2005); Eqrem bej Vlora, *Kujtime* 1 (2001); Clayer, *Në fillimet . . . .*

[901] A complete translation of General Janković's proclamation has been provided in "Appendices."

The advance of the invading armies alarmed the Albanians. Early October, the newspaper *Liri' e Shqipërisë* (Freedom of Albania) of Sofia, predicting the turn of events, called on the Albanians "to take up the arms and defend the borders of our motherland, seeking autonomy of Albania." The immigrant community newspaper based its appeal on Sami Frashëri's idea that the Albanians had to rise up against the Ottoman Empire to avoid falling into the abyss with it by being treated as an enemy of the Balkan nations.[902]

In the meantime, Austro-Hungarian representatives in Romania telegraphed their government that Albanians had decided to serve in the front—against Greece in the Vilayet of Janina, against Montenegro in Shkodër, facing Serbia in Kosova, and Bulgarian troops in the Vilayet of Manastir.[903] To the outside observer, it occurred as if the Albanians took side with the Ottomans. But the decision to fight was on behalf of Albania, not the empire.

Suggestions that Albanians join forces with the Ottomans were rejected by principal figures of the immigrant communities. Speaking at a meeting of *Vatra*, a newly-formed federation of Albanian organizations, the priest Naum Care stated:

> Turkey, by accepting the demands of the Albanian uprising, made it possible for the existence of the Albanian nationality. This development was a deadly blow to the Balkan countries. Therefore, it seems that our interest lies in cordially cooperating with the Turkish army against the enemies of the empire who are mainly the enemies of Albania.[904]

This opinion was specifically be turned down by Faik Konica and Fan S. Noli.[905]

Well before the war, the Ottoman Empire mobilized Albanians in the military. Leaders of the uprising called from Shkup on all Albanian people to protect their homeland from the threatened invasion, but was unable to provide effective leadership. The absence of an Albanian organization (at least to a level that was seen during the uprising in the summer) meant that volunteers would be better off joining the Ottoman army. The latter had

---

[902] H.P.Sh. 2 (2002), 504.

[903] Czern, Report to Foreign Ministry, encoded telegram, no. 1263, Oct. 6, 1912, HHStA, PA XIV/41, Albanien, XXXIV.

[904] *Ibid.* 50.

[905] *The Albanian Struggle in the Old World and New* (Boston: 1939), 48-49, cited in Skëndi, *Zgjimi kombëtar shqiptar*, 408.

received special training from German experts and was well prepared for war. Nevertheless, defensive efforts would soon prove ineffective. Fifty-thousand rifles that were allegedly shipped to Kosova[906] and handed to local leaders (such as Isa Boletini, Idriz Seferi, and others), for some unstated reasons, were never delivered to defense fighters.[907]

With the outbreak of war, a political initiative nonetheless was taken by patriotic societies, such as *Shpëtimi* (*Alb.*, Salvation) and *Shoqëria e Zezë e Shpëtimit* (*Alb.*, The Black Society of Salvation), which were established in Shkup. Their representatives—including Sali Gjuka, Nexhip Draga, Bedri Pejani, and Mid'hat Frashëri—organized a meeting in the city on October 14 to discuss the Albanian efforts. The group had the approval of Hasan Prishtina, who had joined other leaders of the August uprising in the frontline with Serbia.[908]

The Shkup meeting sent a clear message to the Great Powers:

> Albanians have picked up their arms not to strengthen the domination of Turkey in the Balkans, but to emerge as masters in this land and for the freedom of Albania. Thus, as of today, we declare that whatever our fate may be in battle, Albanians will not accept for the four vilayets other than a single political entity and sovereign.[909]

On October 16, this proclamation was handed over to the European representatives in Shkup, presenting the Albanian attitude about the war, but also about the future of the country as a free state.

During the Balkan War, Albania was not liberated as neighboring countries clamored, but it was invaded by the region's armies rushing to conquer new territories for themselves. Realistically, the Ottoman defeat was not expected, given the capabilities of the imperial army and its superior size and equipment.[910] Within weeks of combat, Bulgarian troops broke the Ottoman

---

[906] H.P.Sh. 2 (2002), 505.

[907] Abdyli, *Hasan Prishtina*, 170-173.

[908] H.P.Sh. 2 (2002), 505; Abdyli, *Hasan Prishtina*, 162.

[909] *Populli*, no. 43, cited in Abdyli, *Hasan Prishtina*, 162.

[910] Ottoman troops stationed in Europe outnumber the Balkan forces by around 30,000; the Ottomans counted at 256,000 men, while the Balkan League had a round 220,000. The Ottoman military was divided into three armies—that of Adrianople (with about 120,000), Manastir (80,000) and that of Janina (with 60,000 soldiers). Up to 60,000 Albanians also served in the Ottoman army. In addition to superiority in numbers, the Ottomans were also better equipped with light and heavy weaponry. Two artillery divisions in Ottoman Europe,

resistance, and the sultan's forces retreated towards Adrianople. Meanwhile, a column of Montenegrin fighters was able to occupy Peja by the end of the third week, while two other columns were nearing Shkodër.[911] On October 15, Serbian troops rushed to the Vranje region, while three days later, a 120,000-strong division launched a fervent attack, moving in three directions: Nish-Manastir-Elbasan, Nish-Manastir-Thessaloniki, and Kurshumli-Prizren-Durrës. Other forces attacked from in the north, marching from Raška towards Mitrovica and Peja and from Javor to Prepolje.[912]

By now, the Ottoman forces had divided in two parts: one on the east, towards Adrianople, and the other in the direction of Shkodër and Janina, opening the way for the Balkan armies to occupy most of the Albanian lands. Claiming a tactical withdrawal, the Ottoman military retreated from most of the troubled areas. The frontlines were left to reserve units (consisting mainly of Albanians) and Albanian volunteers. Kosovar leaders—primarily Hasan Prishtina, Nexhip Draga, Bajram Curri, Isa Boletini, and Idriz Seferi—mainly focused on the frontier area of eastern Kosova, along Podujeva, Kumanova, and Shkup. The resistance, unable to hold for too long, hoped that the Great Powers would intervene to stop the penetration of the Balkan armies. However, Europeans had already begun working on a post-Ottoman Balkans, and the invading forces broke through within about a week.

Resistance fighters caused their enemies substantial losses in the frontline, especially around Podujeva and Kumanova, for which Serbian and Montenegrin armies sought revenge against the civilian population. Serbian special units committed serious crimes against the Albanian population, massacring women, children, and elders. The artillery shelled and razed entire villages to force any of those who survived the massacres out of the country. The Serbian army killed over 50,000 Albanians, while the Montenegrin army massacred around 20,000. Some 150,000 refugees fled to unoccupied parts of Albania or to Turkey. The tragedy was one of a series of genocides against the Albanian people that prompted the condemnation of the civilized world, but for which the perpetrators faced no consequences.[913]

---

which were led by German officers, boasted over 1,000 medium- and long-range grenades, mainly of German manufacturing.

[911] H.P.Sh. 2 (2002), 505.

[912] *Ibid.* 505.

[913] For more about the massacres the Serbian military committed during the invasion, see: Dimitrije Tucović, *Srbija i Arbanija* (Beograd: 1945); Leo Frojndlih, *Golgota shqiptare* (1913).

The Serbian army also captured many of the Albanian leaders assigned to halt the invasion. Hasan Prishtina, Nexhip Draga, Idriz Seferi, Sait Hoxha, and Kasum Seferi, among others, were taken as prisoners to Belgrade, because they refused to sign a declaration of loyalty to Serbia. They were held in prison until May 16, 1913.[914]

For propaganda purposes and to boost the "Serbian patriotic morale," the Serbian government brought thousands of prisoners of war to Belgrade, and paraded them through town, while the military declared the "liberation of Serbian lands from Ottoman occupation." Prince Alexander Karađorđević boasted in front of an excited Serbian crowd: "I would like for thousands of European to come here and see the Albanians we have captured. They will be assured that these people cannot be called humans. The Balkans should definitely be cleared of these beasts."[915]

Karađorđević's statements explain the purpose of the Balkan War: the invasion of the Albanian territory, its partitioning into four parts among the Balkan countries, and the genocide against the Albanian population had to prevent at any cost the Albanian nation from becoming "a dam against pan-Slavism"—a role the Great Powers had openly acknowledged as early as 1878.[916]

The progress of the war put the Great Powers in motion. Austria-Hungary realized that the war had shifted the region's political balance in Russia's favor. The outcome was unacceptable not only to Vienna, but also to its allies of the Tripartite Pact, Germany and Italy, and to Great Britain. As a result, a series of ministerial conferences were held in the Austrian capital throughout October to discuss issues of interest to the dual monarchy. Between October 25 and 30, the discussions focused specifically on the Albanian territory, concluding that it was in Vienna's vital interest to keep Albania regardless of the outcome of the war.[917]

The plan originally proposed an autonomous state that would further the Austrian objectives, but in case the Ottomans were to lose their sovereignty altogether, Albania would become an independent.[918] It was also in the interest of stability for the proposed state to incorporate as much of the Albanian-inhabited areas as possible. Yet, by the time the Austrians conclud-

---

[914] H.P.Sh. 2 (2002), 508.

[915] Abdyli, *Hasan Prishtina*, 171.

[916] For more information see Buxhovi, *Kongresi i Berlinit* . . . .

[917] See *Österreich-Ungarns Aussenpolitik 1908-1914*, no. 4170.

[918] *Ibid.*

ed their conferences, Albania's progressing occupation by the Balkan states shifted the focus to independence.[919] This point of the program was communicated to Germany on October 30 and to Italy on November 3.[920]

When it became clear that the end of the *status quo* was no longer a confidential matter, Berchtold proposed to Russia, on November 17, an exchange of views on the delimitation and internal organization of Albania. Only the establishment of an independent Albania and the security of its territorial integrity was the goal set forth by Austria-Hungary.[921] In the meantime, Rome transmitted its approval on November 21, and sent a detailed response three days later.

Vienna now appeared as the only and safest address for the Albanian in the tragic circumstances. This was confirmed by landowners from Tirana and Durrës who, on November 12, when most of the Albanian vilayets were occupied by the Balkan armies, petitioned Emperor Francis Joseph II for help. They reached out to the Austro-Hungarian monarch to ensure the preservation of Albania's territorial integrity and for full autonomy with the Ottoman state.[922] However, if Turkey, as a consequence of war, would not be able to rule on Albanian soil, they sought to create a kingdom similar to that of other Balkan peoples. Possibly, this kingdom would be modeled after Belgium or Switzerland to maintain the balance in the Balkans.[923]

Another petition to the Great Powers came from İstanbul a week later. The communication called for an intervention to stop the catastrophe that the Albanian people were facing and to find a solution to their national question once and forever. Noting the efforts for independence, the statement requested the respect and support of the Great Powers, as the Albanians were unwilling to accept border changes or permit the Balkan countries to impose their role.[924]

However, Albanians' role as Turkey's "destined companion" did not depend on their willingness. On November 17—after Serbs had reached as far as central Albania and surrounded the city of Durrës—Faik Konitza spoke

---

[919] *Ibid.*

[920]Skëndi, *Zgjimi kombëtar shqiptar*, 410.

[921] See L. Salvatorelli, *La Tripcile Alleanza, storia diplomatica, 1877-1912*, Milano, 1939, 450-452, cited in Skëndi, *Zgjimi kombëtar shqiptar*, 410.

[922] *Ibid.*

[923] *Ibid.*

[924] See the Albanian petition to Pallavicini and his report from Constantinople, Nov. 19, 1912, no. 88, HHStA, PA XXI/47, Türkei XXXXV/6.

out of despair at a meeting of *Vatra* in Boston: "Turkey has been defeated, and Albania is in danger of collapse. What can we, as Albanian patriots, do to save our homeland? We have to ask for help from the Great Powers, so that Albania does not become prey to the predatory neighbors."[925]

Albanian-American sent telegrams to the emperors of Austria and Germany, the king of Italy, the foreign minister of Russia, as well as to state official in France and the United States, with pleas to prevent the partitioning of Albania.

The telegrams and appeals were not enough. But the circumstances made it nearly impossible to take any action on the ground. The Ottoman Empire had already lost the war, and the occupying armies had *de facto* partitioned Albania into four parts. Meanwhile, the top leaders of the Kosova uprising—Hasan Prishtina, Nexhip Draga, Idriz Seferi, and others—who organized the defense of the Albanian territory were captured by the invading Serbs and taken as prisoners of war to Belgrade. In other words, the invasion cut of any domestic political activity among Albanians.

Since conditions at home did not permit political mobilization, the responsibility shifted on the Albanian community in İstanbul and the diaspora to become the spokesperson for their homeland. They took to work for a free state of Albania—whether independent or autonomous. The reigns of high leadership fell naturally to Ismail Qemali, an important Albanian personality who as a career politician and diplomat of the Ottoman Empire could be taken seriously by external factors. Moreover, he had been a principal figure leading to the Taksim Agreement that sparked the Kosova uprising. Now that Hasan Prishtina languished in Serbia's dungeons, Ismail Qemali was the next in line to assume the leadership of the nation.

Speaking of his role in those crucial days for Albania, Ismail Qemali noted that "when the Balkan allies had declared war on Turkey, Bulgarian armies occupied Kirk-Kilisen, and the Serbs took over Shkup, I understood that the time had come for us Albanians to take great measures for our salvation."[926]

Yet, Albania's fate depended on the Great Powers, and the greatest step that Qemali could take was to seek foreign support. He resorted to Vienna for help in saving Albania and securing favorable decisions in any post-war

---

[925] *The Albanian Struggle in the Old World and New*, 50, cited in Skëndi, *Zgjimi kombëtar shqiptar*, 412.

[926] Ismail Qemal Vlora, *Kujtime* (Tiranë: 1997), 369.

settlement. As he prepared to leave İstanbul for a diplomatic journey abroad, Qemali told an Italian newspaper that there was "no solution to the Albanian problem but the Austrian intervention," by both political and military means.[927]

Qemali then travelled first to Romania. Accompanied by Luigj Gurakuqi, a young intellectual from Shkodër, Qemali rallied the Albanians in Bucharest around his plan for Albania's statehood. On November 5, a meeting of activists of the émigré community agreed to form "a steering committee that will take over the country." In addition, a commission was appointed to travel to lobby in the European capitals for "the national land rights of the Albanian people," while a board in Bucharest would coordinate the activities of committees abroad and in Albania. The Bucharest gathering could not decide whether Albania would be autonomous or independent, because this matter remained contingent on future developments of the war and the attitudes of the Great Powers.[928]

Afterwards, Ismail Qemali met in Bucharest with the envoy of Austria-Hungary to Romania, Prince K. E. Fürstenberg, to present him the Albanian position and request for Vienna to take over the role as a defender to Albanians. For this purpose, the Austro-Hungarian envoy informed his government and made it clear to Ismail Qemali that Vienna expected for him to discuss about further steps.[929]

In Vienna, on November 12, senior officials received Ismail Qemali at the Ministry of Foreign Affairs. The Albanian leader spoke only about the possibility of autonomy, proposing an assembly of national representatives who would present a memorandum with the Albanian requests.

Vienna's foreign ministers expressed support for the Albanian national integrity, which they believed would secure peace in Balkans, but refrained from discussing specific issues because of the ongoing war.[930]

The Albanian leader received the final support for his nation's independence days later, on November 17, in a meeting with Berchtold in Budapest. In his *Memoires*, Ismail Qemali wrote that "Berchtold approved my points for the national Albanian issue." The same day, Qemali informed

---

[927]Skëndi, *Zgjimi kombëtar shqiptar*, 412.

[928] *Ibid.* 413.

[929] Eqrem bej Vlora, *Kujtime* 1 (Tiranë: 2001), 314.

[930] See the daily report no. 4398 about Ismail Qemali's visit to the Foreign Ministry of Vienna on November 12 published in *Österreich-Ungarns Aussenpolitik 1908-1914*.

his friends, assuring them that "the Albanian position was secured."[931] He transmitted Berchtold's advice, "it should not be thought about Albania's autonomy, but for an independent country that should be declared in the coming days that would enable Albania to be presented as independent in the upcoming international conference."[932]

Vienna was already set for an independent Albania as the only possible option consistent with the Austro-Hungarian interests to prevent the expansion of Serbia into the Adriatic. The Habsburg state assisted Ismail Qemali and his entourage in their journey from Trieste to Albania. Austrian navy units secured Qemali's ship, while Berchtold telegraphed Ludwig von Rudnay, his vice-consul in Durrës, to notify him of the Albanian leader's arrival. The foreign minister instructed the Austrian representative to assist Qemali with any difficulties he may encounter. Berchtold asked von Rudnay to refrain from any statements on the form of government, but to nonetheless make it clear "that the Austrians would support Albania's independence and [territorial] integrity." This position was also supported by Italy. Ludwig von Rudnay was additionally warned to steer away from the differences that existed between Albanian politicians and to emphasize instead the need for unity. The same message was telegraphed to diplomats of the dual monarchy in Vlora and Janina, too.[933]

While he safely arrived in Durrës, Ismail Qemali did not feel that the town was a secure venue for the assembly that would declare Albania's independence. There were two direct threats coming at once: the Serbian army was not too far and threatened to invade Durrës at any moment, while the Greek Orthodox bishop, Jakovos, stated "he knew and honored only one flag—that of Turkey."[934]

There is no evidence that Ottoman forces hampered or bothered Ismail Qemali, who arrived in Durrës while the port was still free from the Greek blockade and the city under Turkish control. The mayor was Albanian, a gentleman by the name of Mahmut Mahir Efendi, while the most important man in town, Hamid Bej Toptani, was also Albanian. Even the few gendarmes left in the city were all Albanians.[935] As the Ottoman army suffered

---

[931]Skëndi, *Zgjimi kombëtar shqiptar*, 414.

[932] See the daily report about the meeting between Ismail Qemali and Berchtold in Budapest, on November 17, 1912, no. 4399, *Österreich-Ungarns Aussenpolitik 1908-1914*.

[933] *Ibid.*, see Rudnay, Telegram to Berchtold, classified as "top secret," no. 4498.

[934] For more, see Ismail Qemal Vlora, *Kujtime* (Tiranë: 1979).

[935] Eqrem Vlora, *Kujtime* 1, 314.

losses on all fronts, it was unable to bring any trouble. The Ottoman government was unhappy with the course of events and ordered its official to continue their work in Albania. But doing so was as impractical under the circumstances as to force the Porte to ask for Qemali's assistance in rescuing Ottoman troops trapped in southern Albania.[936] Furthermore, there are many indications that some high Ottoman officials had been pleased with the declaration of independence. They were happy because after losing the war with the Balkan states, Western powers could decide to erect an autonomous Albania that would restore Ottoman sovereignty over parts of Europe.[937]

The Albanian leader left Durrës on a southward journey to his hometown of Vlora. On the way, he passed through Kavaja and Fier, where he met the delegates of Kosova, including Riza Bej, members of the Draga and Begolli families, and General Mehmet Pashë Deralla.[938] Finally, at the end of a four-day voyage, on November 26, Qemali entered Vlora accompanied by twenty-seven delegates. Qemali's relative, Eqrem bej Vlora, described the scenery in the city. "A holy ardor of patriotism had conquered my hometown and enthusiasm and joy greeted us everywhere. I was surrounded by eighty-three delegates, Muslims and Christians alike, who had come from all parts of Albania, including those occupied by the invading armies."[939]

Faced with the perils of the ongoing war, Ismail Qemali determined there was no time to wait for the arrival of all delegates. The situation changed rapidly as Balkan forces advanced into the country. Serbs were nearing central Albania, while Greeks threatened to soon meet them from the south. On November 28, 1912, at 2:00 P.M., the Albanian leaders convened at the National Assembly of Vlora.

In the first meeting, thirty-seven delegates attended and the number expanded as each day passed reaching sixty-three people.[940] There were repre-

---

[936] Gawrych, *Gjysmëhëna . . .*, 306.

[937] See Pallavicini's report from Constantinople, Dec. 8, 1912, no. 88 HHStA, PA XXI/47, Tükei XXXXV/6.

[938] Vlora, Eqrem Bej: Kujtime, first volume , Tiranë, 2001, 316.

[939] *Ibid.*

[940] In addition to Ismail Qemali, participants included Luigj Gurakuqi, Sali Gjuka, Bedri Pejani, Rexhep Mitrovica, Vehbi Agolli, Nikollë Kaçori, Jani Minga, Abdi Toptani, Pandeli Cale, Dudë Karbunara, Lef Nosi, Mithat Frashëri, Mehmet Deralla, Hasan Hysen Budakova, Ajdin Draga, Sherif Efendi Dibra, Dhimitër Mbroja, Dhimitër Zografi, Shefqet Daiu, Rexhep

462

sentatives of all Albanian provinces, including the areas occupied by the invading armies. Several delegates also stood in for Kosova, but the most prominent Kosovar leaders were not present on the day of the declaration. Isa Boletini arrived only the following day with 400 fighters.[941] Hasan Prishtina, Nexhip Draga, Idriz Seferi, and many others, had been captured by Serbian troops and taken as prisoners of war to Belgrade. Meanwhile, Bajram Curri's journey to Vlora was cut short by combat against Serbian forces.[942]

The Assembly elected Ismail Qemali as president. In an address to the delegates, he spoke about the past of Albania under Ottoman rule and about the struggle of the Albanians for their rights. Under the circumstances created by the Balkan War, he noted, *"the only way to save Albania was to separate from the Ottoman Empire."*[943] At the close of Qemali's historical speech, the delegates signed a handwritten memorandum memorializing the Assembly's unanimous decision *"that Albania, as of today, should be on her own, free and independent."*[944]

Ademi, Dhimitër Berati, Kristo Meksi, Xhelal Koprencka, Spiro Ilo, Iliaz Vrioni, Hajredin Cakrani, Shefqet Vërlaci, et al.

[941] H.P.Sh. 2 (2002), 510.

[942] *Ibid.* 510.

[943] *Ibid.* 511.

[944] Translated from the Albanian by Robert Elsie in "The Declaration of Albanian Independence," *Texts and Documents of Albanian History*, accessed Feb. 6, 2013, http://www.albanianhistory.net/texts20_1/AH1912_1.html.

CONCLUSION

The National Assembly in Vlora virtually restated the words that George Kastrioti Skanderbeg had uttered at the Convention of the League of Lezha in 1444. Then, "free and independent" meant that Albania belonged to the Christian West, a world and a civilization at whose foundations the people of Arbër stood since antiquity. Under Skanderbeg, Albania faced another world, which came from the East under the banner of Islam.

While the Albanians alone clashed their swords with the Ottomans, other European nations kept their only hopes in the castles of Arbër, praying that they continued to defend the West. When, several decades later, the invaders from the East crushed the post-Skanderbeg resistance, Albania was the last Balkan country to fall under Ottoman rule. However, five centuries later, the peninsula's small country became the last to secede from the oriental empire.

Skanderbeg's homeland declared its independence when the Ottoman state was in the throes of death. Days after rebels in the city of Shkup forced the Young Turks regime to accept Albania's independence, neighboring Serbia, Montenegro, Greece, and Bulgaria invaded the country in a hustle to undo once and for all that which days before appeared as the cornerstone of an Albanian state within its natural ethnic proportions.

Creating their own state was a difficult task for the Albanians, not because they wished to remain an inseparable part of the Ottoman Empire (even though they embraced Islam and rose to the higher ranks of the empire, the Albanian people preserved their ethnicity, language, and historical heritage with an inclination towards the Western civilization). The efforts for a nation state were hindered by the Ottomans, who believed that, because the majority of Albanians had converted to Islam, the empire could permanently maintain its European possessions. In the meantime, the resurrection of the state of Arbër disturbed the Slavic-Orthodox neighbors, too, who had often fought against Albanians during medieval times.

The period prior to Albania's independence were marked by events that gave rise an irreversible current of pan-Slavic nationalism. Since the turn of the 18th century, the Tanzimât reforms and later the Easter Crisis created the opportunity for the first Slavic-Orthodox states to emerge in Ottoman Europe. Meanwhile, Albanians as well resorted, although not promptly, to the national identity to secure their future among European nations. The independent nation state was a condition to that.

Albanian efforts for statehood were faced with double challenges: from the one side, with the Ottomans; and, on the other hand, with the hegemonic neighbors. This required that the Albanians made great strides, and the intellectual elite were the first to realize the needs of the people. The development of the common language and cultural and national emancipation could lead the nation the right way—that is, to separate from Ottoman Empire and to prevent territorial losses to the neighboring countries.

The national renaissance, or Rilindja Kombëtare, virtually found the magical formula when it proclaimed the common language and culture as the basis for the Albanian national identity. Meanwhile, religions were made a part of a "common spiritual pluralism," which assisted the national cause. The motto "Feja e Shqiptarit âsht Shqiptaria" (Alb., "The Faith [i.e., religion] of the Albanian is Albanianism") became the worthiest and only principle that would secure the future, albeit with difficulty, of the ethnic group.

Based on this formula, the leaders of the national movement conceived the aspirations for self-government, which they first promoted in the era of the Albanian League of Prizren. This nationwide organization pointed out the Albanian determination to defend the territorial integrity of the ethnic group, demonstrating at the same time the ambition to build the national state. Albanian leaders hoped to accomplish the goal gradually and in conformity with the political circumstances and regional developments, which required extreme caution with the Ottoman Empire and the Great Powers of Europe. And, the continent's empires were well aware that Albania was the only county that could be used as a barrier against pro-Slavic and expansion of Russian influence in Balkan.

The Rilindja period—it span from the Tanzimât reforms to the Young Turks Revolution that come to an end with the Ferizaj Convention, in July 1908—represents likewise the most controversial phase in Ottoman history. At home, regional despotism was replaced by an absolute monarchy; on the international arena, the 1856 Peace Conference of Paris welcomed the Ottoman state into European concert and guaranteed the empire's territorial integrity against foreign intervention. However, it was the relentless movements of the Slavic-Orthodox peoples that eroded the Ottoman state internally, diminishing its territorial extent and ensuring its eventual collapse in the Southeast European region.

These developments obviously also affected the Albanians, culturally and politically. On the earlier aspect, people believed it essential to express its nationality as a conglomerate of multiple identities (religious, ethnic, regional, etc.); on the political field, the Albanians rallied for autonomy within the empire, demanding that way the proposed entity known as Ottoman Albania, a precondition to European Albania, the independent state that would appear when the sultan's regime departed from the old continent.

Owing to Russian support, neighboring peoples began to formulate political programs for their nation states and, with the outset of the 19ᵗʰ century, the Balkan countries began secede, one after the other, from the Ottoman Empire (Serbia, Montenegro, and Bulgaria become autonomous principalities before attaining the full sovereignty; Greece achieved independence at once). However, in addition to breaking off from the padishah, the neighboring Slavic-Orthodox also heralded their ambitions to expand territorially by adding Albanian lands to their states. The Albanian people were inevitably compelled to meet the challenge of nationalism in order to demonstrate they are an ancient European people and as such they are the master of the ethnic Albanian territory encapsulated in the four vilayets (Kosova, Shkodër, Manastir, and Janina). At the same time, leading activists began to work on an Albanian political program, which intended to maintain the balance of three parties: Albanians, Ottoman Empire and European Great Powers. Such a thing appeared unattainable.

The Albanian national movement faced multiple difficulties, because it countered the social, cultural, and political realities of Ottoman Empire. The Sublime Porte considered most of the ethnic group as a part of the Ottoman nationality (millet-i osman), since the majority of Albanians converted to Islam. Meanwhile, the sultan viewed Albania—this was the norm at least during the reign of Sultan Abdul Hamid II—as a "bastion of Islam in Europe," on whom the empire's future depended. For thirty-two years on the throne, Abdul Hamid made all the efforts to prevent and combat national revival and self-government in Albania.

In the struggle against the Hamidian regime, the Albanians had great hurdles to overcome: sustaining a process of cultural emancipation based on the Albanian language and consolidating the national identity over religious and regional and social differences was not an easy task. The Albanians were soon challenged by Islam and Ottomanism as the main pillars of the Ottoman state.

The Tanzimât reforms played a principal role on this unpredictable road. During nineteenth century, the Ottoman Empire undertook a series of changes favoring the Christian peoples in the Balkans. However, the Albanians could not be left aside as the ethnic group's intellectual elite soon proved through its expansive activity in İstanbul. Headed by the Frashëri brothers (Abdyl, Sami, and Naim), Albanian activists adopted the platform of Rilindja Kombëtare that served the national movement as a guide to Albania's statehood until the proclamation of independence in 1912. The 1876 constitution afforded the ethnic community great leverage when the first Ottoman parliament convened for a brief period. The imperial assembly held debates over administrative reforms pursuant to the Ottoman commitments to the Great Powers. On their part, Albanian deputies, Abdul Frashëri and Mehmet Ali Vrioni, proposed that the four Albanian vilayets be unified into a single self-governing entity. This request gained international legitimacy when, two years later, the Albanian League of Prizren worked to create a self-governing state within Ottoman Empire.

Albanian intellectuals in İstanbul received great encouragement from the activity of the Albanian diaspora in Italy, Rumania, Egypt, and other countries. The nationalist sentiment that spread among the Slavic-Orthodox peoples of the Balkans (and the efforts to divide from Ottoman Empire) had already induced the emergence of Albanian nationalism among émigré communities.

In the 1840s, the Arbëreshë of Italy increasingly emphasized the ancient history of Albanians and their identity of a European people. Jeronim de Rada and Dhimitër Kamarda authored prominent literary and academic works that greatly influenced Rilindja Kombëtare. Meanwhile, Naum Veqilharxhi, from Korça, became active among Albanian expatriates in Bucharest, Romania. Hi wrote a memorandum, calling on his compatriots of the Orthodox faith to work for the development of the Albanian language and education. Inspired by the Romanian movement for independence, where Albanians had their share of contribution, Veqilharxhi believed in consolidating the Albanian identity through education. While in Bucharest, he invented a unique alphabet for the language and published a primer book that fellow activists then distributed in his home country, too.

Veqilharxhi's activity is rightly considered as the beginning of Rilindja Kombëtare. The movement continued afterwards with the İstanbul Commit-

468

tee, led by Sami Frashëri. Many other patriots, including Vaso Pasha and Hoxha Tahsini, served in the group. Their work became very popular when they founded Shoqëria e të shtypurit shkronja shqip (The Albanian Print Press Society), the organization that published important literary works, non-fiction, and textbooks in the Albanian language. The İstanbul intellectuals, moreover, conceived the political program of the Rilindja movement.

The Albanians were able to maintain a single position by identifying the nation with the language. They considered faith as a spiritual aspect that did not affect one's national identity. Sami Frashëri's maxim was that the Albanians, whether Christians or Muslims, are first Albanians. Hence the metaphor that "the religion of the Albanian is Albanianism" rightfully become a driving force of the national renaissance.

This patriotic formula, along with the political demands for Albanian autonomy within Ottoman Empire, reach universal acceptance by nearly all groups. Albanians from diverse backgrounds became increasingly more conscious of the need for action based on the national identity. Following this path, Albanians could accomplish two objectives at once: they could protect their ethnic territory, and could attain equality with others by creating their own state.

The sultan was opposed to the Albanian movement. To secure his throne, Abdul Hamid relied on handouts to conservative landlords and religious hardliners, which presented the empire as the Albanians' only hope of protection from the hostile neighbors. However, Rilindja Kombëtare was determined to fight for the national identity even through cooperation with the empire-wide opposition to the sultan. This becomes particularly evident with the appearance of Young Turks. Ibrahim Temo, an Albanian, was one of the founders of the most important opposition organization, meanwhile Ismail Qemali, Hasan Prishtina, Hoxha Tahsini, and others also aligned with the Young Turks. They propagated Ottomanism as a new civil patriotism erected on the unity and equality of all Ottoman nationals, regardless of religion, language, or ethnicity. The platform also promised to remove the Albanians from the infamous millet-i osman category, bringing the people hope of equality and freedom to express their true cultural and national identity.

The Albanians provided a valuable contribution to the opposition movement, notwithstanding from the fact that they conflicted with Young Turks as soon as the political group seized the power. The Ferizaj Convention, held in Kosova in July 1908, was crucial for the victory of the Young Turk Revolution, after delegates send an ultimatum to Abdul Hamid, compelling him to rein-

state the imperial constitution. The move was righteous and constructive, for it closed the chapter of Islamism, noted for the great suffering of the Albanian people. Sultan had for decades manipulated the wealthy and the orthodox Islamic clergy to obtain their support, while he made continuous concessions to Slavic-Orthodox peoples under the pressure of the Balkan countries and the Great Powers. Albanian discontent culminated in 1903, when Abdul Hamid accepted the Mürzsteg Agreement—a reform package imposed by Austria-Hungary and Russia, effectively terminating Ottoman sovereignty in the European part of the empire. The following years were a period of crises, including the Balkan wars and the retreat of the Ottoman Empire.

Well before the turmoil ensued, Balkan countries intended to divide the region of Macedonia among them. But as the Albanians stood on their way, Serbia, Bulgaria, and Greece first subsidized armed groups to destabilize the region and prevent plans for Albania's independence. Under the influence of the neighbors, Albanian activists also steered off track, temporarily detouring from Rilindja's plan for an open movement for autonomy. Albanians became active in the movements of other nations, joining "liberation" chetas, although they served the Slavic plans to partition and occupy Albania. The Ilinden Uprising in 1903 warned that Albanian cause could easily vanish and lose its momentum.

The trend came to end, however, with the Yong Turk Revolution. Even though the new regime soon came against the Albanian interests, the contribution that the ethnic group gave prior and during the revolution was originally beneficial. This initial freedom, lasting through mid-1909, was the heyday, marking the period of the greatest national and political progress the Albanians ever achieved under the Ottoman Empire. Twenty-six Albanian deputies won seats in the free parliamentary elections, following the promulgation of the constitution. In addition to pursuing their national program, Albanians also assumed the leadership of the opposition in the Ottoman parliament. Meanwhile, the educated class worked to develop the national culture and language, particularly by improving education. They opened Albanian schools, while Albanian and Turkish languages become mandatory at all institutions, including Greek religious schools. Activists formed cultural associations and clubs, published newspapers and books, including textbooks for the Albanian schools.

One of the greatest achievements was apparently the standardization of the alphabet at the Congress of Manastir. The gathering was organized in 1908 by the city's literary club, which invited representatives from all Albanian associations, at home and abroad; activists from Romania, Egypt, and Unites States were also present. The Congress of Manastir remains a celebrated event not only for its impact on the language, but for the political message as well. By sanctioning the Latin alphabet, the Albanians reiterated their pro-Western and European orientation. Moreover, they reaffirmed the goals of Rilindja Kombëtare for an independent state of Albania, after the withdrawal of the Ottoman Empire from the continent.

The alphabet marked the start of discord with the Young Turks. The imperial government, allied with Islamist conservatives, supported an Albanian alphabet using Arabic letters. Angered by the Manastir decision, the Sublime Porte reverted to despotism, combating the Albanian language and national education. A 1910 state decree banned not only clubs and newspapers, but Albanian schools as well. The authorities prohibited the teaching of Albanian language in Turkish and Greek state schools alike.

The Young Turks launched an unforgiving campaign against the Albanian vilayets, targeting even the right of local self-government that certain regions had enjoyed for centuries. Increased taxes, counterinsurgency actions, a new military draft (that now included Ottoman subjects of all religions), and the disarmament of the population created a wide gap between the Albanians and the Young Turks. Protests and uprisings motivated by the situation soon reached wide proportions.

The Young Turks initiated military expeditions to "restore order" in the Albanian vilayets, disrespecting in this way their promises. They not only had the support of nationalist and traditionalist forces in the country, but Russian backing as well. The tsar encouraged the Ottoman government "to disarm the unruly Albanians" and for this provided money to İstanbul. In the meantime, neighboring states blamed the Albanians for persecuting other ethnic groups and demanded that the Sublime Porte take rough measures against "the savages." Simultaneously, the Balkan monarchies tried to engage some of the Albanian landlords and the fanatic nobility to fight for the return of Abdul Hamid. Serbia and Montenegro reached a deal with local leaders n Kosova and the Mbi-Shkodër highlands in northern Albania, promising them weapons and money for a fight against the Ottoman Empire. And, as attested during the 1910 and 1911 uprisings, Belgrade and Cetinje were in fact able to use the Albanian movement for their own purpose.

The warlike orientation justified the Young Turks in taking even greater action. During the spring of 1909, they tightened their grasp on power: after Abdul Hamid failed to reestablish the absolute power, the Young Turks

471

removed him from the throne and reinforced their own position. In 1910 then, the Porte dispatched to Kosova the army commanded by Şevket Turgut Pasha to suppress the Albanian uprising.

Nevertheless, the national movement continued to oppose the Young Turks regime. Finally, the decisive events sparked in 1912 in Kosova. A new uprising came as a product of Albanian leaders rather than induced by Serbia and Montenegro as it had been the case in the earlier years. The first step was the Taksim Agreement, named after the quarter of the Ottoman capital where leaders of the national movement gathered in February 1912. Headed by Ismail Qemali and Hasan Prishtina, participants agreed to work on two objectives: to overthrow the centralist-nationalist regime and to provide for an Albanian autonomy.

By early August, the Albanians achieved the first goal. They forced the Young Turk government to resign and the CUP-dominated parliament (recently elected) was dissolved three days later. On August 18, Ottoman authorities accepted a fourteen-point memorandum, known as Hasan Prishtina's Program. The provisional government of Gazi Ahmed Muhtar Pasha accepted the requests, granting the status of a nationality to the Albanians and opening the way to the autonomous government, the proposed entity that foreigners then called Ottoman Albania.

The 1912 uprising was the first instance where the national movement successfully combined political efforts with military resistance. With the exception of Hasan Prishtina, the participants of the Tasim meeting did not fulfill their duties since they could not initiate an insurgency in central and southern Albania. Nevertheless, Albanians in those regions were in cohesion with their compatriots, when the uprising took place in Kosova. There were local revolts outside the vilayet, too, showing support for the Kosovar position in negotiations that began with Ottoman officials. Ismail Qemali, who was abroad to obtain armament and diplomatic support for the uprising, gave his support for the Kosovar demands, too. Initially, Qemali had made some controversial statements on the rebellion in a way that threatened to undermine Hasan Prishtina's work. The latter was already facing many internal setbacks: on the one side, landlords enticed from Serbian agents called for the return of Abdul Hamid; on the other side, an opposition group demanded solely the overthrow of the "bad government," and failed short of supporting autonomy. The solidarity of Albanians outside Kosova and Qemali's endorsement were hence decisive for the uprising, even though it did not spread to all Albanian vilayets. An agreement was reached with the Ottomans and, alt-

472

hough it did not directly mention autonomy, ethnic Albanians gained a number of fundamental rights.

Ultimately, the deal was so unacceptable to Albania's adversaries as to bring them to war against the Ottoman Empire. Serbia, Greece, and Bulgaria had already announced their readiness to resort to arms when they founded the Balkan Alliance in early 1912. Thus, after the Sublime Porte accepted Hasan Prishtina's Memorandum, the regional countries initiated a conflict with the only goal being to partition the Albanian territories after the alliance's victory over the Ottomans.

Once the conflict, known as the First Balkan War, began, the Albanians took to arms under Ottoman command, hoping to defend their motherland. Doing so, however, they risked retaliation from neighbors in case of defeat. At the same time, they also faced the sluggish morale of Ottomans. The imperial army did stand firm against the Balkan Alliance. Ordering maneuvers to supposedly concentrate forces around Shkodër in the north and around Janina in the south, the Ottomans permitted Serbian, Montenegrin, Bulgarian, and Greek armies to rapidly occupy nearly all of the Albanian territories.

Various historians debate to this day about the actual reasons of the Ottoman withdrawal. It was well-known that the Ottoman Empire was prepared to face Balkan countries, even more so if the fronts continue to remain open for a long time, alerting the Europeans who would not permit Russia's allies to impose their hegemony by force. Whereas, by choosing to retreat "tactically," Ottoman forces caused an unprecedented tragedy.

The resistance of Albanian units, consisting of volunteers and reserve forces, was not sufficient to halt the Slavic and Greek assault. Invading armies unleashed into Albanian lands massacring not only the helpless defenders, but the unarmed population, too. Once they crossed the border, overrunning the Merdar checkpoint in Kosova, and reached the Albanian shores, Serbian forces committed the second genocide within forty years (the first having occurred during the Russo-Turkish war, in the winter of 1877-1878, when Serbia forced hundreds of thousands of Albanian to flee their homes in Toplica, Kurshumlia, and Prokupa).

The regional alliance occupied almost all of Albania during the Balkan War. Serbian and Montenegrin forces seized resistance leaders. Hasan Prishtina, Nexhip Draga, Idris Seferi, and others were taken to the Belgrade prison, and the burden fell on Albanian leaders residing in İstanbul to wage the political and diplomatic war for the salvation of Albania.

Therefore, Ismail Qemali and Luigj Gurakuqi headed a delegation to Austria-Hungary. They stopped on the way in Bucharest, where a meeting was organized to discuss Albania's future. Participants failed to define the desired political status, but they entrusted Ismail Qemali to seek Austria-Hungary's help to save their homeland. On November 17, this time in Budapest, the Albanian leader met with Foreign Minister Berthold, who guaranteed the support of dual monarchy. The Austro-Hungarian dignitary advised Qemali that Albanians must declare their independence before the Great Powers were to meet to resolve the Balkan matter (an international conference was planned for early December).

As of the Budapest meeting, the Albanians entered the most difficult stage of their struggle for statehood. Ultimately, on November 28, 1912, delegates gathered at the National Assembly in Vlore passed a great monumental act: Albania was declared a free and independent state after centuries of Ottoman rule. The historic meeting held in the free coastal town in southern Albania concluded a process that began in the then-occupied north. In the words of Hasan Prishtina, "the Balkan Wars caused for the honor to belong to Vlora, not Kosova, and for a lesser Albania to be created instead of a greater Albania."

APPENDIX
TABLES AND EXCERPTS

Early Ottoman Census Data

TABLE 1. NUMBER OF TIMARS IN ALBANIAN SANJAKS

Sanjak	Timars
Pashasanjak of Shkup (Trk.: Üsküb)	344
Sanjak of Vuçitërn (Trk.: Vıçıtırın)	317
" " Prizren	225
" " Shkodër (Trk.: İşkodra)	53
" " Dukagjin (Trk.: Dukacin)	-
" " Elbasan	138
" " Ohër (Trk.: Ohri)	342
" " Vlora (Trk.: Avlonya)	439

Sanjaks not appearing on this table are mentioned in Chapter 1.

TABLE 2. 1530-1533 CENSUS DATA FOR THE SANJAK OF VUÇITËRN

Kazas	Kasabas	Vital and miscellaneous statistics	
Novobërda	Vuçitërn	Population: 26,573	*Sanjakbeys*: 1
Prishtina	Prishtina	*Avarız*(tax)-paying	*Kadıs*: 4
Bellasica	Janjeva	households: 13,780	*Zaims*: 5
Vuçitërn	Novobërda	Villages: 1084	Spahis: 293
	Bellasica	Muslims: 283	*Dizdars*: 1
	Trepça	Mosques: 4	Garrisons: 48
	Lower Trepça	Masjids: 10	*Mera* fiefs: 60
	Bellobërda	Monasteries: 42	Baths: 2
	Koporiq	Churches: 11	Caravanserais: 2

TABLE 3. ALBANIAN NAMES IN DARDANIA[945]

Dardania Field (eastern Dardania)	Dukagjin Plateau (western Dardania)
Gjerekare: Berisha, son of Branko; Radonja, son of Berisha	*Peja*: Gjura, the son of Geg Peter; Pavle Arbanas; and Nikola Arbanas; Peter, son of Gjon; Nikola, son of Piso, and Nikola's brother, Gjon; Domenik; Radashan Liku[946]
Gllareva: Kojica, son of Gjon; Radislav, son of Gjon	
Vuçitërn: Radivoje, son of Gjonesh; David, son of Shlava; Radica Arbanas [*i.e.*, the Albanian]; Gjoniqi, etc.	*Deçan village*: Radovan, son of Gjon; *bashtina* [*i.e.*, inherited property] of Nikolla Gjeçi [Gjech]
Obrica: Gershad Arbanas, brother Stepan, and Gershad's own son, Raho; Millosh, Berisha's brother, and Millosh's son, Gjura	*Gjakovica (Gjakova) village*: Nikza, son of Nika; Nikolla, son of Mira; Gjon, son of Gega; Bobza, son of Pal [*i.e.*, Paul]; Shteplo, son of Mela; Mira, a widow
Shtërpce: Petro, son of Arbanas	
Kuçica: Todor, son of Arbanas, and Todor's son, Bodan; Branislav, son of Arbanas	*Kosuriq*: Nikolla, son of Nika
	Uça: Lazar, Dimitri's brother; Dimitri, son of Gjon; Gjon, Andria's brother; Gjura, son of Gjon; Gjon, Tidor's brother
Lower Tushila: Novak, son of Arnaud	
Klladoronica: Radihna, son of Arbanas; Radac, son of Arbanas	*Cërni Potok*: Gjon, son of Nikolla; Leka, son of Peter; Dimitri, Leka's brother; Nenko, son of Gjon; Nikolla, son of Gjon; Dimitri, son of Gjon; Gjon, son of Dimitri; Gjin, son of Meksha; Gjin, son of Zahar
Strellica: Petro, son of Arbanas, and brother Novak	
Shipitulla: Petko Arbanas; Mihal Arbanas, and brother Radko	
Çikatova: Radovan, son of Gjin	*Dujak*: Nenko, son of Gjin; Radich, son of Gjin; Gjin, son of Meksh; Gjin, son of Nikolla
Gernçare: Berisha, son of Gjon	
Sarban: Vlkoslav, son of Medunas, and brother Lesh	*Netrobishta*: Drago Arabanas and his brother, Nikolla; Gjin, son of Gjura (Gjursha)
Prunda: Nikola Arbanas and brother Radislav	
Verba: Branko Arbanas; Millosh Arba-	*Krushevica*: Gjergj, son of Radich;

NOTES

[945] [Phonetic spelling as used by the author in the Albanian has been retained.—Translator]
[946] Rizaj, *Kosova gjatë shekujve . . .*, 462.

476

Dardania Field (eastern Dardania)	Dukagjin Plateau (western Dardania)
nas	Gjergj, son of Dimitri; Branko, Gjon's
Llovisha: Dujko, son of Lesh, and brother Brajan	brother, and Branko's son, Vuk; Nikoll, Gjergj's brother; Dimitri, son of Span
Lesser Obrinje: Kin Arbanas; Bogdan, son of Gjin	*Sllojan village*: Nikolla, son of Gjon; Nenad, son of Arbanas; Radisav, son of
Shtimle: Andria, son of Arbanas; Dhimitri, son of Gjin	Gjon; Miha, son of Arbanas
Nerodime: Radislav, son of Gjon	*Dobriçadoll* (present-day Dobër, Gjakova): Progon, son of Lika; Gjin, son
Sadrina: Pribina, son of Gjon; Dobizhva, son of Gjin	of Nikolla; Gjergja, son of Progon; Gjon, Gjura's brother; Peter, son of Gjin;
Zllatare: Petro, Arbabas	Maria, a widow
Bojac: Ivko, son of Gjon	*Kovalica*: Pal, son of Gjin; Gjin, son
Sojevo: Radisav, son of Gjon	of Nikolla; Andria, son of Gjin
Gjinovc: Branko, son of Gjon	*Romica*: Branko, son of Gjin; Gjon,
Upper Tërpeza: Gjin, son of Rankos	a pauper
Kashtanjeva: Dimitri, son of Gjon; Dragan, son of Gjon; Ivan, son of Kalajan, and Ivan's son, Gjin	*Lepovac*: Gjon, son of Andria; Gjin, son of Vuk; Gjin, son of Bërdo; Gjon, son of Stepan; Gega Todori; Gjeç, son of
Sellce: Smil, son of Leshin, and Smil's son, Rasho, and brother, Vasil; Nikolla, Smila's brother	Gjon; Gjon, son of Meksha
	Cermian: Boshko, son of Gjin
	Gllogjan: Progon, son of Grubaç [Grubach]
Podgorce: Vlkuslav Arabanas; Radisavi, son of Gjon	*Lower Petërç*: Nenko Arnavut
Grbavc: Vlladko Arbanas and son Novak	*Trakaniq*: Dejan, son of Gega
Kllokot: Bogdan, son of Gjon; Rashko, son of Gjon	*Vraniq*: Gjin, son of Nikolla; Nenko, son of Gjin; Gjin, son of Andreja;
Pasjan: Dabizhiv, son of Gjon, and brother Dimitri	Nenko, son of Progon; Andria, son of Leka; Progon, son of Gjon; An-
Ovçareva: Bogdan, son of Milan, and Bogdan's sons Pertro and Gjin; Bogdan, son of Gjin	dria, son of Muriq [Murich; *i.e.*, Maurice]; Pepa, son of Leka; Pepa, son of Mara; Leka, Gjon's brother;
Lower Bërnica: Danko Arbanas; Prijezda, son of Danko	Leka, son of Todor; Mara, a widow; Neka, a widow
Tirinc: Dimitri, son of Gjon; Dimitri's son Vuçko, and brother Jovan	*Kraçor*: Gjin, son of Gega, and Gjin's son, Andreja; Gjergj, son of Gjin;
Llaple: Millosh, son of Gjin; (another)	Ilia, son of Drech; Gjon Arbanas;

Dardania Field (eastern Dardania)	Dukagjin Plateau (western Dardania)
Millosh, son of Gjin	Gjon Çiragjini
Suvodo: Gjon Arbanas	*Banja*: Gjon, son of Pop, and Gjon's son,
Bresje: Millosh, son of Gjin; Radihna,	Radovan
son of Gjon	*Rudnik*: Nikolla, son of Arbanas, and
Vërban: Radinha, son of Gjon	Nikolla's son, Radisav; Stepan, son
	of Llesh
	Upper Beliqa: Nikolla, son of Arbanas
	Leskovc village: Dimitri, son of Nikolla;
	Dimitri Arnavut, etc.[947]

In addition to the communities listed above, there were Albanian names in the Upper and Lower Leshnica villages of eastern Dardania (consisting of fifteen and twenty-one household).[948]

---

[947] Pulaha, "Të dhëna onomastike mbi elementin shqiptar të krahinave të Sanxhakut të Shkodrës në fund të shekullit XV," *Studime historike* 4 (1972) [Tiranë]: 175-185.

[948] H. Hađibegić, et al., *Oblast Brankovića*, cited in Rizaj, *Kosova gjatë shekujve . . .*, 432, 434.

Letter of Pjetër Budi to Cardinal Gozzadino[949]

Your Illustrious and Reverend Lordship,

I, Pjetër Budi, bishop of Zadrima, was born in Gur i Bardhë, a fortress of Ematia [*i.e.*, Mat] in Albania, to the old house of Budi of Macedonia and in my youth I was virtually at all times in service of several bishops of our country, under whom I pursued the study of these few sciences until I was twenty-one, since at that time I had become a minister and was at the same time sent to the province of Serbia among those Catholic peoples. There I stayed for about twelve years, until the latest provincial synod, which was held in the said province of Serbia at the good initiative of monsignor Tomasso Orsino, archbishop of Tivar, at which [synod], with the approval all the clergy of those peoples, I was made vicar general of Serbia, and later I was enforced once again in the same office (at the time) of the visit of Monsignor Bizzi, successor of the said archbishop, and in exercise of that office, for a period of seventeen years, as much as I was able to, I did not cease to help and console with all zeal those peoples, as well as the ministers themselves, with spiritual examples, by always writing spiritual books in their language, for those of Serbia as well as those of Albania, as it is seen today in all of those regions. Recently, I was asked many times by some magnates of those peoples of Albania, and especially by two Turk [*i.e.*, Muslim] chieftains, close relatives of mine, who are the heads of all those regions, to come to these areas to meet with the above-mentioned and lord knight Bertucci, who is like our general custodian, for all those Christian peoples, whether of the kingdom of Bosnia, or of Albania, and together with them to reveal their desire to His Holiness or another powerful Christian. On the other hand, having in mind the severe damage to the sacred Catholic faith, which is held with little respect from some of those believers and (inspired) from the zeal to give notice to His Holiness to [find a] cure everything, I gladly departed to come to the source of grace and mercy: this happened in 1616. And, immediately after I arrived here, with many prayers and memorials, I did not fail to bring [the plan] to the attention of the memory of the Blessed Pope Paul V, but since I do not know well the affairs of Rome and since I did not find the above-mentioned knight Bertucci (who at the time had been sent by his

---

[949] [Retranslated from an Albanian translation. Archaic style has been retained for accuracy purposes.—Translator]

Order in Germany to his Cesarian Majesty or for the same matters) and having no one else to rely on, I was unable to do anything at that time.

The province of Albania is the one that is situated to [the western] end of Macedonia, and has the Adriatic Sea to the west, is surrounding by Greeks to the east, and [the ecclesiastic province of Serbia] to the north. It is ruled entirely by the Turks and, in certain lower regions, is oppressed to the greatest extent. This province contains fourteen bishoprics, which for many years have been vacant and without shepherds, except for those of Stefania[ka] and Alban and, in present times, two other recent appointees, that is I and another in Lezha. These peoples, having remained for so long without spiritual governance, have fallen into such an unenlightenment and ignorance such that they daily depart from the Catholic faith and embrace the Greek schism or Mahometism [i.e., Islam], especially when they are subjected more than others to the Ottoman tyranny. And those who are not so oppressed live catholically, as is the case in particular with the Kelmendi, who live in the mountains above Lake Shkodër and reach the number of 6,000 warriors, valuable and unwavering men, whom the Turk has never been able to rule or obtain haraç payments from. They live with their arms at hand, as do the peoples of Kuç and Piper, their allies, together with those of Marković, who may reach the same number of fighting men; [there are also] many other peoples and communities around Shkodër, who are full of desire to see their liberation one day. On the other hand, towards Kruja, are the Dukagjinis, who rose against the Turks thirty years ago and reach that same number of 6,000 warriors, all bearing their own arms. These are unwavering and valuable men that the world may have, they are well-trained in military discipline, and they live in highlands above Lezha and between Shkodër and Kruja. Until now, they have caused great damages to the Turks. They have destroyed castles and towns of the Turks and have constantly been victorious in all battles against the Turks, their main enemy. And these are all Catholic peoples and very obedient to the Holy Roman Church.

There are, on the other part, by the borders of Macedonia and Bulgaria, other peoples that were called the lands of Skanderbeg, that is, Matia [i.e., Mati], Brenda, Kurbin, Tamadheja, and Çermenika, located along the highlands above Kruja and Elbasan, although mixed with Turks [i.e., Muslims], with a Christian majority, men not less mighty and warriors, and all of them armed (with hand weapons) reach the number of 5,000 warriors. All of them have a great desire to see one day the flag of a Christian prince who moves at least to fast their hands and help them unite with [Europe] against

480

the Turks, to oust him from the country. Furthermore, they shall move they see that a prince has hoisted his flag at a main fortress of Albania and in such a case 30,000 thousand combat-ready Albanians shall rise.

The heads of such peoples are mostly relatives of mine and very close friends, such that even the Turkish (Muslims) chieftains of those areas have revealed their souls. And with those heads a manner has been planned to capture the fortresses of those areas, as the said knight Bertucci is aware for all details, the time and the manner . . .

To further continue my communication, I shall recount to Your Illustrious Lordship that, when I departed from those peoples, both peoples' leaders and [Muslim] chieftains, asked me repeatedly, to reveal by all means to His Holiness, Your Lordship, or to another Catholic prince, this desire of theirs and to come to their aid with men and other matters necessary for war, although, to feed the people, the country has an abundance and needs no aliments. But it needs only a prince to support it with men, especially men of command, and with ammunitions because they are sufficient to resist the Turkish enemy with their own forces; however, for greater security, they need a prince, who would be their president or lord, to be able to furnish them with the necessary articles. Since three years have now passed and the said peoples have not received any news on this matter (and regarding) their desires [*i.e.*, demands], they have recently sent, disguised as a student, a nobleman from the bishopric of Sapa, named Nikollë Leka, who knows very well the cities of Shkodër and Lezha and is in good terms with the above-mentioned peoples of Kelmend and Dukagjin [. . .]

There are other peoples in the lowlands of Shkodër, in Drisht: Pultians, Saptians, and Sardenians; in Lezha, Kruja, and Durrës; [there are] inumerous peoples, all of them Catholics, although mixed with Turks (Muslims), Christians by majority, and all of them armed [and] reaching the number of 8,000 warriors, filled with the desire to have someone come to their aid to liberat them; so are not only the Christians, but also the [Muslim] chieftains, and (those) who have denied faith, because they can no longer endure the Ottoman tyranny, and therefore each desires to be liberated once (and for all) from such a misery or [they wish] to die fighting.

Therefore, he who would have knowledge of the communities and people of Albania and how easily the main fortresses may be taken from the Turks, I am assured, knowing that, knowing the exact and easiest way to become lord of the above-mentioned provinces, he would not waste even one hour of his time without executing those sacred undertakings. And, whoever becomes lord of the said fortresses, comes and becomes even lord of Macedonia, Bulgaria, Serbia, and Greece. The Turk will have been destroyed and ruined if Albania is taken from him because there is no region other than ours through which more damage and annihilation could be caused to the Turks... And for this, one is convinced for many reasons. First and foremost, because the fortresses that shall be taken by the Christians cannot be seized by war and can be held with small garrisons, and for so long as there shall be ammunition and supplies, [the fortresses] shall not fall by no means: mines, attacks, or any other way. Those (fortresses) shall be seized at different times as to permit intervening months in between, during which necessary aid may be taken delivered. The fortresses are close to each other, such that our aid could be delivered over one day and night, unless the Turk comes through the sea to reoccupy those fortresses, (but) he will have to sail from far, and even if he comes through the sea, he shall have no ports to disembark his men because all ports shall be taken and held by Christians; moreover, the Christian fleet shall halt the [Turkish] advance to the region. On land, the Turk cannot reach here because, in the highlands, along the Albanian-Greek border, there are gorges and canyons everywhere, such that even if a whole world were to come, it would never pass through to ruin those lands of ours; so narrow are the pathways such that every province is bound by very harsh mountains and with such passes that one hundred men could equal to and defy 10,000. The country is also fertile and has all types of foods; the air is very soft, from the best and most excellent that could be found on Earth and usually [people] reach ninety or hundred years of age. The interior is filled with all types of prey, with excellent wines, oils, quality wheat, and animals in abundance; there are many rivers and forests, lakes with plenty of fish and of all varieties; in other words, internally and externally, and from all sides, [the country] is a paradise on Earth. Now it is the time is the most appropriate to execute this undertaking, since the country has unfurnished with Turks, as all of them have gone to war against the Poles. And, if this undertaking were carried out, it would be a lifesaver for the Poles, and the Emperor himself because, upon learning of the Albanian expedition, His Cesarian Majesty will inevitably direct his weapons against the Turks and the Poles will not make peace (as they would) otherwise.

The said peoples await my personal notification to learn what decision His Holiness hath taken in regards to this desire of theirs, and they ask me that I return with a positive response; and now I will have to console the minds, with this virtuous and sacred position of this higher and much virtuous pontiff, who has supported this excellent matter, so that a good start may be found, since this good news, will bring great joy to those peoples. And, so that this sacred plan must not be discovered by the enemies, I shall bring to those peoples some full pardons with certain blessings for those communities, as it may please His Holiness, and I shall distribute my books printed at the order of our lordship, such that my return shall not attract suspicion . . .

In other words, once I arrive in those communities, I shall again put everything in line and I ensure His Holiness that, for any of His orders, we shall all be ready to fully carry out the order to die for the holy Catholic faith, although, with divine help, we will seize those fortresses with the agreement of those Turks who remain in the fortresses, as we have agreed with them to carry out everything without military confrontations; and, once we will have seized the said fortresses, then, the gallery of His Holiness jointly with those of Malta will, once they reach the shores, disembark the first aid supplies and soldiers to deploy as guards of the said fortresses . . .

I pray, therefore, to Your Illustrious Lordship to condescend and give a thorough consideration and to give our lordship notice for purposes of making this sacred decision because, if the undertaking is made, all Christendom will rush to lend a hand. But, the start has to occur much clandestinely and without military maneuvers; and, once the two main fortresses of Albania are taken, His Holiness shall become lord of all the country, where all the spoils and chattel that is found in Albania (as extracted) from the very rich Turks, reach millions of forints, and these shall serve as useful earnest money to spend for new advances and profits; moreover, there shall be discovered other treasuries that are now hidden in the said province of Albania and are contained in intact gold mines, which shall yield great and valuable fruits for the entire country. But above all, it is necessary that I arrive to expedite and organize the necessary matters for this deal, hence everything for the glory of God and for the growth of the Holy Catholic faith and in service of Christendom and for the destruction of the tyrannical Turk. And with that [said], with the good grade of Your Most Illustrious Lordship, I humbly kiss your hand.

> Your Illustrious Lordship's very humble servant,
> Pjetër Budi, bishop of Zadrima.
> In Rome, September 15, 1621.

Abedin Pasha's Letter

Confidential Letter to the Heads of the Albanian League by Abedin Pasha

My name and my inclusion in the Sultan's government by the governor of Selanik demonstrate His Majesty's concern for our nation and this deserves attention.

You have been informed in Selanik about my as appointment minister of the foreign affairs. I have never dreamed of things of this nature. But, I have always desired that this important position be occupied by a friend of Albania, who would be able to defend the political state of the country and present it in all of Europe.

Therefore, Almighty God astonishingly honored all of my prayers and I was appointed to such an office, which is of great importance for our national cause. In the name of God and with the help of the Almighty, I hope to carry out and fulfill my duties. Like our brothers, I also have taken it upon myself to work through all my life and endeavor for the good and *the fate of our fatherland, Albania.* You could imagine my present sentiment and to believe it, now that I am in this office. I pray that you may convey my advice because there are some of those who wish to compromise the fatherly government of His Majesty, the Sultan. He desires to protect you.

For many days now a conference has convened in Berlin to resolve the Greek issue. Owing to the commitment of our government, which has taken preliminary measures, I am highly convinced that the results of the meeting will not be to the detriment of the Albanians, *because you will benefit from the Great Powers' intention to maintain Albania as an important factor.* Since I am profoundly convinced that the Greek issue, which brings such grave concerns to our country, will be resolved properly, I ask of you that during the talks in Berlin you refrain from any action that could contradict our goals. Until the final word is said on the key matters of the Albanian issue, you should think only of justice and negotiations. Should you have no time to send your special delegation to deliver you wishes, then the best option is for you to collect signatures and send them as soon as possible to Berlin. This way, you shall present your work before the European audience. *Myself, I have collected signatures here in İstanbul and I am sending them so that you may add your signatures.*

I shall notify you that the illogical claims the Montenegrins have recently made on the Albanian territory will not have the support of the Great

Powers. I am convinced that this issue, too, will soon be resolved in our favor. I will inform you once I have received any news on this regard.

The main desire of His Majesty, the Sultan, when He appointed me as minister of foreign affairs, was to demonstrate that his great heart will always beats for Albania and that Albania is vitally tied to the general interests of the state. *I wish to remind you that Turkey's existence in Europe is closely linked to Albania's existence.* This is a vital matter, the same for both sides, Albania as well as the Porte. *All the intentions and positions of the Porte are for Albania to remain strong and important. This is also the wish of the Great Powers, which have an interest in the Ottoman [presence] in Europe.* The Sublime Porte, messieurs, will protect you from the greed of your neighbors and you will create a high barrier against those who wish to expand at our expense.

Albania must become an important factor because her present role is great for us. March, thus, ahead united and strong, together with your brother of the non-Muslim faith, for they are also sons of your land.

This is the logic of the situation and the desire of His Majesty. Any decision or behavior of yours that would oppose His Majesty would be a fatal mistake for you and that would be used by Turkey's enemies, who are your enemies, too.

Abedin Pasha

The Frashëri-Vrioni Memorandum

[. . .]

The Greek nation has won its independence and now seeks to annex Epirus and Hellenize the Albanian people thereof. The Greek government has not ceased and will not cease to use all possible means to reach its goal. In fact, the Greek government has for a while financially supported bandits, using them to incite the Christian Albanian population to rise against [Muslim Albanians] and the Porte.

[Such were the intentions] of General Givas when he crossed the Greek border in 1854, followed by a myriad of gangs. His partisans terrorized the people only in order to have them side with [the Greeks].

The criminal endeavors were ineffective. They failed to change the people's mind.

Such attempts were repeated in 1866, but did not yield any success. Then, the Greek government formed "revolutionary" committees in various parts of Epirus and Thessaly, giving the inhabitants large quantities of armament and ammunition. In addition, the Greek gangs were led by officers of the Greek army and supported by regular Greek troops. Nevertheless, in 1878, Epirus peasants were the first to repel the attackers at the Battle of Ligoris.

Realizing once more that it could not impose its will upon the people, the Greek government changed to the present strategy . . . . Today, the Greek government endeavors to reach its goals through diplomacy and, in the memorandum Mr. Delian delivered to the Congress, demands that Epirus, Thessaly, Macedonia, and even Constantinople be given to Greece!

While the Congress did not accept the Greek demands, it promised the Hellenic kingdom someway the districts of Preveza, Narta[sic], Margarita, Paramitra, Parga, and Janina to the Kalama River, without the slightest regard to the rights of the Albanian people of those territories.

Fortunately, this position formulated in Berlin was not final and has not taken effect.

The rights of the Albanians, nonetheless, have been endangered and have received no recognition, despite the telegrams of protest delivered to the Congress of Berlin, and parts of [Albania] were ceded to Serbia and Montenegro.

If old and new maps and geographic foundations were to be given any consideration, one may easily see and understand what an injustice was done to the Albanians. A man, of the least informed, knows that the Albanians are an older people than the Greeks. Epirus has been an integral part of Albania since ancient times and was never held by the Greeks. The works of world historians, from Heredotus and Thucydites to Strabo, attest to this historic fact, while modern geography books agree with the ancient writers.

One of the greatest propaganda absurdities that the Greek have been disseminating fabricates that the inhabitants of Janina and Narta, who have knowledge of the Greek language, are Greeks. Today Epirus has more than 600,000 inhabitants, a small part of which speaks Greek. In fact, the group relatively comprises of 74,000 inhabitants. This indicates that they are not of Greek origin, but that the [Hellenic] alphabet and trade have exerted their influence on that part of the population. The world today is aware of what language the inhabitants of those areas speak and that they are ethnic Albanians. Furthermore, if the language spoken must determine to which state a territory will belong, we ought to change the maps of Asia, Europe, and the world at large. Should we define citizenship on a linguistic basis, we would have to begin with Greece, annexing the 210,000 of its inhabitants who today speak Albanian within the present Greek borders; then, we ought to take 160,000 Albanians from Italy, 150,000 from Serbia, Montenegro, Bulgaria, and Dalmatia [Zadar (Alb.: Zara); then part of Austria-Hungary], and so on. This is the logic that Greece relies on today. One may wonder where it would take us.

Even though Serbia and Montenegro were given entire districts, such as Shpuza, Podgorica, and Vranje, we, the Albanians, believe that we ought to refrain from action for that would endanger the respect of the Congress of Berlin, which we value so highly. The loss of those territories is not of the same gravity and value as the present Greek claims. These would be catastrophic for us. One must by no means forget that the Serbian and Montenegrin annexation of the said territories has brought great difficulties and turmoil that continue to this day. The decisions broke the perpetual harmony that the two people had enjoyed until then. This was hence a mistake.

The value of Epirus cannot be compared to the territories lost in the north. The importance of Epirus is much greater since key Albanian ports, including Preveza, Narta, and Parga, are situated there. Albania has no other harbors that could rival [those of Epirus]. Moreover, the areas are of vital strategic importance, among the most valuable in Albania.

Should those areas be given to the Greek, as he now persistently demands, [the decision] would touch the hearts of every patriot willing to defend his country above all. If the keys to Albania are handed to another people, this would serve as a starting point to seize all of Albania. Thereby, the most strategic areas would be given to a state, which has for a long time taken a hostile stance against us. This would bring us such a diminishment that no people gripped by patriotic feelings could endure.

It is well-known that the Albanian farmers subsist on their arid, mountainous pastures. In wintertime, the flocks graze in Preveza, Parga, Margariti, and all the way to Janina. If those areas are to be given to Greece, the Albanians would have no place to overwinter their livestock and would be forced to sell it. Has any thought been given to such a situation? This would inflict a people with having no basis to subsist. The said areas that the Greeks demand are the only in the region that provide food for the Epirus population.

This is the truth and the reason behind the territorial claims since the Greeks are well aware of the said benefits. . . .

The Albanians have their own homeland, language, nation, and tradition, they have preserved throughout many centuries of aggression from Rome, Byzantium, Venice, and other foreigners. How may one justify for an ancient and renowned nation to be unjustly denied its independence?

The Albanian people today count over 2,300,000 souls. Notwithstanding the intentions of the neighboring countries or the threats the people face, Albanian patriots are united with one another by oath—to fight for their goals and defend the Porte along with their homeland, language, and nation. The Albanians also think that internal reforms are requisite for success. For those reason, they have pledged [to fight against the Greek annexation of] Preveza, Narta, Janina, and other Albanian districts. Should such a thing happen—i.e., for the Greeks to occupy our territories—the Albanians would rather wish to die in the battlefield.

Your Majesty's government of Germany is erected on justice and reason. We are convinced and that the German government will be active and address our concerns properly. In doing so, it will honor our goals, which are founded in justice and equality.

The German government will not permit that the path of reforms and progress, which we are determined to follow, be closed for us and that we be kept from prosperity. Because that would force us to follow the path of bloodshed—war.

This is our hope, which we invest in geniality, an attribute that is largely present among the German people.

The delegates of the Albanian people:
Mehmet Ali Vroni,
Abdyl Frashëri.

Proclamation of the Serbian Army, 1912

[The letter was written in colloquial Albanian using the Cyrillic alphabet]

To All Tribes in Albania, Brothers:

Everyone knows that nothing on the face of the earth may happen without the blessing of the Almighty.

In the name and with the help of Allah, we have taken off and are coming to you. We are coming to the land of yours and ours that the Ottomans have occupied for five hundred years and over, but we are not coming to do you harm, but we are coming to relieve you of the harm.

You see yourselves, brothers, what the Ottomans (Young Turks much worse) [have done to do you]. There is no [evil] they do not force on you. Their army and guns razed your homes, scorched villages, treaded on your families, filled their prisons with your sons, and nowhere, not even in your own homes, did they leave you in calm. [They are causing] injustice, which the Albanian cannot endure, and moreover, they take your sons and send them to Annatolia and Arabia to shed blood for them.

For those reasons, and many such needs, you have risen and fought bravely against them, but what happened? Since they were not able to halt you by means of guns and rifles, they resorted to deception, promising with good words what you demanded, but in reality not [living up to their word].

They [suppressed you by means of violence], brothers, but in the name and the might of God, we are taking on the war where you left off, and in the name of God, all of the needs for which you have so bravely fought shall be fulfilled when we arrive amongst you.

We are coming to you, brothers, bringing you peace and justice, and to ensure that the ancient trinity, ancient people, ancient honor, and ancient glory are brought back to their place, where they once were in the ancient ages; and we will shed our blood for these sacred things of yours just as we do for those of ours.

Have no doubts, brothers; for the faith of God, we are not coming to do you harm; we are coming with the honor of the highlands and with good intentions. Have no doubts that it will be otherwise; you will have your own faith, your traditions, and self-government as you please and as Albania has had since Leka [Dukagjini].

For our faith in God, we shall forget all evil that has occurred thus far, and we shall permit no other than way but for everyone to enjoy [true freedom of] faith, honor, and property, and for no one to cause harm to another.

We shall fire our guns on those who fire on us and, God willing, we shall scorch that house and village that fires their guns against us, and the one that welcomes us brotherly, we shall embrace brotherly, as the brother embraces his brother, because we are seeing eye to eye on the faith in God, justice, and humanity, and [together] we are fighting against the others.

We give our word on this and we hail to you, to inform you that the time has come, brothers, for the country of the Ottomans to break up, and for us, as well as for you, to live in brotherhood with each other, owing to King Peter who has directed for this message and assurance to be delivered to you.

Brothers, in the name of the King, we are delivering to you this message along with our [reaffirmation of] our faith in God. We have now paid our indebtedness to God and to the people. For our faith, the Almighty is our witness; and may God the Almighty judge whoever may become the cause of bloodshed.

To our [faithful] meeting, brothers!

Teşrin-i Evvel 1328 [October 1912]
In Podujev[a]
Commander of the Serbian Army
Božidar Janković

BIBLIOGRAPHY AND ARCHIVE SOURCES

Archive sources, books, major scholarly articles, and periodicals have been listed here. Detailed citations, including references to newspaper articles and suggested readings, have been included in the notes following each chapter.

Archives

HHStA—Haus-Hofund Staatsarchiv, Politisches Archiv, Wien [Austrian State Archive, Vienna]: *Albanien* III-XXXVIII (1871-1918); *Grichenland* I, II, VI; *Montenegro* I, XVII; *Serbien* I, III, XIX; *Türkei* IV, VIII B, XV, XXX, XXXIII, XLV[45].

PA AA—Politisches Archiv des Auswärtigen Amts, Bonn [The Political Archive of the German Foreign Office, Bonn]: [Protocols and documents of the Congress of Berlin, including contemporary diplomatic acts of the Ambassadors' Conference of the Congress of Berlin, 1878-1881]

Diplomatic Documents

Bittner, Ludwig, et al. *Österreich-Ungarns Aussenpolitik von der bosnischen Krise 1908 bis zum Kriegsausbruch 1914.* Vols. 1-8. Wien: 1930.

K. und K. Ministerium des A☐ussern [Austro-Hungarian Foreign Ministry]. *Diplomatische Aktenstücke betreffend die Ereignisse auf dem Balkan.* Wien: 1914.

____. *Diplomatische Aktenstücke über die Reformaktion in Mazedonien 1902-1906.* Wien: 1906.

____. *Diplomatische Aktenstücke über die Reformaktion in Mazedonien 1906-1907.* Wien: 1907.

Komjáthy, Miklósné, ed. *Protokolle des Gemeinsamen Ministerrates der Österreichisch Ungarischen Monarchie (1914-1918).* Budapest: 1966.

Lepsius, Johannes, et. al. *Die Grosse Politik der Europäischen Kabinette 1871-1914.* Vol. 1-40. Berlin: 1927.

Books

Abdylhamiti, Sulltan [Sultan Abdul Hamid II]. *Kujtimet e mia nga politika.* Shkup: Logos, 2010.

Adanır, Fikret. *Die makedonische Frage. Ihre Entstehung und Entwiklung bis 1908.* Wiesbaden: 1979.

Akademia e Shkenca e Shqipërisë. *Historia e Popullit Shqiptar* III. Tiranë: 2007.

Akademia e Shkencave e Shqipërisë. *Historia e Popullit Shqiptar.* Vols. I-II. Tiranë: 2002.

Akademia e Shkencave RPSh. *Historia e Popullit Shqiptar.* Vols. I-II. Prishtinë: Rilindja, 1969.

Anonymous. "Annali Ragusini anonimi intem Nicolai de Ragina, Diegessit Sp. Nodilo." *Monumenta Spectania Historiam Slavorum Meridionalium* XIV. Zagrabiae: 1883.

Anonymous. *Le grand Castrioto d'Albanie.* Paris: 1799.

Antivarino. *Historia Scanderbegi, edia për quadom Albanensem, etc.* Venetiis: 1840.

Babinger, Franc. *Mehmet pushtuesi dhe koha e tij.* Prishtinë: 1982.

Babinger, Franz. *Das Ende der Arianiten.* München: 1960.

Babinger, Franz. *Ewlija Tschelebis Reisewege in Albanien.* Berlin, 1930.

Balcanicus [Stojan Protić]. *Albanski problem i Srbija i Austrougarska.* Beograd: 1913.

Bardhi, Frang. *Skëndrbeu. apologji.* Tiranë: 1962.

Barleti, Marin. *Rrethimi i Shkodrës.* Tiranë: 1962.

Barleti. *Skënderbeu.* Prishtinë: 1968.

Barletius, Marinus. *De Obsidione Scodrensi.* Venetiis: 1504.

Barletius, Marinus. *Des aller Streytpasten un teürsten Fürsten und Herrn George Castrioten genannt Scanderbeg Hercogen zu Epiro und Albanine ect.* II Latein Beschreiben und yetz durch Joannem Pinacianum Newlich vertteütscht, Augspurg Durch H. Steiner. 1533.

Barletius, Marinus. *Historia de Vita et Gestis Sconderbergi Epirotarum Principis.* ect. Impressum Romae per B (erdamus) V(vitabus).

Bartl, Peter. *Albanien: vom Mittelalter bis zur Gegenwart.* Regensburg: 1995.

Bartl, Peter. *Die Albanische Muslime zur Zeit der Natianlenunabhängigkeitsbewegung 1878-1812.* Wisbaden, 1968.

Belegu, Xhafer. *Lidhja e Prizrenit dhe veprimtaria e saj 1878-1881.* Tiranë: 1939.

Biçoku, K. and J. Kastrioti: *Gjergj Kastrioti Skënderbeu*. Bibliogafi 1454-1835, vol. I, Tiranë: 1997.

Biçoku, Kasem. *Kastriotët në Dardani*. Prishtinë: 2009.

Bismarck, Otto von. *Gedanken und Erinnerungen*. Stuttgart/Berlin, 1920.

Boekh, Katrin. *Von den Balkankriegen zum Ersten Weltkrieg. Kleinstaaten-politik und ethnische Selbestimmung auf dem Balkan*. München, 1996.

Boev, B. *Balkanska Federacija*. Beograd: 1904.

Boue, Ami. *La Turqie d'Europe* I. Paris: 1840.

Bourcart, J. *L'Albanie et les Albannais*. Paris: 1921.

Bozbora, Nuray. *Shqipëria dhe nacionalizmi shqiptar në Perandorinë Os-mane*. Tiranë: 2002.

Bozhari, Koço. "Lufta shqiptaro-turke në shekullin XV." *Burime bizantine*. Tiranë. 1967.

Buda, Aleks. *Shkrime historike*. Vols. I-II. Akademia e Shkencave, RPSSh: Tiranë: 1968.

Buxhovi, Jusuf. *Kongresi i Berlinit 1878*. Prishtinë: 2008.

Buxhovi, Jusuf. *Nga Shqipëria Oosmane te Shqipëria Evropiane*. Prishtinë: 2010.

Buzuku, Gjon. *Meshari*. Vols. 1-2. Prishtinë: 1986.

Cana, Zekeria. *Lëvizja kombëtare shqiptare në Kosovë 1908-1912*. Prishtinë: 1979.

Cana, Zekeria. *Socialdemokracia serbe dhe çështja shqiptare 1903-1914*. Prishtinë: 1986.

Cana, Zekeria. *Shpalime historike*. Prishtinë: 1982.

Chlumecký, Leopold von. *Östereich-Ungarn und Italien*. Wien: 1904.

Chlumecký, Leopold von. *Österreich Ungarn und Italien. Das Westbalkan-ische Problem Und Italiens Kampf Um Die Vorherrschaft in Der Adria*. Leipzig/Wien: 1907.

Clayer, Nathalie. *Në fillimet e nacionalizmit shqiptar*. Tiranë: 2009.

Cvijić, Jovan. *Balkansko poluostrvo i južnoslovenske zemlje: osnovi antropo-grafije*. Beograd: 1966.

Demiraj, Shaban and Kristaq Prifti. *Kongresi i Manastirit ngjarje me rëndësi historike në Lëvizjen Kombëtare Shqiptare*. Tiranë: 1968.

Dodoni, Visar. *Memoriet e mija: Kujtime nga zhvillimet e para të rilindjes së kombit shqiptar*. Bukuresht: 1930.

Dragoj, Nuri. *Shqiptarët dhe Grekët*. Tiranë: 2009.

Durham, Edith. *Brenga e ballkanasve*. Tiranë: 2005.

Faensen, Johannes. *Die albanische Nationalbewegung*. Wiesbaden: 1980.

Frangu, Dhimitër. *Lufta e turqve kundër Skënderbeut*. Tiranë: 2000.

Frashëri, Kristo. *Lidhja e Prizrenit*. Tiranë: 1956.

Frashëri, Kristo. *Rilindja kombëtare shqiptare*. Tiranë: 1962.

Frashëri, Kristo. *Skënderebu: jeta dhe vepra*. Tiranë: 2002.

Frashëri, Mehdi. *Historia e lashtë e Shqipërisë*. Tiranë: 2000.

Frashëri, Midhad] Mali Kokojka. *Naim Be Frashëri*. Sofia: 1901.

Frashëri, Naim. See Jokl.

Frashëri, Naim. *Vepra 1*. Prishtinë: 1986.

Frashëri, Sami. *Shqipëria ç'ka qënë, ç'është e ç'do të bëhetë?* Bukuresht: 1899.

Garašanin, Ilija. *Načertanje*. Beograd: 1906.

Gawrych, George. *Gjysmëhëna dhe shqiponja: Sundimi Otoman, Islamizmi dhe Shqiptarët 1874-1913*. Tiranë: 2007.

Gawrych, George. *Ottoman Administration and the Albanians, 1908-1913*. Michigan: 1980.

Gegaj, Athanas. *Arbëria dhe Gjergj Kastrioti Skënderbe 1405-1468*. Tiranë: 1995.

Geschke, A. *Die Deutsche Politik in der mazedonischen Frage bis zur Tükischen Revolution von 1908*. Danzing, 1932.

Glenny, Misha. *Historia e Ballkanit 1804-1999*. Tiranë: 2007.

Gopčević, Spiridon. *Stara Srbija i Makedonija*. Beograd: 1980.

Grameno, Mihal. *Kryengritja shqiptare*. Vlorë: 1925.

Gjini, Gaspër. *Skopsko prizrenska biskupija kroz stolječa*. Zagreb: 1986.

Hadži-Vasiljević, Jovan. *Albaska liga: Arnautska kongra i srpski narod u Turskom carstvu 1878-1882*. Beograd: 1908.

Hadži-Vasiljević, Jovan. *Arnautski pokret u XIX veku*. Beograd: 1905.

Hadži-Vasiljević, Jovan. *Četnicka akciza u Staroj Srbiji i Makedoniji*. Beograd: 1928.

Hadži-Vasiljević, Jovan. *Pokreti arnauta zua vreme srpsko-turskih ratova 1876-1878*. Beograd: 1922.

Hahn, J. G. *Albanesiesche Studien*. Vol. 1-2. Wien: 1853-1854.

Haselmayer, Fr. *Diplomatissche Geschihte des zweiten Reiches von 1871-1918*. München: 1926.

Hasluck, F. W. *Chrisianity and Islam nder the Sultans*. Oxford: 1929.

Haxhiu, Ajet. *Hasan Prishtina dhe lëvizja patriotike në Kosovë*. Tiranë: 1964.

Heaton-Armstrong, Duncan. *Gjashtë muaj mbretëri 1914*. Tiranë: 2001.

Hrabak, Bogumil. "Arbanaški prvak Isa Boletinac i Crna Gora 1910-1912." *Istorijski zapisi 1927-1977*. Titograd: 1977.

Inalxhik, Halil. *Perandoria Osmane 1300-1600*. Shkup: Logos, 2010.

Ippen, Theodor A. *Beitregä zur inneren Geschihte Albaniens im XIX Jahrhundert*. München/Leipzig: 1916.

Ippen, Theodor A. *Novibazar und Kossovo*. Wien 1892.

Ippen, Theodor A. *Skutari und di Nordalbanische Küstenebene*. Sarajevo, 1907.

Izzet Pascha, Ahmet. *Denkwüdigkeiten des Marschalls Izzet Pascha*. Leipzig: 1927.

Jäckh, Ernst. *Im tükiscen Kriegslager durch Albanien*. Heilbronn: 1911.

Jacques, Edwin. *Shqiptarët: Historia e popullit nga lashtësia deri në ditët e sotme*. Tiranë.

Jastrebov, J. S. *Stara Srbija i Albanija*. Beograd: 1904.

Jireček, Konstantin. "Albanien in der Vergangenheit." Ludwig von Thallóczy, ed. *Illyrisch-albanische Firschungen* 1 (München/Leipzig: Von Dunker Humbolt, 1916): 63-94.

Jireçek, Konstandin. *Historia e Serbëve* II. Tiranë: 2010.

Jokl, Norbert, transl. "Die Bektaschi von Naim Bej Frasheri." *Balkan Arich*. 2 (Leipzig: 1926): 226-256.

Jorga, Nicolae. *Geschihte des osmanischen Reiches*. Vols. I-II. Gotha: 1908-1909.

Josef von Hamer. *Historia Turskog Osmanskog Carstva*. Vols. I-III, Zagreb: 1979.

Jovanović, Jovan. *Borba za narodno ujedinjenje 1903-1908*. Beograd: 1938.

Kaleshi, Hasan. "Turski pokušaji za revidiranja zakonika Leke Dukađinija i ukidanje autonomije albanskih plemena u XIX veku." *Zbornik Obićanjo pravo i samouprave na Balkanu i u susednim zemljama* 1. Beograd: 1974. 389-410.

Kaleshi, Hasan. *Disa aspekte të luftës për alfabetin shqip në Stamboll. Gjurmime albanologjike* I (Prishtinë: 1969).

Kaleshi, Hasan. *Prve truske-srpske stamparije i poceci stampe na Kosovu*. Beograd: 1969.

Koleci, Niko. *Kryengritja e përgjithshme shqiptare kundër sundimit turk në vitin 1912*. Tiranë: 1962.

Kumanudi, Kosta. *Pogled nga ulogu Rusije i Austrije u istocnom pitanju*. Beograd: 1903.

Londres, Albert. *Komitaxhinjtë ose terrorizmi i Ballkanit*. Tiranë: 2009.

Lose, I. *Die wölkerrechtlichen u politischen Bezihungen Albaniens zu Italien*. Würzburg: 1930.

Mach, Richard. *Der Machtbereich des bulgarichen Exarchts in der Türkei*. Leipzig: 1906.

Mihacević, Lovro. *Crtice albanske povjesti.* Sarajevo: 1912.

Milojević, Milan D. *Balkanska ravnoteza.* Beograd: 1913.

Montran, Robert. *Historia e Perandorisë Osmane.* Tiranë: 2003.

Murzaku, Thoma. *Politika e Serbisë kundrejt Shqipërisë gjatë luftës ballkanike 1912-1913.* Tiranë: 1978.

Naçi, Stavro. *Pashallëku i Shkodrës.* Tiranë: 1964.

Nemezov, N. *Značaj arnautskog pokreta.* Sarajevo: 1910.

Nopca, Franjo. *Prinosi staroj povjesti Sjevere Albanije.* Sarajevo: 1910.

Novotny, A. *Österreich, die Türkei und das Balkanproblem im Jahre des berliner Kongresses (Quellen und Studien zur Geschihte deer Berliner Kongresses 1878).* Graz/Köln: 1957.

Ostrogorski, Georgije. *Historia e Perandorisë Bizantine.* Tiranë: 2002. 382.

Ostrogorski, Georgije. *Istoria Vizantije.* Beograd: 1964.

Pandevski, Manol. *Politićki partii i organizacii vo Makedonija 1908-1912.* Shkup: 1965.

Pango, Petraq. *Kujtime nga lëvizja për çlirimin kombëtar 1878-1912.* Tiranë: 1962.

Pavlović, M. *Pokret u Bosni i u Albaniji protiv reforma Mahmuda II.* Beograd: 1913.

Pllana, Emin. *Kosova dhe reformat në Turqi.* Prishtinë: 1978.

Pollo, Stefanaq, Selami Pulaha, eds. *Akte të Rilindjes Kombëtare Shqiptare 1878-1912.* Tiranë: 1978.

Pollo, Stefanaq. *Shpallja e pavarësisë së Shqipërisë.* Tiranë: 1962.

Popović, Dimitrije. *Borba za Narodno ujedinjenje 1908-1914.* Beograd: 1936.

Prela, Zef. *Mbi politikën austro-hungareze në Shqipëri në çerekun e fundit të shekullit XIX.* Tiranë: 1960.

Prela, Zef. *Problemi shqiptar dhe politika austro-hungareze 1897-1912.* Tiranë: 1962.

Pribram A. F. *Die politischen Geheimvertrage Österreich-Ungarns 1879-1916.* Wien: 1920.

Prishtina, Hasan. *Nji shkurtim kujtimesh mbi kryengritjen shqiptare 1912.* Bari: 1925.

Pushkolli, Fehmi. *Mbrojtja Kombëtare Shqiptare e Kosovës 1878-1990.* Prishtinë: 1991.

Puto, Arben. *Historia diplomatike e çështjes shqiptare 1878-1926.* Tiranë: 2003.

Qosja, Rexhep. *Çështja shqiptare: historia dhe politika.* Prishtinë: 1994.

Rakić, Milan. *Konsulska pisma 1905-1911.* Beograd: Prosveta, 1985.

Rizaj, Skender. *Kosova gjatë shekujve XV, XVI dhe XVII.* Prishtinë: 1982.

Rrahimi, Shukri. *Vilajeti i Kosovës*. Prishtinë: 1969.

San Guliamo, A. *Briefe über Albanien*. Leipzig: 1913.

Schubert, Peter. *Die albanische Frage und ihr Einfluss auf Siherheitslage des Balkans*. Eberhausen: 1996.

Schubert, Peter. *Zündstoff im Konflikfeld des Balkans: Die albanische Frage*. Baden-Baden: 1997.

Schwartz, Stephen. *Islami tjetër: Sufizmi dhe rrëfimi për respektin*. Prishtinë: 2009.

Siebertz, Paul. *Albanien und die Albanesen*. Wien: 1910.

Sienkevič, I. Grigorevna. *Albanija v period vostacnog krizisa*. Moskva, 1956.

Sienkevič, I. Grigorevna. *Osvobotitelnoe dvizenie albanskog naroda v 1905-1912*. Moskva: 1959.

Skëndi, Stavro. *Zgjimi kombëtar shqiptar*. Tiranë: 2000.

Šufflay, Milan. *Histori e Shqiptarëve të veriut*. Prishtinë: 2009.

Šufflay, Milan. *Srbi i Arbanasi: njihova simbioza u srednjem veku*. Beograd: 1925.

Tahiri, Abdyl. *Hasan Prishtina*. Prishtinë: 2003.

Tomić, Jovan. *Austrougarska i arbanasko pitanje*. Beograd: 1913.

Trotsky, Leon. *The Balkans Wars*. New York: 1980.

Thallóczy, Ludwig von, ed. *Illyrisch-albanische Forschungen*. Vols. I-II. München/Leipzig: Von Dunker Humbolt, 1916.

Thengjilli, Petrika. *Shqiptarët midis Lindjes dhe Perëndimit 1506-1750*. Tiranë: 2003.

Uebergrsberger, H. *Russlands Oreintpolitik in den letzten zweihunderten*. Stuttgart,1913.

Vaso, Pashko. *Vepra 1*. Prishtinë:1989.

Veizi, Fane. *Kongresi i Lushnjës*. Tiranë: 1959.

Verdho, Liljana. *Skënderbeu në shtypin e lëvizjes kombëtare*. Tiranë: 2008.

Verli, Marenglen. *Kosova sfida shqiptare në historinë e një shekulli*. Tiranë: 2007.

Vlora, Eqrem bej. *Aus Berat und vom Tomor*. Sarajevo: 1911.

Vlora, Eqrem bej. *Die Wahrheit über das Vorhehen der Jüngurken in Albanien*. Wien: 1911.

Vlora, Eqrem bej. *Kujtime I (1885-1912)*,Tiranë: 2001.

Vlora, Eqrem bej. *Kujtime II (1912-1925)*. Tiranë: 2001.

Vlora, Qemal Ismali. *Kujtime*. Tiranë: 1997.

Vllamasi, Sejfi. *Ballafaqimet politike në Shqipëri 1897-1925*. Tiranë: 1990.

Wendel, Herman. *O Jugoslaviji, Italiji i Albaniji*. Beograd: 1921.

Williams, Georg Fred. *Shqiptarët*. Tiranë: 1934.

Zamputi, Iniac. *Dokumente të shekujve XVI-XVII për historinë e Shqipërisë.* Vol. I (1507-1592). Tiranë: 1989.

Zeki Pasha. *Moje uspomene iz Balkanskog rata 1912.* Beograd: 1925.

Zinkeisen, J.W. *Geschihte des osmanischen Reiches in Europa* V. Gotha, 1857.

Articles and Periodicals

Benna, A. H. "Studien zum Kultursprotektorat Österreich-Ungarns in Albanien in Zeitalter des Imperialismus (1888 1918)." *Mitteilungen des Österreichische Staatsarchivs* 7 (Wien: 1954): 13-47.

Buda, Aleks, et al. "Dokumente rreth kryengritjeve shqiptare kundër pushtuesve osman në vitet 30 të shek XV." *Studime historike* I. Tiranë: 1967.

Cana, Zekeria. "Reaksioni xhonturk kundër shkollës dhe shkrimit shqip në pragun e Kryengritjes së Kosovës më 1910." *Gjurmime albanologjike* I (Prishtinë: 1969).

Chlumecký, Leopold von. "Die Italo-Albanesen und die Balkanpolitik." *Österreichische Rundschau* IV (Wien: Nov.1905-Jan.1906): 331-352.

Chlumecký, Leopold von. "Die Jungtürken und Albanien." *Östereichische Rundschau* 26 (Wien: Jan.-Mar. 1911): 268-274.

Ippen, Theodor A. "Beiträge zur inneren Geschihte Albaniens im XIX Jahrhunderten." Ludwig von Thallóczy, ed. *Illyrisch-albanische Firschungen* 1 (München/Leipzig: Von Dunker Humbolt, 1916): 342-358.

Ippen, Theodor A. "Das religiose Protektorat Österreich-Ungarns in der Turkei." *Die Kultur* 3 (Wien: 1901-1902): 298-310.

Ippen, Theodor A. "Italien und die albanesische Frage." Featured article. *Die Grenzboten* 60 (Leipzig: 1901): 289-259.

Kaleshi, Hasan and Hans-Jürgen Kornrumpf. "Das Wilajet Prizren. Beitrag zur Geschichte der türkischen Staatsreform auf dem Balkan im 19. Jahrhundert." *Südost Forschungen* 26 (München: 1976): 176-238.

Kissling, H. J. "Zur Frage der Anfänge des Bektaschitums in Albanien." *Oriens* 15 (Leiden: 1910): 281-286.

Malt. J., ed. "Neuer Beitrag zur inneren Geschichte Südalbaniens in der 60-er Jahren des 19. Jahrhunderts-Bericht des k. k. Consuls in Janina de data 24 Juni 1868." *Südost Forschungen* 16 (München: 1957): 435-444.

Pollo, Stefanaq. "Shqipëria në vitet 1900-1912." *Buletini i Universitetit Shtetëror* (Tiranë: 1965).

Prela, Zef. "Aspekte ekonomike të depërtimit paqësor të Austro-Hungarisë në Shqipëri 1900-1912." *Studime historike* 2 (Prishtinë: 1966).

Rappaport, A. "Mazedonien und di Komitadschis." *Berliner Monatshefte* 8 (Aug. 1930): 731-747.

Raschdau, L, ed. "Durchführung der Berliner Kongresakte 1880-1881." *Deutsche Rundschau* 147 (Berlin: Apr.-May-June 1911): 222-248.

Sienkevič, I. Grigorevna. "Mladotureckaja revolucija 1908 i albansko nacionalnoe dvizenie." *Sovetskoe vostokovednie* 1 (Moskva: 1958).

Stadtmüller, Georg. "Die albanische Volkstumgeschihte als Forschungsproblem." *Leipziger Vierteljahrsschrift für Südosteuropa* V (1941): 58-80.

Stadtmüller, Georg. "Die Islamisierung bei den Albanern." *Jahrbücher für Geschichte Osteuropas* 3 (1958): 404-429.

Stadtmüller, Georg. "Landschaft und Geschichte in Albanisch-epirotischen Raum." *Revue Internationale des Études Balkaniques* III (Belgrade: 1937-38): 345-370.

Strauss, Johann. "Das Vilayet Janina 1881-1912: Wirtschaft und Gesellschaft in einer 'geretteten Provinz'." *Türkische Wirtschafts und Sozialgeschichte (1071-1920)*. Hans Georg Majer, Raoul Motika, eds. Wiesbaden: 1995. 297-313.

Šufflay, Milan. "Die Kirchenzustände im vortürkischen Albanien: Die Ortodoxe Durchbruchszone im katolischen damme." Ludwig von Thallóczy, ed. *Illyrisch-albanische Firschungen* 1 (München/Leipzig: Von Dunker Humbolt, 1916): 299-342.

Thallóczy, Ludwig von. "Die albanische Diaspora." *Illyrisch-albanische Firschungen* 1 (München/Leipzig: Von Dunker Humbolt, 1916): 299-341.

Thopia, Karl. "Das Fürstentum Albanien (Eine zeitgeschihtliche Studie)." Ludwig von Thallóczy, ed. *Illyrisch-albanische Firschungen* 2 (München/Leipzig: Von Dunker Humbolt, 1916): 219-287.

Vishko, Ali. "Një tentativë e qeverisë turke për reforma në krahinat shqiptare kah fillimi i vitit 1912." *Përparimi* 2 (1967).

Vlora, Ekrem Bej]. "Ziele und Zukunft der Albanesen." [Albanian Memorandum]. *Österreichische Rundschau* 15 (Wien: 1908): 391-406.

Vukanović, Tatomir P. "Arbanaski ustanci 1826-1832." *Vranjsi glasnik* V (Vranje: 1969).

Wigand, G. "Das Albanische in Attika." *Balkan Arich.* 2 (Leipzig: 1926): 167-225.

Zavalani, Fehmi. "Komiteti Shqiptar i Manastirit dhe ngjarjet tjera." *Përpjekja shqiptare* 3-5 (Tiranë: 1937).

Jusuf Buxhovi

KOSOVA
Volume 2

Printed by
"PROGRAF"
Prishtina, Kosova

Buxhovi, Jusuf
    Kosova: (The Ottoman Empire)
Jalifat Publishing, 2013
Houston, Texas
www.jalifatpublishing.com

Volume 2

ISBN 978-0-9767140-6-4
ISBN 978-0-9767140-8-8